THE HANDBOOK OF
INTERNATIONAL
FINANCIAL
MANAGEMENT

THE HANDBOOK OF INTERNATIONAL FINANCIAL MANAGEMENT

Editor
Robert Z. Aliber
Graduate School of Business
University of Chicago

Dow Jones-Irwin
Homewood, Illinois 60430

Dow Jones-Irwin is a trademark of Dow Jones & Company, Inc.
All rights reserved. No part of this publication may be
reproduced, stored in a retrieval system, or transmitted,
in any form or by any means, electronic, mechanical,
photocopying, recording, or otherwise, without the prior
written permission of the publisher.

This publication is designed to provide accurate and
authoritative information in regard to the subject matter
covered. It is sold with the understanding that the
publisher is not engaged in rendering legal, accounting, or
other professional service. If legal advice or other expert
assistance is required, the services of a competent
professional person should be sought.

*From a Declaration of Principles jointly adopted by a Committee
of the American Bar Association and a Committee of Publishers.*
Project editor: Lynne Basler
Production manager: Bette K. Ittersagen
Compositor: Bi-Comp, Incorporated
Typeface: 11/13 Times Roman
Printer: R. R. Donnelley & Sons Company

Library of Congress Cataloging-in-Publication Data

The handbook of international financial management / editor, Robert Z.
  Aliber.
    p.   cm.
  Includes index.
  ISBN 1-55623-019-2
  1. International finance. 2. Banks and banking, International.
I. Aliber, Robert Z.
HG3881.H267 1989
332.1'5—dc20   89–31636
                      CIP

Printed in the United States of America

1 2 3 4 5 6 7 8 9 0 DO 6 5 4 3 2 1 0 9

NOTES ON THE AUTHORS

Niso Abuaf is a manager with Salomon Brothers Inc., New York, formerly a vice president and financial economist, Chase Manhatten Bank.

Robert Z. Aliber is a professor of international economics and finance at the Graduate School of Business, University of Chicago.

John F. O. Bilson is a senior vice president with the Chicago Corporation.

Joseph Bisignano is assistant manager, Monetary and Economic Department, Bank for International Settlements, Basle, Switzerland.

Lawrence J. Brainard is a senior vice president with Bankers Trust Company, New York.

Brendan Brown is with the Mitsubishi Finance Company, London.

Mark T. Campbell is a manager with Arthur Andersen & Co., Chicago.

Thomas F. Cargill is a professor of economics, University of Nevada-Reno, Reno, Nevada. Recently he has been a visiting scholar at the Federal Reserve Bank of San Francisco and the Federal Deposit Insurance Corporation.

John F. Chown is president of John F. Chown Limited, tax consultants, London.

Ian A. Cooper is senior lecturer and Baring Research Fellow, London Graduate School of Business Studies.

Howard S. Engle is a partner at Arthur Andersen & Co., Chicago.

Ellen Evans is a financial analyst with Salomon Brothers Inc., New York.

Hans Genberg is a professor of economics at the Graduate Institute of International Studies, Geneva.

Christine R. Hekman is an associate professor at the Peter F. Drucker Graduate Management Center, the Claremont Graduate School, Claremont, California.

Philippe Jorion is an associate professor of international business, Columbia University.

Maurice Levi is Bank of Montreal professor, Faculty of Commerce and Business Administration, University of British Columbia, Vancouver.

Richard Levich is a professor of finance and international business, Stern School of Business, New York University.

John Lipsky is a director in the Bond Market Research Department of Salomon Brothers Inc., New York.

Michel G. Maila is a vice president with Bank of Montreal, Toronto.

Kate Phylaktis is a senior lecturer of international business, City University, London.

Cecilia G. Reyes is a doctoral candidate in finance at the London Graduate School of Business Studies.

Nicholas Sargen is a manager with Salomon Brothers Inc., New York.

Stephan Schoess is president of Hedge, Inc., Chicago.

Roy C. Smith is a clinical professor of finance and international business, Stern School of Business, New York University, and a limited partner (retired general partner), of Goldman, Sachs & Co., New York.

Clyde P. Stickney is The Signal Companies professor of management, The Amos Tuck School of Business Administration, Dartmouth College.

Thomas J. Trebat is program officer for international economics at the Ford Foundation in New York. He was previously a vice president of Bankers Trust Company, New York.

Christian C. P. Wolff is a professor of finance at the University of Limburg, Maastricht, The Netherlands.

Geoffrey Wood is a professor of economics, City University, London.

Josef Zechner is an assistant professor, Faculty of Commerce and Business Administration, University of British Columbia, Vancouver.

INTRODUCTION

Few events illustrate the integration of world financial markets more than the near-simultaneous meltdown in equity prices in New York, London, Frankfurt, and Tokyo in October 1987. The opening prices in the New York Stock Exchange were keyed to closing prices in the London Stock Market. In turn, the opening prices in London were strongly affected by the pattern of closing prices in Tokyo earlier in the same day. Price movements in Tokyo at the beginning of each day's trading were sharply affected by stock price movements in New York on the previous day—which was about three hours earlier. The paradox is that the economic climate and prospective economic developments in Japan and in Great Britain in October 1987 were significantly different from the economic development that led to the sharp decline in the U.S. stock market. Nevertheless, within a few days, equity price indexes in virtually every industrial country had declined by 20 to 30 percent.

The significance of the November 1987 worldwide collapse in equity prices was that financial market events in Western Europe and Japan had an obvious, direct, and powerful impact on U.S. financial markets. Since the end of World War I, increases in U.S. interest rates induced sympathetic increases in interest rates in many foreign financial centers as investors shifted funds among markets in the search for higher returns; similarly, decreases in interest rates on U.S. dollar assets led to decreases in interest rates in various foreign markets. But for 60 years this traditional relationship between changes in interest rates in the United States and changes in interest rates in other countries had been asymmetric—changes in interest rates in Great Britain, Germany, and

Japan had a trivial impact on interest rates on U.S. financial assets. In international financial relationships, the United States was the "Giant Among Nations." And as Keynes quipped, when the United States sneezed, the rest of the world caught pneumonia.

In the summer of 1987, however, increases in interest rates on German mark securities and on Japanese yen securities—and the prospect of further increases in interest rates in Germany and Japan—induced investors to sell U.S. dollar securities and move their funds into assets denominated in the Japanese yen, the German mark, and other foreign currencies. As a result, interest rates on U.S. dollar securities increased—and the U.S. dollar depreciated further in the foreign exchange market. In turn the increase in U.S. interest rates—and the prospect of further increases—triggered the sales of U.S. equities by both U.S. and foreign investors. The near-simultaneous decline in prices of equities in New York and other financial centers reflects the substantial increase in cross-holdings of equities; thus, U.S. investors have diversified their portfolios and acquired billions of dollars of equities denominated in the currency of another industrial country. Much earlier, investors resident in Canada, Great Britain, and other industrial countries had acquired substantial volume of U.S. dollar equities. And beginning in the early 1980s, investors resident in Japan had acquired billions of U.S. bonds, deposits, and equities.

The increase in the importance of Western Europe and Japan in the international financial economy is evidenced in several ways—one is the increase in their share of national income of the combined OECD countries, which reflects both their more rapid growth and the appreciation of their currencies relative to the U.S. dollar. Thus, the Japanese share of OECD national income was increased throughout the 1970s and 1980s. Over the same period, Germany's share in the combined national incomes of the OECD countries also increased. The increase in the importance of Western Europe and Japan in the international *financial* economy also reflects the more rapid increase in the value of Japanese equities and those of Western Europe relative to the value of U.S. equities. Like the comparison of the gross domestic products of each country, this comparison reflects the fact that economic growth rates in these other industrial countries in the 1960s and 1970s generally were higher than those in the United States.

The combination of more rapid increases in the national incomes of Western Europe and Japan than in the United States, the more rapid increase in the market value of their equities, and the appreciation of their currencies have meant that the return to U.S. investors on foreign equities—and on foreign bonds—has exceeded the return on U.S. bonds. As a consequence, U.S. investors were attracted to foreign equities. And at the same time, investors based in other countries increased their demand for U.S. securities as a way to diversify their currency-mix wealth holdings.

The closer integration of national financial markets has also been associated with three major institutional developments. The first is the development of new financial instruments. These include: bank deposits denominated in the U.S. dollar, the Japanese yen, the British pound, the German mark, and the Swiss franc; Eurobonds; interest rate swaps; futures contracts in foreign exchange; foreign exchange swaps; zero-coupon bonds; and bonds with interest payable in one currency that are convertible into another currency. More new financial instruments have been developed in the 1980s than in any previous decade.

The second factor in the closer integration of financial markets is the liberalization of national financial regulations; this phenomenon is global, although the scope of deregulation and the direction in individual countries differ, largely because of national differences in the pattern and mix of financial regulation. This liberalization has relaxed interest rate ceilings, reduced reserve requirements, and relaxed barriers to geographic expansion and to expansion of the product line of particular institutions, and so forth. Liberalization has affected both the terms on particular securities and the activities of particular types of financial institutions—boundaries have declined.

The third factor in the closer integration of national financial markets is the increased cross-penetration of foreign ownership, exemplified by the sharp increase in the number of foreign banks and foreign security firms in New York. Similarly there has been a large increase in the number of foreign banks and brokerage firms in London and Tokyo. The buzzword is globalization, exemplified by the efforts of banks and other financial institutions headquartered in the United States, Great Britain, Japan, and several other countries to establish worldwide presences.

These three developments—new financial instruments, financial deregulation, and globalization—are responses to two different developments. The first of these was the remarkable development of computers and information technology, which greatly reduced the cost of coordinating trading in different centers and of organizing portfolios that are designed to reduce risk of particular investors. The second development was the surge in the inflation rate in the United States and other industrial countries, which had two significant impacts (1) the prices of various financial assets began to vary significantly in response to changes in national inflation rates and changes in interest rates in various countries, and (2) the costs of national regulations began to increase significantly.

As inflation and the costs of these regulations increased, the economic payoff for circumventing these regulations increased correspondingly.

One objective of *The Handbook of International Financial Management* is to document the developments in national financial markets—international financial markets are the constellation of national markets. The second objective is to discuss the opportunities and challenges for corporate financial managers in this new financial environment, including the capital-budgeting decision, the cash management decision, the portfolio decision—in an international context. One of the unique international financial decisions is the debt denomination-decision. Should firms denominate debt in their domestic currency or in one of a number of foreign currencies?

The *Handbook* is organized into four parts. The chapters in Part 1 cover the institutional changes and developments in financial markets and in financial centers, and especially the development of new financial instruments. The chapters in Part 2 deal with regulatory and accounting issues that affect international financial transactions. The chapters in Part 3 discuss the traditional issues of financial management in a world in which exchange rates change abruptly and by a large amount—and in which nominal interest rates on comparable assets denominated in different currencies differ sharply. Recent changes in the international financial environment are discussed in Part 4.

Richard Luecke suggested that I organize this *Handbook*. Cathy Coursey was extremely helpful in maintaining a busy correspondence with the authors. And these authors—former students and colleagues—have been both supportive and patient in their willingness to participate.

Robert Z. Aliber

CONTENTS

PART 2
REGULATORY PRACTICES—THE RULES

PART 3
THE MANAGEMENT DECISIONS

PART 4
THE ENVIRONMENT

APPENDIXES

PART 1

FINANCIAL MARKETS AND INSTITUTIONS— THE PLAYERS

CHAPTER 1

THE INTERNATIONAL DEBT MARKET

John Lipsky
Nicholas Sargen
Ellen Evans

THE 1980s: DECADE OF BOND FINANCE

International capital markets have undergone profound changes in recent years as a consequence of volatile interest rates and exchange rates, oil price shocks, and large and unstable balance of payments conditions in both developed and developing countries. During the 1970s, banking flows dominated international capital movements, as the massive Organization of Petroleum Exporting Countries (OPEC) current account surplus was recycled through the international banking system. In the medium-term arena, LIBOR-based (London interbank offered rate) floating-rate syndicated bank loans emerged as the key instrument of international finance, and the developing countries enjoyed much greater access to bank finance than they had in the past. By comparison, bond issuance played a subordinate role in providing cross-border finance.

This situation changed fundamentally during the early 1980s. The debt problems of the developing countries became critical, causing commercial banks to slow their international lending. At the same time, industrial country borrowers increasingly turned to bond markets to finance large or rising government deficits: during the first seven years of this decade, most industrial countries experienced a tripling of their public sector debt outstanding, and some countries—notably, the United States, France, Italy, and the Netherlands—saw government debt quadruple. In addition, corporate debt outstanding ballooned, as businesses increased their leverage in the face of falling interest rates. On the lending side, preferences shifted from bank deposits to fixed-income securities as payments surpluses shifted from OPEC to countries such as Japan, West Germany, and Taiwan.

By 1983, bond issuance had displaced syndicated loans as the principal vehicle of international finance (see Figure 1–1). Since then, the gap has widened fairly steadily: during 1986, medium-term syndicated loans totaled $54 billion, while gross new international bond issuance amounted to a record $221 billion—five times greater than the magnitude at the start of this decade.

Until 1987, international bond issuance (consisting of Euro-bonds and foreign bonds) had been the most rapidly growing sector of the world bond market. Nonetheless, the international sector still accounts for only about 10 percent of the world bond market, as the domestic bond markets of the leading industrial countries have also expanded significantly.

FIGURE 1–1
Gross New Volume of International Bonds and Bank Lending, 1980–1987
(U.S. Dollars in Billions)

	International Syndicated Bank Loans	International Bonds	
		Total	Floating Rate Notes
1980	$79.9	$ 38.5	N.A.
1981	91.3	47.2	$ 7.5
1982	90.8	71.5	11.3
1983	60.2	73.3	15.4
1984	53.2	108.6	34.5
1985	54.2	165.5	56.1
1986	54.2	220.8	48.8
1987	76.2	173.2	11.4

Source: OECD, *Financial Statistics Monthly,* and Salomon Brothers Inc.

The rapid buildup of debt and high volatility of interest rates and exchange rates have placed a premium on the marketability of capital market instruments, giving rise to the securitization of a wide range of financial instruments. Deregulation of financial markets in the United States resulted in increasing pressures on commercial banks to remove underperforming assets from their balance sheets. This resulted in the securitization of the U.S. mortgage market, with mortgage pass-throughs and other securities collateralized by mortgages. In the international arena, securitization was associated with the rapid growth of the floating-rate note market, the proliferation of note issuance facilities, and the emergence of a Eurocommercial paper market.

Increased financial market volatility has also contributed to a whole new technology for risk management. This is apparent in the widespread use of interest rate and currency futures and options. These instruments have enabled issuers and investors to alter their currency and interest rate exposure without reallocating their portfolios. Moreover, as the maturities of these contracts have been extended, arbitraging of yield curves has become prevalent worldwide: today, more than ever before, there is a tendency for interest rate parity to hold at the long end of the maturity spectrum, as well as at the short end.

These emerging trends of internationalization, securitization, and financial innovation have pushed against preexisting barriers in national capital markets, culminating in the deregulation of financial markets worldwide. Even though the United States and Britain have been at the forefront of deregulation efforts, the last few years have seen important liberalizations of financial markets in several other countries including Japan, West Germany, France, Switzerland, and the Netherlands. These liberalizations have resulted in the introduction of new financial instruments in these markets, such as floating-rate notes, zero-coupon bonds, and currency and interest rate swaps, and have permitted greater access to foreign investors and issuers. In addition, withholding taxes on domestic fixed-income securities have been eliminated in a number of these countries.

As barriers between national capital markets have been reduced, competition among financial institutions and financial centers has become more intense. This, in turn, poses a challenge to the continued rapid growth of the Eurobond markets. The Euro-dollar bond market, in particular, suffered a sharp setback in 1987 as a result of problems of illiquidity in the floating-rate note sector and intense competition among underwriters, as well as the weakness of the U.S. dollar. Consequently, the role of the Euro-bond market is now being reexamined by market participants.

This chapter describes the size and composition of the world bond market, identifying key characteristics of the principal national bond markets, as well as the role that the Eurobond market plays in linking them. Linkages between markets are examined, first from the perspective of issuers and then from the perspective of investors. The chapter concludes by assessing areas in which arbitrage across markets has become nearly perfect, as well as by identifying areas in which market imperfections persist.

SIZE AND COMPOSITION OF THE WORLD BOND MARKET

As of year-end 1987, the nominal value of outstanding publicly issued bonds in the world's 13 major bond markets exceeded $9.4 trillion, or more than three times the size at the beginning of the 1980s (see Figure 1–2). Approximately two thirds of these issues represent direct or indirect debt obligations of central, state, or local government entities, while the remaining third are corporate bonds, debt issued by other nongovernmental entities, and international bonds. Eurobonds account for the bulk of all international bonds: foreign bonds—issued by nonresidents in domestic capital markets such as the U.S. Yankee, U.K. Bulldog, Japanese Samurai, and Swiss franc sectors—represent one third of the international total. Private placements comprise a separate category of fixed-income securities, and totaled $1.2 trillion outstanding at the end of 1987.

In terms of currency of denomination, there are three major blocs: the U.S. dollar sector, consisting of the U.S. bond market and the closely-linked Canadian bond market, is by far the largest, accounting for half of all outstanding publicly issued fixed-income securities. The Japanese bond market is the second largest, with outstandings of $2.1 trillion, or 22 percent of the total. The third

FIGURE 1-2
Size of Major Bond Markets at Year-End 1986 (Nominal Value Outstanding, Billions of U.S. Dollars Equivalent)[a]

Bond Market	Total Publicly Issued	As Percent of Public Issues in All Markets	Central Government	Central Government Agency and Government Guaranteed	State and Local Government	Corp. (Including Convertibles)	Other Domestic Publicly Issued	International Bonds[b] Foreign Bonds	International Bonds[b] Euro-bonds	Private Placement Unclassified
U.S. dollar	$4,165.7	44.3%	$1,335.2	$945.1	$776.3	$658.5	$16.0	$55.1	$379.5	$364.8
Japanese yen	2,120.6	22.6	1,236.2	153.5	54.0	157.3	412.7	41.0	65.9	346.9
Deutschemark	811.5	8.6	191.7	34.6	23.6	1.6	456.0	104.0	—	328.4[c]
Italian lira	540.1	5.7	415.5	24.6	—	5.4	91.3	1.8	1.5	—
French franc	336.8	3.6	98.9	160.5	3.6	62.8	—	3.1	7.9	—
U.K. sterling	332.7	3.5	258.6	—	0.2	19.4	—	6.6	47.9	—
Belgian franc	196.8	2.1	97.0	60.4	—	7.6	27.0	4.4	0.4	—
Canadian dollar	192.9	2.1	78.4	0.1	63.4	31.3	0.7	0.8	18.2	—
Swiss franc	171.7	1.8	9.1	—	10.5	35.2	36.4	80.5	—	58.1
Danish krone	171.2	1.8	49.8	—	—	—	117.9	—	3.5	—
Swedish krona	160.6	1.7	68.7	—	2.4	12.8	76.6	—	0.1	—
Dutch guilder	128.4	1.4	77.3	—	3.9	29.8	—	12.1	5.3	92.2[c]
Australian dollar	73.6	0.8	28.5	13.8	—	12.9	—	—	18.4	25.9
Total	**$9,402.6[d]**		**$3,944.9**	**$1,392.6**	**$937.9**	**$1,034.6**	**$1,234.6**	**$858.0[d]**		**$1,216.3[c]**
Sector as Percent of Public Issues in All Markets		100.0%	42.0%	14.8%	10.0%	11.0%	13.1%	9.1%		

a Exchange rates prevailing as of December 31, 1987; ¥121.025/US$, DM1.5698/US$, Lit1,172.0/US$, Ffr5.322/US$, £0.5301/US$, C$1.299/US$, Sfr1.2905/US$, Dkr6.051/US$, Skr5.754/US$, Dfl 1.7662/US$, A$1.3889/US$, and ECU 0.762/US$.
b Includes straight, convertible and floating-rate debt.
c In addition, there exists an unspecificable amount of privately placed issues of the private sector.
d In addition, there was $33.8 billion of outstanding ECU-denominated Eurobonds at year-end 1987.

Source: Salomon Brothers Inc.

major bloc is the West European sector, which includes markets whose currencies are closely linked through the European Monetary System. The strongest linkage is among bond markets within the deutsche mark (DM) bloc, namely, the West German, Dutch, and Swiss bond markets: their currencies are considered to be nearly perfect substitutes and, as a result, yields in these markets are very closely arbitraged. Yields in major West European bond markets, such as the U.K. sterling and French franc sectors also have links to the deutsche mark bloc, but their yields tend to fluctuate more independently of the deutsche mark sector.

DISTINCTIVE FEATURES OF NATIONAL BOND MARKETS

It is tempting to think that no matter where in the world one invests, "a bond is a bond." In fact, however, there are numerous differences among international fixed-income markets. The principal differences relate to the mix of public- and private-sector debt, the procedures used for distributing debt instruments, and variations in tax and regulatory treatment among the major financial centers.

U.S. Bond Market

The U.S. bond market, the most developed and least regulated market for fixed-income securities, serves as a yardstick against which other national bond markets can be compared. A distinctive feature of the U.S. bond market is the presence of a well-developed corporate sector. In fact, until the mid-1970s, corporate bond issuance in the United States far exceeded that of the federal government. This situation has changed markedly since then, however, as a result of the massive buildup of U.S. government debt: during the 1980s, the federal government has accounted for about 30 percent of all debt issued in the United States, compared with only 7 percent in the early 1970s. In addition, between 1980 and 1987, federal agency debt tripled, mainly reflecting a quintupling of mortgage pass-through securities, while municipal debt doubled. The sector of the U.S. corporate bond that has grown the most rapidly in recent years is the high-yield or "junk" bond market.

As a result of these developments, the government sector now dominates the U.S. bond market, not only in size but also in its influence on other sectors. U.S. corporate paper or debt of federal agencies and municipalities is typically priced in terms of their yield "over or under the U.S. Treasury curve." This not only reflects the role of U.S. Treasuries as the riskless asset in the system but also the existence of actively traded issues throughout the maturity spectrum. The liquidity of the U.S. Treasury market is enhanced by the existence of a well-developed futures market for Treasury securities.

The U.S. system for issuing government debt is based on a system of regularly scheduled auctions. Each new issue is under-written by market makers—there are currently 42 primary dealers—and the full issue amount is always allocated. Conse-quently, the determination of issue price is left entirely to the market. Similarly, prices of U.S. Treasuries in the secondary market are determined by market forces, and, as such, are highly influenced by new developments, especially the release of U.S. economic statistics. Bid/ask spreads are the narrowest of any of the world's bond markets—usually only $\frac{1}{32}$ of a point on actively traded issues.

A noteworthy feature of the secondary market for U.S. government securities is the existence of actively traded issues throughout the maturity spectrum. This enables market makers to construct a well-defined yield curve for U.S. Treasuries, from which prices of less actively traded issues can be interpolated. This serves as the basis for constructing yield curves in the corporate sector, although the pricing of U.S. corporate debt is also heavily influenced by assessments of credit risk and call risk. By compari-son, outside the United States, trading of government bonds is confined to a small number of issues, and there is very little issuance of nonbank corporate debt.

British Gilt Market

At present, the government bond market that most closely resem-bles the U.S. system is that for British gilts—the oldest fixed-income market in the world. However, prior to October 1986, U.K.

authorities generally issued gilts directly to the public at a fixed price. Unsold bonds were held by the Bank of England "on tap" and were sold to market makers at a later date—and often at a different price. As a result, the Bank of England, rather than market makers, assumed the price risk. In May 1987, following the so-called Big Bang, which reformed the market's institutional structure, a new gilt auction system was introduced. This system closely resembles the U.S. model except that the Bank of England reserves the right to allot less than the full issue amount under exceptional circumstances (see Figure 1–3). This means that the Bank of England retains some control over price.[1] In addition, market makers are not required to bid at auctions.

The Big Bang also altered the institutional structure of the gilt market by eliminating the distinction between market makers (or "jobbers"), who previously had been prevented from dealing with the public, and brokers, who had been prevented from making markets. In response, the number of dealers in the gilt market rose from 2 before October 1986 to 27 after that date, including foreign firms. Although these changes have fundamentally altered the method of distributing government debt to the public, the impact on secondary market trading is less noticeable: the gilt market, like the U.S. Treasury bond market, remains highly sensitive to news developments, and has long exhibited a fairly high degree of price volatility. Bid/ask spreads are also low—usually $\frac{1}{16}$ of a point on liquid issues.

Japanese Bond Market

Compared to the U.S. and U.K. markets, the Japanese government bond market is significantly more regulated. The primary market yield on government bonds is negotiated between the ministry of finance and an underwriting syndicate of leading financial institutions. Until the mid-1970s, members of this syndicate were required to hold new issues for at least one year, after

---

[1] For the time being, the auction system will supplement rather than replace the established tender system. In the longer term, however, the tender system could eventually be replaced by a series of quarterly auctions.

FIGURE 1–3
The U.K. and U.S. Auction Systems

Name of System	New U.K. System Auction	Current U.S. System Auction
Method of allotment	Stock allotted at price bid	Stock allotted at yield bid
Market makers bid	Price	Yield
Noncompetitive bids	Up to £100,000 at average price	Up to US$1,000,000 at average yield
Type of issues sold	Short-, medium-, long-; current-coupon issues	2,3,4,5,7,10,30 years at present, current coupons
Approximate announcement date	Several weeks in advance	Regularly scheduled throughout the year
Final details announced	A minimum of one week in advance	6–8 days in advance
When-issued trading	Yes	Yes
Size	£1–1¼ billion	Up to US$10 billion
Settlement	Same-day payment for bids of more than £100,000; next-day payment for bids of up to £100,000; next-day delivery	4–10 days
Restrictions on bidders	None	Only market makers may bid
Market makers required to bid	No	Yes
Partly paid issues	Yes	No
Entire amount allotted	Not necessarily	Yes
Restrictions on take-up by individual market makers	The Bank may limit individual bidders to 25% of an issue	No
Other long-term funding in addition to auctions	Yes	No
Issues reopened	The Bank may issue additional tranches by tap or auction 28 days or more after auction	Possible in successive regularly scheduled auctions
Bids submitted (local time)	10:00 AM GMT	1:00 PM EST

which they could be resold to the Bank of Japan. This system came under strain in the second half of the 1970s, when public sector deficits rose to as high as 8 percent of gross national product (GNP). In addition, the government realized that if the inflationary consequences of large budget imbalances were to be avoided, a secondary market had to be developed, in which government paper could be placed with nonbank investors.

In response to these considerations, reforms were introduced in the late 1970s and 1980s. An auction system for the distribution of two- and four-year government bonds was introduced, and more recently for 20-year bonds. Nonetheless, the government still plays an active role in determining the cost of government debt issuance. Yields on most new 10-year issues—which are the principal financing instrument—are still negotiated, and yield differences between new and outstanding issues remain, although they are considered smaller than in the past.

The secondary market, on the other hand, reflects to a much greater extent the free play of market forces. Bond syndicate members are no longer required to hold newly issued bonds for at least one year, and the pace of trading volume in the over-the-counter secondary market has increased by five-fold since 1984. There has been a large flow of funds into institutions that invest in and actively manage fixed-income securities. In addition, the pricing of bonds has become much more responsive to both domestic and international economic or political developments. Consequently, the volatility of the Japanese government bond market, which had been remarkably low by international standards during the first half of the 1980s, has risen sharply in the past two years (see Figure 1–4).

Lack of liquidity continues to be a problem. Actively traded securities are not available across the maturity spectrum. For example, the Japanese government sector does not include a well-developed market for Treasury bills, as bills are not regularly issued at market rates in significant quantities. Furthermore, most trading activity tends to be concentrated in the benchmark 10-year issue. The benchmark effect in Japan—in which the most actively traded issue commands a premium versus other similar issues—is by far the most pronounced of any market. For example, during 1987 the spread between nonbenchmark Japanese government

FIGURE 1-4
20-Day Yield Volatility of Japanese Government Benchmark Series

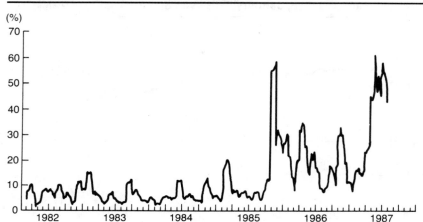

bonds and the benchmark issue averaged 25 basis points, and on several occasions exceeded 60 basis points (see Figure 1–5 on next page). In contrast, the spread between "off-the-run" issues in the U.S. Treasury market and the benchmark issue is typically less than 10 basis points.

To improve market liquidity and efficiency, the Japanese government has encouraged the development of a futures market. The futures contract, which began trading on the Tokyo Stock Exchange in October 1985, has already become the most active coupon futures contract in the world. Nonetheless, despite the tremendous success of the contract, the arbitrage between the cash and futures market is far from perfect. Since the contract began trading, there has been a tendency for the price of the futures contract to be expensive relative to the cash market, in that a long cash/short futures position has, at times, yielded a rate of return substantially greater than the cost of financing the cash position.[2]

The Japanese Ministry of Finance has also proposed changes to foster the development of a Japanese corporate bond market.

---

[2] Reasons for this situation are discussed in Nicholas Sargen et al., *Trading Patterns in the Japanese Government Bond Market* (Salomon Brothers Inc) October 1986.

FIGURE 1–5

Ten-Year Japanese Government Bond Yields—Benchmark Series versus Nonbenchmark Average, January 1983–September 1986

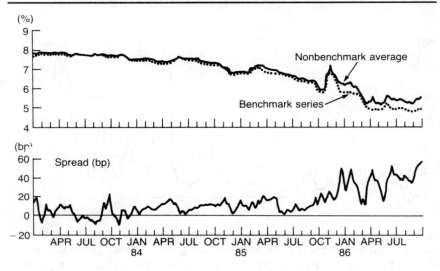

Even though Japan has become the world's largest creditor nation, Japanese corporations have raised more capital overseas through the issuance of stocks and bonds than domestically, while obtaining the vast majority of financing through borrowings from domestic banks. Japanese corporations have found issuance procedures far simpler and interest rates generally lower in Euroyen and Swiss franc bond markets. This reflects the tedious registration procedures and controls on issue volumes and interest rates that have plagued the domestic market. The new proposed procedures would halve the time necessary to receive approval for issuance and greatly simplify filing procedures.

Developing a domestic corporate bond market will not be easy: the Euroyen market, which has also been liberalized recently, has shown strong resilience. Nevertheless, the largest potential demand for Japanese corporate yen-denominated bonds is in Japan. Deregulation will likely raise the share of domestic issuance at the expense of the Euroyen market, and once shelf registration comes to Japan, the domestic market should become a more important site for corporate bond issues.

West German Bond Market

Although West Germany boasts the largest economy within Western Europe, its government bond market ranks fifth overall and third within Europe in outstandings. This reflects the relatively low level of public deficits in the past decade, the existence of a tax on secondary market trading of West German securities, and the unique method of financing the public sector through the banking system. The latter situation has evolved because of the presence of universal banking in West Germany: banks are permitted to engage in securities activities, including underwriting, as well as traditional banking activities.

The tradition of bank financing is evident in the large volume of outstanding bank bonds and Schuldscheine (certificate of indebtedness placed with banks), which are largely issued to finance the public sector. At the end of 1987, Schuldscheine accounted for less than 30 percent of total West German debt, down from 58 percent in 1980. Bank bond issuance has also slowed in recent years, although this sector remains the largest component of the deutsche mark bond market. The two principal forms of bank bonds, mortgage and commercial bonds, are considered similar in credit quality to securities issued by the federal government because of their legal structure: both are collateralized fixed-income securities with a first charge on the prime assets of the issuing banks.

Only recently has the federal government begun to rely more heavily on the bond market than on bank financing. Public authority bonds—issued by a syndicate of German and foreign banks—accounted for approximately 65 percent of total publicly issued outstanding debt at the end of 1987, compared with only 40 percent in 1981.

The West German government bond market also differs from other major government markets in the importance of international investors. In recent years, foreign investors have been the principal buyers of new issues, accounting for up to 80 percent of sales. In part, this can be attributed to the existence of transfer taxes on secondary market trading of West German securities. A tax of 0.2 percent is levied on West German investors, while nonresidents pay only half this amount. The lower rate for foreign investors also accounts for the active international market for West German securities in London.

The recent imposition of a 10 percent withholding tax on domestic West German bonds from 1989 on is likely to dampen foreign investor demand for these securities. The tax may also present a serious impediment to the evolution of Frankfurt as an international financial center.

Market Conventions

Apart from these basic differences in market size, distribution procedures, and tax and regulatory treatment among the major financial centers, there are also more subtle variations in the conventions used to conduct transactions in these markets. For example, in most Eurobond markets—as well as in the domestic markets of the United States, Japan, and Canada—almost all bond trading takes place over-the-counter. In the United Kingdom and West Germany, however, the stock exchange plays a major role. Accrued interest may be handled in different ways—for example, the familiar price-plus-accrued trading used in the Eurobond and many domestic markets, or "flat" trading in the West German Schuldscheine sector. Yields to maturity are calculated in the following ways: on an annual compounding basis in the Euromarkets and most continental government markets; semiannually in the United States, Canada, the United Kingdom and Australia, and other domestic markets; and on a semiannual, simple-interest basis in Japan.

Similarly, there are significant market-to-market differences in procedures for custody, settlement, new issues, government regulation, permissible maturity ranges, withholding taxes, and access to markets by foreign investors and borrowers. These differences are summarized in the Appendix to this chapter.

ROLE OF THE EUROBOND MARKET

In view of the ongoing efforts to liberalize the domestic financial markets in many industrial countries, the role of the Eurobond markets is widely debated. Since its origins in the early 1960s, the Eurobond market has thrived, mainly because it has offered both issuers and investors a refuge from tax and regulatory barriers in competing financial centers. Consequently, the Eurobond market has provided a means of arbitraging yields in the various national bond markets.

Evolution of the Eurobond Market

The birth of the Eurobond market is commonly traced to 1963, when the United States passed the Interest Equalization Tax (IET). Following World War II, European and other foreign borrowers increasingly turned to the U.S. capital market, raising a total of $14 billion in the Yankee market in 1963. However, in response to the concerns of U.S. authorities about capital outflows from the United States, President John F. Kennedy proposed a tax—the IET—to equalize the cost of borrowing in Europe and the United States. The rate was set high enough to choke off the Yankee bond market, except to Canadian borrowers and international organizations that were exempt from the tax. As a result, foreign borrowers turned to the Eurodollar bond market as a source of funds. Also, in the mid-1960s, the Eurobond market benefited from a voluntary credit restraint program in the United States; this program encouraged overseas subsidiaries of U.S. corporations to tap international markets for funds.

The evolution of the Eurobond market since the 1960s has been influenced primarily by currency fluctuations, changes in tax and regulatory procedures, and factors affecting the overall liquidity of the market, as well as by shifts in global payments imbalances. Although commercial banks played the predominant role in recycling surplus funds from the OPEC countries in the 1970s, the Eurobond markets served as vehicles for financing industrial country borrowers—especially governments and state enterprises of European countries—as well as for international financial institutions, such as the World Bank and the regional multilateral lending institutions (see Figure 1–6). By comparison, issuance by U.S. corporations—though remaining moderate throughout the 1970s—picked up considerably during the 1980s, as the U.S. dollar strengthened. In 1986, U.S. corporations were the principal borrowers in the Euromarkets, often achieving lower borrowing costs than available in the U.S. capital market.

FIGURE 1–6

Gross Issuance in the Eurobond Markets, 1963–1987 (In Billions of U.S. Dollars)

	1963–1969	1970–1979	1980–1987
Eurobonds, total	$11.8	$92.8	$650.1
U.S. companies	4.5	10.6	138.4
Other companies	2.8	33.1	⎧
Governments and			412.8
state enterprises	4.0	39.8	⎩
International			
organizations	0.5	9.23	98.8

Source: Morgan Bank, *World Financial Markets*, March 1978 and July 1984 issues, and Salomon Brothers Inc. for 1980–1987.

Currency Considerations

The importance of currency movements to this market is apparent from Figure 1–7 which shows the currency composition of new issues in the Eurobond market from 1977 to 1987. Until 1987, the share of Eurodollar bond issuance ranged from a low of 52 percent in 1978—a period of dollar weakness—to a high of 81 percent in 1982, following the dollar's rebound. Since then, the share of Eurodollar bonds has steadily declined. During 1987, the U.S.

FIGURE 1–7

Currency Composition of New Eurobond Issues, 1977–1987

	1977–1979	1980–1984	1985	1986	1987
U.S. dollar	62.2%	79.6%	69.7%	62.8%	41.8%
Japanese yen	0.6	1.0	5.2	10.1	16.6
Deutsche mark	25.7	7.7	8.4	9.2	10.1
British pound	1.6	3.5	4.2	5.8	11.6
European currency unit	0.8	3.0	5.5	4.1	5.5
Canadian dollar	2.1	2.2	2.3	3.2	4.4
Australian dollar	—	—	2.4	2.7	6.6
Other	7.0	2.9	2.3	2.1	3.9

Source: Morgan Bank, *World Financial Markets* and Salomon Brothers Inc.

dollar share fell to only 42 percent as a result of both the plunge of the dollar and rising U.S. interest rates.

For the most part, issuing trends are determined by investors' preferences for currencies: borrowers can now easily alter their currency and interest rate exposure through the use of swaps (see the next section). The investor base in the Eurobond market is often more diverse than that available to issuers in domestic capital markets. In addition, these investors, primarily European, Japanese and, more recently, U.S. financial institutions, as well as retail investors—the so-called Belgian dentists—are particularly sensitive to fluctuations in relative currency values. As a result, currency fluctuations also affect yield relationships, not only between U.S. dollar and non-U.S. dollar issues but also between Eurodollar bonds and those issued in the domestic U.S. market.

Impact of Withholding Taxes

A major challenge to the Eurobond market occurred in 1984, when the United States, Canada, and several European countries, including West Germany and France, repealed withholding taxes on purchases of domestic securities. Prior to July 1984, a 10 percent withholding tax applied to purchases of U.S. securities by foreign investors. However, a U.S. treaty allowed U.S. corporations to circumvent the tax by issuing bonds through their affiliates in the Netherlands Antilles. Consequently, an anomaly existed in which some U.S. corporations—usually high grade institutions—could borrow more cheaply in the Euromarket than in the U.S. bond market, and often at yields below those on U.S. Treasuries (see Figure 1–8).

The July 1984 decision by the U.S. government to remove the 10 percent withholding tax made U.S. government securities and domestic U.S. corporate bonds more attractive to foreign investors. It also fundamentally altered the spread relationships between domestic and Eurodollar bonds. Thus, yields on U.S. Treasuries fell below those of Eurodollar bonds following the repeal of the withholding tax. At the same time, yield spreads between Eurodollar bonds and comparable domestically issued corporate bonds narrowed, but were not completely eliminated. One reason is that

FIGURE 1–8

10-Year Eurodollar versus 10-Year U.S. Treasury (Yields and Spread,
Weekly Dates, January 6, 1983–January 14, 1988)

Source: Salomon Brothers Inc.

Eurobonds are issued in "bearer" format, while domestic corporate bonds are registered. Investors are willing to pay a premium
for bearer bonds, both to remain anonymous and to protect against
the possibility of a reimposition of withholding taxes.

The effect of the repeal of withholding taxes in the United
States, West Germany, and other European countries is apparent
in the stepped-up purchases of government securities by foreign
investors: purchases of U.S. Treasuries by Japanese investors, in
particular, soared immediately after the U.S. withholding tax was
repealed. Government securities, rather than Eurobonds, now
represent the principal fixed-income foreign asset acquired by
international investors.

Nonetheless, contrary to earlier forecasts that elimination of
the U.S. withholding tax would lead to the demise of the Euromarkets, gross issuance of Eurobonds continued to soar in 1985 and
1986. Apart from direct cost savings, issuers are attracted to the
Eurobond markets by the relative ease with which deals can be
brought to market. Issues can be arranged in a few days, without
having to go through complicated and time-consuming registration
procedures.

The principal drawback of the Euromarkets for U.S. investors is that Eurobonds must be "seasoned." That is, because Eurobonds are not registered with the Securities and Exchange Commission, U.S. investors generally cannot buy them in the primary market, but must wait a specific period until primary distribution is complete. Consequently, there is a different investor base for pre- and post-seasoned Eurobands.

Problems of Illiquidity

Issuance of the U.S. dollar floating-rate note (FRN) market—the largest sector of the FRN market—declined by 20 percent in 1986, after rising steadily for 10 years. Several factors were responsible for this reversal, including investors' increasing preference for fixed-rate debt in a declining interest rate environment. First, aggressive underwriting practices in the primary market drove coupons on sovereign notes below the London interbank offered rate, thereby significantly reducing the appeal of these securities to traditional commercial bank investors. Second, other new forms of floating-rate finance, such as Eurocommercial paper and fixed-rate debt matched with interest rate swaps, offered attractive rates to issuers.

A crisis in the perpetual sector at year-end 1986 further weakened investor confidence in much of the FRN market. Perpetual issuance by commercial banks surged in late 1985 and in 1986 in response to new central bank regulations in several countries, such as the United Kingdom, Canada, Australia, France, and the United States. These regulations treat certain forms of perpetuals as primary capital. Nearly $8.5 billion of these securities was brought to market in 1986, accounting for roughly one quarter of the total Eurodollar FRN market. The perpetuals incorporated different put features and a wide range of provisions in the event of nonpayment of dividends. Late in the year, growing concern about the degree of investor protection dampened market liquidity and led to dramatic price declines. Weakness in this sector spread to dated FRNs, bringing an unprecedented lack of liquidity to the secondary market and limiting new issues in the FRN market. During 1987, gross issuance of Eurodollar FRNs dwindled to less than $4 billion, or less than one tenth the 1986 amount.

The Eurobond markets, more generally, have suffered from increasingly intense competition among underwriters, causing market makers to reassess whether the resulting sharp narrowing in underwriting and dealing spreads is sustainable over the longer term. This situation has cast a pall over the Eurobond markets and the willingness of individual securities firms to maintain a high profile in the market. The market undoubtedly faces a period of further retrenchment immediately ahead. Nonetheless, it will continue to serve as a major source of finance for sovereigns, multilateral lending institutions, high-grade multinational corporations, and international banks.

SWAP ARBITRAGE IN INTERNATIONAL CAPITAL MARKETS

In addition to the Eurobond market, the development of currency and interest-rate swap markets has greatly expanded the breadth and depth of arbitrage across the world's major capital markets. Swap contracts enable market participants to take advantage of cheaper funding in one market, and then convert the resulting liability to the desired interest-rate and currency exposure. Similarly, by using swaps, payments on attractively priced securities can be converted to a wide range of interest-rate and currency profiles.

Swap contracts are agreements between two parties to exchange interest payments of differing character—fixed or floating interest rates and/or denominated in different currencies—based on a notional principal amount for a specified period. In general, no principal is exchanged up front or at maturity.

In the most common type of interest rate swap, one counterparty makes payments based on a fixed rate of interest, while the other party's payments are referenced off a floating-rate index such as a three- or six-month LIBOR. Nondollar interest rate swaps have also become increasingly common: these involve the exchange of fixed-rate payments denominated in a currency such as the yen, for variable payments referenced off a common floating-rate index in that currency, such as CD or interbank deposit rates.

Cross-currency interest-rate swaps involve the exchange of payments in different currencies and also on different interest rate bases, that is, from fixed to floating rates. Typically, this transaction involves the exchange of nondollar fixed-rate interest payments for U.S. dollar-denominated floating-rate interest payments.

Motives for Swaps

An increasing number of market participants use swaps to change the interest rate or currency exposure in attractively priced assets: Investors swap payments on mortgage, Eurobond, floating-rate note, high-yield or real estate securities to generate returns far above those available for comparable credits on traditional investment vehicles. The main motivation of swap counterparties, however, has been the opportunity to exploit differential borrowing advantages to raise funds cheaply. Typically, fixed-rate bond markets have tended to require a wider quality spread between higher- and lower-rated counterparties than is typical of floating-rate markets. Although the higher-rated issuer often borrows more cheaply than does the lower-rated issuer in both markets, the former participant generally enjoys a greater advantage in the bond market. Conversely, the lower-rated issuer usually faces less of a quality differential in the floating-rate market. If each borrower raises funds in the market in which it has a relative advantage, the resultant interest payments can be swapped to achieve cheaper funding for both.[3]

A wide range of factors leads to disparities in the pricing of debt across capital markets. These include regulatory barriers to capital mobility such as exchange controls or withholding taxes; relatively greater risk aversion among investors in bond markets; differences in the taxes imposed on interest and capital income; and differences in the information available to investors and lenders in different capital markets, that, in turn, affect perceptions of credit risk. As a result, at any point in time, borrowers can often

---

[3] See also Ellen Evans and Gioia Parente, "What Drives Interest Rate Swaps," Salomon Brothers Inc., 1987.

achieve substantial cost savings by choosing one capital market over another (see Figure 1–9).

The Euro-Australian bond market, which has grown very rapidly in recent years and is almost completely swap-driven, illustrates these considerations. The cost savings available to a borrower in the Euro-Australian dollar bond market generally reflect the arbitrage of structural barriers and differing credit preferences across markets. An Australian withholding tax imposed on foreign holders of private placements issued by Australian borrowers restricts these entities' access to international capital markets. In addition, Australian entities launching public issues pay much larger yield premiums in the Euro-Australian dollar bond market than in the Eurodollar bond market. Shorter-term note issuance facilities and Eurocommercial paper offer even lower premiums.

This yield differential largely results from differences in each sector's investor base: Investors in the Euro-Australian dollar market tend to be retail-based, while institutional investors comprise a larger share of the other sectors. At the same time, well-known international borrowers pay much lower spreads in Euro-Australian dollars, as a result of the recent increase in international demand for high-yielding assets such as Australian dollar bonds. Consequently, non-Australian entities can often lower the cost of borrowing U.S. dollars by issuing Australian dollar-denominated bonds and entering into a currency swap to convert the final payment stream to U.S. dollars. Similarly, Australian entities are often able to lower the all-in cost of debt by borrowing U.S. dollars and swapping into their local currency.

Growth of Swaps

The increased utilization of interest rate swaps in an asset/liability context has caused the volume of these swap agreements to soar. According to the International Swap Dealers Association (ISDA), the notional volume of U.S. dollar interest-rate swaps—the largest interest-rate swap market—transacted in the second quarter of 1987 rose to approximately $68 billion, an increase of roughly 40 percent over the 1986 period. The notional volume of outstanding interest-rate swaps was estimated at $313 billion at year-end 1986,

FIGURE 1–9
Medium- to Long-Term Financing Alternatives—All-in Borrowing Costs for AA Credits, July 24, 1987
(Semiannual-Bond-Equivalent Basis)

	Fixed Rate					Floating Rate[a]			
	3 Years	5 Years	7 Years	10 Years	30 Years	3 Years	5 Years	7 Years	10 Years
U.S. dollar									
Domestic bond (Ind)	8.45%	8.70%	9.10%	9.35%	10.10%	-10bp	-26bp	-20bp	-16bp
Euro straight	8.30	8.75	9.25	9.55	NA	-25	-21	-5	-4
Euro FRN[b]	NA	NA	NA	NA	NA	5	5	5	5
Domestic MTN	8.45	8.70	9.10	9.35	NA	-10	-26	-20	-16
Euro MTN	8.50	8.75	NA	NA	NA	-5	-21	NA	NA
Foreign currency (Swapped to U.S. Dollars)									
Euro-Canadian	8.55%	8.93%	9.24%	9.45%		-13bp	-14bp	-17bp	-16bp
Euro-Sterling	NA	8.93	9.52	9.93		NA	-13	9	22
Euro-Deutschemark	NA	9.27	9.86	9.90		NA	18	41	24
Euroyen	NA	9.48	9.90	10.32		NA	38	45	61
Foreign Swiss franc	NA	9.50	9.80	9.91		NA	40	35	25
Euro-ECU	NA	9.03	9.32	9.58		NA	-5	-10	-5
Euro-Australian	8.15	8.71	NA	NA		-51	-36	NA	NA
Yankee Australian	8.17	8.72	NA	NA		-49	-35	NA	NA
Yankee New Zealand	8.11	NA	NA	NA		-54	NA	NA	NA
Reference rates									
U.S. Gov't.	7.81%	8.13%	8.40%	8.58%	8.83%				

[a] Represents fixed-rate debt swapped into floating-rate exposure; basis-point spreads are quoted above/below six-month LIBOR.
[b] Indicative quotes for AA sovereign borrower; shown for comparison purposes. ECU European currency unit. FRN Floating-rate note. MTN Medium-term note. NA Not available.

nearly as large as the nominal value of outstanding Eurodollar bonds.

The volume of nondollar interest rate swaps has also risen dramatically over the past two years: market participants estimate that interest rate swaps denominated in deutsche marks currently account for one third to one half of the total DM100 billion interest-rate and currency swaps executed by West German banks and subsidiaries by the end of May 1987. By comparison, in 1986 interest-rate swaps represented only about 10 percent of the total swap transactions by these institutions. Similarly, yen interest-rate swap transactions have ballooned from an estimated ¥3 trillion in 1986 when the market began, to approximately ¥5.5 trillion in the first four months of 1987. In this market, a city bank typically swaps floating-rate liabilities into longer-term fixed-rate funds, with a long-term credit bank as a counterparty.

FIGURE 1-10
New Issue Currency Swap Activity, 1981-First Half 1987 (U.S. Dollars in Billions)

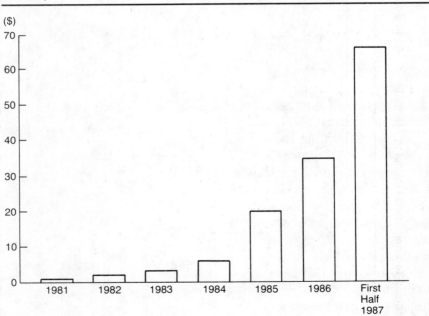

*Annualized

The currency swap market has also continued to expand rapidly: in 1986, the volume of new international bonds swapped at the time of issuance by the issuer to another currency rose by 80 percent to $35 billion from $19 billion in 1985. This pace has continued in 1987: Preliminary estimates for 1987 show currency swap-driven international issuance rising to $55 billion, nearly double the previous year's figure, although the issuance of new debt has declined by almost one quarter (see Figure 1–10). This represents more than 30 percent of total new issuance during the year, twice the share in 1986. Other currencies swaps linked to outstanding assets and liabilities also continue to climb. According to the best estimates of market participants, such transactions account for up to two times the volume of currency swaps associated with new debt issues; this suggests that the total value of currency swaps executed during 1987 may have reached as much as $165 billion.

INVESTING IN INTERNATIONAL BONDS

Just as borrowers are interested in obtaining the lowest all-in cost of finance, investors in international fixed-income securities typically are seeking to maximize their overall rate of return for a given degree of risk tolerance. The strategies that individual investors pursue vary depending on their underlying objectives, views about the direction of interest rates and exchange rates, and willingness to accept interest rate and currency risks.

Throughout the 1970s, many multicurrency fixed-income portfolio managers followed a "one-dimensional" investment strategy. If they thought a particular currency would strengthen, they bought bonds denominated in that currency. Conversely, they tended to avoid those securities denominated in currencies that they expected to weaken. To the extent that these portfolio managers were successful in anticipating trends in the foreign exchange markets, such a strategy worked well.

During the 1970s, exchange rates were generally more volatile than interest rates, so it made sense to focus on the currency dimension. Moreover, there was usually a positive relationship between currency strength and bond price movements, with the result that the performance of fixed-income markets tended to reinforce the profit from a correct currency forecast. From 1976 through 1978, for example, the DM, Swiss franc, and yen were among the best performing currencies, and their respective fixed-income markets rallied virtually throughout this period. At the other extreme, foreign investors either in dollar bonds in 1976–79, or in the U.K. sterling fixed-income market in 1975–76, would have seen their portfolios' value decimated by severe foreign exchange losses reinforced by sharp bond price declines.

In recent years, however, the "pick a currency" approach would have been much less successful. During the 1980s, interest rate differentials have been a key determinant of currency movements; thus, a strong rally in bonds denominated in a particular currency was frequently accompanied by foreign exchange losses. For example, U.S. dollar bonds posted the largest price gains of any major market during the worldwide rally that took place in 1985 and 1986. However, this sharp relative decline of dollar interest rates also contributed to the dollar's 60% depreciation against the yen and major continental currencies. Consequently, yen and DM-denominated bonds generated a much better overall return than did the dollar sector during this period. By comparison, during 1987 U.S. dollar-denominated bonds underperformed non-dollar bonds for both currency and interest rate reasons. The dollar continued to depreciate sharply even though interest rate differentials widened in favor of the dollar.

Separating Currency and Interest-Rate Exposure

In essence, then, a multicurrency investment manager is now confronted with portfolio decisions that are at least two-dimensional: they involve expectations for both exchange rates and interest rates. Figure 1–11 shows strategies that may be appropriate depending on the mix of interest-rate and exchange-rate outcomes. For example, if interest rate differentials favoring the dollar are expected to widen and the dollar to strengthen (Quadrant 1), an appropriate strategy would be to increase the weight of nondollar bonds in the portfolio, but to short the currencies versus the dollar. Conversely, if interest rate differentials are expected to narrow while the dollar weakens (Quadrant 3),

FIGURE 1-11
Exchange Rate and Interest Rate Movements

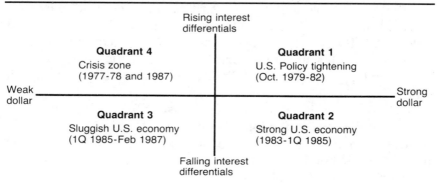

a strategy of acquiring dollar-bonds and shorting the U.S. dollar would be appropriate. In this respect, it may make sense for investors to separate their currency and interest-rate decisions.

Fully Hedged Bonds

Fully hedged bonds provide a means by which investors can eliminate currency risk completely while diversifying their bond-market exposure. The entire stream of coupon and principal payments in a foreign currency is sold forward for the home currency. For example, a U.S. investor buying a fully hedged gilt would sell forward the stream of receipts denominated in sterling for U.S. dollars. This would eliminate the currency exposure of the investment, and at the same time, transform the yield to that of a U.S. dollar-denominated security. The transaction, in effect, represents the application of interest rate parity to the long end of the maturity spectrum. However, because the investor has acquired a foreign bond, the price risk is that of the foreign bond—in this example, a British gilt.

The motive for purchasing a fully hedged bond is to take advantage of anomalies arising when the arbitrage is not perfect. For example, in the mid-1980s, British gilts fully hedged into U.S. dollars occasionally offered as much as a 50-100 basis point pickup in yield over a U.S. Treasury. As long as investors consider gilts and U.S. Treasuries to have comparable credit risks, purchase of such an asset would be highly attractive. The arbitrage arises from the pricing of the long-dated forward currency contract based on differentials in Eurointerest rates (e.g., between Eurodollar bond yields and Eurosterling bond yields). These may differ from interest-rate differentials for securities in domestic bond markets; for example, yields on U.S. Treasuries versus those on British gilts.

One factor limiting the widespread use of fully hedged bonds is the lack of liquidity in the long-dated forward exchange market. In the event an investor wishes to liquidate a position before the maturity of the bond, significant transactions costs may be incurred in unwinding the original position.

Rolling Hedge

Figure 1–12 illustrates a situation where an investor can arbitrage yield curves between the U.S. and nondollar bond markets, while removing most of the currency exposure through the use of

FIGURE 1–12
U.S. Treasury and West German Government Bond Yield Curves

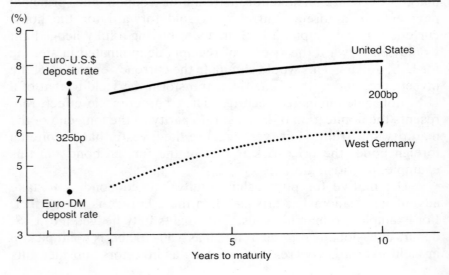

short-term rolling hedges. In this example, a U.S. investor buys a 10-year West German government bond, effectively surrendering 200 basis points in yield relative to 10-year U.S. Treasuries. At the same time, deutsche marks are sold for U.S. dollars three months forward to cover principal plus interest for the three months. The investor thereby picks up the short-term interest rate differential of 325 basis points, more than offsetting the loss in yield at the long end of the curve.

This strategy provides exposure to the West German bond market, such that the investor stands to gain as long as West German bonds outperform U.S. Treasuries (in local currency terms), or the two yield curves retain their relative shapes. The strategy eliminates most, but not all of the currency risk, in that the investor is still exposed to any changes in principal valuation. By the same token, the investor does not face the problem of illiquidity associated with fully hedged bonds, because the market for short-term currency forwards is substantially more liquid than for long-dated forwards. Apart from providing potential yield enhancement, investments in currency hedged foreign bonds may provide investors with a means of capturing the diversification benefits of foreign bonds.[4]

Indexing

In addition to "active" strategies in which investors attempt to benefit from expected currency and interest-rate movements, it has become more common in recent years for investors to pursue passive strategies. Consequently, index returns are increasingly being used as a comprehensive representation of "market performance," against which fund managers can compare the returns on their portfolios. In the United States, indices such as the Salomon Brothers Broad Grade Investment Index and the Shearson-Lehman Brothers Index are commonly used yardsticks for comparing performance in the U.S. bond market, as well as for formulating asset allocation decisions.

---

[4] See Vilas Gadkari, *The Role of Currency-Hedged Bonds in International Fixed-Income Diversification* Salomon Brothers Inc., June 1987.

FIGURE 1–13
Salomon Brothers World Government Bond Index

	Annual Return					
	Local Currency Terms			U.S. Dollar Terms		
	1985	1986	1987	1985	1986	1987
World Government Bond Index	16.23%	13.52%	4.85%	27.27%	23.05%	18.41%
United States	20.94	15.73	1.93	20.94	15.73	1.93
Canada	21.91	14.19	3.62	14.79	15.72	10.01
West Germany	10.61	7.99	37.18	42.02	37.18	29.38
Japan	8.68	10.78	5.96	36.84	40.09	38.11
United Kingdom	12.13	11.86	15.51	40.20	14.76	46.58
Switzerland	5.80	5.93	4.56	34.26	34.99	32.59
Netherlands	10.09	7.63	7.55	42.60	36.34	32.11
France	16.43	14.39	5.84	50.52	34.10	26.60
Australia	7.03	19.58	18.84	-12.06	16.63	29.00

As bond market performance has become more important on a worldwide scale, the need has arisen for an accurate, replicable fixed-income benchmark. Salomon Brothers' World Government Bond Index provides a comprehensive measure of the total return performance of the domestic government bond markets in each of nine countries—the United States, Japan, the United Kingdom, West Germany, France, Canada, the Netherlands, Australia, and Switzerland—and a weighted average of the nine countries. Total returns are reported on a monthly basis, both in local currency terms and in U.S. dollar terms, to assess the extent to which performance is affected by currency and interest-rate movements (see Figure 1–13).

SUMMARY AND CONCLUSIONS

As a result of the rapid growth of the Eurobond market, the evolution of interest-rate and currency swaps, and the liberalization of domestic financial markets, fixed-income markets throughout the world have become increasingly linked in the 1980s. Issuers in the international fixed-income markets now routinely consider all available sources of finance irrespective of currency or interest-rate structure—whether fixed or floating—to obtain the cheapest all-in cost source of funding. Similarly, international investors have become significant buyers of fixed-income securities throughout the world. The influence of foreign investors is especially apparent in the U.S. Treasury market in recent years and is also a significant factor in the British gilt market, the West German government bond market, and other European markets. Consequently, the U.S. Treasury yield curve now provides a basis for assessing relative values in the fixed-income markets around the globe, as well as in the U.S. corporate sector.

The process of bond market integration, however, is still not complete. Several barriers remain that effectively limit the substitutability of bonds issued in the various national markets and those issued in the international markets. Capital controls and withholding taxes remain in a number of countries, and, in the case of West Germany, a withholding tax was reimposed in 1989. Similarly, registration requirements apply to bonds issued in the United

States and other countries, and Eurobonds are affected by seasoning requirements. In addition, investors' willingness to hold foreign securities are strongly influenced by perceptions of credit risk, which vary considerably across countries, as well as by tax accounting and regulatory considerations. Furthermore, some investors—especially retail investors and Japanese institutions—are more oriented by current yield considerations, while most large institutional investors tend to be "total rate-of-return" oriented.

As a result, pricing anomalies often appear across different bond markets, creating arbitrage opportunities for lenders and borrowers. For the most part, the arbitrage that takes place through the Eurobond market, swap markets, and other derivative instruments is generally effective in narrowing cost or yield differentials, particularly in those instances in which bonds are actively traded. Arbitrage opportunities are often seen as windows of opportunity that open and close over relatively short periods. In some cases, however, pricing anomalies persist, especially when markets or sectors lack depth and breadth. Consequently, prices observed in the marketplace may not always reflect perfect arbitrage.

APPENDIX

U.K. Denominated Bonds

	U.K. Gilts	Euro-Sterling Bonds
Market size (year-end 1987)	£137 billion $258 billion	£25 billion $47 billion
Issuing process	Tender system supplemented with an experimental auction system May 87. New system modeled on US Treas. system.	International underwriting syndicate
Issue size	£800–1,250 million	£30–100 million
Maturity at issue	1–30 years (to 37 years if index-linked; a few perpetuals).	Usually 5–10 years
Call features	None	Variable
Liquidity	Excellent	Variable
Dealing size	£1 million	£½ million
Dealing spreads	$\frac{1}{16}$–$\frac{1}{8}$ point	½ point
Interest; day count	Semiannual; Actual/365	Annual; $\frac{30}{360}$
Settlement	1 business day	5 business days
Custody	Physical, through the Central Gilt Office.	Euroclear, Cedel
Quotron ticker	UKTG	—
Seasoning (U.S. resident)	40 days	3 months
Withholding tax (U.S. resident)	None. U.S. investors must apply for exemption from 27% tax on all but FOTRA or Section 99 Gilts.	None
Ex-dividend date	37 days before interest payment date. Some issues have a "special ex-dividend" period of three weeks before the ex-dividend date.	

Japanese Yen-Denominated Bonds

	Japanese Government Bonds	Euro-Yen Bonds
Market size (year-end 1987)	¥150 trillion $1.2 trillion	¥8 trillion $70 billion
Issue size	¥100–2,500 billion	¥5–100 billion
Issuing process	10-year currently issued via fixed allocation syndicate. Auction of some 10-year issues since 1987. Other maturities issued via auction.	International underwriting syndicate
Maturity at issue	2–20 years	5–12 years
Call features	Some bonds issued with call provisions, but no bonds have been called.	Variable
Liquidity	Good in benchmark issue. Current 10-year benchmark #89.	Good in latest sovereign issue.
Dealing size	London: ¥1–10 billion Tokyo: ¥1–20 billion	¥100–500 million
Dealing spreads	Benchmark: 1 bp with dealers, 1½ bp with customer liquid nonbenchmark: 2 bp off-the-run: 5–7 bp.	¼–½ point
Settlement	Regular settlement days on 10th, 20th and last day of month. Proposal to change settlement days to 5th, 10th, 15th, etc.	5 business days
Interest; day count	Semiannual; Actual/365 (No leap) Quoted on a simple yield basis.	Annual; $^{30}/_{360}$
Custody	Citibank Tokyo	Euroclear, Cedel
Quotron ticker	YEN	—
Seasoning (U.S. resident)	40 days	3 months
Withholding tax (U.S. resident)	20% tax on interest reduced to 10% for U.S. investors. Must file for exemption.	None

Deutsche Mark-Denominated Bonds

	Government Bonds (Bunds)	Euro-Deutsche Mark Bonds
Market size (year-end 1987)	DM301 billion $191 billion	DM163 billion $103 billion
Issuing process	Underwritten by a fixed syndicate.	International underwriting syndicate.
Issue size	DM1–4 billion	DM100–1,500 million
Maturity at issue	2–30 years	5–20 years
Call features	Non-callable	Usually callable
Liquidity	Good	Fair
Dealing size	DM1 million	DM250,000
Dealing spreads	⅛–⅜ point	½–¾ point
Settlement	2 business days	5 business days
Interest; Day count	Annual; $^{30}/_{360}$	Annual; $^{30}/_{360}$
Custody	Book entry via custodian bank.	German bank, Euroclear, Cedel.
Quotron ticker	BUND Bundesrepublic BUNB Bundesbahn BUNP Bundespost	—
Seasoning (U.S. resident)	40 days	3 months
Withholding tax (U.S. resident)	None. U.S. investors need not file for exemption.	None

CHAPTER 2

FOREIGN EXCHANGE: TRANSACTIONS IN SPOT, FORWARDS, SWAPS, FUTURES, AND OPTIONS

Niso Abuaf
Stephan Schoess

Foreign-exchange transactions have become more and more important for importers, exporters, international and multinational corporations, and financial institutions as well as individuals. We review some basic concepts of the foreign-exchange market, explore the nature of various foreign-exchange transactions, and examine the properties of exchange-rate quotes and their relationships to each other. Finally, we discuss some of the risks involved in foreign-exchange transactions.

THE FOREIGN-EXCHANGE MARKET

Foreign exchange is foreign money in the form of notes and demand deposits. For obvious reasons, U.S. dollar-denominated notes and demand deposits are foreign exchange for residents outside the United States. British pound-denominated notes and demand deposits are foreign exchange for residents outside the United Kingdom.

In the foreign-exchange market participants exchange bank deposits denominated in one currency for bank deposits denominated in another currency. The exchange of bank notes constitutes only a very small fraction of total foreign-exchange market activities. As such, we ignore it here. The foreign-exchange market is primarily an over-the-counter market linked by telecommunication equipment such as telephones, telexes, and computers. Exchange-traded instruments such as futures and options, however, have been gaining market share. The market is the largest financial market in the world: average daily volume is estimated to be in excess of U.S. $250 billion.

The participants of the foreign-exchange market include individuals, international investors, importers and exporters, international corporations, financial institutions, and central banks. Financial institutions, primarily commercial banks, and, increasingly, other financial institutions, account for the large majority of all foreign-exchange transactions. The international money center banks execute orders for their customers and act as brokers. Most of these banks, though, see their main function as dealers/market makers. In their dealer role, banks make two-sided markets and are prepared to trade at any time with other market-making banks. Together, their foreign-exchange trading activities help to even out the temporary excesses of supply or demand that inevitably emerge from thousands of individual transactions executed each day.

Foreign-exchange transactions are executed by participants for a variety of purposes. Historically, most participants used the foreign-exchange market to finance some underlying commercial transaction, such as payment for imported goods. Recently, foreign-exchange transactions associated with capital-market operations—such as the issuance of debt abroad or the purchase of foreign financial assets—have surpassed transactions based on commercial activity. In addition, foreign-exchange transactions are used for hedging purposes. Hedging involves either the purchase or sale of foreign exchange to offset an exposed position or the deliberate assumption of an exchange risk in an effort to offset a similar risk in the opposite direction. Arbitrage transactions are usually executed by financial institutions. Foreign-exchange arbitrage describes activities that lead to profits from pricing inefficiencies in the market. These activities are, by definition, riskless only with respect to changes in exchange rates. As in any other market, speculative activities are an important component of foreign-exchange transactions. Speculation involves the intentional assumption of foreign-exchange risk (in the form of a long or short position) with the objective of generating profits from anticipated changes in exchange rates. Interventions by central banks are at times a very important component of foreign-exchange transactions. Central banks buy and sell foreign exchange to influence general money-market conditions, the level of exchange rates, and the volatility of exchange rates. Any intervention in the domestic money market affects the foreign-exchange market.

FOREIGN-EXCHANGE TRANSACTIONS

Foreign-exchange transactions involve the exchange of two currencies. When the deal has been agreed upon, the involved participants arrange for settlement. Settlement takes place in the two countries whose currencies are being used. In a transaction involving U.S. dollars and German marks, settlement is accomplished by payment of German marks in West Germany against payment of U.S. dollars in the United States. The currencies are actually delivered as debits and credits. The dealing center, that is, the place in which the deal is made, has to be distinguished from the settlement centers.

Spot Transactions

The most common transaction in the interbank market is a spot transaction.

Settlement
By convention, the agreed payment date, or "value date" as it is known, is two business days after the day the transaction is originated. The reasons for this custom are practical and administrative. The foreign-exchange market must overcome time differences of up to 24 hours. Therefore, a standard spot value date of either the same day (today) or the next business day (tomorrow) would be infeasible in most cases.

To be an eligible value date, the settlement date must be a business day in the countries of the currencies being traded. The same holds for the definition of a business/working day. Because of time-zone differences, settlement on any given working day will first be accomplished in the Far East, then in Europe, and lastly in the United States.

There are several exceptions to the two business days settlement rule:

1. If a foreign-exchange spot transaction involves the U.S. dollar and the first of the two days is a holiday in the United States but not in the other settlement center, the first day is counted as a business day for settlement purposes.
2. Spot transactions involving the Canadian dollar and Mexican peso versus the U.S. dollar are settled one business day after the transaction is originated.
3. Fridays are not part of the business week in most Middle Eastern countries, though Saturdays and Sundays are. For a typical spot transaction originating on Wednesday, the settlement for the non-Middle Eastern currency would occur on Friday while the Middle Eastern currency settles on Saturday.

Spot Rate Definition.   The spot rate is the price at which spot transactions are facilitated in the interbank market. In general, all quotations are only good for immediate dealing. At times, a specific spot quote given by a bank indicates whether the bank wants to increase or reduce its position in a particular currency. For example, if a bank owns more Swiss francs than it believes to be optimal, the bank sets its quote to discourage sellers of Swiss francs and encourage buyers of Swiss francs.

Quotation.   With the exception of the British pound and some related currencies such as the Australian and New Zealand dollars, exchange rates are expressed in direct quotes in the interbank market. Direct (European) quotes express exchange rates as the amount of domestic (non-U.S.) currency units per foreign currency unit. Usually, the foreign currency unit is the U.S. dollar. For direct quotes, the domestic (non-U.S.) currency is called the quoted currency and the foreign currency is the base currency. Depending on the value of the domestic currency relative to the foreign currency, direct quotes have been between zero and six decimal places. Typical direct quotes are

$$\text{DM} \quad 2.2110/\$$$
$$\text{Can\$} \quad 1.3760/\$$$

The British pound and related currencies are always expressed in indirect quotes. Indirect (American) quotes express exchange rates as the amount of foreign currency units per domestic currency unit. Historical reasons account for expressing the value of the British pound in indirect quotes. Until World War I, and to a certain extent also between the world wars, the British pound was the cornerstone of the international monetary system. All countries expressed the value of their respective currencies vis-à-vis the British pound. As the political, economic, and financial power moved from London to New York, countries started to express the value of their currencies in terms of the U.S. dollar. However, the tradition for quoting the British pound was not altered. In addition, the British pound remained a nondecimal currency until the early 1970s. A direct quotation for the British pound would have been extremely awkward. Typical indirect quotes (for non-Americans) are

$$\$ \ .4523/\text{DM}$$
$$\$ \ .7267/\text{Can\$}$$

Obviously, direct quotes and indirect quotes are not independent from each other. The relationship between them is reciprocal: 2.2110 is approximately the reciprocal of .4523 ($1 \div 2.2110 \approx .4523$). A direct DM/$ quote for a German trader is an indirect quote for an American trader. The following table illustrates this:

	Direct Quote		Indirect Quote	
German:	DM	2.2110/$	$	.4523/DM
American:	$	.4523/DM	DM	2.2110/$
Canadian:	Can$	1.3760/$	$	.7267/Can$
American:	$	.7267/Can$	Can$	1.3760/$
British:	—		$	1.4275/£
American:	$	1.4275/£	—	

Cross Rates.   The general practice of the foreign-exchange market is to quote the value of any currency with respect to the U.S. dollar. Once the rates for two currencies, such as the German mark and the Canadian dollar, are known in terms of the U.S. dollar, the price of the German mark in terms of the Canadian dollar as well as the price of Canadian dollar in terms of the German mark can be calculated. An exchange rate that is calculated based on two other exchange rates is called a cross rate. For the example cited earlier, the following holds:

$$DM/Can\$ = \frac{DM/\$}{Can\$/\$}$$

$$Can\$/DM = \frac{Can\$/\$}{DM/\$}$$

Given the spot rates of DM 2.2110/$ and Can$ 1.3760/$, we can calculate the following direct quotes:

$$\text{Germany: } \frac{DM\ 2.110/\$}{Can\$\ 1.3760/\$} = DM\ 1.6068/Can\$$$

$$\text{Canada: } \frac{Can\$\ 1.3760/\$}{DM\ 2.2110/\$} = Can\$\ .6223/DM$$

Following European custom, these quotes are expressed as DM 160.68/Can$ 100 and Can$ 62.23/DM 100. Cross-rate quotes are given for 100 units of the foreign currency. This practice reduces the number of decimal places used in the quotation. With spot rates of DM 2.2110/$, Can$ 1.3760/$, and $ 1.4275/£ the following cross rates can be calculated:

	Direct Quotes		Indirect Quotes	
Germany	DM	160.68/Can$ 100	Can$	62.23/DM 100
Canada	Can$	62.23/DM 100	DM	160.68/Can$ 100
Germany	DM	315.62/£ 100		—
Britain		—	DM	315.62/£ 100
Canada	Can$	196.42/£ 100		—
Britain		—	Can$	196.42/£ 100

Exchange-Rate Changes. Because of the floating exchange-rate system, exchange rates, just like other asset prices, change continuously. Suppose the DM/$ rate changes from DM 2.2110/$ to DM 2.1850/$. For any exchange-rate quote, a decrease (increase) of the numerical value of the quote indicates an increase (decrease) in the value, that is, an *appreciation* (*depreciation*) of the quoted currency. An appreciation of the quoted currency automatically implies a depreciation of the base currency.

Changes in the exchange rates are often expressed as indicated earlier. They are also expressed in basis-point changes, changes in ticks, and percentage appreciations or depreciations.

A basis point refers to the last digit in a European (direct) quote used in the interbank market. A change in the DM/$ rate from DM 2.2110/$ to DM 2.1850/$ is a 260 basis-point decrease of the spot rate. (2.1850 − 2.2110 = −.0260 = −260 basis points).

A tick refers to the last digit in an American quote. In the preceding example, the change of the quotes from Dm 2.2110/$ to DM 2.1850/$ corresponds to a change of the American quotes from $ .4523/DM to $ .4577/DM. This is a 54-tick increase in the exchange rate. (.4577 − .4523 = .0054 = 54 ticks).

Changes in exchange rates are often expressed in percentage appreciations and depreciations. If the German mark appreciates against the U.S. dollar, the U.S. dollar depreciates against the German mark. However, the percentages of appreciations and depreciations are not identical. For small exchange-rate changes these differences can be ignored. The following calculations demonstrate this point:

	DM/$	$/DM
Ending Rate (a)	2.1850	.4577
Starting Rate (b)	2.2110	.4523
Difference (a) − (b)	−.0260	+.0054
Percentage change: $\dfrac{(a) - (b)}{(b)} \times 100$	$\dfrac{-.0260}{2.2110} \times 100$	$\dfrac{.0054}{.4523} \times 100$
Result	−1.176%	+1.194%

The results indicate that the U.S. dollar depreciated against the German mark by 1.176 percent, whereas the German mark appreciated against the U.S. dollar by 1.194 percent. Notice also that the percentage appreciation of one currency always has to be larger than the percentage depreciation of the other currency.

Bid-Ask Spreads. Typically, a bank quotes two-way prices: the price at which it will buy (bid) and the price at which it will sell (ask/offer). Regardless of the terms used in the quote, a match with a bank's quotation can be arranged only if another party does exactly the opposite of what the bank is doing. The size of bid-ask spreads depends on the currencies involved, their volatilities, the time of day, and the liquidity in the market. The more uncertainty and the less the liquidity, the larger the bid-ask spread. Spreads reimburse banks for their costs and risks incurred in their foreign-exchange transactions. Typical spreads in the spot market for DM/$ and Can$/$ quotes are

DM: 2.2107/13

Can$: 1.3760/65

If a bank is quoting the preceding figures, this means that a customer can buy German marks from (sell U.S. dollar to) the bank at DM 2.2107/$ and can sell German marks to (buy U.S. dollars from) the bank at DM 2.2113/$. At the same time, the bank sells German marks (buys U.S. dollars) at DM 2.2107/$ and buys German marks (sells U.S. dollars) at DM 2.2113/$. The conventional quotation needs explaining when the "big figure" is being straddled. A quote of DM 2.2195/05 is to be interpreted as: bid 2.2195, ask 2.2205.

As explained earlier, spreads reimburse banks for their costs and risks. A bank's income for a $1 million round-trip transaction can easily be computed. The bank has to pay DM 2,210,700 for $1 million. It receives DM 2,211,300 for selling $1 million. Total profits equal DM 600, or roughly $271.37 (converted at the mid-point of bid/ask spread). The percentage transaction cost can be directly calculated using the following formula:

$$\text{Percentage transaction cost:} \quad \frac{(\text{Ask} - \text{Bid}) \times 100}{(\text{Bid} + \text{Ask}) / 2}$$
(round trip)

Given bid/ask quotes for DM/$ and Can$/$ transactions, the bid/ask prices for the cross-rate quote of DM/Can$ (or Can$/DM) can be calculated:

	DM/$	Can$/$
Bid	2.2107	1.3760
Ask	2.2113	1.3765

DM/Can$ bid: 2.2107/1.3765 = DM 160.60/Can$ 100
DM/Can$ ask: 2.2113/1.3760 = DM 160.70/Can$ 100

To buy Canadian dollars, a German participant first buys U.S. dollars in exchange for German marks, and then sells U.S. dollars in exchange for Canadian dollars. To sell Canadian dollars, a German participant first sells Canadian dollars in exchange for U.S. dollars and then sells U.S. dollars in exchange for German marks.

Correspondingly, the calculation for Can$/DM quotes is

Can$/DM bid: 1.3760/2.2113 = Can$ 62.23/DM 100
Can$/DM ask: 1.3765/2.2107 = Can$ 62.27/DM 100

In general, given two quotes (A and B) the following formula for cross-rate spreads applies:

$$\text{cross-rate spread (\%)} = (1 + \text{spread A(\%)})(1 + \text{spread B(\%)}) - 1$$

Spreads for quotations of currencies that trade on a continuous basis are much narrower than those of currencies traded infrequently or in smaller volume. Whether the use of a cross-rate is more advantageous than using the U.S. dollar depends on the size of available spreads. In general, coping with one spread rather than two is preferable. However, some of the crosses are traded infrequently. It is therefore possible that the cross-rate spread is larger than the sum of the spreads in the two quotes against the U.S. dollar.

A customer should always shop for the best quotes available. Typically, a customer calls at least 3 and no more than 10 dealers to get the best available quote. For the multitude of currencies traded, the speed of quotations, the size of transactions, as well as narrow spreads and constant liquidity are the prime selection criteria for choosing the right partner in foreign-exchange transactions.

Forward Outrights

A forward-outright transaction differs from a spot transaction in that the value (settlement) date is more than two business days in the future. The maturity of a forward contract can be a few days, months, or even years. Maturities of exactly one week, one month, or two months are called even dates. All other maturities are odd dates. Active trading in the interbank market is ordinarily limited to even-date maturities. Trading for odd dates is primarily between banks and their customers. Forward contracts with settlement dates identical to currency futures and options contracts are also considered even-date contracts and are actively traded in the interbank market.

A forward contract is an agreement to exchange a specified amount of foreign currency at a future date. The exchange rate is fixed at the time the forward contract is agreed. No accounts are debited or credited until settlement date.

Settlement

Generally, the settlement date for any forward contract is determined according to the following: first, one finds the proper spot value date for the specific currencies in the foreign-exchange market.

Second, if the spot value date is, for example, October 3, the one-day forward contract settles October 4, the one-week contract on October 10, the one-month contract on November 3, and the two-month contract on December 3. A full calendar month is used, regardless of the number of days in that particular month.

Third, if the settlement date determined is a holiday in either or both settlement centers, the next eligible business day (going forward rule) will be the settlement date.

Fourth, if the going-forward rule carries over into the next week, month, or year, the rule of going forward to the next eligible day does not apply. Instead, the eligible date is determined by the going-backward rule. Thus, settlement will be on the last eligible date in the particular week, month, or year.

The last business date of a month is particularly important in financial markets due to many standard payments occurring on that day. If these payments are denominated in foreign currencies, firms might want to hedge the associated foreign-exchange exposure. In this sense, the last business day of a month, quarter, and year is an often-used, standard forward value date.

Forward Rate

Definition. The forward rate is the price at which forward transactions are facilitated in the interbank market. There is a unique forward rate for each maturity date. As for spot quotes, forward quotes are only good for immediate dealing. Transaction costs, that is, bid-ask spreads associated with forward contracts, are larger than those on spot transactions. Moreover, the spreads tend to increase with the length of a forward contract as well as the volatility of the currencies involved.

Quotation. Forward exchange rates can be quoted in three distinct ways. The comments made on spot-rate quotes concerning direct/indirect quotes, quoted/base currencies, basis points/ticks, spreads, and cross rates apply equally to forward exchange rates. Bank traders normally quote forward rates as outright quotes to corporate customers and correspondent banks seeking to buy or sell a currency for a particular future date. Outright quotes are either in the form of direct quotes or indirect quotes. The following table shows direct and indirect quotes for rates of the German mark and Canadian dollar against the U.S. dollar:

	Direct DM/$	Indirect $/DM	Direct Can$/$	Indirect $/Can$
Spot	2.2107/13	.4522/24	1.3760/65	.7264/67
1 month	2.2055/63	.4532/35	1.3776/83	.7255/59
2 months	2.2016/24	.4540/43	1.3791/99	.7246/51
3 months	2.1973/81	.4549/52	1.3809/19	.7236/42
6 months	2.1837/48	.4577/81	1.3868/78	.7205/11
12 months	2.1574/90	.4631/37	1.3982/02	.7141/52

In the interbank market, banks quote forward rates in basis point or tick differences to the spot rate (swap rates or points). The swap rates for the direct and indirect outright quotes in the preceding table are as follows:

	Direct DM/$	Indirect $/DM	Direct Can$/$	Indirect $/Can$
Spot	2.2107/13	.4522/24	1.3760/65	.7264/67
1 month	52/50	10/11	16/18	9/8
2 months	91/89	18/19	31/34	18/16
3 months	134/132	27/28	49/52	28/25
6 months	270/265	55/57	108/113	59/56
12 months	533/523	109/113	222/237	123/115

Several things should be noted. First, the swap rates are not exchange rates but exchange-rate differentials. Second, swap rates ignore the appropriate place of the decimal point in relation to the spot rate. In general, the last digit of a swap rate corresponds to the last digit in the corresponding spot rate. Third, because swap rates are exchange-rate differentials, simply taking the reciprocal of swap rates does not enable one to go from direct to indirect quotes and vice versa. Fourth, all swap-rate quotes are positive numbers.

Fifth, in the preceding example bid quotes are larger than ask quotes for DM/$ and $/Can$ quotes and smaller for $/DM and Can$/$ quotes. This distinction determines whether swap rates have to be added to or subtracted from the current spot rate to determine the forward-outright quote. Independent of whether direct or indirect quotes are used, the following rules apply: If the swap-rate bid is greater than the ask quote, the swap rate has to be subtracted from the current spot rate to determine the forward-outright quote. For a dealer to make money, the bid rate has to be always lower than the offer rate. If the swap points are quoted such that the left side is larger than the right side and if the swap points are added to the spot rate, then there is the possibility that the calculated forward-outright bid is greater than the forward-outright ask. Because this should not happen, the swap points have to be subtracted from the spot rate. If the swap-rate bid is smaller than the ask quote, the swap rate has to be added to the current spot rate to determine the forward-outright quote. These rules are demonstrated for the DM/$ and $/DM quotes as follows:

DM/$

	Bid	Ask
Spot	2.2107	2.2113
1 month	2.2107 − .0052 = 2.2055	2.2113 − .0050 = 2.2063
2 months	2.2107 − .0091 = 2.2016	2.2113 − .0089 = 2.2024
3 months	2.2107 − .0134 = 2.1973	2.2113 − .0132 = 2.1981
6 months	2.2107 − .0270 = 2.1837	2.2113 − .0265 = 2.1848
12 months	2.2107 − .0533 = 2.1574	2.2113 − .0523 = 2.1590

$/DM

	Bid	Ask
Spot	.4522	.4524
1 month	.4522 + .0010 = .4532	.4524 + .0011 = .4535
2 months	.4522 + .0018 = .4540	.4524 + .0019 = .4543
3 months	.4522 + .0027 = .4549	.4524 + .0028 = .4552
6 months	.4522 + .0055 = .4577	.4524 + .0057 = .4581
12 months	.4522 + .0109 = .4631	.4524 + .0113 = .4637

At times, the middle rate for a currency in the forward market is identical to the middle rate available in the spot market. This means that the forward price is at par with the spot price. The swap rate might then be expressed as −7/+7 or 7P7. This means that the quoting bank is willing to buy forward at a seven-point discount to spot and willing to sell at a seven-point premium to spot. Equally, a quote of 14/00 or 14/P shows that the quoting bank is willing to buy the forward at a 14-point discount and willing to sell at par with spot.

The third way to quote forward rates is in annualized forward premiums or discounts. If a currency is less (more) expensive in the forward market than in the spot market, the currency is said to be trading at a forward discount (premium).

Forward premiums and discounts can be calculated only with respect to the base currency. That means that in DM/$ quotes, the forward premium or discount of the U.S. dollar vis-à-vis the German mark can be calculated. In $/DM quotes, the forward premium or discount of the German mark vis-à-vis the U.S. dollar is calculated.

To use a common denominator, premiums and discounts are annualized. For this, the Euromarkets use two bases: a 360-day year or a 365-day year. The 365-day year is used for the British pound, the Irish pound, the Kuwaiti dinar, and the Belgian franc. All other currencies are dealt on a 360-day basis. The Belgian franc is also dealt on a 360-day year if both parties involved are non-Belgian. At times, banks in their dealings with customers use a 365-day year for the Canadian dollar though interbank dealings are on the basis of 360 days.

Premiums and discounts can be calculated with respect to the current spot or the forward-outright rate. Views regarding the correct approach differ. The choice should depend on the particular transaction. It often is suggested that if a forward contract is used to hedge a forward commitment, the forward rate should be used as the base. If, however, a forward contract is used to hedge a current foreign-currency-denominated investment, the spot rate should be used as the base. Premiums and discounts in interbank market transactions are usually calculated on the base of the forward rate. The formula for the calculation of annualized premiums/discounts (AP/D) is:

$$AP/D = \frac{Forward\ Outright - Spot}{Spot\ or\ Forward\ Outright} \times \frac{360\ or\ 365}{n} \times 100$$

where n is the length of the forward contract in days.

Premiums and discounts can be calculated using bid or ask prices or the middle rates. The following tables show the calculation for annualized premiums and discounts for DM/$ and Can$/$ quotes using a 360-day year, bid prices, and the spot rate as the base:

DM/$

1 month	$AP/D = \dfrac{2.2055 - 2.2107}{2.2107} \times \dfrac{360}{30} \times 100 = -2.8225\%$
2 months	$AP/D = \dfrac{2.2016 - 2.2107}{2.2107} \times \dfrac{360}{60} \times 100 = -2.4698\%$
3 months	$AP/D = \dfrac{2.1973 - 2.2107}{2.2107} \times \dfrac{360}{90} \times 100 = -2.4246\%$
6 months	$AP/D = \dfrac{2.1837 - 2.2107}{2.2107} \times \dfrac{360}{180} \times 100 = -2.4427\%$
12 months	$AP/D = \dfrac{2.1574 - 2.2107}{2.2107} \times \dfrac{360}{360} \times 100 = -2.4110\%$

	Can$/$
1 month	$AP/D = \dfrac{1.3776 - 1.3760}{1.3760} \times \dfrac{360}{30} \times 100 = +1.3952\%$
2 months	$AP/D = \dfrac{1.3791 - 1.3760}{1.3760} \times \dfrac{360}{60} \times 100 = +1.3517\%$
3 months	$AP/D = \dfrac{1.3809 - 1.3760}{1.3760} \times \dfrac{360}{90} \times 100 = +1.4244\%$
6 months	$AP/D = \dfrac{1.3868 - 1.3760}{1.3760} \times \dfrac{360}{180} \times 100 = +1.5698\%$
12 months	$AP/D = \dfrac{1.3982 - 1.3760}{1.3760} \times \dfrac{360}{360} \times 100 = +1.6134\%$

The results indicate that the U.S. dollar trades at a forward discount against the German mark, whereas it trades at a forward premium against the Canadian dollar. As explained later, a currency trades at a forward premium (discount) against another currency if its money-market rate is lower (higher) than the corresponding money-market rate of the other currency. Typically, interest rates on DM-denominated deposits are lower than corresponding interest rates on U.S.-dollar-denominated deposits. Interest rates on Canadian-dollar-denominated deposits are higher than those on U.S.-dollar-denominated deposits. Hence with respect to the U.S. dollar, the German mark is typically trading at a forward premium while the Canadian dollar is trading at a forward discount.

Forwards (Classical Swaps)

Banks active in the interbank market find trading forward-outright contracts relatively risky. Consequently, they use them infrequently. Instead, banks trade in the interbank market on the basis of a transaction known as a swap. This swap is a different transaction from the more recently introduced capital-market cross-currency swap, which we discuss in a later section.

A swap transaction involves the simultaneous purchase and sale of a certain amount of foreign currency for two different value dates. In a swap position, the amount of the foreign currency bought always equals the amount of the same foreign currency sold. Only delivery dates for the purchase and sale differ. There are basically four swaps:

1. The purchase of spot against the sale of forward.
2. The sale of spot against the purchase of forward.
3. The purchase of short-term forward against the sale of longer-term forward (forward-forward swap).
4. The sale of short-term forward against the purchase of longer-term forward (forward-forward swap).

A swap transaction does not create a foreign-exchange exposure. It does, however, create an interest-rate exposure as participants effectively borrow one currency and lend the other. A change in relative interest rates during the life of the swap thus influences profits and losses.

A swap transaction can be either a pure swap or an engineered swap. A pure swap is arranged as a single transaction with a single counterparty. An engineered swap is arranged in two transactions with two different counterparties. Because the two transactions of an engineered swap might be closed at different times, both the spot rate and the swap rate are of importance.

Banks engage in swap transactions for three major purposes:

1. To change the currency denomination of a transaction from one currency to another and back again.
2. To move a given currency deal forward or backward in time.
3. To take views on changes in interest rates as a component of their overall trading or global funding strategy.

As an example for the first use, assume that a bank is unable to lend a particular currency. The bank borrows another currency, sells that currency spot against the needed currency, and simultaneously sells the latter currency forward. Through swap transactions, banks can produce or manufacture any desired currency.

As an example for the second use, assume that a bank sold forward outright a currency to its corporate client. The bank could hedge its exposure by buying the currency forward in the interbank market. Because of the (credit) risks involved, interbank forward-outright deals are rare. Instead, the bank buys the currency spot and then uses a swap transaction which sells the currency spot and buys it forward. The swap market helps to shift the forward exposure to a nearer date.

Banks also use swap transactions to profit from anticipated changes in interest differentials. Suppose, for example, a bank expects the foreign interest rate to decline within a month. The decline in the foreign interest rate might lead to an appreciation or depreciation of the foreign currency. To speculate on either would be risky. But the reduction in the foreign interest rate will surely increase the forward premium (or reduce the forward discount). The bank, therefore, expects to be able to sell the foreign currency at a higher premium (lower discount) in a month. The bank enters into a swap transaction selling the foreign currency spot and buying it forward. If the change in interest rates occurs, the bank reverses the swap for a profit.

Corporations also use the swap market for the preceding reasons. In addition, they enter swap arrangements to alter maturity dates of previous obligations. Assume, for instance, a company bought forward foreign exchange to cover an account payable due in six months. Five months later it becomes obvious that the payment is not due for another three months. The corporation enters into a swap agreement selling one-month forward and buying three-months forward the foreign currency (forward-forward swap).

By definition, a swap transaction implies a zero net foreign-exchange position. However, the maturity of various cash flows may not be matched. If interest-rate differentials are fully reflected in forward premiums and discounts, a swap transaction with matched cash flows does not generate profits. The profits are derived from deliberately mismatching cash flows in anticipation of changes in interest-rate differentials. To lock in profits (or limit losses) after a change in an interest-rate differential has occurred, banks usually square the cash flow positions.

Settlement
Settlement dates for either leg of swap positions are determined according to the rules for spot and forward settlement dates.

Swap Rate Definition.   The swap rate is the price at which swap transactions are facilitated in the interbank market. There is a unique swap rate for each maturity structure of the two components. This implies that the spot-three month swap rate usually differs from the three to six month swap. As stated earlier, the swap rate is not an exchange rate but an exchange-rate differential, that is, the difference between the rates of exchange used in the two trades. For most practical purposes, the level of the spot rate itself is not very important. What matters are the premiums and discounts to spot received or paid.

To the extent that time elapses between the initial swap with unmatched cash flows and the one generated to square the cash flows, changes in the spot rate may have a significant influence on the level of the swap rate. (A 3 percent interest differential between the German mark and the U.S. dollar gives a swap rate of 600 points at a spot-rate level of DM 2.0000/$. The same interest differential gives a swap rate of 900 points at a spot-rate level of DM 3.0000/$.)

Quotation.   Swap rates are quoted in two distinct forms. The previous comments made on spot and forward quotes apply equally to swap rates. Swap rates are most often quoted in basis-point differentials. We discussed the mechanics in the previous section. Suppose, the current DM/$ and Can$/$ quotes are as follows:

	DM/$	*Can$/$*
Spot	2.2107/13	1.3760/65
1 month	52/50	16/18
2 months	91/89	31/34
3 months	134/132	49/52
6 months	270/265	108/113
12 months	533/523	222/237

The spot-six month DM/$ swap rate of 270/265 means the bank is prepared to swap out German marks (sell German marks spot, buy German marks forward) at a cost of 265 basis points. The bank is willing to swap in German marks (buy German marks spot, sell German marks forward) at a net benefit of 270 basis points. The corresponding quote for a 6–12 month forward-forward swap is 263/258. (533 − 270 = 263; 523 − 265 = 258).

The spot-six month Can$/$ swap rate of 108/113 means the bank is prepared to swap out Canadian dollars at a net benefit of 113 basis points. The bank is also willing to swap in Canadian dollars at a cost of 108 basis points. The corresponding quote for a 2–12 month forward-forward swap is 191/203 (222 − 31 = 191; 237 − 34 = 203).

The second way of quoting swap rates is in equivalent annualized interest-rate differentials. This is done because in a swap transaction a bank is effectively borrowing one currency and lending another currency for the period between the two value dates. The calculation is based on the following (simplified) formula:

$$\text{Swap Rate (\%)} \quad \frac{\text{Swap Rate}}{\text{Spot Rate (or Forward Rate)}} \times \frac{360 \text{ or } 365}{n} \times 100$$

where n is the number of days in the swap.

Using the preceding rates for a spot-six month swap and the spot rate as a base, the following results can be calculated:

DM/$ bid:

$$\text{Swap rate (\%)} = \frac{.0270}{2.2107} \times \frac{360}{180} \times 100 = 2.443\%$$

DM/$ ask:

$$\text{Swap rate (\%)} = \frac{.0265}{2.2113} \times \frac{360}{180} \times 100 = 2.397\%$$

Can$/$ bid:

$$\text{Swap rate (\%)} = \frac{.0108}{1.3760} \times \frac{360}{180} \times 100 = 1.570\%$$

Can$/$ ask:

$$\text{Swap rate (\%)} = \frac{.0113}{1.3765} \times \frac{360}{180} \times 100 = 1.642\%$$

The quoting bank is willing to swap out German marks (Canadian dollars) at a net cost (yield) of 2.397 percent (1.642 percent). It is willing to swap in German marks (Canadian dollars) at a net yield (cost) of 2.443 percent (1.570 percent).

Short Dates

Short-date forward contracts are defined in numerous ways. They are foreign-exchange transactions with maturities less than a month, or with maturities less than a week; or transactions with maturities before spot. In this section, transactions with value dates before spot are covered.

Spot-value dates are normally two business days after the transaction is agreed upon. This leaves some room for deals with value dates before spot, such as value date today and value date tomorrow (next business day). Because of existing time-zone differences among the major dealing centers, deals with value dates before spot are often not feasible. Deals for value today can only be done for currencies whose settlement time zones are substantially behind the time zone of the dealing center. For example, a Canadian dollar/U.S. dollar or even a German mark/U.S. dollar deal struck in Tokyo could be done for value today. The time-zone difference in this example is sufficient to process all the necessary documentation for settlement. On the other hand, a Japanese yen/U.S. dollar deal struck in New York could not be done for value today. Foreign-exchange transactions for value tomorrow (next business day) are more often possible than for value today. Subject to these constraints, foreign-exchange transactions with value dates before spot are possible for certain currencies and certain countries.

In the interbank market, most of the short-date transactions are done in the form of swap agreements. These swaps include, from today until tomorrow (overnight or O/N), and from tomorrow until the next business day (tom/next). The tom/next swap is often referred to as the "rollover swap" in the United States. Depending on the definition for short dates, other swap transactions such as spot/next, spot a week, spot a month can be included.

Short-date swaps are primarily used for swapping out of overbought or oversold positions. For example, an overbought position in pound sterling for spot delivery can be dealt with in two ways. The bank can move spot delivery backwards with a tomorrow/next swap transaction. In this case, the bank would buy the foreign currency for value date tomorrow and sell it for spot. The bank can also move the spot delivery forward with a spot/next swap transaction. Here the bank sells pound sterling for spot and buys it forward for settlement of the first business day after spot.

Settlement

Settlement dates for short-date transactions are implied by their names. Depending on the particular swap transaction the value dates are either today, the next business day after today (tomorrow), the spot-value date, or any day after spot. The value dates after spot are determined the same way as settlement dates for forward contracts.

Swap Rate

Quotation. Short-date swaps work just like every other swap. However, these swap rates have to be used differently as they are used to calculate forward-outright (better: backward-outright) rates before spot. Assume the following spot and swap rates for German mark/U.S. dollar transactions:

	DM/$
Spot	2.2107/13
O/N	11/7
T/N	5/3
1 month	52/50

Suppose the spot delivery date is Thursday and the current (Tuesday) spot rate is 2.2107/13. The outright rate for Tuesday and Wednesday delivery—rates before spot—have to be calculated. The swap rates have to be worked backwards in time to a date before spot. This does not mean that instead of subtracting swap rates (if bid is larger than offer) they are now added to spot rate. It means that bid/ask swap rates are switched and then added to or subtracted from the spot rate according to the general rules. The following table describes the procedure:

	Quotes	Reversal	Calculation	Outright
Spot	2.2107/13			2.2107/13
O/N	11/7	7/11	bid 2.2107 + .0007 = 2.2114	2.2114/24
			ask 2.2113 + .0011 = 2.2124	
T/N	5/3	3/5	bid 2.2107 + .0003 = 2.2110	2.2110/18
			ask 2.2113 + .0005 = 2.2118	
1 month	52/50	N/A	bid 2.2107 − .0052 = 2.2055	2.2055/65
			ask 2.2113 − .0050 = 2.2065	

To rely constantly on short-date swaps is risky. For one, swapping into and out of positions on a daily basis creates extra transaction costs and other back room operational costs. Also, short-date swap rates are at times affected by special factors such as tax payment dates and month-end dates (ultimo).

Option Forwards

An option-forward contract is defined as a forward-outright contract where the delivery date is at the option of the customer. As in a normal forward-outright contract, the parties agree at the time of the deal on the size of the transaction, the currencies involved and the exchange rates involved. The delivery date is fixed between any two dates.

Settlement
Settlement for the option-forward contract is two business days after the exercise of the option. The determination of the settlement date corresponds to settlement dates of spot contracts.

Option-Forward Rates

Quotation. In quoting rates for option-forward contracts, banks consider the possibility that customers exercise the option at the worst possible time. Suppose the following DM/$ rates are quoted:

	DM/$	DM/$ Outright Quotes
Spot	2.2107/13	2.2107/13
1 month	52/50	2.2055/63
2 months	91/89	2.2016/24
3 months	134/136	2.1973/81
6 months	270/265	2.1837/48
12 months	533/523	2.1574/90

A customer wants to buy U.S. dollars (sell German marks) forward with the time option from spot to three months. Suppose the bank quotes the U.S. dollar at the three months forward rate. The customer exercises for spot delivery. The customer can sell spot German marks at the full forward premium. Obviously, the bank has to take the worst case into account. The bank, therefore, would quote the current spot price. Suppose, on the other hand, that the customer wants to sell U.S. dollars (buy German marks) forward with the same time option. Suppose the bank quotes the U.S. dollar at the spot rate. The customer exercises for three-month forward delivery and is able to sell the U.S. dollars in three months at no forward discount (buys the German marks at no premium). To avoid this situation, the bank would quote the customer the three-month forward price. Thus for a spot-three month option-forward transaction the minimum spread would be 2.1973/2.2113. Minimum spreads for other possible option-forward contracts are:

Spot–1 month	2.2055/2.2113	1 month–2 months	2.2016/2.2063
Spot–2 months	2.2016/2.2113	1 month–6 months	2.1837/2.2063
Spot–3 months	2.1973/2.2113	3 months–6 months	2.1837/2.1981
Spot–6 months	2.1837/2.2113	3 months–12 months	2.1574/2.1981
Spot–12 months	2.1574/2.2113	6 months–12 months	2.1574/2.1848

Why would customers ever enter foreign-exchange transactions with such wide spreads? The alternative to an option-forward contract is to enter a forward-outright contract with a "best guess" maturity date and then roll over the forward contract with short-date swaps to the exact delivery date. However, this technique might require many swap transactions for which the customer pays a spread each time. Because spreads are usually relatively large on short-date swaps as well as influenced by extraordinary circumstances, the alternative of the option-forward contract is often superior.

Cross-Currency Swaps
In this section we discuss the recently introduced cross-currency swaps. These are different from the classical swaps discussed earlier in that they have interim cash flows and are typically of larger tenor. Because they have been traded by the capital-market groups of commercial and investment banks, they have also been called capital-market swaps.

A currency swap is an exchange of cash flows, in different

currencies and over time, between two parties. In a typical currency swap, parties exchange principal in one currency for principal in another currency at the outset, and re-exchange these principals at maturity. Usually, and unlike the classical swap, the initial and final rates of exchange are identical. To account for this, there are interim interest payments reflecting market rates in the respective currencies to service the principal amounts. The interest payments are set according to a predetermined rule.

To illustrate, assume that party A and party B enter into a five-year German mark/U.S. dollar swap at an exchange rate of 2.0000 DM/$, a 5 percent DM interest rate, and a 10 percent $ interest rate, with yearly interest payments. If party A initially receives $1 million, it must initially pay DM 2 million. At maturity, party A pays back the $1 million and receives back the DM 2 million. Naturally, party B has the other side of these transactions. In addition, since party A is the original receiver of the $1 million, it services this principal amount by making $100,000 (10 percent of $1 million) yearly payments to party B for five years. Similarly, since party B is the original receiver of DM 2 million, it makes DM 100,000 (5 percent of DM 2 million) yearly payments to party A for five years.

There are many variants to the preceding transaction, particularly because the markets have been evolving very rapidly. Specifically, the interim interest payments can be floating or fixed for either or both of the currencies. If so, the swap can take on various names such as fixed to floating or floating to floating cross-currency, annuity or coupon cross-currency, or cross-currency interest-rate swaps. Because the usage of these names is not standard, it is best to clarify specific meanings in case of doubt.

On some rare occasions, the interim payments might also amortize the principal, and the swap is called amortizing. There are also forward swaps where the swaps are entered into at some future date, and options on swaps where the holder of the options has the right but not the obligation to buy or sell a swap.

Currency swaps evolved from parallel or back-to-back loans arranged between two companies in different countries. These were popular in the United Kingdom in the late 1960s and early 1970s as a means of financing investment abroad without violating foreign-exchange regulations.

To illustrate, suppose a British firm wants to invest abroad but cannot obtain the foreign exchange due to government controls. It can, however, make a British pound loan to a U.S. company operating in the United Kingdom. The U.S. company in exchange makes a U.S. dollar loan, outside of the United Kingdom to the British company, which invests the proceeds as it pleases. This is virtually identical to a cash collateralized foreign-exchange loan where the British company deposits cash with a British bank in the United Kingdom and borrows U.S. dollars from the foreign subsidiary of the British bank. This enables the British company to invest abroad and the U.S. company to invest in the United Kingdom with neither incurring foreign-exchange risk.

Parallel loans suffer from several problems. First, default by one party does not release the other from making its contractually obligated payments. Second, although the loans offset one another, they remain on the balance sheet for accounting and regulatory purposes. Third, documentation requirements are extensive. Swaps were developed in the early 1980s to overcome these problems. The documentation of a currency swap does not include an initial exchange of principal, and as such is an off-balance-sheet instrument. Usually, the initial exchange of principal takes place as a separate foreign-exchange transaction. Differences in regulatory, accounting, legal, and supervisory domains notwithstanding, swaps and parallel loans have identical cash flows. Because of the offset feature though, swaps have lower credit risk than back-to-back loans.

Ignoring the initial exchanges, both treasury and capital-market swaps are similar to forward contracts. The only difference is that the capital-market swap has interim interest payments. This renders a capital-market swap less risky than a forward, and this is probably why these swaps have extended the maturities of long-dated currency cover.

Traditionally swaps were used to transform the currency base of liabilities, hence the name liability swap. These were made popular by the historic Swiss franc/U.S. dollar and German mark/U.S. dollar currency swaps between IBM and the World Bank in 1981.

The World Bank wanted to borrow Swiss francs because Swiss franc interest rates were much lower than U.S. interest rates, and the World Bank's own forecast of the dollar/franc exchange rate pointed to a much stronger dollar than that dictated by the interest-rate parity theorem. That is, the World Bank was willing to take on a Swiss franc liability, regardless of the exchange risk. In addition, the World Bank could also lend Swiss francs to various developing countries. It, however, did not want to borrow through the relatively small Swiss market because the World Bank was afraid that the size of its debt issue would be relatively large. In addition, as it had issued Swiss franc debt several times before, it had an inkling that the market's appetite for its debt was saturated. What the World Bank really wanted was to raise money in the United States and convert that to a synthetic Swiss franc liability.

On the other hand, IBM thought that by raising money in Switzerland and swapping it into dollars, it could get a slightly better rate than in the United States. There are several possible reasons for this: Swiss investors probably thought more favorably of IBM than American investors (the name effect); they wanted to diversify their portfolios with IBM stock (the portfolio effect); and regulatory considerations (such as Securities and Exchange Commission rules making it cheaper to raise money in the Euromarkets than in the United States). Regardless of the reasons, it was wise for IBM and the World Bank to raise money in Switzerland and the United States, respectively, and then swap their liabilities into their preferred currencies.

The very process of exploiting arbitrage opportunities eliminates them. That is, if IBM can borrow at lower cost in Switzerland than in the United States because of its perceived name, after a while it would flood the Swiss market with its debt obligations, drive up its borrowing costs, and no longer find it profitable to borrow in Switzerland.

If this were the major driving force behind currency swaps, the market should have contracted. On the contrary, this market is estimated to have grown from $1.5 billion in 1981 to $40 billion in notional principal in 1986. This suggests that swaps are possibly driven by tax or regulatory considerations rather than the name effect. It is noteworthy that most of these swaps are typically associated with Eurobond issues.

Arbitrage opportunities also exist when taxes or other regulations are present. For instance, Japanese, Australian, and New Zealand domestic interest rates are higher than their Euro counterparts for various reasons such as withholding taxes or simple regulations elevating interest rates. This creates an opportunity to borrow in these currencies in the Euromarkets and then swap into dollars. The buyers of these currencies can, in turn, invest them in their respective countries, earning the domestic country-Euro market edge.

Asset swaps use the same principles as liability swaps. The difference is that they are used to transform the currency make-up of assets rather than liabilities. For instance, investors wishing to invest in Australian companies but not wanting to subject themselves to Australian dollar exchange-rate risk can buy Australian bonds and swap their revenue streams into U.S. dollars, or some other currency, creating what is called a synthetic security. On the other side of the transaction, there may be an investor who buys a non-Australian dollar-denominated Eurobond, swapping the revenue stream into higher-interest bearing Australian dollars, regardless of the exchange risk.

Just like other foreign-exchange instruments, swaps can be used to hedge import payments, export receivables, foreign-dividend payments, debts and investments, and to speculate. As arbitrage opportunities disappear, and tax and regulatory loopholes are closed, this swap usage will probably become more prevalant.

Because swaps effectively reduce market imperfections, they tend to reduce the risks associated with the operation of the financial system. Thereby, they render a more efficient functioning of the system and make available transactions that were not available before. Were it not for cross-currency swaps long-dated forward contracts would probably not be feasible.

Futures

Futures contracts traded on organized futures exchanges are conceptually similar to forward contracts traded in the interbank market. The distinction lies in the contract specifications, as well as in the organization and operation of the marketplace. A foreign-exchange futures contract contains the obligation to buy (long) or sell (short) a specified amount of a foreign currency at a presently specified price. Futures contracts on foreign currencies are traded on the International Money Market (IMM, a subdivision of the

Chicago Mercantile Exchange), the London International Financial Futures Exchange (LIFFE), and various other (secondary) exchanges such as the Singapore International Monetary Exchange (SIMEX) and the MidAm Exchange in Chicago (a subsidiary of the Chicago Board of Trade). Though contract specifications as well as trading and clearing procedures differ among the exchanges, the following describes the fundamental differences between exchange-traded futures contracts and over-the-counter-traded forward contracts.

Traded Currencies
In the over-the-counter (interbank) market, forward contracts are traded in almost every conceivable foreign currency. The number of currencies traded on exchanges is limited and includes the German mark, Japanese yen, British pound, Swiss franc, French franc, Canadian dollar, the Australian dollar, and the European Currency Unit. However, trading in these currencies is so liquid in the interbank market that these currencies make up well over 90 percent of all foreign-exchange trades.

Base Currencies
Though most foreign-exchange transactions in the interbank market use the U.S. dollar as one of the currencies involved, cross-currency deals, that is, deals that do not include the U.S. dollar, are possible. On the other side, all futures contracts use the U.S. dollar as the base currency. Cross-currency futures contracts are not traded at this time.

Contract Size
The size of interbank market transactions is negotiable and usually fixed in U.S. dollar terms. Contracts on futures exchanges are standardized and fixed. In addition, the size of the contracts is determined in terms of the foreign (non-U.S.) currency. For example, the size of the German mark contract on the IMM is DM 125,000. Deals can, therefore, only be done for DM 125,000 or multiples of it.

Maturity Dates
Transactions for any maturity date are possible in the over-the-counter market. The length of the contract is determined by the

two involved parties. For most interbank transactions, though, the length of contracts is standardized, that is, contracts for one week, one month, or two months are the norm. Contrary to this, futures contracts have a fixed delivery date (and last trading date). For example, on the IMM, delivery dates are always on the third Wednesday of the expiration month (June, September, December, March). The last trading day is the preceding Monday.

Trading Hours
Trading in the interbank market can take place 24 hours and seven days a week. Liquidity on Saturdays and Sundays and during off-hours is limited. Trading on organized exchanges is limited to the peak hours on weekdays only. This severely limits the use of exchanges during volatile periods to participants with no access to the interbank market. Exchanges are reducing this disadvantage by expanding trading hours and by linkages with other exchanges covering different time zones.

Quotations
In general, European quotes are used in the interbank market. For example, the exchange rates for German mark/U.S. dollar transactions are given in DM per U.S. dollar. Exchanges use American quotes because the contracts are fixed in units of the foreign (non-U.S.) currencies. As in the interbank market, exchanges quote a two-sided market with bid-ask prices.

Transaction Costs
Quoted prices in the interbank market are not directly comparable to exchange quotes. Orders in the interbank market are executed flat. No commissions are added to purchase orders at the offer price nor deducted from sell orders at the bid price. On exchanges, orders are executed at the best available price. Commissions are then added to the total purchase price or subtracted from the amount of the sale.

Delivery
In practice, almost all forward-outright contracts in the interbank market are settled by delivery of the underlying currencies. In contrast, only a very small percentage of futures contracts are

delivered. Most positions in futures contracts are reversed before the delivery date by entering into the exact opposite of the original transaction.

Decentralization/Centralization

Dealers in the interbank market transact their business on a private, one-to-one basis. This implies that quoted prices deviate among participants. Price dissemination is decentralized. On the other side, members of a futures exchange operate around a common trading pit, openly calling out their bids and offers. At any point in time, there is (should be) only one best bid and one best offer price. In this sense, futures price dissemination is centralized.

Lines of Credit/Margins

Any party in a foreign-exchange transaction faces the risk that the counterparty will not fulfill its obligations. To limit this risk, interbank-market participants establish lines of credit with each other for foreign-exchange dealings. These lines of credit reflect the creditworthiness of the counterparties. The foreign-exchange position with each counterparty is thus limited. The credit risk is established with the direct counterparty.

To evaluate the credit risk involved in futures trading, the creditworthiness of the original counterparty is irrelevant. The risk is managed by a margining system. Exchange-market participants must post a good-faith deposit. This initial margin guarantees the performance of each contract. The financial integrity of exchange-traded contracts is further enhanced by a clearinghouse system in which the exchange and its membership assume the opposite side to each contract and thereby share the responsibility for its fulfillment.

The initial margin is complemented by a variation margin. The clearinghouse collects on a daily basis additional funds from losers and pays those funds into the account of winners. This process of marking-to-market on a daily basis guarantees that the clearinghouse and its members are only at risk for the dollar value of the current trading day's price variation.

The distinction between realized and unrealized gains and losses is important. The initial margin represents the participant's equity. If subsequent exchange-rate changes generate unrealized gains, the equity in the account is increased by the amount of that gain. Equity over and above the amount of initial margin required to carry one's position is the account excess. The excess may be used to increase the net position or may be withdrawn from the account. Should the account incur a net loss, the equity is reduced by the amount of the loss. If no excess equity is available to cover the loss, the trader is required to deposit additional equity to the account in the form of variation margin. If the contracts are liquidated, that is, unrealized losses are converted to realized losses, there would be no need to deposit additional margins.

Market Size

Aside from the spectacular growth of trading in foreign-currency futures contracts, the exchange market is small compared to the interbank market. Futures exchanges provide access to the foreign-exchange market to participants who otherwise would not be able to use the interbank market due to their credit risk. In addition, futures exchanges provide a centralized price dissemination function unavailable in the over-the-counter market.

Options

Foreign-currency option contracts are relatively new instruments. They are traded both on organized exchanges and in the interbank market. An option gives the buyer the right—but not the obligation—to buy (call option) or sell (put option) a given amount of foreign exchange at a predetermined exchange rate (strike price). For this right, the buyer pays the seller (writer) a premium.

Options on financial instruments, like foreign exchange, are insurance contracts and should be viewed and analyzed as such. Like any insurance contract, the option also has a terminal date called the expiration date. If the option may be exercised before the expiration date, it is called an American option. If the option can only be exercised on the expiration date, it is called a European option.

The premium for a call and put option is determined by several variables: the difference between spot and strike prices, time until expiration, domestic and foreign interest rates, and the expected volatility. Volatility is defined as the annualized standard deviation of daily exchange-rate changes. The precise mathematical solution of European option prices was first developed by Black and Scholes.

Basic arbitrage techniques such as conversions (buy put, sell call, and buy a forward contract) and reversals (sell put, buy call, and sell a forward contract) maintain (approximate) the correct price relationship between puts and calls of the same exercise price through the foreign-exchange market. Other techniques such as boxes (buy puts and calls with one strike price and sell puts and calls with a higher or lower strike price) maintain (approximate) the correct price relationship between puts and calls with different strike prices through the interest-rate market.

As of now, the language in the foreign-currency option market is not standardized. Participants should be aware that a U.S. dollar/German mark call option could either be a call option on the German mark (against the U.S. dollar) or a call option on the U.S. dollar (against the German mark). Again, differences exist between standardized contracts traded on exchanges and the practice in the over-the-counter market. On most exchanges, call and put options refer to the right to buy or sell foreign (non-U.S.) currencies against the U.S. dollar. In general, call and put options in the over-the-counter market refer to the right to buy or sell U.S. dollars against foreign (non-U.S.) currencies.

According to the definitions of calls and puts, the premium quotations also differ. For call and put options on the German mark against the U.S. dollar, premiums are quoted as U.S. cents per unit of German mark. On the other hand, for call and put contracts on the U.S. dollar against the German mark, premiums are quoted in terms of German pfennigs per U.S. dollar.

Options are very versatile tools for speculative, trading, and hedging activities. Their specific risk-return characteristics allow for limited downside risk while retaining unlimited upside profit potential. These instruments offer both multicurrency investors and international corporations important new tools for dealing with a range of currency-exposure problems. Currency options are attractive both for the corporation and the investor because they are, in essence, insurance policies against unexpected movements in exchange rates. (More details on foreign-currency options are available in Chapter 16.)

RELATIONSHIP BETWEEN EXCHANGE RATES

Spot, forward, swap, futures, and option prices are not independent from each other. In practice, all of the exchange rates are determined simultaneously along with the relevant interest-rate differentials between countries. The following describes the arbitrage conditions which ensure these relationships.

Arbitrage Conditions

Assume the following hypothetical scenario: Interest rates for one-year German mark deposits are 5 percent. The corresponding rates for U.S. dollar deposits are 10 percent. The current spot rate is DM 2.0000/$.

An investor has two choices: first, to invest $100 in the U.S. money market at 10 percent interest, and end up with $110 a year from now. Second, to convert the U.S. $100 into German marks at the current spot rate of DM 2.0000/$, and invest the converted funds (DM 200) in the German money market at 5 percent interest, and end up with DM 210 a year from now.

Which alternative would the rational investor choose? This depends on whether DM 210 is more or less valuable than $110 a year from today. This, however, is unknown today as the spot rate one year from today is unknown. The future spot rate that would make an investor indifferent between receiving U.S. $110 or DM 210 a year from now can be easily calculated. This future spot rate is DM 1.9091/$ (DM 210/$110).

Instead of leaving the German mark position open and facing an exchange-rate exposure, an investor could cover the DM 210 by selling the German marks forward today with a one-year forward contract. As long as the one-year forward rate does not equal DM 1.9091/$, arbitrage opportunities exist.

Suppose the one-year forward rate is DM 1.8500/$. The German mark is relatively expensive in the forward market. Based on this scenario, the rational investor would convert U.S. $100 into DM 200 at the current spot rate and would sell forward the expected sum of DM 210 at the rate of DM 1.8500/$. This covered transaction would ensure a total receipt of $113.51 at the end of the year compared to $110 for the domestic transaction. This profit opportunity would entice all investors to buy German marks against U.S. dollars in the spot market and to sell German marks in the forward market. This would lead to an appreciation of the spot value of the German mark—the spot rate (DM/$) falls—and to a depreciation of the forward value—the forward rate (DM/$) rises—until no more profit opportunities exist.

Suppose, on the other hand, that the one-year forward rate is DM 1.9500/$. The German mark is relatively cheap in the forward market. Based on this scenario, the rational investor would convert DM 200 into $100 at the current spot rate and would buy forward the expected sum of $110 at the rate of DM 1.9500/$. This covered transaction would ensure a total receipt of DM 214.50 at the end of the year compared to DM 210 for the alternative transaction. This profit opportunity would entice all investors to sell German marks against U.S. dollars in the spot market and to buy German marks in the forward market. This would lead to a depreciation of the spot value of the German mark—the spot rate (DM/$) increases—and to an appreciation of the forward value—the forward rate (DM/$) falls—until no more profit opportunities exist.

This arbitrage condition determines only the relative difference between spot and forward rates. It does not determine the level of either rate. This arbitrage condition holds for any level of exchange rates and is manifested in the interest-rate parity theorem.

Interest-Rate Parity Theorem

The interest-rate parity theorem relates forward premiums and discounts of specified maturities to the money-market interest differentials on similar assets denominated in different currencies. As explained earlier, the spot-forward relationship is set by covered, or riskless, interest arbitrage.

For any exchange rate defined as domestic currency units per foreign currency unit, interest-rate parity can be formulated as follows:

$$\frac{F - S}{S} \cdot A = \frac{r_D - r_F}{1 + r_F} \text{ , or}$$

$$\frac{S - F}{F} \cdot A = \frac{r_F - r_D}{1 + r_D}$$

where

$$F = \text{forward rate}$$
$$S = \text{spot rate}$$
$$A = \text{annualization factor (365 or 360/number of days for forward contract)}$$
$$r_D = \text{domestic money-market rate}$$
$$r_F = \text{foreign money-market rate}$$

The arbitrage condition according to interest-rate parity only holds if the maturity dates for the money-market investments match those of the forward contracts. This requires that a one-month deposit rate has to be used in conjunction with a one-month forward rate, a six-month deposit rate with a six-month forward rate, and so on. In a previous section the annualized forward discounts of the U.S. dollar against the German mark were calculated. The results are repeated here:

$$1 \text{ month } AP/D = -2.8225\%$$
$$2 \text{ months } AP/D = -2.4698\%$$
$$3 \text{ months } AP/D = -2.4246\%$$
$$6 \text{ months } AP/D = -2.4427\%$$
$$12 \text{ months } AP/D = -2.4110\%$$

Based on these numbers, a general observation can be made: forward discounts on the U.S. dollar decline as the maturity increases. This means that the spread between U.S. dollar and comparable German mark interest rates narrows as time to maturity increases.

Interest-rate parity does not have to hold precisely because arbitrage transactions are associated with certain transaction costs, no matter how small. Two transaction costs have to be considered before covered interest arbitrage activities are undertaken. First, buying and selling foreign exchange in the spot and forward-outright market are associated with transaction costs, exemplified by bid-ask spreads. Second, covered interest arbitrage involves lending and borrowing activities for which bid-ask spreads exist. Both spreads have to be taken into account before an arbitrage transaction.

The arbitrage condition requires that the alternative investments are identical except for their respective currency denomination. In the preceding example, an investment in a U.S. asset was compared with an asset in Germany. These assets, however, are not identical. For one, the credit risk of the respective issuing banks in the United States and Germany might differ. There is also political risk. The American investor faces the potential risk that the German government may make repatriation of German mark assets impossible on the maturity date. The German investor faces the potential risk that the U.S. government may make repatriation of U.S. dollar assets impossible. In practice, the conditions of interest-rate parity are only met in the Euromarkets. Deposits denominated in U.S. dollars and German marks and issued by the same bank in London or any other offshore center are identical except for the currency denomination. The credit risk is the same as well as the political risk.

For the major international banks, foreign-exchange operations and Euromarket activities are viewed as components of overall asset and liability management. Foreign-exchange traders and Eurodeposit traders sit side by side. If any divergence of forward premiums/discounts develop from interest-rate differentials, both traders react. Forward quotations and Eurodeposit rates are adjusted instantly.

TYPES OF RISKS

Several risks are associated with any foreign-exchange transaction.

Exchange-Rate Risk
When a corporation or bank buys or sells foreign currencies, an exposure called an "open position" is created. Until the time that position can be "covered" by selling or buying an equivalent

amount of the same foreign currency, the firm is exposed to the risk that the exchange rate might move against it.

Management limits the open position dealers may take in each currency. Though practices vary, limits are given for "overnight" positions and often also—though with wider limits—for "daylight" positions.

Interest-Rate Risk

Interest-rate risk arises whenever there are mismatches (called gaps) in the maturity structure of a participant's foreign-exchange book. The foreign-exchange book is the complete tally of all outstanding spot, forward, and swap contracts. This problem is identical to the interest-rate risk of domestic assets and liabilities.

The swap market is primarily used to even out gaps in the interest-rate structure of foreign-currency-denominated assets and liabilities.

Credit Risk

Whenever a firm enters a foreign-exchange contract, it faces a risk, however small, that the counterparty will not perform according to the terms of the contract. In this sense, there is a credit risk, though no credit is extended. To limit this risk, a careful evaluation of the creditworthiness of the counterparty is essential.

Another, and potentially more harmful form of credit risk, called delivery risk, stems from the time-zone differences on settlement days. Inevitably, a U.S. bank selling sterling, for example, must pay British pounds to a counterparty earlier in the day than it is credited with U.S. dollars in New York. In the intervening hours, a company can go into bankruptcy or a bank can be declared insolvent.

Political Risk

At one time or another, virtually every country has interfered with international transactions in its currency. Interference might take the form of regulation of the local exchange market, restrictions of foreign investments by residents, or limits on capital inflows from or outflows to other countries. Participants in the foreign-exchange market should carefully analyze the potential of exchange controls to minimize possible harm.

CHAPTER 3

INTERNATIONAL MONEY AND SWAP MARKETS

Brendan Brown

The international money market is a loose term, widely used, but variously defined. The broadest definition encompasses all short-term debt markets in international monies (those monies which enjoy significant international custom—either from investors, or borrowers, or both). Examples of short-term debts that are traded include bank deposits, bankers' acceptances, commercial paper, Treasury bills, short-term floating rate notes, and various synthetic instruments involving swap markets; for example, synthetic floating rate notes.

The narrowest definition would restrict the term *international money market* to offshore markets in bank deposits where the buyers and sellers (alternatively, borrowers and lenders) are predominately nonresidents of both the offshore center and of the country issuing the currency in question. By this definition, the international money market would be quite small, essentially being restricted to the Euromarkets in London and Luxembourg. An in-between definition would include all short-term debt markets in which there was significant international business relative to domestic business. For example, Eurodollar commercial paper, but not domestic U.S. commercial paper, would fall under this definition.

DEFINING INTERNATIONAL TRANSACTIONS

A schema can be drawn up of the various international transactions in money and credit markets where these are distinguished by their degree of internationality.[1] The transactions are differentiated on the basis of three criteria: first, residence of the debtor (bank in the case of a deposit) relative to the country issuing the given currency; second, residence of the investor relative to the country issuing the given currency; and third, residence of the debtor relative to the residence of the investor.

On the first criterion, the transaction is either onshore (for example, a dollar deposit in the United States, dollar commercial paper issued by a U.S. borrower) or offshore (a dollar deposit in London, dollar commercial paper issued by a European corporation). On the second criteria, the transaction is either domestic (a U.S. investor buying dollar paper issued by any debtor) or foreign (a non-U.S. investor buying dollar paper issued by any debtor). On the third criterion, the transaction is either internal (where the residence is the same for debtor and investor—for example, a British investor buying a deposit in any currency with a British bank or other debts in any currency issued by a British borrower). Or the transaction could be external (where the residence is different for debtor and investor—for example, a British investor buying any debt, in pounds or in any other currency, issued by any non-British debtor).

Within this schema are five possible categories of transactions. *Onshore-internal* transactions are those in which both the investor and debtor reside in the country issuing the given currency; for example, a U.S. resident buying Eurocommercial paper in dollars issued by a U.S. corporation. For an *onshore-external* transaction, the debtor, but not the investor, resides in the country issuing the given currency; for example, a German resident buying Eurocommercial paper in dollars issued by a U.S. corporation. In an *offshore-internal* transaction, the investor and borrower reside in the same country but use a foreign currency: for example, a

---

[1] See B. D. Brown, *The Forward Market in Foreign Exchange* (London: Croom Helm, 1983), chapter 6.

Japanese corporation placing dollar funds with a Japanese bank. For an *offshore-external/domestic* transaction, the currency of denomination is issued by the country of residence of the investor, but not of the borrower: for example, a British investor buying Sterling commercial paper issued by a Swedish borrower. In an *offshore-external/foreign* transaction, the investor and borrower reside in different countries, but neither resides in the country of issuance of the currency used. Examples include the purchase of a deutsche mark deposit at a Luxembourg bank by a French investor, or a British investor buying dollar Eurocommercial paper issued by Gaz de France.

This last transaction—offshore-external/foreign—is the basis of the narrowest definition of international money market. In practice, the volume of such transactions is only a small share of total volume under wider definitions, as shown by the data on international banking flow shown in Tables 3–1 and 3–2. Table 3–1 shows the external position—liabilities and assets outstanding to nonresidents—of banks reporting to the Bank for International Settlements with respect to the countries shown. For example, German nonbank investors in June 1987 had $30.3 billion of deutsche mark-denominated deposits with banks outside the Federal Republic of Germany; U.S. nonbank investors had $195.2 billion of dollar deposits with banks outside the United States (not very dissimilar relative to the German total as a proportion of respective GDPs). Both these deposit totals fall under the definition of *offshore-external/domestic* transactions— as do the interbank loans in deutsche marks (DM) from the Federal Republic ($85.8 billion) and in dollars from the United States ($308.4 billion). The nonbank totals can be compared with those in Table 3–2; they show that nonbank *offshore-external/foreign* deposits in DMs and dollars amounted to $45.0 billion and $240.7 billion respectively.

Further examples of the range of international monetary transactions can be drawn from Tables 3–1 and 3–2. Table 3–2 shows that offshore-internal loans outstanding from banks in the industrialized countries to nonbanks at the end of June 1987 amounted to $43.7 billion in deutsche marks and $236.9 billion in U.S. dollars. Offshore-internal deposits with banks in the industrialized countries from nonbanks amounted to $11.4 billion in DMs

TABLE 3–1
External Position of All Reporting Banks vis-à-vis Individual Countries,
June 1987 (In $ Billions)

	Assets		Liabilities	
	Bank	Nonbank	Bank	Nonbank
Belgium-Luxembourg	168.5	15.7	158.2	17.4
France	128.2	18.7	116.3	10.4
in Ffrs	6.2	1.6	5.9	1.4
Germany	64.0	53.2	132.0	40.8
in DMs	41.3	40.0	85.8	30.3
Italy	74.8	25.4	54.8	5.9
Netherlands	43.2	17.3	64.6	19.8
Spain	12.5	10.9	28.0	4.8
Sweden	19.2	8.8	9.8	1.6
Switzerland	50.4	11.8	250.0	20.5
in Sfrs	12.8	2.4	53.0	3.7
United Kingdom	373.1	24.7	477.1	26.2
in £s	22.1	4.0	23.6	5.1
Canada	36.7	19.4	34.2	12.2
Japan	405.9	25.5	245.8	5.6
in yen	59.7	8.0	49.9	1.4
USA	376.1	124.9	355.4	211.4
in $	327.2	111.3	308.4	195.2
Hong Kong	147.5	9.6	141.5	15.9
Singapore	116.1	2.0	109.6	2.9
Cayman Islands	104.5	5.5	110.6	5.0
Bahamas	92.1	7.2	105.8	3.9

Source: "International Banking and Financial Market Developments," Bank for International Settlements, October 1987.

and $58.8 billion in U.S. dollars. Table 3–1 shows that nonbank nonresidents held $40.0 billion of DM deposits in the Federal Republic, while nonbank non-U.S. residents held $111.3 billion of dollar deposits with U.S. banks—both amounts falling under the heading of onshore-external transactions.

Our focusing in these and previous examples on the U.S. dollar and deutsche mark is not accidental. As the world's number one and number two international monies respectively, the amount of international business in them is greater than in other currencies. Also promoting the use of offshore-external/domestic transactions

TABLE 3–2

Currency Breakdown of Reporting Banks' Positions in Industrial Countries, June 1987 (In $ Billions)

	With Respect to Nonresidents (External)			With Respect to Residents (Internal)	
	Nonbank Assets	Nonbank Liabilities	Official Deposits	Nonbank Assets	Nonbank Liabilities
In foreign currency					
U.S. dollar	260.3	240.7	77.5	236.9	58.8
Deutsche mark	77.5	45.0	20.6	43.7	11.4
Swiss franc	21.2	10.4	5.1	42.2	3.8
Japanese yen	17.3	8.2	9.4	10.6	5.6
British pound	6.5	9.5	1.1	3.9	2.9
French franc	4.4	4.0	0.6	4.9	2.3
Netherlands florin	4.0	3.4	1.6	5.2	1.7
Belgian franc	1.6	6.4	0.2	1.0	0.8
Italian lira	3.4	1.4	0.2	1.0	1.0
European currency units	12.0	3.7	1.8	7.0	3.0
Unallocated*	14.4	12.1	2.1	14.4	12.5
In domestic currency					
U.S. dollar	107.9	69.7	57.1		
Other	180.2	94.0	51.7		
Memo:					
Banks in other reporting countries	217.1	199.4	46.2		

* Includes positions of U.S. banks, for which no figures are available.

Source: Bank for International Settlements.

in these two currencies are the regulations imposing extra costs on doing domestic compared to offshore business (for example, reserve requirements and deposit insurance).

IMPORTANCE OF INTERBANK TRANSACTIONS

We shall return to the distinction between the various international money market transactions (using the given criteria) in our discussion of arbitrage relationships. Meanwhile, however, there is a further striking observation to be made from Table 3–1—in addition to the one already made about the importance of international transactions other than those under the heading offshore-external/foreign, which underlies the narrowest concept of international money market. This concerns the huge scale of interbank transactions. For example, banks outside the United Kingdom had $477 billion of deposit liabilities to U.K. banks in June 1987, while U.K. banks themselves had $373 billion of deposit liabilities outstanding to foreign banks. What lies behind such huge totals?

One factor is market making. As in all markets where dealers act as principals in satisfying orders by taking inventory positions themselves—rather than refusing to deal until a transactor in the opposite direction can be found—a substantial amount of business is between the dealers (here, banks) themselves. A bank in London, for example, asked to quote for a large three-month dollar deposit, and having its quote accepted, would seek to lay off its exposure to interest-rate risk (the risk that three-month rates can fall) by finding a would-be borrower of three-month funds. Often, the most readily obtainable borrower is another bank just "hit" in the opposite direction, that is, satisfying a demand for three-month fixed-rate credit and anxious to minimize the time during which it is at risk to a rise in interest rates.

Sometimes the resulting interbank transaction in the preceding example is between two banks in London. But frequently the counterpart is a bank in another center—often in the United States as the deepest money market in dollars is in New York City. Similarly, in the offshore markets in deutsche marks, inventory positions are often laid off in the deeper money market in Frankfurt, explaining a significant share of the interbank positions outstanding in the Federal Republic as shown in Table 3–1. As a general proposition, the amount of interbank business between an offshore center and the relevant onshore market is more important (relative to total business in the offshore center) the thinner the natural business offshore (nonbank borrowers and lenders wishing to do business there).

Market making, however, cannot explain the large net positions that various countries have with respect to the international interbank market. For example, in the deutsche mark market, German banks at the end of June 1987 had a net creditor position of DM 44.5 billion with respect to banks abroad. Taking all currencies together, U.K. banks had a net creditor position of $105 billion with respect to foreign banks; banks in the United States, by contrast, had a small net debtor position of $20.5 billion with respect to foreign banks. Swiss banks had a huge net creditor position of $199.6 billion while banks in Japan had a huge net debtor position (vis-à-vis foreign banks) of $160 billion.

The net creditor position of German banks in the DM market arises from the giant current account surpluses of the Federal Republic in the mid-1980s. The principal counterpart to these were short-term capital outflows driven by the demand for DM financing from the private nonbank sectors in other European Monetary System (EMS) countries (where the attraction of DM loans was their low nominal interest cost in comparison with domestic loans). In the main, the DM borrowing occurred via the intermediation of the banking sector in these countries, as illustrated by the large volume (DM 43.7 billion) of "internal" Euro-DM loans to nonbank entities (resident in the same country as the bank making the loan) shown in Table 3–2. An example of the underlying transactions would be Italian corporations (especially small and medium-sized ones) borrowing in DMs from a local Italian bank with which they had established relationships, the bank in turn borrowing DMs either from a bank in Germany or in a Euro-DM center (probably London or Luxembourg).

In principle, the Italian bank in the preceding example could have obtained DM funds either directly from the nonbank sector in the Federal Republic (an offshore-external/domestic transaction) or in Italy itself (an offshore-external/foreign transaction), rather than from foreign banks. In practice, however, the net flow of arbitrage funds in DMs from the Federal Republic to satisfy net demand for DM credit by the nonbank sector in other countries is most likely to come in the form of lending abroad by German banks. These banks, with their established relationships with foreign banks, have an edge over the German nonbank sector. They can more readily and cheaply take advantage of any arbitrage opportunity that arises when DM interest rates are higher outside the Federal Republic than within (this condition reflects net excess demand abroad for DM credit at the prevailing DM interest rate). Moreover, the nonbank sector in EMS partner countries of the Federal Republic would hardly become a large net supplier of DM funds, given the same interest rate advantage in favor of their domestic currency that encourages local corporations to borrow in DMs.

Just as balance of payments developments lie behind German banks' net creditor position in relation to foreign banks, they lie behind the net debtor position of banks in the United States. Before the United States's current account swung into huge deficit, U.S. banks had a large creditor position with respect to foreign banks. A corollary of the deficit has been large capital inflows into the United States, some of which have come via the banking sector. The resulting rundown and subsequent reversal of the U.S. banking sector's creditor position has occurred in a number of ways.

For example, relatively high dollar interest rates induced nonbank sectors abroad to repay dollar loans from banks outside the United States; these banks, in turn, have had less recourse to funds from New York banks. Also operating in the same way has been the reduced official balance of payments financing needs of foreign governments (a counterpart to the widening of the U.S. current account deficit), meaning that some have reduced their outstanding dollar borrowing from banks in the offshore market. Investors outside the United States, attracted by high U.S. interest rates, increased their holdings of offshore dollar deposits, meaning that banks in the offshore market have had a reduced need for loans from the New York money market.

In contrast to the United States and Federal Republic, the net position of U.K. banks with respect to foreign banks (or the Bank for International Settlements (BIS) reporting area) has little to do with balance of payments developments. Rather, the main factor in the large creditor position of U.K. banks with respect to foreign banks in the rest of the BIS reporting area is London's success in attracting large pools of nonbank deposit business and also deposits from banks outside the BIS reporting area (hence not included under bank positions in Table 3–1, but included under this heading in Table 3–3). London's comparative advantages in obtaining these large pools of funds outstrips its advantages in finding nonbank foreign loan customers; the resulting surplus is absorbed to a large extent in the form of net lending to foreign banks within the BIS reporting area.

Tables 3–3 and 3–4 show that the pools of funds London attracts include: first, deposits from central monetary institutions that choose London as the number one center in which to place reserves held in the form of Eurodeposits. Second, U.S. nonbank residents may well place over half their holdings of Eurodollar

TABLE 3–3
External Position of U.K. Monetary Sector and Other Financial Institutions, June 1987 (In $ Billions)

Analysis by Sector	United Kingdom	
	Liabilities	Claims
Sterling		
Liabilities to/claims on:		
Central monetary institutions	3.7	1.7
Other banks	33.5	27.6
Other nonresidents	34.1	26.9
US dollars		
Liabilities to/claims on:		
Central monetary institutions	41.7	13.0
Other banks	313.2	352.3
Other nonresidents	141.4	107.9
Other currencies		
Liabilities to/claims on:		
Central monetary institutions	24.9	3.9
Other banks	178.1	173.4
Other nonresidents	37.4	58.6

Source: Bank of England.

TABLE 3–4

External Position of U.K. Monetary Sector and Other Financial Institutions, June 1987 (In $ Billions)

Analysis by Country	United Kingdom Liabilities		United Kingdom Claims	
	Pounds	Foreign Currency	Pounds	Foreign Currency
BIS Reporting area				
Belgium Luxembourg	2.5	39.8	4.5	41.7
France	4.3	31.9	6.2	31.3
Germany	1.4	50.8	0.5	28.2
Italy	1.5	14.0	2.1	28.6
Netherlands	4.2	17.5	2.3	13.7
Spain	1.4	12.4	1.6	7.7
Sweden	0.4	3.1	1.0	7.0
Switzerland	8.4	84.0	1.9	15.2
Japan	1.2	66.4	1.8	140.5
United States	4.5	161.2	3.0	122.2
Other industrial	7.4	26.6	5.5	44.7
Hong Kong	2.2	20.8	1.9	28.9
Singapore	1.7	12.9	1.0	25.9
Caribbean	3.5	41.5	2.4	32.5
Others				
Bermuda	0.8	7.4	0.1	1.4
W. Europe	3.4	9.5	1.8	14.6
Australia	0.5	1.5	1.4	7.3
New Zealand	0.3	0.7	0.4	2.7
South Africa	0.7	0.9	0.7	7.3
Organization of Petroleum Exporting Countries	6.8	35.0	4.1	6.5
Taiwan	0.3	14.7	0.0	1.2
Other non-oil Less Developed Countries	7.4	27.3	6.5	49.4
Eastern Europe	0.6	6.7	1.9	18.0

Source: Bank of England.

deposits in London (for the total U.S. nonbank holdings amounting to $195 billion, see Table 3–1). Third, banks outside the reporting area—largely in the Third World and in Caribbean offshore centers—use London as the number one market for placing Eurodollar deposits. The Caribbean centers are to a large extent recycling deposits they themselves have received from, say, Latin America.

TABLE 3–5
Swiss Fiduciary Business, December 31, 1986 (In Sfr Billions)

	Banks' Fiduciary Deposits from Abroad	Banks' Placement of Fiduciary Deposits with Banks Abroad
BIS area	44.4	150.2
Belgium	4.0	19.7
West Germany	4.6	4.9
France	7.3	12.3
United Kingdom	10.0	46.0
Italy	9.2	1.2
Japan	0.4	0.4
Canada	1.0	3.2
Luxembourg	1.2	35.9
Netherlands	1.5	21.0
United States	4.0	2.1
Others	1.2	3.3
Other W. Europe		
Greece	3.5	0.1
Monaco	0.7	0.7
Spain	3.1	0.1
Turkey	2.1	0.2
Others	1.9	0.7
Other industrialized countries		
Eastern Europe	0.1	0.1
Caribbean	22.1	9.8
Latin America	9.8	1.4
Middle East	31.4	0.7
Africa	5.9	0.4
Asia	7.0	0.5
Others	0.0	0.4

Source: Swiss National Bank.

The position of London as a large net lender to banks in the reporting area should not disguise the fact that it is a large debtor of Swiss banks and to a much smaller extent of German banks. But these debtor positions are in large part offset by London's creditor position with respect to Japanese banks. Some part of the Swiss banks' net creditor position with respect to foreign banks can be explained as a counterpart to Switzerland's continuing large current account surplus (the nonbank sector in many European countries being a net borrower of low-interest-rate francs—see Table 3–2). A large part of the creditor position can be explained by the role of Swiss banks as fiduciary agents (see Table 3–5), whereby they place their customers' funds in the Eurodeposit market under the name of the bank, but at the customer's risk.

Japanese banks' large net indebtedness to foreign banks, especially in London, is in contrast to Japan's role as the number one creditor nation. Long-term capital exports from Japan, however, far outstripped the current account surplus through the mid-1980s, the balance being financed by short-term capital inflows via the banking sector. And already, before the years of large surplus, Japanese banks were major borrowers abroad to finance Japan's international trade. Some of the long-term capital outflows from Japan created direct counterpart short-term capital inflows through the banks. For example, there were large-scale purchases of U.S. Treasury securities on a hedged basis—the investor either financing the purchase by borrowing short-term dollars or by buying yen forward against dollars, which would induce arbitrage inflows of short-term capital via the banks.

INTERNATIONAL LIQUIDITY CRISIS

The large net creditor and debtor positions of various centers vis-à-vis foreign banks is highly relevant to understanding what would be the impact of a liquidity crisis on international capital flow. The most likely trigger to a liquidity crisis is a sudden increase in the perceived risk of lending to banks, perhaps induced by a major default, say, of a bank or a large debtor. In response, banks would curtail their lines of credit to other banks and in particular to foreign banks, as any lifeboat operation launched by national authorities might well provide a lower order of rescue for foreign lenders (depositors) than for domestic depositors. In the process of contraction of cross-border interbank lending, countries whose banking systems are heavily indebted abroad would suffer an outflow of capital, and the scope of central banks in these countries to act as lenders of last resort could be limited by a shortage of foreign-exchange reserves.

Among the countries in the BIS reporting area, Japan stands out as the country with the largest net indebtedness to foreign banks. In an international liquidity crisis, Japanese banks could find it impossible to renew all external credits falling due, and request accommodation from the Bank of Japan which would dip into its foreign-exchange reserves. Many of the banks refusing to renew credits would be in London, given the large indebtedness of Japanese banks in the London Euromarket—see Table 3–4. These London banks in turn would be subject to a withdrawal of credits by banks in Switzerland, the Federal Republic, and the Caribbean who themselves have net creditor positions in London.

The withdrawal of credits by Swiss banks has somewhat different currency implications from those by other major groups of banks. This follows from the fact that the Swiss franc is not a reserve currency and so the repatriation of funds to Switzerland, whether by banks on their own account, or in their capacity as fiduciary agents for clients, would have no counterpart in an official sale of francs by the central bank in the debtor country (here debtor refers to the external position of the banking sector). Hence the Swiss franc would come under upward pressure.

By contrast, the withdrawal of credits by German banks would trigger large official sales of the deutsche mark; thus, dampening its appreciation in the foreign exchange market. Much of the German banks' foreign lending to other banks is in DMs (see Table 3–1) and is to an ultimate debtor in other EMS countries. Central banks there would accommodate a new withdrawal of DM orders either by drawing down DM reserves or by using official lines of DM credit with the Bundesbank under EMS arrangements.

Hence, the Swiss franc might well be stronger than the deutsche mark in an international liquidity crisis. A simple reading of Table 3–1, which shows a large net creditor position for banks in London relative to foreign banks in the BIS reporting area, would suggest that the pound could also be strong in a liquidity crisis. There are, however, other considerations pointing in a different direction. First, banks in London have a large net indebtedness to banks outside the reporting area, some of which would themselves be in the front line of credit withdrawal and, in turn, be forced to meet this by reducing balances with U.K. banks. Second, London's role as deposit-taker from central banks could be in jeopardy, if these respond to increased banking risks by moving funds to the United States—either into Treasury bills or into U.S. banks. (Later we discuss why U.S. banks might be considered safer than London banks.) Third, a large share of the nonbank U.S. resident-held deposits in London could be repatriated (again based on the view that U.S. banks are safer—an extra inducement here being the deposit insurance that U.S. nonbank residents would enjoy at home). Fourth, U.K. registered banks—the ultimate constituency of the Bank of England in its role as lender of last resort—do not have a worldwide net creditor position vis-à-vis foreign banks in the reporting area. (In Table 3–6 the figures for U.K.-registered banks include the positions of branches abroad.)

This last point can be elaborated. The general assumption is that in an international liquidity crisis the appeal to the lender-of-last-resort function is based on nationality rather than residence. Thus a branch of a British bank in New York suffering a run on its deposits would look to its head office, which in turn would look to the Bank of England, rather than to the U.S. Federal Reserve, for accommodation. One implication is that international deposits with a bank of nationality X, where that nation's banking system is heavily indebted (or a net basis) to foreign banks and has a large volume of deposits outstanding in foreign currencies, and where the central bank of nation X has a low level of foreign-exchange reserves, are particularly exposed to danger in an international liquidity crisis.

Conversely, international deposits with a bank of nationality Y, where that nation's banking system has a creditor position with respect to foreign banks (on a net basis) and conducts most of its external deposit and loan business in Y's currency, and where the central bank of nation Y has a high level of foreign-exchange reserves, have a low exposure to danger in an international liquidity crisis. In broad terms, Swiss, German, and U.S. banks, all

TABLE 3–6

Net International Assets of Banks by Nationality of Ownership, September 1986 (In $ Billions)

Parent Country of Bank	Net Claims	Related Offices	Other Banks	Vis-à-vis Nonbanks	Official Institutions	CDs and Other Securities
Austria	− 0.4	—	− 7.5	− 7.5	− 0.2	− 0.2
Belgium	− 0.8	1.7	−13.2	13.1	− 2.2	− 0.2
Luxembourg	− 0.1	− 0.1	3.6	− 3.6	—	—
Canada	−11.1	8.2	− 2.0	− 8.6	− 4.5	− 4.2
Denmark	− 0.5	3.3	− 7.2	3.8	− 0.3	− 0.1
Finland	− 1.5	− 0.3	− 8.6	7.0	0.4	—
France	10.3	− 6.4	−18.1	45.4	− 8.1	− 2.1
Germany	56.0	−11.6	57.6	24.7	−11.9	− 2.8
Italy	− 2.4	− 1.0	−19.0	23.9	− 1.0	− 5.3
Japan	56.9	−17.4	−67.3	202.7	−23.7	−37.4
Netherlands	5.0	− 0.3	7.4	3.8	− 5.0	− 1.5
Spain	1.2	0.2	6.2	− 4.9	—	− 0.3
Sweden	0.4	0.6	− 9.0	11.3	− 0.2	− 2.3
Switzerland	21.2	−27.0	48.7	6.3	− 6.9	0.1
United Kingdom	−10.5	0.8	14.2	13.0	−10.8	−27.7
United States	21.5	24.2	60.1	3.7	−34.4	−32.1

* Banks' holdings of CDs (for banks in the United States only) less banks' issues of CDs and other securities.

in varying degrees, fall under this heading. Thus, in a crisis, there would be a tendency for depositors to switch funds, in whatever currency, toward banks of those nationalities, increasing the pressures on countries lacking such safe banking systems.

Of several factors favoring the United States as a recipient of funds in an international liquidity crisis, the second and third are not shared to the same degree by the Federal Republic or Switzerland. First, U.S.-registered banks and their branches elsewhere in the BIS reporting area have a large net creditor position in relation to foreign banks (see Table 3–5). The apparent contradiction with Table 3–1, where banks in the United States are shown having a small debtor position, can be explained by the large number of foreign-owned banks in New York funding themselves abroad, and by the importance of U.S. bank branches abroad that not only have a rich deposit base among U.S. nonbank customers but also are net lenders to foreign banks.

Second, U.S. banks do by far the greatest proportion of their international deposit and loan business in U.S. dollars—a proportion substantially larger than that done for international business in marks and francs by German and Swiss banks respectively. Third, insofar as an international liquidity crisis is accompanied by an increased demand for highly liquid nonbank investments, U.S. Treasury bills and bonds stand out from alternatives in other currencies. If the increased demand for U.S. bills and bonds has some counterpart in reduced demand for deposits in nondollar currencies, the U.S. balance of payments would be strengthened thereby.

The last two factors stem from the U.S. dollar's position as the world's number one international currency. This also gives the United States an asymmetric advantage over even Switzerland and the Federal Republic in geographically concentrated liquidity crises. For example, suppose a run were to develop on a big Swiss bank—as occurred in the Chiasso crisis of 1977.[2] International depositors with the bank in dollars or other nonfranc currencies would be unlikely to find suitable alternative placements for all

---

[2] See B. D. Brown, *The Flight of International Capital* (London: Croom Helm, 1987), p. 392.

their withdrawn funds inside Switzerland whether they incurred exchange-rate risk and switched into franc investments or added to dollar deposits with the other Swiss banks. These banks might lend them to the bank with problems as part of a lifeboat operation sponsored by the Swiss National Bank. Thus, some net outflow of funds from Switzerland would be probable, accommodated by the Swiss National Bank acting directly as lender of last resort (in dollars) to the bank with problems.

By contrast, were an isolated run to develop on a large U.S. bank, as occurred, for example, in the Continental Illinois Bank crisis of 1984, international dollar deposits withdrawn would likely be replaced in alternative investments inside the United States (including deposits with other banks), so deep are the markets for these, and no exchange-rate risk would be involved in the transfer. There could be some net capital outflow on account of the withdrawal of international nondollar deposits from the bank in trouble. For example, depositors in deutsche marks with the U.S. bank would most likely look to reinvest the funds outside the United States and the U.S. banking system. But, as already explained, this source of outflow (foreign currency deposit withdrawal) is likely to be particularly low in the case of the United States.

DEFAULT RISK AND COVERED-INTEREST ARBITRAGE

The ultimate risk in an international liquidity crisis is that one or more countries—most likely those whose banking systems are heavily indebted abroad—will declare a standstill on foreign credits. Historical precedents include most of the belligerent countries in early August 1914 at on the outbreak of World War I, Germany and many of the central European countries in the summer and autumn of 1931, and Mexico in August 1982.[3] The risk of such a moratorium or standstill, however slight, is present in all international investment transactions and stems from the possibil-

---

[3] See B. D. Brown, *Monetary Chaos in Europe* (London: Croom Helm, 1988), chapter 1.

ity of not only an international liquidity crisis but also of a national
economic or political crisis.

So-called political risk—the risk of moratorium, standstill, or
exchange restrictions being imposed and so inflicting loss on the
creditor—varies between the different broad categories of international transactions described at the opening of this chapter. In
onshore-internal and onshore-external transactions, only one political risk is present—that the country issuing the currency in
question will impose restrictions. By contrast, in offshore-internal,
offshore-external/domestic, and offshore-external/foreign transactions, two political risks are present—that the country issuing the
currency and the debtor's country of residence might impose
restrictions.

For example, a French resident holding a deposit in francs
with a bank in France (an onshore-internal transaction) is subject
to one political risk, that France might impose exchange restrictions limiting the convertibility of the deposit into foreign currency.
The nonresident holder of the franc deposit in France is similarly
subject to political risk, but this is not identical in form or
magnitude to that faced by the resident. In particular, exchange
restrictions might be introduced with respect to resident but not
nonresident funds; if they are introduced with respect to both, the
loss inflicted on the nonresident is probably greater than on the
resident given the considerable scope for the latter to use
"blocked" funds on purchasing domestic goods and services.

A British investor in dollar commercial paper issued by an
Italian corporation (an offshore-external/foreign transaction) is
subject to two distinct political risks. First, Italy could impose
restrictions on resident debtors making the payments in freely
convertible currency. Second, in extreme circumstances, the
United States might impose restrictions on the transfer of
dollars—and all offshore dealings in dollars at some point involve a
funds transfer within the political jurisdiction of the U.S. authorities—to certain categories of nonresidents. For example, during
World War II transfers of U.S. dollar funds to residents of the Axis
countries and of the neutrals became subject to license.

A U.S. investor in the same Italian commercial paper (an
offshore-external/domestic transaction) would also be subject to
the dual political risk, but of a somewhat different nature. In

particular, the risk of the United States interfering with the transferability of funds by residents is less than for nonresidents. An Italian investor in the same commercial paper (an offshore-internal transaction) would be subject to U.S. political risk to a greater degree than the U.S. investor; but the Italian investor would be less at risk from Italian action, in that blocked lira funds could be used at home.

Political risk is one factor that explains international interest-rate differentials, particularly between deposits and other debt instruments denominated in the same currency. For example, one element in the interest-rate differential in favor of Eurodollar deposits in London or Paris over those in New York could be political risk (where comparison is made for rates paid by banks of similar credit rating). There is the remote possibility that in an international liquidity crisis, for example, the convertibility of deposits in London or Paris could be restricted. Other elements to be considered are the greater liquidity of dollar money markets in the United States than offshore and uncertainty whether the Federal Reserve's role as lender of last resort would extend fully to the offshore liabilities of U.S. banks.

When comparing interest-rate differentials between currencies, exchange-rate expectations are likely to dwarf political risk as an explanatory variable. For example, the rate differential between dollar deposits in New York and deutsche mark deposits in Frankfurt reflects foremost the expectation of dollar depreciation against the mark. In addition, the differential might incorporate a combination of positive or negative risk premiums—two of which are exchange risk and political risk. This combined premium is compensation for investors at the margin distorting their portfolios away from neutrality. Such a distortion has a counterpart, in general equilibrium, in balance of payments financing requirements. The neutral portfolio is that which any given investor would hold if the expected rate of return, adjusted for exchange-rate change, were identical on all currencies. The determination of the neutral weights for each involves trade-offs between minimizing variability of the portfolio's purchasing power, minimizing the portfolio's exposure to political risk, and obtaining hedges against other risks to which the investor might be subject. For example, dollar-based investors could justify some holding of deutsche marks as a hedge against the recession risks to which their equity holdings are subject because the mark tends to rise against the dollar in a U.S. recession.

When comparing covered interest-rate differentials between currencies, political risk is not an element. To illustrate this point, it is useful to outline the transactions involved in covered arbitrage, say, between the dollar and deutsche mark money markets. In effect, the arbitrage spans three markets—the dollar deposit, the deutsche mark deposit, and the mark-dollar swap market. In a three-month mark-dollar swap transaction for $100,000, the transactor buys (or sells) $100,000 spot against marks and simultaneously sells (or buys) $100,000 three-month forward against marks; the swap rate is quoted as a margin—the difference between spot and forward rate—for a given reference spot rate. These three markets form a triangle, in the sense that any transaction in one market can be replicated by effecting transactions in the other two. For example, instead of lending marks for three months, the investor can swap marks into dollars, and lend dollars for three months. Strictly speaking, the investor would also have to sell forward for marks the interest due on the dollar loan. Alternatively, instead of swapping marks into dollars, the dealer can lend marks and borrow dollars to the same equivalent spot value, buying the dollar interest due forward against marks. Instead of lending dollars for three months, the investor can swap dollars into marks and lend marks for three months; again effecting a small supplementary forward transaction.

Covered interest arbitrage involves spotting an opportunity where a transaction can be more cheaply effected indirectly (at the other two corners of the swap-deposit triangle) than directly (at the corner of the same triangle). In practice, arbitrage opportunity only occurs at the most illiquid corner of the triangle—sometimes the swap market, sometimes the less liquid of the two deposit markets.[4] The amount of saving obtained by arbitrage is described as the covered interest margin between the two currencies and this varies according to whether we are looking from the borrower's or lender's viewpoint (or from the swap buyer's or swap seller's)

---

[4] Brown, *The Forward Market*, chapter 5.

viewpoint, on the assumption that bid-offer spreads in all markets are significant.

Political risk can be present in covered interest arbitrage; in certain situations the arbitrager could suffer loss from the imposition of exchange restrictions or debt moratoria. However, often the political risks in the two "legs" of the arbitrage operation are offsetting. For example, consider the German investor who spots an arbitrage opportunity in the form of depositing U.S. dollars in New York and swapping deutsche marks into dollars, rather than depositing marks in Frankfurt. He assumes political risk in the first transaction. Some of the risk, however, is shed in the second transaction; the party that buys dollars forward from the investor (as part of the swap deal) undertakes to deliver deutsche marks forward, even if dollars meanwhile have become subject to restriction. Thus, political risk is not an element in the covered interest-rate differential between the Frankfurt and New York money markets. Other factors such as relative liquidity, capital and reserve requirements on banks, and convenience considerations are responsible. For instance, at the margin, German investors may be willing to suffer a lower return at home than that which could be obtained via covered interest arbitrage, owing to the convenience of having funds near at hand.

Nor is political risk usually present in covered-interest arbitrage between two Eurodeposit markets in one center. For example, consider covered arbitrage between the Eurodollar and Euromark market in London. Instead of placing a deposit in marks, the investor who swaps these into a dollar deposit assumes no additional political risk. Both the Euromark and Eurodollar deposit in London are subject to the risk of U.K. restrictions; the assumption of U.S. political risk and the shedding of German political risk in the deposit switch is reversed in the forward mark-dollar transaction which is one part of the swap deal. In practice, covered-interest margins rarely exist between Eurodeposit markets in one center; convenience considerations, for example, that are important in explaining covered margins between domestic centers are not highly relevant to comparison within a center. Moreover, because Euromarkets are usually narrower than their domestic counterparts, banks might be more successful in closing arbitrage gaps before becoming subject to capital and reserve requirements.

NEW SWAPS, NEW ARBITRAGE

The conventional swap market at the heart of covered-interest arbitrage is only a distant relative of currency and interest-rate swap markets; first developed in the 1980s, they revolutionized international financial markets. In a straightforward interest-rate swap, borrower A with a fixed-rate liability enters into an arrangement with borrower B who has a floating-rate liability outstanding in the same currency, whereby A will pay B's interest outgoings as they fall due and conversely. In effect, the swap transforms B's liability from a fixed rate to floating rate and A's liability from floating rate to fixed rate. An essential condition for the interest-rate swap to be profitable for a borrower is that A has a comparative advantage (relative to B) in raising fixed-rate finance (perhaps because A's name is especially popular with international investors).

In a straightforward currency swap, say, for U.S. dollars against deutsche marks, borrower A with a fixed-rate liability outstanding in deutsche marks enters into an arrangement with borrower B who has a floating rate liability in U.S. dollars, whereby A will pay B's interest due and effect repayment of B's loan at maturity while B will pay A's interest due and effect repayment of A's loan at maturity. Such an arrangement would be advantageous if B wants to borrow fixed-rate marks, and yet, A has a comparative advantage in tapping the fixed-rate market.

The innovation of currency and interest-rate swaps has introduced an array of new arbitrage opportunities possible in money and bond markets. From the viewpoint of investors, the most important new opportunity is the so-called asset swap. As an alternative to direct purchases of floating-rate assets—whether floating-rate notes, commercial paper (rolling this over on maturity), or deposits (again rolling over)—an investor can create a synthetic floater by purchasing a fixed-rate bond and simultaneously entering into an interest-rate swap.

For example, investor A might spot an arbitrage opportunity to buy $1 million of a three-year fixed-rate bond outstanding of corporation X, with a credit rating of a single A, and simultaneously enter a three-year interest rate-swap. This would involve paying fixed-rate interest due on counterparty B's fixed-rate liability and receiving from B floating-rate interest set with reference to the London Interbank Offered Rate (LIBOR). The margin above LIBOR, which A would receive on the resulting synthetic floater, might be attractive compared to what could be obtained from a direct purchase of single A floaters in the market. Or, if these are not available, the margin could be compared to what the theoretical margin on a single A floater should be; it is calculated by adding the normal margin that single A borrowers must pay over AA borrowers to rates in the market for AA-rated floating-rate notes.

It may be asked how an asset-swap opportunity can exist for the investor without a simultaneous opportunity for corporation X to buy back its own fixed-rate bonds, refinance itself on a floating-rate basis (probably via a bank credit), and enter into an interest-rate swap to convert its floating-rate liability into a fixed-rate liability. Often, size is a barrier to arbitrage by the corporation. In buying back a whole issue, X would drive up the price of outstanding bonds and thereby eliminate any arbitrage opportunity.

Sometimes corporation X could even make a new fixed-rate issue on terms that permit some large investors to immediately enter into an asset swap. This could occur where the issue can be sold at two prices—a higher one to small retail investors and a lower one to the large institutional investors; alternatively, X might see some advantage, albeit at some cost, in obtaining a wide distribution of its paper between banks who buy it as part of an asset swap, perhaps with a view to expanding its scope to obtain bank financing in the future.

Usually, though, asset-swap opportunities are in the secondary fixed-rate market, and in its more illiquid sector (for single A corporate paper, for example), where the absence of ready demand means that at times a big offer of notes in a given issue might drive its price down to a level attractive for synthetic floating-rate note creation. The possibility of asset swaps does, however, set a lower limit to how far the yield on floating rate notes can fall relative to LIBOR even in the case of top-rated issues, although in practice this is never likely to be reached. For example, in the secondary market the margin below London Interbank Bid Rate (LIBID) on a five-year U.S. dollar floating-rate note issue for the United Kingdom could not widen so far that it would be highly profitable for the investor to instead purchase a five-year fixed-rate dollar issue of the United Kingdom and enter into an interest-rate swap (receiving floating-rate interest and paying fixed-rate interest).

Weighing against asset swaps ever being profitable for prime rated paper is lack of widespread nonbank demand for floating-rate notes and the limited interest of banks in taking paper onto their books at only fine margins above LIBID or at rates below LIBID. The lack of nonbank demand can be explained by such investors' preference for keeping the floating-rate section of their portfolios in short-maturity paper—for example, commercial paper and bank deposits—having already usually large amounts of long-maturity paper through their involvement in fixed-rate paper. In view of the fact that their own credit rating is usually less than prime and that they would have to pay a significant margin above LIBOR for long-term funds, banks can hardly justify buying large amounts of top-rated floaters.

Just as the possibility of asset swaps sets a lower limit to the yield on floaters relative to LIBOR, the possibility of the borrower obtaining floating-rate finance indirectly—by issuing fixed-rate paper and entering into an interest-rate swap (whereby the borrower pays floating and receives fixed interest)—rather than by a direct issue of a floating-rate note, sets an upper limit. In practice, prime borrowers usually find that the margin at which they could issue a floating-rate note is above the upper limit. Sometimes, however, there are exceptions. For example, during a period of considerable inflation uncertainty, nonbank investment demand for floating-rate notes could rise sharply, meaning that margins on even top-rated new issues could fall below the upper boundary.

Sometimes political or other considerations can swing a borrower in favor of making a jumbo floating-rate note issue even at a rate relative to LIBOR somewhat above the theoretical upper limit. For example, the United Kingdom made a jumbo issue in 1986 for $4 billion at a rate relative to LIBID which was widely perceived as higher than what could have been achieved from a series of fixed-rate issues (perhaps in different currencies) together with swap transactions. It would not, however, have been possible to make a jumbo issue of similar size in the fixed-rate market (hence the need for a series of issues) given the much greater risks incurred by issuing banks in the fixed-rate than in the floating-rate market, and the narrowness of the swap market. If it were known that the United Kingdom were in the market to conclude $4 billion worth of swaps, this would turn the rates there against it. Politically, the U.K. government did not want to be seen as having again become a frequent borrower abroad because the Conservatives had attacked foreign borrowing by the prior Labour government. Instead, a lightning jumbo issue was preferred. An additional consideration could have been unwillingness to enter into huge swap commitments, thus assuming counterparty risk.

Counterparty risk is greater in currency swaps than in interest-rate swaps; the two principal amounts of equal value when the swap is contracted may be of very different value by the end. The significant counterpart risk in currency swaps explains why some apparent arbitrage opportunities involving a crossing of currency frontiers can remain open. In principle, if currency swaps were riskless, then the following parity conditions should hold between, say, Eurodollar and Euromark bond markets of whatever maturity. It should not be cheaper in market equilibrium for a wide range of borrowers to issue a fixed-rate bond in DMs, swap the fixed-rate DMs into floating-rate dollars, and swap the floating-rate dollars into fixed-rate dollars, than issuing a fixed-rate dollar bond. Nor must the opposite inequality be broken (meaning that indirect financing via the dollar is cheaper than fixed-rate financing in marks).

Specifically, the spread that borrowers in the DM bond market must pay above German government yields less the DM currency swap rate (for DM fixed rate to $ floating rate) plus the dollar interest-rate swap should lie within a tight margin of the spread which the same quality of borrower would have to pay above U.S. Treasury bonds. Note that swap rates are expressed relative to government-bond yields, with LIBOR taken as reference point. For example, a five-year DM currency swap rate of 15 points means that a floating-rate dollar liability on which interest is payable at LIBOR can be swapped into fixed-rate DMs at 15 percentage points above the German government-bond yield.

The preceding statement of interest-rate parity between the bond and swap markets can be extended to include intermediation via three rather than two swap markets. Instead of swapping fixed-rate DMs directly into floating-rate dollars, the arbitrager could swap fixed-rate DMs into floating-rate DMs (a DM interest-rate swap), and then swap floating-rate DMs into floating-rate dollars (a so-called LIBOR–LIBOR swap). The arbitrager could go one step farther. Instead of effecting the LIBOR–LIBOR swap, for the given maturity of five years (a floating-rate dollar liability being swapped for a floating-rate mark liability), the arbitrager could effect a conventional six-month swap (borrowing dollars for six months and lending marks for six months is equivalent to selling dollars six months forward against marks, which in turn is equivalent to a spot sale of dollars against marks plus a conventional dollar-mark six-month swap in which dollars are simultaneously bought spot and sold forward), rolling this over at maturity throughout the five-year period. Here the distant relationship of currency and interest rate swaps to the conventional swap reveals itself.

The two interest-rate parity theorems described involving first, the interest-rate swap market and the floating-rate note market and second, currency plus interest-rate swaps and yield spreads in two bond markets of different currency denominations, are essentially statements of static equilibrium conditions. They are analagous to the better-known interest-rate parity theorem relating the conventional swap rate to interest rates in two money markets of different currency denominations. The dynamics of arbitrage—the relative extent by which swap rates and bond yields adjust under the pressure of arbitrage from an initial disequilibrium position—is not within the scope of this chapter. Nor are the separate constraints on arbitrage possibilities that arise from the possibility of producing currency and interest rate swaps synthetically—at least for maturities up to around two years—by transactions in the interest-rate and currency futures markets.

CHAPTER 4

THE ART OF
CENTRAL BANKING

Joseph Bisignano

The practice of central banking in any country depends on the structure of its financial institutions and markets, its economic and political history and, to some degree, prevailing academic economy orthodoxy. No doubt, it also depends on the personalities of the individuals who exercise central banking policy. This chapter describes what some have referred to as the "art" of central banking from several of these vantage points, with particular emphasis on the United States, but with considerable illustration drawn from the financial structures and policy execution in other large industrial countries.

Concentrating attention on central banking in the United States is obviously of greatest interest to American financial analysts, corporate treasurers, and the like, but such focus carries with it two potential handicaps. First, viewing central banking in general from a U.S. vantage point obscures the fact that money and capital markets abroad are in many cases considerably less well developed than those in the United States. There is a tendency for U.S. economists and financial analysts to casually extrapolate U.S. institutional and financial market experience in their interpretation of financial market events abroad and to view foreign central

The views expressed here are those of the author and not necessarily those of the Bank for International Settlements. My thanks to John Kneeshaw and Palle Andersen for helpful comments and to Robert Z. Aliber for over the years always asking me interesting questions.

banking policy in this light. Second, until very recently it has been common to view the United States as a "closed economy," that is, with only modest international trade in goods although with considerable trade in financial assets. From a monetary policy perspective the status of the trade balance or foreign-exchange value of the dollar was not often viewed as being of first-round importance; domestic economic considerations tend to dominate the published monetary policy records of the United States. As a result, the exchange rate has been viewed more as a potential constraint than as an explicit objective in most circumstances. Such a vantage point may strongly slant the view of foreign central bank policy considerations. This chapter can broaden the reader's perspective of the practice of central banking.

This chapter is organized into five parts: the first considers the goals of monetary policy. The second section considers central bank instruments, that is, the mechanisms by which central banks attempt to influence not only short-run interest rates, the growth of money and credit but also the behavior of economic activity and prices in the medium to longer run. Because the instruments of monetary policy are dependent on the characteristics of money and capital markets, this section also briefly describes the money and capital markets of some of the larger economies. The third section describes the changing views of the monetary "transmission mechanism," that is, the channels through which monetary policy alters economic behavior. The exchange rate is the subject of section four. Here the debate over the efficacy of central bank intervention in the exchange markets is summarized, and some attention is given to the increased internationalization of securities markets. Lastly, section five reviews some of the policy issues raised for central banks by the liberalization, innovation, and internationalization in banking and finance. The supervisory and regulatory issues raised by these developments are also given some attention.

THE GOALS OF MONETARY POLICY

In establishing goals for monetary policy, central banks are immediately confronted with the problem of determining what is achievable in the short run and sustainable in the longer run. In influencing the growth of money and credit and the level of interest rates on short-term marketable financial assets, central banks have the ability to expand nominal aggregate demand considerably in the short run. The rise in nominal demand translates itself into an increase in real output and prices. The monetary influence on prices, however, is normally transmitted with a considerably longer time lag than the influence on real output. In this respect, then, the gains from expansionary monetary stimulus arrive early and the costs, to the degree that monetary policy is excessive, arrive later in the form of a higher price level. The speed with which monetary expansion is reflected in prices depends on a variety of factors, such as the degree of labor and capacity constraints in the economy, the impact of expansionary monetary policy on the exchange rate, and, in a difficult to specify but highly important manner, the credibility of the central bank in the eyes of the private sector. Here credibility is defined as the ability of the central bank to convince the private sector that it views price stability as a prominent long-term objective and is pursuing appropriate policies to achieve that objective. Central banks might be considered then to engage in both fire fighting and fire prevention, the former the short-term concern with the cyclical status of real aggregate growth, and the latter the pursuit of long-term price stability.

An example of central bank goals is contained in the following statement from the Federal Reserve publication, *Purposes and Functions:*

> The Federal Reserve contributes to the attainment of the nation's economic and financial goals through its ability to influence money and credit in the economy. As the nation's central bank, it attempts to ensure that growth in money and credit over the long run is sufficient to encourage growth in the economy in line with its potential and with reasonable price stability. In the short run the Federal Reserve seeks to adapt its policies to combat deflationary or inflationary pressures as they may arise. And as a lender of last resort, it has the responsibility for utilizing the policy instruments available to it in an attempt to forestall national liquidity crises and financial panics.[1]

---

[1] *The Federal Reserve System: Purposes and Functions* (Washington, D.C.: Board of Governors of the Federal Reserve System, 1984).

Contrast the preceding statement of goals with those of the Deutsche Bundesbank, which places special emphasis on price stability:

> But in the interaction between the various economic policy decision-makers—Parliament, the Federal Govenment, the central bank, management and labour—the Bundesbank must always regard its function as guardian of the currency, as laid down in the Act, as its *primary task*. That is why the Bundesbank Act has not only made the central bank independent of instructions from the Federal Government; in addition, the basic obligation contained in the Act for the Bundesbank to support the general economic policy of the Federal Government is expressly linked to the condition that this does not create insoluble conflicts with the primary task performed by monetary policy (Bundesbank Act, Section 12).[2]

The fire fighting versus fire prevention analogy in the case of the United States is easily extracted from the first quote by noting the phrases "attempts to ensure . . . reasonable price stability" and "adapt its policies to combat deflationary or inflationary pressures."

Three questions are raised in the practical pursuit of both short- and long-run goals. The first is whether the central bank ought, or indeed is able, to establish a clearly articulated and implementable "rule" defining how it will pursue its goals. Since the early 1970s a number of countries have established explicit monetary growth targets, sometimes referred to as "intermediate targets," which express policy intentions over a period of usually one year. The increased liberalization of financial markets and deregulation of banking, together with the pronounced internationalization of money and capital markets, have made the use of such targets increasingly more difficult. (This issue is considered in some depth in a later section.) Alternatively, the central bank may not wish to strap itself to any one policy rule and instead prefer to use discretion in the execution of policy. This hardly implies that

---

[2] *The Deutsche Bundesbank: Its Monetary Policy Instruments and Functions,* Deutsche Bundesbank Special Series No. 7 (Frankfurt: Deutsche Bundesbank, 1982), p. 9.

the employment of a policy rule prevents the use of practical day-to-day discretion in executing policy, but rather that the "reaction function" of the central bank may be less tightly tied to the behavior of any single credit or monetary aggregate, or financial asset price, implying that there will be no explicit publicly known constraint on the growth of the balance sheet of the central bank, money, or a particular financial asset price.

The second practical question raised in pursuing central bank goals is determining what can be used as an indicator of the central bank's policy stance. This question often is stated in terms of whether one judges policy by a quantity or a price, the quantity being a monetary, credit, or reserve aggregate and the price some interest rate or exchange rate under the short-run influence of the central bank, often a very short-term money-market rate. Academics have conducted extensive debates over what is the appropriate indicator of monetary policy. As it is the asset side of the central bank's balance sheet that is generally under the control of the central bank, and the short-term interest rate is the result of the interaction of the demand for credit from the central bank with the available supply, it is argued by some that short-term interest rates are an improper indicator of the central bank's "tightness" or "ease." Those who concentrate on the interest rate, the price of credit, argue that the price of credit is the chief concern of the central bank in the very short run, and, possibly, the quantity of credit or money only indirectly or over a longer span of time. (The interest rate of most concern is the one the central banks can most immediately affect, usually a short-term rate in the interbank market.)

The third practical problem of central bank goal achievement can be called the "targets and instruments problem," namely that the central bank can have only as many targets as it has instruments to achieve them. Having a greater number of targets than instruments will probably result in policy conflicts. If, for example, a central bank in the short run wishes to reduce aggregate domestic demand because it fears potential overheating of the economy but also desires to prevent currency appreciation, it may be frustrated in achieving these goals by relying on the domestic short-term interest rate. A rise in interest rates aids the achievement of the former but not the latter, and the reverse with a reduction in short-term interest rates.[3]

Because of the greater ease in altering monetary policy than fiscal policy, both in reaching a decision and in implementation, and because of the illusion at times that real output and employment gains can be obtained and secured by a further easing in monetary policy with little danger to price stability, monetary policy in almost all countries at one time or another has been the easy lever to pull to provide short-run stimulus to aggregate demand. In addition, given the difficulty in judging the appropriate monetary policy in many circumstances and the variable time lags involved between the provision of monetary stimulus and the appearance of output gains, monetary policy may suffer from an endemic weakness leading to its overuse. In short, the bias is often toward greater use of monetary stimulus to achieve employment or output goals which may either not be achievable or whose attainment may be only transitory.

To show how monetary policy goals in some countries have changed over time, consider the following statement from the Bank of Canada's *Annual Report* for 1982. It pointedly summarizes the shift in emphasis on attainable central bank goals, a view probably shared by other central banks:

> Probably never before in human history had the living conditions of so many people improved so rapidly. One of the contributory factors was the success of public policy in the major industrial countries in maintaining an environment favourable to economic growth. That policy arose from a strong commitment of government to high levels of employment and output and involved a great readiness of governments and central banks to move quickly to stimulate fiscal and monetary policies whenever there were signs of economic recession. . . .
>
> The events of the last dozen years or so have exposed some

---

[3] A targets-instruments problem was evident in the United Kingdom in the spring of 1988. As expressed in an article in the *Financial Times:* "The dilemma to which these disagreements are witness is, as the Bank of England reminded us last week, the conflict between the buoyancy of domestic demand and that of sterling. With just one instrument, the interest rate, a choice has to be made." See "Interest Rate Dilemmas," *Financial Times,* May 16, 1988.

problems with this policy prescription. The principal difficulty with financial stimulation is that it is hard to get it right, and a persistent tendency toward overdoses has increasingly guided cost and price inflation rather than an increase in employment and output. This was the principal cause of the worldwide surge of inflation in the early 1970s. . . .

Since then another limitation on financial stimulation as an instrument of economic policy has become more and more evident. This is that its beneficial effects cannot be counted on in a society that lacks confidence in the future value of its national money. When people have expectations or fears of high and rising inflation they tend to see in stimulative financial policy evidence that their expectations or fears are warranted. The actions that they then take to protect themselves push up costs and prices (including interest rates) and reduce the benefits to employment and output that the financial stimulation was undertaken to achieve."[4]

A further possible impediment to the pursuit of conservative monetary stimulus is the macroeconomic policy stance of the central government treasury and the budgetary position of the government. Only in a very few countries are central banks truly politically independent of the treasury. Given the frequent need to finance governments via debt finance, central banks have often provided the avenue by which governments partially finance themselves. One may, in fact, view central banks as having a central role in the conduct of fiscal policy—in particular, debt management policy. Whereas the treasury determines the division of government finance between taxation and government debt issuance, the central bank determines whether the private sector will hold government paper in the form of interest-bearing marketable securities (at least in developed economies) which are not usable as means of payment or as noninterest-bearing (until recently in most countries) means of payment in the form of coin, currency, or bank deposits. The central bank may also alter the composition of public debt held by the private sector by engaging in open market operations in government securities by varying maturities. The natural link between monetary policy and debt

---

[4] *Annual Report of the Governor to the Minister of Finance* (Ottawa: Bank of Canada, 1982), p. 6.

management policy has caused one prominent economist to conclude "there is no neat way to distinguish monetary policy from debt management, the province of the Federal Reserve from that of the Treasury. Both agencies are engaged in debt management in the broadest sense, and both have powers to influence the whole spectrum of debt".[5]

The inflationary experience of the 1970s has considerably tempered the short-term output goals of many central banks. That experience has resulted in a greater emphasis on medium-term objectives. The decade of the 1970s saw aggregate price inflation greatly influenced by the behavior of commodity prices, particularly oil. Nonetheless, one policy lesson of the decade was that monetary policy in several large economies was overburdened and overstimulative. The presumed trade-off between inflation and unemployment appeared to worsen, with fewer employment gains obtainable with more expansionary monetary stimulus. Considerable academic literature in monetary economics during the 1970s and 1980s focused on a revival of the proposition of the long-run neutrality of money, that is, that in the *long run* the equilibrium demand for and supply of goods and services could not be influenced by a change in nominal quantities, i.e., by the nominal quantity of money, but only by price-adjusted, "real," variables. Many academics retreated from earlier advocacy of activist monetary policy to one of emphasizing the greater independence of real economic activity from monetary stimulus in the long run, and even in the shorter run, as the private sector uncovers the policy obligations of the central bank and discounts the inflationary consequences of excessive monetary stimulus. The public, they argued, has been made more aware of the inflationary consequences of rapid monetary growth. It was argued that central banks have only a limited ability to stimulate nominal aggregate demand with expansionary monetary policy, particularly when the private sector is aware of the policy rule of the central bank, which it can partially uncover by closely viewing the actions of the monetary authorities. Although the academic argument that antici-

---

[5] James Tobin, "An Essay on the Principles of Debt Management," in *Fiscal and Debt Management Policies* (Englewood Cliffs, N.J.: Prentice-Hall, 1963) pp. 378–455.

pated monetary stimulus had no impact on real economic activity may have been taken to the extreme, it partially succeeded, along with the lessons gained from a decade of high and volatile inflation, in convincing economists and financial analysts in and outside central banks that price stability should receive renewed emphasis as the paramount goal of central banks.

THE INSTRUMENTS OF MONETARY POLICY

Central banks are able to influence economic activity by virtue of the simple fact that there is a demand for their liabilities, currency demanded by the general public, and reserves held with them by the banking system. Reserves are demanded either because of reserve requirements placed on banks, as settlement balances, or for precautionary reasons—given that the private sector may wish at any time to convert non-risk-free bank deposits into currency. Considerable debate has taken place about the necessity of reserve requirements for reasons of monetary control, with the negative camp arguing that reserve requirements are simply a tax on banks and unnecessary to control the growth of the money stock. A residual demand for central bank liabilities (so-called base money or the monetary base) would exist in any case because banks have a precautionary demand for currency given the likelihood and stochastic nature of deposit withdrawals. Most central banks impose some form of reserve requirements on their banking systems; one exception being Belgium.[6] However, changes in reserve requirements in most countries are altered infrequently and in many cases only in exceptional circumstances. This author tends to view reserve requirements more as a tax on the banking system and less as a necessary or efficient means of controlling the growth of the liabilities of the banking system.

A useful starting point in discussing the instruments of mone-

---

[6] A comparative study of banking deregulation in Europe, touching on the issue of reserve requirements, is Ernst Baltensperger and Jean Dermine, "Banking Deregulation in Europe," *Economic Policy: A European Forum,* April 1987, pp. 64–109.

The Balance Sheet of the Central Bank

Assets	*Liabilities*
Loans to the banking system	Currency
Domestic securities	Reserve deposits
Foreign exchange	
Gold	
Monetary base	Monetary base

---

tary policy, to which we later append specific examples, is to consider the stylized balance sheet of the central bank.

Given a demand for its liabilities, the central bank influences the short-term price of credit—the interest rate—by expanding or contracting the supply of base money by adjusting the size of the asset side of its balance sheet and by altering the composition of these assets. Thus, there can be both a volume or liquidity effect and a substitution effect on interest rates. The liquidity effect is an obvious one—the short-term interest rate is likely to decline with an increase in the monetary base. The substitution effect is of considerable importance to the efficacy of monetary policy, a subject to which we return several times in the course of this chapter. The substitution effect involves the question of whether the central bank can alter the price of a financial asset—for example, short-term or long-term interest rates or the exchange rate—by altering the composition of its balance sheet and in doing so the composition of interest-bearing and noninterest-bearing assets in the hands of the nonbank public.

Consider the example of a central bank that conducts monetary policy through the control of its domestic securities portfolio, say, short- and long-term government debt. Should the central bank purchase short-term paper and at the same time sell long-term debt out of its portfolio by an equal amount, so as to leave the monetary base unchanged, will this have an effect on the relationship between short- and long-term interest rates? The answer depends on how substitutable short- and long-term debt are in the portfolios of the private sector. If the two assets are poor substitutes for one another, the open market operation tends to lower short-term rates and raise long-term interest rates. On the other hand, if the assets are good substitutes, so that the private sector is relatively indifferent to the maturity composition of its portfolio of government debt, the operation has little or no effect on the term (maturity) structure of interest rates.

A similar question of financial asset substitution concerns the important question of central bank intervention in the foreign exchange market. Intervention has as an objective the desire to influence the exchange rate, either to smooth rate movements in the event of perceived excessive volatility or to achieve a particular exchange-rate level. Leaving aside for the moment the effect of intervention on exchange rate expectations, intervention in the exchange market in most cases affects the monetary base in the same manner as monetary operations in the domestic money market, where, in the U.S. context, the central bank purchases or sells short-term government debt. (In some cases exchange-market intervention is undertaken through a treasury exchange rate stabilization fund. The general point still applies.) In the case of foreign-exchange intervention, the central bank may choose to purchase foreign exchange, leaving domestic residents holding more domestic financial assets and fewer foreign assets. The extent of any effect on the exchange rate depends on the degree of substitutability of domestic for foreign assets in private portfolios. Although this subject is covered in more detail later, we should mention at this point that central banks often "sterilize" foreign-exchange intervention, meaning that to leave the monetary base unaffected by the exchange-market intervention the central bank performs an opposite and offsetting operation in the domestic money market. The practical reason for such an operation is often to prevent exchange market intervention from having any significant and undesired impact on short-term money market interest rates. The question of substitutability of alternative financial assets, be they different because of maturity or currency of denomination, should be kept in mind in considering the ability of the central bank to alter relative prices of financial assets, either returns on debt instruments or exchange rates.

In addition to central bank operations in domestic money and foreign-exchange markets, control of the growth of money and bank credit may take place through four additional avenues. First, the banking system may have direct access to loans from the central bank or facilities for discounting of government paper or commercial bills. Central banks may alter the quantity of credit made available to banks, in some cases with explicit lending limits, or it may alter the price at which this credit is made available; for example, the official discount rate. Second, the central bank may impose explicit credit ceilings on individual banks, constraining explicitly the growth of their assets or liabilities. Third, access to foreign credit by banks or the nonbank sector may also be restrained. Lastly, bank balance sheets may be explicitly constrained by the imposition of ceilings on deposit or lending rates. Thus, aside from central bank operations in open money and capital markets, and changes in reserve requirements, the control of the growth of bank credit may be achieved through restrictions on the price (e.g., deposit rates) or quantity of credit made available by banks to the nonbank sector, through control of the quantity or price of credit from the central bank to the banking system and via restrictions on the availability of credit by banks or the nonbank sector from foreign sources.

Before describing the primary monetary and credit control techniques used in some of the major economies, we should note that five elements impinge to some extent on the monetary control instruments employed by central banks and the constraints placed on their use: the structure, depth, and ongoing liberalization of domestic money and capital markets; the formal use of monetary targets; financial structure—specifically, the financial integration of commercial bank and security services within the banking system; the formal commitment of the central bank to an exchange rate system, such as the European Monetary System; and the financial openness of the domestic money and capital markets.

The U.S. financial system is almost unique in having well-developed and liquid money and capital markets for both government and many private-sector securities. Because of the depth and liquidity of the market in short-term federal government securities, the central bank can readily influence the federal funds rate—the rate at which banks trade central bank reserves with one another—through open market purchases and sales of government paper. In practice the federal funds rate is managed in the short run with the use of repurchase agreements, a temporary injection of liquidity via the purchase of government paper; later this is reversed when the securities are repurchased by a bank or securities dealer. Considerable financial intermediation in the United States also takes place outside the banking system, both in the domestic commercial paper and corporate bond markets. In recent years previously nonliquid bank assets have been repackaged in securitized form, for which secondary markets have been developed. In addition, a considerable menu of short-term financial assets compete as short-term investments and, more recently, as means of payment, with interest-bearing and non-interest-bearing bank deposits. Again we note the issue of asset substitutability. Short-term monetary policy aimed at controlling a specific monetary aggregate must contend with the interest-sensitive portfolio behavior of the nonbank public, which may quickly alter its demand for short-term bank liabilities in response to a change in interest rates on short-term nonbank marketable financial assets.

Both Germany and Japan display some sharp contrasts to the United States in the structure of their financial markets and the instruments used in implementing monetary policy. The German financial system is characterized by the large role of universal banks, which, unlike banks in the United States and Japan, conduct both commercial and investment banking and security brokerage activities. Banks in Germany also accept deposits and extend loans of medium- to long-term maturity. These activities are reflected in the structure of the German bond market, where approximately 70 percent of the outstanding bonds on the domestic market are issued by banks, and the remainder mainly consist of long-term obligations of the public sector. The direct issuance of bonds by the corporate sector in the domestic market is relatively insignificant.[7] Similarly, the short-term money market in Germany is notable for the relative absence of domestic short-term instruments that might be considered good substitutes for bank deposits.

---

[7] A recent description of the German capital market is Willy Friedman and Heinz Hermann, "Recent Changes in Capital Markets in Germany," in *Changes in the Organization and Regulation of Capital Markets* (Basle, Switzerland: Bank for International Settlements, 1987).

For example, of the seven large industrial economies, Germany is the only one that does not have money market mutual funds or an active market in commercial paper because of a tax on securities turnover. The lack of liquid domestic short-term financial assets outside the banking system is obviously of some benefit to the central bank in controlling the money supply because asset substitutability is considerably more limited than, say, in the United States.

Two major structural changes in Japanese financial markets have helped shape the interaction between the central bank and private money and capital markets. First, after 1974 in response to the decline in corporate investment attributable to the first oil price shock, the Japanese corporate sector found itself with excess funds, which it placed in the emerging Gensaki market, a repurchase market that yielded returns higher than those on regulated bank deposits. Second, the enormous rise in the stock of government debt necessitated changes in the issuance procedure and the development of a secondary market. Hence the development of a liquid short-term money market and a large secondary market in government securities enhanced the ability of the central bank to influence interest rates more directly in open security markets and also created substitutes for rate ceiling-regulated bank deposits.

Japan provides a classic example of the managed transition of a large economy, initially dependent on indirect financial intermediation via a tightly regulated banking system, with tight controls on deposit and lending rates and quantitative limits on credit from the central bank, developing into a deregulated, market-oriented financial system. In the process of change, the banks and the previously bank-dependent corporate sector have emerged with considerable access to international credit, while the central bank has shifted from control by quantity constraints to market-oriented monetary control techniques, designed to influence open-market interest rates. Because the corporate sector prior to liberalization had no access to foreign funding, stock issuance was limited, and money and capital markets were underdeveloped and subject to government restrictions; banks were the main source of credit to the corporate sector aside from internal funding. To direct credit to the corporate sector at relatively low rates of interest, the authorities closely regulated deposit rates and provided ready access for the 13 city banks to central bank credit via the discount window, where funds were available at a rate lower than the interbank loan rate. As an example of the tightness of control over bank funding, the issuance of certificates of deposit by banks was prohibited. On the loan side, banks were restricted as to the permissible maturity of loans made available to the nonbank sector. The large city banks made primarily short-term loans, while trust banks made long-term loans and were able to issue long-term bank bonds. Another notable feature of the Japanese financial system still evident today is the large postal saving system, which, given the tax-free saving accumulation by individuals until April 1988, was a major conduit for funds channeled to the Ministry of Finance's Trust Fund Bureau; they were then allocated by the government to desired public and private projects.

The development of the secondary bond market in Japan, necessitated by the rapid growth in government debt after the first oil-price shock, was one of the early cracks in the tightly controlled bank funding and loan markets, as it provided a market rate of interest which competed directly with regulated bank deposit rates. As a result, large corporate customers shifted funds from the bank deposit market to the government securities repurchase, or Gensaki, market. By 1976 the government officially recognized the Gensaki market, implemented prudential guidelines, and in 1979 the issuance of large CDs was permitted.[8] Since the late 1970s Japan has had a flurry of deregulation and innovation in its financial markets, including the opening up of the domestic market to foreign competition. Banks and corporations may freely borrow abroad, and other financial institutions, particularly insurance companies, have considerable ability to invest in foreign securities. Interest-rate ceilings on bank deposits have also been considerably relaxed. With the regulation of money and credit via price rather than quantity, monetary control procedures have also had to adapt.

---

[8] A short review of the development of Japanese financial markets since the early 1970s may be obtained in Thomas F. Cargill, "Japanese Monetary Policy, Flow of Funds, and Domestic Financial Liberalization," *Economic Review*, pp. 21–32, Federal Reserve Bank of San Francisco, Summer 1986; an extensive survey of Japanese banking and the pre- and post-liberalization financial system is available in Robert A. Feldman, *Japanese Financial Markets: Deficits, Dilemmas, and Deregulation* (Cambridge, Mass.: MIT Press, 1986).

Because of the continued absence of a large and liquid market in short-term government securities, hampered by the government sale of short-term Treasury debt at below market rates directly to the Bank of Japan, and the small quantity of such paper in private hands, open-market operations in government securities to some extent are still rather limited. Another anomaly of the Japanese capital market is that, because of restrictions and administrative difficulties in issuing corporate debt in Japan, a very considerable amount of corporate debt is issued in the Eurobond market, where the so-called Euroyen segment has seen enormous growth in recent years.

Monetary and credit control techniques are dependent on both the institutionalization of official monetary aggregate targeting and the official or unofficial constraint imposed by exchange rate commitments. With respect to targeting, the desired degree of "automaticity" of policy response to deviations of actual money growth from target determine to what extent central banks may desire to actively intervene in the money markets. In this regard it is notable that very short-term money-market rates in Germany and Japan often appear rather stable when compared with the behavior of U.S. short-term rates (see Chart 4–1).

Although most central banks consider the achievement of monetary control to be essential to the achievement of price stability, in recent years the use of formal monetary targeting has been on the decline. Two factors principally account for the disenchantment with official monetary targeting: the effects on the demand for money induced by financial innovation and deregulation, and the related unanticipated decline in the velocity of money—the ratio of nominal gross national product (GNP) to money following the reduction in inflation and short-term interest rates around 1982 (see Chart 4–2). These problems have been particularly acute for the United States but have also arisen in other countries. Canada is one such example. In late 1975 the Bank of Canada announced a specific target for the growth of M1, defined as the sum of currency and chartered bank demand deposits held by the public. In November 1982 the Bank officially abandoned this monetary target. The following is an excerpt from the Bank's *1982 Annual Report:*

The announcement by the Bank of Canada last November that it no longer has a specific target for the monetary aggregate M1 was interpreted in some quarters as indicating a fundamental change in the Bank's approach to monetary policy and in the current thrust of that policy. Neither is true. The decision was a purely practical one arising from the impact on M1 of recent major changes in the forms in which money balances are being held in Canada. . . .

The combination of inflation, high interest rates, computer-based technology, and competition among financial institutions has resulted in innovations in financial services that have permitted Canadians both to reduce appreciably the average size of balances they hold for making payments and to hold more of those balances in interest-earning forms not included in M1. . . .

As a result of these innovations, a substantial reduction has taken place in the growth of M1 relative to that which one would have

CHART 4–1
Daily Interest Rates since the Louvre Accord

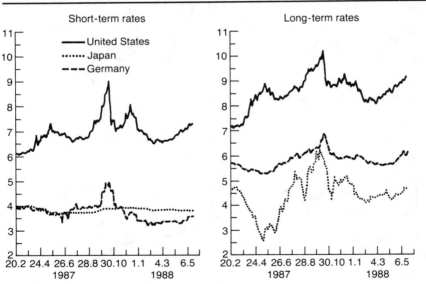

Three-month U.S. CD, three-month Gensaki and three-month Frankfurt interbank rates. 10-year U.S. Treasury notes, 10-year Japanese Government Bonds, German Public-Sector Bonds

CHART 4–2
Velocity of Money

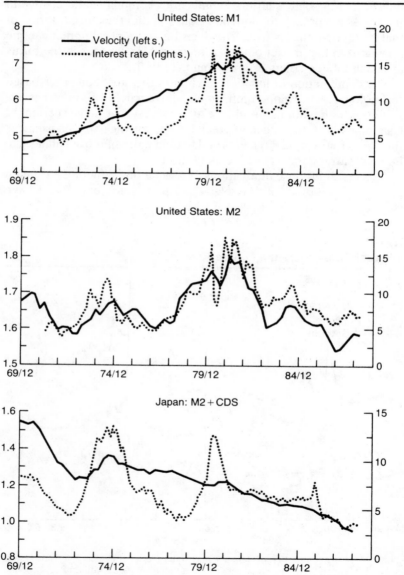

Interest rates, U.S.: 3–T commercial paper; JP: Call money; GB and DE: 3–T. Interbank; CA: 3–T. Finance Company paper

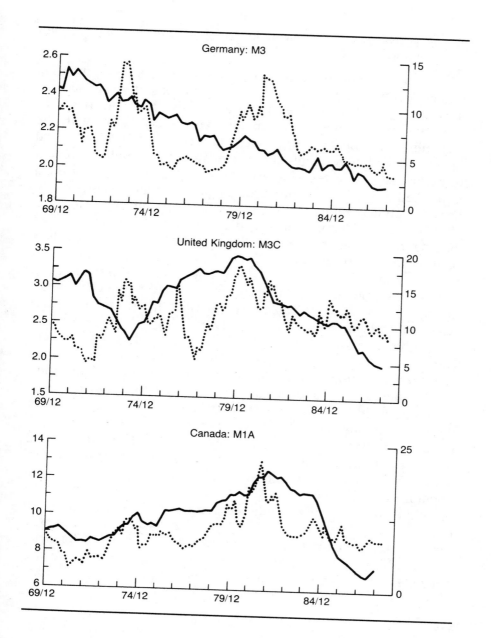

expected, given movements in total expenditures in the economy and interest rates.[9]

Canada is not alone in having had difficulty in committing official central bank policy to the achievement of a specific monetary growth objective. The Bank of England and the U.S. Federal Reserve have both publicly expressed concern with the instability of monetary aggregates caused by deregulation and financial innovation, resulting at times in either the abandonment of particular aggregates as intermediate targets or in placing them in the nether world of monitored aggregates. In any event, central bank targeting of monetary aggregates has certainly not caused the abandonment of very short-run discretionary policy in favor of automatic rules tied to the behavior of observed money growth in relation to some preannounced target. The deemphasis of monetary targeting has meant that short-term interest-rate policies in several countries have been less precommitted to specific monetary growth objectives. Table 4–1 describes the status of central bank monetary targeting as of mid-1988.

Although monetary targets have been deemphasized in recent years, exchange rate constraints or objectives have received increased attention. Note the distinction between central bank policy aimed at controlling a quantity, the stock of money balances in private hands, and policy aimed at influencing a relative price, the exchange rate, via control over a short-term rate of interest. In the case of control over the stock of money balances, the central bank is primarily attempting to influence domestic portfolio preferences, preferences between monetary (primarily bank deposit) and nonmonetary financial assets. In the case of an exchange rate objective, on the other hand, the central bank is attempting to influence both domestic and foreign portfolio preferences, not only for short-term monetary assets, but for a wide range of financial assets. Shifts in asset preferences in the latter case hence are dependent on financial conditions in both domestic and foreign

---

[9] *Annual Report of the Governor to the Minister of Finance*, Bank of Canada, 1982, pp. 25 and 27. For a discussion of the instability of monetary velocity in U.S. contexts see *Monetary Targeting and Velocity: Conference Proceedings*, Federal Reserve Bank of San Francisco, December 1983.

security markets and it may require cooperation or coordination with foreign monetary authorities to achieve specific exchange rate objectives. Control of a domestic monetary aggregate may be less subject to the vicissitudes of foreign portfolio preferences than attempts to influence the exchange rate, although this obviously depends on the specific circumstances. The instruments that monetary authorities choose for implementing monetary operations in the domestic money markets or operations in the foreign-exchange markets, depend to some degree on whether the dominant objective is a monetary aggregate or the price of foreign exchange. And the ability of the central bank to influence either depends on the substitutability between domestic and foreign assets, in the portfolios of both residents and foreign investors.

We do not comment on the other factors mentioned previously which influence the monetary control instruments employed by the central banks other than to repeat the argument that asset substitutability, either between similar marketable debt instruments of different maturity, different assets of similar maturity, or between domestic and foreign financial assets, is a major consideration in the choice of operating instruments.

Any discussion of the operating control procedures of central banks should begin with the recognition that in the very short run the primary objective of most central banks is to maintain stable conditions in domestic money markets. The often repeated academic criticism of the U.S. central bank is that the attempt to maintain stable money market conditions has often led to an inflationary bias in policy, and possibly to an amplification of business-cycle fluctuations. Reluctance to raise interest rates in a business-cycle upswing, and reluctance to lower them in a cyclical downswing has increased, so the argument goes, the peak-to-trough movement in interest rates and real economic growth, causing a "boom-bust" business cycle. (Recall that for a good part of the postwar period the U.S. banking system operated under constraints on deposit rates, which, when binding, resulted in disintermediation and a curtailment in credit supply from banking institutions, particularly to the housing industry.) Excessive "fine-tuning" of money-market conditions has been a standard, although at times narrowly focused, criticism of Federal Reserve monetary operating procedures.

TABLE 4–1
Monetary and Credit Aggregates: Objectives and Rates of Expansion (In Percentages)

Countries	Monetary or Credit Aggregate[1]	Objective[2] for 1986[3]	1987[3]	1988[3]	Monetary or Credit Expansion Target Period[4] 1986	1987	Change over Four Quarters[5] 1987 QI	1988QI
United States	M_1	3–8%	—	—	15.6%	6.3%	16.8%	3.9%
	M_2	6–9	5½–8½%	4–8%	9.4	4.0	9.5	4.1
	M_3	6–9	5½–8½	4–8	9.2	5.3	8.6	5.4
	TDND	8–11	8–11	7–11	13.3	9.8	11.9	9.2
Japan	M_2 + CDs	8–9	11–12	12	8.3	11.8	8.8	12.1
Germany	CBM	3½–5½	3–6	—	7.7	8.1	7.7	8.3
	M_3	—	—	3–6	7.3	6.1	7.4	6.0
France	M_2	—	4–6	4–6	4.9	4.1	3.8	3.1
	M_3	3–5	3–5	—	4.5	9.2	5.2	8.1

United Kingdom	M0	2–6	2–6	1–5	5.8[6]	5.8[6]	4.4	5.2
	M3	11–15	—	—	20.7[6]	20.7[6]	19.5	20.9
Italy	CPS	7	5–9	6–10	11.4	10.2	13.4	9.9
	M2	7–11	6–9	6–9	9.4	8.4	10.2	7.0
Spain	ALP	9½–12½	6½–9½	8–11	11.9	14.0	11.5	13.8
Switzerland	CBMA	2	2	3	2.0	3.0	3.2	1.3
Netherlands	DM2	5½–6	11–12[7]	—	9.6	13.6[7]	6.9	n.a.

[1] TDND = total domestic debt of nonfinancial sectors; CBM = central bank money; CPS = credit to nonstate sector; ALP = liquid assets in the hands of the public; CBMA = adjusted monetary base; DM2 = contribution to M2 creation by banking system (the increase in bank credit to the private sector and in long-term bank credit to the public authorities minus the increase in banks' long-term liabilities).
[2] For TDND in the United States, monitoring range only; for M2 + CDs in Japan, projection only.
[3] Periods running from the fourth quarter to the fourth quarter for the United States, Japan (except 1988, second quarter to second quarter), Germany and France; and from December to December for Italy, Spain, and the Netherlands. For the United Kingdom, 12-month periods ending in March. Annual averages for Switzerland. In the United Kingdom the 1986 target for sterling M3 (subsequently renamed M3) was suspended in October 1986.
[4] Calculated on the same basis as the objective.
[5] Based on quarterly averages.
[6] Twelve months to March 1987 and 1988.
[7] For a period of 24 months ending in December 1987.

Source: Bank for International Settlements, *Annual Report*, June 1988.

The demand/supply aspects of short-term central bank operating procedures can be characterized as follows: for a given demand for reserves, via the control of the asset side of its balance sheet the central bank can choose to control one of two things, a quantity or a price, that is, the quantity of reserves, or in the short run their price, the short-term rate of interest.

The Bank Reserve Market (Money Market)

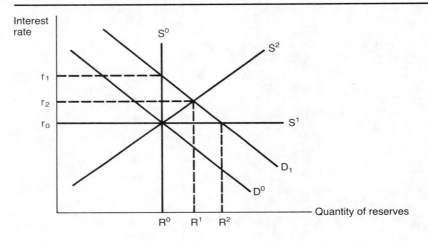

Very short-term monetary policy and the techniques by which it is achieved are basically questions about the slope and intercept of the central bank's reserve supply function. Consider a simple diagrammatic exposition. Given the demand schedule for reserves by banks, D_0, the short-term money market interest rate is r_0 for each of the supply curves shown in the Bank Reserve Market diagram. Supply curve S_0 is drawn under the assumption that the central bank is intent on fixing the short-run reserve supply at R^0, regardless of the demand for reserves, and will allow the short-term interest rate to adjust to clear the money market. Supply curve S^1 is drawn under the assumption that the central bank wishes to maintain the short-term interest rate at r_0 and will supply whatever quantity of reserves is required to do so; in this case the quantity of reserves (and of money) is demand determined. The last supply curve, S^2, slopes upward to the right; in it the incremental cost of reserves rises with an increase in supply. This may be the case, for example, where borrowing from the central bank may be provided at a graduated rate, or where the central bank provides some disincentive to borrow, increasing the explicit price or some "shadow" implicit price for the increased provision of reserves.

Consider the rate smoothing operation as one where in the very short run the central bank accommodates all reserve demands at the rate r_0—that is, via the supply function S^1. An increase in reserve demand, say, due to an exogenous increase in loan demand by the private sector, shifts the demand curve up to the right to D^1, resulting in an increase in total reserve supply to R^2, with no change in the interest rate. The central bank may follow such a policy in the short run because it believes the increase in reserve demand to be transitory and will in a short time return to D^0.

In the case where the central bank is completely "non-accommodating", the supply curve S^0, a rise in demand can only be eliminated by permitting the money market rate to rise to r_1. If the increase in reserve demand is indeed transitory, this means that the short-run money market rate may fluctuate over a wide margin, r_0 to r_1. Such volatility may be considered by the central bank to be undesirable and excessive. Alternatively, the central bank may wish to dampen fluctuations or smooth money market rates by satisfying some, but not all, of the increase in reserve demand. The upward slope to the supply curve S^2 may be produced in a variety of ways, by direct central bank discouragement of frequent borrowing from the discount window, by the use of a graduated discount rate, or by the partial provision of the additonal reserves through purchases of securities in the money market. This latter approach, the supply curve S^2, limits the swing in the short-term money-market rate, with the short rate rising to only r_2 from r_0. This induces banks in turn to limit credit provision by raising its cost to the private sector. If the additional reserve demand is indeed transitory, the market rate returns to r_0, and only modest movements in short-term rates have occurred.

Which supply of reserves function a central bank ought to institute to implement the desired degree of control of reserves and short-term rates depends on the answer to two questions: first, can the central bank identify transitory fluctuations in reserve (or money) demand and, second, what purpose is served, or damage inflicted, by permitting short-term interest rates to move within a wide margin in the short run? Excessive smoothing or stabilization of short-term money-market rates may result in a demand-driven money supply, in which the central bank acts passively to shifts in reserve demand. Over an extended period of time such a policy may cause the central bank to lose control over reserve and money growth, which may amplify aggregate demand movements and in time lead to an inflationary bias in policy. On the other hand, if an increase in the demand for reserves can be identified as transitory, or if the increase in reserve demand is desired by the central bank, it may serve little purpose to gyrate the short-term money-market rate. For any fixed supply of reserves in the *very short run*, there will always be a tendency for an increase in demand to cause the short-term rate to overshoot its long-run equilibrium given by the long-run supply curve S^2, causing the short-term rate to first move to r_1 and then to decline to r_2. To eliminate the volatility caused by a fixed short-run supply of reserves, the central bank may intentionally accommodate the reserve demand, but at a marginally higher rate.

One argument against short-run central bank reserve accommodation is that inertia is a characteristic of human behavior. Slowness to react to rapid reserve (money) growth can lead to the provision of greater liquidity in a cyclical upswing than is desirable for long-term price stability. In addition, it is difficult to know what is the "appropriate" nominal interest rate. (It is similarly difficult to determine the appropriate "real," price-adjusted interest rate and nearly impossible to control it except over short periods.) Nominal interest rates contain both a "real" component and a component to compensate for inflationary expectations. The real component may indeed be cyclically related to economic activity, and a rise in the real rate may be desirable to curtail excess demand for goods and services. Dampening of interest rate movements may, therefore, prevent short-term interest rates from playing their appropriate role of allocating goods to their most efficient use. So runs the debate over short-term interest rate policy behavior of the central bank.

Actual central bank reserve control operations may to some degree be described in the demand/supply mold pictured earlier. Under the so-called federal funds rate operating procedure, the

Federal Open Market Committee (FOMC) "selected a narrow band . . . for the funds rate that it believed consistent with its intermediate monetary traget and the broader objectives of monetary policy. This implied that the Federal Reserve, through open-market operations, varied non-borrowed reserves essentially dollar-for-dollar with changes in required reserves."[10] Such an operating procedure requires the central bank to have some understanding of the demand for money and, in turn, the demand for reserves, to choose that federal funds rate which would produce the desired quantity of the money stock. In a sense, the central bank is instituting policy by "reading off the demand curve," selecting that interest which would produce a quantity of money close to the targeted objective.

Since the 1970s the Federal Reserve has followed several short-run monetary control procedures. In October 1979 the federal funds rate operating procedure was dropped and replaced by the so-called nonborrowed reserves operating procedure, in which the central bank established short-run targets for the provision of reserves through open-market operations. Under this procedure the Federal Open Market Committee was required to estimate which interest rate would be consistent with its targets for monetary growth. Given this figure, an estimate of borrowing from the discount window was made. The money target was used to approximate the demand for required reserves, via the known reserve requirement ratios, and added to this was an estimate of "excess reserves" (basically a precautionary reserve demand). From the sum of required and excess reserves, implying total reserve demand, was subtracted estimated borrowed reserves, yielding the nonborrowed reserve target.

The Federal Reserve's nonborrowed reserve operating procedure may be interpreted as putting some positive slope in the

---

[10] Brian F. Madigan and Warren T. Trepeta, "Implementation of U.S. Monetary Policy," in *Changes in Money-Market Instruments and Procedures: Objectives and Implications* (Basle, Switzerland: Bank for International Settlements, March 1986), p. 242. Note that in the U.S. context, total reserves are defined equally as reserves borrowed from the central bank (borrowed reserves) and reserves supplied through open market operations (nonborrowed reserves); total reserves can also be broken down into their required component implied by reserve requirements (required reserves) and a nonrequired component (excess reserves).

reserve supply schedule shown in the preceding diagram. During the reserve control period, nonborrowed reserves were kept close to target, which was easy enough, because nonborrowed reserves could be directly controlled by open-market operations. Monetary growth in excess of the predetermined, short-run path quickly resulted in a tightening of money-market conditions, because the pressure of reserve demand could not be automatically relieved via the Federal Reserve's discount window, where excessive borrowing is actively discouraged.

The success of the nonborrowed reserve "experiment" is still in debate. During its implementation, from October 1979 to October 1982, it resulted in both higher and more volatile short-term interest rates. It is credited by some as having been the control framework needed to reduce monetary growth in the United States and reduce the rate of inflation. It is, at the same time, criticized by "monetarists" as not having been a true implementation of monetarist principles, which arguably may be interpreted as a supply curve such as S^0 in the diagram, that is, with strict short- and long-run control over total reserves, or the sum of total reserves plus currency, the monetary base.

After October 1982 the Federal Reserve switched to a procedure of targeting borrowed reserves, which may be loosely interpreted as a modified federal funds operating procedure, in which there is much less automaticity in market interest-rate responses to deviations of money growth from target, but still more than was permitted under the strict federal funds rate operating procedure. The evaluation of monetary operating procedures in the United States is complicated by the fact that in 1987 the Federal Reserve abandoned the use of M1, basically currency plus checkable deposits, as an intermediate target, placing greater emphasis on broader monetary aggregates. With the demise of M1 as an explicit target, the Federal Reserve has placed less emphasis on monetary aggregates in the implementation of policy and more emphasis on the short-run developments in financial markets, the real economy, as well as in prices and exchange rates. The current status of monetary targeting in the United States is best captured by the official statement of monetary policy objectives for 1988:

> In light of the experiences of recent years, which have been marked by large swings in velocity, the ranges (for the monetary aggregates)

for 1988 were widened somewhat. There is continuing "noise" in the relationship of money growth to economic activity; in addition, velocity of money is sensitive to changes in market rates of interest. This sensitivity means that even small changes in rates, caused by variations in spending or prices, can have sizable effects on the quantity of money the public wishes to hold. Combined with an uncertain outlook for the economy and inflation, this implies that wider ranges are needed to encompass possible outcomes for monetary growth consistent with satisfactory economic performance in 1988.[11]

Financial market activity and central bank monetary control techniques in Japan have evolved rapidly since the late 1970s, when financial liberalization began in earnest. Prior to the 1970s Japan's financial system was characterized as having one very distinctive feature, that of an "artificially low interest rate policy."[12] Such a policy was aimed at allocating the large pool of private savings to the corporate sector at below-market interest rates. To accomplish this goal, credit by the Bank of Japan to the banking sector was strictly rationed, primarily through the discount window, deposit rates at banks were regulated, and loan rates were not determined in competitive markets.[13]

As mentioned earlier, one of the few markets in Japan that was free of official regulation in the late 1970s was the Gensaki market, where higher rates attracted corporate funds from bank deposits. In addition, higher rates on postal saving accounts increased the funding difficulties of the large city banks. As a result of these emerging competitive pressures, commercial banks were permitted to issue certificates of deposit in 1979, with secondary market trading commencing in the following year. In addition, the domestic money market was opened to foreign participation again in

---

[11] "1988 Monetary Policy Objectives: Summary Report to the Congress on Monetary Policy pursuant to the Full Employment and Balanced Growth Act of 1978," February 23, 1988, Board of Governors of the Federal Reserve, p. 3. A graphic analysis of the borrowed reserve operating procedure is available in Daniel L. Thornton, "The Borrowed Reserves Operating Procedure: Theory and Evidence," *Review*, Federal Reserve Bank of St. Louis, January/February 1988, pp. 30–54.

[12] See Shoichi Royama, "The Japanese Financial System: Past, Present, and Future," *Japanese Economic Studies*, Winter 1983–84, pp. 3–32.

[13] Ibid., p. 8.

1979, with foreigners allowed to enter the Gensaki and CD markets. These measures increased the arbitrage activities between the Euroyen rate and rates in the domestic short-term financial markets, which further increased with the liberalization of foreign-exchange controls in 1980. The important Foreign Exchange and Foreign Trade Control Law, passed in 1980, permitted Japanese banks to borrow and lend foreign exchange domestically and abroad and gave residents the ability to freely obtain foreign exchange.[14] A significant opening up of domestic short-term financial markets to greater competitive pressures domestically and internationally thus occurred at the turn of the 1980s. Further liberalization continued following the Japan–United States Yen/Dollar Committee Report in 1984; the report recommended a series of future liberalization measures. With the removal of yen-swap limits in 1984, Japanese, U.S., and Euro short-term financial markets were considered by the Bank of Japan to be "virtually integrated."[15]

Some appreciation of the extensive liberalization of Japanese money and capital markets and the relaxation of constraints on Japanese foreign portfolio investment is necessary to understand the considerable change in financial markets that confronts the Bank of Japan's attempts to control monetary and credit growth and to influence short-term interest rates.[16] The growth of the open market, as opposed to the interbank market, and the interaction of this market with foreign short-term markets has induced the Bank of Japan to seek new ways of directly intervening in domestic short-term markets. Much of the central bank's actions directed at affecting money-market conditions continue to take place in the

---

[14] Two useful reviews of financial liberalization in Japan are Sena Eken, "Integration of Domestic and International Financial Markets: The Japanese Experience," *Staff Papers,* International Monetary Fund, September 1984; and "Characteristics of Interest Rate Fluctuations amidst Deregulation and Internationalization of Finance," The Bank of Japan, Research and Statistics Department, Special Paper No. 126, October 1985.

[15] See Bank of Japan, "Characteristics of Interest Rate Fluctuations," p. 6.

[16] To quote the Bank of Japan study on this point, "a question may arise that if the share of the yen call and bill markets tends to decline in the short-term financial markets as a whole in Japan . . . the Bank of Japan's ability to control short-term interest rates may be weakened (in particular the removal of the yen swap limit may become a loophole for the Bank of Japan's management of the financial market)." p. 7.

call and bill markets. Changes in the official discount rate and reserve ratios are the second avenue for influencing money-market conditions. Although there is a sizable secondary market in long-term government debt in Japan, a short-term government securities market is still in its infancy, as mentioned earlier due to the fact that the bulk of short-term government paper resides with the Bank of Japan. Since 1981 the Bank of Japan has sold Treasury bills to money-market dealers, who in turn sell them to financial institutions. However, operations in Treasury bills are still largely limited to sales; bill purchases are restricted by the unavailability of a significant supply in private portfolios. On the other hand, the Bank of Japan has engaged in purchases of long-term government bonds with the intent of providing long-term liquidity to the banking system, as opposed to short-term fine-tuning operations.

The discount facility with the Bank of Japan remains an active tool of monetary management, although, given the development of the short-term money market since the late 1970s, it is not as dominant an instrument as previously. As in the United States, the discount rate in Japan is kept below the call and bill rates, and hence some measure of direct credit rationing to the banks must be imposed. This is effected through the use of credit lines primarily with the major city banks. These credit lines are established partly on the basis of the net worth of the individual banks.

Sales and purchases of private bills have remained the primary instruments of monetary control, but with the rapid growth of the open market interest rates in the interbank market, the yen call and bill market rates, which were directly influenced by Bank of Japan activity, began to have less influence over movements in open-market interest rates. For this reason, the Bank of Japan has begun to diversify its open-market operations into CDs and prospectively commercial paper. In December 1988 it also introduced changes in procedures which relied more on market forces to influence interbank rates at maturities of over 7 days.

The continuing deregulation of domestic financial markets and the liberalization of funding access and portfolio investment in foreign markets has increased the allocative efficiency of capital in Japan. At the same time, nonetheless, it may present problems for monetary control reminiscent of those encountered in the United States during the 1970s and 1980s when restrictions on deposit rates were removed and banks were permitted to offer transaction accounts with market-related rates of interest. The removal of interest rate ceilings on large-scale deposits in October 1985, the reduction in their minimum size from yen 1 billion to yen 100 million in April 1987, the reduction in the minimum size of CDs and the development of money-market certificates have greatly expanded the investment opportunities in short-term instruments both for institutional investors and individuals. The removal in April 1988 of the small savers' tax exemption, which permitted tax-free interest income on saving deposits of less than yen 3 million, likely increased the attractiveness of money-market certificates. However, the efficiency provided by financial deregulation can be expected to be offset somewhat, at least in the short run, by greater difficulty in interpreting previously reliable monetary aggregates, as the substitutability of components of these aggregates with nondeposit short-term portfolio investments increases.

In Germany the Bundesbank's monetary control procedures have had to be adapted to changes in the domestic financial markets to a much lesser extent. German financial markets are quite open and liberalized, yet the structure of the long-term capital market is very different from that in the United States or Japan. In contrast to the Japanese banking system prior to 1979, there are few official restraints on deposit or loan interest rate setting in Germany. The Bundesbank is not empowered to impose quantitative ceilings on bank lending nor ceilings on deposit rates. Recent changes in central banking operating procedures in Germany were more in the nature of fine-tuning adjustments than fundamental alterations in open-market policy.[17] The changes have been primarily aimed at reducing the role of adjustments in administered interest rates on borrowing from the central bank and increasing the utilization of open-market instruments to inject or withdraw reserves from the banking system. To some degree the use of the

---

[17] A detailed treatment of recent central bank operating procedures in Germany is contained in H. J. Dudler, "Changes in Money-Market Instruments and Procedures in Germany," in *Changes in Money-Market Instruments and Procedures: Objectives and Implications* (Basle: Bank for International Settlements, March 1986).

main market intervention instrument, security repurchase agreements, was adopted because of its greater ease of implementation and because it improved the ability of the central bank to convey to the market its true intentions. Changes in the interest rate on the central bank's short-term financing facility for "Lombard" credit were thought in the past to have received excessive market attention, hampering its use as a tool for short-term interest rate and reserve management. The effect was to cause the Lombard rate to become a floor for the call money rate. The procedures for fine tuning the money market were altered in 1984 when the Bundesbank restricted the use of Lombard credit and began to provide the bulk of the banks' liquidity needs by securities repurchase agreements.

The switch from the provision of short-term liquidity to the German money market through Lombard credit to the provision by revolving repurchase agreements is an example of a change in monetary policy enhancing short-term money-market management flexibility. It does not represent a change in techniques likely in the longer run to influence the ability of the central bank to achieve longer-term monetary growth objectives. Refinements in procedures used for repurchase agreements continue to be made.[18]

As emphasized earlier, a central bank's ability to control any particular monetary aggregate depends to an important degree on financial asset substitutes for bank deposits available in the marketplace. An argument can be made that in recent years those countries which have had the most success in controlling targeted aggregates have been the countries that have had limited domestic short-term financial asset substitutes with deposit instruments. Germany can to some degree be characterized as belonging to such a group, as its domestic money market provides few short-term asset competitors with bank deposits. Even with limited short-term asset substitutability, however, Germany in 1988 chose to replace its target for central bank money, consisting of banks' required

---

[18] "The Bundesbank's Transactions in Securities under Repurchase Agreement," *Monthly Report of the Deutsche Bundesbank*, May 1983, pp. 27–28. Also see "Recent Developments with Respect to the Bundesbank's Security Repurchase Agreements," *Monthly Report of the Deutsche Bundesbank*, October 1985.

minimum reserve holdings with respect to their domestic liabilities at 1974 reserve ratios plus notes and coin in circulation, with one for a broad aggregate, M3, composed of currency, sight deposits, time deposits, funds borrowed for less than four years, and savings deposits at statutory notice. One reason for the move to a broader monetary aggregate was that currency, which forms a large part of the central bank money aggregate in Germany, is sensitive to interest rates, in contrast to the situation in some other countries. Low interest rates during 1987 and/or the expectation of deutsche mark appreciation increased the demand to hold currency. The difficulty of accurately identifying the sources of shifts in the demand to hold the targeted aggregate has over time weakened countries' commitments to formal monetary or reserve targeting.[19] And the reduced ability of these targeted aggregates to accurately reflect the stance of monetary policy has increased the need for central banks to have flexible operating instruments.

CHANGING VIEWS OF THE MONETARY TRANSMISSION MECHANISM

Views on the manner in which monetary policy alters economic behavior have changed with the increased mobility of financial capital both domestically and internationally. The removal of interest rate ceilings on deposits and the elimination of explicitly imposed constraints on either the asset or liability side of commercial-bank balance sheets (e.g., the "corset" in the United Kingdom, the "encadrement du crédit" in France, regulation Q in the United States, and deposit-rate ceilings in Japan) have meant that

---

[19] A thriving infant industry has existed at central banks and international economic institutions which over the entire period in which monetary targeting has been in force attempted to identify the causes of instability in the demand by the private sector to hold money balances. The ongoing developments in financial deregulation and the large decline in interest rates in the industrial countries following 1982 have caused large movements in the velocity of money which are not easy to identify empirically. An excellent study of the international behavior of the velocity of money can be found in Peter Isard and Liliana Rojas-Suarez, "Velocity of Money and the Practice of Monetary Targeting: Experience, Theory and the Policy Debate," in *Staff Studies for the World Economic Outlook* (Washington D.C.: International Monetary Fund, 1986).

the market-determined price of credit and not restrictions on its availability, or quantitative rationing, has increasingly become the mechanism by which credit is allocated in most industrial economies. In addition, the international allocation of credit via the price mechanism has been enhanced by the removal of exchange controls, either partially or completely, in several countries since the 1970s (e.g., the United Kingdom in 1979, Japan in 1980, and partially in France in 1987). The move to a financial world where interest rates and exchange rates are more market determined has also meant that the incidence of monetary policy has changed. No longer, for example, is it expected that the housing industry will be the first and hardest hit in the United States by a restrictive monetary policy due to the disintermediation of funds out of deposit institutions into marketable, nonbank, financial assets caused by market rates exceeding deposit rate ceilings. At the same time increased international capital mobility in an environment of floating exchange rates has caused the traded goods and import-competing sectors to bear a greater burden in the real economic adjustment to a change in monetary policy, even for countries which viewed themselves as relatively closed. The insular views of many policymakers in the United States have changed dramatically during the 1980s in response to the enormous, and largely unexpected, real currency appreciation/ depreciation cycle which followed a combination of expansionary fiscal-restrictive, anti-inflationary monetary policy at the turn of the decade. The resulting large current-account deficits and shift of the United States from a net creditor to that of a major net international debtor have significantly altered policy views on how open the U.S. economy is and have caused a revaluation of what economists call the "transmission mechanism."

A long-lived academic battle has been waged over whether the impact of monetary policy is transmitted through its effect on the quantity (or price) of credit or the quantity of money. Viewed from the point of view of the balance sheet of the commercial banking system, a noneconomist might argue that the debate is a rather arid one, because credit is simply the assets side of the balance sheet and money the liabilities side. Trouble sets in for the money school when the question is asked whether all deposit liabilities, or only some of them—for example, those which can be used as transactions media, checking accounts, and the like—count as money. Because of the increased ease of convertibility of nontransactions deposits into sight deposits, the issue has been settled, at times for only brief periods, by empirical analysis, determining whether, for example, the demand for money could be explained by such determinants as income and interest rates. The Federal Reserve's recent abandonment of M1 as an intermediate monetary target and the Bundesbank's switch from central bank money to M3, a very broad aggregate, suggests that the definitional problems of the money school persist. The credit school suffers from similar problems, as it is not certain which credit aggregate is most relevant to the central bank, for example, bank credit or a broad aggregate encompassing credit extended by several financial institutions and marketable financial paper. In recognition of this school the Federal Reserve officially monitors a very broad debt measure, defined as "total domestic debt of the nonfinancial sectors." Both schools suffer from the practical problem that their preferred aggregate, broad monetary, or credit (debt), is at times difficult to control with the available arsenal of central bank instruments.

With this in mind, let us focus on the price of credit, particularly the very short-term rate of interest over which the central bank has some influence. There is no doubt that central banks are aware that they control only the supply of reserves, the asset side of their balance sheet, and that the interest rate is jointly determined by the interaction of central bank supply and private market demand for central bank liabilities. They are also aware that in the long run the price of money, the inverse of the price level, is a "monetary phenomenon." Central banks need to assume responsibility for the rate of inflation. Nonetheless, in the short-to-intermediate run the central bank has significant influence over the short-term rate of interest. How is this influence transmitted to the demand and supply of goods and services?

The first transmission avenue is via the cost of bank reserves. A tightening in the reserve market induced by the central bank raises the marginal cost of funds to banks, the interbank rate, which in turn may lead to an increase in funding and in loan interest rates. If deposit rate ceilings are in force, the transmission mechanism may effect both a rise in price and a restriction on supply once ceiling rates are approached. Changes in the cost and availability of credit have in the past been very effective in Japan owing to the employment of constraints on bank deposit and lending rates, as suggested in a recent study by the Bank of Japan:

> Changes in interbank interest rates influence the amount of credit extension by financial institutions via changes in the profitability of providing credit and thereby influence the money supply. However, the prospective further liberalisation of deposit rates as well as the proliferation of "spread-banking" is likely to imply a gradual decline in the importance of this supply-side influence which is dependent on the inflexibility of interest rates on bank lending. On the contrary, increasing emphasis is expected to be placed on the demand influences, as interest rates influence the spending activities of the private sector.[20]

As mentioned in the quotation, another avenue of monetary transmission is directly from the bank reserve market to the short-term open money market; for example, in the United States this includes the short-term Treasury securities market, the secondary market in CDs, and commercial paper. Because individuals and institutions often trade between assets of similar short-run maturity, the considerable substitutability between short-term assets would imply that a tightening in the bank reserve market would feed into other short-term interest rates. Such arbitrage activities in Japan, specifically between the interbank market and the open market, were enhanced by the creation of a CD market, the deregulation of Gensaki transactions by city banks, and the entry of securities firms in the yen call and bill markets in the early 1980s. Nonetheless, there has been concern at times that open-market rates in Japan have not responded quickly to changes in interbank rates; hence the desire of the Bank of Japan to encourage arbitrage between these markets. The U.S. federal funds market has for some time been well integrated with other short-term money markets, so that reserve restraint is usually quickly trans-

---

[20] Toshihiko Fukui, "The Recent Development of the Short-term Money Market in Japan and Changes in the Techniques and Procedures of Monetary Control Used by the Bank of Japan," Special Paper no. 130, The Bank of Japan, Research and Statistics Department. January 1986.

mitted to short-term interest rates, particularly bank funding and loan rates.

Even though the short end of the term structure of interest rates may normally quickly reflect rate movements in the interbank market, it is not at all certain that long-term interest rates will be similarly affected. Chart 4–1 displays representative short- and long-term interest rates in the United States, Japan, and Germany from the period of the Louvre Accord in early 1987 to May 1988. As can be seen from the chart, there appears to be considerable coincident movement in short-term and long-term interest rates in the United States during the period. Some relationship is also apparent in the German markets. In contrast, 1987 was a very unusual period for the Japanese long-term government bond market as long rates fluctuated over a wide margin, while short-term interest rates moved within a very narrow range. The unusual volatility in the Japanese bond market was argued by some to have resulted from a change in institutional investor preferences between U.S. and Japanese government bonds due to "shifts in Japanese investor confidence regarding the value of the U.S. dollar and to changing perceptions about Japanese monetary policy."[21] Indeed, the long-term market in some countries appears at times to be "unhinged" from developments in the short-term money markets.

Central bank influence on the medium- to long-term market via activity in the interbank market is at best quite modest and cannot always be relied on to produce the intended effect. This has increasingly become the case with the further internationalization of bond markets during the 1980s.[22] Table 4–2 displays the breakdown between resident and nonresident purchases and sales in the German bond market. Until 1985 there was only modest interest by foreigners seen in the German bond market. Since then, there has been both considerable growth and volatility in foreign participation. In 1986, for example, of the DM 104 billion bonds

---

[21] See N. Sargen, K. Schoenholtz, and B. Alcamo, "Japanese Bond Market Volatility and International Capital Flows," Salomon Brothers Inc., Bond Market Research, August 1987.

[22] The Bank of Japan, "Characteristics of Interest Rate Fluctuations," pays particular attention to the interrelationship between U.S. and Japanese bond markets, concluding that "the yields on long-term bonds have increasingly tended to fluctuate freely and largely."

issued in the German bond market DM 59 billion were purchased by nonresidents. In 1987 foreign purchases were very substantial during the first half of the year and completely dried up in the second half. Although financial asset prices are largely determined by the demand to hold the existing stock of assets, and only secondarily by the flow, or change in supply, shifts in nonresident investor preference can have a significant impact on a country's long-term bond rates. The domestic market transmission mechanism via short- to long-term bond yields is increasingly becoming a tenuous one. Long-term bond markets are increasingly international markets, with domestic interest rates becoming dependent on nonresident investor preferences. The development of new financial instruments such as currency swaps have increased the globalization of financial markets and may probably further reduce the ability of central banks to influence their domestic long-term interest rates.

Further complicating the understanding of long-term interest rate determination is the fact that the common paradigm economists often use in explaining long rates, the so-called expectations model of the term structure of interest rates, has been difficult to establish empirically. This model, which is actually an arbitrage equilibrium condition, suggests that the yield on a long-term bond ought to roughly equal the average of the current plus expected future short-term interest rates, over the same horizon as that of the long bond. To the extent that the central bank influences current and expected future short rates, it can be said to influence the long rate. Recent research unfortunately has not supported the expectations argument. Particularly during the period from 1979, when the Federal Reserve changed monetary operating control procedures, movements in long-term interest rates in the United States appear more difficult to explain and too volatile vis-à-vis the volatility in short-term rates to be consistent with the expectations theory of the term structure.[23]

It thus appears that central banks increasingly confront move-

---

[23] See Olivier J. Blanchard, "The Lucas Critique and the Volcker Deflation," *American Economic Review,* pp. 211–15, May 1984; and Robert J. Shiller, "The Volatility of Long-Term Interest Rates and Expectations Models of the Term Structure," *Journal of Political Economy,* pp. 1190–1219, December 1979.

TABLE 4–2
Sales and Purchases of Bonds in the Federal Republic of Germany (In DM Billions,)

| Period | Total Sales 1 | Sales of Domestic Bonds[1] Issues | | | Sales of Foreign Bonds[2] 5 | Memo Item Balance of Transactions with Non-residents[3] 6 |
		Total 2	Banks 3	Public Authorities 4		
1980	52.6	45.2	41.5	4.9	7.3	– 7.0
1981	73.1	66.9	70.5	– 2.6	6.2	– 7.7
1982	83.7	72.7	44.8	28.6	11.0	– 8.7
1983	91.3	85.5	51.7	34.4	5.7	+ 5.1
1984	86.8	71.1	34.6	36.7	15.7	– 1.9
1985	103.5	76.1	33.0	42.7	27.5	+ 4.0
1986	103.8	87.5	29.5	57.8	16.3	+42.7
1987	113.0	88.2	28.4	59.8	24.8	+10.1
1st qtr	49.7	42.5	15.3	27.2	7.2	+15.9
2nd qtr	22.1	13.9	5.3	8.7	8.1	+ 3.9
3rd qtr	28.6	19.9	6.5	13.3	8.7	– 9.2
4th qtr	12.7	11.9	1.3	10.6	0.8	– 0.5

Purchases

	Total Purchases	Banks[4]	Domestic Nonbanks[5]			Nonresidents[6]
			Total	Domestic Bonds	Foreign Bonds	
	7	8	9	10	11	12
1980	52.6	19.1	33.2	29.1	4.1	0.3
1981	73.1	17.4	57.1	51.5	5.7	− 1.5
1982	83.7	44.8	36.7	24.5	12.2	2.3
1983	91.3	37.6	42.9	36.4	6.5	10.8
1984	86.8	23.0	50.0	34.2	15.8	13.8
1985	103.5	32.5	39.5	15.9	23.7	31.5
1986	103.8	32.4	12.4	− 0.3	12.7	59.1
1987	113.0	43.6	34.4	11.3	23.1	35.0
1st qtr	49.7	12.3	14.2	8.7	5.6	23.2
2nd qtr	22.1	7.2	2.9	− 4.3	7.2	12.0
3rd qtr	28.6	12.6	16.5	7.7	8.8	− 0.5
4th qtr	12.7	11.6	0.8	− 0.7	1.6	0.3

1 Net sales at market values plus/less changes in issuers' holdings of their own bonds.—2 Transaction values.—3 Purchases of domestic bonds by nonresidents less sales of foreign bonds to residents (col. 12 less col. 5); — = capital exports. + = capital imports.—4 Including the Bundesbank; book values.—5 Residual.—6 Net purchases (+) or net sales (−) of domestic bonds by nonresidents; transaction values. Discrepancies in the totals are due to rounding.

Source: *Report of the Deutsche Bundesbank for the Year 1987*, p. 50.

ments in long-term interest rates over which, particularly in the short run, they have little ability to influence. There rates may appear unusually volatile given movements in domestic short-term rates and are increasingly influenced by exchange rate expectations and by activity in foreign financial markets. In 1987 and 1988 the term structure behavior which appeared to be particularly puzzling was that in the German bond market. Between the end of 1986 and March 1988 the yield on government securities with one month to maturity fell from about 4.5 percent to about 3.2 percent. Long-term bonds with 10 years to maturity, however, were relatively unresponsive to the decline in short rates, remaining between 6 and 6.5 percent. The behavior of long-term rates in Germany appeared difficult to explain given the low rate of inflation, the modest growth in aggregate demand, the strength of the deutsche mark against the U.S. dollar and, in contrast, the significant flattening of the term structure in Japan, which was also experiencing low inflation and an appreciating currency. Chart 4–3 plots the difference between long- and short-term interest rates for the United States, Japan, and Germany, displaying the sharp difference in the steepness of the term structure between the German and Japanese bond markets.[24]

The ability of monetary policy to directly alter financial wealth is another avenue of the monetary transmission mechanism. Here too, however, there is considerable uncertainty and continued debate over the reliability and the degree of impact of changes in short-term rates on wealth and, in turn, on aggregate expenditures. Changes in short-term money-market interest rates induced by a

---

[24] The behavior of long-term interest rates in Germany in 1987 was explained by the Bundesbank as follows: "The upward trend of interest rates in the capital market which lasted until autumn last year was in conspicuous contrast to the Bundesbank's interest rate and liquidity policy stance in the money market, which, taken as a whole, fostered a further decline in short-term interest rates. . . . In their behaviour in the financial markets investors and borrowers alike seemed to assume that the scope for further interest rate reductions is virtually exhausted. This assessment is backed by the historical experience that market interest rates below 6 percent have never lasted long in Germany. This experience is based in turn on the fact that such a far-reaching reduction in the inflation rate as at present has never continued for an extended period in recent decades. A renewed increase in prices has been followed sooner or later by the interest rate level." *Report of the Deutsche Bundesbank for the Year 1987*, p. 48.

CHART 4–3
Yield Curves (Long Rates Minus Short Rates)

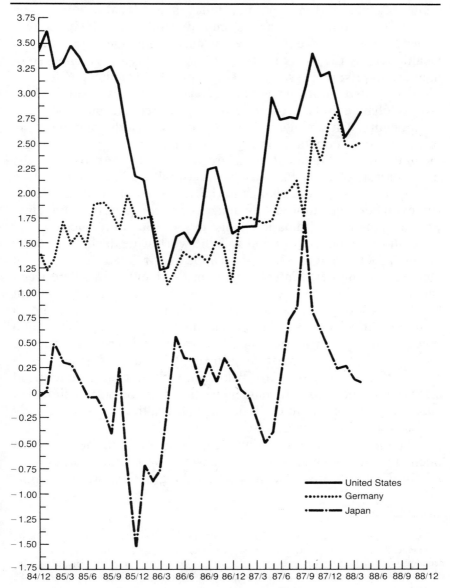

tightening or easing in the reserve market may alter the present discounted value of longer-dated financial assets. Whether a tightening of policy, for example, induces a "wealth effect" on domestic consumption or investment depends on whether current expenditures are more influenced by current income or the stock of wealth held by the private sector. As private wealth is composed of financial assets, real assets (housing, household capital goods), and the discounted future wages and salaries, it is not at all obvious how a change in short-term rates can alter the sum of these components. The change in the value of the wealth components in response to a monetary policy change may be of opposite sign, yielding little adjustment in aggregate wealth. Presumably the transmission of monetary policy via wealth effects takes place principally through the change in the valuation of financial assets. But even here the empirical evidence is not completely convincing. Probably the most dramatic change in the value of financial assets to occur in the postwar period was the worldwide decline in equity prices in October 1987, which appeared related to the large increase in long-term interest rates in the United States between January and October of that year—with long-term government bond rates rising from just over 7 percent to over 10 percent in October. Surprising to most financial analysts, the expectation of a recession in 1988 was disappointed—real GNP growth averaged over 4 percent in the fourth quarter of 1987 and the first quarter of 1988.[25] The absence of a significant cutback on aggregate demand after an enormous loss in financial wealth in October 1987 should at least shake our belief in the reliability of wealth effects induced by changes in money and bond-market conditions.

The increase in international capital mobility in the 1980s has opened up a new avenue of the transmission mechanism, at least for the United States, which, while making the export and import

---

[25] See, for example, "Recession Likely in 1988," *The Pocket Chartbook,* Goldman Sachs Economic Research Group, October 1987. The careful analysis of the Goldman Sachs economists, based largely on previous relationships between wealth and private saving, caused them to conclude "The collapse in stock prices makes it likely that the U.S. economy will experience a recession next year. Consumers are apt to increase their savings in response to a high loss in net worth and heightened uncertainty about future developments." p. 1.

competing sectors more sensitive to shifts in monetary policy, may dampen the adjustment in the domestic demand-oriented sector, such as housing, due to the moderating impact on interest rates arising from monetary policy induced capital inflows. In a world of highly mobile international capital, a tightening of monetary policy may generate a considerable short-term capital inflow which dampens the rise in domestic interest rates, while producing a currency appreciation. Hence the incidence of monetary policy, compared to a regime of limited capital mobility, is likely to shift from interest-rate-sensitive sectors to exchange-rate-sensitive sectors. The degree of the incidence of policy shifts falling on the export and import competing sectors obviously depends on the openness of the economy to international trade in goods and services. In the stylized world of perfect capital mobility even modest shifts in domestic interest rates induce offsetting capital flows which reduce the domestic interest rate movement, throwing the burden of adjustment on another relative price, the exchange rate, and hence on the export sector. In such a world it can be argued that monetary policy is equivalent to exchange-rate policy.

Greater openness to trade in the economy and a greater degree of capital mobility in an environment of floating exchange rates may also considerably alter the ability of monetary and fiscal policy to stimulate economic growth. A fiscal expansion financed by debt issuance should in the short run raise interest rates and income. However, a rise in interest rates induces a capital inflow, appreciating the domestic currency and, over time, reducing international trade competitiveness, leading to a trade deficit. In time, then, the stimulus to income provided by fiscal spending is offset by the trade deficit. Monetary policy, on the other hand, gains dominance as a stimulator of aggregate demand. A monetary expansion in the short run lowers domestic interest rates, which induces a capital outflow and a depreciation of the domestic currency. The increase in international trade competitiveness, in turn, promotes exports and increases aggregate demand. As mobility in international capital implies that domestic and international interest rates cannot depart from each other for long (abstracting, of course, from differences in inflation and expectations of exchange-rate movements), the capital outflow causes domestic interest rates to rise and return to the world level. In the meantime there has been a

TABLE 4–3

Responses of Capital Flows (Net) to a 1 Percent Increase in Interest Rates (In Billions of the Local Currency)

Countries	Domestic Interest Rate		Foreign Interest Rate	
	Short run	Long run	Short run	Long run
United States	11.1	55.6	− 5.3	− 38.8
Germany	9.6	39.2	− 3.5	− 52.8
Japan	11,283.0	4,898.0	−1,227.0	−4,871.0

Source: Adapted from Table 4.15 in Guy V. G. Stevens et al., *The U.S. Economy in an Interdependent World: A Multicountry Model,* Washington, D.C.: Board of Governors of the Federal Reserve System, 1984.

considerable improvement in domestic output due to the exchange-rate-induced stimulus provided to the export sector.[26]

International capital mobility in a world of floating exchange rates is thus both a blessing and a curse for monetary policy. The effectiveness of monetary policy in affecting aggregate output, at least in a stylized textbook sense, should increase, and the sectoral impact of policy should change, the greater the degree of capital mobility. However, market expectations of future exchange rate adjustments induced by small differentials in interest rates may cause major shifts in capital flows, increasing the difficulty of the central bank in maintaining an independent interest-rate policy and possibly complicate the control of domestic liquidity. An example of the sensitivity of capital flows to a change in domestic and foreign short- and long-term rates of interest is given in Table 4–3. An illustration of the role of exchange rate expectations in inducing movements in interest rates and capital flows is provided by Yoshio Suzuki of the Bank of Japan in describing financial market

---

[26] This analysis of monetary and fiscal policy under floating exchange rates and capital mobility is the so-called Mundell-Fleming model; see J. Marcus Fleming, "Domestic Financial Policy under Fixed and under Floating Exchange Rates," *Staff Papers,* pp. 369–79, International Monetary Fund, November 1962; and Robert A. Mundell, "Capital Mobility and Stabilisation Policy under Fixed and Flexible Rates," *Canadian Journal of Economics and Political Science,* pp. 472–85, November 1963.

behavior in the early 1980s, a period of strong U.S. dollar appreciation:

> The volatility of long-term market interest rates can be explained by four factors related to expectations theory. First, as interest rates in the United States became volatile, so did expectations of short-term interest rates in Japan. The mechanism is this: as interest rates in the United States rise, the market believes that the Bank of Japan will prevent the interest spread from widening due to fear of yen depreciation; as a result, the market bids short-term interest rates up. . . . Third, government policy changes have combined with arbitrage to move long-term rates. Between April and October 1982, for example, the Bank of Japan's policy to prevent depreciation of the yen raised interbank rates; through arbitrage, this induced the increase in interest rates in open markets such as Gensaki and CDs, which in turn affected current long-term interest rates, though to a smaller extent. Fourth, exchange-rate volatility has generated large-scale inflows and outflows of international capital, which, when used to purchase or sell domestic assets, has induced movements in interest rates."[27]

Floating exchange rates and interest-rate-sensitive capital flows have increasingly made the external sector a major component of the monetary transmission mechanism. The resulting international financial interdependence has increased the call for greater coordination of macroeconomic policies between countries.

THE DEBATE OVER THE EFFECTIVENESS OF FOREIGN-EXCHANGE MARKET INTERVENTION

Short-run monetary policy in the United States is usually equated with adjustments in the discount rate and open market operations, the direct purchase or sale of U.S. government securities, and the short-term liquidity injections or withdrawals through repurchase

---

[27] Yoshio Suzuki, *Money, Finance, and Macroeconomic Performance in Japan* (New Haven, Conn.: Yale University Press, 1986), p. 71.

agreements and matched sale-purchase arrangements. The short-term policy stance of the Federal Reserve is very often equated with the current level of the federal funds rate. Short-run monetary operations in other countries take a variety of forms. In Canada, for example, the primary short-run policy influence on the level of bank reserves is the central bank management of the daily transfer of government deposits between chartered banks and the central bank. The Bank of Canada also quite regularly intervenes in the foreign exchange market, focusing considerable attention on the Canadian dollar/U.S. dollar exchange rate. Like the Bank of Canada, the Swiss National Bank does not conduct significant open-market operations in the domestic money market. Rather, short-term foreign-exchange swaps are conducted with Swiss commercial banks, providing or withdrawing reserves as is consistent with short-term objectives for interest rates and intermediate objectives for the monetary base, essentially the sum of currency and bank reserves less end-of-month refinancing credit. The Banque de France has over time shifted from discount procedures to tender procedures in both government securities and private paper, as the primary means of controlling the growth of bank reserves but also intervenes regularly in the foreign-exchange markets to stabilize the exchange rate in a way that is consistent with its commitment to the European Monetary System.[28] As in many other countries, foreign-exchange flows are potentially a major determinant of bank liquidity in France; but the Banque de France offsets those flows which would produce undesired conditions in domestic money markets.

What fundamental differences does it make to the level of bank reserves, short-term interest rates, or the exchange rate, if a central bank chooses to conduct reserve-supplying operations in the domestic money market rather than the foreign-exchange market, or the reverse? From viewing the stylized balance sheet earlier, it is clear that central banks can choose to alter the maturity, debtor (public versus private debt), or currency of

---

[28] Regarding the operations of the Banque de France in the interbank market, see M. Lagayette, "La Réforme du Fonctionnement du Marché Interbancaire et des Modalités d'Intervention de la Banque," *Bulletin Trimestriel,* pp. 45–48, Banque de France, December 1986–January 1987.

denomination composition of its assets, all of which have an identical impact on the size of the balance sheet. Any differences between such operations in their influence on interest rates (short versus long, or Treasury bills versus commercial bills) or exchange rates (e.g., deutsche mark/U.S. dollar versus lira/dollar) depends on the substitutability of these assets in private portfolios. The question therefore is whether a change in the composition of the stocks of financial assets in private hands alters the relative prices (interest rates and exchange rates) of these assets. The answer is an empirical one and depends specifically on the alternative assets one is considering in determining the intervention vehicle.

In a broad sense, one can say that open-market operations and foreign-exchange operations are identical; both can be used to alter the reserves of the banking system. They are also similar in that both are likely to influence the domestic interest rate and the exchange rate. Thus, the definition of "pure" or "clean" floating of the exchange rate as the absence of direct intervention in the foreign-exchange market is one more confusing economic metaphor, as the intervention might just as well take place in the domestic money market with possibly a similar impact on the exchange rate.[29] Although open-market operations in practice are usually thought to have a greater effect on the domestic interest rates than foreign-exchange operations, and the latter to have a larger effect on the exchange rate than open-market operations, the dominance of either is largely an empirical question of asset substitutability.

Exchange market intervention may take the form of the purchase of foreign exchange with domestic currency. The foreign currency could then be used to buy interest-bearing, marketable foreign securities. Hence the operation is simply one of an exchange of domestic money for foreign securities, having the effect of increasing the foreign security component on the asset side of the central bank's balance sheet. Should the central bank wish to

---

[29] A clear, if mildly technical, analysis of the relationship between foreign exchange intervention and domestic open market intervention is Jüng Niehans, *International Monetary Economics* (Baltimore: Johns Hopkins University Press, 1984), chapter 12. The criticism of the usual definition of "pure floating" is Niehans'.

neutralize the growth in its balance sheet due to the exchange market intervention, it could carry out an offsetting reserve operation of selling domestic securities, thereby draining reserves from the banking system. The net result of the two interventions, so-called sterilized intervention, is to increase the private market's holdings of domestic securities and reduce private holdings of foreign securities, with the result of leaving the size of the central bank's balance sheet unchanged.

In practice most central banks routinely engage in some form of offsetting domestic open-market operations or similar reserve contraction/expansion activities to moderate the reserve impact of the inflow or outflow of foreign-currency movements on domestic liquidity, with the aim of stabilizing short-term money-market conditions. As mentioned several times, whether an intentionally designed sterilized foreign-exchange operation alters the exchange rate or the domestic, or foreign, interest rate depends critically on the substitutability of domestic and foreign bonds in private portfolios. If the two securities are perfect substitutes, there is no change in either the exchange rate or interest rates. At this point the conditions for perfect asset substitutability should be made explicit in the case of domestic versus foreign securities. If asset holders are "risk neutral," such that the difference between the expected returns on the two bonds is equal to the expected rate of change in the exchange rate—implying that no special premium is demanded for holding a foreign-currency-denominated bond—the foreign and domestic securities are considered perfect substitutes. In such a case, the currency composition of the total supply of bonds, which the central bank can effect by sterilized intervention, has no direct impact on the exchange rate. In this sense only nonsterilized intervention, where the central bank alters the ratio of interest-bearing debt to non-interest-bearing financial assets in private portfolios (e.g., money for bonds) and directly expands or contracts its balance sheet, can move the exchange rate.[30]

---

[30] A detailed analysis of asset substitutability and foreign exchange market intervention is contained in Lance Girton and Dale W. Henderson, "Central Bank Operations in Foreign and Domestic Assets under Fixed and Flexible Exchange Rates," in *The Effects of Exchange Rate Adjustments*, ed. Peter B. Clark, Dennis E. Logue, and Richard James Sweeny (Washington D.C.: Department of the Treasury, 1974).

Perfect asset substitutability implies that it is an illusion to suppose that the central bank has two independent policy instruments, intervention in the domestic open-money market and intervention in the foreign-exchange market. Yet the empirical evidence on sterilized intervention is far from conclusive. To date much of the academic work on the effects of sterilized intervention on the exchange rate concludes that except for the very short run it is ineffective, although exceptions can readily be found.[31] Nonetheless, many central banks very actively engage in sterilized foreign-exchange intervention. One empirical justification for intervention has been the work by the Bank of Canada on the efficiency of the foreign-exchange markets. The study by Longworth, Boothe, and Clinton concluded that the foreign exchange market for the Canadian dollar was not efficient, where efficiency is defined to exist "if participants take account of all available information when forming expectations about future exchange prices such that there are no systematic ex ante opportunities to earn above-normal profits."[32] The authors' argument runs as follows:

> We tested the joint hypothesis known as the "speculative efficiency hypothesis" which states that: (i) markets are efficient; (ii) risk premiums are constant; and (iii) transactions costs are negligible. . . . If the markets were efficient and risk premiums were constant, exchange rates would move in line with the relevant information available to the market. Intervention would then be justified only if the authorities had information on the economic fundamentals that was superior to that held by other actors and if that information could not be published readily. . . . The rejection of the joint condition (market efficiency and constant risk premiums) is important, whether the evidence is interpreted to imply market inefficiency or the existence of a time-varying risk premium. With either

---

[31] The study by de Graume, Fratianni, and Nabli found that sterilized intervention in the case of Germany had a significant ability to alter the time path of the exchange rate; see Paul de Graume, Michele Fratianni, and Mustapha K. Nabli, *Exchange Rates, Money and Output: The European Experience,* (London: The Macmillan Press Ltd., 1985). However, the study by Maurice Obstfeld found that German sterilized intervention was of little consequence in altering exchange-rate behavior; see "Exchange Rates, Inflation, and the Sterilization Problem: Germany: 1975–80," pp. 161–89, *European Economic Review,* March–April 1983.

[32] David Longworth, Paul Boothe, and Kevin Clinton, "A Study of the Efficiency of Foreign-Exchange Markets," Bank of Canada, p. i, October 1983.

interpretation, the case for an active exchange market policy is open.[33]

The study by the Bank of Canada essentially concluded that financial assets denominated in different currencies were not perfect substitutes, and hence there is a role to be played by official intervention, even if sterilized by offsetting reserve operations in the domestic money markets. However, it would be misleading to interpret such studies to imply that sterilized intervention, or even nonsterilized intervention alone, can be aimed at pegging exchange rates at levels which fundamentals, such as inflation and interest differentials, suggest cannot be maintained. Rather, intervention is often aimed at smoothing movements in exchange rates in an attempt to influence short-term exchange rate expectations and to prevent cumulative movements in exchange rates from leading to "band-wagon effects" or self-fulfilling expectations. These intentions are expressed in the Bank of Canada's *1985 Annual Report:*

> Foreign exchange market operations by the Bank of Canada, as agent for the Exchange Fund Account of the Minister of Finance, continued to be oriented toward promoting orderly market conditions by dampening excessive movements in the exchange rate. . . . For a period in early 1986 a more aggressive strategy was adopted to counter intensified pressure on the Canadian dollar. Forceful intervention in the exchange market was coordinated with actions by the Bank of Canada in the Canadian money markets.[34]

During the early 1970s there was a strong theoretical and doctrinal strain in academic arguments suggesting that, because of the rise in international capital mobility, financial assets were becoming almost perfect substitutes, implying a limited role for official exchange market intervention. Since that time there has been an increasing amount of empirical work which comes out in favor of the absence of perfect substitutability and hence of the effectiveness of sterilized intervention.[35] The state of the art seems

---

[33] Ibid., p. i and p. 6.

[34] *Annual Report of the Governor to the Minister of Finance and Statement of Accounts for the Year 1985,* Bank of Canada, 28 February 1986, p. 39.

[35] The study by Deborah J. Danker et al. concluded that, in the case of the U.S. dollar, perfect substitutability could be rejected vis-à-vis Germany and Canada but not with respect

at present to reside with the conclusion of one influential exchange-rate modeler that, "There is, of course, no question that dollar and foreign-currency assets are imperfect substitutes."[36]

Exchange market intervention in many countries might be best described as "leaning against the wind" intervention, that is, short-run resistance to appreciation or depreciation that might be expected to lead to cumulative disturbances which would affect aggregate demand or price behavior. Recognizing the limited, short-run effectiveness of sterilized intervention, a conclusion reached in the 1983 Jergensen Report, many observers believe that intervention is useful in stabilizing short-run exchange market expectations.[37] This argument may be supported by the increasingly accepted proposition that in the short run there appears to be the tendency for exchange rates to overshoot their long-run equilibrium levels, partly because in response to changes in monetary stimulus, prices of financial assets adjust quickly while goods prices tend to display considerable inertia. In the short run an expansionary monetary policy can be expected to result in a decline in the domestic short-run interest rate and a depreciation of the domestic currency. However, the domestic currency is likely to depreciate to the point where a future appreciation is expected, equal to the differential between foreign and domestic interest rates. (Such an expectation would be consistent with the expected return on domestic and foreign assets, evaluated in either currency, being equal.)[38] The potential for movements in exchange

---

to Japan. They tentatively concluded that sterilized intervention is effective. See Deborah J. Danker et al., "Small Empirical Models of Exchange Market Intervention: Applications to Germany, Japan, and Canada," Staff Studies No. 135 (Washington D.C.: Board of Governors of the Federal Reserve System, 1985).

[36] Rudiger Dornbusch, "Equilibrium and Disequilibrium Exchange Rates," in *Dollars, Debts and Deficits* (Cambridge, Mass.: MIT Press, 1987), p. 52.

[37] "Report of the Working Group on Exchange Market Intervention," chairman Phillippe Jurgensen, published by La Documentation Française, Collection des Rapports Officiels, March 1983, Paris.

[38] The so-called overshooting hypothesis is often associated with the work of Rudiger Dornbusch, "Expectations and Exchange Rate Dynamics," *Journal of Political Economy*, pp. 1161–76, December 1976. Note that overshooting is not a phenomenon unique to exchange rates but is a common characteristic of all asset markets. For a discussion of this asset market behavior, see Jüng Niehans, "The Appreciation of Sterling: Causes, Effects, Policies," Center Symposia Series, No. CS-11, Center for Research in Government Policy and Business, Graduate School of Management, University of Rochester, 1981.

rates beyond some presumed equilibrium level, leading to possible, cumulative, destabilizing expectations of future exchange-rate movements, may create the need for the central bank to actively intervene in the exchange markets. At the same time, to prevent such interventions from disrupting short-term money-market conditions, and in an effort to limit departures of targeted monetary aggregates from desired levels, short-term intervention may be routinely sterilized.

There is little disagreement that in the long run significant adjustments in exchange rates cannot be achieved through the use of sterilized interventions but require major adjustments in monetary and/or fiscal policy. Monetary policy corrections in this regard are characterized as expansion or contraction in the monetary base. Whether the adjustment in the monetary base occurs via an expansion in domestic credit—for example, purchases or sales of domestic financial assets in the open market—or an expansion in foreign credit—purchases or sales of foreign-denominated assets— is in the long run a question of second order depending on the institutional structure of the financial system. To effect a significant change in either interest rates or exchange rates requires a change in the ratio of money to bonds held by the private, nonbank sector and not simply a change in the currency composition of the latter.

The preceding discussion of foreign-exchange market intervention concerns the role of what might be called short-term exchange rate smoothing or leaning against the wind operations by the central bank. Such operations should be considered to be a component of short-term monetary management. A much broader concern is raised by prolonged foreign-exchange market intervention aimed at correcting what central banks judge to be a significant currency "misalignment." Prolonged intervention also involves the question of what is the optimal quantity of international reserves for the world economy. The large effective exchange rate (i.e., weighted average) appreciation of the U.S. dollar up to early 1985 and its subsequent considerable depreciation into 1988 (see Chart 4–4) gave rise to a series of coordinated efforts by central banks and finance ministers at first to effect a depreciation of the dollar and later to attempt to moderate its decline (the Plaza Agreement of September 1985, the Louvre Accord of February

CHART 4–4
Effective Exchange Rates, 1981–1988 (Monthly Averages, December
1980 = 100)

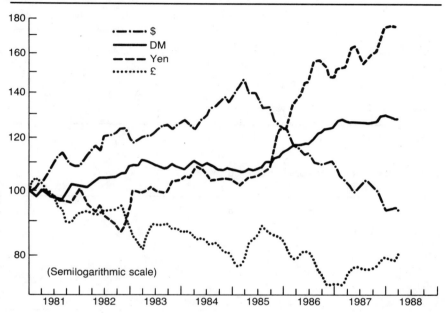

1987).[39] The currency misalignment during the 1980s had resulted in
a major trade and current-account deficit on the part of the United
States and major surpluses for several large industrial economies,
as well as some of the newly industrialized economies, such as
Taiwan, South Korea, Singapore, and Hong Kong. The combination of current-account imbalances and major currency intervention was the cause of a significant growth in international reserves,
in particular, in foreign exchange.

As seen in Table 4–4, the growth of total international reserves
excluding gold, primarily foreign-exchange reserves, has been very
rapid since 1982, amounting to a 73 percent increase for the

[39] A description of these coordinated central bank agreements and the activity in the
exchange market surrounding them may be obtained in the annual reports of the Bank for
International Settlements for the years 1986 to 1988.

TABLE 4–4
**Official Holdings of Reserve Assets by Industrial Countries, Year-End
1980–87** (In Billions of SDRs)

	1981	1982	1983	1984	1985	1986	1987
Total reserves excluding gold	185.1	184.4	205.0	224.5	227.4	248.9	319.4
	(0.4)*	(−0.3)	(11.2)	(9.5)	(1.3)	(9.5)	(28.3)
Foreign exchange	159.6	153.2	167.9	183.9	187.3	209.8	282.6
	(−3.1)	(−4.0)	(9.6)	(9.5)	(1.8)	(12.0)	(34.7)

* Percentage change from previous year in parentheses.

**Foreign Exchange Reserves: G-7
Countries** (In Billions of SDRs)

Country	End-1985	End-1987
United States	11.7	9.2
Japan	20.3	53.3
Germany	35.5	51.4
United Kingdom	8.9	27.2
France	22.1	20.9
Italy	12.8	19.6
Canada	1.4	4.4

Source: *International Financial Statistics*, International
Monetary Fund, May 1988.

industrial countries. Foreign exchange holdings rose by almost 35
percent in 1987 alone, in considerable part due to central bank
foreign-exchange intervention in support of the U.S. dollar, necessitated by the decline in private foreign capital inflows into the
United States. At the end of 1987 the combined foreign exchange
reserves of Japan and Germany were equivalent to almost the
entire foreign-exchange reserve holdings of the Group of Seven
(G-7) countries combined at the end of 1985.

It has been common in discussions of official reserve growth to
measure the quantity of international reserves in relation to total
imports, with imports used as a measure of economic openness.
Chart 4–5 presents the ratios of total official reserves less gold to
imports for all industrial countries, as classified by the Interna-

CHART 4–5
Nongold Reserves to Imports

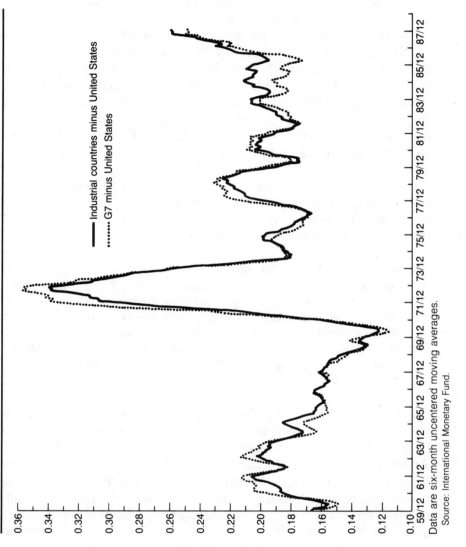

Data are six-month uncentered moving averages.
Source: International Monetary Fund.

tional Monetary Fund, less the United States and for the G-7 countries, again less the United States. The data presented are monthly, measured as six-month moving averages. Two things are readily apparent. First, contrary to expectations held before the move to floating exchange rates in 1973, nongold reserve holdings by central banks in the industrial countries, in relation to imports, have been generally higher during the period since the collapse of the fixed exchange rate system than before. Second, in relation to total imports nongold reserves have increased significantly in 1986 and 1987 and at the end of 1987 were at their highest level since 1973.

It had been anticipated that the regime of floating exchange rates would greatly reduce the demand by central banks to hold large quantities of reserves, as payments imbalances would be eliminated by changes in exchange rates.

> It does not follow, of course, that the problem of international liquidity vanishes altogether under floating. If there are official interventions in the exchange market, as there probably always will be, there is some need (or demand) for reserves. But since under floating the authorities are not restricted in their interventions by a rigid barrier, unless they restrict themselves, which would be tantamount to giving up the float, the need for reserves cannot be greater under floating than it is under the adjustable peg.[40]

One obvious reason for the continued demand for official reserves during the period of floating is the fact that the current "regime" of floating exchange rates has been a managed system. Additionally, industrial economies during the 1970s have been subject to a number of external shocks, such as the rise in oil prices, which may have increased the official demand for international reserves. Recent periods of large international trade imbalances, exchange market turbulence, and currency misalignment resulting in significant reserve accumulation and currency inter-

---

[40] See Gottfried Haberler, "How Important Is Control Over International Reserves?" reprinted in *Selected Essays of Gottfried Haberler,* edited by Anthony Y. C. Koo (Cambridge, Mass.: MIT Press, 1985), p. 212.

vention have all contributed to the holding of large stocks of foreign exchange reserves by central banks.

Several studies have attempted to determine whether the demand for international reserves is related to a limited set of explanatory variables and whether such a relationship is stable. The variables often used to explain reserve demand include the level of imports, the average propensity to import, and the variability of a country's balance of payments. Generally these studies have concluded that, with the exception of the 1972–73 period, reserve demand relationships have remained stable during the period of the 1960s and 1970s.[41] A recent study, utilizing data extending to 1984, concluded that the disturbances observed in financial markets in the early 1980s have not altered the stability of the demand for international reserves by developed countries but "appear to have been most destabilizing for the demand for reserves by the developing countries."[42]

The growth of international reserves is of considerable concern if it leads to excessive growth of private liquidity. A considerable portion of the growth in foreign-exchange reserves since 1986 has been related to official central bank exchange-market intervention. This intervention has largely been related to central bank attempts to prevent too rapid or excessive movements in exchange rates vis-à-vis the U.S. dollar. As most central banks sterilize exchange market interventions by performing reserve offsetting operations in the domestic money market, one might argue that exchange-market intervention has not led to excessive growth in monetary aggregates and private market credit. Such a judgment may be shortsighted, however, as domestic money-market operations since the mid-1980s have also often had an exchange-market objective, in addition to objectives related solely to domestic economic conditions. As it is clearly difficult, if not impossible, to attribute central bank reserve creation operations in the domestic

[41] These conclusions were reached by H. Robert Heller and Moshin S. Khan in "The Demand for International Reserves under Fixed and Floating Exchange Rates," *Staff Papers*, International Monetary Fund, pp. 623–49, December 1978.

[42] See José Saul Lizondo and Donald J. Mathieson, "The Stability of the Demand for International Reserves," *Journal of International Money and Finance*, pp. 251–82, September 1987.

money markets specifically to either the achievement of domestic or external objectives, one can only loosely conjecture the degree to which rapid growth in domestic money and credit has been due to exchange market considerations. It does appear, nonetheless, that in some countries strong growth in monetary aggregates during 1986 and 1987 can be attributed to lower short-term interest rates and exchange market intervention, with lower interest rates partly a result of the attempt to achieve exchange-rate policy objectives. It is thus disquieting to observe the rapid growth in monetary aggregates in some countries during 1986 and 1987, growth which has taken place pari passu with the growth of their international reserves. Chart 4–6 displays the behavior of monetary growth in Germany and Japan during the 1986–87 period, together with targeted ranges in the case of Germany, and projections in the case of Japan.

CHART 4–6
Actual and Projected or Targeted Growth Rates of Money

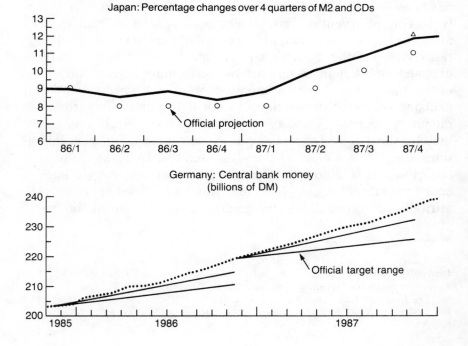

FINANCIAL LIBERALIZATION AND INNOVATION: SOME POLICY ISSUES FOR CENTRAL BANKS

Changes observed in financial instruments, markets, and institutions since the mid-1970s have fundamentally changed and are continuing to change the processes by which credit is intermediated in industrial economies. Such phrases as *nonbank banks, money versus near-money, securitization,* and *off-balance-sheet banking* signal that traditional definitions of what is "money" and what is a "bank" have been undermined by the flurry of financial liberalization, innovation, and internationalization in financial activities and technology. The long-run goals of central banks may have remained the same; however, the intermediate financial objectives by which these goals are best attained are certainly less obvious than they were just a few years ago. Central banks face the problem of having fewer direct controls on the activities of banks in an environment of increased financial-asset price volatility and uncertainty. Although new financial instruments have been created which provide more scope for risks to be hedged or transferred, they may at the same time be the source of increased volatility in asset prices. (See Table 4–5 for a summary of some of these new financial instruments.)

The factors contributing to these trends (financial liberalization, deregulation, and the development of new financial instruments and markets) have been mentioned at various places in this chapter. Such factors include the height and volatility of interest rates induced by inflation during the 1970s, which created a need for hedging instruments and induced individuals to economize on the use of noninterest or low-interest-bearing financial assets; the growth of government debt, which has stimulated the development of secondary markets in government paper, increasing competition with deposit instruments and gradually inducing the elimination of deposit rate ceilings; the increased internationalization of banking and securities business, encouraged partly by the removal of exchange controls and restrictions in domestic money and capital markets, leading to increased competition and giving rise to the development of new instruments (e.g., currency swaps) and new financing facilities (e.g., note issuance facilities); and improved

TABLE 4–5
New Financial Instruments on Interest Rates and Foreign Exchange

Instrument	Date of First Appearance	Date of Market Maturity	Trading Volume or New Contracts 1987 (in millions)	Outstanding Positions or Open Interest at End-1987 (in billions of U.S. dollars)	Intermediaries (Arrangers)	Principal Users of Market
FUTURES						
Foreign currency	1973	1979–81	20.5[1]	11.9[1]	Organized exchanges	Nonbanks (banks)
Interest rate	1975	1979–81	97.5[1]	345.6[1]	Organized exchanges	Depends on instrument
Equity indices	1981	1983–84	25.5[1]	17.2[1]	Commercial banks	Commercial banks/ investment banks/ institutional investors
Forward rate agreements	early 1980s	1985–86	n.a.	n.a.	Commercial banks	Commercial banks
OPTIONS						
Foreign currency, traded on exchanges	1978[2]; 1982[3]	1985–86	7.0[1]	32.1[1]	Organized exchanges	Nonbanks
Interest rate, traded on exchanges	1980[2]; 1985[3]	1986	23.3[1]	115.7[1]	Organized exchanges	Nonbanks
Over-the-counter foreign currency options	existed for many years	1984–85	3.1[4]	n.a.	Commercial and investment banks	Nonbanks
Over-the-counter interest rate options	existed for many years	1984–85	n.a.	n.a.	Commercial and investment banks	Nonbanks
SWAPS						
Foreign currency swaps[5]	late 1970s	1982–83	(40–45)[e6]	100–150[e]	Commercial and investment banks	Nonbanks and banks
Interest rate swaps[7]	late 1970s	1982–83	224.0	675.0	Commercial and investment banks	Nonbanks and banks

e = estimate. n.a. = not available.
[1] On U.S. exchanges only. [2] Netherlands. [3] United States and elsewhere. [4] Source: Federal Reserve Bank of New York: *Summary of Results of U.S. Futures Foreign Exchange Market Turnover Survey in March 1986*. Sales of foreign currency options over the counter reported by 123 banking institutions and 13 nonbank financial institutions. Over-the-counter purchases were equal to $5.2 billion. [5] Source: Bank of England, *Quarterly Bulletin* (February 1987). [6] Swaps arranged during 1986, in billions of U.S. dollars. [7] Value of notional principal amounts of interest rate and currency swaps reported by domestic U.S. banks (worldwide consolidated) in billions of U.S. dollars. Positions may be double-counted (Source: U.S. call report).

Source: H. Bockelmann, Die neuen Finanzinstrumente—Chancen und Risiken, Colloque du Groupement International pour l'Etude des Problèmes de l'Epargne, Zürich, 20 May 1988.

computer and telecommunications technology, which has permitted more rapid and efficient international trading of securities and management of financial resources through the employment of the new tools and instruments of modern finance theory (e.g., options pricing, portfolio insurance).[43] At the same time there have also been three significant competitive forces acting on commercial banking, with the pressure of such competition dependent on the institutional structure of banking and securities markets within countries; the first, the increased competition stemming from the growth and flexibility of securities markets; the second, the increased competition coming from foreign banking penetration into domestic markets; and the third, competition deriving from banklike or securities firms offering various types of traditional banking service. Both the competitive forces acting on banking and the mélange of innovations, liberalizations and deregulations of banking and nonbanking finance have altered several aspects of central banking activities and concerns.

Rather too briefly, we can summarize by saying that the preceding factors have had an impact on the definitions of money, the relationship between reserve creation and money creation (the "money multiplier"), the statistical stability of the demand by the private sector to hold bank deposit transactions media, the monetary transmissions mechanism, the payments mechanism, the efficacy of existing banking regulations and supervisory practices, and the adequacy of existing bank capital.[44] The combination of these problem areas is now causing central bankers in some countries to take a much broader view than they did earlier of how

---

[43] A general review of this subject is contained in J. David Germany and John E. Morton, "Financial Innovation and Deregulation in Foreign Industrial Countries," *Federal Reserve Bulletin,* October 1985; with specific reference to Japan, see Yoshio Suzuki, "Financial Innovation and Monetary Policy in Japan," *Monetary and Economic Studies,* Bank of Japan, June 1984; and Yoshio Suzuki, "Financial Reform in Japan—Developments and Prospects," *Monetary and Economic Studies,* Bank of Japan, December 1987. For an analysis of the causes of financial innovation and a description of some of the new instruments used in international banking, see *Recent Innovations in International Banking,* Bank for International Settlements, April 1986.

[44] How financial innovation has affected several of these areas of central bank concern is analyzed in Jacques J. Sijben, "Financial Innovation, Monetary Policy, and Financial Stability," *Kredit und Kapital,* Number 1, pp. 45–66, 1988.

their financial markets ought to be reorganized, regulated, supervised, and capitalized.[45] It is also producing considerable rethinking of how best to formulate intermediate-run monetary policy in a deregulated financial world.

Consider only the example of the changing nature of customary commercial banking business. In the United States many banks are now heavily involved in securities brokerage, underwriting, and contingent liability creation activities. Many large banks are creators but not the ultimate holders of commercial loans, having developed substantial loan sale business with regional and international banks. Banks in the United States are also increasingly involved in the underwriting of some municipal bonds. One area of major concern to central banks has been the enormous growth in so-called off-balance-sheet business, essentially the creation of contingent bank liabilities such as letters of credit and interest rate swaps, liabilities which do not initially involve an extension of credit and hence do not constrain the utilization of existing capital. Such liabilities carry risks which, because they are contingent, are difficult for supervisors or debt-rating agencies to judge. For U.S. commercial banks, standby letters of credit alone have grown from less than US$20 billion in 1976 to US$150 billion in 1985.[46] The *American Banker* estimated for the five largest American banks that off-balance-sheet commitments totaled US$1.2 trillion at the end of 1986.[47] The largest segment of these commitments were reported to be related to futures and options contracts. The growth of off-balance sheet banking has raised the presumption that banks now confront greater risks than they did in traditional on-balance-sheet banking. (The presumption may be justified, but the evidence for such a conjecture is not always readily apparent. Some studies suggest, for example, that the credit standards for standby letters of credit extended by U.S.

---

[45] See, for example, E. Gerald Corrigan, "Financial Market Structure: A Longer View," in *Annual Report,* Federal Reserve Bank of New York, pp. 3–54, 1986.

[46] See Barbara Bennett, "Off Balance Sheet Risk in Banking: The Case of Standby Letters of Credit," *Economic Review,* pp. 19–29, Federal Reserve Bank of San Francisco, Winter 1986.

[47] "Off-Balance Sheet Items Are Piling Up," *American Banker,* pp. 1 and 15, 1 May 1987.

banks are higher than those for loans in recognition of the nature of risks on contingent liabilities.)[48]

The changing composition of aggregate risks taken by banks, as well as perceptions of an increase in risk due to greater financial asset price volatility, the increased internationalization of banking, and the decline in capital ratios of some large banks have led central banks and supervisory authorities in the Group of Ten countries plus Luxembourg (the Basle Committee on Banking Regulations and Supervisory Practices), to propose an initiative which would lead to a greater convergence of measures and standards of bank capital adequacy. The proposals call for risk-based capital measures such that "bank capital adequacy is assured by a method that is explicitly and systematically sensitive to the risk profile of individual banking organizations. All assets and certain off-balance sheet items (translated into balance sheet equivalents) are assigned to appropriate risk categories. This permits the relevant banking authorities to establish different capital requirements for various classes of assets and, as appropriate, to include certain off-balance sheet activities."[49] The proposals for an internationally agreed on system of measurement and standards for bank capital adequacy have been recognized by U.S. regulators and supervisors as desirable given the problems of asset quality faced by U.S. banks, the increased volatility in financial markets, the growth of off-balance-sheet financing techniques, and the changes that have taken place in financial technology.[50]

Financial innovation and deregulation have also, as mentioned earlier, greatly undermined the policy usefulness of previous definitions of money and led to a significant reduction by countries in the use of intermediate monetary targets. For lack of an obviously better alternative, greater short- and medium-term mone-

---

[48] See Bennett, "Off Balance Sheet Risk," p. 26.

[49] David Spencer and Allan Murray-Jones, "Capital Adequacy: Toward a Level Playing Field," *International Financial Law Review,* pp. 19–23, March 1988.

[50] See statement by William Taylor, Staff Director, Division of Banking Supervision and Regulation, Board of Governors of the Federal Reserve System, before the Subcommittee on General Oversight and Investigations of the Committee on Banking, Finance and Urban Affairs, House of Representatives, 12 April 1988.

tary policy discretion and finetuning of money-market conditions has been employed by central banks in recent years. As the sectoral impact of monetary policy has changed, with the external sector now a major element in the transmission mechanism even in the United States, greater policy attention has been devoted to exchange rate behavior, both as a potential policy target and information variable. The growth of securitized finance, the increased direct intermediation through capital markets and the repackaging for market sale of previously nontraded financial claims, may also change the transmission mechanism and the incidence of monetary policy. The greater institutionalization of trading in some financial assets, such as equities, and the increase in international portfolio investment may increase the speed with which disturbances in one financial center are transmitted to foreign markets and their impact. These changes in financial assets, markets, and institutions suggest that the greater integration of international finance may have reduced the ability of any one central bank to independently control the domestic volume of credit and money and the level and stability of interest and exchange rates. Hence, the integration of world money and capital markets appears to be spurring the need for greater cooperation and coordination of macromonetary policies and greater harmonization of regulatory and supervisory standards.

CHAPTER 5

THE STRUCTURE OF THE INTERNATIONAL BANKING INDUSTRY

Robert Z. Aliber

The international banking industry is characterized by several stylized facts. The first is that the industrial structure of banking differs sharply among the major countries. As Figure 5–1 shows, three national patterns are evident. One, perhaps the most typical, is that four or five banks account for 80 or 90 percent of total bank deposits; the banking industries in Canada, Great Britain, and Switzerland conform to this pattern. The second pattern is illustrated by Italy and Japan, where banking is less concentrated; the 10 largest banks account for less than 50 percent of total bank deposits. Banking is least concentrated in the United States, where there are nearly fifteen thousand banks, more than in all other countries combined.[1]

A second stylized fact is that the banks in each country are extensively regulated, compared with firms in most other industries; banks are subject to constraints on the mix of assets and on the maximum size of the loan to any one borrower. Banks must

---

[1] The data from *The Banker* include the assets of those banks in the top 500 on a global basis. The larger the number of banks in a country, the more banks that are not included in the sample of *The Banker;* hence the market shares of the largest banks are overstated. This argument probably is significant only for the United States.

FIGURE 5–1
Industrial Structure of Commercial Banking (In Percentages)

Market Share of Banks	Largest Bank	Three Largest	Five Largest	Ten Largest
United States	10%	20%	28%	42%
Canada	24	65	93	—
Japan	06	17	28	47
United Kingdom	22	58	79	94
Germany	12	27	40	64
Switzerland	29	75	86	96
France	18	50	74	92
Italy	11	28	44	74

Source: *The Banker*, various issues.

hold reserves at the central bank, their deposits are subject to interest rate ceilings, and are limited as a multiple of their capital. The entry of banks into new markets is constrained. Similarly, the products or services that banks can sell are limited.

A third stylized fact is that the returns earned by firms in the banking industry do not seem inconsistent with the textbook model of a competitive industry, perhaps because there are few, if any, monopoly elements in banking. Nothing a bank produces is patentable—indeed the products of various banks are nearly perfect substitutes for each other, and hence "commodities." As Figure 5–2 shows, commercial banking is much less concentrated than many other industries when viewed in the global context; there are substantially fewer firms in most other industries, such as

FIGURE 5–2
Structure of International Industries (In Percentages)

Market Share Firms	Banking	Autos	Chemicals	Metals	Petroleum
Largest	3%	19%	9%	15%	12%
Three largest	7	36	21	28	31
Five largest	10	46	31	36	43
Ten largest	17	63	48	52	60

Source: *The Banker, Fortune*, various issues.

autos, petroleum, metals, and chemicals. If bank deposits are viewed as a proxy for the sales of each firm, then, the largest 5 banks in the world account for 10 percent of total bank sales, and the 10 largest banks account for 15 percent of the sales of the largest 500 banks.

The fourth stylized fact is that a large number of firms in the banking industry have brand name recognition—Citibank, Bank of America, Chase, Morgan Guaranty, Deutsche Bank, Societe General (both in France and Belgium), Banque Nationale de Paris, Barclays, Bank of Tokyo, National Westminster, Bank of Montreal, Dai-Ichi Kangyo, Fuji—the reader of the *New York Times* or the *Manchester Guardian* or the *Nihon Keizai Shimbum* might recall the names of 25 to 50 banks headquartered in any of 10 or so countries. That there are so many well-known firms in a "commodity business" is a paradox—typically commodity businesses are characterized by small anonymous firms. (We discuss international competition in Chapter 6.)

The fifth stylized fact is that the relationships among firms in the banking industry are complex—banks compete with each other for deposits and for loans, they participate jointly in syndicated loans and in service bureau activities, and they borrow and lend with each other. Interbank transactions are extensive, and have no good counterpart in other industries except, perhaps, petroleum.

The sixth stylized fact is that international trade in the products of banks is modest, especially at the retail level; most residents of most countries purchase their bank deposits from a banking office located in their neighborhoods, and virtually all of these banking offices are branches of banks headquartered within that country.[2] Indeed, international trade in banking is significantly less extensive than international trade in most consumer goods and

---

[2] International banking is a broad term that includes three or four distinct activities. The largest is offshore banking—banks sell deposits and make loans in a currency other than that of the country in which the banking office is located. Export banking involves extension of credit to customers based in countries other than those of the country in which the bank is located; export banking and wholesale banking are somewhat overlapping sets. Foreign banking involves sale of deposits in a domestic currency by banks headquartered in a foreign country; thus as an example, the sale of British pound deposits in London by United States, Swiss, and German banks. This chapter primarily is about foreign banking.

in many service industries, such as airline travel, shipping, and movie rentals. Wholesale banking, which involves the extension of credit to business firms, is much more international than retail banking.

The seventh stylized fact is that the share of foreign banks in the several domestic markets appears to be negatively related to concentration of firms in these markets; the share of foreign banks in the several national deposit and loan markets is larger, the smaller the scope of concentration.

The size of distribution of banks by country of charter or passport, as shown in Figure 5–1, does not provide an accurate view of the competitive structure in the banking industry in an international context for several reasons. The first is that many of the largest banks headquartered in each country compete for deposits and loans in other countries through branches and subsidiaries. Thus, 15 percent of the U.S. market for commercial and industrial loans is supplied by the U.S. branches and subsidiaries of banks headquartered in the United Kingdom, Germany, Japan, and other foreign countries. Moreover, banks headquartered in the United Kingdom, Germany, Japan, and a few other foreign countries compete for U.S. dollar loans and U.S. dollar deposits from their branches in London, Luxembourg, and other offshore financial centers. Similarly, U.S. banks compete for deposits and loans in other countries from their offshore offices, and to a much lesser extent, from their head offices.

Banks headquartered in each country compete with foreign banks in three distinct markets—the U.S. market, the German market, the offshore market, and third-country markets. The U.S. banking market is subject to U.S. regulation, and the German market is subject to German regulation. The entry of U.S. banks into the German market is regulated, and entry of German banks into the U.S. market also is regulated; both markets are protected. The offshore market largely is unregulated, except that the banks headquartered in most countries are subject to indirect regulation of the activities of their branches in the offshore market as an extension of domestic regulation. National banking markets, especially the retail deposit market and the retail loan market, are partially segmented from each other. Hence, the markets in which banks compete are partially overlapping, and partially segmented.

That consumers in most countries buy their banking services or products from offices (e.g., plants) in their neighborhoods, just as they buy their groceries in their neighborhoods, suggests that proximity is important in the relationship between the buyers of bank deposits and the banks that produce these deposits. Buyers of bank deposits are involved in many transactions with their banks within in a year. Transaction costs increase with distance and explain why the buyers of the various products or services of banks transact with a nearby office; the greater the distance from the customer to the banking office, the higher these costs—and especially when currency is to be deposited or withdrawn from a bank. Banks establish plants close to their customers as a way to minimize the costs of economic distance.[3] Proximity does not explain why the banking offices in each country are almost always owned by domestic firms.

Regulation has had a significant impact on the number of firms and the number of plants in the banking industry by raising costs and forestalling the expansion of the more efficient firms. The regulatory factors that affect the structure of the industry include limitations on entry and limitations on takeovers, and a large number of portfolio-diversification requirements and interest-rate ceilings.

Contemplate the structure of the banking industry in a world with one uniform set of national banking regulations and one national currency. The number of firms in the industry would be smaller, and some marginal banks would have merged. The number of plants in the industry would be smaller. Each firm would have more plants; the decline in the number of firms would be larger in percentage terms than the decline in the number of plants. The spatial distribution of plants would differ. Most consumers, especially those in smaller countries, probably would have access to a larger number of plants within a given market area; however, a few consumers would have access to fewer plants, because cross-

---

[3] Changes in technology—the rapid expansion of automatic teller machines (ATMs)—reduce the significance of the proximity argument. The ATMs are owned by a service bureau, and used by the customers of many different banks. As a result, proximity to a plant will become less significant in the choice of the bank.

subsidization from plants in large cities to plants in small cities would be less extensive, a result of the more competitive structure of the industry. The costs of some banks would be lower; a larger number of banks would achieve scale economies. Competition in the larger national markets would be more extensive, and firms not previously extensively involved in these markets would enter them to increase size; obtaining target volume of deposits is easier in a large market than in a small one.

The differences between the structure of the banking industry and the structure contemplated in a world of unified regulation might reflect national differences in regulation, or protection.[4] The structure of the banking industry might reflect that the banks fail to expand their plants in foreign countries because there is no financial incentive to do so. The lack of financial incentive might reflect that the costs of banks are similar, and that few if any banks have cost advantages that would enable them to compensate for the costs of economic distance. Formal or informal barriers limiting the entry of foreign banks into national markets would be redundant; even in the absence of these barriers, banks would not expand abroad. Banks headquartered in one country are likely to expand abroad only if they have an economic advantage relative to their host country competitors; this is the necessary condition. But these banks expand abroad only if entry into the foreign market is not restricted or constrained; freedom to enter is a sufficient condition.

The determinants of the size distribution of banks by country are discussed in the next section of this chapter. Then the structure of the banking industry in a unified currency world is discussed. The third section reviews the investors' evaluation of banks.

---

[4] The proximity argument suggests that with the existing payments technology most customers buy their banking services and products from nearby banking offices. As a result, the thrust of this chapter is with "the right of establishment" of foreign firms rather than with the ability of residents of individual countries to buy services and products from banking offices located in other countries. A study of the purchase of products of banks located in other countries would involve a compilation of exchange controls along the lines of *Exchange Arrangements and Exchange Restrictions*, published annually by the International Monetary Fund.

THE DETERMINANTS OF THE SIZE
DISTRIBUTION OF BANKS BY COUNTRY

The size distribution of banks by country of charter differs, even though the hierarchical structure of banking and the financial services industry in each country is similar. Each institution is ranked in one of three tiers within this structure by the "moneyness" of its liabilities. The central bank is at the apex of the structure; the central bank produces high-powered money from the viewpoint of the monetary analyst and a risk-free asset from the viewpoint of individual investors or depositors—or at least an asset free of default risk. Commercial banks are at the next tier in this hierarchy; they produce demand deposits, which are transferred in money payments. The investor is concerned—modestly—with the default sensitivity of the liabilities of each bank and with any differential in default sensitivity. Nonbank financial intermediaries produce near monies that have the liquidity of money but are not directly transferrable as means of payment.

The ability of a bank or any other financial institution to expand its size—to acquire more assets—is determined by its skill in marketing its liabilities; in this sense banks sell deposits and buy high-powered money in the form of currency and of deposits at the central bank.[5] Banks pay interest on their deposit liabilities to induce investors to buy these liabilities—they seek to obtain high-powered money so they can buy more income-earning assets. By limiting the supply of high-powered money, the central bank limits the size of the banking system.

A bank can increase its share of the total market for bank deposits by increasing its marketing expenditures—by selling its liabilities at a lower price (e.g., paying a higher interest rate on its deposit liabilities), by improving the perceived quality of its product (e.g., the safety of its deposits), by enhancing the conve-

---

[5] The terminology in this paragraph is unconventional. Thus the unique product aspect of a bank—one that carries the bank's own brand name—is its liabilities. Banks "produce" deposits (and in the process they "create" credit). Each bank produces or sells deposits, just as drug companies produce aspirins, vitamins, and Valium. All of the bank's assets are identified with someone else's brand name.

nience and reducing the costs of using its deposit liabilities in payments, and by advertising. Just as a drug company seeks to optimize its marketing expenditures by choosing between nonprice advertising and various price-cutting promotions, so a bank seeks to optimize between reliance on price-cutting and nonprice promotions. The key question is whether an increase in the interest rate paid on deposits or an increase in marketing expenditures has a larger impact in increasing the volume of deposits. The ability of a bank to increase its marketing expenditures depends on its success not only in managing the institution at a low cost but also as an investor, which comprises several arguments—its ability to acquire a portfolio of assets whose total return is high relative to their risk, to cope with transformation risk (e.g., managing the yield curve), and to integrate its liability management activities with its asset management activities.

The liability management activities of a bank involve marketing and promotion; the bank's brand name is important, especially to large (and hence uninsured) depositors. In contrast, the asset management activity primarily involves risk appraisal. The liability management and the asset management activities are linked in several ways—the transformation risk is associated with the shape of the yield curve and changes in its shape are important because the maturity of bank assets is longer than the maturity of liabilities. The two sides of the bank's balance sheet can be viewed as being aspects of a vertically integrated firm, with the sale of deposits the upstream activity and the purchase of loans the downstream activity. Even though many customers of the bank are on both sides as buyers of deposits and sellers of loans, households are the major depositors, while business firms are the primary borrowers; the deposit business is more of a retail business. Price competition in the wholesale market is more extensive than in the retail market.[6]

---

[6] One implication is that the return or profit rate on capital committed to the wholesale credit activity might be lower than the return on the less competitive national activity of selling deposits. The dilemma may be more apparent than real; theory suggests that the bank might reallocate resources from the less profitable activity to the more profitable activity as a way to enhance total return. The complication is that if the deposit market is oligopolistic, then any firm that increases its investment in this activity may induce a response from other firms, so that total returns decline.

Residents of each country can choose among a very large number of monies and near monies; the choice involves at least four dimensions. One dimension involves the liquidity or moneyness of the assets they might acquire; a second involves the default sensitivity of the firm that produces these assets; the third involves the currency of denomination of these assets; and the fourth involves the venue of issue of these assets. A particular risk is identified with each of these dimensions; in some cases the risk is institution-specific, and in other cases, investor specific. For example, the currency denomination risk is specific to each investor. Each of these differences affects the risk attached to each particular liability, and some of these differences affect the cost of producing the liability. Investors choose among the available money and near monies on the basis of currency preferences, the return on the liabilities offered by particular institutions, the default-sensitivity risk associated with liabilities of each institution, and where they wish to hold their funds.

The traditional analysis of the size distribution of banks highlights the trade-off between the factors that lead toward a reduction in the number of banks so that economics of scale and of scope are fully realized, and the factors that constrain this tendency, especially regulation. Scale economies may be relevant for many of the inputs to banking—marketing and advertising for deposits, management of risk appraisal, diversification, and management of payments. The conventional wisdom is that scale and scope economies can be realized at a reasonably low level of bank size relative to the size of the largest banks. Small firms coexist with large firms in many segments of the industry. The idea of scale economies is associated with manufacturing production, and with efficient utilization of an indivisible unit of capital equipment or an indivisible factor. However, the economies of scale in marketing may only be achieved at a substantially larger scale; unit costs may continue to decline for large increases in marketing expenditures. Regulation may forestall the tendency toward a reduction in the number of banks through mergers and acquisitions. Moreover, the availability of lender-of-last-resort facilities and of deposit insurance also enhance the ability of smaller institutions to maintain market share.

Banks are extensively involved with other banks in a variety of credit activities. The extensive interbank transactions reflect that individual banks differ in the location of their offices or in their capital and perceived strength to depositors or in the strength of their marketing skills relative to their investment skills. Perhaps, the single most important factor in explaining interbank transactions is that banks differ in their abilities to sell deposits, because their credit standing differs; thus banks with the highest credit standing sell deposits at the lowest interest rates, and in turn, lend the funds to banks considered somewhat riskier. These banks with the lower credit standing borrow—on the margin—from the banks with the superior credit standing rather than from the public, as a way to reduce their total costs of funds. In turn, banks with the superior credit rankings lend to other banks because the returns are high relative to the risks. One implication from the pattern of interbank transactions is that the banks most likely to establish plants abroad are those with the strongest ability to sell deposits—those with the superior credit standing.

Banks are affected by a large number of portfolio regulations, including reserve requirements, capital deposit regulations, interest rate ceilings, loan limits, and portfolio mix requirements. To the extent these regulations—such as reserve requirements and portfolio mix requirements—limit the income of banks, the size of the banking industry is smaller than it would otherwise be. Similarly the higher the capital deposit requirements, the lower the profitability of banks, and the smaller the size of the banking industry. To the extent these regulations limit price or nonprice competition, the average bank is smaller, and there are more banks in the industry.

Domestic portfolio regulations may handicap the ability of a bank based in one country to expand its plants in other countries, and especially its ability to establish plants to sell deposits. The source country bank needs a sufficiently large market share so that scale economies can be obtained, and especially scale economies in marketing. Achieving these scale economies may be especially difficult in those national markets characterized by a small number of banks.[7] Moreover, portfolio regulation may limit the ability of the potential entrant to increase market share by cutting price.

---

[7] The problem of entry into a foreign market is affected by whether the media markets within a country are national or regional. The more national these markets the more powerful the economies of scale argument in detering the entry of foreign firms.

The demarcation of the world into multiple currency areas also may affect the structure of the industry. Thus exchange controls adopted as a supplement to monetary policy or exchange rate policy may indirectly protect domestic firms. And domestic banks may have a marketing advantage in the sale of their liabilities because they have preferred access to their central bank for liquidity.

Scale and scope economies have a number of implications for the extent of concentration in the banking industry; they follow from the combinations of assumptions about the size of the national banking market and the minimum efficient size. One implication is the more extensive the scope of regulation in a country, the larger the number of banks in that country. A second implication is that for any given set of bank regulations, the smaller the banking market within a country, the smaller the number of banks; national income may be a proxy for the size of the banking market. A third implication is that for a country of given national income, the larger the number of separate regional banking markets, the larger the number of banks. A fourth implication is that if the banking markets in various countries differ in size, the larger the geographic size of the country, the larger the number of banks and their average sizes.

Data on the size distribution of banks by country are shown in Figure 5–3. The deposits/assets of a particular bank and those of its country of origin by charter are not fully congruent; the deposit data include all foreign and offshore deposits. In contrast, the country data include only domestic deposits—those of foreign banks as well as of domestic banks. These data may suggest that the efficient-size banking unit is smaller than it is for two reasons. The first is that some of the banks in several countries may occupy niches; these institutions are likely to be smaller than other banks, and hence lead to a downward bias in the average size institution. The second is that in countries with a small number of banks, the authorities may have constrained mergers despite the presence of scale economies.

The number of banks in each country accounting for 80 percent, 90 percent, and 95 percent of total bank deposits is shown in Figure 5–3; in the United States, 67 banks account for 90 percent of deposits while in other countries 90 percent of deposits are accounted for by a much smaller number of banks. The second set

FIGURE 5-3
The Industrial Structure of the Banking Industry

	United States	Canada	Japan	United Kingdom	France	Germany	Italy	Nether-lands	Sweden	Belgium	Switzer-land
Banks											
80 percent	47	4	25	6	7	19	14	4	4	5	9
90 percent	67	5	39	8	10	28	19	4	5	6	7
95 percent	85	6	43	11	12	35	23	5	5	8	10
Slope											
No. 2/No. 1	53	88	89	95	92	77	81	95	93	70	91
No. 5/No. 1	38	50	80	39	60	55	73	36	30	55	19
No. 10/No. 1	23	n/a	53	7	17	34	32	n/a	n/a	6	n/a
Average											
Top 5	106,653	51,857	211,483	87,135	127,521	91,358	58,347	50,118	22,172	38,274	55,806
Top 10	80,650	n/a	177,926	51,470	78,842	72,487	48,174	n/a	n/a	n/a	31,141
Top 20	55,046	n/a	139,066	n/a	n/a	46,209	n/a	n/a	n/a	n/a	n/a
1977											
Largest/total	.11	.24	.07	.23	.13	.28	.23	.29	.29	.33	.17
No. 1–3/total	.29	.63	.18	.57	.32	.78	.57	.74	.82	.92	.37
No. 1–5/total	.38	.92	.30	.79	.47	.92	.79	1	.97	—	.51
No. 1–10/total	.56	—	.51	.97	.72	—	.93	—	—	—	.76
Numbers in											
80 percent	32	5	22	6	13	4	6	4	3	—	12
90 percent	51	5	34	7	19	5	9	5	4	—	16
95 percent	63	6	43	9	24	6	12	5	5	—	20

	C1	C2	C3	C4	C5	C6	C7	C8	C9	C10	C11
Slope											
No. 2/No. 1	.87	.91	.88	.88	.81	.99	.77	.92	.91	.94	.61
No. 5/No. 1	.38	.53	.81	.39	.54	.22	.26	.39	.12	.43	—
No. 10/No. 1	.27	—	.58	.08	.33	—	.08	—	—	—	.20
Average											
Top 5	47,732	21,715	32,524	23,034	32,425	14,217	36,866	10,795	15,187	33,646	195,229
Top 10	34,759	—	27,886	14,041	24,764	—	21,725	—	—	—	14,528
Top 20	22,358	—	21,138	—	15,787	—	—	—	—	—	9,137
1982											
Largest/total											
No. 1–3/total	.098	.26	.06	.22	.12	.27	.18	.25	.11	.28	.29
No. 1–5/total	.26	.63	.18	.61	.29	.73	.51	.57	.31	.79	.77
No. 1–10/total	.35	.90	.29	.83	.42	.84	.74	.85	.48	.96	.96
No. 1–10/ total	.51	—	.49	.93	.66	.95	.92	—	.74	—	—
Numbers in											
80 percent	44	5	23	5	18	5	7	5	13	4	4
90 percent	73	5	35	8	27	8	10	6	18	4	4
95 percent	92	6	47	14	35	11	13	7	23	5	5
Slope											
No. 2/No. 1	.97	.72	.93	.89	.69	.93	.92	.69	.87	.90	.93
No. 5/No. 1	.44	.49	.80	.41	.52	.20	.47	.51	.67	.16	.19
No. 10/No. 1	.28	—	.61	.05	.27	.07	.14	—	.31	—	—
Average											
Top 5	81,850	48,116	77,089	68,900	57,137	32,766	87,066	23,626	37,174	33,646	16,084
Top 10	59,693	—	65,871	38,693	44,195	18,439	53,922	—	28,572	—	—
Top 20	38,828	—	50,577	20,794	28,015	—	29,417	—	17,926	—	—

Source: *The Banker*, selected issues.

of figures illustrate the "slope" of the size of banks with respect to their ranking on the hit parade; these data include the share of bank deposits accounted for by the largest bank, the ratio of the size of the fifth largest bank to the largest bank, and the ratio of the size of the tenth largest bank to the largest bank. The third set of figures show the size of the average bank based on the size of the 5 largest, and then the 10 largest banks, and the 20 largest banks.

One inference from Figure 5–3 is that the smaller the country, the larger the share of the market accounted for by the largest five banks. One of the surprises is the difference among countries in the size distribution of banks; in small countries, the fifth largest bank accounts for a smaller share of deposits relative to the largest bank. In Japan the 10th largest bank is about half as large as the largest bank; in most other countries, including the United States, the 10th largest bank is substantially smaller than the largest—and this factor seems pervasive across countries. Because of its size, the United States has more banks and more larger banks.

THE STRUCTURE OF THE BANKING INDUSTRY IN A UNIFIED CURRENCY WORLD

Consider the industrial structure of banking in a hypothetical world with only one currency and without regulations that would forestall the expansion of banks so that they achieve scale economies. Regulations would not be country-specific, or affect the size distribution of banks. Because the regulatory costs associated with banking would be smaller, a larger share of the credit flows would occur through banks. The number of banks would be smaller because more banks would achieve scale economies; the increase in the number of banks sufficiently large to achieve scale economies would dominate the increase in the size of the banking industry. The number of banking offices would be smaller; each bank probably would have a larger number of banking offices.

The structure of the banking industry in this hypothetical world would reflect technological factors, and especially the minimum size of the firm associated with scale and scope economies. The location of banking offices would be determined by the location of depositors and borrowers, by the costs of producing similar banking services at a more distant location, and the costs of "arbitraging" the nearby high-cost banking offices and the distant low-cost banking offices. Because national wage rates would differ, the production of bank services might be more labor intensive in the banking offices in some countries than in others.[8] The national identity of banks would be determined by the costs of capital to firms headquartered in different countries; banks headquartered in those countries identified with a low cost capital would have an advantage.

The offshore banking market has several of the features of this hypothetical world. Competition among banks in the offshore market is extensive; there are more than three hundred offshore banks in London, and more than fifty in Luxembourg, Singapore, Frankfurt, and most other major offshore centers. The interest rates that each bank pays on its deposits depend on investors' assessment of the risk attached to its deposits, and the volume of deposits it wishes to sell. Entry of banks into the offshore market by establishing branches in offshore financial centers such as London and Luxembourg is virtually unrestricted by host-country regulation. Moreover, the activities of these branches are almost completely free of regulation by the authorities that directly manage the offshore banking jurisdiction. There are some differences between this hypothetical world and the world of offshore banks; one major difference is that banks operating in the offshore market do so through branches. A second difference is that deposits and loans in the offshore banking market are denominated in 1 of 10 or 15 national currencies; however, the interest rates on deposits and loans by currency differ by the cost of foreign-exchange swap and transaction costs—and these transaction costs are trivial. Most of the inputs to the production function of bank branches in the same offshore center are similar; their wage rates and space rents are comparable. The activities of offshore branches of banks headquartered in some countries are subject to

---

[8] Consider the location of the telephone operators at the distant end of your 1-800 calls. Frequently these operators are in Oklahoma or South Dakota; wage differentials dominate the incremental distance costs.

regulation by the authorities in the countries where the banks are chartered, especially capital-deposit requirements, and perhaps to a lesser extent, portfolio regulations. Similarly, differences among countries in the cost of capital to firms headquartered in particular countries also affect the ability of their offshore branches to compete in the offshore market.

The maximum interest rate that each bank can offer on offshore deposits, given the interest rate on offshore loans, is a function of the capital-deposit requirement and the spread between the interest rate on deposits and the interest rate on loans. The higher the capital-deposit requirement and the higher the spread between the interest rate on deposits and the cost of capital, the lower the maximum interest rate that the bank can pay on its deposits. The demand for the deposits of an individual bank is a function of the estimates of the risk attached to its deposits as well as of the interest rate offered on these deposits. Although a higher capital-deposit requirement means the maximum interest rate is lower, the higher capital-deposit requirement may mean that the risk attached to the deposits is lower.

The implication of the assumption of a universal technology, similar wage rates, and national differences in the cost of capital is that market shares of banks headquartered in different countries in the offshore market should reflect differences in the cost of capital and in the risk attached to their deposits.

INVESTORS' EVALUATIONS OF BANKS

One financial aspect of the theory of the firm is that firms expand when their cost of capital is below the anticipated profitability on a potential new investment. This proposition has several implications—one is that the firms within an industry most likely to expand, and to expand most rapidly, are those with the lowest cost of capital. The rationale is that firms compete in many of the same factor markets, and a firm with a cost-of-capital advantage is favorably positioned relative to its competitors. Another implication is that firms are agents of their shareholders, and the signals about whether a firm should expand are given to the firm's managers by investors.

The implication is that the lower the cost of capital to an individual bank, the more rapid the rate at which this bank can expand. This cost-of-capital argument is linked to the credit reputation of the bank; in the absence of regulation, each bank would choose the ratio of capital to total deposits that would minimize the total cash outflows associated with maintainence of a particular level of loans. The more attractive a bank's liabilities are to depositors, the lower the interest rate the bank pays on its liabilities, and the greater the profitability. Thus, some banks trade on their names and act to protect the value of their names.[9]

One unique aspect of banking is that the industry is highly leveraged, more so than almost any other industry; leverage is measured by the reciprocal of the ratio of capital to deposits. However, a very high level of capital-deposit ratio may lead to higher total costs. Those banks with the higher levels of capital-deposit ratios may be able to sell their deposits at lower interest rates, because the "buffer" between the losses a bank might incur and the losses to depositor is larger, the higher the level of the capital-deposit ratio; hence the risk to the holder of deposits is lower. Those banks with a lower cost of capital are able to increase market share because they can pay a higher interest rate on their deposits, or to increase their expenditures associated with the marketing of deposits. A major difference among banks headquartered in various countries is their cost of capital, which is country-specific. Moreover, within individual countries, there may be industry-specific costs of capital; these could reflect differences in anticipated growth rates of particular industries or differences in the variability of their earnings.

Banks headquartered in countries identified with low costs of capital are in an advantageous position to enter the domestic markets of banks headquartered in countries identified with high costs of capital; the first group of banks have a competitive advantage not shared by the second group of banks. The differences in the cost of capital among banks headquartered in the various countries may be country-specific—thus the relationship

---

[9] These banks also use their name advantage to sell "lines-of-credit"—which is a source of fee income which does not affect required reserves or their interest payments.

among the costs of capital for firms headquartered in different countries might differ systematically by country.

One approach to comparing the cost of capital to banks headquartered in various countries is to compare their price-earnings ratio—the lower this ratio, the lower the cost of capital. An alternative approach is to compare dividend yields; this alternative is less compelling because dividend-payout ratios may differ across countries.

Estimates of the cost of capital of banks headquartered in seven large industrial countries are summarized in Figure 5–4 for the 1975–1987 period. Summary data also are shown for the price-earnings ratios for all firms in each of these countries. One

FIGURE 5–4
The Cost of Capital to Banks by Country 1975–1987

	Price-Earning Ratio	
1987	*Bank P/E*	*Country P/E*
Japan	74.04	45.70
Italy	20.48	21.00
Switzerland	11.27	14.30
Canada	8.60	17.60
United Kingdom	7.25	13.40
United States	7.16	14.10
Germany	—	14.70
WORLD	19.90	18.20
1986	*Bank P/E*	*Country P/E*
Japan	58.71	25.90
Italy	21.45	26.20
Switzerland	12.87	14.40
United Kingdom	10.33	12.10
Canada	8.00	15.30
United States	7.46	13.70
Germany	—	16.70
WORLD	17.30	15.00
1985	*Bank P/E*	*Country P/E*
Japan	51.04	25.90
Switzerland	9.43	11.40
United States	8.14	9.90
Italy	7.98	18.10
Canada	7.10	17.80
United Kingdom	6.45	11.10
Germany	—	13.50
WORLD	13.70	11.90

FIGURE 5–4 (continued)

	Price-Earning Ratio	
	Bank P/E	Country P/E
1984	*Bank P/E*	*Country P/E*
Japan	25.01	25.10
Switzerland	9.97	12.60
Italy	8.48	—
United States	6.26	12.20
Canada	6.23	27.50
United Kingdom	4.43	10.40
Germany	—	15.00
WORLD	9.30	13.90
1983	*Bank P/E*	*Country P/E*
Japan	27.00	22.20
Germany	15.40	11.20
United Kingdom	10.38	9.80
Switzerland	9.73	10.90
Canada	6.73	10.90
United States	5.80	10.10
Italy	3.95	—
WORLD	9.10	11.50
1982	*Bank P/E*	*Country P/E*
Japan	33.91	18.20
Germany	15.40	8.50
Italy	12.53	—
Switzerland	10.00	10.70
United States	6.15	7.70
Canada	5.13	8.60
United Kingdon	3.48	8.30
WORLD	9.40	9.20
1981	*Bank P/E*	*Country P/E*
Japan	30.60	16.10
Switzerland	13.83	12.50
Germany	10.63	7.40
Italy	9.45	—
Canada	7.50	8.60
United States	5.78	9.10
United Kingdom	2.70	6.20
WORLD	8.90	9.10
1980	*Bank P/E*	*Country P/E*
Japan	23.50	19.20
Switzerland	14.23	13.20
Germany	9.40	9.00
Canada	6.48	8.70
United States	5.24	7.40
Italy	3.45	—
United Kingdom	3.35	5.40
WORLD	8.30	8.40

FIGURE 5–4 (concluded)

	Price-Earning Ratio	
	Bank P/E	Country P/E
1975	*Bank P/E*	*Country P/E*
Italy	21.20	—
Japan	19.03	14.00
Germany	14.27	9.70
Switzerland	6.60	6.30
United Kingdom	2.10	3.10
United States	—	8.10
Canada	—	6.80
WORLD	9.80	7.70

Notes:

1. Banks used in Bank P/E ratios:

United States	*Canada*
Citicorp	Royal Bank of Canada
Bank of America	Bank of Nova Scotia
Chase Manhattan	Bank of Montreal
Bankers Trust	Canadian Imperial Bank
JP Morgan	*Germany*
Chemical Bank	Commerzbank
First Chicago Corp.	Deutsche Bank
Switzerland	Dresdner Bank
Schwiez Bankverein SBS	*Italy*
Schwiez Bankgesell. UBS	Banca Commerciale Italiana
Schwiez Kreditanstalt	Credito Italiano
United Kingdom	MedicoBanca
National Westminster	Banca di Roma
Lloyds Bank	*Japan*
Barclays Bank	Dai-Ichi Kangyo Bank
Midland Bank	Fuji Bank
	Mitsubishi Bank
	Mitsui Bank
	Industrial Bank of Japan
	Daiwa Bank
	Bank of Tokyo
	Sanwa Bank
	Sumitomo Bank

2. The 1975 edition of *Capital International* does not include North American companies.
3. The 1970 edition of *Capital International* does not include P/E ratios and yields for individual companies.
4. The date of each ranking in the heading is the first day of the year or the last day of the previous year.

Source: *Capital International* (Geneva: Capital International Perspective SA), various issues.

inference from the data is that national differences in price-earnings ratios are substantial. A second is that the ranking of price-earnings ratios for banks in each country and for all firms in each country are similar but not identical. A third is that the range of price-earnings ratios for banks is larger than the range for countries—with the implication that there is a significant bank industry effect; in general, however, the price-earnings ratios for banks within each country are lower then those for all firms in the country.[10]

The ranking of banks by country by dividend yield is generally inverse to the ranking by price-earnings ratio (See Figure 5–5.) The dividend yields for banks headquartered within a country are generally higher than those for all firms headquartered within that country. From the viewpoint of any one bank, a low dividend yield is an advantage, for the cash-flow requirements of meeting the needs of shareholders are minimal. Cash can be used for payment of interest to depositors.

Banks headquartered in Japan, Italy, and Switzerland consistently appear toward the top of the price-earnings ratios and the low dividend-yield ratios. The price-earnings ratios of banks headquartered in all countries have increased; however, the increase in the price-earnings ratios for banks headquartered in other industrial countries has been greater than for banks headquartered in the United States. The implication from both the comparisons of the levels of price-earnings ratios and the rate of increase in the price-earnings ratios is that banks headquartered in Japan should be expanding their offices abroad. One extension of this argument is that banks headquartered in the United States might have been at the forefront of foreign expansion of the 1960s because U.S. banks then had a cost-of-capital advantage. And another is that U.S. banks now can sell their foreign offices to banks with lower costs of capital.

---

[10] The price-earnings ratio for each country includes the price-earnings ratio for the banks headquartered in each country. The more appropriate approach would involve adjusting the price-earnings ratio for each country to exclude the price-earnings ratios for banks. The weights of banks in each country's price-earnings ratio differ; the smaller the country, the larger the weight.

FIGURE 5–5
Dividend Yields of Banks by Country

1987	Bank Yield	Country Yield
Japan	0.05	0.70
Switzerland	2.43	1.90
Italy	2.45	1.70
Germany	3.53	2.80
United States	4.05	3.60
United Kingdom	5.30	4.20
Canada	5.40	2.90
WORLD	1.90	2.60
1986	*Bank Yield*	*Country Yield*
Japan	0.63	1.00
Switzerland	2.37	1.90
Germany	2.40	2.70
Italy	2.63	2.10
United States	4.61	3.80
Canada	5.35	3.10
United Kingdom	6.03	4.40
WORLD	2.30	3.20
1985	*Bank Yield*	*Country Yield*
Japan	0.74	1.00
Italy	2.40	3.60
Switzerland	3.40	2.70
Germany	5.10	3.90
United States	6.19	4.70
Canada	6.55	3.60
United Kingdom	7.10	4.50
WORLD	2.80	3.80
1984	*Bank Yield*	*Country Yield*
Japan	1.65	1.30
Italy	2.85	3.10
Switzerland	3.17	2.50
Germany	4.73	3.70
United States	6.05	4.50
Canada	6.05	3.20
United Kingdom	7.65	4.80
WORLD	3.90	3.80
1983	*Bank Yield*	*Country Yield*
Japan	1.66	1.70
Italy	2.30	2.50
Switzerland	2.57	2.90
Germany	3.30	4.90
United States	6.26	5.00
United Kingdom	6.48	5.50
Canada	6.53	3.90
WORLD	4.20	4.50

FIGURE 5–5 (concluded)

	Bank Yield	Country Yield
1982	*Bank Yield*	*Country Yield*
Italy	0.98	1.60
Japan	1.45	1.70
Switzerland	3.60	3.50
Germany	4.17	6.30
United States	6.28	5.80
Canada	7.13	4.60
United Kingdom	7.25	6.10
WORLD	3.90	5.00
1981	*Bank Yield*	*Country Yield*
Italy	1.48	1.90
Japan	1.74	2.00
Switzerland	2.83	2.90
Canada	5.20	3.90
United States	6.28	4.90
United Kingdom	7.02	6.40
Germany	7.83	6.40
WORLD	4.00	4.70
1980	*Bank Yield*	*Country Yield*
Japan	1.89	2.00
Switzerland	2.93	2.80
Italy	3.93	2.60
Canada	5.93	3.80
United Kingdom	6.13	6.70
Germany	6.67	5.90
United States	6.70	5.70
WORLD	4.20	5.10
1975	*Bank Yield*	*Country Yield*
Japan	2.05	2.90
Italy	2.68	2.70
Switzerland	4.13	4.40
Germany	4.50	4.80
United Kingdom	10.08	11.60
United States	—	5.10
Canada	—	5.40
WORLD	3.90	5.40

Source: *Capital International*, various issues.

REGULATION, PROTECTION, AND
THE STRUCTURE OF BANKING

The differences between the number of banks that might exist in the hypothetical world described earlier and the larger number that actually exist could reflect either regulation or protection. Some of the protection is explicit in the form of exchange controls or restrictions on entry, and some would be implicit and associated with the national boundaries. Most of the bank deposits produced in each country are produced by domestically owned banks—and most of the bank loans are from domestically owned banks.

Domestic residents may be constrained from buying products or services produced abroad by tariffs or quotas; bank depositors may be constrained by exchange controls from holding deposits issued in foreign banks. Foreign banks may be precluded by regulation from establishing de novo branches or subsidiaries, and from buying established domestic banks. The usual approach to the identification of protection in banking is to develop a list of the types of regulations that particular countries have adopted. Exchange controls are frequent, especially among the developing countries.

The contrast between the share of foreign-owned banks in the domestic market for deposits and loans in the United States, and in most other industrial countries is sharp. The limited presence of foreign banks in the domestic banking business in many countries—especially those countries characterized by extensive concentration in banking—might reflect one of several different factors. One is that the few banks have achieved substantial scale economies, and that the foreign banks are dissuaded from entry because the prospect of achieving comparable economies is low. A second possible explanation is that competition among the host-country banks is so intense that the profits in banking are below the cost of capital of the source-country banks. A third possible explanation is that the anticipated profits on host-country banking are high, and that the entry of foreign banks is somehow restricted by a variety of formal or informal regulations.

The presence of restrictions on entry of foreign banks should be distinguished from the effectiveness of these regulations; the implication is that the restrictions were adopted as a precautionary device to keep foreign banks from "knocking at the door" rather than because they were at the door.[11]

If the cost-of-capital argument is the necessary condition for entry into an established foreign market, the sufficient condition is that the source-country firm not be at a substantial profitability disadvantage. One reason the foreign bank would be at a profitability disadvantage is the cost of economic distance; a second is the difficulty in achieving scale economies comparable to those of host-country banks, and especially in marketing of deposits. Foreign banks can enter a national market through a takeover of established banks or through establishment of new offices; where the national market is characterized by a small number of firms, takeovers are unlikely. Banks establishing new offices encounter handicaps in achieving scale economies comparable to those realized by the established banks. The result is that foreign banks are much more likely to enter those countries characterized either by several regional markets, or a large number of domestic banks, or both. Hence the structure of the industry might reflect economic factors rather than regulation.

One approach toward replicating the efficiency of banking in each country is the size of the spread between the interest rate that banks pay on deposits and the interest rate they charge on loans. This spread reflects and includes the cost of capital, much as in the offshore market; this spread also includes the cost of domestic regulation and the costs of managing the sale of domestic deposits. These data are replicated in Figure 5–5. These data do not lead to the conclusion that there is a significant association between the number of banks in each country and the size of the deposit-loan spread.

The theory of international banking explains the ownership structure in the banking industry—and why banks headquartered in one country establish offices in other countries. Most of the approaches to the theory of international banking are extensions of

---

[11] Richard Dale, *The Regulation of International Banking,* Cambridge: Woodhead-Faulkner, 1984.

the theory of direct foreign investment.[12] Two major approaches to the theory of international banking can be summarized. One approach, sometimes called the gravitational pull approach, is that banks establish foreign offices to follow the move of domestic firms into foreign markets. One motive is that the banks want to reduce the likelihood that the foreign banks will begin to gain shares of the foreign business of these firms, which might be the "thin entering wedge" in a new business relationship, or because they have a valuable set of information on their clients and can satisfy the needs of these clients at a lower cost than the host-country banks can.

The second approach toward the theory of international banking is that banks expand abroad when they have a capital market advantage over their host-country competitors. There are two aspects of this advantage—one is why this advantage exists, and the second involves the implications of this advantage for the industrial structure of the industry. The advantage reflects that national capital markets are partially segmented. This advantage means that source-country banks pay a higher price than host-country banks for a particular host-country income stream, because the source-country firms place a higher value on this income stream in the host country than host-country banks. Hence, the factors making it possible for source-country firms to pay a higher price for host-country income streams also explain why source-country banks expand abroad. This capital market view relies on perfect market assumptions, in that source-country firms compete with host-country firms on comparable terms in both product markets and in factor markets, with the exception that source-country firms have a cost-of-capital advantage. The implication of the perfect market assumption is that source-country firms expand abroad only because they have an advantage that compensates for their unique costs of economic distance. This advantage is an equity market advantage; firms including banks headquartered in low-interest-rate countries have a lower cost of capital.

---

[12] Robert Z. Aliber, "International Banking: A Survey," *Journal of Money, Credit, and Banking,* October 1984, pp. 661–78.

The gravitational pull approach focuses on the asset side of the bank's balance sheet; banks wishing to make loans to their clients investing abroad can source the funds necessary for these loans in the interbank market or they can establish offices to sell deposits.[13] In contrast, the capital market advantage centers on the liability side of the bank's balance sheet; other things being equal, the capital-market advantage means that the source-country bank is able to pay a higher interest rate on deposits than the host-country bank.

The implication of the capital-market view is that the necessary condition for the entry of a bank into the foreign market by establishing offices to sell deposits is that the cost of capital of the source-country bank is below the cost of capital for host-country banks, and by more than enough to compensate for the costs of economic distance. Moreover, because banking is so highly leveraged, this cost-of-capital advantage must be substantial, as high leverage means that the capital has a modest weight in the total supply of funds to banks. Nevertheless, a cost of capital advantage of two to three percentage points could translate into a nontrivial difference in an average weighted cost of funds.[14]

CONCLUSION

The thrust of this chapter is to examine the industrial organization of the banking industry on a worldwide basis. The activities of banks can be segmented into the production and sale of deposits and the purchase of loans and investments. International banking

---

[13] The stylized fact is that a large part of international banking loans are funded in the interbank market. Most of the foreign banks in London do not have a significant volume of British pound deposits; similarly most of the foreign banks in New York do not have a significant volume of U.S. dollar deposits.

[14] Consider the combination of the impacts of a capital-deposit ratio of 10 percent and a cost-of-capital advantage of 3 percentage points. If the deposit interest rate averages 5 percent, then the source-country banks might be able to pay an interest rate 30 basis points higher than the host-country banks. These examples are sensitive to the spread between the deposit interest rate in the host country and the cost of capital to host-country banks.

traditionally has been primarily concerned with the purchase of loans and investments. One characteristic of the sale of deposits is that individuals prefer to deal with banking offices in their neighborhoods; the costs of dealing with banking offices at some distance are too high. Banks find it expedient to site offices near clusters of people—and most of these banking offices are operated by domestic firms. In most countries, foreign-owned firms account for less than 5 percent of the banking offices and total deposits.

Hence the key question is whether domestically owned firms's near-monopoly in producing bank deposits reflects one or several economic factors, or whether the small share of foreign-owned banks in the production of deposits in most countries reflects protection. Economic factors that might dissuade foreign banks from entry include low anticipated profitability, perhaps because foreign-owned banks would find it difficult to achieve scale economies and also because the cost of capital of the host country is low.

The key presumption of this chapter is that banks expand their foreign offices and their retail activities in the production of deposits when they have a cost-of-capital advantage relative to their host-country competitors. Whether banks actually expand depends on whether they can obtain scale economies in the host country comparable to those of the domestic banks.

REFERENCES

Aliber, Robert Z. "International Banking: A Survey." *Journal of Money, Credit, and Banking,* October 1984, pp. 661–78.

Dale, Richard. *The Regulation of International Banking.* Cambridge: Woodhead-Faulkner, 1984.

Economic Council of Canada. *Efficiency and Regulation: A Study of Deposit Institutions.* Ottawa, 1975.

The Economist. London. selected issues.

Fieleke, Norman S. "The Growth of U.S. Banking Abroad: An Analytical Survey." in *Key Issues in International Banking.* Boston: Federal Reserve Bank of Boston, 1977.

Office of Technology Assessment, Congress of the United States. *International Competition in Services,* esp. chap. 3, "International Competition in Banking and Financial Services." Washington, D.C.: U.S. Government Printing Office, 1987.

Pecchiolo, R. M. *The Internationalization of Banking: The Policy Issues*. Paris: Organization for Economic Cooperation and Development, 1983.

Terrell, Henry S., and Sydney J. Key. "The Growth of Foreign Banking in the United States." In *Key Issues in International Banking*. Boston: Federal Reserve Bank of Boston, 1977.

Walter, I. *Barriers to Trade in Banking and Financial Services*. London: Trade Policy Research Centre, 1985.

CHAPTER 6

INTERNATIONAL COMPETITION IN BANKING AND FINANCIAL SERVICES

Office of Technology Assessment,
Congress of the United States

Over the postwar period, few international businesses have grown as rapidly as banking. For 20 years or more, rates of expansion on many measures have been in the range of 20 percent per year. National capital markets have become more tightly integrated, mirroring linkages among banks and other financial institutions. More than 150 U.S. banks maintain branches overseas; Citicorp alone operates in more than 90 countries. Foreign banks have reciprocated, opening new offices throughout the United States.

Truly international capital markets have led to a broad range of new financial products. Many of these new products have been introduced in the so-called Euromarket. This offshore or external market, relatively free of the restrictions and regulations that governments normally place on financial transactions, has become a highly desirable alternative for businesses seeking to place or to raise funds. Because the Euromarket is efficient, costs for both lenders and borrowers are low. Firms can issue financial instruments (e.g., bonds, notes, or commercial paper) in dollars or almost any other currency. In a typical transaction, the London office of the U.S. securities firm Prudential Bache raised a total of 4.3 billion yen (about $16.7 million) early in 1985 for the Japanese robotics manufacturer Dainichi Kiko through placements with seven institutional investors in Europe.[1]

Two primary forces lie behind much of the growth and change in international banking: deregulation, and new technologies. The United States has been a leader in both, with generally positive impacts on U.S. international competitiveness in financial services. (Although this chapter focuses on companies that identify themselves as banks, boundaries between banks and other financial firms have blurred; there are no longer hard and fast distinctions by firm or by product.) Laws and regulations constraining banks have been relaxed or repealed. Looser regulation means opportunities for new products. Deregulation, by increasing competition, also drives down profit margins, inducing some banks to take greater risks in the hope of maintaining profitability. Governments everywhere stand behind the safety and stability of their banking systems; plainly, deregulation only goes so far. Governments also continue to influence banking activities as they pursue macroeconomic policy and control of the money supply. The relationships between public and private sectors in banking are unique among industries.

Financial service firms have been major users, but not originators, of postwar advances in computer and communications systems. Thus technology—the other major driving force—has been an independent factor. Deregulation permits firms to broaden the scope of their financial activities; technical advances make it possible to do so efficiently, and on a global scale. Banks turned to computer technology, first, to help manage their vast flows of paperwork. Strategic applications came later, complementing back-office automation with banks looking to technology for help in escaping from government regulations; offshore Eurobanking, perhaps the preeminent example, began in the early 1950s, but it was electronic funds transfers that freed offshore markets from fixed geographic locations, opening them to worldwide participation.

---

[1] W. Dawkins and Y. Shibata, "A Japanese Upset for Venture Capitalists," *Financial Times,* 28 October 1986, p. 28.
Dainichi Kiko entered bankruptcy the next year.

Today, a large American company can arrange a loan in Tokyo or place a security denominated in yen and swap the currency into dollars to be spent in the United States (or marks to be spent in Germany), at the same time swapping a fixed interest rate for a variable rate—a transaction that, while not unheard of, would have been unusual as recently as 1980. Funds flow across national boundaries as never before, and national financial systems have become tightly interwoven. Once, the effects of a major failure would have been isolated within the bank's home country; today, they could ripple around the world. While steps taken in the past few years have allayed much of the immediate concern over stability of the world financial system, future developments could easily lead to renewed fears of worldwide banking collapse.

This chapter examines competition in international financial services, in both offshore and onshore markets. (Onshore banking refers to operations in national markets by foreign-owned banks— for instance, Japanese banks in the United States.)

The sections that follow highlight four major points:

1. The maze of U.S. banking regulations—implemented by the states as well as by federal agencies—exerts wide-ranging impacts on the international competitiveness of the U.S. financial services industry. Rapid expansion of international banking makes these impacts much more important than just a few years ago, but policymakers give them little consideration. Our analysis indicates a need for the policymaking process to reflect, on a routine rather than exceptional basis, the impacts of federal policies on the international competitiveness of the U.S. financial services industry.

2. Regulators confront moving targets as technological change and competitive pressures lead to continuous restructuring in world financial markets. Increasingly integrated but decreasingly regulated markets pose greater dangers of instability and world banking collapse. National regulations intended to protect depositors and ensure stability have self-limiting effects; in a competitive world, they drive banks to seek unregulated markets and unregulated prod-ucts—a dynamic that can lead to greater risks. U.S.

leadership in seeking greater international coordination of banking supervision and banking regulation could help move the system toward a more stable footing. (To some extent, the decrease in regulation has been accompanied by an increase in supervisory oversight by government bodies—i.e., by monitoring rather than control.)

3. External markets have grown as providers of capital search for higher returns, while corporate borrowers seek lower financing costs. Not long ago, corporations went to the Euromarkets for bank loans to support their foreign subsidiaries. Today, they look to these markets for securitized financing—bonds and stocks, commercial paper that can be traded in secondary markets—to finance domestic as well as foreign operations. Securitization—the replacement of loans by marketable securities—has permanently changed the environment for international competition. The consequences make competitive life more difficult for U.S. banks.

4. Only the Japanese seem in a position to challenge American financial services firms. As Japan's financial markets become more fully integrated into the world system—in part as a result of prodding by the U.S. government—Japanese financial institutions will mount major competitive challenges. While it is too early to predict the outcomes, it is not too early to take account of this new source of competition in implementing federal policies. For example, it is not at all clear that U.S. pressure aimed at opening up Japan's capital markets is in the longer-term interest of the U.S. financial services industry.

In such a world, can the federal regulatory and supervisory system continue to cope? This chapter suggests that, at the very least, the system needs modification to bring national and international considerations into better balance.

As they have evolved since the 1930s, U.S. banking policies, at both state and national levels, have generally been focused quite narrowly on the particular problems of a particular time. The policies themselves emanate from a bewildering assortment of state and federal authorities (including, at the national level, the

Comptroller of the Currency, the Federal Reserve Board, and the Federal Deposit Insurance Corporation (FDIC)). Rarely have either state or federal agencies examined the possible impacts of their actions on the international competitive standing of U.S. banks, even though in many cases these impacts are real and apparent. The FDIC, for instance, establishes premium levels with little effort at coordination with other governments; yet international differences in these premiums alone could place U.S. banks at a competitive disadvantage.

One policy option would establish mechanisms for monitoring and coordinating the actions of federal agencies as they affect the international competitiveness of the U.S. banking industry. This is not to suggest that these impacts should dictate policy, but that they should take their place with other considerations as a normal part of the policymaking process.

National banking regulations exist in part to foster confidence in the security of deposits and in the continuing viability of the system as a whole. But continuing restructuring of world financial markets, driven in part by advancing technology, can quickly make the regulations of any one country obsolete. New products, many of them securities, continually stretch the boundaries of the permissible. With sources of interest income remaining more heavily regulated than fee-earning services, banks develop new products that replace loans with other sources of earnings. As banks and other institutions develop new forms of financing, regulatory officials find themselves chasing moving targets. When the regulatory agencies react to their innovations, the banks move off in another direction.

In the United States, the responsibility for monitoring and for implementing regulatory policies shifts between agencies as new forms of financing spring up, with ultimate authority becoming diffused and confused. The problem is little different in other national markets. Internationally, the situation is still messier; regulatory structures, where they exist, remain poorly developed. The growth of offshore markets makes regulations in any and all countries less effective because financial institutions have more ways of avoiding them. Although the banks themselves benefit from a stable international environment, they have been more concerned with narrow questions that affect their ability to compete with one another. Banks and national governments are in similar positions: individually, they can do little to preserve stability internationally.

In this climate, governments have begun to consider methods for coordinating and harmonizing their regulatory and supervisory practices. The Federal Reserve and other U.S. authorities have opened discussions on the possibility of international rules for external markets. Recent proposals for a bilateral agreement with the United Kingdom (U.K.) on capital requirements may be a first step toward broader arrangements.[2] Our analysis points not only to the need for continuing such talks, but to the need for a thorough study of sources of possible instability.

Although coordination of regulations might help, national interests inevitably differ and widespread agreement may be hard to achieve. At this point, it is not even clear that appropriate international forums for negotiation exist. Over the past few years, the Basel Committee, an advisory group of central bankers and supervisory officials from fewer than a dozen major nations, has provided a place for discussion, but the committee would not necessarily be the proper setting for negotiations among governments.

What then of U.S. international competitiveness in banking? Securitization—replacement of bank loans by securities as preferred sources of corporate financing—has made deep and permanent changes in the competitive environment. Investment banks have become much more prominent in international markets because of their experience in structuring new securities issues; rapid growth has led U.S. investment banks, which remain small compared to commercial banks, to seek new capital—sometimes foreign—to keep pace with market expansion. At the same time, where permitted, U.S.-based commercial banks have plunged into investment offerings (regulations restrict this in the United States). U.S. commercial banks have also sought other sources of income

---

[2] See D. Lascelles, "Britain and U.S. Agree on Landmark Banking Pact," *Financial Times*, 9 January 1987, p. 1, and related stories on pp. 6 and 18.

to supplement their international lending. Some of these fee-based products—for example, foreign exchange trading and interest rate swaps—could turn out to be riskier than anticipated.

OTA's analysis suggests that the competitive changes caused by securitization threaten the competitive position of individual banks more than that of the U.S. industry as a whole. Indeed, relative to foreign industries, the American financial services industry has done well in the rapidly shifting competitive environment of the past few years. American banks have been able to take advantage of learning and experience in their deregulated home market ahead of major foreign competitors; some of the latter have invested in the United States primarily to gain experience. From all recent signs, U.S. international competitiveness in banking and financial services will remain strong. This does not mean, of course, that all American banks will do well internationally. This is an industry with many competitive firms. Some do well in some markets, some do well in others. Products are similar, and technology—though not the expertise to use it—is easy to come by. New financial services arise in part as banks struggle to differentiate themselves and become something other than purveyors of commodity-like products. No one can count on decisive sources of advantage or sure success in the future.

There seems only one real threat to the competitive rank of the U.S. financial services industry—Japan. Japanese banks, almost invisible 15 years ago, have become major players on the international stage. Because of continuing and massive bilateral trade surpluses with the United States and other industrial nations, Japan has become a huge international creditor, particularly in dollar-denominated financial assets. Japanese banks now hold more international deposits than their American counterparts, and far surpass any other national industry. The competitive thrusts of Japanese banks show greater sophistication today than even two or three years ago.

Yet Japanese competition has thus far made few major differences for U.S.-based financial institutions. American banks have been aggressive, innovative, and efficient—qualities that have enabled them to maintain their international position in an increasingly deregulated global environment. Could all this change, in the way it did for industries manufacturing automobiles or consumer electronics? Could the Japanese exploit new competitive opportunities to carve out ever-larger shares of international markets? Do their onshore investments in the United States represent competitive strategies aimed at the home markets of American banks? While not impossible, and while some signs point in this direction, parallels between markets for financial services and manufactured goods can easily be overdrawn.

Banking has been a highly competitive international industry for decades, with many firms from many countries competing in at least some parts of the market. In such industries, few of the forces affecting competitiveness, in isolation, make a big difference (the way technical skills do in the commercial aircraft industry, or scale economies once did in automobile production). American banks have not been insular or insulated; they have capitalized effectively on advantages where they could find them, just as foreign banks have. Competition between the United States and Japan seems bound to intensify, with the pace largely controlled by Japan's willingness to liberalize its financial markets. The competitive threat is real, but careful monitoring of relative positions seems the appropriate response for the moment.

GROWTH AND COMPETITION IN INTERNATIONAL FINANCIAL SERVICES

Banking—the second-oldest service—was also one of the earliest to be traded internationally. Trade in goods still requires financing, but international banking today hardly resembles the industry of even a decade ago. Looser regulatory structures have bred greater competition among more banks in more parts of the world. No longer can banks live comfortably within sheltered regional or national markets. Protective barriers offered one of the few sources of decisive advantage in a business with many able competitors, quick to copy good ideas. Although much of the business continues to revolve around trade-related instruments like letters of credit and banker's acceptances, new products—particularly those sold in lightly regulated or unregulated external mar-

TABLE 6–1
Growth Rates of International Banking Compared to World Trade

	Annual Rate of Growth		
	1966–73	*1973–80*	*1980–84*
Total international banking deposits[a]	30.0%	24.4%	6.6%
Total world exports	9.2	25.2	−1.5

[a] Equal to the sum of domestic and foreign currency liabilities to nonresidents of all banks worldwide, plus their foreign currency liabilities to residents.

Source: *Annual Report, Bank for International Settlements* (Basel, Switzerland: Bank for International Settlements, various years); *International Financial Statistics* (Washington, D.C.: International Monetary Fund, various years).

kets—have grown at an explosive pace. Here, the banks that have gotten in first have generally been able to maintain leading positions.

Market Dynamics

International banking deposits (as defined in Table 6–1) have grown much faster than world trade (i.e., total world exports of goods and services). In most countries, international banking has also grown more rapidly than domestic banking; for the nations of the Organization for Economic Cooperation and Development (OECD), the ratio of foreign to domestic liabilities more than doubled during the 1970s, and has continued to rise, albeit more slowly.[3] During the 1970s, banks everywhere found their profitability slipping in traditional markets. Early responses included heavy lending to newly industrialized and less developed countries (NICs and LDCs), and to Eastern Europe. Rising oil prices meant large

---

[3] M. Pecchioli, *The Internationalization of Banking: The Policy Issues* (Paris: Organization for Economic Cooperation and Development, 1983), p. 16.

To take a different kind of indicator, the number of major banks having offices in banking centers outside their home countries increased from about 300 in 1970 to 550 in 1980—*The Bankers' Almanac and Yearbook*, 1970–71 and 1980–81 (New York: I.P.C. Business Press Limited).

trade surpluses in some countries and large deficits in others; banks could get funds from oil exporting countries, extend loans to importing countries, and expect handsome profits. These loans grew to become a significant part of the portfolios of many major banks before the shortcomings of the strategy became clear to all.

During this period, American banks did about 27 percent of the total syndicated lending to these countries, about the same as their percentage of worldwide assets.[4] Worldwide recession and falling oil prices, along with less than prudent loans, make repayment of principal and in some cases the interest on many of these obligations uncertain. In worst case defaults, the capital of even large money-center banks could be wiped out, leading to a crisis at the lending bank or banks; beyond ongoing risks of defaults, the major implication for competitiveness is that banks with high levels of risky international debt have limited strategic options.

Big banks take most of the business in international financial services; perhaps two dozen firms with headquarters in the OECD nations account for more than half of all cross-border lending, and some 60 percent of lead managements of bonds and other securities issues.[5] Among these banks, positions have been changing. As Figure 6–1 shows, the assets of the largest Japanese banks have been growing steadily, and now exceed those of their American

---

[4] "International Bank Lending Trends," *World Financial Markets* (New York: Morgan Guaranty, July 1985), pp. 5, 7.

By the end of 1986, Brazil's foreign debt stood at about $108 billion and Mexico's at $100 billion. Among countries seeking rescheduling, these two are followed by Argentina ($50 billion), Venezuela ($35 billion), and the Philippines ($27 billion). Major lenders to these countries include Citicorp (the largest single lender to Brazil and Mexico), Manufacturers Hanover, BankAmerica, and Chase; each of these banks has loans outstanding to Brazil that total more than half of its shareholders' equity. Ten or more U.S. banks have outstanding Latin American loans totaling more than their equity. See P. Truell, "Citicorp's Reed Takes Firm Stance on Third-World Debt," *Wall Street Journal* 4 February 1987, p. 6; "Risks of Foreign Banks in Latin America," *Financial Times,* 25 February 1987, p. 4; E. N. Berg, "Brazil's Debt: A Key Juncture," *New York Times,* 3 March 1987, p. D1.

U.S. banks are particularly affected by Latin American debt problems, with Western European banks exposed in Eastern Europe, and the Japanese in Indonesia. In lending to Brazil, Japan follows the United States, with outstanding long-term loans of $8.8 billion, compared with $18.6 billion for American banks.

[5] P. Mentre, "The Fund, Commercial Banks, and Member Countries," Occasional Paper 26, International Monetary Fund, April 1984.

FIGURE 6–1
Relative Asset Shares of the World's Largest Banks[a]

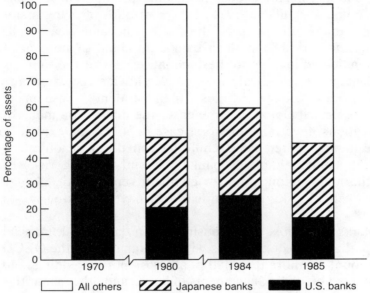

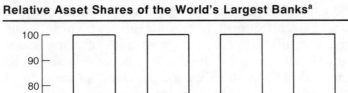

[a] 300 largest banks for 1970–84, 500 largest for 1985.
   Source: 1970–84: *The Banker* (various issues); 1985: "30th Annual Survey of the World's Top 500 Banks: Part II," *American Banker*, 30 July 1986, pp. 36–44.

counterparts. The relative shifts visible in Figure 6–1 reflect macroeconomic factors such as differing economic growth rates and currency exchange values, among other things, with the increase in U.S. asset share between 1980 and 1984 largely a consequence of the strength of the dollar during that period.

Cross-border assets paint much the same picture. At the beginning of 1986, Japanese banks for the first time held more international deposits than U.S. banks—a gap that widened quickly during the year as the dollar weakened. Banks from other countries trail far behind. The rapidly rising assets in the Japanese financial system stem in large part from Japan's consistently high trade surpluses over the past half-dozen years. It is this growth in assets that, more than any other factor, points toward greater competitive challenges by Japanese banks.

In 1984, the latest year for which comparable data are available, Citicorp remained the largest financial institution in the world as measured by assets, with $190 billion, followed closely by five Japanese banks, the largest of which was Dai-Ichi Kangyo, at about $170 billion.[6] Measured in this way the dominance of Japanese banks as a group appears overwhelming. When measured by profits, however, Citicorp was far ahead, earning almost a billion dollars, compared to runner-up Barclays (British) at $600 million. National Westminster (another British bank), Chase Manhattan, and Manufacturers Hanover all reported greater profits than the Japanese leader, Sumitomo, which earned less than $400 million.

American banks have generally moved the fastest into fee-based services, many of which generate profits that do not translate into assets. This accounts for some of the disparity between asset and profit measures. Data presented later in the chapter show that U.S. financial institutions have large and often increasing shares of markets for major international banking products. American banks also tend to have many more foreign branches: by Sumitomo's count it has only 40 foreign branches, compared with over 1,800 for Citicorp. In summary, the big U.S. banks, although certainly not dominant, remain competitively strong.

Competition among banks is only part of the story. U.S. banks have new rivals who have entered from outside the financial services industry—not only corporations that place their own commercial paper, but also companies expanding into financial services from other industries. Some, like the major department

---

[6] "International Banking: Wooing the Customer," *The Economist,* 22 March 1986, p. 6; "30th Annual Survey of the World's Top 500 Banks: Part II," *American Banker,* July 30, 1986, pp. 36–44. In 1985, Dai-Ichi Kangyo became the biggest bank in the world as measured by assets, and in 1986 the biggest bank holding company as measured by assets, surpassing Citicorp.

All measures of bank size and profitability reflect dramatically shifting exchange rates, as well as differing accounting principles and banking practices.

Most Euromarket transactions involve the U.S. dollar, but participants (buyer, seller, underwriter) need not have their main businesses in the United States. Likewise, an American bank might underwrite a corporate bond in London denominated in yen that is sold to a French bank and raises money for a Brazilian firm; U.S. laws prohibit commercial banks from underwriting such an issue here.

stores with their charge cards, and automobile companies with their financing subsidiaries, have been extending consumer credit for years—and earning healthy profits from these parts of their businesses. More recently, companies like Sears—which purchased Dean Witter in 1981—have sought to use their marketing skills and network of outlets to enter retail markets for financial services. Thus far, entrants from other industries have not had much impact internationally, nor have mergers between financial and nonfinancial firms been outstandingly successful; frequently, profits of the merged units have fallen.

Onshore and Offshore Banking

Funds move internationally in two markets, onshore and offshore. In an *onshore* transaction—for example, when an American corporation arranges to borrow yen in Tokyo—foreigners participate through national markets. Onshore banking also takes place when foreign-owned financial institutions enter domestic markets—when a Japanese bank opens offices in San Francisco or New York, or buys an American bank. In *offshore* markets, financial transactions take place largely beyond the regulatory reach of the government issuing the currency of the transaction—the case when an American corporation borrows dollars (or yen) in London. Offshore markets, often called Euromarkets because much of the activity continues to take place in European financial centers, tend in practice to be largely free of regulation by any and all governments; they need have no fixed geographic location, and today could almost be viewed as existing in the telecommunications infrastructure.

In either onshore or offshore markets, flows of funds can be direct or intermediated. In the first case, a broker brings together a buyer and seller of securities (e.g., stocks or bonds). Direct flows of funds in the foreign sector of national capital markets mostly involve bonds. In intermediated transactions, a financial institution, usually a bank, borrows by issuing its own liabilities and lends the money to others.

Today, onshore markets for foreign bonds, concentrated in Switzerland, the United States, and Japan, total about $30 billion; continuing regulatory constraints have slowed growth, contrib-

TABLE 6–2
Companies with Shares Traded on Foreign Markets, by Home Country

Headquarters of Issuing Company	Number of Companies		
	December 1983	December 1984	June 1985
United States	84	85	85
Japan	49	65	81
United Kingdom	13	25	33
Federal Republic of Germany	17	22	26
Other	73	131	175
	236	328	400

Source: *Euromoney*, various issues.

uting to expansion in other financial instruments. Onshore markets for equity (stock) have begun to expand rapidly, although remaining small compared to foreign-bond markets. While the shares of relatively few corporations are listed on exchanges outside their home countries—Table 6–2—the numbers have been headed steeply upward, especially among the biggest companies; the 400 firms traded on foreign markets as of mid-1985 may have represented a quarter of the total capitalization of their home-country stock markets.[7] It should soon be possible to buy or sell any major stock at any time of day or night through an exchange in Europe, North America, or Asia. The emergence of foreign markets for stocks promises to be a big step toward fuller integration of capital markets internationally, with dramatic consequences for the underwriting business.

Onshore banking through direct investment has also been expanding, spurred by a loosening of regulatory constraints in

[7] "The Corporate List," *Euromoney*, February 1986, pp. 168–169.
In 1983, corporations raised $83 million through new equity issues in markets outside their home coutnries—a financing mechanism almost unheard of previously. New Euroequity issues totaled $306 million in 1984, $3.2 billion in 1985, and the same amount in the first six months of 1986. See Q. P. Lim, "Equities Enter the Eurobound Age," *Euromoney*, October 1985, p. 262; and S. Lohr, "Turning to Europe for Equity," *New York Times*, 21 August 1986, p. D1.

countries including Japan, Canada, Sweden, Taiwan, and Australia. Figure 6–2 shows the steady expansion of foreign bank lending in the United States. New York, as a major international banking center, has been home to many foreign bank offices for years: Bank of Tokyo's New York office was founded in 1880. But expansion

FIGURE 6–2
Lending in the United States by Foreign-Owned Banks

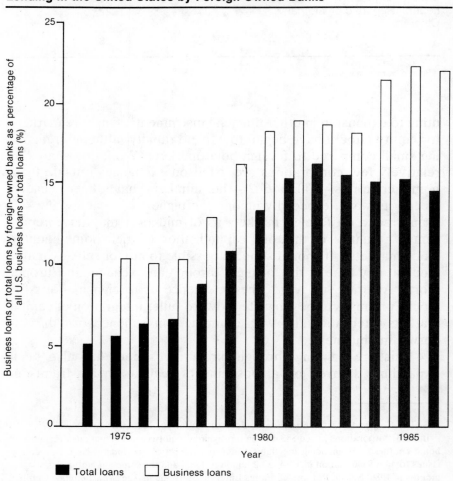

Note: Percentages for December of each year, except June 1986.
Source: Federal Reserve Board, unpublished data, November 1986.

elsewhere, and particularly in retail banking, is a newer phenomenon; Japanese banks have become much more visible in California (Sumitomo Bank of California, California First, Bank of California). In 1975 the foreign assets of U.S. banks (outbound banking investment) greatly exceeded the assets of foreign banks in the United States (inbound); since then, outbound growth has been slow compared to inbound, and today inbound and outbound banking investment are about equal.[8] Box 6–1 summarizes reasons for the growing foreign bank presence in the United States, while a later section looks more closely at the strategies of Japanese banks.

The external or offshore markets function quite differently. Eurodollar bonds, to take an example, are denominated in dollars but bought and sold outside the United States, typically in London. Most Euromarket transactions involve the U.S. dollar, but participants (buyer, seller, underwriter) need not have their main businesses in the United States. Likewise, an American bank might underwrite a corporate bond in London denominated in yen that is sold to a French bank and raises money for a Brazilian firm; U.S. laws prohibit commercial banks from underwriting such an issue here.

Although London has traditionally been the center of the offshore market, Singapore and New York have seen rapid growth in recent years. Fierce competition has led to reduced operating costs and rapid expansion. In 1965 the Eurodollar market was less than 10 percent as large as the domestic U.S. financial market— $12 billion versus about $170 billion. By 1983 the Eurodollar market had surpassed $800 billion, more than half the size of the U.S. domestic market. Direct financing, mainly Eurobonds, has been growing considerably faster than the intermediated transactions that also take place in external markets. (Lack of regulations and reporting requirements in offshore markets means that their size can often be estimated only roughly.)

Expanding external markets go hand in hand with newer banking products that facilitate international flows of capital. Telecommunications links (Box 6–2) have spurred growth in

---

[8] Federal Reserve Board, unpublished data.

BOX 6–1
Foreign Banks in the United States

Figure 6–2 shows that foreign banks increased their onshore business in the United States quite rapidly during the 1970s. Some of this growth has followed naturally from rising international trade and expansion in foreign economies. Have competitive shifts played a part? Answers to this question begin with the reasons that foreign banks invest in the United States.

The first of these, as in so many industries, is the size and lucrative nature of the U.S. market. New York City is the world's largest center for financial services. Any bank that sees itself as multinational will seek customers among American corporations, along with access to a base of dollar deposits and the discount window of the Federal Reserve System. Not only is the banking infrastructure more advanced here than elsewhere, but financial services have been deregulated ahead of other parts of the world. Foreign banks establish or expand U.S. operations in part to gain experience in a comparatively deregulated environment, one they expect to spread to their home country and to other markets within which they do business.[1] Differences in national regulations also create strategic opportunities; for instance, the mix of U.S. and foreign regulations that apply to branches and agencies in the United States may result in lower costs for some financial service products—e.g., business loans—for some foreign banks. Other reasons for investing in the United States include the following:

- Foreign banks, many of which operate on a nationwide basis in their home markets, may feel that they will have advantages over less-experienced U.S. institutions as interstate banking spreads.
- Until passage of the 1978 International Banking Act and subsequent legislation, foreign banks were treated differently than American banks, arguably to their benefit. Moreover, U.S. antitrust policy has made it easier for foreign banks to purchase troubled financial institutions, or bank units sold for strategic reasons—a quick and easy entry to fundamentally profitable markets. For example, when Bankers Trust decided to deemphasize retail bank-

ing in the New York City area in 1979, it sold most of its 106 branches to three foreign banks.[2]
- Some foreign banks, less burdened by risky debt in developing countries than their American competitors, have greater strategic freedom.
- Just as American banks followed American corporations overseas, Japanese and some European banks have moved into the United States to serve their corporate clients.
- Finally, entering the United States will make sense for any bank with reason to believe it can compete; initial entry into the U.S. market serves as a test. Rapid expansion can follow if the bank finds itself to be highly competitive, or if the fluid environment here should shift in its favor.

Despite the *possible* sources of advantage mentioned above, the U.S. operations of foreign banks have seldom been particularly profitable.[3] While there are many reasons for foreign banks to seek an onshore presence in the United States, there is little evidence that the expansion illustrated in Figure 6–2 points to competitive advantages over U.S. banks. And of course these banks are not selling services supplied from overseas, but services produced here with the aid of U.S. workers, the U.S. banking infrastructure, and, often, U.S. capital.

[1] See, for example, K. A. Grossberg, "Japan Checking Out U.S. Banking Revolution," *Wall Street Journal,* Feb. 6, 1986, p. 24.
[2] E. Compton, "Bank Leumi Trust, National Bank of North America, and Barclays" in *Inside Commercial Banking,* 2d ed. (New York: Wiley, 1983), pp. 93–94, 199.
[3] See, for example, N. Gilbert, "Foreign Banks in America: They're Still Coming," *Euromoney* August 1985, pp. 150–156. Of course, banks, like firms in any industry, sometimes choose to sacrifice profits to buy market share.

interest rate and currency swaps. (Swaps, explored more fully later in the chapter, involve the exchange of one financial asset or obligation for another.) The annual volume of outstanding interest rate and currency swaps has grown beyond $300 billion. With these and other new banking products (e.g., standby letters of credit, also described later), banks earn fees for their services rather than

BOX 6-2
Technology in Banking: Electronic Networks and
Cash Management Systems

As in so many of the services, new technologies in banking mean, first and foremost, applications of digital computers and telecommunications systems. Banks have been leaders in applications since computers began to spread in the business world. Today, back-office paperwork functions—e.g., check processing—are highly automated; transactions processed overnight a few years ago can be handled immediately. Larger financial service firms continue to invest hundreds of millions of dollars annually in new software and hardware, with much of the investment now going to support new products rather than the automation of existing operations. Fault-tolerant systems cut down on errors, with some banks investing millions of dollars for backup systems that may never be used—but if needed, could save far greater sums (see the Bank of New York example below).[1]

Banks are also learning to use computers analytically—for risk analysis and decision support—as well as for routine transaction processing. Simple computer programs can calculate a range of possible repayment schedules for proposed loans; complex programs analyze price trends of thousands of Eurobonds each day. Software developed by Bankers Trust reputedly gives the company's foreign exchange traders a 10 second advantage over the competition, enough time to execute four or five trades. Soon, expert systems will be available in the form of computer programs that embody the decision rules followed by experienced foreign exchange traders. The expert system will never be as good as the true human expert, whose storehouse of experience leads to judgments and intuitions that cannot be reduced to rules the computer can follow (ch. 8). But expert systems will help the inexperienced to learn, the inexpert to perform better, and the true expert to avoid errors. Among those recently surveyed, about 20 percent of American financial institutions had already begun to install expert systems, with another 40 percent planning to do so over the next few years.[2]

Networks.—Banks communicate and transfer funds through computers linked to form value-added networks (VANs, ch. 5). Member banks can transmit messages both domestically and across national borders via SWIFT (Society of Worldwide Interbank Financial Telecommunications), which began operations in Europe in 1977 and now links nearly 2,000 locations in over 50 countries. Jointly owned by more than a thousand banks, the SWIFT system currently handles almost a million messages each day.

SWIFT transmits messages between banks, but not funds. These are the province of other computer networks. Normally, any international transfer involving dollars will make use of CHIPS (Clearing House Interbank Payments System), controlled by a dozen large New York banks (the clearinghouse banks) and connecting 140 U.S.- and foreign-owned institutions, all in New York City. (Three of the clearinghouse banks—Marine Midland, National Westminster Bank U.S.A., and European American Bank—are subsidiaries of foreign companies.) CHAPS, a similar network in the United Kingdom, serves the large London banks. In a typical transaction:

- Bank A in London has a correspondent relationship with Bank B in New York and wishes to transfer funds to Bank D in Tokyo which has a correspondent relationship with Bank C in New York. B and C are CHIPS members.
- After message traffic between A and B concerning the transaction, perhaps over SWIFT, B enters codes for itself and for the receiving bank C into its CHIPS terminal, along with the sum to be transferred and the identity of bank D.
- The message goes to the central CHIPS computer, where it is stored temporarily.
- The sending bank B must next transmit a verification for the release of funds. The central computer then debits the CHIPS account of B, and credits the account of the receiving bank C (retaining a permanent record). Bank C informs Bank D that the transaction has been completed.

Normally, each of the 140 banks will settle its account with CHIPS at the end of the business day. Final settlements use

BOX 6–2 (*continued*)

FedWire—another network, this one operated by the Federal Reserve System. FedWire, which links about 6,300 financial institutions in the United States, nets transactions immediately.

Many other networks also provide electronic funds transfer services, with about 60 automated clearinghouses (ACHs) currently operating in the United States. In contrast to CHIPS, most ACH transactions are relatively small. They also provide services to firms outside the banking industry—e.g., direct deposits of employee paychecks. Other computer networks provide quotations and execute trades of commodities and securities. Nonfinancial firms can tap into almost any of these systems with an electronic cash management system, as discussed below.

Multinational banks commonly operate private international networks for communications between branches—e.g., Manufacturers Hanover's Geonet. A common pattern consists of service centers in major financial markets, from which further spokes fan out. Hongkong and Shanghai Bank, for instance, operates a telex network linking more than 100 offices in over 60 countries based on leased lines (cable and satellite) and switching centers in Hong Kong, Britain, the United States, Bahrain, and Australia. The company also has a newer computer network, only partially completed, which operates at much higher speeds. Independent vendors such as GEISCO, Telenet, and Tymnet—all of which offer specialized services for banks—provide a further set of alternatives for message communications and securities transactions.

The greater the speed with which message, clearing, and settlement systems function, the greater the opportunities for banks to make profits on certain kinds of transactions. On the other hand, when the time lags between messages, clearing (transactions booked), and settlement (payment made) decline, financial institutions have less chance to take advantage of floats, the de facto interest-free loans made possible by these lags.

Implications for Stability.—Computer networks are never foolproof. A highly publicized failure cost the Bank of New York about $5 million during a 2-day span in November 1985. The bank, which does a very large business in government securities, normally receives and makes payments on these securities almost simultaneously. A software error in the firm's system left it liable for payments without receiving the corresponding credits. Before discovering the problem, the bank ran up a $32 billion overdraft with the Federal Reserve. The $5 million in interest charges came to about 5 percent of the bank's annual earnings.[3]

As message, clearing, and settlement networks evolve toward greater complexity and greater speed, the probabilities of system failures may not rise, but their consequences certainly will. When, for instance, payments moved through the mail, failure of a bank might be a process taking weeks. Regulatory authorities could monitor the situation and intervene if appropriate. Now a bank could fail almost instantaneously.

Cash Management.—For many years, banks provided services to corporations in exchange for the interest-free use of funds on deposit. With rising interest rates, corporations began to view this as a bad bargain; today, corporate treasurers manage their cash balances and short-term asset much more aggressively, as they have always managed long-term funds. Banks have been faced with the loss of more than the interest income. Many of their traditional customers now have the ability to manage their own cash, should they choose to do so. Typically, the banks have restructured their products and accounts in response, and introduced new computer-based technologies to offer corporations a package of cash management services that can handle not only currency, collections, and disbursements, but transactions in commercial paper, short-term notes, and foreign exchange.

For a multinational corporation (MNC), the cash management system will aggregate information from, and move funds among, branches and subsidiaries around the world. In effect, the bank helps the corporate treasury operation improve its efficiency—for instance, by sweeping all idle cash into an investment account on a daily basis.[4] The bank gives up the use of the higher balances the corporation once maintained, but gets fees for the new services it provides. The corporation gets an integrated package, without having to put the system together itself (although some do). Already, cash management systems may provide direct access to market quotations and

BOX 6–2 (concluded)

execution of buy and sell orders. In principal, a company can centralize almost all its cash management functions at a single treasury work station (a computer terminal or PC). Thus far, perhaps a thousand treasury work stations have been installed worldwide—most of them in the United States; as experience accumulates, they will probably become much more popular.

MNCs and other large corporations deal with many banks, most or all of which must participate for a cash management system to function efficiently. The major U.S. commercial banks pioneered integrated cash management services, at home during the 1970s and internationally beginning in the early 1980s. Differences in tax laws and banking regulations, as well as restrictive telecommunications policies, have led to complications abroad, with many foreign banks reluctant to participate. At present, for example, Japan's Ministry of Finance permits a computer link between a corporation and a bank, but prohibits electronic funds transfers; the Ministry plans to remove this restriction once Japanese banks have become more competitive in cash management technologies. While the larger European banks have also begun to develop their own systems, their software remains far behind the best U.S. practice. A survey of 60 large multinational banks, with headquarters in Japan, North America, and Europe, revealed that many depend heavily on American cash management technology.[5]

[1] On backup systems, and applications mentioned in the next paragraph, see R. B. Schmitt, "The Technology Gamble," *Wall Street Journal*, Sept. 29, 1986, p. 10D.

New technologies used in retail banking—e.g., automatic teller machines (ATMs)—have more visibility but little to do with international competition. Their main effect is on the price and quality of retail services domestically.

[2] "The Future of Technology in the Financial Services Industry," *American Banker*, Apr. 14, 1986, p. 14. Coopers and Lybrand, which conducted the survey, found that more banks than insurance companies, brokerage firms, or investment houses expected to use new technologies like expert systems as competitive weapons. An analyst at Arthur D. Little has estimated that 35 percent of the largest U.S. financial institutions will install prototype expert systems during 1987, compared with 5 percent in 1986—W. M. Bulkeley, "Computers Take on New Role As Experts in Financial Affairs," *Wall Street Journal*, Feb. 7, 1986, p. 23. For further examples of expert systems applications, see B. J. Feder, "The Computer As Deal Maker," *New York Times*, Aug. 14, 1986, p. D2; also, L. Kehoe, "White Collar Robots Go To Work," *Financial Times*, Aug. 5, 1986, p. 9.

[3] J. M. Berry, "Computer Snarled N.Y. Bank," *Washington Post,* Dec. 13, 1985, p. D1. Trading in government securities averages about $200 billion daily.

[4] RJR Nabisco (formerly RJ Reynolds) says it saves $20 million annually through cash management techniques. For instance, the company can now match a need for Deutsche marks 6 months in the future to pay for German tobacco machinery with an expected inflow of marks from overseas subsidiaries. Previously, it would have purchased a forward contract from a bank to lock in the price of the machinery in dollars. See "How the Last Became First," *Euromoney,* February 1986, p. 39.

[5] "New Directions in European Cash Management," Business International, 1985. While most banks in most countries, including the United States, had developed their own software, 16 of the 60 worldwide chose Chemical Bank's BankLink. Outside the United States, software from National Data Corp., also an American firm, was the second choice to BankLink. Of the four Japanese banks surveyed, none had developed their own software, all looking instead to U.S. suppliers.

The survey painted a similar picture for network services. GEISCO, a General Electric subsidiary, supplied VAN services to half the overseas banks, and more than half the American banks. Overseas, local post, telegraph, and telephone authorities (PTTs) were second to GEISCO, with other U.S. firms, such as ADP, also providing services both in the United States and abroad. Four U.S. banks maintained private networks, but only 2 of 34 foreign banks.

A survey of corporate treasurers internationally ranked Citibank at the top of commercial banks providing electronic cash management services, followed by three other U.S. banks—BankAmerica, Chase, and Chemical. See "Corporate Finance," *Euromoney,* March 1985.

interest. As Figure 6–3 shows, fees have been growing relative to interest as a source of revenues for U.S. banks. The shift toward fees is probably greater for international banking than for domestic operations.

Securitization

Perhaps the most striking and most significant change in financing practices—a change that has accompanied the rise of external markets, and contributes to the growth of fee-based services— stems from securitization. A company seeking financing can, in general, do so either by borrowing from a financial institution or by issuing a security such as a bond or stock. Likewise, those with money to invest can deposit funds in a financial institution or buy securities directly. Securitization refers to the growing tendency for those on both sides—funds seekers and investors—to choose securities, and for these securities to be traded in secondary

FIGURE 6–3
Growth in Fee Income Relative to Interest Income for U.S. banks

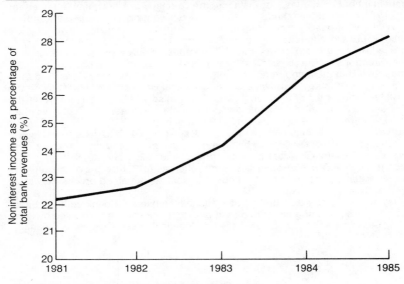

Source: *Federal Reserve Bulletin*, September 1986, p. 627.

markets. Banks can securitize existing loans by selling the right to collect the interest and principal. Individuals securitize when they purchase shares in a money market mutual fund as an alternative to demand deposits.

Securitization reduces the demand for traditional financial services, particularly by larger customers; a corporation that once borrowed from a bank may now issue commercial paper directly. And in some cases, the bank's intermediary role—bringing together investors and those looking for financing—declines. But in other cases, even with securitization the bank continues its traditional functions, particularly those of managing the sizes, risks, and maturity of assets and liabilities; financial intermediaries collect small deposits and make large loans (and use demand deposits to fund term loans), and substitute their own creditworthiness for that of the borrower.

INTERNATIONAL BANKING STRATEGIES

Profitability in banking has been dropping—see Figure 6–4.[9] While competition has intensified in lending, the traditional core of the business, loans have been diminishing relative to fee-earning services as a source of earnings. Regional and national markets, once comfortably segregated, have been opened to new entrants, domestic and foreign. Securitization has cut into customary sources of profit. With more intense competition, particularly in familiar lines of business, banks have searched for new strategies that might help them earn profits at accustomed levels.

Broadly speaking, deregulation has pushed financial institutions into riskier endeavors as they have sought to avoid the devolution of banking into a commodity-like service. They have developed new products, sought out new onshore and offshore markets, and, where possible, tried to move from commercial banking into related services—notably, securities trading and investment banking. In an industry like this, with many able competitors, competitive success normally comes through the accretion of small advantages. How well U.S. banks do in finding new and profitable markets will be perhaps the single most important factor in determining their future competitiveness. Regardless of whether the industry as a whole rises or falls relative to others in the world, some American banks will probably do quite well, and some might do quite poorly.

New and/or Rapidly Growing Product Markets

Banks that can identify and develop new products ahead of the competition can often generate relatively large returns, at least until their rivals catch up. Even then, product differentiation may

---

[9] No comparative data more recent than that in the figure is available. Both the largest and the smallest U.S. banks showed further drops in profits during 1985; although average profit levels for all U.S. banks rose in 1985, reversing a five-year decline, Continental Illinois' return to profitability accounts for the entire gain. See D. J. Danker and M. L. McLaughlin, "Profitability of U.S.-Chartered Insured Commercial Banks," *Federal Reserve Bulletin*, September 1986, p. 618.

Because of differing accounting rules, absolute values of return on equity across countries have little significance.

FIGURE 6–4
Return on Equity in Banking, Five Countries

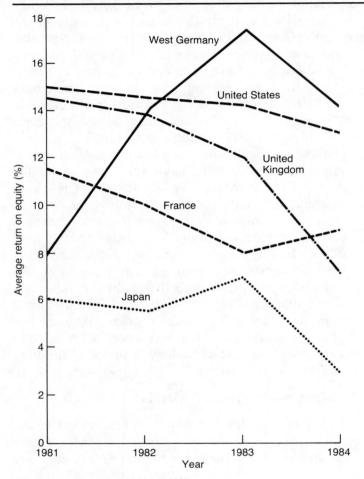

Source: *The Economist,* 22 March 1985.

offer continuing competitive advantages. Thus innovative financial products have been central elements in the strategies of American banks. Most of these products are not so much new ideas as existing products that have seen rapid growth because the combination of market conditions (inflation, exchange rate instability, deregulation, the Euromarkets, securitization) and new technologies (computer networks, telecommunications) makes them attractive both for financial firms and their customers.

The pervasiveness of regulations complicates innovation in this industry. Government policies in both the United States and Japan, for instance, have restricted the spread of automated teller machines (ATMs). U.S. regulations generally allow withdrawals in two or more states, but deposit-taking across state boundaries has been limited by restrictions on both bank holding company activity and interstate banking. Japan permits ATM use only during certain hours, thus curbing one of their principal attractions—around-the-clock access. In both cases, regulations limit the advantages that innovating banks can expect.

Other innovations have come in direct response to regulation. In the 1970s, high U.S. interest rates, combined with regulatory limits on the interest banks could pay on deposits, led to the creation of money market mutual funds. Reserve requirements on deposits in the United States, and restrictions on capital movements here and elsewhere, contributed to the expansion of the Euromarket relative to more regulated capital markets during the 1970s and 1980s.

When new banking products circumvent existing regulations, national governments may respond by reinterpreting legislation or passing new laws. Alternatively, regulatory authorities may view the innovation as desirable, and perhaps liberalize the rules further. Internationally, deregulation has proved contagious: multinational corporations (MNCs) and other major bank customers can often choose the country and the banks—thus the regulations—with which they wish to deal. National governments that fear the loss of valued customers then must liberalize their own regulatory structures. After fixed commissions were abolished on the New York stock exchange, trading volumes rose; the London exchange was eventually forced to follow suit. Liberalization of the London financial market, in turn, has brought in new business from Paris and elsewhere on the continent, with liberalization in many parts of Europe following.

Deregulation has also spread to Japan. Until recently, Japanese corporations could not issue Euroyen bonds (bonds denominated in yen and sold in the Euromarket). Japanese corporations seeking to participate in the Euromarket were forced into other currencies, where Japanese banks tended to be less competitive. The government's decision to permit a Euroyen market (corporations still must meet certain financial tests) represents a concession to this reality. Still later, the authorities permitted an offshore market to develop in Japan (operations began in December 1986).

Eurobonds and Euronotes

Eurobond issues grew at about 30 percent per year between 1975 and 1985—Figure 6–5. New Eurobond and Euronote issues totaled about $136 billion in 1985 and an estimated $180 billion in 1986.[10] Lack of regulation in the Euromarkets means lower issuing costs for the banks, and lower margins for customers. Customers as well as banks may be able to bypass domestic constraints; South Korean firms, for instance, have sought medium-term financing in the Euromarket because inflation, uncertainty, and government restrictions have prevented the development of a medium-term domestic bond market in Korea.

Eurobonds come in three varieties: (1) traditional fixed-rate bonds; (2) floating-rate notes (FRNs—issued with maturities up to seven years and paying interest at rates periodically adjusted to reflect prevailing short-term rates); and (3) convertible Eurobonds (which bear fixed rates but can be converted into equity shares of the issuing firm—in recent years these have never exceeded about 10 percent of the total market). As Figure 6–5 indicates, new FRN issues have grown especially quickly: first marketed in 1978, by 1984 they accounted for 40 percent of the Eurobond market.

Table 6–3 shows that U.S. financial services firms have had by far the greatest share of the Eurobond issue market, doing even better in the rapidly growing FRN segment. American firms manage nearly 60 percent of issues denominated in dollars, and about two thirds of all Eurobond issues for U.S. corporations. (Box 6–3 expands on the significance of the dollar as the primary currency of international trade.)

---

[10] "Key Figures," *Euromoney*, February 1986, p. 170; "International Bonds: A Profitable Year for Borrowers," *Financial Times*, 29 December 1986, p. 13.
Shorter maturity bonds are known as notes.

FIGURE 6–5
Growth of the Eurobond Market

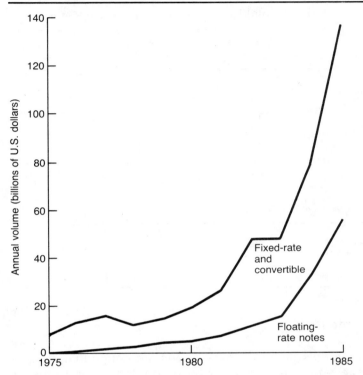

Sources: *Euromoney,* various issues. "Recent Innovations in International Banking," Bank for International Settlements, Basel, Switzerland, April 1986, p. 163.

Trade Financing and Other Fee-Earning Services
One of the oldest international services provided by commercial banks, trade financing, continues to expand. Such traditional businesses as letters of credit (LCs), whereby banks endorse their customer's creditworthiness, are now carried out largely through the telecommunications infrastructure. Clients can request LCs electronically, using standard formats, with many of the communications handled via SWIFT or such U.S.-based data processing organizations as GEISCO and ADP. Paperwork costs have been cut, and the process is now much quicker—a matter of hours

TABLE 6–3
Eurobond Issue Managers by Country

	Percentage Share of New Issues, 1984		
	Floating Rate Notes	*Fixed Rate Notes*	*Overall*
United States	53%	35%	44%
Federal Republic of Germany	3	20	12
Switzerland	11	8	11
United Kingdom	13	6	10
France	11	4	8
Japan	2	10	8
Subtotal	93%	83%	93%
Others*	7%	17%	7%

* Includes smaller issue managers from countries listed, as well as countries not on the list.

Source: *Euromoney*, various issues.

BOX 6–3
The Rule of the Dollar

Many of the world's financial transactions are denominated in U.S. dollars, even when the parties have no relationship to the United States. Trade between Japan and North Korea, for instance, has commonly been conducted in dollars. While the continuing importance of the dollar creates competitive advantages for U.S. banks, these advantages are small, and will no doubt decline further in the years ahead.

Why is the dollar so commonly used? Many of the reasons are historical. Before World War II, the British pound had been the world's primary currency for international transactions. But the major European currencies did not return to convertibility until 1957. The dollar has kept its role since, in part because the United States provides an unmatched banking infrastructure, with well-developed markets for holding short-term balances, in addition to political and economic stability. Moreover, the volume of international capital flows involving American companies, particularly during the 1950s and 1960s, also made it natural to continue using dollars. But decisions by residents of other countries to use the dollar—or any currency other than their own—depend on relative attractiveness, and most of these factors have less weight today than in earlier years. As market participants have diversified across currencies, the deutsche mark (DM) and the yen have slowly gained in market share. Indeed, the yen has become almost as popular as the DM, one among many signs of the integration of Japan's financial system into the world system.

What advantages, if any, accrue to financial institutions doing business in their home currency? The first point is this: the more open and better developed the market, the less the advantages for domestic banks. Even in such countries as the United States, however, regulatory/administrative factors tend to tip the scales a bit. A second factor, related but distinct: domestic banks normally dominate the clearing (payment) system in their currency. Other banks bear costs (through their balances with members of the clearing system, as well as the fees they pay for services). For such reasons, domestic banks tend to have a competitive edge—small but potentially significant—in transactions involving their home currency. Even in the free-for-all external markets, U.S. ownership helps in attracting U.S. dollar deposits, while German bank branches do better in attracting DM deposits. With continuing deregulation, and movement toward globally integrated financial markets, such advantages will probably continue to erode. Even so, as pointed out at many places in this chapter, banking is a highly competitive business; a superior position must be built piece by piece, and each piece counts.

rather than weeks. (Citibank claims it can issue a letter of credit in a matter of minutes.) While the United States led in automating this process, some European banks, especially in Scandinavia, have developed competitive systems.

Standby letters of credit (SLCs) also substitute a bank's credit standing for that of the client. The market for SLCs—agreements to lend money should other prospective lenders refuse to do so—grew from almost nothing in the early 1970s to nearly $150 billion by 1984. Five large banks—Citicorp, Manufacturers Hanover, BankAmerica, Chemical Bank, and Bankers Trust—account for more than a third of the U.S. total. Foreign banks, too, have been quite active in SLCs, with Barclays' New York branch reporting that in some months its letter of credit business exceeds its loans.

The fees a bank can charge for SLCs depend in part on market judgments of the bank's riskiness; if a bank has a high credit rating, its guarantee is worth more. Because of their exposure in developing countries, U.S. banks have been viewed as relatively risky; many have been hard-pressed to compete with their Japanese and European counterparts. (Of the major U.S.-based banks, only Morgan Guaranty still has the coveted AAA rating.) Indeed, Japanese banks have recently backed tax-exempt state and municipal bonds in the United States, including issues by Michigan, and by the cities of Chicago and Philadelphia.

A banker's acceptance (BA) guarantees payment of a trade debt. These time drafts can be traded in a secondary market which, in the United States, amounts to about $80 billion annually. More than half of this represents third-country BAs, involving neither U.S. imports nor exports. The third-country portion of the market reflects not only the prominence of the U.S. dollar in international trade, but also the ability of U.S. financial institutions to capture business from banks in other nations willing to deal in dollar obligations. Thus, the recent announcement by the Japanese government that it will allow a yen-denominated acceptance market may or may not represent much of a threat to American banks. To the extent that the yen makes inroads on dollar-denominated BAs, banks based in Japan have something of an advantage. Still, even in a yen acceptance market, U.S. banks might be able to remain competitive because of their accumulated experience.

Financial swaps enable two parties with advantages in different segments of the market to exchange (swap) their obligations. Banks earn fees for arranging these transactions—another example of the growing importance of noninterest income. New variations have fostered enormous growth in the market. Recently, much of the expansion has been in cross-currency interest-rate swaps. For an example, consider that a Japanese firm seeks fixed-rate financing in dollars, while an American company wants floating-rate financing in yen. If the Japanese firm can borrow yen relatively cheaply, and the American firm dollars, they are able to swap their interest rate obligations to their mutual benefit. The bank serving as intermediary absorbs the credit risk of each party. Many actual transactions become much more complicated than this example, involving three or more currencies and other complexities.[11] Because these transactions involve only a contingent liability on the part of the bank, they remain off the balance sheet, although some larger banks have begun to take swaps onto their books by offering a swap to one party even if no counterparty has yet been found.

U.S. commercial and investment banks have been leaders in the market for swaps, where success depends on efficiency, inventiveness, and quick response. Citicorp alone accounted for some $25 billion in swaps in 1985. Only one British investment bank (SG Warburg) and one French bank (Paribus) have established positions comparable to even the smaller U.S. players. Banks have developed the swap market largely in response to the needs of their clients. For commercial banks, these are mostly corporations. The leading investment banks—which include Salomon Brothers, First Boston, and Goldman Sachs—often arrange swaps for other financial institutions, especially savings and loan associations.

Many of the financial products discussed earlier—banker's acceptances, SLCs, swaps—share a common characteristic: they do not appear on the books of the bank, but the bank guarantees the credit of other parties. Regulators have been concerned over the growth of these possibly risky activities; governments require banks to maintain reserves of capital against their assets (mainly loans, but also treasury and other securities), in part to protect consumers and other depositors. To the extent that banks develop

---

[11] In March 1986, American Express raised 20 billion yen in the Euroyen market, which it swapped into $109 million and then into securities denominated in eight different currencies, some of these securities at floating rates and some at fixed rates—L. Wayne, "New Broader Role for Finance Officers," *New York Times,* 20 October 1986, p. D6.

and market financial products without creating assets on their balance sheets, they avoid these requirements (and the associated costs). A bank that guarantees a loan may be able to collect a fee almost as large as the interest it could have earned if it had made the loan itself. Likewise for a swap, the bank guarantees payment of interest by both parties but neither of the swapped instruments becomes an asset or liability of the bank.

Regulatory authorities have looked askance at this de facto loosening in control. In most cases where governments have begun to count such items against capital requirements, they have viewed SLCs, swaps, and other guarantees as much smaller risks than loans. But the fact remains that, at this point, no one is in a position to judge the real risks: growth in many of these markets has been very rapid, and experience remains limited. In general, the United States has been slower than other industrialized countries to extend capital adequacy requirements to off-balance-sheet items. U.S. policy, therefore, seems to have had the effect of inducing American banks to market off-balance-sheet products more aggressively than their foreign competitors. So far, the result has been to help U.S. banks capture large shares of these markets.

Movement into Investment Banking

Many commercial banks see attractive strategic opportunities in investment banking—trading in securities, underwriting stock and bond issues, and arranging mergers and acquisitions. Investment banking holds out the prospect of recovering lost profitability: commercial banks do well to earn 15 percent on equity, while rates of return above 30 percent are far from unknown among investment banks (which do not take deposits or make loans). An American commercial bank contemplating a move into investment banking faces two sets of obstacles, the first legal and political, the second organizational.

The Glass-Steagall Act and other U.S. legislation bars firms from engaging in both commercial and investment banking in the United States (although American firms can do so overseas). While Japan maintains restrictions similar in some respects to those imposed in the United States, few other foreign governments maintain this regulatory separation; in countries including the Federal Republic of Germany, Switzerland, and the Netherlands, so-called universal banks underwrite corporate securities, offer mutual funds, and engage in the full range of stock brokerage activities. The freedom granted U.S. commercial banks to function as investment banks abroad has been one of the factors spurring expansion of the Euromarket (where, however, American investment banks have performed better than commercial banks in managing Eurobond issues, products similar to those investment banks work with at home).

In recent years, commercial banks have moved into new businesses domestically that test the limits drawn by U.S. law. Often, the courts have been asked to decide the merits of the arguments for a liberal interpretation of the restrictions, as put forward by commercial banks, versus the stricter standard suggested by investment banks. (The much smaller investment banks have not sought to move into commercial banking.) Two current examples:

1. Should Bankers Trust be permitted to broker commercial paper for its corporate clients? A Federal Appeals court in December 1986 ruled in favor of Bankers Trust, overturning a district court finding that had reversed a Federal Reserve decision. The Securities Industry Association quickly signaled its intent to appeal to the Supreme Court.
2. The Federal Reserve is expected to decide in 1987 whether commercial bank holding companies will be permitted limited underwriting of municipal revenue bonds and certain other securities.*

As these examples suggest, and as discussed in more detail in a later section on "Policy Issues" below, the separation of commercial and investment banking in the United States has been slowly breaking down, in part because new banking products blur some of the traditional distinctions. But if the erosion of Glass-Steagall and other restrictions continues, as it no doubt will, U.S. commercial banks face another obstacle in moving into investment banking—differences in organizational patterns and managerial style suggested by the saying that "bankers live off their assets,

---

* In 1987, the Federal Reserve permitted commercial bank holding companies to engage in the limited underwriting of municipal revenue bonds and certain other securities.

merchant bankers [i.e., investment bankers], live off their wits."[12] In the United States, managing a combined organization means reconciling such differences, a process that will take time and during which other opportunities might slip by. Plainly, greater freedom from legal restrictions would lead the larger commercial banks to venture further into investment banking. Some would probably be successful. Others might have trouble mastering new and unfamiliar lines of business, perhaps eventually withdrawing to more familiar territory.

Finding Profitable Market Segments in Commercial Banking

Onshore Retail Banking

Overseas retail banking has seemed a relatively conservative choice for banks seeking greater profits. Here, size by itself seldom provides much of an advantage, but new products, good service, and aggressive marketing hold out the promise of substantial rewards. Indeed, foreign banks have moved into the United States no doubt feeling they could offer better quality services and/or undercut their rivals' costs. The rapid spread of credit card services (e.g., Visa, MasterCard), now offered around the world through joint ventures owned by participating banks, provides another example of international expansion in retail banking.

Particularly in countries with stable regulated markets, nomi-

---

[12] See P. L. Zweig "Some Big Banks Find Entering New Fields A Tough Transition," *Wall Street Journal*, August 13, 1986, p. 1.

Unlike manufacturing companies, financial services firms depend on no raw materials or manufactured inputs to produce their end products. They do depend on people—the bank's employees. In international banking especially, the skills that employees bring to and develop on the job—and the ways in which the organization deploys these people and their skills—can make a great deal of difference for competitivenes. In this, banking is not unlike other knowledge-based service industries.

In recent years, banks have sought greater numbers of specialists in fields like bond trading, currency transactions, and swaps. Increasingly, they have hired people from graduate schools of business to fill such positions, rather than promoting from lower positions within the bank—O. Bertrand and T. Noyelle, "Changing Technology, Skills and Skill Formation in French, German, Japanese, Swedish and U.S. Financial Service Firms: Preliminary Findings," report to the Center for Educational Research and Innovation of the Organization for Economic Cooperation and Development, August 1986, pp. 47–48.

nally competing banks have often been happy to fall into patterns of peaceful coexistence. When American banks have been able to enter such markets, their efficiency advantages have sometimes led to profit levels well above those of their local rivals.[13] On the other hand, U.S. banks have not done very well since being admitted to the Canadian market in 1980. Earlier government restrictions barred foreign banks from establishing subsidiaries, branches, or agencies in Canada, and limited them to a 10 percent holding in a chartered bank. The result was high prices and profits for Canadian banks.[14] Since 1980, foreign banks have been permitted to expand in Canada, but with restrictions—e.g., on the number of branches permitted—that continue to limit their ability to compete with Canadian banks. Citicorp, the largest foreign bank in Canada, has only eight branches. Foreign entrants have been largely denied access to a low-cost deposit base; U.S. banks have not been able to earn the high profits that might be expected in a protected retail market. Nor is Canada the only country in which liberalization has been structured in such a way as to limit the opportunities available to U.S. and other foreign banks.

Citicorp, Chase, and a few British and Japanese banks have been the only entrants pursuing retail banking on anything approaching a worldwide scale. Citicorp has major efforts underway in Europe and elsewhere, and has been quick to introduce new retail banking products in seeking greater market share. In Britain, Citicorp's more efficient systems help it process mortgage applications in 10 days, compared with a month for local competitors; Citibank claims to undercut the costs of its rivals by 50 percent in some lines of business.[15] Other U.S. banks have been quite

---

[13] For example, Citibank has reportedly earned a substantial portion of its worldwide profits in Brazil—20 percent in 1983—where a grandfather exception permitted it to remain after the Brazilian market was closed to other foreign entrants. See I. Walter, "International Competitive Distortions in Banking and Financial Services," draft for Trade Policy Research Centre, London, March 1984, p. 12.

[14] After-tax return on capital to Canadian banks averaged 12.9 percent, compared to 9.1 percent for eight large New York banks—*Efficiency and Regulation: A Study of Deposit Institutions* (Ottawa: Economic Council of Canada, 1975).

[15] "Citicorp's Gutsy Campaign to Conquer Europe," *Business Week,* July 15, 1985, p. 47. Also see P. L. Zweig, "The Elusive Consumer," *Wall Street Journal,* September 29, 1986, p. 34D. Citicorp has retail banking operations in 34 countries, Chase in 25.

selective in entering retail markets abroad; Citicorp has been alone in expressing interest in acquiring a small Japanese bank as a wedge into Japan's retail market. Citicorp's strategy is predicated in part on technological superiority leading to lower costs. But to succeed in retail banking, a foreign entrant must also develop a detailed knowledge of local conditions—knowledge at least equal to that of the competition. This is a task that demands a strong commitment over time, even if the new entrant begins by buying an existing bank or hiring experienced people locally. Citicorp gets advantages from being a major commercial lender in many countries. This appears to be one reason it has been able to expand in overseas markets despite being perceived as a foreign presence—a far more serious disadvantage in retail than in commercial banking.

Commercial Lending to Small and Medium-Sized Firms

In recent years, banks both in the United States and overseas have been placing much more emphasis on lending to smaller companies. Foreign banks in the United States lend to small businesses here; Citicorp's branches in many of the 90-some countries in which it operates are said to be eagerly pursuing the loan business of firms with sales in the $25 million and up range. The reasons begin with securitization, and the increasing self-sufficiency of large corporations. When these corporations go directly to the capital markets, banks may still provide guarantees, and sometimes distribution services, but margins tend to be thin. Smaller companies, less known and perceived to be more risky, still need the services of a bank to raise money.

Financial institutions in different countries have developed this portion of the market differently. In Japan businesses depended much more heavily on bank loans after the war than on equity. But by the 1970s, as Japanese economic growth continued, larger corporations could finance much of their expansion through reinvested earnings. Toyota, admittedly an extreme case, has generated so much cash the company has sometimes been called the Toyota Bank. As Figure 6-6 shows, the drop in bank lending in Japan compared to other sources of corporate funds has been dramatic. Faced with rapidly declining demand for loans from their major customers, Japanese banks have sought to lend to the small businesses they once ignored.

FIGURE 6–6
Sources of External Financing for Japanese Corporations

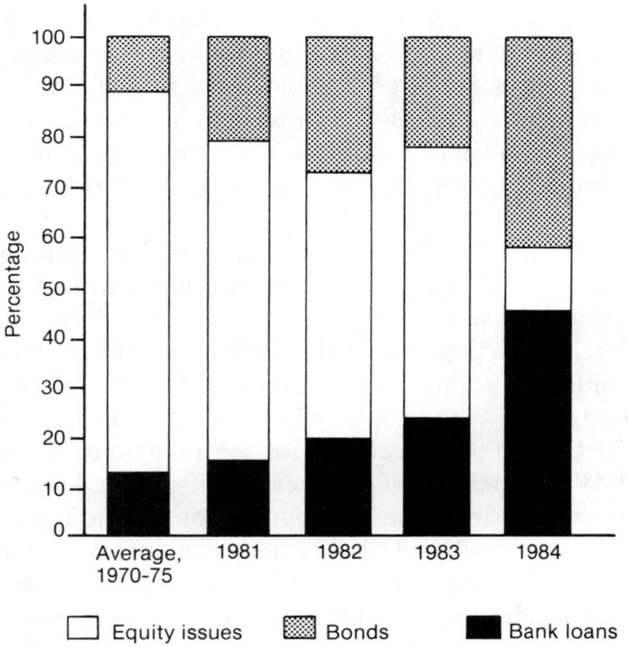

Source: "Survey of Japanese Financing and Banking," *The Economist,* December 8, 1984, p. 21.

The Future

Competitive strategy for any commercial bank seeking to expand internationally hinges on its view of the coupling among its services. Will a bank that offers a broad range of products be able to reduce its costs? Will it reap marketing advantages, perhaps be able to lock in its clients? Will a corporation that uses Morgan Guaranty as a lead manager in the Eurobond market also borrow money from Morgan domestically? If the answers to these questions turn out to be yes, then banks able to offer a comprehensive package of services will be well-positioned to grow and compete in international markets. By the same token, a bank with an extensive worldwide network of branches, agencies, representative offices, and subsidiaries is better placed to develop and market a wide range of financial products. On the other hand, no matter the efforts of banks to maintain ongoing "relationships" with clients, customers all over the world seem to be shopping for banking services more extensively than in earlier years. Relationship banking is in part simply a reaction to such trends, including securitization. Although some U.S. banks no doubt have success in locating profitable areas of foreign commercial banking, this is plainly not a strategic route open to all. Those that already have a broad and deep foreign presence—notably Citicorp—seem most likely to prosper through continued penetration of new onshore banking markets.

Furthermore, any strategy aimed at finding and exploiting unusually profitable lines of business depends on doing so before other financial institutions seize the same opportunity. Banking expertise is widespread, particularly in the OECD countries. The history of LDC lending demonstrates the point. Many regional U.S. banks, deciding there were profits to be made in loans to the developing world, set up offices overseas for the first time. Even without the Third World debt crisis, lower returns would have followed simply from the increase in competition. Lending to medium-sized businesses in Canada holds a similar lesson: after the market opened to American banks, fierce competition among Canadian, U.S., and other foreign banks kept profits low. Even though they lobbied hard and ultimately with some success for greater access to the Canadian market, American banks have been disappointed with the results. They have also won concessions from Japan's Ministry of Finance (MOF). This enables U.S. banks to expand their activities in Japan, but here as well, competition promises to hold down profitability. The point is a general one: in an era of deregulation, profits will be low in many or most of the markets seen as new opportunities for American financial service firms.

Moreover, concessions overseas often go hand in hand with losses of previous advantages. Onshore foreign banks in Japan recently won the right to enter the trust business. The Japanese government has granted licenses to six U.S. and three other foreign banks. These foreign banks now have a strategic option not open to the biggest Japanese banks. But other recent policy decisions—for example, permitting Japanese corporations to issue Euroyen bonds—mean that, in at least some cases, Euroyen bonds placed by Japanese banks will supplant Eurodollar bonds that would otherwise have been handled by American banks.

Future competition in international banking promises to be fierce, with many entrants having similar capabilities seeking to establish themselves in new and growing markets (geographic as well as product). American banks do have sources of competitive advantage, primarily their experience in a deregulated and competitive environment, and in applications of technology. Foreign institutions have advantages of their own such as the financial clout of the big Japanese banks to set against them.

JAPANESE COMPETITION: TWO SCENARIOS

Over the past decade, U.S.-based financial institutions have grown rapidly. In terms of assets, however, Japanese banks have grown much faster, as Figure 6–1 shows. The astounding expansion of Japanese manufacturing industries has pulled Japan's financial institutions onto the world scene, with banks following their corporate customers abroad. Although banks from countries like Britain and West Germany are strong in some parts of the market, only the Japanese pose a real threat over the foreseeable future to the U.S. position in financial services.

This section sketches out two possible scenarios for the rivalry between U.S. and Japanese banks. In the first, regulatory constraints and other factors built into the Japanese system slow international expansion, blunting many of the competitive thrusts of Japan's banks. In the second scenario, more rapid deregulation by Japan's government leads to concerted attacks on international markets by financial institutions largely free to pursue strategies of their own choosing, and with the financial muscle to succeed more often than not. On balance, we view the second scenario as more likely, but the critical decisions will be made within the Japanese government, where they will emerge from the interplay of political and bureaucratic forces. Liberalization in Japan means still more intense competition in international banking, competition to which U.S. and Japanese banks bring differing sets of strengths. At the least, competitive life for U.S. firms will be more difficult.

Constrained Growth

Japan's large continuing current-account surpluses have been accompanied by rapid growth in international assets, both financial and nonfinancial. Management of these assets has become the responsibility of Japanese financial institutions, especially the banks, which have grown proportionately. Despite their size, the sense has remained, in some circles, that Japanese banks, while undeniably major players, have not yet become fully competitive with European and American banks internationally. Some of their rivals do not perceive the Japanese to be good bankers, claiming that they lack the skills and experience that are the strengths of U.S. and European financial firms. Japanese banks, for instance, must compete for the best graduates of the best universities with other industries and with government ministries—a sharp contrast with the United States, where investment banks, especially, can often pick and choose, competing only with one another. All this could change, but in the constrained growth scenario the change will come slowly.

Japan also has a currency that has not been widely used to denominate international transactions. The dollar remains the currency of choice in offshore financial markets, and, to a lesser degree, in trade (see Box 6–3). To the extent that these patterns continue, American financial services companies have a source of ongoing if modest advantage, while Japanese banks face a competitive hurdle. The Japanese, of course, understand this. Why have they not taken steps to make the yen more acceptable in international business circles? That is, given Japan's presence in world commerce, why has the European market not developed faster? Only in 1986—although the relative asset growth of Japan's banks has been visible for years—did the Ministry of Finance permit an offshore European market in Tokyo.

The reluctance of Japan's government is understandable. An open door for Japanese financial institutions to participate in international markets, and for the yen to become more widely used, necessarily implies opening Japan's *domestic* financial markets to foreigners. Indeed, this move would have to come first. For the yen to be a major currency internationally, both foreigners and Japanese must have greater freedom to move funds into and out of

Japan, to maintain accounts of all kinds, and to otherwise enter Japanese financial markets—as has been the case in dollars in the United States for years.

The MOF, one of the most powerful agencies in the Japanese government, although slowly loosening its grip on financial and monetary affairs, has no wish (at least in this scenario) to take liberalization nearly as far as it has gone in the United States. Japanese officials view "guidance" of the banking system as one of the critical elements in their country's postwar economic boom. With the postal savings system an important source of financing for Japan's budget deficits and outstanding debt—at interest rates low by world standards—the MOF has little enthusiasm for liberalization, which would raise the cost of servicing that debt. Furthermore, a wholesale loosening would make domestic monetary policy more difficult to implement, and leave the Japanese economy more vulnerable to ill-conceived monetary and fiscal policies elsewhere in the world—a decidedly unpleasant prospect to MOF officials.

Large Japanese corporations see things differently. Regardless of their view of the past, today most would argue that the closed nature of Japanese financial markets limits their strategic opportunities and competitive prospects. Corporations want to control their own financing, without interference from the government. The constrained growth scenario, therefore, hinges on the MOF surrendering its authority only grudgingly, and more often than not prevailing over corporate interests and other government agencies—for example, the Ministry of International Trade and Industry—that favor liberalization.

Indeed, the MOF appears to be split internally on this issue, with some factions advocating more rapid change. But the interplay of forces within the Japanese government, and the policies that emerge, tell only part of the story. Even assuming more freedom for Japan's banks, will they be able to increase their competitive presence as rapidly as Japanese manufacturing firms? Analogies do exist between Japan's growing competitiveness in financial services and past successes in manufacturing. But none of the analogies is particularly close. The constrained growth scenario treats the competitive precedents with skepticism, emphasizing the differences between financial services and the typical Japanese strategy in manufacturing (build scale at home; find attractive market niches overseas; export from a secure base in Japan, seeking greater market share; invest in foreign markets only when forced by political pressures and the threat of trade barriers).

In the constrained growth scenario, two key differences weaken the parallels with Japan's past competitive successes. First, U.S. banks are not easily outflanked. These are not steel companies, domestically oriented and comfortably ensconced behind barriers created by transportation costs thought high enough to keep out foreign products. Nor automakers, with an international perspective and many foreign investments, but with domestic products perceived as uniquely suited to U.S. market conditions. Nor even computer companies, with technological leads that shrank much faster than expected.

Banking was an international business before Columbus; Japanese banks have been participants for more than a hundred years. For several decades, American financial firms have won out in world markets against able foreign competitors through aggressive strategies and innovative products. Moreover, American banks compete strongly among themselves. Those that survive domestic competition are well-placed to compete internationally. Even more, an increasingly permissive U.S. regulatory environment has taught them how to maintain high levels of customer satisfaction without compromising efficiency. Finally, the U.S. industry benefits from a home market that is the center for new applications of computer hardware and software technologies, as well as telecommunications. Thus, to successfully attack the U.S. banking industry, any competitor must put together a coordinated strategy that can be effective on multiple dimensions; for example, offshore markets, business lending, retail banking, investment and brokerage activities, and applications of new technology. Those accepting the constrained growth scenario see little indication that the Japanese (or anyone else) have the capabilities to succeed in such an endeavor.

There is a second difference. The structure of this industry differs markedly from manufacturing sectors, where Japanese companies could begin by creating efficient production systems to supply domestic markets. When they identified market niches abroad—such as small, black-and-white televisions—Japanese firms could export and sell at low prices, taking advantage of their domestic base and local labor force. This is decidedly not the case in a service like banking. To compete, Japanese financial firms must maintain operations in world banking centers such as London and New York. They have to rely on the same labor pool and confront the same cultural traditions as others. They cannot depend on their strength at home, but have to develop competitive advantages in markets not only far away but also in the backyards of their strongest competitors. This is a new and different competitive environment for the Japanese, one in which success promises to be elusive.

For all these reasons, then, in the constrained growth scenario, Japanese competition will be slow to develop. Competitive thrusts by Japanese banks will be isolated, with little cumulative effect. U.S. financial service firms will maintain their international leads. The MOF, a conservative force within the Japanese bureaucracy, will not abandon the tools it believes are responsible for a favorable macroeconomic environment. Japanese financial markets will open only slowly. Meanwhile, the U.S. regulatory climate will remain conducive to American success.

Rapidly Mounting Competitiveness

What would it take to invert the preceding picture? More than anything else, ways in which Japan's banks could turn the enormous increase in Japanese-held financial assets to competitive advantage. Although this overseas asset growth cannot be attributed solely to the efforts of Japanese banks, the fact is that the assets are there, and Japanese banks (and others) have the opportunities (or problems) of managing them.

Not only have the largest Japanese banks grown bigger, but more Japanese banks are also now powerful enough to be serious players internationally; by some measures, Daiwa, ninth among Japanese banks, is larger than Chase. With expansion come new sources of competitive advantage: Japanese banks can pursue more strategies simultaneously, undertake more activities independently, without the need for correspondent banks or syndicates. Moreover, their asset holdings will continue to grow, at least for the next several years. Although Japan's exports have slowed somewhat, her trade surplus remains large; Japanese financial claims on the world will continue to mount.

Thus far, however, the Japanese approach to their overseas assets has been a conservative one, emphasizing safety. Funds have been held in foreign bank deposits, or invested in Treasury bills and notes, denominated in local currencies. While prudent, such strategies sacrifice many opportunities for greater earnings. A number of signs now point to a more active posture by the Japanese.

Almost any scenario that sees a rapidly expanding Japanese presence in international banking must begin with foreign direct investment in manufacturing. For 30 years, Japanese manufacturers have been very aggressive in seeking out export markets and in guaranteeing their supplies of raw materials (iron ore) and energy (coal and petroleum). Until recently, most of their other international ventures have been tentative and small in scale. Japanese investments in Western Europe remain a small fraction of U.S. investments there (a cumulative $11 billion, versus $107 billion for the United States).[16] Until the last few years, both business and government in Japan have directed their attention to internal development; electronics and automobile firms, for example, began building plants in the United States only after trade-related political pressures built to very high levels.

Now, of course, the picture is changing rapidly. Japanese manufacturing firms have stepped up their foreign investments and begun to establish truly multinational operations. In this, they are following in the footsteps of American firms—footsteps 30 or 40 years old. Just as American firms invested in Europe to assure continued access to markets there, Japanese companies now find themselves seeking to avoid incipient trade restrictions in both Europe and the United States. And, again like American firms before them, Japanese companies now see stronger ties with their foreign customers as a competitive necessity.

---

[16] "Japanese Investment in Europe," *Financial Times*, 13 November 1986, sec. III. Department of Commerce estimates placed U.S. foreign direct investment at 41 percent of the world total in 1981, compared to 7 percent for Japan. *International Direct Investment: Global Trends and the U.S. Role* (Washington, D.C.: Department of Commerce, 1984), p. 45.

Expansion abroad has inescapable consequences for the Japanese financial system, and for the government. Historical parallels suggest that Japanese banks will seek to expand overseas, following on the heels of manufacturing investments. U.S. banks moved abroad to service customers setting up offices and factories around the world. American companies preferred, and still prefer—all else equal—to deal with American financial institutions. But if the banks do not offer their services overseas, companies find alternatives in foreign banking industries. American banks had little choice but to follow their customers. Japanese banks have the same choice—or lack of choice. They, too, will follow their customers into foreign markets.

Providing familiar services to familiar customers in a foreign setting does not make an international bank, or an international industry; much more is necessary, beginning with accommodating government policies in both home and host countries. In general, favorable host-country policies already exist. Japanese manufacturers are moving into markets where other foreign firms—financial firms included—have been comfortable for years. Japanese government policies, as discussed above, seem a different matter. Indeed, the future policies of the MOF and other Japanese agencies will be perhaps the single most critical factor in determining rates of international expansion by Japanese banks.

With trade friction and political pressure mounting on many fronts, financial liberalization is but one of a series of policy questions facing Japan's government. For years, other countries have objected to export-led growth in Japan, and demanded reciprocal access to markets there. Beyond this, other countries have begun pressing the Japanese to behave more like a major world power. Japan's corporations, meanwhile, face stronger competition in their traditional export markets from developing countries—South Korea, Taiwan, and even Brazil. With Japanese manufacturers responding to new pressures in part through rapid increases in foreign investment, financial institutions, by every indication, wish to become more active not just in financing for Japanese corporations, but also in the entire range of banking services supplied internationally. Both manufacturing and banking sectors will press their views on the Japanese government—arguing that financial liberalization is necessary, and must come quickly. The real questions, then, concern the government's response.

As yet, the MOF has not been willing to move very far on domestic matters—a precondition for international expansion, for reasons outlined earlier. Still, many signs in both official reports and in the Japanese press indicate that the ministry will not try to stall liberalization indefinitely. MOF officials, like their counterparts elsewhere in the government, have many times acknowledged—to be sure, in vague and noncommittal ways—the need for Japan to take its rightful place among the world's economic powers.[17] Given changing attitudes elsewhere in Japan's government (and in some parts of the MOF), it is a reasonable presumption that, although the ministry may be able to fight a rear guard action, ultimately it will have to give way. In this second scenario, the MOF gives way sooner rather than later.

The major Japanese banks, foreseeing the eventual outcome on the policy front, clearly plan to be ready; they are attempting to gain experience, as quickly as possible, in the somewhat arcane ways of international banking. They still have a good deal to learn. Will Japanese banks be able to establish foreign branches and subsidiaries that can compete head-to-head with long-established and aggressive rivals? On such matters, the jury will be out for a number of years. But few today would underestimate the ability of Japanese firms in *any* industry to master the intricacies of international competition. And of course, the banks will not be alone. With the new foreign investments by Japanese manufacturing firms, Japanese financial institutions have a ready-made customer base, solid ground on which to build.

This leaves, finally, the question of whether the world will continue to rely on the U.S. dollar. The answer, in this scenario, is that it makes little real difference. The primacy of the dollar is not all that important for American financial firms. Non-U.S. banks compete effectively in offshore dollar markets already. Indeed,

---

[17] For example, "International Banking's Pending Issues Suddenly Unfold," *Japan Report,* Joint Publications Research Service JPRS-JAR-86-018, 19 December 1986, p. 58—an interview with Takotomo Otsu, International Finance Bureau, Ministry of Finance, translated from *Ginko Jihyo,* 16 September 1986.

banks from quite a large number of countries compete successfully in whatever markets they choose to enter, even if they cannot manage a presence across the board. Beyond this, the dollar will not necessarily retain its dominance over the longer run. Other currencies—notably the yen—could make inroads. This would, once again, require policy changes in Japan, but Japanese economic strength makes growing prominence for the yen inevitable.

In this scenario, then, Japanese competitiveness in international financial markets steadily increases. Japan's government raises its profile internationally, making clear its intent to protect the interests of Japanese banks should an international debt crisis arise. Major U.S. banks, vulnerable because of their exposures in the developing world, find the competitive balance tilting toward the largest holders of international deposits in the world.

It is too early to predict outcomes. But competition between the United States and Japan in financial services will certainly intensify. The competition will differ in many ways from that in manufacturing industries, but past experience suggests that it would be better for U.S. bankers and U.S. policymakers to err on the side of overestimating rather than underestimating the Japanese threat. Policymakers in the U.S. government tempted to urge their Japanese counterparts to liberalize rapidly might first think through the full range of possible consequences.

POLICY ISSUES

Governments everywhere regulate banking; in some places they own the banks. Rules set by governments determine the products offered, and, indirectly, the profits that are possible. Banking is a very special industry. Banks provide the mechanisms for creating, transferring, and storing money—essential for the exchange of goods and services. All industrial market economies have relatively complex and sophisticated banking systems. Banks are also special because of their role as depositories of savings and other financial assets. All governments take steps to protect consumer deposits. Finally, governments implement monetary policy through the banking system—in the United States, a process centering on the Federal Reserve Board (FRB). The special nature of banking means deregulation—permitting banks and banklike firms to respond more directly to market incentives—does not go too far. Deregulation tempts banks into riskier lines of business. But customer safety, and public perceptions of safety, keep governments involved in the banking industry, just as governments continue to regulate some aspects of the airline industry.

Given the special relationship between the government and the banking system, should federal agencies support U.S. banks internationally? If so, when and how? Or should the primary concern of policymakers be domestic financial services? In reality, such distinctions are false. As the scenarios for Japanese competition suggested, competitive ability depends in part on domestic policies—a fact of life in this and many other industries, although one that the U.S. government has seldom acted on, or even acknowledged.

Domestic Regulations

Separation of Commercial and Investment Banking

Although administrative and judicial decisions have widened the scope of activities permitted commercial banks, and the banklike businesses that compete with them, the Glass-Steagall Act and other U.S. laws and regulations continue to enforce a separation between investment and commercial banking. Few other countries divorce these two activities.

The argument for following much of the rest of the world in permitting universal banking begins with the steadily increasing integration of national capital markets, and the growth of hybrid products such as floating-rate notes that combine features of commercial and investment banking services. With securitization, investment banking products tend to replace commercial banking products. To be competitive in investment banking, moreover, now demands large amounts of capital—capital that U.S. commercial banks have, and U.S. investment banks need. Mergers and acquisitions involving U.S. investment banks—including the recent purchase by Sumitomo of a share in Goldman Sachs—have been driven by these requirements for capital. Finally, say the advocates of relaxation, the view that combining commercial and investment banking leads to potential conflicts of interest—the original reasoning behind Glass-Steagall—is no longer true, if it ever was (as shown in part by the lack of such problems in universal banking in Europe).[18]

The case for maintaining the separation with little or no change rests on a different logic. Removing the restrictions would work to the benefit of large commercial banks—many of which have made major errors in judgment in recent years. The implication? Relaxing Glass-Steagall and other restrictive policies might simply give big banks more room to make big mistakes, perhaps requiring new government interventions to resolve.

Whether one likes it or not, however, the walls between commercial and investment banking are crumbling. Policymakers must first ask, given continuing efforts by commercial banks to expand into these activities, whether it will be possible to continue enforcing the separation indefinitely. After all, commercial banks seek to move into investment banking in part to counter the thrusts of other financial and nonfinancial firms into their own territory—thrusts made possible by deregulation in the United States over the past decade.

In a climate of contagious deregulation can the barriers between commercial and investment banking hold? Our analysis suggests that, in the long run, they cannot. The analysis also suggests that the regulatory separation has had only limited significance for the international competitiveness of the U.S. financial services industry (helping in some ways, hurting in others)—but that a policy of attempting to preserve the separation indefinitely could be inefficient if not counterproductive.

U.S. banks continue expending effort and resources in finding ways to circumvent the rules—effort that might better be directed elsewhere. The questions then become: When and how should the rules be relaxed? Should policymakers permit gradual and selective entry by commercial banks into some but not all currently prohibited businesses? Or should the prohibitions simply be dropped at some agreed time? It may be time for Congress to confront these issues more directly.

---

[18] For the historical background, see I. Walter, *Barriers to Trade in Banking and Financial Services* (London: Trade Policy Research Centre, 1985).

Regulation of Interstate Banking

The other major division imposed on the banking industry by U.S. legislation, in the form of the McFadden Act, together with subsequent laws restricting bank holding companies, has been geographic: banks were not to expand across state lines. Here, judicial rulings, legislative changes, and technological developments have combined to undermine many of the prohibitions written into the law, as these affect wholesale and international banking.

Indeed, at this point, permitting unlimited interstate banking would make little difference for the international postures of U.S. banks, with one exception. In several parts of the United States, existing small to medium-sized banks have begun to merge into super-regional firms—often taking advantage of legal provisions that favor their expansion over existing money-center banks. Although few do much overseas business currently, some will probably grow large enough to support operations in say, London—and in doing so, recapturing customers lost to correspondent and money-center banks. (NCNB, of North Carolina, is one of only six U.S. banks with membership on the London Stock Exchange.)

While the emergence of these super-regional banks will take time, they could eventually provide a source of new vitality, helping the U.S. industry maintain its competitive position. In sum, there seems little reason based on international considerations for Congress to consider changes in the laws governing interstate banking.

The Banking Infrastructure

The Federal Reserve Board (FRB), along with agencies such as the FDIC, maintains a dual relationship with the U.S. banking system. On the one hand, as a regulator, the board sets rules under which banks must operate. On the other hand, the FRB also supplies banking services—notably clearing and settlement for member banks, a critical part of the nation's banking infrastructure. How well government agencies fulfill their functions as instrinsic parts of the banking system helps to determine the competitive position of the U.S. industry.

When a Korean firm borrows dollars, the transfer of funds from the lender's account to that of the borrower normally takes place through the CHIPS system, while the net settlement between banks involves FedWire (Box 6–2). FedWire, CHIPS, and the other elements in an efficient transfer system have played key roles in maintaining the dominant position of the dollar in world commerce. By legislation, the FRB's FedWire system is to be a break-even service.[19] In recent years, the board, in its role as regulator and provider of net settlement services, has acted in ways that insulate FedWire from competition. For instance, the FRB has imposed caps on daylight overdrafts regardless of whether the overdrafts are on FedWire or a competing service. Banks, needing to carefully monitor their overdrafts, have tended to give more of their business to FedWire, at the expense of private competitors.[20] Fewer rivals for FedWire could mean less pressure to keep prices low and reliability high—the principal issue for policymakers.

The possibility of conflicts between the FRB's concern for its own profitability and its regulatory responsibilities will exist so long as the FRB acts both as competitor and regulator; given the importance of FedWire and other portions of the banking infrastructure for the nation's competitive position, maintaining the efficiency of this infrastructure becomes an ongoing policy issue of some significance. If anything, the Monetary Control Act of 1980, which requires the FRB to cover its costs, may encourage the board to use its regulatory power to reduce competition, and, with it, the efficiency of the payments process.

Safety and Stability of the Financial System

Like the FRB, the FDIC provides services to the U.S. banking industry—deposit insurance, for which banks pay an annual premium—while also functioning as a regulatory body. In practice, the FDIC may act to protect all deposits, even those in overseas branches, given its overriding concern with preventing bank failures in the first place. The FDIC's policy of protecting banks to

---

[19] In 1984, the board reported that FedWire had become largely self-supporting, and that its wire transfer services as a whole had made a $3.5 million profit. *Seventy-first Annual Report, Board of Governors of the Federal Reserve Board* (Washington, D.C.: Federal Reserve Board, 1985), p. 194.

[20] See J. W. H. Watson, "Fed Drives Out Competitors in Bank Fund Transfers," *Wall Street Journal*, 13 March 1986, p. 30. Bankwire, founded in 1952, and by 1971 jointly owned by some 200 U.S. banks, ceased operations in February 1986.

protect depositors means that new financial products may, like overseas deposits, get the benefits of the FDIC umbrella even though in principle outside its coverage (and even though no premiums are paid). Standby letters of credit, for example, create contingent liabilities for the bank. If the borrower fails, the liability becomes a real one. A deposit insurance program that prevents bank failures has the effect of insuring SLCs as well, even though the FDIC's legal obligations may not extend this far (a question at present unanswered).

SLCs are only one of many examples where the FDIC's nominally domestic guarantees can affect international competition. But it would be wrong to suggest that FDIC protection creates major competitive advantages for U.S.-owned banks. Other industrialized countries are no more likely to let their large banks fail than is the United States. The issues revolve around the implicit subsidies provided by such guarantees.

Governments everywhere stand behind their financial systems. In doing so, they help their banks compete. Unless governments collect fees or premiums reflecting the risk of failure, they are subsidizing these banks. Subsidies may well be justified, considering the benefits to the public at large, but they nonetheless raise the question of distortions internationally. Movement toward standardizing practices across countries—for example, tying premiums to the protection actually provided, thus reducing subsidy levels, or reducing uncertainty as to the immediacy of payment in the event of a failure—would be a significant step toward a level playing field. Another step would be to pursue international agreements aimed at coordinating regulatory and supervisory practices, thereby reducing the need for either implicit or explicit insurance. Put another way, international coordination of regulatory practices can reduce the potential for distortions in financial markets. International agreements aimed at standardizing such practices, although they might take years to achieve, merit high priority as a U.S. negotiating objective.

Problem loans to developing countries raise similar issues. Some of these loans pose potential threats to the solvency of large U.S. banks. How far should the federal government go toward lessening these threats? The Baker Plan—a U.S. initiative proposed by former Treasury Secretary James Baker, calling for joint action by the banks, the borrowing countries, and multinational lending institutions such as the World Bank—would help the borrowing countries service their debt, thereby reducing risks for the banks. But perhaps more effective government policies could have kept the banks out of their present troubles. LDC loans also raise the questions of coordinating policies toward loss reserve requirements—currently stricter in the United States than in Japan, for example.

Given the trends outlined in this chapter, policymakers may wish to consider risk-related insurance premiums as an alternative to other forms of regulatory interventions in the financial services industry. The Third World debt situation provides perhaps the strongest argument for such an approach. The problem, of course, lies in making the judgments about riskiness, particularly for new or different ventures. Still, that is what insurance is all about.

Does the United States Need a New Approach to Banking Regulations?

The U.S. deposit insurance system, the regulatory separation between investment and commercial banking, and restrictions on interstate banking all stem from legislation passed in the aftermath of the banking collapse of the 1930s. The laws have been modified over the years, but with no fundamental shift in philosophy. In the practice of banking, however, change has been sweeping—both internationally and domestically, for example, the rise of nonbank banks. Perhaps it is time for Congress to consider comprehensive new banking legislation.

Reasons for considering a new approach begin with interactions between spheres of regulatory and supervisory practice once largely independent, but no longer so. For example, lifting the Glass-Steagall restrictions would force changes in FDIC insurance; otherwise, the insurance umbrella would, in effect, be stretched over a wide range of risky activities for which it was never intended. Banks with FDIC coverage would be competing with uninsured nonbanks, that could legitimately protest unfair competition. One alternative would be to switch the basis for regulation from an institutional focus (i.e., regulating what a particular type of institution can do) to functional regulation. Commercial banks might then be permitted activities currently denied them under

Glass-Steagall (and other current laws), but in turn directed to treat funds from different sources differently. For example, individual depositors could be protected by requiring banks (and nonbanks) to invest funds from small depositors only in short-term Treasury securities, and to give such depositors priority in the event of a voluntary or involuntary liquidation—thereby reducing or eliminating the need for insurance to protect consumers.

Future Policies: Negotiating Objectives

Data for Analysis
The federal government collects a great deal of data on international banking compared with other service industries; unfortunately, none of it measures international banking activity in ways that correspond to exports and imports in other industries.[21] Because existing data can offer little guidance for policymakers on probable consequences of changes in either foreign or domestic policies, banking and other financial services deserve high priority in any effort to improve data collection and analysis relating to trade in services. In the absence of such information, policymakers might, in fact, wish to de-emphasize liberalization of trade in financial services simply because the consequences for the U.S. economy cannot be predicted.

Dealing with Restrictions Abroad
U.S. financial services firms face severe restrictions in many foreign countries.[22] Some governments simply deny entry to foreign banks, or limit the businesses they can pursue; until recently,

---

[21] *Trade in Services: Exports and Foreign Revenues* (Washington, D.C.: Office of Technology Assessment, September 1986). The special problems posed by measuring trade in financial services are summarized on p. 40, with OTA's own estimates for foreign revenues in commercial banking on pp. 56–58. These estimates suggest that the foreign revenues (not exports of U.S. banks) probably exceeded $12 billion in 1984, but the underlying date are too weak to place a great deal of confidence in this or any figure.

[22] For details, see "National Treatment Study: Report to Congress on Foreign Government Treatment of U.S. Commercial Banking and Securities Organizations, 1986 Update," Department of the Treasury, Washington, D.C., December 1986. Also; earlier Treasury Department national treatment studies (in 1979 and 1984); *International Trade in Services: Banking* (Paris: Organization for Economic Cooperation and Development, 1984); and "Direct Sources of Competitiveness in Banking Services," prepared for OTA by J. G. Kallberg and A. Saunders under contract No. 533-5640, pp. 5.5–5.47.

Sweden prohibited any foreign bank office from accepting deposits or making loans. Some countries deny foreign-owned banks full access to the central bank discount window; foreign banks must often use clearing systems controlled by their local competitors.

There are cases in which U.S. banks can engage in activities denied to local banks. Until the early 1980s, only foreign banks in Japan could make foreign currency loans to Japanese borrowers—a lucrative business. Opening the market to Japanese banks has hurt onshore firms. But in general, foreign government policies limit U.S. banks compared to their local rivals, with restrictions on the type of foreign presence—branches, subsidiaries, agencies—making it difficult for U.S. banks to operate as integrated multinationals. Australia, Canada, Finland, New Zealand, Norway, and Sweden, among others, permit foreign banks to establish subsidiaries but not branches. This imposes more of an arm's-length relationship than other organizational forms. Some countries limit transfers of funds across their borders. Negotiations that would help American banks integrate their worldwide operations deserve high priority.

Unfortunately, the 1978 International Banking Act removes a potential level for U.S. negotiators. So long as the law is in place, the United States cannot really threaten to reciprocate when other countries place burdensome restrictions on U.S.-owned institutions. A credible threat of reciprocity in banking regulations, even if never called on in practice, could be a negotiating advantage for the United States. Congress may wish to consider amending the International Banking Act to this effect.

International Coordination
Each country has its own banking regulations, with many differences. South Korean companies seeking to expand have a difficult time raising money in part because of restrictions on Korean banks. And if a Korean bank tries to float bonds in the United States for a Korean corporation, it faces restrictions that limit the foreign portfolio holdings of American purchasers. For such reasons, the Korean company is more than likely to go to the Euromarket, where neither Korean nor U.S. regulations apply. Similarly, a multinational corporation does business with banks wherever it can make the best deal. U.S.-based MNCs borrow

from European or Japanese banks if lower capital ratio requirements permit better terms than American banks can offer. European banks and governments, meanwhile, argue that their tighter supervision of off-balance-sheet activities handicaps them unfairly in markets for, say, floating-rate notes.

The dilemma is plain. Asymmetries in regulations induce banks to move their operations elsewhere—for example, to offshore markets. If national governments maintain their regulations unchanged, their domestic banking industries lose business and their regulatory agencies lose control. They can either try to extend their regulatory grasp to the offshore market or liberalize domestically. Offshore markets cannot be unilaterally regulated, but U.S. policymakers have nonetheless sought at times to have it both ways. The FRB's decision in 1981 to permit U.S. and foreign banks to establish international banking facilities (IBFs) in the United States represents an attempt to compete with offshore markets by permitting lightly regulated Eurodollar-like markets here. But in part because IBFs still must live with more regulations than competing offshore establishments, growth has been slow. Attracting more of this business to the United States would mean relaxing regulations that the FRB considers important for the stability of the U.S. banking system.

Where banks and their customers meet in international capital markets, then, banks press their governments for treatment at least as lenient as their foreign rivals, or seek agreements that impose tighter standards on those rivals. U.S. banks argue for higher capital ratios elsewhere or lower ones in the United States. But the function of such regulations is to preserve stability—an objective difficult to question so long as regulations do not unnecessarily sap efficiency. All this suggests that, difficult as it may be to achieve, international coordination of policies toward banking should be a paramount goal—that this is one industry where the hoary notion of a level playing field has real meaning as a policy objective; there is no reason to permit large financial institutions or large MNCs to play off governments—each with good reasons for regulating financial services—against one another.

U.S. policymakers should continue balancing the need for safety and stability in the nation's banking system—and the ability to pursue monetary policy—against the benefits of a more liberal and presumably more efficient banking system worldwide. Policy-makers may also find it time to begin considering whether to move beyond coordinated national policies toward supranational supervision and regulation of financial services.

CONCLUDING REMARKS

International banking has grown very rapidly in the postwar period. U.S. financial services firms have been preeminent over much of this time, although banks from other countries have often grown faster. These strides by foreign banks do not mean that the competitive abilities of American financial institutions have diminished so much as that other economies have been expanding rapidly, and their banking industries are becoming stronger.

Banks compete not only with one another, but also with their customers. Businesses turn to banks for financing needs ranging from cash management and short-term revolving credit to the structuring of complex financial packages for capital expansion and overseas investment. Large corporations need financial institutions relatively less than smaller companies. Multinationals have the capability to manage their own cash and market their own commercial paper, although they may need banks for access to the clearing system or for insuring their paper. As a corporation's own cash management system improves, its banks must maintain an edge or lose business; if the banks get better, the corporate treasury operation will, too.

Electronic cash management is possible only because of developments in computer and communications systems; data processing and telecommunications technologies help integrate world capital markets, make new banking products possible, and provide faster and cheaper delivery of traditional banking services. As electronic messages have replaced paper and the telephone, the amount of information available to bankers making decisions on loans or currency transactions has increased enormously.

Innovations in financial products and in the technology for delivering services have helped American banks maintain their competitive positions. U.S.-based institutions have dominated in markets for new products such as interest rate swaps and Eurobonds. They have adapted rapidly to securitization; when it comes to technologies used in trading securities, American firms lead the rest of the world by substantial margins. In many markets, U.S. banks have been successful despite inherent disadvantages; examples include banker's acceptances for third-party trade, and securities underwriting in foreign currencies.

At the same time, foreign banks have dramatically increased their presence in the United States (although expansion has slowed in the last several years). Does this imply lagging competitiveness by U.S. banks in their home market? We have found little evidence to suggest such an interpretation; foreign banks come here in part to gain experience in a highly competitive, deregulated, and technologically advanced industry; the very fact that U.S. financial services firms remain highly competitive internationally attracts foreign banks seeking to learn from U.S. experience. As in other industries, the size and wealth of the nation's economy attracts foreign firms.

Many of the forces that have worked to the advantage of U.S. competitiveness in the past promise to continue to do so. But competitive patterns can and will change. Americans—both as individuals and as corporate officers—may think first of Merrill Lynch or Chase Manhattan when it comes to financial services, whether domestic or international. Japanese feel the same way about Nomura Securities and Fuji Bank. Nonetheless, U.S. automakers, who once bought all their steel from American steelmakers, now purchase overseas as well. Today, American corporations increasingly seek financing on the world market.

Competition among the world's major banks has tended to keep differences in the price and characteristics of services relatively small. Still, banks differ in corporate strategy, in marketing skills, and in production efficiency. Seldom are these differences large enough to enable banks from one country to quickly or easily take business from foreign rivals who have comfortable working relationships with major customers. Over time, they do have a cumulative impact on market share and other indicators of competitive success.

But the financial institutions in the advanced industrial economies will probably not diverge very much in the factors that determine competitive outcomes. Market forces will keep them close together (in the absence of massive changes in the world economy). Innovations in banking products and in back-office production technologies diffuse with considerable speed. Other governments are following the U.S. lead in deregulating financial markets. Both forces—technology and deregulation—point toward increasing convergence. If anything, the competition that already exists in the United States and in offshore markets—and the multinational character of U.S. banks—will give them ongoing opportunities to attract customers based in foreign countries. American banks that take advantage of these opportunities should continue to do well internationally.

The forces at work in financial services will also lead to greater cross-penetration of major markets, both domestically (in the form of regional and perhaps nationwide banking) and internationally. Moves by banks like Citicorp and Chase into regional U.S. markets find their analogs in competition in Tokyo and London, as well as New York, among banks and securities houses from many countries. British banks are moving in the same directions as American banks—and for many of the same reasons. The deregulation of the London stock exchange, the Big Bang of October 1986, will surely speed the convergence of financial services offered by U.S. and British firms (although London is currently behind in technology).

Deregulation in Japan has been slower, with Japanese banks less willing than their American counterparts to test the limits of existing laws and regulations. Even so, banks in Japan have been pushing for greater freedom of action for some time. In 1979, for example, arguing that restrictions on managing issues overseas only applied to public offerings, the wholly owned Swiss subsidiary of Fuji Bank took the lead role in managing a Swiss franc private issue for a Japanese construction company. These and subsequent thrusts by Fuji and other Japanese banks led to the de facto reinterpretation of parts of Section 65 of Japan's Securities and Exchange Law controlling the separation of commercial and investment banking in Japan.[23]

---

[23] W. Hayden, "Internationalizing Japan's Financial System," *Japan's Economy: Coping with Change in the International Environment*, D. I. Okimoto, ed. (Boulder, Colo.: Westview Special Studies Series, 1982), pp. 99–100.

Internationally, with so many players in each market, price competition will continue to be intense. Customers will be able to switch easily among competing banks; the banks will be under constant pressure to hold down prices. Real or threatened competition will keep margins low, making financial services unprofitable by the standards of the late 1970s—not only in major world markets, but also in many markets previously viewed as local or regional. In this competitive milieu, the leading banks from each country may well change. The big banks in the major industrial countries will be carrying the burdens of past mistakes for years to come; loan portfolios weighted down with Third-World debt limit their strategic options. Emerging super-regional banks in the United States, with stronger balance sheets, may be able to take international business away from larger banks that must avoid new risks. At the same time, regional banks—in the United States, Japan, and elsewhere—will face much stronger competition in their traditional markets. As a result, the high profit levels of regional and super-regional banks will probably diminish.

Governments affect competitive dynamics in this industry through regulatory and supervisory policies, directly and indirectly. All governments view banking as a special industry. In seeking to protect depositors, particularly individuals for political reasons, they inevitably have an interest in the fortunes of individual banks. But national regulations have become increasingly difficult to maintain; when one country deregulates, others may have little choice but to follow. With national regulatory structures growing more porous, real dangers of instability on a global scale follow. Given ongoing integration in world financial markets, it may be time to seriously consider supranational regulation of those markets.

Governments not only regulate, some own and operate financial institutions. Although postal savings banks, for example, may have no direct presence internationally, they can nonetheless affect competitiveness indirectly. Japan's postal savings system—the largest depository institution in the world—makes the Japanese government cooler than it might otherwise be toward liberalization. By increasing competition for deposits—and, in effect, giving Japanese savers access to the higher market interest rates set internationally—liberalization would force the postal savings system to pay out more in interest.

As Japanese manufacturing firms continue to invest in other countries, Japanese banks will follow. As they do, they will mount more substantial and more sophisticated competitive challenges to the leading American financial firms, in this aided by Japan's very large holdings of foreign assets—a legacy of many years of trade surpluses. At this point, many of the decisions that will determine the pace and force of this challenge remain matters of domestic Japanese politics; if those advocating rapid change in Japan's own financial markets win, further penetration of Japanese banks into international financial markets will come quickly; if the conservative Ministry of Finance manages to hold onto most of its control over Japan's domestic markets, the pace will be slower.

What then of the outlook for U.S. financial service firms? Deregulation and new competition will, as always, make for winners and losers. Some foreign banks may continue growing faster than American banks, if only because they service faster-growing economies. Japanese firms like Nomura Securities will continue expanding in the United States to serve Japanese (and American) clients. Leading U.S. institutions will report profits below traditional levels, some of the super-regional banks will flounder, some large banks may shrink dramatically. Mergers, possibly involving some of the biggest banks—U.S., Japanese, European—will continue.

By several measures, particularly in asset size, U.S. banks have lost ground in recent years. Given the ongoing shift in international banking from lending to fee-based services, these losses—and the gains by Japanese banks—are not so serious as they would otherwise be. But a major competitive challenge to the American financial services industry is coming from the Japanese. The outcomes may be in doubt, but not the gravity of the threat to U.S. competitiveness.

CHAPTER 7

INVESTMENT AND
MERCHANT BANKS

Roy C. Smith

International transactions involving loans and securities have occurred more or less continuously since the 15th century, when both commerce and conflict between the city-states of Europe had to be financed by means other than taxes. Those who provided the finance, like the Medicis of medieval Florence, had to be well connected with decisionmakers, maintain a wide network of sources of information and influence, and possess an exquisite sense of timing. They had to be clever, be able to react quickly, and be—or at least appear to be—unquestionably sound themselves. Though the business was imperiled by the intrigues of others as well as the risk of the market, for those who could compete in it successfully the rewards could be very great. Banker-adventurers have been closely involved with, or at least not far behind, most of the great events of modern European history and, especially, its colonial period. Financial skills have always been in demand, and many of the functions performed today are not so different from those carried out 500 years ago.

However, the scale and the volume of transactions, the speed at which they are conducted, and the vast array of products now available is far beyond anything our financial forefathers could have imagined. So is the extent to which the international component of finance has grown and become institutionalized.

The great players are no longer private banking houses but

substantial financial institutions whose activities span the globe. They come from America as commercial and investment banks; from Europe as merchant banks, banques d'affaires, and universal banks; and from Japan as long-term credit banks, city banks, trust banks, and securities firms. Though in some countries regulations require separation between deposit taking and loan making on one hand, and securities underwriting and trading on the other, such regulations do not apply beyond the borders of the countries involved. The world beyond one's own borders is often referred to in financial parlance as "offshore," where national regulations do not apply. For regulatory purposes, it is a stateless world. There various banks compete in Eurobond and equity securities and international investments of all types.

In recent years the volume of bond and equity financing conducted in the Euromarkets and involving transactions between national markets has grown very rapidly. Linkages between markets have increased to an extent that conditions in one market affect those in others, leading us to conceive of world financial markets as having become "globalized." In the case of major industrialized countries, barriers to cross-border financial transactions have declined to almost nothing. Deregulation of the financial services sector in many countries has led to increased competition and exposure to international markets. Prodigious improvements in telecommunications have made it possible for markets to become integrated. These developments have greatly expanded the range of alternatives available to those from all over the industrialized world who seek to raise money or invest it (see Chart 7–1).

Major markets for securities, foreign exchange, and commodities have come to be centered in New York City, London, and Tokyo and trading between these markets in almost all instruments goes on around the clock. The international securities business has become large, complex, diverse, highly competitive, and risky. As in the days of the Medicis, to survive today's players must continue to be able to adapt to changes in the marketplace, particularly the international market in which traditional regulatory orderliness does not apply. The 1980s have been and the 1990s will continue to be times of great competitive and strategic repositioning by the world's major financial institutions and providers of financial services.

CHART 7–1
Causes and Consequences of Globalization

Caused by
- Deregulation abroad
- Greater institutionalization abroad
- Success of Euromarkets
- Integration of markets
- Technology and know-how

Led to
- Increased cross-border investments
- Wider range of alternatives for clients
- Three-market capability
- Need for larger firms
- Greater risk exposure
- Greater commitment of capital overseas
- Management complexities

EUROPEAN ORIGINS

Banking in Europe has an extremely long, rich, and varied history. From widely different origins, banks of many types have evolved through time into what are thought of today as investment and merchant banks. In medieval Italy various northern cities developed deposit banking from pawnbrokering and money changing. These banks became skilled in transferring money required for trade between Tuscany and other parts of Europe. They established branches or agencies in France, Spain, Belgium, Holland, Germany, and Britain. To secure advantages in these foreign areas, including profitable export concessions and currency exchange, the Italians were persuaded to advance funds to English and other monarchs who quite frequently defaulted, often bringing down whoever was then holding the king's paper. As the Italians faded, merchants from the south of Germany took their place in the 16th century. The famous Fuggers of Augsburg were merchants who traded all over Europe through "factories," or branches containing a warehouse and a countinghouse in various countries.

The Fuggers are credited with developing the system of financial intermediation in which they would borrow from wealthy depositors to lend to others. Other merchants, such as the Rothschilds of Frankfurt, goldsmiths, and public notaries became increasingly active as financial intermediaries through the 18th and 19th centuries when they came to be called merchant bankers. Often the transactions financed by the banks were international and involved trade with colonial areas frequently short of credit.

By the 19th century, most of such houses had left the commercial aspects of their business behind to specialize in the seemingly more profitable and less risky business of lending, usually against good collateral, to support trade between other parties. Often clients would ask their merchant bankers to "accept," or guarantee, receivables due from customers of the client or the client's own obligations to make payment for goods or services so these notes could be discounted for cash at banks. In the United Kingdom virtually all of today's merchant banks are designated accepting houses authorized to do business with the Bank of England. Many great names of finance, such as Rothschild, Baring, and Lehman, began as merchants who later became bankers.[1]

Raising Funds and Managing Money

In addition to financing trade and commerce, merchant bankers often performed other services for their clients. For those needing money for capital investments they arranged loans in the form of secured or promissory notes which they sold to investors, many of whom were purchasers of the trade paper which was also sold by the bank. For those with large fortunes seeking good quality investments, they offered advice and found opportunities. Some German bankers, many of whom were descendants of Jewish merchants and goldsmiths from Berlin, Hamburg, Frankfurt, and the Rhineland, evolved as private bankers to monarchs, governments and large corporations which were constantly seeking funds, and to wealthy families whose money required skillful management. Names such as Warburg and Bleichroder, along with Rothschild, are those of prominent European private bankers who have

---

[1] Charles P. Kindleberger, *A Financial History of Western Europe* (Winchester, Mass.: Allen & Unwin, 1985), pp. 42–46, 81–82.

survived to the present. Other European banks, especially the Swiss, specialized in money management of funds left in the bank's custody by wealthy families and individuals. Political disruption, wars, and economic restrictions resulted in large amounts of private wealth flowing into Switzerland during this century where it could be left with the large universal banks in Zurich or Basel, or with the smaller, more specialized and intimate private banks such as Pictet, Hensch, and Lombard Odier which today are located mainly in Geneva.

In the latter part of the 19th century a type of bank specializing in investments in industry, called banques d'affairs, developed in France and Belgium. Banks such as the Banque de Paris et de Pays-Bas (Paribas) made loans and invested their own and client funds in securities, including common stock, in many companies included on its large list of industrial corporate clients. Because of the substantial amount of capital required for these investments, only the larger banks developed industrial portfolios to any significant degree. Elsewhere in Europe, the larger German, Swiss, and other continental banks that engaged in all aspects of banking from deposit taking to investment management came to be called universal banks. These, especially the German universal banks, have made substantial investments in their industrial clients, especially during the periods after the world wars.

INVESTMENT BANKING IN THE UNITED STATES

Two main tasks to be accomplished by investment bankers in the United States during the 19th century were the establishment of networks and connections through which European capital could be channeled into the United States, and the organization of an internal American securities distribution system.

Several prominent London banks such as Baring Brothers and Rothschilds were represented in the United States by the 1840s, in the latter case by the wealthy, socially prominent, and powerful figure of August Belmont. London connections were vital to any ambitious American financial house and several of these located representatives in England to look after their business there and to widen their circle of acquaintances. Alexander Brown of Baltimore organized in the early 1800s the London firm of Brown Shipley, headed by one of his sons, and branches in New York and Philadelphia headed by other sons. The New York firm ultimately became Brown Brothers & Harriman.

Another American, George Peabody of Boston, founded his own firm in London after representing others there for many years. He accepted as a partner in 1854 one Junius S. Morgan, a dry-goods merchant of Boston. On Peabody's retirement to pursue a second career as a philanthropist, for which he was offered (but declined) a knighthood by Queen Victoria, the firm's name was changed to J. S. Morgan & Co. The firm, which later became known as Morgan Grenfell & Co., was represented in New York and Philadelphia by Junius' son, J. Pierpont Morgan, who had set up his own firm in 1860. The younger Morgan went on to become the most important and celebrated investment banker in United States' history. Morgan's firm distributed stocks and bonds of U.S. corporations in Europe, and later of European governments and corporations in the United States. It also organized some of the largest corporations in America—such as U.S. Steel in 1901—by merging several independent producers into a new giant, capitalizing the new company with both debt and equity, and underwriting the sale of these securities to investors through syndication operations in the U.S. and Europe. Much of what investment bankers in the United States do today, including mergers and acquisitions, the distribution of various securities, and restructuring and recapitalizing underperforming companies, was first done before World War I. J. P. Morgan and his associates operated in a totally unregulated, unprotected environment that created many opportunities as well as many hazards for bankers. The relationships between bankers and clients were extremely close, with bankers and their partners occupying several seats on the boards of directors of client companies and participating actively in management decisions. Rapidly growing, capital-intensive businesses benefited from these relationships, because through the sponsorship of these better known financiers they could have access to the markets for working and investment capital.[2]

---

[2] Vincent P. Carosso, *Investment Banking in America* (Cambridge, Mass.: Harvard Univ. Press, 1970), pp. 29–75.

In the 1860s, a number of Jewish banking firms with German origins, some of which had prospered during the Civil War by selling U.S. government securities to investors in Germany, began to rise in prominence. Among these were J. & W. Seligman, Kuhn Loeb, Lehman Brothers, and Goldman Sachs. All of these firms had strong European connections which they were able to employ successfully in distributing U.S. securities. The Jewish firms were especially active around the turn of the century in selling securities of retailing and light manufacturing companies. Goldman Sachs and Lehman Brothers are credited with devising the first initial public offerings of common stock in the United States with issues by General Cigar Manufacturing Co. and Sears, Roebuck & Company in 1906.[3]

The general distribution of securities in the United States developed slowly. The main activity of the domestic brokerage business was the sale of U.S. government securities, particularly those issued to finance wars. The U.S. Treasury floated a $16 million war bond in 1813, most of which could not be sold to the public and had to be purchased by three wealthy New Yorkers. The Civil War produced somewhat better results. The first national brokerage effort was undertaken by J. Cooke, who sold large quantities of Civil War bonds through a national sales organization. Subsequently he applied his organization to the sale of municipal and some corporate, mainly railroad, securities. The Cooke firm failed in 1873 in one of the periodic panics that characterized 19th-century American finance. Other competitors, however, rose in its place including the First National Bank of New York, which was founded in 1863 and was active in investment banking and securities distribution until 1933.

After 1900 there was sufficient investment capital available in the United States for large issues to be completely taken up by U.S. investors. Indeed, in the period between the world wars, the U.S. market accommodated substantial issues of foreign securities, many of which were issued by Latin American governments that ultimately defaulted. To manage such large issues of securities, the "underwriting syndicate" was devised. Such syndicates

---

[3] Ibid., pp. 1–28.

were formed by grouping a hundred or so securities firms into tiers, according to the financial capacity and prestige of individual firms, to purchase as a group an entire issue of securities for resale over a period of time, in an orderly manner, to institutional, individual, and overseas investors.[4]

The twenties were boom years, especially for the issuance of new corporate and investment company securities. Private banks like J. P. Morgan and Kuhn Loeb dominated the new issues business, but well capitalized securities affiliates of the major commercial banks, such as First National Corporation and Chase Securities Corp., were also quite active in bringing new issues to the market as well as in secondary market trading. During the feverish period of the late twenties, many excesses occurred. Ultimately, the stock market crash of October 29, 1929, triggered the collapse of financial markets in other countries, and a combination of nonresponsive monetary policies and restrictive trade legislation helped to bring on the Great Depression of the 1930s. Banks were blamed for causing the crash and subsequent hard times. Concerned by the collapse of banks around the country and inspired by the activist administration of newly elected President Franklin Roosevelt, the Congress passed legislation that had major effects on the banking and securities businesses in the United States.

The trauma of the Great Depression, with its contraction of world trade and numerous sovereign defaults, caused a 30-year hiatus in international banking. The international environment of the 30s and 40s, characterized by waves of nationalism, socialism, and militarism was far less conducive to international finance than had been the previous 115 years of the Pax Britannica. Free market mechanisms were perceived to have failed and governments assumed an unprecedented role in regulating economies. Bankers, wounded by bank failures and loan defaults, and now subject to extensive government regulation, largely accepted their new role as managers of financial "public utilities" providing liquidity and services under careful supervision of regulators.

When the United States emerged from isolationism to fund the

---

[4] Ibid., pp. 51–78.

Allied war effort and subsequently to reconstruct an economically devastated Europe through the Marshall Plan, the U.S. government, not the banks, was the provider of the funds. Governments, in cooperation with one another, created the World Bank and the IMF at the Bretton Woods conference in 1944. These new institutions were to have the principal role in lending to developing countries and to prop up currencies. In the 50s and early 60s, U.S. capital was exported abroad through direct foreign investment of U.S. multinational corporations, which attracted the banks again to the foreign environment. This environment expanded dramatically during the 60s and 70s.

The so-called Glass-Steagall provisions of the 1933 Banking Act required all banking institutions to discontinue participation in the corporate securities business. This resulted in the formation of two separate and distinct banking industries in the United States made up of commercial banks and investment banks. The former were subject to either state or federal bank regulation, and were allowed to make bank loans, and to accept deposits (which were entitled to U.S. government insurance up to a maximum amount through the Federal Deposit Insurance Corporation (FDIC), also created in 1933). Commercial banks were also entitled to borrow from the Federal Reserve, which would act as a lender of last resort. Investment banks, so named because they dealt in investment securities, were not banks at all. They were underwriters, brokers, and dealers in negotiable securities. With the exception of U.S. government and certain municipal securities, commercial banks were not permitted to participate in these businesses. Investment banks and other securities firms were made subject to regulation by the Securities and Exchange Commission, as provided for in the landmark 1933 and 1934 Securities Acts which were enacted after the stock market crash of 1929. Although denied access to the banking business, securities firms were allowed to finance customer purchases of securities under margin rules promulgated by the Federal Reserve and to underwrite issues of commercial paper, or short-term promissory notes, sold by top-rated corporations to raise working capital. Commercial banks were not, initially, deemed eligible to participate in the commercial paper business, which became exclusive to investment banks and

those corporations large enough to issue their ov
The provisions of the Glass-Steagall Act, howe
outside the United States, where vigorous cor
banks and investment banks in both the banking
businesses has been going on for more than a decade.

Many changes have occurred over recent years which have affected the divisions of labor between commercial banks and the various investment and merchant banking organizations around the world. In the United States the securities business has grown much more rapidly since 1975 than the banking business, and many commercial banks, seeking to enter this promising field, have endeavored to secure changes and liberalizations to the Glass-Steagall Act. As of the end of 1988, banks have succeeded in forcing the erosion of the act in many significant areas (including the ability to enter the commercial paper business and to underwrite a limited amount of corporate bonds and related securities), but the main prohibitions against unrestricted underwriting of corporate securities and engaging in the brokerage business remain. Major banks strongly oppose these restrictions and have engaged in vigorous efforts to promote a major legislative change to the Glass-Steagall Act. For the past several years such efforts have had the support of the Treasury Department and more recently the Federal Reserve Board, though Congress has been substantially divided on the issue.

BANKING DIVISIONS IN JAPAN

During the American occupation of Japan following World War II, occupation authorities made a number of major reforms in the structure of Japanese industry. The large industrial and financial holding companies called *zaibatsu* were broken up, in the interest of restricting anticompetitive and politically powerful monopolies. At the same time an equivalent of the Glass-Steagall Act was inserted into the Japanese commercial code as Article 65, and accordingly, since 1947 Japanese commercial banking has been separate from investment banking which is conducted exclusively by securities firms. These are dominated in Japan by four large

TABLE 7–1
Comparison of Market and Book Value of Certain Japanese Firms with Financial Firms from Other Countries

World Rank by Market Value	Market Value 12/31/87 ($ billions)	Book Value 12/31/87 ($ billions)	Ratio of Market Value to Book Value
1 SUMITOMO BANK	58.9	5.3	11.1
2 FUJI BANK	55.6	5.1	10.9
3 DAI-ICHI KANGYO BANK	55.3	4.8	11.5
4 MITSUBISHI BANK	48.6	4.9	9.9
5 INDUSTRIAL BANK OF JAPAN	46.4	3.5	13.3
6 SANWA BANK	44.2	4.5	9.8
7 NOMURA SECURITIES	38.4	8.8	4.4
8 MITSUI BANK	28.4	2.9	9.8
9 LONG TERM CREDIT BANK	27.5	2.7	10.2
10 TOKAI BANK	27.3	3.0	9.1
13 BANK OF TOKYO	17.9	3.0	6.0
14 DAIWA SECURITIES	15.8	4.3	3.7
16 NIKKO SECURITIES	14.5	3.9	3.7
20 YAMAICHI SECURITIES	11.8	4.1	2.9
22 Union Bank of Switzerland	10.1	7.6	1.3
23 American Express	9.8	4.6	2.1
27 Deutsche Bank	8.4	7.1	1.2
28 Swiss Bank Corp.	8.4	6.9	1.2
29 National Westminster Bank	8.1	9.2	0.9
31 Credit Suisse	6.8	5.2	1.3
32 J P Morgan	6.5	5.0	1.3
33 Barclays Bank	6.1	7.7	0.8
34 Citicorp	5.9	8.8	0.7
38 Hong Kong Shanghai Bank	4.4	4.3	1.0
60 Societe Generale	3.1	3.2	1.0
70 Salomon Brothers	2.6	2.8	0.9
72 Merrill Lynch	2.5	3.3	0.8
73 Bankers Trust	2.4	2.9	0.8
98 Chemical Bank	1.9	3.0	0.6

Source: *Euromoney.*

retail brokerages, Nomura, Daiwa, Nikko, and Yamaichi. These firms had been associated with zaibatsu before the war but were reconstituted afterward as independent companies. Each has about 100 branch offices throughout Japan handling securities transactions for individuals, institutions, and corporations. Between them, the "big four" as they are known, account for approximately 40 percent of commissions earned and a higher percentage of underwriting managerships. Article 65, like the Glass-Steagall Act, does not apply outside Japan, but the administrative jurisdiction of the Ministry of Finance does and the activities of banks and securities firms, though liberalized greatly, are still subject to strict regulation.

It is generally assumed that the amendment or abolition of the Glass-Steagall Act will result in a similar change in the Japanese Article 65, which has also been subject to controversy and challenge in Japan. Many foreign banks have already been able to bypass restrictions preventing them from participating in the securities business in Japan, and this has put further pressure on the Japanese government to provide similar advantages for Japanese banks by amending Article 65. Many new financial services have been introduced in Japan over the past few years, and the banks and securities firms have fought over which should have rights to which businesses. Because of the booming stock market, fixed commission structure, and the enormously increased importance of Japan as a financial center, the securities firms have grown more rapidly than banks. Today the principal firms are not only equivalent in size to the formerly all-powerful banks, but they are also much larger, in terms of the market value of their capitalization, than any investment or merchant bank elsewhere in the world (see Table 7–1).

CHANGES IN THE UNITED KINGDOM— THE BIG BANG

From the early 19th century to the start of the First World War, the United Kingdom was the dominant financial power in the world. However, two world wars, from both of which it emerged a weakened victor, and the loss of its colonial empire, hastened Britain's decline relative to the rising powers of America, Japan and continental Europe.

From the end of the Second World War through 1979, the United Kingdom labored under exchange controls designed to defend an overvalued pound. But even as the U.K.'s economy diminished in world stature and sterling declined in international importance relative to the dollar as a reserve currency, London, because of its accumulation of know-how and its hands-off attitude regarding the regulation of offshore financial transactions, emerged as the world capital of the Euromarkets.

In 1979, with the election of Margaret Thatcher as prime minister and the abolishing of exchange controls, a vigorous decade in the British economy began. It ushered in a period when the cloistered domestic capital markets were opened to the rigors of international competition. As a result of an antitrust action filed against the stock exchange in London by the previous Labor government, the Conservative government negotiated a settlement whereby the stock exchange would make important changes to its rule book. That settlement led to what came to be known as the "Big Bang."

Previous stock exchange rules had permitted the exchange to treat itself as a closed shop. As in the case of "Mayday" in the United States, when negotiated as opposed to fixed-rate brokerage commissions were introduced on the New York Stock Exchange on May 1, 1975, the rule change was forced by a threat of an antitrust action against the exchange by the government. Unlike Mayday, however, the Big Bang required that the entire stock exchange system for dealing in debt and equity securities be scrapped and rebuilt.

First, negotiated commission rates were required.

Second, brokers and jobbers, or market makers (roughly equivalent to specialists on the New York Stock Exchange) would no longer be restricted to performing only their respective functions, or acting in a single capacity. Members could now act in a dual capacity, if they wished, as both brokers and jobbers (or as broker/dealers in U.S. terms).

And third, foreign and other nonmember securities firms could join the exchange and compete for business against British firms. The Big Bang also resulted in the market for government bonds (called gilt-edged securities, or gilts) being totally recast to resemble closely the U.S. system of having numerous authorized primary market dealers trading directly with the central bank. In addition, the stock market was to be rebuilt along the lines of the U.S. National Securities Dealer Quotation (NASDAQ) system for electronic over-the-counter trading. Within a year following the rule changes, the trading volume on the London Stock Exchange had more than tripled, customers admitted receiving better and more advanced services, and the floor of the exchange itself was virtually deserted as trading became almost totally electronic. The pressure on profits for the many firms competing for business in the London Market has been extreme, however, especially in the period following the market crash of October 19, 1987.

Though the commercial banking and securities functions are now separately regulated in the United Kingdom, there are no prohibitions against banks engaging in underwriting, brokerage, and trading of securities and most have gone into these businesses through subsidiaries.

Explosions similar to Big Bang have been heard around the world as financial markets were deregulated in the early 1980s in Canada, Australia, Germany, France, and to some degree in Switzerland.

FREER ACCESS TO MARKETS BY FOREIGNERS

Prior to 1980, foreign firms were restricted from participating in indigenous markets just about everywhere. After Mayday in 1975, the New York Stock Exchange (NYSE) permitted foreign firms to become members, and a few (mainly Japanese) did. With negotiated rates, however, most non-U.S. securities firms had only a limited incentive to join. They could save the expense of a large operation in New York, and still get very competitive executions of orders for their customers by shopping their business around among increasingly competitive, service-oriented U.S. brokers. Very few firms actually expected to challenge the U.S. investment bankers on their home ground, so they really did not need to be NYSE members.

Some Swiss, German, French, and British banks (and other European banks through minority interests) had owned securities affiliates in the United States before the passage of the International Banking Act of 1978 and were, therefore, grandfathered to conduct both banking and securities businesses in the United States. However, most foreign banks large enough to be able to finance a large-scale operation in the United States were, like their U.S. counterparts, prevented from participating in the securities business. A few firms, such as Paribas (one of the grandfathered banks) and S. G. Warburg (a British merchant bank) who jointly purchased a majority interest in A. G. Becker in 1976, have attempted to compete in the U.S. domestic investment banking business. The Paribas-Warburg venture was not successful, however, as the Becker firm (then called Warburg-Paribas-Becker) failed and was ultimately liquidated into Merrill Lynch in 1983.

In Europe the Big Bang was seen both as a success (from the standpoint of users of capital market services) and as a wave of the future. In its wake, liberalizations permitting foreign participation in national markets occurred in Germany and France, and in Switzerland local underwriting practices were relaxed sufficiently to allow foreign firms to have a bigger share of participations in Swiss franc-denominated issues led by the big three Swiss banks.

In Japan the opening of the Japanese capital markets to foreign issuers and securities firms had been progressing gradually since the mid-1970s. Foreign investment bankers were permitted to open branches that were licensed to engage in certain aspects of the securities business in Japan in the early 1980s. As the Japanese became large-scale exporters of capital, international firms rushed to open branches in Tokyo, and pressure was applied to open the stock exchange to foreign membership. This was granted in 1986, when six non–Japanese firms were allowed to join—three American investment banks (Merrill Lynch, Goldman Sachs, and Morgan Stanley), two British merchant banks (S. G. Warburg and an affiliate of Robert Fleming & Co.), and a British-based stockbroker owned by Citicorp (Vickers da Costa). Subsequently to the initial opening of the exchange to foreign membership, 16 additional memberships were granted to foreign firms, including some controlled by non–Japanese commercial (or universal) banks. Though it appears that the Japanese authorities did not wish to grant highly controversial concessions to foreign banks that they could not offer to their own banks, banking authorities in many countries threatened to deny or rescind licenses granted to Japanese banks in their countries unless reciprocal privileges were extended to their banks in Japan.

Foreign Ownership of Firms

The rapid growth of the securities business during the 1970s and 1980s placed heightened importance on the ability of firms to raise capital. In the United States there had been earlier investments in

the capital stock of investment banks by foreign firms. Credit
Suisse, one of the big three Swiss banks, had invested through its
60 percent subsidiary Credit Suisse First Boston in a 39 percent
interest in First Boston Corporation in 1978. (Subsequently, in
1988, Credit Suisse First Boston and First Boston were merged
into a new holding company 44.5 percent owned by Credit Suisse.)
Lehman Brothers had sold a minority interest to Banca Commer-
ciale Italiana in the early 1970s which remained until the acquisition of Lehman by Shearson American Express in 1984. Both of
these investments were made at times when the American firms
were suffering earnings and capital problems. A minority interest

TABLE 7–2
**International Holdings of Certain Investment and Merchant Banks on
December 31, 1988**

	Percent	Owned by
U.S. Investment Banks		
Shearson Lehman Brothers	13.0	Nippon Life Insurance
Goldman Sachs	12.5	Sumitomo Bank
Paine Webber	18.0	Yasuda Life Insurance
Drexel Burnham	25.3	Banque Lambert Group
First Boston	100.0	CS-First Boston (44.5% owned by Credit Suisse)
Wertheim & Co.	50.0	J. H. Schroder
Aubrey G. Lanston	100.0	Industrial Bank of Japan
C. J. Lawrence	100.0	Morgan Grenfell & Co.
Merchant Banks and U.K. Brokers		
Credit Suisse First	60.0	Credit Suisse
Boston	34.0	First Boston
Morgan Grenfell	5.0	Deutsche Bank
Hoare Govett	100.0	Security Pacific
Vickers da Costa	100.0	Citicorp
Scrimgeour Kemp-Gee	100.0	Citicorp
L. Messel	100.0	Shearson Lehman Brothers
Laurie & Milbank	100.0	Chase Manhattan
Simon & Coates	100.0	Chase Manhattan
Philips & Drew	100.0	Union Bank of Switzerland
James Capel	100.0	Hongkong Shanghai
Savory Milln	100.0	Swiss Bank Corp.

Source: *Economist*, annual reports.

in Dillon Read was held by a Swedish group until the firm was sold to the Travelers Insurance Group in 1983. After Salomon Brothers' acquisition by Phibro in 1983, a substantial minority interest in the firm was held for a time by Minorco, a major South African-controlled corporation. By the mid 1980s other U.S. firms were raising capital by selling interests to foreign institutions. The Industrial Bank of Japan acquired a government bond dealer, Aubrey G. Lanston, in 1986. Goldman Sachs sold a 12.5 percent nonvoting limited partnership interest to Sumitomo Bank; Shearson Lehman Brothers sold a 13 percent interest to Nippon Life, Paine Webber sold a 25 percent share to Yasuda Life, and Nomura Securities had been involved in unfruitful discussions to acquire a 50 percent interest in Kidder Peabody.

In Britain the buildup to Big Bang saw 19 of the 20 largest brokerage firms sell out entirely to buyers from the United States, Germany, and Switzerland as well as to British institutions. Among these were the acquisition of Philips and Drew by the Union Bank of Switzerland, which also was reported to have agreed to purchase the merchant bank, Hill Samuel, though the transaction was aborted. Security Pacific acquired a controlling interest in Hoare Govett. Swiss Bank Corporation acquired Savory Milln, and Deutsche Bank secured a 5 percent interest in Morgan Grenfell. All of the top jobbers were also sold. Other merchant banks have also found themselves the target of open market purchases by unwanted parties. Table 7–2 shows the international holdings of major competitors in the global securities business as of the end of 1987.

BUILDUP OF OVERSEAS OPERATIONS

In the early part of the 1980s, international transactions expanded very rapidly. The Eurobond market, inspired by a strong dollar and falling interest rates, became extremely active in both the issuance of new securities and in secondary market trading. Several very large issues were launched, including a $1 billion issue of convertible debentures for Texaco in 1984, the largest such issue ever. New types of securities proliferated, many linked to interest rate or currency swaps. Transactions in nondollar securities also expanded, especially after the dollar began to fall in 1985. International issues of equity securities became very common and were in great demand. Firms also foresaw a substantial increase in the volume of business in the U.K. bond and equity markets following the Big Bang.

For those firms seeking to carve out a secure position in various European markets, a vast expansion of personnel, facilities, and commensurate overhead was required. Many U.S. firms saw the expansion of the Euromarkets and the unique opportunities associated with Big Bang to be very attractive and moved accordingly. Some U.S. firms had already become active in U.K. corporate finance—including mergers and acquisitions, and equity and real estate financings—and expected to increase their participation in these profitable areas over the next few years. For several U.S. houses, a tripling or quadrupling in the size of their London operations over a two-to-three-year period would be necessary. At the same time many of these firms were not only expanding rapidly in Tokyo, where trading with large financial institutions became a major business opportunity, but also evaluating new opportunities to set up or expand in Frankfurt, Zurich, Toronto, Paris, and Sydney. German, Swiss, and French banks expanded their London operations during this period but not to the same extent as the U.S. firms. Japanese securities firms were mainly concentrating their efforts in London in handling the considerable volume of business brought to them by their Japanese clients, both corporate issuers and institutional investors, but they also had their eyes on banking operations in London, for which all four of the major firms had received licenses by the end of 1987.

Some buildup in the United States by European and Japanese houses also took place during this period. British merchant banks added to their U.S. staffs, and some like Kleinwort Benson acquired modest-sized government bond dealers and swap specialists. Five major European banks grandfathered to conduct investment banking operations in the United States (Deutsche, Dresdner, Paribas, Union Bank of Switzerland, and Swiss Bank Corp.) stepped up their activities through subsidiaries, but none had yet become a major factor in the securities business in New York. Japanese firms, while concentrating on Japanese business in the United States, were making some progress with U.S. clients. A few new issues of U.S. corporate bonds were led by Japanese houses, and all of the "big four" had become primary market government bond dealers by the end of 1987.

During the 1980s non–U.S. firms, however, were not visible in the more lucrative areas of U.S. investment banking such as managing issues of common and preferred stock, arranging mergers and acquisitions, leveraged buy-outs, junk bonds, or real estate financing. Even when the clients were non–U.S. corporations, the investment bankers handling these transactions were almost always U.S. firms. These highly specialized transactions were dominated by the top 5 to 10 U.S. firms which had the capital, the infrastructure, the contacts, and the know-how to remain on the leading edge of these rapidly changing, complex, high value-added and accordingly, very profitable activities.

In Japan the attraction of a dynamic local market and a huge flow of investment capital overseas drew many securities firms from Europe and the United States to expand their operations in Japan considerably. Under the best of circumstances, expanding a foreign firm's staff in Tokyo is difficult. It is especially difficult when it has to be done very quickly and at the same time that all of one's competitors are also expanding in Japan. Nevertheless, most firms managed to do it, though perhaps not in all cases with maximum efficiency.

Following the acceptance of the original firms into membership in the Tokyo exchange, participation of foreign firms in underwritings and government bond auctions increased. At the same time, however, the Japanese authorities instituted a reduction of stock exchange commissions for those generating large volumes, which reduced the revenues of the foreign firms whose business in Japanese securities was almost entirely institutional. Meanwhile, of course, the yen-dollar exchange rate was rising rapidly as were occupancy and all other expenses of foreign firms in Tokyo. After the first year's experience most would agree that the Tokyo market had become too expensive and too competitive for all but the major firms.

International Investment Banking Services

There are now a large number of different international investment banking products and services. Most of these are well integrated with their domestic market equivalents. Indeed, the words *domestic* and *international* are fading from use for certain services, such as the issuing of long-term debt or structuring portfolios for institutional investors. However, it is helpful in keeping track of the great variety of services now offered by the various firms from around the world, to think of a division between home-country clients and foreign clients, as well as the traditional division between services to those requiring capital and those requiring investments for capital.

Home-country clients, from the United States, Europe, and Japan, have all seen a great proliferation of financial services that have considerably increased the range of alternatives available to them when, for example, they are planning a debt financing. The choice is no longer between the bond market and a bank loan. For borrowers today, the choice is between several capital market alternatives in the home market and several more alternatives from international markets. These latter include straight debt financing in one's own currency, financing in another currency swapped into the home-country currency, or floating-rate financing converted into fixed-rate financing by means of an interest-rate swap. Bond issues can be sold with detachable warrants that provide for the purchase by the holder of other securities of the issuer, either additional debt securities or equity securities. There often can be as many as a dozen viable, price-competitive financing alternatives that the issuer must consider in making a selection. The range of issuers that are acceptable to the international markets has also expanded greatly since 1980; no longer must an issuer be a large, well-known corporation to be able to launch a Eurobond offering. In fact, many alternatives and ideas are provided to all sorts of potential issuers by aggressive, opportunistic bankers. So many alternatives backed by so much competitive energy has resulted in a great deal of international financing being completed in recent years, particularly in the Eurosecurities markets as Chart 7–2 indicates.

Many investment bankers believe they must maintain a first-rate capital markets team capable of offering a fully internationalized array of financing alternatives to keep from losing their traditional home-country clients. Others with fewer traditional clients see opportunities for themselves in the situation. In any case, as clients have been drawn to the tempting offerings of a globalized marketplace, those bankers who have missed leading them there have been forced to follow along.

The same has been true of investor clients who, having

CHART 7–2
Volume of New International Bond Issues (1963–1987)

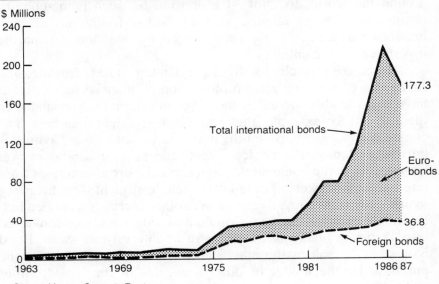

Source: Morgan Guaranty Trust.

discovered international portfolio diversification, require the same support services as when they are investing domestically. Investment research and a willingness to make secondary markets in issues are the most important of these. If U.S. brokers are not going to provide these services at a quality level at least as good as their foreign competitors, their share of the home-country institution's commission volume will decline as business is directed to foreign firms. Institutional investors, particularly private pension funds, have expanded their international investments enormously in recent years, as Table 7–3 indicates, so that it has become equally important for both defensive and opportunistic reasons for firms offering services to investors to internationalize their businesses.

As bankers regard nonhome-country clients, they think in terms of three services: (1) executing transactions in the banker's home-country for the nonhome-country clients; (2) executing

TABLE 7–3
Foreign Assets of Private Pension Funds ($ Millions)

	1980	1985	1990 (estimated)
United States	$3,300	$27,000	$129,300
United Kingdom	9,700	34,400	84,200
Japan	400	7,600	47,200
Netherlands	1,500	5,400	15,900
Canada	2,000	4,100	9,000
Switzerland	1,300	1,700	6,900
Rest of world	n/a	1,500	6,400
W. Germany	500	1,000	3,500
Ireland	300	700	1,400
Australia	0	500	3,700
Belgium	275	500	1,100
France	75	200	600
Total	$19,350	$84,600	$309,400

Source: Inter Sec Research Corporation.

transactions in third countries for them; and (3) executing transactions in the nonhome-country client's own national market.

When a U.S. firm issues bonds in the United States for the Kingdom of Norway (called Yankee bonds) or assists a Swiss client in selling shares of IBM, then the firm is performing the first category of these services. Home-country international services are the easiest to provide, and probably the most profitable for the bankers. The competitive field is smaller and the firm's domestic reputation is, perhaps, the most important factor in the awarding of the business to the banker. These services have been performed in one form or another for many years, particularly in the United States. British merchant banks have also provided foreign clients with British banking, corporate finance, money management, and underwriting services for many years, although the demand for sterling denominated "Bulldog" bonds and other strictly British services has been modest. The Japanese securities firms owe their great international development of the past 10 or 15 years to the provision of Japanese market services to clients in Europe and the

United States. Brokerage services in Japanese shares have been by far the most important of these, but the issuance of yen-denominated bonds in the Tokyo market ("Samurai" bonds) and the listing of shares on the Tokyo Stock Exchange have also been active businesses.

The execution of services in third countries, particularly the stateless one in which the Euromarkets flourish, is an important part of the international business of all bankers. Originally there was a competitive advantage associated with the arrangement of issues denominated in the bankers' own home currency. Eurodollar issues became associated with U.S. firms, Euro-Canadian dollar issues with Canadian firms, and Euroyen with the Japanese. Though this is still true on the whole, these divisions are much less adhered to today. The markets have become exceedingly competitive, and participants now quote actively in all major currencies. Also, the arrangement of Euro transactions for nonhome-country clients has become quite common. It is not unusual for a Japanese firm to win a dollar mandate from a Swedish issuer, nor for a Euroyen issue for a French company to be bought by a British firm. In the Euromarket, anything goes!

With so many participants, however, and so much emphasis on transactional relationships, price competition can be severe. The advantage goes to those competitors who have very close relationships with issuers (such as the Japanese securities firms have with their Japanese clients) or are capable of placing large amounts of bonds, usually with home-country or otherwise captive investors. The Swiss banks manage very large sums of money for investment clients who are traditional buyers of Eurobonds, especially Eurodollar issues. When the dollar is attractive to these investors they are very active buyers of Eurodollar bond issues brought by American corporations. During such times U.S. and Swiss firms rank high in the Eurobond league tables. On occasions, such as during 1986–1988, when Japanese corporations are eager to escape restrictive new issue practices in their home market by issuing securities in the Euromarkets, and/or when Japanese investors are eager to buy Eurosecurities of Japanese and other companies, the Japanese securities firms rank high in the league tables.

In addition to Eurobonds, banks today offer international equity underwritings. These can be arranged through the traditional Eurobond syndication method, or they can involve home-country issues with international tranches. If Nestlé wants to sell shares outside of Switzerland, it can have its banker organize a distribution by inviting a group of international underwriters to purchase the shares just as if they were Eurobonds. If Sears, Roebuck wants to sell a new issue of common stock, its U.S. investment banker may suggest that it provide for a portion of the issue, perhaps 15 percent, to be sold to overseas underwriters through a separate but simultaneous offering to broaden the company's base of international shareholders and to attract worldwide demand for the issue as opposed to just U.S. demand. When the British government was disposing of some of its industrial holdings in conjunction with its policy of privatization, foreign tranches were provided in the United States, Canada, Japan, and continental Europe for some of the larger issues.

In such cases, it was necessary to integrate the underwriting systems in different countries to make the transaction work. In the case of the $12 billion issue of British Petroleum shares that was caught up in the stock market crash of October 1987, the underwriting systems were integrated in such a way that the foreign underwriters who participated in the two-week underwriting of the issue in the United Kingdom caused the four U.S. underwriters to suffer losses, estimated at $200 million after taxes, on the transaction. Similar foreign tranches, not always involving similarly linked underwriting risks, have been arranged for privatization offerings in France, Germany, and Singapore. Foreign underwriters also participated in the Japanese syndicates underwriting issues of Nippon Telegraph and Telephone and Japan Air Lines shares.

The most difficult form of international services for a firm to offer successfully are services that are to be executed in national markets of nonhome-countries. Well-entrenched, effective national competition is difficult to dislodge. As previously noted, the European banks permitted to perform investment banking services in the United States have not achieved a significant market share even though they have been competing in the United States for many years. In Japan, Germany, France, and Switzerland foreign competitors have faced much the same story. In Britain, however, where Big Bang weakened the hold of British firms on their historical businesses, and allowed foreign firms much greater opportunity to offer new and competitive products and services to clients in the United Kingdom, freer and greater competition has been the result. Foreign firms can perhaps hope to secure in a few years time a prominent share of the market for securities market services in the United Kingdom. Recent deregulation of securities markets in Canada and Australia may have a similar effect on foreign competition in those markets in the future.

COMPETITIVE STRATEGIES OF MAJOR FIRMS

The securities business has experienced many changes in the past decade. Markets have become globalized creating a much broader range of financial alternatives for users of services. To be an effective competitor today, a firm must be able to provide a full range of expensive international capabilities. Competition in some sectors of the market, such as the Eurobond area, is intensified by the substantial increase in the number of participants. Increasingly, firms must use their own capital to take positions in tightly priced issues. On the other hand, the demand for capital market services as a whole has grown at a far faster rate than has the demand for banking services during the past several years. More and more transactions, once considered the natural business of commercial banks, are migrating to capital markets in securitized form where more competitive pricing can be obtained. Financing for working capital, inferior credits, and collateralized transactions can now be more cheaply obtained in the markets. Increasingly, investment bankers are being attracted to transactions in which they invest their own capital in bridge loans that are ultimately repaid from a sale of securities. Commercial banks, on the other hand, have made substantial investments to increase their capital market capabilities.

In some countries there is also increasing erosion of barriers requiring the separation of banking from securities businesses. Further deregulation in these areas is expected in the United States and in Japan. Home-country competition will increase for those firms that have had the benefits of membership in a small oligopoly that dominates the securities business in their country. Competition will come from other ambitious securities firms seeking to improve their shares of market in an environment in which it is much easier to do business with the traditional clients of other firms. It will come also from other providers of financial services, such as commercial banks in the United States, which have previously been excluded from dealing in securities by regulation, and from a variety of foreign firms who will continue to expand in the home markets of others or acquire positions in firms that are already well established.

Investment banks and merchant banks have always taken pride in their ability to "live by their wits." Many have survived for a hundred years or more in a business that is risky and unpredictable because they have done just that. The premium has been greater on the professional talent and flexibility of the firm, than on the availability of capital. These conditions will no doubt continue into the future, but the globalization of markets, the corresponding internationalization of firms, changes in the competitive climate, and the need to be active and competent in a large number of fields and territories will certainly increase the importance of capital and the managerial abilities of major firms in the future. Equally, major firms will have to refine their competitive strategies to make the most of their strengths and comparative advantages and the least of their weaknesses and comparative disadvantages. Each firm will find itself sufficiently different from others to justify a custom-made strategy just for itself. There will be room, in this context, for a lot of variety among the players each of whom, however, will do well to heed the words of Casey Stengel, the celebrated American baseball manager who advised, "If you don't know where you're going, you might end up someplace else."

Table 7–4 is a partial list of those investment banks, merchant banks, and others who might aspire, by the year 2000, to end up as one of a small and powerful world financial oligopoly and whose competitive strategies today must reflect that ambition. Not all will achieve the goal.

TABLE 7-4
Principal International Securities Dealers in 1986 ($ millions)

	Assets	Net Income	Capital	Assets ÷ Capital	Employees
UNITED STATES					
Investment Banks[a]					
Salomon Brothers	$ 78,164	$ 516	$3,209	24.1	7,800
Merrill Lynch	53,013	454	2,865	18.5	47,900
Shearson Lehman	53,978	316	3,122	17.4	25,004
Goldman Sachs	38,794	NA	1,985	19.5	6,049
Morgan Stanley	29,190	201	901	32.3	4,312
Kidder Peabody	21,840	NA	684	31.9	6,866
Commercial Banks					
Citicorp	191,355	1,058	9,060	21.0	88,500
Chase Manhattan	94,766	585	4,280	22.1	47,480
Morgan Guaranty	74,643	872	5,130	14.6	14,518
Chemical Bank	58,712	402	3,120	18.9	20,993
Bankers Trust	53,735	428	2,721	19.9	11,069
JAPAN					
Securities Firms					
Nomura	17,844	1,347	5,094	3.5	9,445
Daiwa	8,506	263	1,540	5.7	NA
Nikko	14,991	600	2,899	5.2	8,398
Yamaichi	13,246	516	2,301	5.7	7,512
Banks					
Mitsubishi	203,869	514	4,984	40.8	13,345
Sumitomo	173,509	456	3,937	44.0	13,733
IBJ	160,886	412	3,296	48.8	5,447
LTCB	115,529	219	2,423	48.1	3,357
Bank of Tokyo	111,489	334	3,678	30.1	13,569
HOLLAND					
Amsterdam Rotterdam	62,986	190	2,134	29.6	23,489
Algemene	66,944	240	3,329	20.3	29,043
SWITZERLAND					
Investment Banks					
CSFB	3,261	140	520	6.3	1,023
Universal Banks					
UBS	93,756	478	5,353	17.5	19,900
SBC	85,453	418	6,344	13.6	15,775
GERMANY					
Universal Banks					
Deutsche Bank	131,861	550	5,176	25.5	50,590
Dresdner Bank	101,226	260	3,433	29.8	36,769
Commerzbank	75,460	210	2,509	30.2	25,658
FRANCE					
Banques d'Affaires					
Paribas	93,240	260	2,332	40.0	28,000
Commercial Banks					
BNP	142,533	464	4,492	31.7	58,623
Credit Lyonnais	132,692	299	2,598	51.0	54,557
Soc. Generale	116,554	413	3,383	34.5	43,655
CCF	32,173	56	608	52.8	12,504
UNITED KINGDOM					
Merchant Banks					
Barclays	116,596	911	5,493	21.3	110,000
Montagu/Midland	78,519	357	2,984	26.3	67,534
Kleinwort Benson	14,506	76	776	18.7	3,500
Morgan Grenfell	5,819	47	390	14.9	NA
SG Warburg Securities	4,084	60	337	12.2	NA
Baring Bros.	3,381	11	302	11.3	1,500

[a] First Boston included under Switzerland: Credit Suisse First Boston.

Source: Annual reports.

SUMMARY

The recent rapid rise in international investment banking is a resumption of a trend which began in the early 19th century and continued uninterrupted to the eve of the Great Depression. In the 1980s, half a century later, this resumed trend is driven with unprecedented force by deregulation, competition, and telecommunications innovations. The separation of investment from commercial banking, decreed in the 1930s, is now being dismantled while rapid innovation in financial instruments increases the scope of investment banking services.

In the 1970s, in the United States, and in the 1980s in the United Kingdom and Japan, significant deregulation has allowed foreigners freer access to domestic securities markets. This has complemented the simultaneous rise in the Euromarkets in globalizing securities markets. At the same time, investors have acquired an appetite for internationally diversified portfolios. Through foreign acquisitions, expanding overseas operations, and crossing the dividing line between investment and commercial banking, about 50 banking houses throughout the world have emerged as serious competitors to provide the full range of international investment banking services. These banking houses are striving to become one of the truly global investment powerhouses by the year 2000.

CHAPTER 8

THE REGULATION OF FINANCIAL MARKETS

Thomas F. Cargill

During the 1980s there has been a virtual explosion of interest and debate about the regulation of financial markets among economists, policymakers, and market participants. Questions about the objectives and the effectiveness of financial regulation were increasingly raised during the 1970s when inflation and high interest rates rendered the then-existing structure of regulation incapable of providing an efficient and stable financial environment. As a result, there has occurred a major transition in the national's financial institutions and markets along with a major shift in the government regulations imposed on financial transactions. The transition of finance and regulation is referred to as "deregulation," "financial reform," or "financial liberalization" because financial markets and regulation now permit a far greater degree of competition than previously.[1] The transition of financial markets and financial regulation is not unique to the United States, however. Similar financial reforms have been ongoing for a number of years in other developed economies such as Australia, Canada, France, Ger-

---

[1] Thomas F. Cargill and Gillian G. Garcia, *Financial Reform in the 1980s* (Stanford, Calif.: Hoover Institution Press, 1985) provide a broad overview of financial reform in the United States.

many, Japan, and New Zealand as well as in many developing economies such as Indonesia, South Korea, and Taiwan.[2]

The objective of this chapter is to provide an overview of financial regulation by considering several aspects of government intervention in the financial markets. Given that finance and financial markets both in the United States and elsewhere are in transition, our discussion often considers several of the aspects from a historical perspective.

The objective of the chapter is carried out in seven sections. First, we discuss the basic responsibilities of financial markets in the overall economy and the fundamental rationale that accounts for the acceptance of some minimal role for government intervention in at least some financial markets even in the context of a competitive market system. Second, we discuss the specific objectives implicit in the current structure of financial regulation and draw attention to the underlying behavior of the authorities responsible for financial regulation from two perspectives: first, the role of the regulatory authority as an exogenous entity that attempts to correct "market failure" to promote the "public good" and second, the role of the regulatory authority as an entity that both influences, and is influenced by, the regulated entity or entities in ways that may produce financial regulation conflicting with the public good. Third, we summarize the institutional structure of financial regulation. Fourth, we discuss the shift in the focus of financial regulation during the past decade from restraining competitive forces to now permitting competitive forces a greater role in the financial system than previously. Fifth, we discuss the transition of financial markets and financial regulation from an international perspective. Sixth, we discuss three major issues facing

---

[2] The financial transition in other countries is discussed in Hang-Sheng Cheng, ed. *Financial Policy and Reform in Pacific Basin Countries* (Lexington, Mass.: D.C. Heath and Company, 1986); M. A. Akhtar, *Financial Innovations and Their Implications for Monetary Policy: An International Perspective* (Basle, Switzerland: Bank for International Settlements, 1983); and Yoshio Suzuki and Hiroshi Yomo, eds., *Financial Innovation and Monetary Policy: Asia and the West* (Tokyo: University of Tokyo Press, 1986). Thomas F. Cargill and Shoichi Royama, *The Transition of Finance in Japan and the United States: A Comparative Perspective* (Stanford, Calif.: Hoover Institution Press, 1988) provide a comparative study of financial reform in Japan and the United States.

regulators of financial markets that are challenging their ability to support an efficient and stable financial environment. Seventh, we present some brief concluding comments.

FINANCIAL MARKETS, THE ECONOMY, AND GOVERNMENT INTERVENTION

This section provides an overview of the major financial markets that constitute the financial system and the responsibilities of the financial system in the overall economy. We also look at the unique characteristic of a subset of the financial markets that provides the fundamental rationale for government intervention in the financial system even in the case of a perfectly competitive economy.

Financial Markets and the Financial System. The two general categories of financial markets that together constitute the nation's financial system are direct and indirect financial markets.

In the direct financial market, the ultimate lender or surplus unit directly assumes the risk of the financial obligation issued by the ultimate borrower or deficit unit.[3] Direct markets are characterized by the maturity of the financial obligation with obligations of one year or less traded in the money market while obligations with a maturity greater than one year are traded in the capital market. Money and capital markets themselves are further divided into new issue and secondary markets.

In the indirect financial market, a third entity referred to as a financial institution serves as an intermediary between the ultimate lender and borrower and fundamentally changes the nature of the financial transaction. The ultimate lender accepts a financial obligation drawn on the institution rather than the ultimate borrower and as a result, indirect finance increases the flexibility of financial obligations in terms of denomination, maturity, and risk. Indirect markets are divided into two groups—depository and nondeposi-

---

[3] A deficit unit is defined as an economic unit whose borrowing from all financial markets exceeds lending; a surplus unit is defined as an economic unit whose lending to all financial markets exceeds borrowing.

tory financial institutions—depending on the financial obligation used by a given institution to obtain funds. Depository institutions (commercial banks, savings and loan associations, savings banks, and credit unions) issue deposit obligations many of which represent the major component of the nation's money supply. About 75 percent of the money supply consists of transactions deposits (demand deposits, negotiable orders of withdrawal or NOW accounts, automatic transfer service or ATS accounts, and credit union share drafts) issued by depository institutions. Nondepository institutions issue obligations such as casualty and life insurance policies, finance paper, and pension plans; these are not normally regarded as part of the money supply.

Direct and indirect markets account for about 75 and 25 percent of the flow of funds from lenders to borrowers in any given year, respectively, and simultaneously satisfy the varied financial needs of households, business, government, and foreigners.

Basic Functions of the Financial System.   The financial system as a collection of financial markets has essentially four functions to perform.

1. The financial system should provide an efficient transfer of funds from surplus to deficit units.
2. The financial system should be adaptable to the changing needs of the economy in terms of the sources and level of economic growth.
3. The financial system should remain sound and viable in the face of adverse economic events.
4. The financial system should provide an environment that permits the monetary authority to effectively control credit and money without disproportional impacts on different sectors of the financial system.

Fulfillment of these four functions is a necessary condition for sustained and noninflationary economic growth. History provides many examples to illustrate the adverse effects resulting from a poorly functioning financial system. The Great Depression provides the clearest example of what happens when the financial system becomes unstable. Even though considerable debate remains about the initiating causes of the Great Depression, there is little doubt that the series of bank runs and subsequent bank failures from 1929 through 1933 played a major role in sustaining the depressed economy throughout the decade.[4]

On a smaller scale, the financial disruptions of the 1970s reflected by "credit crunch" periods and disintermediation of funds from indirect to direct markets had important adverse impacts on the economy. In addition, monetary policy had a disproportionate impact on the banking system because of the rapid growth of financial innovations by nonbank financial institutions and the declining membership base of the Federal Reserve.[5] Member banks were thus becoming a smaller part of the money supply process.

Evolution of Monetary Standards and Government Regulation of Some Financial Markets.   Several specific considerations rationalize the current level of government regulation of financial markets that we discuss later; however, these themselves are derived from a single basic rationale that is fundamentally rooted in the historical evolution of an economy's monetary standard. Monetary standards have naturally evolved in ways that introduce externalities related to the actions of specific financial markets and as a result, rationalize some degree of government intervention if a stable monetary and financial environment is to be achieved.

Monetary standards have progressed through three stages: commodity standards, representative commodity standards, and fiat or credit standards. Commodity and representative commodity standards were the first to emerge; they depended on the supply of some commodity such as gold or silver to determine the money supply. Although these systems required little government regulation, they provided a monetary standard that was resource using (the base commodity had alternative uses and resources were

---

[4] Milton Friedman, and Anna J. Schwartz, *A Monetary History of the United States, 1867–1960* (Princeton, N.J.: Princeton University Press, 1963).

[5] Member banks were required to meet reserve requirements imposed by the Federal Reserve and nonmember banks were required to satisfy reserve requirements imposed at the state level; however, state-imposed requirements were generally less restrictive than those imposed by the Federal Reserve. There was a continual decline in the membership base of the Federal Reserve during the 1970s as an increasing number of banks opted for nonmember status to operate under a less restrictive reserve requirement system.

required to secure increases in the base commodity over time) and was not adaptable to the changing needs of economic growth as the supply of the base commodity had little direct relationship with the needs of trade. As a result, the market had an incentive to develop substitutes for commodity money; these were fiat or credit based in the sense that they were supported by promises to pay rather than by a 100 percent commodity reserve.

Consider how a fractional reserve system evolved from a commodity representative standard in which gold certificates backed by a 100 percent gold reserve circulated as money. Institutions that held the gold and issued the certificates were not depository institutions in the modern sense and functioned merely as warehouses for gold; however, they evolved into modern depository institutions when they recognized that they could enhance profits by issuing promises to pay (bank notes or deposits) in excess of their gold reserve whenever they advanced funds to borrowers. Past experience indicated that only a fractional reserve of the commodity money would be required to meet conversions of promises to pay into gold or to meet adverse clearings with other depository institutions. The public found the promises to pay were more convenient than commodity money and were willing to treat the promises to pay as money as long as it believed they could be redeemed into the base commodity. Hence from society's point of view, the fractional reserve system reduced the opportunity cost of the resources devoted to the money supply and provided a money supply that was more responsive to the needs of trade. Monetary standards eventually developed to the current stage where all aspects of the money supply became fiat or credit based, including the reserves held by depository institutions.

Although a fiat-based system offered a more efficient and adaptable money supply, it introduced important externalities associated with the actions of individual banks. The evolution of the fractional reserve system gave banks in the aggregate the ability to expand and contract the money supply and influence the overall value of money; however, there was no reason why an individual bank would consider the impact of its own actions on other parties. Hence, there was no assurance that a stable money supply would be forthcoming and no assurance that a determinant value of money would be achieved.

In 1959 Milton Friedman argued that this situation eventually generated "economic counterfeiting" and that in the absence of some government regulation that ensured government control over the quantity of money, a fiat or credit system was not consistent with a stable financial and monetary environment.[6] According to Friedman, government had the right to impose reserve requirements on depository institutions to provide a basis for the conduct of monetary policy directed toward controlling the supply of money and hence, the value of money.

Friedman focused on the need to impose some degree of regulation to achieve control over the money supply; however, the introduction of fiat elements into the money supply justified government regulation to limit risk taking by depository institutions and to limit contagion effects from the failure of one or several depository institutions. The failure of a few institutions could adversely impact other depository institutions in the context of fractional reserves because not only can the public not easily distinguish between good and bad institutions but also depository institutions in a competitive environment tend to assume high levels of risk in the pursuit of profit, and some unregulated institutions may conduct fraudulent activities. Instability among depository institutions adversely impacts other financial markets in rapid succession as they occupy the central position in the financial system given their role in the money supply process. Thus, aside from monetary control considerations, the stability of the financial system required some degree of government intervention to limit risk taking and to limit contagion in the case of local shocks to the banking system.

Recognition that the natural evolution of fiat or credit elements into the money supply process rationalized some minimal role for government intervention in some financial markets, however, did

---

[6] Milton Friedman and Anna J. Schwartz, in a 1986 paper, provide an updated discussion of the rationale for government intervention in the financial system. Arthur J. Rolnick and Warren E. Weber "New Evidence on the Free Banking Era," *American Economic Review* 73 (December 1983), pp. 1080–91, and Lawrence H. White, *Free Banking in Britain* (Cambridge: Cambridge University Press, 1984), present a somewhat different perspective and suggest that the historical evidence does not provide a strong argument for government intervention.

not prevent intense debates about the form and degree of government regulation. Considerable differences of opinion persist about the type, the extent, and the effectiveness of government intervention in the financial system.

SPECIFIC RATIONALES FOR FINANCIAL REGULATION

The fundamental rationale for some degree of government regulation for at least some segment of the financial system (depository institutions primarily) has provided a foundation for the evolution of specific objectives of financial regulation directly related to the four functions of a financial system. At the current time, financial regulation is broadly concerned with the following four objectives: to provide for an efficient flow of funds to finance economic growth; to provide financial markets with sufficient flexibility to adapt to the changing needs of surplus and deficit units; to ensure the stability of financial markets in the face of adverse economic events and to protect depositors; and to provide a financial environment that permits effective monetary control by the monetary authority.

Even though these objectives rationalize the major regulations directed toward financial markets, regulation has also been used to achieve objectives unrelated to the efficiency, adaptability, soundness of financial markets, or with the effectiveness of monetary control procedures. In the United States for example, financial regulation has been used to support and subsidize residential mortgage credit. The special treatment of thrift institutions (savings and loan associations and savings banks) relative to other institutions with respect to portfolio restrictions, interest rate ceilings, and tax policy has been an important component of the social contract to support the housing sector. Although the social contract has been weakened to some extent by the deregulation process of the past few years, financial regulation continues to encourage a greater flow of funds into housing than would otherwise occur in a more competitive environment.

Throughout the financial history of the United States each of the above objectives at one time or another has played an important role in the evolution of financial regulation. At the same time, the stability of financial markets has occupied the greatest attention of the regulatory authorities in the United States and elsewhere. The majority of regulatory changes have been designed to ensure the soundness and stability of depository institutions and to ensure the confidence of the public that deposits will remain a viable component of the money supply.

Theories of Regulatory Behavior. The discussion to this point has taken the view that the regulation of financial markets is rationalized on the basis of the externality or public good character of financial institutions whose obligations constitute an important part of the money supply. That is, financial regulation exists because of "market failure." The market failure view suggests that government responds to the collective and implicit request of market participants to establish regulations that provide a greater degree of financial stability and efficiency than would otherwise be the case. Even though some market participants bear the cost of regulation, the benefits to the many justify the regulation of financial markets for the public good. For example, the externalities introduced by the evolution of fractional reserves justifies the imposition of reserve requirements on depository institutions to ensure effective monetary control, it justifies portfolio regulations to limit risk, and it justifies lender of last resort services by the monetary authority and government deposit insurance to limit contagion. In regard to direct financial markets, the registration and reporting requirements imposed on issuers of securities contributes to a more efficient market environment and hence, contributes to the public good even though some members of the market bear the cost of regulation.

The market failure view regards government as an exogenous entity, providing regulation to improve the market's efficiency and stability. The extensive growth of government regulation in general since the 1930s has been rationalized on this basis. There is no clearer example of the importance of the market failure view than the establishment of financial regulation during the Great Depression. The then-accepted view of the Great Depression argued that the banking system in an environment without interest rate ceilings and other portfolio restrictions assumed more risk than was prudent for institutions whose deposit liabilities were the major component of the nation's money supply. In addition, the absence of meaningful registration and reporting requirements for issuers of securities in the direct money and capital markets and the close relationship between commercial and investment banking permitted activities in organized money and capital markets that rendered them inherently unstable in the face of any adverse economic event.

Thus, the absence of extensive government regulation of the financial markets preceding the start of the Great Depression permitted the markets to develop in ways that were fundamentally unsound. The resulting market failure increased the susceptibility of the financial markets to any adverse economic event and as such, the failure of financial markets to remain viable during the Great Depression rationalized a major increase in the degree of government intervention.

In recent years economists have found the market failure view an unsatisfactory approach to explain regulatory policies. George Stigler was one of the first to seriously question the market failure view and suggested that it offered little, if any, useful insight about the existence or the evolution of regulatory policy.[7] Stigler argued that on close inspection regulation responded more to the interests of the regulated entity than to the public interest. The "special interest" or the "many special interests" approaches to regulatory policy regard the regulatory authorities as suppliers of regulation and special interest groups as demanders of regulation. These approaches suggest that regulatory policies may conflict with the public interest as they are more likely to be designed to maintain a given special interest's market share than to impose regulation that truly benefits the public.

Public choice theory has extended the special interest view and incorporated the fact that regulatory authorities have an independent existence and operate to maximize their own objective function which may even include the regulator's concept of the public interest. The regulatory objective function is complex and

---

[7] George Stigler, "The Theory of Economic Regulation," *Bell Journal of Economics* 2 (Spring 1971), pp. 3–21.

may include a variety of factors such as special interest groups, the public interest, and most important, the survival and growth of the regulatory authority itself. Like the special interest view, the public choice view suggests that the resulting set of regulations may conflict with the public interest.

STRUCTURE OF THE REGULATION OF FINANCIAL MARKETS

The institutional structure of financial regulation has remained relatively constant since it was established by the reforms enacted during the 1930s; however, the regulations imposed on financial transactions have significantly changed during the past decade.

Structure of Financial Regulation; Multiplicity of Regulatory Authorities. Compared to other countries, the United States possesses a large number of governmental entities responsible for the regulation of financial markets. Although the multiplicity of regulatory authorities is partly accounted for by the dual system of intermediation finance in which depository institutions can elect to operate under either a state or national charter, there still exists a relatively larger number of regulatory authorities at the federal level than is to be found in most other countries.

The public choice view of regulation can provide some insight into why the regulatory structure in the United States has evolved to incorporate many authorities often with overlapping responsibilities. As new segments of the financial system emerged and gained increased importance in the flow of funds, there also emerged two sets of forces that made it unlikely that the new financial activity would be regulated by an existing authority. First, those responsible for the new activity, recognizing that some degree of government regulation was unavoidable, would support the establishment of a new regulatory authority rather than have its activities regulated by an existing authority. The newly regulated activity would receive more attention from a new regulatory authority because it would not have to compete for attention with other regulated activities already influenced by an existing regulatory authority. Second, even though an existing regulatory authority would want to incorporate the new activity, existing regulated activities would resist incorporating the new activity to prevent dilution of their established shares of influence over the existing regulatory authority.

Hence, from a public choice point of view, there is considerable pressure for a new financial market to generate a new regulatory authority. There is, however, one problem with this approach. Although it offers some insights into the evolution of multiple regulatory authorities in the United States, it is unable to account for the small number of separate regulatory authorities in other countries. Perhaps the explanation is to be found in the greater emphasis in the United States on a formal governmental structure representing all interests in society than is found in most other countries. In any event, the fact remains that the United States possesses a large number of regulatory authorities by any reasonable standard.

The multiplicity of regulatory authorities has been increasingly blamed for inefficient and inconsistent financial regulation, especially in light of the fact that financial institutions are becoming more similar and competition between direct and indirect markets more intense as a result of the financial reform process. In 1984 the Busk Task Group on Regulation of Financial Services chaired by former Vice President George Bush released a report that examined many of these issues and recommended a major consolidation of the regulatory authorities responsible for overseeing the activities of the banking industry. The 1984 Bush Report was the most recent example of several studies recommending a consolidation of regulatory authority; however, like the earlier studies, the Bush Report has had little impact on the structure of financial regulation in the United States.

Structure of Financial Regulation: The Regulatory Authorities.   The institutional structure of regulation in the United States reflects the decomposition of financial markets into indirect-depository institutions, indirect-nondepository institutions, and direct securities markets.

In intermediation finance, several regulatory authorities at the federal level deal primarily with depository institutions such as the Board of Governors of the Federal Reserve System, Comptroller of the Currency, Federal Deposit Insurance Corporation, Federal Home Loan Bank Board, the Federal Savings and Loan Insurance Corporation, National Credit Union Administration, and the Regional Federal Reserve Banks. The regulation and supervision of the depository institutions is regarded as the most important overall responsibility of financial regulation because their transaction deposit liabilities represent the major component of the nation's money supply. In addition to the federal regulatory authorities, every state has some duplicate regulatory agency or agencies focusing primarily on state-chartered depository institutions.

Figure 8–1 illustrates the multinature of the U.S. regulatory structure in terms of the various regulatory entities that oversee the activities of banks and their holding companies. The table would increase in complexity if we were to add the other major depository institutions—savings and loan associations, savings banks, and credit unions—since they involve regulatory agencies in addition to those listed in Figure 8–1.

In regard to nondepository institutions such as finance companies, life insurance companies, and pension funds, there exist other state and federal regulatory authorities. For instance, finance companies are regulated primarily at the state level; however, because consumer lending is subject to several federal regulations regarding truth in lending, finance companies are also subject to federal regulation. Life insurance companies are regulated at the state level. Pension funds are regulated at the state level and as a result of the 1974 Employee Retirement Income Security Act are also under federal jurisdiction.

In regard to direct money and capital markets, the Securities and Exchange Commission (SEC) regulates a wide range of activities on organized securities markets. The SEC regulates the activities of securities dealers, requires the registration of securities issued in organized markets, and imposes financial reporting requirements on issuers of securities. In addition to regulating activities in direct financial markets, the SEC also concerns itself with the banking industry in two respects: first, many bank holding companies issue shares subject to SEC registration and reporting requirements. Second, despite the regulated separation between commercial and investment banking, commercial banks have made

FIGURE 8–1
Existing Regulation of Banks and Their Holding Companies

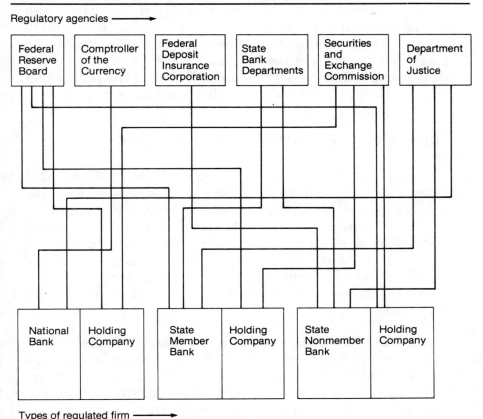

Source: Task Group on Regulation of Financial Services: *Blueprint for Reform: The Report of the Task Group on Regulation of Financial Services*. Washington, D.C.: GPO, 1984.

recent inroads into the securities industry by offering security brokerage services.

Organized futures markets in agricultural products have long been in existence; however, the past decade has witnessed a rapid growth in futures markets for financial instruments such as Treasury bills, Treasury bonds, large bank certificates of deposits, Eurodollar time deposits, stock market indexes, and other financial assets. The Commodities Futures Trading Commission regulates a wide range of activities in futures markets for financial instruments.

In addition to regulatory authorities directly concerned with the financial markets, other government agencies also concern themselves with activities in the financial system. Specifically, the Justice Department and the Federal Trade Commission are frequently involved with bank merger and holding company acquisition activities and with truth in lending regulations, respectively.

SHIFT IN REGULATORY FOCUS IN THE 1980s

The reforms enacted in the wake of the collapse of the financial system during the Great Depression established much of the current structure of financial regulation. Most of the regulatory authorities discussed earlier and listed in Figure 8–1 were established by a series of legislative events during the 1933–35 period. Even though there have been few major institutional changes in financial regulation, the 1980s have witnessed a dramatic shift in the focus of financial regulation with regard to competition.

Financial Regulation prior to the Start of Financial Reform. Until 1979 and 1980 when the financial reform process was firmly established, the regulatory policies directed toward intermediation financial markets were primarily designed to limit risk taking by depository institutions and to limit contagion when one or a small number of institutions failed. This was accomplished by a variety of policies: portfolio restrictions that segmented various depository institutions, regulations and supervision that ensured a minimal level of asset quality, regulations on entry and exit, restrictions on product and geographic operations of depository institutions, separation of commercial and investment banking, restrictions on interest rates that could be offered to attract deposits (Regulation Q), and federal deposit insurance. Many of these sharply limited the degree of competition among depository institutions as well as limited the degree of competition between direct and indirect financial markets. Thus, the regulatory authorities focused on ensuring the soundness of intermediation finance even if this restricted competition and thereby limited the efficiency and adaptability of financial institutions.

This preoccupation with safety and soundness was a natural response to the experiences of the Great Depression. The collapse of the banking system was attributed to the excessive levels of risk that banks had assumed in the late 1920s in an environment of competition without extensive government regulation and supervision. Banks aggressively competed for funds in an environment without restrictions on deposit rates and as a result were forced to acquire higher yielding but also high-risk assets. With few restrictions on the uses of bank funds, banks become involved in real estate and stock markets and made high-risk commercial loans that were imprudent for institutions whose deposit liabilities represented the major component of the nation's money supply. In addition, the lack of a meaningful financial disclosure framework for securities markets increased the potential for practices that weakened the foundation of financial markets.

In contrast, regulatory policies directed toward the securities markets were not designed to limit risk and limit competitive forces. The new rules and regulations that emerged from the financial reforms of the 1930s were designed to make the securities markets more efficient and less subject to price manipulation by providing an easily accessible financial disclosure framework to market participants. In addition, regulations forced a sharp separation between commercial and investment banking limiting the risk exposure of commercial banks.

Thus, regulations adopted differing approaches to indirect and direct financial markets. Competitive forces were restricted in the indirect financial markets to reduce risk taking by institutions that issued deposit money; in contrast, competitive forces were encouraged in the direct markets. The basic rationale for this dual approach was based on the recognition that depository institutions stood at the center of the financial system because their deposit liabilities served as money. The level of system risk was regarded as directly related to depository institution risk and the experiences of the Great Depression seemed consistent with this view. Unfortunately, the dual approach provided the basis for much financial instability in the 1970s when inflation and high interest rates became a prominent feature of the United States economy.

Emergence of Structural Problems in the Late 1960s. Of the many structural problems that emerged in the late 1960s and early 1970s, Regulation Q ceilings on deposit rates and portfolio constraints on thrifts that specialized in mortgage lending were especially important.[8] By 1966 Regulation Q limited the deposit rate that federally insured banks, savings and loan associations, and savings banks could offer on savings and time deposits. Banks had been prohibited from paying explicit interest on demand deposits since 1933.

Both Regulation Q and thrift portfolios did not become a problem until after 1965 when the United States entered into an inflationary period that was not reversed until the early 1980s. As the rate of inflation gradually increased after 1965 until reaching almost 20 percent per annum in 1980, interest rates in the money and capital markets frequently exceeded by a large margin the Regulation Q ceilings imposed on depository institutions (see Figure 8–2). The large differentials between regulated and unregulated interest rates induced large transfers of funds from various financial institutions to the direct money and capital markets where the funds could earn a market rate of interest. The emergence of money market mutual funds after 1971 made it relatively easy to transfer even small deposits to the direct money and capital markets. The resulting disintermediation process threatened the variability of depository institutions and adversely affected the supply of mortgage and consumer credit.

The portfolio limitations on thrift institutions dictated that thrifts would allocate the major part of their asset portfolios to fixed-rate long-term residential mortgages; however, their sources of funds were becoming increasingly short-term and market-sensitive. The traditional strategy of financing long-term loans with savings and time deposits exposed thrifts to new problems when interest rates rose and became more volatile.

In addition to the structural problems in the financial system,

---

[8] Savings and time deposits at commercial banks were subject to Regulation Q as a result of the 1933 Banking Act; however, savings and time deposits at thrifts were not subject to Regulation Q until 1966. The 1933 act also prohibited banks from paying interest on demand deposits.

FIGURE 8–2
Differential between Unregulated and Regulated Interest Rates for the United States, 1975–1985

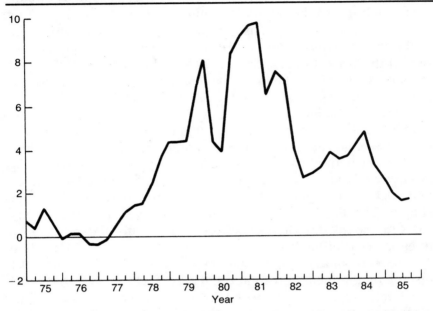

Note: The unregulated interest rate represented by three-month Treasury bill rate. The regulated interest rate represented by Regulation Q ceiling for bank saving deposits.

the Federal Reserve System found it increasingly difficult to control the money supply by the late 1970s. It became widely accepted by the late 1970s that monetary control was a necessary condition to bring the inflation rate down; however, the financial innovations that had been ongoing during the 1970s weakened the traditional relationship between the Federal Reserve's instruments and the money supply.

A crisis in the real and financial sectors of the economy was in the making by 1979: the inflation rate had reached an unprecedented level of almost 20 percent, the price of gold had exceeded $800 per ounce, the value of the dollar on foreign-exchange markets was declining, Chrysler Corporation was in need of a large federal bailout, increasing concerns about not only the fragility of some large banks but also the soundness of thrift institutions were being raised. In addition, it was widely recognized that many of the financial innovations designed during the past decade to circumvent binding regulations that limited profit opportunities had exposed financial institutions to new risks threatening the viability of the entire financial structure. The passage of the 50th anniversary of the Great Depression in 1979 added to the mood of fear for the soundness of the financial system and rekindled memories of bank runs and failures during the Great Depression.

The high inflation rates of the 1970s and their impact on unregulated interest rates in direct financial markets were ultimately recognized as the fundamental source of the financial system's structural problems. In addition, it became widely recognized that inflation could only be brought under control if the Federal Reserve significantly reduced the growth rate of the money supply. The Federal Reserve argued, however, that the growing role of nonbank depository institutions and demand deposit substitutes made it difficult to effectively control the money supply as commercial banks were the only depository institutions subject to reserve requirements. In addition, the Federal Reserve argued that its effectiveness to control money was reduced because of the declining membership base as banks opted to give up their membership status to operate under a less restrictive state-imposed reserve requirement system.

The Initiation of Regulatory Reforms. The financial reforms are ensured on four fronts.

First, the Federal Reserve announced new operating procedures in October 1979 emphasizing control over the monetary aggregates as a necessary strategy for lowering the inflation rate.

Second, the Federal Reserve announced new measures of the monetary aggregates in February 1980 that incorporated the major financial innovations of the past decade and thus incorporated nonbank depository institutions into the money supply process.

Third, the Depository Institutions Deregulation and Monetary Control Act of March 1980 initiated structural changes in the financial system that were on a par with those made during the reforms of the Great Depression. The 1980 act significantly enhanced the competition between all depository institutions by allowing all depository institutions to issue a new interest-bearing transaction account or NOW account. The act granted thrift institutions limited diversification powers to make consumer loans, to offer credit cards, and to offer fiduciary services to reduce their reliance on mortgages. The act initiated a phaseout of Regulation Q interest rate ceilings to be completed over a six-year period as well as eliminated or modified other forms of interest rate restrictions in the financial system. In terms of monetary control, the 1980 act introduced a new reserve requirement system designed to enhance the Federal Reserve's control over the money supply. All federally insured depository institutions were now required to meet Federal Reserve-determined reserve requirements. In turn, all federally insured depository institutions would have equal access to Federal Reserve services on a fee-paying basis.

Fourth, the Garn–St Germain Depository Institutions Act of October 1982 further increased the degree of competition among depository institutions by providing greater asset diversification powers to thrift institutions and introducing new deposit instruments not subject to interest-rate ceilings.

These actions have significantly redirected the focus of financial regulation by removing key constraints on competitive behavior and thereby increasing the role of competitive and market forces. The reform process, however, is far from complete. Significant geographic and product-line restrictions limit competition among depository institutions, demand deposits remain subject to a zero-interest-rate ceiling despite the removal of all other deposit-rate ceilings, commercial banks retain a virtual monopoly over commercial transaction deposits because other depository institutions cannot offer demand deposits as a normal source of funds and profit-seeking entities cannot hold NOW accounts, and finally, there continues to exist a sharp separation between investment and commercial banking.

The transition of finance has yet to be completed in the United States and as of the late 1980s, two major areas of concern remain.

First, the thrift industry has continued to weaken along with the ability and willingness of federal regulatory authorities to deal with the problem. As of 1989 several hundred thrift institutions were permitted to remain in operation despite negative net worth positions and several hundred more thrift institutions were operating with net worth positions of no more than 3 percent of assets. The Federal Savings and Loan Insurance Corporation, which insures the deposits of the majority of thrift institutions, is insolvent itself, since its reserves are insufficient to close the insolvent thrift institutions. By early 1989, the thrift problem had reached major proportions with no easy solutions in sight. Estimates of the cost for dealing with the problem range from $100 billion and upward and, as such, the solution will involve taxpayer resources. The newly elected Bush administration has offered a bail-out plan, but at the time of this writing, it is too early to see how the proposal will fare with Congress and the federal regulators. In any event, the solution will likely involve some reorganization of the regulatory structure and new financial regulations, which may or may not be consistent with the effort to liberalize financial transactions.

Second, the banking industry and the bank regulators have intensely pressured Congress to repeal the 1933 Glass-Steagall Act which separates commercial from investment banking. At the time of this writing, the Glass-Steagall restrictions remain in force; however, it is likely that Congress will in the near future significantly expand the diversification powers of banks. The repeal of Glass-Steagall in the light of the thrift problem has raised a number of concerns about expanding the powers of the banking industry, especially when federal regulators must bear some of the responsibility for letting the thrift situation become a major problem.

Nonetheless, the removal of key regulatory constraints on portfolio behavior has significantly increased the degree of competition in the financial system. In this respect, it is useful to draw some comparison with the reforms of the 1930s. The financial reforms of the 1980s and the 1930s shared a common concern for the stability of the financial system and the conduct of monetary policy; both responded to a crisis situation. The major difference, however, resides in the fact that the reforms of the 1930s were designed to limit competition among financial institutions whereas the reforms of the 1980s have been designed to remove key constraints on competitive behavior. In fact, some of the constraints on competitive behavior that have been removed or relaxed during the 1980s had originally been imposed by the reforms of the 1930s.

AN INTERNATIONAL PERSPECTIVE ON FINANCIAL REGULATION

The regulation of financial markets in other countries has also experienced a shift similar in orientation to that of the United States. Many countries found that the new economic and technological environment of the 1970s rendered their rigidly controlled financial structures ineffective and sometimes unstable. In addition, they found that the conflicts between the new environment and the existing structure of financial regulation made it increasingly difficult for the monetary authority to carry out its basic responsibilities of economic stabilization. Like the United States, the regulatory authorities recognized that the solution to these problems revolved around the removal, or the relaxation, of key constraints on competitive behavior among market participants.

The international character of the process has been emphasized by several recent conferences that brought together government officials, academics, central bankers, and others to discuss the transformation of finance and money. The Bank for International Settlements in December 1983 focused on the financial changes occurring in the developed economies of Austria, Belgium, Canada, France, Germany, Italy, Japan, the Netherlands, Spain, Sweden, Switzerland, the United Kingdom, and the United States.[9] The Federal Reserve Bank of San Francisco in December 1984 focused on the financial changes occurring in developed and developing economies of the Pacific Basin Region.[10] The Bank of Japan in May 1985 held its Second International Conference in which much of the discussion focused on the financial and monetary changes occurring in a wide range of economies, both developed and developing.[11]

The underlying theme of these and other attempts to access the changes in financial regulation taking place during the past decade is readily apparent. Despite differences among countries in economic and social structure and the stage of economic develop-

---

[9] M. A. Akhtar, *Financial Innovations and Their Implications for Monetary Policy.*

[10] Hang-Sheng Cheng, ed., *Financial Policy and Reform in Pacific Basin Countries.*

[11] Yoshio Suzuki, and Hiroshi Yomo, eds., *Financial Innovation and Monetary Policy: Asia and the West.*

ment, domestic financial markets are becoming increasingly competitive and regulatory authorities are less inclined to impose regulations that restrain competitive forces. In addition, the financial markets of many countries are rapidly becoming internationalized as restrictions on the inflow and outflow of capital are being relaxed.

ISSUES IN THE REGULATION OF
FINANCIAL MARKETS

There is little doubt that a major change in the focus of financial regulation has been in progress during the past decade; although many of the more serious structural problems of the financial system have been addressed and the financial system has become more competitive, significant regulatory issues have been raised by the transition of finance. Three appear particularly important: the regulatory-market conflict, the moral hazard of current government deposit guarantees, and the regulatory implications of rapid internationalization of finance. Even though the following discussion focuses on these issues from the perspective of the United States, they are important for many countries currently in the process of restructuring financial regulation.

The Regulatory-Market Conflict. One of the most significant behavioral characteristics of financial markets during the 1970s was the ability of market participants to innovate and introduce new financial assets and services that circumvented regulations limiting profit opportunities. NOW accounts, repurchase agreements, bank holding company-related commercial paper, Eurodollar deposits, and money market mutual funds were all instruments introduced by the market that rendered existing regulations on portfolio behavior less effective. In response, the regulatory authorities frequently extended the range of regulation to encompass the new innovations to reestablish the effectiveness of regulatory policies. But this only induced more innovation, which in turn induced more regulation.

Thus, the conflict between the market and the regulatory authority is essentially a Hegelian dialectical sequence of regulation, innovation, reregulation, and reinnovation.[12] The dialectical character of the process suggests that the evolution of an equilibrium or stationary regulatory structure is uncertain. It may not exist or if it does exist, it may evolve only after a long period of time.

The intensity of the regulatory dialectic depends partly on the degree to which existing regulations limit profit opportunities for market participants; for example, in terms of interest rates the intensity of the regulatory dialectic is a direct function of the size of the differential between unregulated and regulated interest rates. It also depends on the ability of market participants to innovate which itself is dependent on many factors, one of the most important being the degree to which computer technology is applied to financial transactions. The importance of the regulatory dialectic has increased immensely during the past decade along with the application of advanced computer technology to financial transactions. Computerization has dramatically reduced the per unit cost of financial transactions and has made it easier to introduce new financial assets and services that are not subject to existing regulations. As a result, the degree to which a given regulation limits profit and thus induces a financial innovation has declined and will decline further as the continuing advances in computer technology are applied to financial transactions.

This has raised an important issue with respect to the effectiveness of any regulation that limits profit making in the financial system. In addition, it raises a serious issue for monetary control since central banks, like the Federal Reserve, rely on a monetary control mechanism rooted in the regulation that depository institutions must satisfy minimum reserve requirements. Reserve requirements are a form of financial regulation that limits profit and as a result induces market participants to shift to financial assets not subject to reserve requirements.[13]

---

[12] Edward J. Kane, "Accelerating Inflation, Technological Innovation, and the Decreasing Effectiveness of Banking Regulation," *Journal of Finance* 36 (May 1981), pp. 355–67.

[13] Edward J. Kane has emphasized the implications of the regulatory dialectic for the regulation of financial markets. Eugene E. Fama has emphasized the implications of the dialectic for the conduct of monetary policy. Thomas Mayer, in "Federal Reserve Policy since October 1979: A Justified Response to Financial Innovation?" paper presented at the Second Surrey Monetary Conference, April 1987, provides an interesting summary of the issues with respect to monetary policy.

The Moral Hazard of Government Deposit Guarantees. In many respects, federal deposit insurance represents the most significant reform to emerge from the Great Depression. Many arguments can be offered to support a reduced level of government regulation in the financial system; however, few would suggest abandonment of federal deposit insurance. It has greatly reduced the range of contagion in the financial system by making it less likely that the failure of one or a few depository institutions can adversely impact other institutions or markets.

At the same time, a serious problem has emerged with the current structure of deposit insurance because it is based on a fixed-percentage-rate premium applied to an institution's total deposits. The fixed-rate premium is insensitive to the risk of the individual institution and thus encourages risk taking. Even though the moral hazard of fixed-rate premium deposit insurance was not a major issue when depository institutions had limited portfolio opportunities, it has become important in a more competitive financial environment because financial institutions now have the opportunity to assume greater risk than previously.

Various proposals have been suggested to deal with the moral hazard of deposit insurance ranging from the establishment of variable insurance premiums related to some measure of risk to variable capital-asset requirements related to some measure of risk.[14] At the time of this writing, however, there are no definite plans to substitute a risk-sensitive insurance system for the current system.

Internationalization of Finance. The internationalization of finance has been a major characteristic of financial change during the past decade. The shift from a fixed to a floating exchange rate system, the growth of international trade, and the relaxation of restrictions on inflows and outflows of capital by many countries as a part of their financial reform process have contributed to a rapid internationalization of finance.

This has been most clearly reflected by the growth of international banking and the even more rapid development of the

---

[14] Federal Deposit Insurance Corporation, *Deposit Insurance in a Changing World* (Washington, D.C.: Federal Deposit Insurance Corporation, 1983).

Eurocurrency markets. International banking has become increasingly unified as a result of the development of international clearing and financial telecommunication systems such as SWIFT and CHIPS, which permit banks to clear transactions across nations. In addition, U.S. banks have greatly expanded their foreign operations at the same time that foreign banks have become increasingly important in the U.S. banking industry.

International banking activities, whether reflected by U.S. banking activities in other countries or foreign bank activities in the United States, have been handled by the same regulatory structure as domestic banking activities. However, the rapid internationalization of finance and the increased networking of banking across national boundaries have raised serious issues for financial regulators. Regulators must now have access to reliable information on both the borrower's ability to repay (traditional credit risk) as well as the financial and real environment of the country in which the loan is made (country risk).

In response to this concern and especially in light of the recent international debt problems, regulatory authorities have attempted to develop procedures for assessing bank risk in an international setting. Representatives from the Federal Reserve, the Comptroller of the Currency, and the Federal Deposit Insurance Corporation meet frequently to determine country risk for selected countries to aid regulators in judging the foreign activities of domestic banks. In addition, the United States has brought pressure on other countries to increase cooperation among the regulatory authorities in different countries, to develop a common framework for assessing the risk of international banking operations, and to strive for a more unified approach to bank regulation.[15]

CONCLUDING COMMENTS

This chapter has provided an overview of the salient features of the regulation of financial markets. Financial regulation is based on the view that some financial markets are inherently different than

---

[15] Kane (1987) has emphasized the importance of adopting a common regulation approach among countries to remove incentives for banks to shift to less regulated environments.

markets in general because of the externality or public good character of their operations. Despite the current efforts to increase the range of competitive forces in financial structures in the United States and elsewhere, financial regulation remains committed to limiting risks taken by depository institutions and to providing an environment for effective monetary control.

The regulation of other financial markets has been less concerned with limiting risk and more concerned with enhancing the efficiency of financial transactions by imposing registration and reporting requirements on issuers of securities and preventing price manipulation.

It is likely that this dual aspect of the regulatory attitude toward depository institutions and direct money and capital markets will continue because the financial obligations traded in direct markets are not regarded as part of the money supply, while at the same time, the depository institutions play the central role in the expansion and contraction of the nation's money supply. Given that modern monetary standards are fiat based and direct market instruments are not yet close substitutes for deposit money, financial regulation will treat depository institutions differently than other financial markets.

REFERENCES

Akhtar, M. A. *Financial Inovations and Their Implications for Monetary Policy: An International Perspective.* Basle, Switzerland: Bank for International Settlements, 1983.

Cargill, Thomas F., and Gillian G. Garcia. *Financial Reform in the 1980s.* Stanford, Calif.: Hoover Institution Press, 1985.

Cargill, Thomas F., and Shoichi Royama. *The Transition of Finance in Japan and the United States: A Comparative Perspective.* Stanford, Calif.: Hoover Institution Press, 1988.

Cheng, Hang-Sheng, ed. *Financial Policy and Reform in Pacific Basin Countries.* Lexington, Mass.: D. C. Heath and Company, 1986.

Fama, Eugene E. "Banking Regulation in the Theory of Finance." *Journal of Monetary Economics* 6 (January 1980), pp. 39–58.

Federal Deposit Insurance Corporation. *Deposit Insurance in a Changing World.* Washington, D.C.: Federal Deposit Corporation, 1983.

Friedman, Milton. *A Program for Monetary Stability.* New York: Fordham University Press, 1959.

Friedman, Milton, and Anna J. Schwartz. *A Monetary History of the United States, 1867–1960*. Princeton, N.J.: Princeton University Press, 1963.

————. "Has Government Any Role in Money?" *Journal of Monetary Economics* 17 (1986), pp. 37–62.

Kane, Edward J. "Accelerating Inflation, Technological Innovation, and the Decreasing Effectiveness of Banking Regulation." *Journal of Finance* 36 (May 1981), pp. 355–367.

————. "Competitive Financial Reregulation: An International Perspective." In *Threats to International Financial Stability,* ed. Richard Fortes and Alexander Swoboda. Cambridge: Cambridge University Press, 1987.

Mayer, Thomas. "Federal Reserve Policy since October 1979: A Justified Response to Financial Innovation?" In *Monetary Policy and Financial Innovations in Five Leading Industrial Countries*, ed. Stephen Brown. London: Macmillan, 1988.

Rolnick, Arthur J., and Warren E. Weber. "New Evidence on the Free Banking Era." *American Economic Review* 73 (December 1983), pp. 1080–91.

Stigler, George. "The Theory of Economic Regulation." *Bell Journal of Economics* 2 (Spring 1971), pp. 3–21.

Suzuki, Yoshio, and Hiroshi Yomo, eds. *Financial Innovation and Monetary Policy: Asia and the West*. Tokyo: University of Tokyo Press, 1986.

Task Group on Regulation of Financial Services. *Blueprint for Reform: The Report of the Task Group on Regulation of Financial Services*. Washington, D.C.: GPO, 1984.

White, Lawrence H. *Free Banking in Britain.* Cambridge: Cambridge University Press, 1984.

PART 2

REGULATORY PRACTICES— THE RULES

CHAPTER 9

EXCHANGE CONTROLS: THEORY AND EVIDENCE

Kate Phylaktis

A country's right to impose controls on international capital movements has never been challenged. Indeed, capital controls enjoy a place of honor in the International Monetary Fund (IMF) Articles of Agreement (Article VI) as an adjunct to borrowing from the fund when capital outflows are occurring. The tendency to use capital controls has been following cycles at least among the developed countries. Most European countries retained well into the 1950s a complex structure of controls on international capital movements introduced before World War II. However, as the European economies grew in strength, the restrictions were dismantled, and toward the end of 1958 the major industrial countries made their currencies convertible de facto.

The process of liberalization was reversed during the 1960s. The development of the Eurodollar market, the growth of multinational corporations, and the intensification of international banking ties resulted in international capital becoming more mobile. This international financial integration had reduced the maneuvering room for monetary authorities and encouraged a resumption of controls on international capital movements. The discriminatory controls in trade in goods which were eased at the time were substituted with discriminatory controls in trade in financial assets.

The process of liberalization was resumed in the mid-1970s and has continued since then. The United States dismantled controls in 1974; Germany, Switzerland, and Japan gradually reduced controls over the years; the United Kingdom abolished them in 1979; and France, under the pressure of its European Economic Community (EEC) partners, is currently reducing its capital controls. A similar attempt to liberalize capital controls has also been made by some developing countries, for example, Argentina, Chile, and Uruguay.

This new wave of liberalization is due to several causes: first, to the general tendency toward less official intervention in financial and goods markets; second, to the realization that with the development of multiple financial assets which are highly substitutable, it is difficult to devise a comprehensive system of capital controls; and third, to the consequences of the oil price shocks. The oil importing countries were subjected to a huge resource transfer to the oil exporting countries. To alleviate the adjustment process, they dismantled controls in an attempt to attract capital inflows and finance their huge current-account deficits.

This chapter begins by looking at the arguments put forward by both developed and developing countries for using capital controls as a policy instrument. First, we classify the various types of controls. Second, we analyze the effects of controls on the rate of return of domestic assets and on the interest rate parity.

Third, we examine how exchange rate adjustment is affected by the imposition of capital controls. Effects occur because the interest rate parity relationship is a vital component in the asset market approach to balance of payments analysis. Thus, by making various assumptions concerning the expectations formation mechanism, one is able to trace the effects of exchange controls on the exchange rate under floating-exchange rates, and the effects on official international reserves under fixed-exchange rates.

Fourth, we give an account of the empirical evidence on the effects of capital controls on the observed nominal interest rate differential adjusted for exchange rate changes. Last, we look at the implications of the empirical evidence.

ARGUMENTS FOR CONTROLS

Capital controls have sometimes been used under pegged exchange rates and at other times under floating. They have taken many forms, but almost all with the aim of reducing either capital inflows or capital outflows.[1] In the case of capital outflows, the purpose of the measures has almost always been to protect official resources, and in the case of capital inflows to preserve domestic monetary autonomy. The preceding arguments for controls apply under fixed exchange rates. Under flexible exchange rates, the main purpose of controls has been to prevent the exchange rate from fully adjusting.[2]

In financially repressed economies, however, capital controls have primarily been a complement either to the restrictions that have been placed on domestic financial markets, or to the exchange-rate policies pursued. For example, the imposition of high reserve requirements that gives the Central Bank direct access to loanable funds increases the cost of financial intermediation and the spread between lending and deposit rates. If the reserve requirements are higher than those prevailing in the rest of the world, the cost of domestic credit to a resident will be greater than that of foreign credit, encouraging residents to borrow abroad.[3]

---

[1] There are some exceptions, for example, the investment currency market in the United Kingdom, which aimed at ensuring a zero net outflow by U.K. residents, nonresident funds being left unregulated.

[2] For an elaboration of the effects of controls on the adjustment of an open economy under fixed and flexible exchange rates, see K. Phylaktis and G. E. Wood, "An Analytical and Taxonomic Framework for the Study of Exchange Controls," in *Problems of International Finance*, ed. J. Black and G.S. Dorrance (London: Macmillan Press Ltd., 1984), pp. 149–66.

[3] When there are no market imperfections, arbitrage activities ensure that

$$R_d^L = \left[\frac{F - S}{S} \right] + R_w^L \tag{1}$$

where

R_d^L = interest rate charged on domestic loans;
R_w^L = interest rate charged on foreign loans;
F = forward exchange rate defined as domestic currency; per unit of foreign currency.
S = spot exchange rate defined as above.

The lending interest rate is related to deposit interest rate (R^D) in each of the countries through a spread which in turn depends positively on the required reserve ratio

$$R_d^L = R_d^D + K_d \tag{2}$$
$$R_w^L = R_w^D + K_w \tag{3}$$

Another credit policy common in financially repressed economies is the imposition of interest-rate ceilings on deposits. The higher returns that can be obtained abroad encourage residents to invest their funds abroad.

Thus, such domestic financial regulations lead to a premium (or discount) on the yield on domestic compared with foreign assets, and to capital flows that are considered undesirable. To remedy this situation, the developing countries use capital controls as another form of taxation to offset the direct and indirect taxes implicit in financial system regulations.

A similar situation may arise when a crawling-peg system is adopted. Under such a system a country devalues its exchange rate by a rate equal to the differential between the domestic and foreign rates of inflation. Such a policy can be based on actual (ex post) changes in the price indexes or on anticipated (ex ante) changes. Traditional crawling-peg rules are generally based on ex post changes, while some others, based on preannouncement of schedules for future exchange rate adjustments, are based on ex ante changes. The preannouncement has been used by many Latin American countries, Argentina, Chile, Peru, and Uruguay. In other countries, such as Brazil and Israel, the crawling-peg system entails the preannouncement of the long-run target of maintaining purchasing power parity. Quite often the systematic devaluations are not sufficient to cover the higher domestic inflation rate because the exchange rate is used as an instrument to control inflation rather than to promote exports and discourage imports.

When the crawling-peg rule departs from the purchasing power parity criterion and the exchange rate is not expected to adjust immediately to differential inflation, then investors located

Domestic residents borrow abroad if

$$R_d^L > \frac{F - S}{S} + R_W^L \tag{4}$$

In the presence of reserve requirements, the previous condition is modified to

$$R_d^D + K_d > \frac{F - S}{S} + R_d^W + K_W \tag{5}$$

Given (1), condition (5) is always met if $K_d - K_W > 0$.

abroad perceive a higher return on assets in the domestic country (translated to foreign currency) rather than in their own.[4] These capital flows into the domestic country that increase domestic inflation could be stopped through the imposition of capital controls.

On the whole, however, once imposed capital controls quite often remain in force for long periods even after the reason for imposing them ceases to exist. For example, in the United Kingdom capital controls remained in force for 33 years.

CLASSIFICATION OF CONTROLS

In the analysis that follows, controls have been classified depending on whether they constitute incentives and disincentives for capital flows, or whether they are authorization requirements or outright prohibitions. The first group of measures affects the costs and yields of foreign relative to domestic capital, but preserves the freedom of choice of the domestic decision-making unit, while the quantitative measures of the second group interfere directly with the process of international capital allocation.

Capital controls can be classified according to other criteria such as the type of transactors, that is, whether they affect

---

[4] When the crawling-peg rule departs from the purchasing power parity, the rate of exchange rate adjustment is such that

$$e = \pi_d - \pi_w - \lambda$$

where the π_d and π_w are the domestic and foreign inflation rates respectively and λ the degree of overvaluation. If domestic and foreign interest rates follow the Fisher formulation such that

$$R_d = c + \pi_d$$
$$R_w = c + \pi_w$$

where c is the real interest rate (assumed equal across country), then capital inflows take place as long as

$$R_d > e + R_w$$

which implies $\lambda > 0$.

speculators or interest arbitragers. Such a classification seems very difficult for two reasons. First, some economic agents act as speculators and interest arbitragers at the same time. Second, although various capital controls are directed at one type of market participant, another category might well be affected. The following example illustrates the point: consider a country with fixed exchange rates. Assume speculators become more optimistic about the domestic currency, for example, the deutsche mark (DM). This increases the forward premium on the DM and modifies the behavior of arbitragers, resulting in increases in capital inflows. The authorities impose a tax on nonresident bank deposits to stem this influx of capital. There is a reduction in capital flows. However, if at the same time speculators revise their expectations because they believe that controls can be effective in preventing an inflow, the reduction in capital flows will be greater as the forward rate eases. If on the other hand, they think of this as a last ditch action with little hope of success, they might well revise their expectations upwards, increasing capital inflows.

The classification used in this study has been chosen for two reasons. First, it can be shown that under competitive conditions one can calculate an appropriate price restriction (a negative or positive tax rate) that would have the same restrictive effect on output as any given quantitative restriction. In this way, one can express all restrictions in a tax rate; this facilitates the integration of the study of capital restrictions with that of trade restrictions. Second, price restrictions can be more easily incorporated in the macroeconomic model used to examine the effects of controls on the adjustment process of open economies. The traditional relationship between the price of domestic assets and that of foreign assets is crucial to that model.

The main price restrictions on international capital movements are

1. Discriminatory reserve requirements on banks' domestic and foreign currency liabilities to nonresidents.
2. Cash deposits against funds borrowed abroad.
3. Separate foreign-exchange markets for different international transactions; for example, dual exchange markets or an investment currency market.

4. Reductions in rediscount quotas of banks resorting to excessive foreign borrowing.
5. Prohibition of full interest payments on foreign owned bank deposits.
6. Provision of swap facilities between the control bank and the commercial banks at forward exchange rates more favorable than market rates; that is, an interest rate subsidy on foreign currency holdings.
7. Restrictions on the repatriations of profits, demands, and royalties.

The main quantitative restrictions on international capital movements are

1. Limits on banks' net foreign position or net foreign currency position.
2. The prohibition of the acceptance of deposits in domestic or foreign currency from nonresidents.
3. Ceilings on the foreign or domestic currency bank deposits of individual nonresidents.
4. Prohibition of the repatriation of foreign assets.

ANALYSIS OF CAPITAL CONTROLS

Effects of Capital Controls on the Domestic Financial Market

The effects of capital controls on the domestic capital market can be shown in Figure 9–1 which depicts a capital importing country. SS shows the desired amount of investments held in the country by foreigners at any interest rate. DD shows the net demand for capital at any rate after domestic purchases of assets; it is the difference between stock assets supplied and demand at each interest rate before foreign investors appear. It is downward sloping, reflecting the assumption that (ceteris paribus) net indebtedness increased as interest rates fell. Equilibrium is initially at i_d with foreigners holding OA of claims on the country.

Let us assume that the domestic monetary authorities prohibit the interest payment in full to the foreigners. That reduces the rate

FIGURE 9–1

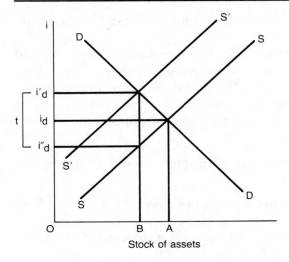

Stock of assets

of return on domestic assets held by foreigners. In Figure 9–1, that causes the SS schedule to shift to the left by the implicit tax rate (t) on the rate of return on domestic assets held by foreigners which is equal to i''_d i'_d. The foreign-held stock of capital is reduced from OA to OB and the domestic interest rate increases to i'_d.

Let us take another example of capital control, the dual exchange markets. The fundamental characteristic of a dual exchange market system is the channeling of international transactions through different foreign-exchange markets—an official exchange market for current-account transactions and a financial exchange market for capital-account transactions. The exchange rate for capital transactions is usually allowed to float freely although some intervention may take place. The exchange rate for current transactions is pegged, and official intervention takes place to prevent the rate from changing.

Under such a system the excess of the financial rate (defined as units of domestic currency per unit of foreign currency) over the official rate represents an effective tax on holdings of foreign assets by residents. That arises from the fact that earnings on foreign investment are (as current-account items) transacted at the official exchange rate and, therefore, the effective rate of return on foreign

FIGURE 9–2

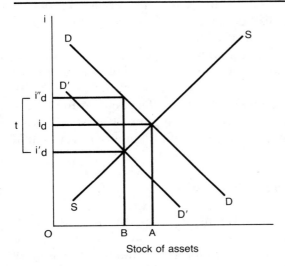

Stock of assets

investment is a function of the proportionate spread between the official and the financial exchange rates.

The effects of this control are similar to those shown in Figure 9–2. There is a shift of the DD schedule to the left by the effective tax (t) on the holdings of foreign assets by residents. The foreign-held stock of capital is reduced from OA to OB and the domestic interest rate falls to i'_d.

All Controls Can Be Expressed as a Tax Rate

Under competitive conditions the following proposition can be made: for each quantitative restriction there is an implicit tax rate that would produce the same restrictive effect. In other words, Bhagwati's proposition for the one-to-one correspondence between tariff and quota is restated.[5] Strict equivalence holds only in the absence of uncertainty.

In Figure 9–1 equilibrium is initially at i_d with foreigners holding OA of claims on the country. Suppose the domestic

---

[5] J. Bhagwati, "On the Equivalence of Tariffs and Quotas," in *Trade, Tariffs, and Growth*, ed. J. Bhagwati (Cambridge, Mass.: MIT Press, 1969).

monetary authorities wish to reduce this. They can either restrict claims to OB (or less), or impose a tax (t) on interest receipts by foreigners equal to $i''_d i'_d$. Either raises the interest rate to i'_d and reduces the foreign-held stock of capital to OB.

Were competitive conditions no longer present then, as Bhagwati shows in the trade case, the one-to-one correspondence between tariff and quota no longer holds; rather, for every quota there is a multiplicity of equivalent tariffs. The reason for this is straightforward; with a monopolistic supplier, the same price (average revenue) can correspond to an infinite number of marginal revenues.

Capital Controls and Interest Rate Parity

This section shows how capital controls (e.g., the prohibition of full interest payments on nonresident deposits and the use of dual-exchange markets) affect international capital movements, by examining how the relationship between the rates of return on assets in domestic and external markets is affected. The arbitrage activities of domestic banks, Eurobanks, and nonbanking institutions ensure that:

1. The rates of return in the national and external markets are equalized.
2. The rates of return in different external markets are equalized through the availability of forward cover in the foreign-exchange market.
3. The rates of return on assets in two different domestic markets are the same.[6]

---

[6] Assume we have two currencies, the U.S. dollar and the deutsche mark; $i_\$$ and i_{DM} are the domestic interest rates on the dollar and the deutsche mark respectively, $i_{E\$}$ and i_{EDM} the Eurocurrency interest rate on the dollar and the deutsche mark. Arbitrage ensures that if $i_\$ = i_{E\$}$, $i_{DM} = i_{EDM}$, $i_{DM} + F_p = i_{E\$}$. If i_{EDM} is higher than i_{DM} because, say, of capital controls, then F_p falls to maintain interest rate parity in Eurocurrency interest rates. For an exposition of the simultaneous determination of the national interest rates, the Eurocurrency rate, and the forward premium, see R. J. Herring and R. C. Marston, "The Forward Market and Interest Rates in the Eurocurrency and National Money Markets," in *Eurocurrencies and the International Monetary System,* ed. C. H. Stern, J. H. Makin, and D. E. Logue (Washington, D.C.: American Enterprise Institute for Public Policy Research, 1976).

The introduction of restrictions on capital flows affects these relationships in the same way as does the existence of transaction costs in the securities and/or foreign-exchange markets. Although the realized rates of return are different from when such "imperfections" did not exist, there is still equilibrium in the markets, in the sense that no unexploited profits are made by making further transactions.[7]

Prohibition of Full-Interest Payments on Nonresident Deposits

Examining the investment alternatives open to a nonresident shows how such a regulation affects the arbitrage relationship between domestic and foreign interest rates.

In the case where there are no capital controls, the return on a deposit held by a nonresident is the interest rate payment i_d plus or minus any capital gain or loss arising from fluctuation in the exchange rates.

$$r = \frac{S_t}{F_t} [1 + i_d]$$

where S_t is the spot exchange rate defined as domestic currency per unit of foreign currency, F_t is the forward exchange rate, regarded as an unbiased prediction of the future exchange rate expected to prevail at the time of the expiry of the deposit, and i_d is the interest rate on the domestic deposit.

The return on a similar deposit held in the nonresident's home country is

$$r^* = [1 + i_f]$$

where i_f is the interest rate on foreign currency deposit. Arbitrage ensures that the return on the domestic and foreign currency deposits is the same. In other words, the interest rate differential is equal to the forward discount on, for example, sterling, if the

---

[7] For elaboration of this concept of equilibrium see J. A. Levich and R. M. Frenkel, "Covered Interest Arbitrage: Unexploited Profits," *Journal of Political Economy* 83 (1975), pp. 325–28.

interest rate in the United Kingdom is greater than that of, for example, the United States.

$$i_d - i_f = \left[\frac{F_t - S_t}{S_t} \right]$$

If the domestic authorities prohibit the interest payment in full to the nonresidents, then the return on a domestic deposit held by a nonresident would be modified to:

$$r_E = \frac{S_t}{F_t} [1 + i_d^E] \quad \text{where} \quad i_d^E = i_d [1 - t]$$

In this case, the interest parity condition is modified to include another term:

$$i_d - i_f = i_d t + \left[\frac{F_t - S_t}{S_t} \right]$$

A "wedge" is interposed.

Dual Exchange Markets

Examining the investment alternatives open to a nonresident once more shows how such an exchange rate system affects the arbitrage relationship between domestic and foreign interest rates. Let us assume Argentina is the domestic country and the United States is the foreign country. Consider the options facing an Argentinian investor. For every peso invested in domestic bonds, the investor gets $(1 + i_a)$ pesos back in one period.

The alternative is to spend the peso on a dollar bond, in which case the investor can buy $1/S^f$ dollars where S^f is the financial peso spot rate. It pays i_{us}/S^f dollars of interest. The Argentinian, however, is forced to convert the interest back to pesos at the less favorable official spot rate S^c_{t+1}, because interest payments are current-account transactions. So it pays $i_{us} S^c_{t+1}/S^f$ pesos of interest. Under the dual exchange rate system the investor could repatriate the principal at the next period's financial peso rate S^f_{t+1}.

Speculative efficiency would ensure that

$$1 + i_a = [ES^f_{t+1} + i_{us} ES^c_{t+1}] \frac{1}{S^f_t} \tag{1}$$

where the operator E denotes market expectations. If it is assumed that $ES^c_{t+1} = S^c_t$ then the preceding condition is simplified to

$$i_a = i_{us} \left[\frac{1}{1+d} \right] + \left[\frac{ES^f_{t+1} + 1 - S^f_t}{S^f_t} \right] \tag{2}$$

$$1 + d = \frac{S^f_t}{S^c_t}$$

If the financial rate S^f never deviated from the official peso rate S^c, then d would be zero and the arbitrage relationship would be reduced to covered interest parity. The domestic rate would be equal to the foreign rate plus expected depreciation. But to the extent that $S^f > S^c$, d represents a positive tax on foreign assets, which must as a consequence pay more to compete with domestic assets. In this analysis expectations about the future financial rate are assumed regressive. If expectations are extrapolative, there would be a capital gain which could offset the tax on the foreign interest rate.[8]

Political Risk

The imposition of controls has another effect on investment decisions other than that of an effective tax. The possible imposition of controls is a type of risk that can be included as an element in the variance of an asset's return. This risk is what Aliber calls political risk, "the probability that the authority of the state will be interposed between investors in one country and investment opportunities in other countries."[9] By the nature of risk, this concept has nothing to do with existing controls per se, but rather relates to the uncertainty of future capital controls.

As in the case of the effective tax, the political risk can lead to a premium (or discount) on domestic compared with foreign assets, which will result in a differential between domestic and foreign

---

[8] See J. M. Fleming, "Dual Exchange Markets and Other Remedies for Disruptive Capital Flows," *IMF Staff Papers*, 21 (March 1974), pp. 1–27. Also see R. Flood, "Exchange Rate Expectations in Dual Exchange Markets," *Journal of International Economics* 8 (1978), pp. 65–77, for an analysis of rational expectations in dual exchange markets.

[9] R. Aliber, "The Interest Rate Parity Theorum: A Reinterpretation," *Journal of Political Economy* 81 (November–December 1973), pp. 1451–59.

interest rates after adjusting for expected exchange rate movements.[10] When the adjusted interest rate differential exactly matches the premium (or discount) arising from controls, there is no incentive for capital flows to take place.[11] Whenever one of the effects associated with controls is altered, however, the premium necessary to equilibrate the market changes accordingly, and capital flows take place until the appropriate interest rate differential is restored.

CAPITAL CONTROLS AND THE ADJUSTMENT PROCESS UNDER FIXED AND FLEXIBLE EXCHANGE RATES

The discussion of the effects of controls on the domestic financial market and on the interest rate parity can be easily incorporated into an asset market approach to the balance of payments. Under fixed exchange rates, the imposition of capital controls enables a country to pursue an independent monetary policy in the short run; under flexible exchange rates, the imposition of capital controls prevents the exchange rate from adjusting to expected inflation rate differentials.[12]

Adjustment Process under Flexible Exchange Rates

The analysis makes use of the model developed by Dornbusch.[13] In such a model a balance of payments disequilibrium is reflected in a money-market disequilibrium. In the short run the interest rate has

---

[10] Other imperfections, such as the existence of exchange risk, can also lead to a premium (or discount) on the yield on domestic compared with foreign assets. Furthermore, the existence of transaction costs in the financial and foreign exchange markets creates deviations from covered interest parity; see J. A. Frenkel and R. M. Levich, "Covered Interest Arbitrage: Unexploited Profits," *Journal of Political Economy* 83 (1975), pp. 325–28; and J. A. Frenkel and R. M. Levich, "Transaction Costs and Interest Arbitrage: Tranquil versus Turbulent Periods," *Journal of Political Economy* 85 (1977), pp. 1209–26.

[11] This statement does not take into account the effects of economic growth. In a world of economies growing at different rates, there could be continuing capital flows, even with an equilibrium interest rate differential, as a result of the expansion of private portfolios containing both domestic and foreign assets.

[12] See note 2.

[13] R. Dornbusch, "Expectations and Exchange Rate Dynamics," *Journal of Political Economy* 84 (December 1976), pp. 1161–76.

to change to restore equilibrium in the money market (Keynesian liquidity preference). How much the interest rate changes depends on the interest elasticity of the demand for money. This liquidity effect, however, is superseded by the change in foreign reserves, so that the domestic interest rate remains equal to the foreign interest rate.

In this framework, the interest rate parity is assumed to hold all the time and the forward rate is assumed to be an unbiased estimate of the expected future spot rate. Under fixed exchange rates, however, the spot exchange rate is held at a fixed parity within an upper and lower band and the forward rate only moves outside the bands when market participants expect a possible official change of parity. For convenience, one can further assume that there is no band around the par value and that the monetary authorities rarely change the parity. In such circumstances the domestic interest rate is equal to the foreign interest rate.

Suppose there is a discrete but unanticipated fall in the money stock. In the short run, the interest rate increases to clear up the money market. Thus, temporarily, the domestic interest rate is higher than the foreign interest rate. This increases the foreign demand for domestic assets, putting upward pressure on the exchange rate. Also, this necessitates interventions in the foreign-exchange market by the monetary authorities to purchase excess foreign currency, resulting in an increase in foreign reserves and an increase in their contribution to the money stock. The total money stock is unchanged, but the division between the foreign and domestic component has changed. The domestic interest falls to the original level because the money supply is restored to the original level.

The adjustment is not yet complete, however, because non-residents are not in equilibrium. They have more domestic bonds than they want to hold at the original level of the interest rate. As they try to get rid of them, the authorities are obliged to buy them to prevent the exchange rate from changing. Thus, in the end everybody has the same portfolio composition as before the monetary shock.

The implication is that independent monetary policy cannot be pursued. Monetary policy is dictated by the world economy (it is assumed that the country is small and not in a position to affect the world interest rate).

The monetary authorities, however, by imposing controls on capital inflows—for example, prohibiting the full interest rate payments on nonresident deposits—can maintain the domestic interest rate higher than the foreign interest rate for as long as the capital control is in action. The authorities gain some degree of monetary independence. At this point the short-run nature of this independence should be emphasized; for the price level consequences of using this independence start to emerge and affect the exchange rate via the purchasing power parity relationship at some stage.

Adjustment under Floating Exchange Rates

Under the floating exchange rate regime, the exchange rate is determined in the long run by the money-market equilibrium and the purchasing power parity. These two conditions simultaneously determine the domestic price level and the exchange rate.

In the short run, however, the purchasing power parity does not hold and the exchange rate is determined by the money-market equilibrium and the interest-rate parity. Whenever the money market is in disequilibrium, the interest rate changes to restore equilibrium. This change in the interest rate is offset by a change in the forward premium so that the interest rate parity is maintained. How the burden of adjustment of the foward premium falls between the forward and spot exchange rate depends on investors' expectations.

Suppose there is a discrete and unanticipated fall in the money stock. In the long run the price level and the spot rate fall by the same proportion. In the short run, however, the price level does not change, and the interest rate increases to clear the money market. The increase in the interest rate has to be offset by a fall in the forward premium on the domestic currency. If investors are assumed to have rational expectations, that is, the forward rate is equal to the long-run exchange rate, the spot exchange rate has to appreciate by more than the forward rate to create an expected exchange-rate depreciation. In the long run, however, as the domestic price level starts to fall, the domestic interest rate returns to the initial level and the spot exchange rate reaches the long-run equilibrium level.

The imposition of capital controls affects the spot exchange rate through the effects of controls on the interest-rate parity. Taking once more the example of the prohibition of full interest payments on nonresident deposits, the interest rate parity condition is modified to include the tax rate implied by the controls (see the preceding section).

$$i_d - i_f = i_d t + \frac{F_t - S_t}{S_t}$$

In this case the interest-rate differential is expanded to include the tax. In a country under flexible exchange rates, the tax is absorbed by the forward premium. How the burden of adjustment of the forward premium falls between the forward and the spot exchange rates depends on investors' expectations.

In the preceding example of a discrete unanticipated fall in the money stock, the imposition of controls on capital inflows causes the exchange rate to appreciate by less in the short run than when there were no controls, assuming that expectations about the exchange rate are not affected by the imposition of controls. Had market participants believed that capital controls would be effective permanently, the appreciation of the exchange rate would have been even less. In the long run, however, as prices adjust to the fall in the money stock, the spot rate comes to be dominated by the purchasing power parity condition.

EMPIRICAL EVIDENCE

The empirical evidence on the effects of capital controls is concentrated on the observed nominal interest-rate differential adjusted for exchange-rate changes. The studies can be divided into two groups. In the first group, the studies analyze the time series properties of the interest-rate differential. Johnston, for example, compared West German domestic and Eurodeutsche mark interest rates between 1973 and 1978.[14] Because exchange risk considerations do not come into this relationship and transaction costs most

---

[14] R. B. Johnston, "Some Aspects of the Determination of Eurocurrency Interest Rates," *Bank of England Quarterly Bulletin* 19 (March 1979), pp. 35–46.

probably are constant, the deviation should reflect capital controls. Johnston found that for the period mid-1975 to end-1977 there was a very close relationship between the rates, but for the period 1973–74 and again in early 1978 when there were capital controls there were substantial deviations.

Otani and Tiwazi used a similar method in their study of the Japanese experience in 1978–81.[15] They compared deviations from interest rate parity when using a three-month Euroyen, and a three-month Eurodollar deposit, with deviations when using a three-month Gensaki bond and a three-month Eurodollar deposit.

The first pair of covered interest rates reflects only transaction costs, while deviations from the second pair reflect transaction costs and capital controls. By thus comparing the two deviations, one can see how they measure the effectiveness of capital controls.

In fact the deviations in the two interest parities were great throughout 1978 (especially in the first quarter) and again in 1980. During both periods capital controls were extensively used. The implementation of the Foreign Exchange Control law in December 1980 resulted in the deviations between the two interest parities disappearing.

One limitation of this way of testing for the effects of capital controls is the lack of distinction between risk and the capital control tax. The second group of studies differentiates between these two effects. Dooley and Isard use a simple model of portfolio behavior to explain the differential between Euromark rates and interest rates within Germany between 1970 and 1974.[16] They consider the behavior of both the German private sector and nonresidents in choosing their portfolio stocks, implicitly taking into account arbitrage possibilities.

Dooley and Isard represent controls by (1) dummy variables; and (2) by using the Wilton-Reid technique to allow the estimated interest differential due to capital controls to shift continuously along a third degree polynomial path. Their work suggests that

[15] I. Otani and S. Tiwazi, "Capital Controls and Interest Rate Parity: The Japanese Experience, 1978–1981. *IMF Staff Papers* 28 (December 1981), pp. 793–815.

[16] M. P. Dooley and P. Isard, "Capital Controls, Political Risk, and Deviations from Interest Rate Parity," *Journal of Political Economy* 88 (April 1980), pp. 370–84.

most of the swing in the interest differential during the 1970–74 period was due to changes in the effective tax imposed by the series of capital controls that were put in place. At times, however, an estimated differential of as much as 2 percent per annum was required, in the context of political risk, to induce nonresidents to hold the excess supply of German debt, given the distribution of wealth between the German private sector and nonresidents.

Classen and Wyplosz use a similar methodology to estimate the impact of capital controls in France during the period 1972–1981.[17] There are two departures from the Dooley and Isard specification. They define asset demands in real terms and they measure controls in a different way. They develop a measure of the tightness of capital controls using a three-step scale proposed by Mathis.[18] They distinguish between restrictions imposed on banks (DB) and nonbanks (DNB) and their values range in absolute terms from 0 to 3, where negative signs correspond to the period when controls were intended to prevent capital inflows. The overall effect is captured in the variable D = DB + DNB. They find that control D had a significant impact. Furthermore, they find that controls on nonbanks are twice as effective as controls on banks. Their interpretation of that result is that banks have ways of circumventing the controls as far as arbitraging between internal and external returns on French assets are concerned.

Phylaktis modifies the Dooley and Isard model in yet another way and applies it to Argentina over the period 1971–84.[19] The model is modified to take account of the absence of external markets for Argentinian assets. Furthermore, the specification of the tightness of capital controls which is based on multistep dummy variables, and the examination of the effects of each capital control on the domestic financial market, make possible the estimation and the discussion of the effective tax of each capital control.

---

[17] E. M. Classen and C. Wyplosz, "Capital Controls: Some Principles and the French Experience," *Annales de l'INSEE* 47–48 (July–December 1982), pp. 629–59.

[18] J. Mathis, "L'evolution des Mouvements de Capitaux à court Terme Framie et l'exteneur de 1967 à 1978," *Economie et Prevision* 2 (1981).

[19] K. Phylaktis, "Capital Controls: The Case of Argentina," *Journal of International Money and Finance* 7 (September 1988), pp. 303–20.

The study finds that only three out of the eight controls used had effects on the observed nominal interest rate differential adjusted for exchange rate changes—the amount of profits as a percentage of capital that can be repatriated, the minimum maturity required for foreign loans and the exchange rate guarantee given to Argentinians for borrowing abroad. The political risk premium associated with prospective controls, however, was found to be highly statistically significant. The importance of the latter is not surprising in view of the lack of credibility which characterized the stabilization policies pursued by the Argentinian government during that time. Phylaktis extended the study to Chile and Uruguay and found similar results to those on Argentina.[20]

CONCLUSION

The imposition of controls on international capital flows have two effects on investment decisions. First, controls give rise to an effective tax similar to the transaction costs that one incurs in buying and selling financial assets and foreign currency like brokerage fees and information costs. Second, the possible imposition of controls, which has nothing to do with existing controls, gives rise to a type of risk which can be included as an element in the variance of an asset's return.

Both effects give rise to a premium (or a discount) on domestic compared with foreign assets, which results in a differential between domestic and foreign interest rates after adjusting for expected exchange rate movements. When the adjusted interest rate differential exactly matches the premium (or discount) arising from controls, there is no incentive for capital flows to take place. This implies that for a continuous effect on capital flows, the monetary authorities should be either continuously broadening the scope of controls or increasing the political risk premium.

Evidence presented in this chapter showed that capital con-

---

[20] K. Phylaktis, "Capital Controls in Argentina, Chile and Uruguay." *International Finance and the Less Developed Countries*, ed. K. Phylaktis and M. Prodham, (London: Macmillan Press Ltd., 1989).

trols have given rise to a premium (or a discount) on domestic compared with foreign assets. What is characteristic of these experiences, however, is the continuous broadening of the controls used.

Taking the example of Germany, between January 1973 and January 1974 there were discriminatory reserve requirements for nonresident bank deposits up to 95 percent as compared with 13 percent for resident deposits. However, capital inflows might not have been affected if nonresidents had bypassed the banks by placing funds with institutions not subject to minimum reserves because they are outside the banking system. During this period, therefore, the German authorities imposed an additional 100 percent minimum reserve requirement against foreign loans contracted by West German companies, making it unprofitable for them to borrow externally (Barderpot Law). This regulation had to widen its coverage to include smaller-sized transactions as time went on.

If one looks carefully at the period after 1978, when the authorities imposed discriminatory reserve requirements once more on the level and growth of deutsche mark liabilities of domestic banks to nonresidents, one notices that the Eurodeutsche mark rate dropped below the domestic interbank rate and subsequently returned to a normal level. The reason could be that this control was not enough to stem the capital inflow. Similar comments can be made about Japan, which has had the most comprehensive system of controls.

In general, in most advanced economies the development in recent years of multiple financial assets that are highly substitutable could be the reason for the liberalization of international capital flows. In such an innovative financial environment, the device of a comprehensive system of controls becomes difficult.

The corollary is that in countries with less developed financial systems, a comprehensive system of controls presents less difficulties. Evidence of the inverse relationship between the degree of financial development and the effectiveness of capital controls is given in Phylaktis.[21] The question which arises in such circumstances is whether the use of controls is a desirable policy

---

[21] See note 20.

instrument. Capital controls in many of these countries are used to prevent domestic entities from escaping the direct and indirect taxes implicit either in financial system regulations or the exchange rate policies pursued. The question then becomes one of the desirability of these financial regulations and exchange-rate policies. Should the monetary authorities interfere in the allocation of credit? Should the authorities allow the exchange rates to become overvalued by defending exchange rates with exchange controls while permitting faster inflation at home than their trading partners are experiencing?

REFERENCES

Aliber, R. "The Interest Rate Parity Theorem: A Reinterpretation." *Journal of Political Economy* 81 (November–December 1973), pp. 1451–59.

Bhagwati, J. "On the Equivalence of Tariffs and Quotas." In *Trade, Tariffs, and Growth,* ed. J. Bhagwati. Cambridge, Mass.: MIT Press, 1969.

Classen, E. M., and C. Wyplosz. "Capital Controls: Some Principles and the French Experience." *Annales de l'INSEE* 47–48 (July–December 1982), pp. 629–59.

Dooley, M. P., and P. Isard. "Capital Controls, Political Risk, and Deviations from Interest Rate Parity." *Journal of Political Economy* 88 (April 1980), pp. 370–84.

Dornbusch, R. "Expectations and Exchange Rate Dynamics." *Journal of Political Economy* 84 (December 1976), pp. 1161–76.

Fleming, J. M. "Dual Exchange Markets and Other Remedies for Disruptive Capital Flows." *IMF Staff Papers* 21 (March 1974), pp. 1–27.

Flood, R. "Exchange Rate Expectations in Dual Exchange Markets." *Journal of International Economics* 8 (1978), pp. 65–77.

Frenkel, J. A., and R. M. Levich. "Covered Interest Arbitrage: Unexploited Profits." *Journal of Political Economy* 83 (1975), pp. 325–28.

————. "Transaction Costs and Interest Arbitrage: Tranquil versus Turbulent Periods." *Journal of Political Economy* 85 (1977), pp. 1209–26.

Johnston, R. B. "Some Aspects of the Determination of Eurocurrency Interest Rates." *Bank of England Quarterly Bulletin* 19 (March 1979), pp. 35–46.

Herring, R. J., and R. C. Marston. "The Forward Market and Interest
Rates in the Eurocurrency and National Money Markets." In *Eurocur-
rencies and the International Monetary System,* ed. C. H. Stern, J. H.
Makin, D. E. Logue. Washington, D.C.: American Enterprise Institute
for Public Policy Research, 1976.

Mathis, J. "L'evolution des Mouvements de Capitaux à court Terme
France et L'exteneur de 1967 à 1978." *Economie et Prevision* 2 (1981).

Otani, I. and S. Tiwazi. "Capital Controls and Interest Rate Parity: The
Japanese Experience, 1978–1982." *IMF Staff Papers* 28 (December
1981) pp. 793–815.

Phylaktis, K., and G. E. Wood. "An Analytical and Taxonomic Framework for the Study of Exchange Controls." In *Problems of International Finance,* ed. J. Black and G. S. Dorrance. London: Macmillan
Press Ltd., 1984, pp. 149–66.

Phylaktis, K. "Capital Controls: The Case of Argentina." *Journal of
International Money and Finance* 7 (September 1988), pp. 303–20.

Phylaktis, K. "Capital Controls in Argentina, Chile and Uruguay." In
International Finance and the Less Developed Countries, ed. K.
Phylaktis and M. Prodham. London: Macmillan Press Ltd., 1989.

CHAPTER 10

ACCOUNTING CONSIDERATIONS IN INTERNATIONAL FINANCE

Clyde P. Stickney

In an international setting, as in a domestic setting, economic considerations should play the dominant role in business decisions. Yet, because accounting affects the manner in which the results of business decisions are reported to investors, creditors, and others, business managers must be cognizant of the impact of the required accounting and weigh its importance in structuring business activities. This chapter explores three accounting issues relevant to international managers: (1) foreign currency translation, (2) hedging foreign exchange risk, and (3) alternative accounting principles across countries.

FOREIGN CURRENCY TRANSLATION

The foreign currency transactions of a U.S. parent company, as well as the operations of foreign branches and subsidiaries, must be translated into U.S. dollars both for preparing financial statements for shareholders and creditors and for measuring taxable income and tax liabilities. This section describes and illustrates the translation methodology and discusses the implications of the methodology for managing international operations.

Functional Currency Concept

Central to the translation of foreign currency items is the functional currency concept. This concept is embedded both in Financial Accounting Standards Board (FASB) *Statement No. 52* which governs financial reporting and in Section 985 of the Internal Revenue Code which governs tax reporting.[1]

Foreign entities (whether branches or subsidiaries) are of two general types:

1. The operations of a foreign entity are a direct and integral component or extension of the parent company's operations. In this case, the U.S. dollar is the functional currency.
2. The operations of a foreign entity are relatively self-contained and integrated within a particular foreign country. In this case, the functional currency is the currency of that foreign country.

FASB *Statement No. 52* sets out characteristics for determining whether the U.S. dollar or the currency of the foreign unit is the functional currency.[2] Exhibit 10–1 summarizes these characteristics. The signals indicating which currency is the functional currency are mixed in some cases, and management judgment is required to determine which functional currency best captures the economic effects of a foreign entity's operations and financial position. As discussed later in this section, management may wish to structure certain financings or other transactions to swing the balance in favor of either the U.S. dollar or the foreign currency as the functional currency. Once the functional currency of a foreign entity has been determined, it must be used consistently over time unless changes in economic facts and circumstances clearly indicate that the functional currency has changed.

FASB *Statement No. 52* provides one exception to the guidelines in Exhibit 10–1 for determining the functional currency. If the

---

[1] Financial Accounting Standards Board, "Foreign Currency Translation," *Statement of Financial Accounting Standards No. 52* (1981).
[2] Ibid., para. 42.

EXHIBIT 10–1
Factors Determining Functional Currency of Foreign Unit

	U.S. Dollar Is Functional Currency	Foreign Currency Is Functional Currency
Cash flows of foreign entity	Receivables and payables denominated in U.S. dollars and readily available for remittance to parent.	Receivables and payables denominated in foreign currency and not usually remitted to parent currency.
Sales prices	Influenced by worldwide competitive conditions and responsive on a short-term basis to exchange rate changes.	Influenced primarily by local competitive conditions and not responsive on a short-term basis to exchange rate changes.
Cost factors	Labor, materials, and other inputs are obtained primarily from the United States.	Labor, materials, and other inputs are obtained primarily from the country of the foreign unit.
Financing	Financing denominated in U.S. dollars or ongoing fund transfers by the parent.	Financing denominated in currency of foreign unit or foreign unit is able to generate needed funds internally.
Relations between parent and foreign unit	High volume of intercompany transactions and extensive operational interrelations between parent and foreign unit.	Low volume of intercompany transactions and little operational interrelations between parent and foreign unit.

foreign entity operates in a highly inflationary country, its currency is considered too unstable to serve as the functional currency, and the U.S. dollar must be used instead.[3] A highly inflationary country is one that has had cumulative inflation of at least 100 percent over a three-year period. Most South American countries and many developing nations fall within this exception and pose particular problems for the U.S. parent company, as discussed later.

The Tax Reform Act of 1986 specifies the methodology for translating foreign currency amounts when measuring taxable income. It borrowed the functional currency concept from *Statement No. 52*. Section 985(b)(1), (2), and (3) of the Code state that

---

[3] Ibid., para. 11.

the U.S. dollar is the functional currency when the activities of a foreign entity (referred to as a "qualified business unit") are conducted "primarily" in U.S. dollars. If such activities are not conducted primarily in the U.S. dollar but "significantly" in a foreign currency, then the foreign currency is the functional currency. Important factors for determining the functional currency are (1) the principal currency in which revenues are earned and expenses are incurred, (2) the principal currency in which the foreign unit borrows and repays its debt, (3) the currency in which the books are kept, and (4) the functional currency of other foreign units of the firm.[4] It has been suggested that the first two factors probably dominate the functional currency determination.[5] The third factor is not discriminating as the books of foreign units are often kept in both U.S. dollars and the foreign currency. The fourth factor envisions consistency in the application of the criteria across economically similar foreign units.

The criteria for determining the functional currency for financial and tax reporting are sufficiently similar that the functional currency for any particular foreign unit is likely to be the same for both reporting purposes.

Translation Methodology—Foreign Currency Is Functional Currency

When the functional currency is the currency of the foreign unit, the all-current translation method is followed. Exhibit 10–2 summarizes the translation procedure for both financial and tax reporting.

Financial Reporting. Revenues and expenses are translated at the average exchange rate during the period and balance sheet items are translated at the end-of-the-period exchange rate. Net income includes only *transaction* exchange gains and losses of the foreign unit. That is, a foreign unit that has receivables and

---

[4] House Report No. 426, 99th Congress, 1st Session 472 (1985); Senate Report No. 313, 99th Congress, 2d Session 457 (1986).

[5] Hals K. Dickenson, "New Foreign Currency Translation and Transaction Rules," *Taxes—The Tax Magazine* (July 1987), pp. 463–77.

EXHIBIT 10–2

Summary of Translation Methodology When the Foreign Currency Is the Functional Currency

	Financial Reporting	Income Tax Reporting
Income Statement	Revenues and expenses as measured in foreign currency are translated into U.S. dollars using the average exchange rate during the period. Income includes (1) realized and unrealized transaction gains and losses, and (2) realized translation gains and losses when foreign unit is sold.	Branch Revenues and expenses as measured in foreign currency are translated into U.S. dollars using the average exchange rate during the period. Income includes (1) realized, but not unrealized, transaction gains and losses and (2) realized transaction gains and losses when the foreign unit remits dividends or is sold.
		Subsidiary Only dividends are included in taxable income, translated using the exchange rate on the date distributed.
Balance Sheet	Assets and liabilities as measured in foreign currency are translated into U.S. dollars using the end-of-the-period exchange rate. Use of the end-of-the-period exchange rate gives rise to unrealized transaction gains and losses on receivables and payables requiring currency conversions in the future. An unrealized translation adjustment on the net asset position of the foreign unit is included in a separate shareholders' equity account and not recognized in net income until the foreign unit is sold.	No translation of balance sheet accounts is permitted or required.

payables denominated in a currency other than its own is presumed to make a currency conversion at the time the account is settled. The gain or loss from changes in the exchange rate between the time the account originated and the time when it is settled is a transaction gain or loss. This gain or loss is recognized during the periods while the account is outstanding.

When a foreign unit is operated more or less independently of the U.S. parent and the foreign currency is therefore the functional currency, only the parent's equity investment in the foreign unit is presumed to be subject to exchange-rate risk. A measurement of the effect of exchange rate changes on this investment is made each period, but the resulting "translation adjustment" is included in a separate account in the shareholder's equity section of the balance sheet rather than being included in net income. The rationale for this treatment is that the investment is presumed to be made for the long term; short-term changes in exchange rates should not, therefore, affect periodic net income. The cumulative amount in the translation adjustment account is taken into consideration in measuring any gain or loss when the foreign unit is sold or liquidated.

Tax Reporting. The amount included in the U.S. tax return of a parent company for earnings of a foreign unit depends on whether the foreign unit is operated as a branch or a subsidiary of the parent.

If the foreign unit is operated as a branch, then the all-current method of translation is followed.[6] However, there are three important differences from the procedures followed for financial reporting:

1. Only realized, or settled, transaction gains and losses from receivables and payables are included in taxable income. Thus, their recognition is delayed for tax reporting relative to financial reporting.
2. An exchange gain or loss is recognized if the exchange rate changes between the time earnings are generated by the foreign branch and a dividend is remitted. This gain or loss is a component of the translation adjustment account for financial reporting but is not recognized for financial reporting prior to complete liquidation of a foreign unit. Thus, exchange gains and losses incurred prior to the remission of earnings as a dividend are recognized earlier for tax than for financial reporting.

---

[6] *Internal Revenue Code*, Sec. 987.

3. There is no translation of the balance sheet for tax reporting.

If the foreign unit is operated as a subsidiary, none of the income of the foreign unit is included in the taxable income of the U.S. parent. Only dividends received from this subsidiary are included. The dividend is translated into U.S. dollars using the exchange rate on the date of distribution.[7] Unlike the case for a foreign branch, no exchange gain or loss arises for exchange rate changes between the time earnings are generated by the foreign subsidiary and the dividend is paid.

Illustration.   Exhibit 10–3 illustrates the all-current method for a foreign unit during its first year of operations. The exchange rate was $1:1 FC on January 1, $2:1 FC on December 31, and $1.5:1 FC on average during the year.

For financial reporting, all assets and liabilities on the balance sheet are translated at the exchange rate on December 31. Common stock is translated at the exchange rate when it was issued; the effects of changes in exchange rates on this investment by the parent are included in the translation adjustment amount. The translated amount of retained earnings is computed by translating the income statement and dividends. Note that all revenues and expenses of the foreign unit are translated at the average exchange rate. The foreign unit realized a transaction gain during the year and recorded it on its books. In addition, an unrealized transaction gain is reflected in the translated amounts for the foreign unit arising from exposed accounts that are not yet settled. Note *a* to Exhibit 10–3 shows the computation of translated retained earnings. The dividend was paid on December 31. Note *b* shows the calculation of the translation adjustment. By investing $30 in the foreign unit on January 1 and allowing the $24.5 of earnings to remain in the foreign unit throughout the year while the foreign currency was increasing in value relative to the U.S. dollar, the parent has a potential exchange "gain" of $35.5. This amount is reported in the separate shareholders' equity account on the

---

[7] *Internal Revenue Code*, Sec. 986.

balance sheet. For tax reporting, the U.S. parent includes $47.5 in taxable income if the foreign unit is operated as a branch and $10 if it is operated as a subsidiary. The taxable income of the branch excludes the unrealized transaction gain but includes a $2.5 gain on the dividend remittance. Note *a* to Exhibit 10–3 shows that the

EXHIBIT 10–3
Translation Methodology When the Foreign Currency Is the Functional Currency

	Foreign Currency	Financial Reporting		Tax Reporting	
Balance Sheet					
Assets					
Cash	FC 10	$2:1FC	$ 20.0	Not Applicable	
Receivables	20	$2:1FC	40.0		
Inventories	30	$2:1FC	60.0		
Fixed assets (net)	40	$2:1FC	80.0		
Total	FC 100		$ 200.0		
Liabilities and Shareholders' Equity					
Accounts payable	FC 40	$2:1FC	$ 80.0		
Bonds payable	20	$2:1FC	40.0		
Total	FC 60		$ 120.0		
Common stock	FC 30	$1:1FC	$ 30.0		
Retained earnings	FC 10		14.5[a]		
Unrealized translation Adjustment	—		35.5[b]		
Total	FC 40		$ 80.0		
Total	FC 100		$ 200.0		
Income Statement					
Sales revenue	FC 200	$1.5:1FC	$ 300.0	$1.5:1FC	$ 300.0
Realized transaction gain	2[c]	$1.5:1FC	3.0[c]	$1.5:1FC	3.0[c]
Unrealized transaction gain	—[d]		2.0[d]	—	—[d]
Remittance transaction gain	—[e]		—[e]	—	2.5[e]
Cost of goods sold	(120)	$1.5:1FC	(180.0)	$1.5:1FC	(180.0)
Selling and administrative expense	(40)	$1.5:1FC	(60.0)	$1.5:1FC	(60.0)
Depreciation expense	(10)	$1.5:1FC	(15.0)	$1.5:1FC	(15.0)
Interest expense	(2)	$1.5:1FC	(3.0)	$1.5:1FC	(3.0)
Income tax expense	(15)	$1.5:1FC	(22.5)	Tax.Inc.	$ 47.5
Net income	FC 15		$ 24.5	(if branch)	

EXHIBIT 10–3 *(continued)*

	Foreign Currency		U.S. Dollars
[a] Retained earnings, January 1	FC 0.0		$ 0.0
Plus net income	15.0		24.5
Less dividends	(5.0)	$2:1FC	$(10.0)
Retained earnings, December 31	FC10.0		$ 14.5
[b] Net asset position, January 1	FC30.0	$1.1FC	$ 30.0
Plus net income	15.0		24.5
Less dividends	(5.0)	$2:1FC	$(10.0)
Net asset position, December 31	FC40.0		$ 44.5
Net asset position, December 31	└──→ $2:1FC		80.0
Unrealized transaction "gain"			$ 35.5

[c] The foreign unit had receivables and payables that were denominated in a currency other than its own. When these accounts were settled during the period, a currency conversion was required and resulted in a realized transaction gain of FC1. This realized exchange gain is recognized for both financial and tax reporting.

[d] The foreign unit has receivables and payables outstanding that will require a currency conversion in a future period when the accounts are settled. Because the exchange rate changed while the receivables/payables were outstanding, an unrealized transaction gain is recognized for financial reporting. It will not be recognized for tax reporting until the accounts are settled in the future.

[e] The foreign unit earned $24.5 during the period. If the $2 unrealized transaction gain is excluded because it is a timing difference, its retained earnings for tax purposes (called earnings and profits) is $22.5. The foreign unit waited until the end of the year to pay out one-third of these earnings as a dividend. Because the foreign currency increased in value during the year, an exchange gain of $2.5 [= (.33 × $22.5) − $10] must be included in taxable income if the unit is operated as a branch.

---

foreign unit generated earnings while the exchange rate was $1.5:1 FC but paid a dividend when the exchange rate was $2:1 FC. By delaying the payment of the dividend and holding the funds in a currency that increased in value relative to the dollar, an exchange gain of $2.5 is recognized. That is, if the FC5 of earnings had been remitted when earned, the dividend would have been $7.5(=$1.5 × FC5). The actual distribution was $10, composed of

$7.5 of earnings distribution (dividend) and $2.5 of exchange gain. When the foreign unit is operated as a branch, the dividend is not included in taxable income. When the unit is operated as a subsidiary, the full amount received of $10 is included in taxable income of the U.S. parent.

Translation Methodology—U.S. Dollar Is Functional Currency

When the functional currency is the U.S. dollar, the monetary/nonmonetary translation method is followed. Exhibit 10–4 summarizes the translation procedure for both financial and tax reporting.

Financial Reporting. The underlying premise of the monetary/nonmonetary method is that the translated amounts reflect amounts that would have been reported if all measurements had originally been made in U.S. dollars. To implement this underlying premise, a distinction is made between monetary items and nonmonetary items.

A monetary item is an account whose amount is fixed in terms of a given number of foreign currency units regardless of changes in the exchange rate. From a U.S. dollar perspective, these accounts give rise to exchange gains and losses as exchange rates change because the number of U.S. dollars required to settle the fixed foreign currency amounts fluctuates over time. Monetary items include cash, receivables, accounts payable, and other accrued liabilities and long-term debt. These items are translated using the end-of-the-period exchange rate and give rise to translation gains and losses. These translation gains and losses are recognized each period in determining net income, regardless of whether an actual currency conversion is required to settle the monetary item.

A nonmonetary item is any account that is not monetary and includes inventories, fixed assets, common stock, revenues, and expenses. These accounts are translated using the historical exchange rate in effect when the measurements underlying these accounts were initially made. Inventories and cost of goods sold are translated using the exchange rate when the inventory items were acquired. Fixed assets and depreciation expense are trans-

EXHIBIT 10–4
Summary of Translation Methodology When the U.S. Dollar Is the Functional Currency

	Financial Reporting	Income Tax Reporting
Income statement	Revenues and expenses are translated using the exchange rate in effect when the original measurements underlying the valuation were made. Revenues and most operating expenses are translated using the average exchange rate during the period. However, cost of goods sold and depreciation are translated using the historical exchange rate appropriate to the related asset (inventory, fixed assets). Net income includes (1) realized and unrealized transaction gains and losses, and (2) unrealized translation gains and losses on the net monetary position of the foreign unit.	Branch The translation procedure is the same as is done for financial reporting. However, only realized transaction gains and losses are included in taxable income. Unrealized transaction and translation gains and losses are not included, nor is any gain or loss on dividend remittances. Subsidiary Only dividends are included in taxable income, translated at the exchange rate on the date distributed.
Balance sheet	Monetary assets and liabilities are translated using the end-of-the-period exchange rate. Nonmonetary assets and equities are translated using the historical exchange rate.	No translation of balance sheet amounts is permitted or required.

lated using the exchange rate on the date the fixed assets were acquired. Most revenues and operating expenses other than cost of goods sold and depreciation are translated at the average exchange rate during the period. The objective is to state these accounts at their U.S. dollar-equivalent historical-cost amounts. In this way the translated amounts reflect the U.S. dollar perspective that is appropriate when the U.S. dollar is the functional currency.

Income Tax Reporting. When a foreign unit is operated as a branch, the translation procedure for the income statement follows the procedure followed for financial reporting with two important exceptions: unrealized transaction and translation gains and losses are not included in taxable income. In addition, unlike the case where the foreign currency is the functional currency, no exchange gains or losses are recognized on dividend remittances.[8] When the foreign unit is operated as a subsidiary, taxable income includes only dividends received.

Illustration. Exhibit 10–5 shows the application of the monetary/nonmonetary method to the data considered earlier in Exhibit 10–3.

For financial reporting, net income again includes both realized and unrealized transaction gains and losses. However, net income in this case also includes a $24.5 translation loss. As Exhibit 10–6 shows, the firm was in a net monetary liability position during a period when the U.S. dollar decreased in value relative to the foreign currency. Because more U.S. dollars are required to settle these foreign-denominated net liabilities at the end of the year than would have been required if the net liability position had been discharged before the exchange rate changed, an exchange loss is recognized.

For tax purposes only, the realized transaction gain of $3 is included in taxable income under a branch arrangement and $10 is included under a subsidiary arrangement.

Implications of Functional Currency Determination

As these illustrations demonstrate, translated financial statement amounts for a foreign unit can be significantly different depending

---

[8] *Internal Revenue Code*, Sec. 986.

EXHIBIT 10-5

Translation Methodology When the U.S. Dollar Is the Functional Currency

Balance Sheet	Foreign Currency		Financial Reporting	Tax Reporting	
Assets					
Cash	FC 10	$2.0:1FC	$ 20.0	Not Applicable	
Receivables	20	$2.0:1FC	40.0		
Inventories	30	$1.5:1FC	45.0		
Fixed assets (net)	40	$1.0:1FC	40.0		
Total	FC 100	$2.0:1FC	$ 145.0		
Liabilities and Shareholders' Equity					
Accounts payable	FC 40	$2.0:1FC	80.0		
Bonds payable	20	$2.0:1FC	40.0		
Total	FC 60		$ 120.0		
Common stock	FC 30	$1.0:1FC	$ 30.0		
Retained earnings	10		(5.0)[d]		
Total	FC 40		$ 25.0		
Total	FC 60		$ 145.0		
Income Statement					
Sales revenue	FC 200	$1.5:1FC	$ 300.0	$1.5:1FC	300.0
Realized transaction gain	2[a]	$1.5:1FC	3.0 [a]	$1.5:1FC	3.0[a]
Unrealized transaction gain	— [b]	—	2.0 [b]		— [b]
Unrealized translation loss	—	Exhibit 10-6	24.5)[c]		—
Cost of goods sold	(120)	$1.5:1FC	(180.0)	$1.5:1FC	(180.0)
Selling and administrative expense	(40)	$1.5:1FC	(60.0)	$1.5:1FC	(60.0)
Depreciation expense	(10)	$1.0:1FC	(10.0)	$1.0:1FC	(10.0)
Interest expense	(2)	$1.5:1FC	(3.0)	$1.5:1FC	(3.0)
Income tax expense	(15)	$1.5:1FC	(22.5)	Tax.Inc.	$ 50.0
Net income	FC 14		$ 5.0	branch	

[a] Realized transaction gains and losses are included in income for both tax and financial reporting.
[b] Unrealized transaction gains and losses are included only in income for financial reporting.
[c] Income for financial reporting includes any unrealized translation gain or loss for the period. The translation gain or loss is based on the net monetary position of a foreign unit during the period. The foreign unit was in a net monetary liability position during a period when the U.S. dollar decreased in value relative to the foreign currency. More U.S. dollars, $24.5, are required to settle the net monetary liability position at the end of the year than if settlement had been made throughout the year before the exchange rate changed. The calculation is shown in Exhibit 10-6.

	Foreign Currency		Financial Reporting
[d] Retained earnings, January 1	FC 0	—	$ 0.0
Plus net income	15		5.0
Less dividends	(5)	$2:1FC	(10.0)
Retained earnings, December 31	FC 10		$ (5.0)

EXHIBIT 10–6
Calculation of Unrealized Translation Loss When the U.S. Dollar Is the Functional Currency

	Foreign Currency		U.S. Dollars
Net monetary position, January 1	FC 0.0	—	$ 0.0
Plus:			
Issue of common stock	30.0	$1:1FC	$ 30.0
Sales for cash and on account	200.0	$1.5:1FC	300.0
Settlement of exposed receivable/ payable at a gain	2.0	$1.5:1FC	$ 3.0
Unrealized gain on exposed receivable/payable	—		3.0
Less:			
Acquisition of fixed assets	(50.0)	$1:1FC	(50.0)
Acquisition of inventory	(150.0)	$1.5:1FC	(225.0)
Selling and administration costs incurred	(40.0)	$1.5:1FC	(60.0)
Interest cost incurred	(2.0)	$1.5:1FC	(3.0)
Income taxes paid	(15.0)	$1.5:1FC	(22.5)
Dividend paid	(5.0)	$2:1FC	(10.0)
Net monetary liability position December 31	(30.0)		$ (35.5)
	└────→ $2:1FC		60.0
Unrealized translation loss			$ 24.5

on the functional currency and related translation method used. Some summary comparisons are as follows:

	Functional Currency	
	Foreign Currency	U.S. Dollar
Net Income	24.5	$ 5.0
Total assets	200.0	145.0
Shareholders' equity	80.0	25.0
Return on assets	12.3%	3.4%
Return on equity	30.6%	20.0%

These differences arise for two principal reasons:

1. Current exchange rates are used in translation when the foreign currency is the functional currency, while a mixture of current and historical rates is used when the U.S. dollar

is the functional currency. Not only are net income and total asset amounts different, but also the relative proportions of total assets made up of receivables, inventories, and fixed assets are different, debt/equity ratios are different, and gross and net profit margins are different. When the all-current translation method is used, the translated amounts reflect the same financial statement relationships (e.g., debt/equity ratios) as when measured in the foreign currency. When the U.S. dollar is the functional currency, financial statement relationships get remeasured (in U.S. dollar-equivalent amounts) and financial ratios differ from their foreign currency amounts.

2. The other major reason for differences between the two translation methodologies is the inclusion of unrealized translation gains and losses in net income under the monetary/nonmonetary method. Much of the debate with respect to the predecessor to FASB *Statement No. 52,* which was *Statement No. 8,* involved the inclusion of this unrealized translation gain or loss in net income. Many argued that the gain or loss was a bookkeeping adjustment only and lacked economic significance. This criticism was particularly justified when no currency conversion was required to settle a monetary item. Also, its inclusion in net income often caused wide, unexpected swings in earnings, particularly in quarterly reports.

As discussed earlier, the manner in which a particular foreign unit is organized and operated affects the determination of its functional currency. In many cases, the signals are mixed, and management judgment is required. For reasons discussed previously, most firms prefer to use the foreign currency as the functional currency because the all-current method generally results in fewer earnings surprises. Some of the actions that management might consider to swing the balance of factors in favor of the foreign currency as the functional currency include:

1. Decentralize decision making into a foreign unit. The greater the degree of autonomy of the foreign unit, the more likely its currency is to be the functional currency. The U.S. parent company can design effective control systems to ensure that corporate objectives are achieved

while at the same time permitting the foreign unit to operate with considerable freedom.

2. Minimize remittances/dividends. The greater the degree of earnings retention by the foreign unit, the more likely is its currency to be the functional currency. It may be possible to get cash out of a foreign unit and into the parent's hands indirectly rather than directly (through remittances or dividends). For example, a foreign unit whose signals about its functional currency are mixed might, through loans or transfer prices for goods or services, send cash to another foreign unit whose functional currency is clearly its own currency. This second foreign unit can then remit it to the parent. Other possibilities for interunit transactions are possible to ensure that *some* foreign currency rather than the U.S. dollar is the functional currency.

3. Denominate borrowing in some currency other than the U.S. dollar. The borrowing need not be in the currency of the foreign unit. Although such a strategy may result in having the second foreign currency be the functional currency, at least the all-current translation would still be used.

4. Transform any U.S. dollar borrowing into some other currency through currency swaps.

In some cases, a firm has no choice but to use the U.S. dollar as the functional currency. This may be because the balance of characteristics of the foreign unit clearly require it or because the foreign unit operates in a highly inflationary country. Because of the possibly significant and often unexpected earnings effects of including the unrealized translation gain or loss in earnings, it is advantageous to neutralize its impact. Because the translation gain or loss usually lacks economic substance, it is not desirable to enter into hedging actions that have economic cost. Rather, a firm should endeavor to manage with a net monetary position as close to zero as possible. Any change in exchange rates when applied to the small net monetary position results in insignificant translation gains or losses.

For most foreign units, cash and receivables are offset by current payables; thus, the net current monetary position is close to zero. However, long-term debt financing is often denominated in the currency of the foreign unit, resulting in a net overall monetary liability position. Some avenues for minimizing the amount of long-term liabilities for the foreign unit that enter into the calculation of the translation gain or loss are as follows:

1. Denominate borrowing in U.S. dollars. Recall that monetary items represent amounts that are receivable or payable in a fixed number of foreign currency units, regardless of changes in exchange rates. U.S. dollar-denominated debt does not satisfy the definition of a monetary item and is, therefore, excluded from the computation of the translation gain or loss.
2. Structure leases for the use of property so they do not qualify as capital leases. Using regular debt denominated in the foreign currency to finance fixed assets increases monetary liabilities. By leasing the asset and accounting for it as an operating lease, the lease obligation is kept off the balance sheet. To treat leases as operating leases, the lessor must assume most of the risk. This means that the lessee is likely paying a larger amount than if the lessee assumed the risks. As stated earlier one must be careful not to incur real economic cost to neutralize a bookkeeping translation gain or loss.
3. Structure a borrowing transaction so that the debt gets reported on the books of some other entity. The myriad off-balance-sheet financing techniques that can be used in a domestic setting may be equally applicable in an international setting and may have the added value of minimizing translation gains and losses.[9]

ACCOUNTING FOR HEDGING TRANSACTIONS

Firms often engage in transactions to neutralize their exposure to exchange (transaction) gains and losses. This might take the form of forward contracts, currency swaps, tax straddles, or other

---

[9] See D. L. Landsittel and J. E. Stewart, "Off-Balance-Sheet Financing: Commitments and Contingencies," in *Handbook of Modern Accounting*, 3d ed., ed. S. Davidson and R. Weil (New York: McGraw-Hill, 1983).

mechanisms. The treatment of gains and losses on these contracts for both financial and tax reporting is discussed in this section. The key issue is whether gains and losses from the neutralizing device should be accounted for and recognized independent of the transaction that gave rise to the need for the neutralizing device or whether the two activities are integrated.

Financial Reporting

FASB *Statement No. 52* sets out the required accounting for forward contracts in foreign currency. These requirements apply to currency swaps and other hedging instruments. Exhibit 10–7 summarizes the required accounting.

A forward contract that does not hedge an exposed position but is entered into as an investment is considered a speculative contract.[10] Such contracts are revalued each period; the change in value since the previous valuation date is recognized as a gain or loss. The revaluation is computed based on the foreign currency amount of the contract and the forward rate available on the market for the remainder of the contract. The contract is essentially marked to market each period.

All other forward contracts are presumed to be entered into to hedge either a specific or general exposed position. Two computations are needed: the initial discount or premium on the contract and the periodic gain or loss. The calculation of these amounts is summarized as follows:

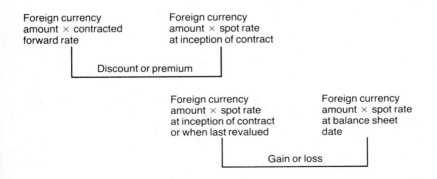

---

[10] FASB, *Statement No. 52*, para. 19.

EXHIBIT 10–7
Accounting for Forward Contracts for Financial Reporting

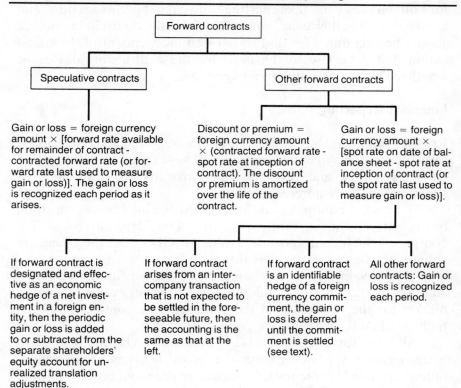

Forward contracts

Speculative contracts

Other forward contracts

Gain or loss = foreign currency amount × [forward rate available for remainder of contract - contracted forward rate (or forward rate last used to measure gain or loss)]. The gain or loss is recognized each period as it arises.

Discount or premium = foreign currency amount × (contracted forward rate - spot rate at inception of contract). The discount or premium is amortized over the life of the contract.

Gain or loss = foreign currency amount × [spot rate on date of balance sheet - spot rate at inception of contract (or the spot rate last used to measure gain or loss)].

If forward contract is designated and effective as an economic hedge of a net investment in a foreign entity, then the periodic gain or loss is added to or subtracted from the separate shareholders' equity account for unrealized translation adjustments.

If forward contract arises from an intercompany transaction that is not expected to be settled in the foreseeable future, then the accounting is the same as that at the left.

If forward contract is an identifiable hedge of a foreign currency commitment, the gain or loss is deferred until the commitment is settled (see text).

All other forward contracts: Gain or loss is recognized each period.

The discount or premium is viewed the same as the discount or premium on any monetary asset or liability: it is amortized over the life of the contract as interest revenue or expense. The effective interest method of amortization is used unless the results from using the straight line method are not materially different.[11]

With the three exceptions discussed next, the gain or loss is recognized each period in measuring net income. Recall from the earlier discussion that unrealized transaction gains or losses are recognized each period as they arise, regardless of whether the all-current or monetary/nonmonetary method of translation is followed. Any offsetting gains or losses on forward contracts are effectively matched against these transaction gains or losses. The net income measure, therefore, indicates the extent to which the exposed position has been neutralized, although few companies provide sufficient detail in their published financial statements for the user to make this assessment.

The three exceptions to the general rule are as follows:

1. If the forward contract is designated as, and is effective as, an economic hedge on the net investment in a foreign entity, then the gain or loss each period is not recognized in determining net income but instead is added to or subtracted from the separate shareholder's equity account for unrealized translation adjustments.[12] Recall that when a foreign unit operates more or less independently of the U.S. parent, the functional currency is usually the currency of the foreign unit and the all-current translation method is used. From the parent's perspective, the foreign unit is viewed more as an investment than as an integral part of the parent's operations. Any effect of exchange rate changes on the parent's investment is not recognized currently because the investment is viewed as a long-term commitment. Thus, the "gain" or "loss" from exchange rate changes is not recognized until the investment is liquidated. Instead they are accumulated in a separate

---

[11] FASB *Statement No. 52*, para. 18.
[12] FASB, *Statement No. 52*, para. 129.

shareholder's equity account. If a parent enters into a formal contract to hedge its exposed position, any offsetting gain or loss on the contract is not recognized in net income each period but is likewise accumulated in the separate shareholder's equity account, based on the matching principle of accounting. To the extent that the gain or loss on the contract exceeds the adjustment from translation, however, that portion of the gain or loss is recognized in computing net income each period.

2. If the forward contract is intended to hedge a long-term intercompany transaction, such as a long-term advance to or from the parent, then the gain or loss is assigned to the separate shareholders' equity account.[13] The rationale for this treatment is that the advance is part of the parent's investment in the foreign unit; the accounting for such advances is, therefore, the same as the accounting for the parent's equity investment.

3. If the forward contract is intended to hedge a foreign currency commitment, then the gain or loss is deferred and included in the measurement of the commitment when it is satisfied.[14] For example, suppose a firm commits to purchase an item of equipment and denominates the price in a currency other than its own. To neutralize its exposed position, the firm takes out a forward contract. Under generally accepted accounting principles, commitments such as these are not usually recognized as liabilities. Poor matching would result if the gain or loss were recognized on the forward contract but the effect of the purchase commitment were not recorded in the accounts until the commitment was satisfied (i.e., the equipment was acquired). To the extent that the forward contract amount exceeds the commitment amount, any gain or loss on such excess is not deferred but recognized currently in determining net income.

---

[13] FASB, *Statement No. 52*, para. 131.
[14] FASB, *Statement No. 52*, para. 21.

It is evident that the required accounting for gains and losses on forward contracts closely parallels the accounting for exchange rate gains and losses (both transaction and translation) that gave rise to the need for a forward contract. The underlying principle is the matching of revenues and gains with associated expenses and losses.

Income Tax Reporting

The tax treatment of forward contracts, currency swaps, tax straddles, and similar instruments has been clarified by the Tax Reform Act of 1986. Exhibit 10–8 summarizes the relevant provisions of the Code.

The major addition to the Code is Section 988. A Section 988 hedging transaction is one that effectively converts nonfunctional

EXHIBIT 10–8
Accounting for Forward Contracts for Income Tax Reporting

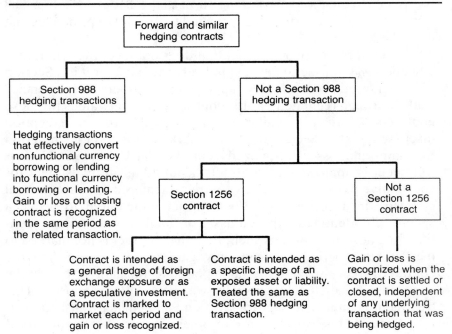

currency borrowing or lending into functional currency borrowing or lending. The general principle underlying Section 988 is that the transaction giving rise to the need for the hedge and the hedge transaction are considered one integrated unit. Any gain or loss on the hedge instrument is recognized in the same period as the gain or loss on the exposed asset or liability. Because transaction gains or losses are usually not recognized for tax purposes (in contrast to financial reporting) until they are closed or settled, the gain or loss on the hedge contract is generally recognized at that time.

Two categories of Section 988 hedging transactions are envisoned: fully hedged and partially hedged. Fully hedged transactions perfectly neutralize an exposed position on an asset or liability. This requires that the amount of the forward contract or other hedging instrument equals the amount of the exposed asset or liability and that the time period underlying each financial contract be the same. In partially hedged transactions, one or both of these criteria are not met. Fully hedged Section 988 transactions follow the rules previously stated. The Internal Revenue Service has not yet issued regulations pertaining to partially hedged Section 988 transactions, but the rules are expected to follow the principles just described.

A forward or other contract that does not meet the criteria for a Section 988 transaction is next judged as to whether it is a Section 1256 contract. Section 1256 applies to contracts in currencies traded through regulated futures contracts. Market values for these contracts are readily available at all times. With one exception discussed next, these contracts are marked to market each period and gains and losses recognized as market values change. This tax treatment is applicable to contracts acquired as an investment for speculative purposes as well as contracts acquired to hedge general exposure in a currency. If the contract is acquired to hedge a specifically identified exposed asset or liability and the firm identifies and accounts for it as such, then the contract is not marked to market each period. Instead, any gain or loss on settling the contract is recognized in the same period as the gain or loss on the exposed asset or liability, usually when the latter is closed. This treatment is similar to that for Section 988 hedging transactions.

A gain or loss on a forward or other contract that is not part of either a Section 988 transaction or a Section 1256 contract is recognized when it is closed or settled independent of the gain or loss on any underlying transaction that gave rise to the need for the contract.

As is the case for financial reporting, the recognition of gains and losses on hedging contracts for tax purposes follows a matching principle. Because transaction gains and losses are generally recognized when settled or closed, offsetting gains and losses on hedging contracts are treated similarly. When the hedging contract can be clearly linked with a specific exposed asset or liability, the matching takes place when the exposed asset or liability is settled. When the linking is not clear-cut, the gain or loss is recognized when the hedging contract is closed. The only exception occurs for publicly traded contracts acquired either for speculative reasons or to hedge general business exposures. These contracts are marked to market each period and any changes in market value recognized as gains or losses as they arise.

ALTERNATIVE ACCOUNTING PRINCIPLES

When analyzing and interpreting the financial statements of a foreign entity, whether it be a subsidiary of a U.S. parent or an unaffiliated foreign firm, recognition must be given to the accounting principles or methods that underlie those statements. Differences in acceptable accounting methods across countries can make intercompany comparisons meaningless. This section discusses the nature and extent of such differences and describes recent efforts toward harmonization.

Differences Across Countries

There have been numerous efforts in recent years both to catalog differences in accounting principles across countries[15] and to

---

[15] Ernst & Whinney, *International Accounting Standards: Synopes, Multinational Comparisons and Disclosure Checklist*, Cleveland, Ohio, 1986; F. D. S. Choi and V. B. Bavishi, "International Accounting Standards: Issues Needing Attention," *Journal of Accountancy* (March 1983), pp. 62–68.

EXHIBIT 10–9
Evolutionary Process of the Setting of Accounting Principles

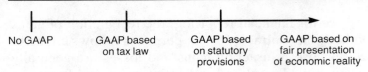

| No GAAP | GAAP based on tax law | GAAP based on statutory provisions | GAAP based on fair presentation of economic reality |

classify countries into various groups based on the nature of the accounting principles or the process through which they are set.[16] Two major drawbacks of these lines of research are as follows:

1. A substantial amount of effort is required to identify the accounting principles followed by various countries around the world. During the last five years, there has been a rapidly increasing degree of harmonization of accounting principles. By the time that studies describing differences in accounting principles are published, the data are usually highly inaccurate.
2. Because of the rapid degree of harmonization, efforts to classify countries according to the nature of the standard-setting process or the resulting specific accounting principles have had mixed results. As discussed later, the standard-setting process in most countries follows a fairly predictable evolutionary process. A specific country's stage in this evolutionary process is a moving target, particularly so in recent years.

Exhibit 10–9 depicts the stages in the evolutionary process of accounting standard setting. In the early stages of economic development of a country, no established mechanism exists for setting accounting principles. Soon after the economic development process begins, however, local governments institute various sales, income, and property taxes. The methods of accounting required for computing tax liabilities often become the methods

---

[16] For a summary and review of these efforts, see A. Belkaoui, *International Accounting: Issues and Solutions* (Westport, Conn.: Quorum Books, 1985), pp. 28–49.

used for financial reporting to creditors, owners, and others. During this phase, most businesses are closely held and use bank financing. Analysis of financial statements tends to focus on the availability of liquid assets relative to the amount of obligations. That is, there is more of a balance sheet than an income statement orientation.

As economic development evolves further, businesses tend to access the public debt and equity markets to a greater extent. Financial statement analysis during this phase shifts more to the income statement and the ability of operations to generate profits and needed cash. During this stage the deficiencies of an income measure defined to raise tax revenues and accomplish certain governmental policy objectives arise. Recognition is given to the need for an income measure that reflects the economic effects of transactions. Generally accepted accounting principles (GAAP) during this phase are typically set by a government legislative process. This occurs both because governmental units have previously been involved in the process of defining the tax base and because the accounting profession within the country is just beginning its own evolutionary development.

As economic development within a country matures, one typically finds sophisticated capital markets and active professional accounting organizations. Deficiencies in using the governmental legislative process to establish acceptable accounting principles become recognized, and standard-setting is turned over to the accounting profession. There is much greater emphasis on accounting principles that capture the economic effects of transactions. Lacking the enforceability of governmentally imposed principles, more effort is devoted to gaining acceptance of accounting principles enunciated by private-sector standard-setting bodies.

Most major countries involved in international business fall into the third and fourth stages of Exhibit 10–9. The United States, United Kingdom, and Canada are probably in the fourth phase. West Germany, France, and Japan are closer to the third stage but rapidly evolving toward the fourth. Most developing nations are in the second or third stages. The wide array of accounting principles that have been cataloged in the studies cited earlier reflect the differing stages of economic development and related evolutionary phases of standard-setting, as well as differences in culture, language, and similar factors. Exhibit 10–10 lists some of the important differences in accounting principles for major trading nations.

Efforts toward Harmonization

Extensive efforts have been made in recent years to harmonize divergent accounting principles. Harmonization is not the same as standardization. Wilson provides the following definition:

> The term harmonization as opposed to standardization implies a reconciliation of different points of view. This is a more practical and conciliatory approach than standardization, particularly when standardization means that the procedures of one country should be adopted by all others. Harmonization becomes a matter of better communication of information in a form that can be interpreted and understood internationally.[17]

Much of the work of harmonization has been undertaken by the International Accounting Standards Committee (IASC). Established in 1973, the IASC is now composed of members from 91 organizations from 66 countries. These members are pledged to exert their best efforts to get pronouncements on accounting standards from the IASC established as the acceptable methods of accounting in their countries. Thus, the pronouncements of the IASC have no enforceability on their own.

The IASC has issued accounting standards on a wide range of topics, including consolidated financial statements, segment reporting, leases, and inventory valuation and cost flow assumption.

Many of these pronouncements do not take a definitive position on a reporting issue. Rather, they describe alternative ways of accounting for a particular item (e.g., income taxes) to enhance understanding of the financial statement effects of the alternatives and the manner in which financial statements prepared on one basis can be reconciled to those prepared on another basis. Harmonization does not eliminate differences in accounting princi-

---

[17] J. A. Wilson, "No Need for Standardization of International Accounting," *Touche Ross Tempo* (Winter 1969), p. 40.

EXHIBIT 10–10

Summary of Alternative Accounting Principles in Major International Trading Nations

Item	United States	Canada	United Kingdom	West Germany	France	Japan
Inventory cost flow assumption	FIFO LIFO Wt. avg.	FIFO LIFO Wt. avg.	FIFO — Wt. avg.	FIFO LIFO Wt. avg.	FIFO — Wt. avg.	FIFO LIFO Wt. avg.
Segment reporting	Sales, income, and assets by product and geographical location	Sales, income, and assets by product and geographical location	Sales, income, and assets by product and geographical location	Not required	Not required	Sales by product and geographical location
Research and development costs	Expensed in period incurred	Expensed in period incurred	Expensed in period incurred	Expensed in period incurred	Deferred and amortized in certain circumstances	Deferred and amortized in certain circumstances
Goodwill arising from business combinations	Amortized over maximum of 40 years	Amortized over maximum of 40 years	Amortized over maximum of 20 years (exposure draft)	No specific maximum period for amortization	No amortization required	Amortization over 5 years
Capitalization of finance leases	Yes	Yes	No	No	No	No
Foreign currency translation	Combination of all-current and monetary/nonmonetary methods	Similar to U.S. but translation gains and losses on long-term debt amortized over life of issue	Similar to U.S.	No specific requirements	No specific requirements	Monetary/nonmonetary method

ples but may be a necessary step in the process of establishing more uniform accounting principles in an international setting. Kirkpatrick states: "Harmonization must be identified as a gradual, though positive, process that with goodwill, common sense and acceptance of user needs, and preparer recognition of these, will pass through the phases of compatibility, comparability, and eventually conformity."[18]

Reporting Requirements for Foreign Registrants in the United States

Foreign corporations desiring to raise capital in U.S. markets are required to conform to two important Securities and Exchange Commission (SEC) requirements:

1. The foreign entity must either (*a*) present a reconciliation, using Form 20F, of net income and balance sheet amounts computed using GAAP of the foreign entity with net income and balance sheet amounts based on U.S. GAAP, or (*b*) if such a reconciliation cannot be meaningfully compiled, then a full set of financial statements and related disclosures conforming to U.S. GAAP must be provided.[19]
2. The financial statements for the most recent three years must be audited in conformance with U.S. generally accepted auditing standards.

The position of the SEC is that differences in accounting principles can be reconciled but differences in auditing standards cannot.[20]

SUMMARY

Accounting issues facing international managers are in different stages of development. Since the issuance of FASB *Statement No.*

---

[18] J. L. Kirkpatrick, "The Gaps in International GAAP," *Corporate Accounting* (Fall 1985), p. 4.

[19] Securities and Exchange Commission, Rule 4-01 (a)(2) [17 CFR 210.4-01].

[20] Securities and Exchange Commission, *Internationalization of Securities Markets* (1987), pp. iv–29.

52, the methods of translating the financial statements of foreign branches and subsidiaries for the purpose of consolidation with a U.S. parent are well settled. Except for operations in highly inflationary countries, most foreign operations are translated using the all-current method. Transaction exchange gains and losses enter into the computation of net income each period, while unrealized translation exchange adjustments are shown in a separate shareholders' equity account and do not affect net income each period. The accounting for forward contracts and other hedging devices for financial reporting has also been settled since *Statement No. 52* was issued.

The method of foreign currency translation and the accounting for hedging contracts for income tax purposes was set out in provisions of the Tax Reform Act of 1986. The treatment of these items for tax purposes closely parallels their treatment for financial reporting except that transaction exchange gains and losses are not recognized for tax purposes in most cases until closed or settled. Given the recent change in the tax law, the Internal Revenue Service has not yet issued full regulations to implement the new tax law.

The topic of international differences in accounting principles is in a stage of rapid change. As capital markets around the world become increasingly more integrated, efforts to harmonize and even conform accounting principles across countries has accelerated. The International Accounting Standards Committee continues to issue new pronouncements that attempt to narrow differences in accounting principles. The IASC has no enforcement power, however, and must rely on the accounting profession within each country to get its pronouncements adopted. The internationalization of securities markets will be a major force in accelerating the pace at which standardization of accounting principles is realized.

REFERENCES

Belkaoui, A. *International Accounting: Issues and Solutions.* Westport, Conn.: Quorum Books, 1985.

Choi, F. D. S., and V. B. Bavishi. "International Accounting Standards:

Issues Needing Attention." *Journal of Accountancy* (March 1983), pp. 62–68.

Dickenson, H. K. "New Foreign Currency Translation and Transaction Rules." *Taxes—The Tax Magazine* (July 1987), pp. 463–77.

Ernst & Whinney. *International Accounting Standards: Synopes, Multinational Comparisons and Disclosure Checklist*. Cleveland, Ohio, 1986.

Financial Accounting Standards Board. "Foreign Currency Translation." *Statement of Financial Accounting Standards No. 52* (1981).

Kirkpatrick, J. L. "The Gaps in International GAAP." *Corporate Accounting* (Fall 1985).

Securities and Exchange Commission *Internationalization of Securities Markets*. Washington, D.C.: Securities and Exchange Commission, 1987.

CHAPTER 11

TAX STRUCTURES AND FINANCE

John F. Chown

Tax management is a central part of international financial management. The object of the exercise is to maximize expected bottom-line profits after tax. Although small differences in tax rates should never dominate a decision on whether to locate a factory in Germany or Italy, they can and should influence how it is financed.

We can regard an international corporate group as a machine for generating cash flows. Each part of it needs to be fed with capital and does, in due course, generate profits. Each part can be financed in different ways in different currencies with different maturities. A systematic analysis, from this point of view, taking full account of currency and interest rate risk and of the tax peculiarities of all relevant countries, often proves rewarding.

Such an analysis should not and need not affect the shape of the underlying business enterprise, where it manufactures, and where it sells. A very useful increase in overall profits can often be achieved by a few subtle decisions on where to borrow, where to invest, and how to route intercompany cash flows.

United States-based corporations have found the ground rules materially different after the Tax Reform Act of 1986. Although this may simplify decisions at a domestic level, it actually makes the task of international tax planners more complex, and more interesting. The reasons are set out briefly in the next section.

Following this, we set out some general principles of international tax planning, and deal specifically with the opportunities for tax efficient corporate finance. In the last section we discuss how recent developments in financial markets affect tax planners.

It is impossible in a general work such as this to set out all the complexities of the tax rules of many countries.[1] The material that is included is intended to give financial managers a feel for the range of problems and opportunities and to encourage them to take an active interest in the work of their tax colleagues. Appendix 1 is a brief summary of the relevant provisions from the Tax Reform Act. Appendix 2 goes into a little more detail on the United Kingdom, a country that persists with irrational and asymmetrical treatment of foreign-exchange gains and losses. A proper understanding of these is useful both in showing the key strategic potential of a United Kingdom subsidiary and giving the flavor of the problems that may arise in many other countries. For the same reason, Appendix 3 discusses some interesting developments in Australia and New Zealand, and Appendix 4 reviews foreign exchange exposure.

INTERNATIONAL TAX PLANNING AFTER THE TAX REFORM ACT

The United States' Tax Reform Act (TRA) of 1986 is probably the most far-reaching change that any country has ever made in its tax system at any time. The stated intention was to provide "a more level playing field," leaving corporations free to maximize pretax profits, assuming that the low-rate broad-based tax system would look after itself. As everyone knows, it is not as simple as that. The implications of TRA will preoccupy general management, as well as tax specialists, for a long time to come.

On the international side TRA is not even intended to be simple. There is meant to be a deliberate bias in favor of investing

---

[1] John Chown, *Tax Efficient Forex Management* (London: Professional Publishing, 1986). This sets out the principles in more detail, and includes more technical material on the tax laws of several countries. Some of the latter, particularly on the United States, have already been overtaken by events.

in the United States. U.S. corporations with international activities are going to have to rethink not only their operations but also the very way they approach the strategic problems of international taxation.

National Approaches to International Tax

Some years ago Professor Sven-Olof Lodin, then at Stockholm University, was asked to take a detailed look at the tax planning practices of multinational corporations. His main task was to see whether the Nordic countries were improperly minimizing taxes (on the whole they were not) but incidentally he found a surprising contrast between American-based and European-based multi-nationals' approach to international taxation.

Typical international tax managers of corporations headquartered in Europe would have an extensive knowledge of the tax systems of all the countries in which their groups did business. They would understand how these foreign taxes interacted with each other and with the tax regime at parent level. They would usually be senior to, or at least more highly paid than, domestic tax managers whose responsibilities were for home-country taxes and would, on best practice, have direct access both to the vice president of finance and to international line management.

In contrast, American corporations' "international tax managers" (if they existed at all) would be subordinates within tax departments whose heads would be mainly, and perhaps exclusively, concerned with United States taxation. The international tax manager would have a detailed knowledge, not of foreign taxes, but merely of how the United States taxes foreign source income.

At one time this actually made sense, but not any more. European companies had to take international tax strategy seriously; American companies did not. The American corporate rate was, at 46 percent plus applicable state taxes, by no means the highest in the developed world, but it was within the normal range. The typical American company with international operations simply took routine advice from the local offices of its auditors on tax liability at subsidiary level, and then cleverly juggled the tax credit mix under the "overall limitation" rules to keep the average foreign source tax charge below the U.S. rate.

This tactic is no longer sufficient. First, it is obviously much harder to get the rate below 34 percent than to get it below 46 percent and, second, the already complex rules governing the types of income excluded from the calculation ("separate limitation") and defining "source" have become more complex. The "controlled foreign corporation" rules are also tightened up and now pick up the extra U.S. tax even if the foreign rate is as much as 90 percent of the U.S. rate.

American companies that pay even a small proportion of their profits as tax to other countries now have to take a leaf out of the books of their European competitors and start discovering the mysteries of strategy in international taxation.[2]

GENERAL PRINCIPLES OF INTERNATIONAL TAX PLANNING

Any corporation trading internationally has to face tax and other legislation in more than one country. Even just exporting involves foreign currency and tariff problems. As soon as the corporation sets up local manufacturing, or assembly plants, or even a local sales office, it is liable to host-country taxes on its profits.

The objective of international financial management is to optimize bottom-line profits, or profits after tax. Managers should not become preoccupied with avoiding tax, but neither must they ignore it. Indeed, the best international tax practice is perfectly compatible with good corporate citizenship.[3] Good international tax planning need not, and generally does not, involve aggressive tax avoidance techniques. The main problem is to ensure that the corporation does not pay tax twice on the same profit, and that it is not more heavily taxed than its local, other American, or third-country competitors.

The first step is obviously to take advantage of the available tax breaks at the local subsidiary level in each country, such as

---

[2] *Journal of Strategy in International Taxation*, London: Professional Publishing Limited.
[3] John Chown and John Humble, "Tax Strategy for Multinationals' Economic and Social Issues," American Management Associations Management Briefing, 1979.

accelerated depreciation and investment tax credits. This can generally be done with no more than competent local CPA advice, and usually without affecting what is being done in other parts of the group. We do have to watch the material differences between countries in what is regarded as acceptable practice.

The Three Strategies

Once we go beyond this, and take a look at strategic international tax planning, we must study how different tax systems fit together. Often the fit is not good, even within the Common Market of the European Economic Community. This can be bad news or good, depending on how well the corporation and its advisers approach and analyze the problem.

The three basic techniques are profit diversion, profit extraction, and profit distribution. How and to what extent can the corporation divert potential profits from a high-tax to a low-tax jurisdiction? What scope is there for extracting profits from the country where they are earned using, for instance, interest, royalties, or management charges? How, having earned profits and paid tax on them, can it distribute them back home to the parent and ultimately to the stockholders with a minimum additional burden?

The key to good international tax planning is for general management to take tax into account before, rather than after, the event, and to bring international tax advisers—whether in-house or professional—into strategic discussions rather than leaving them to make the best of decisions already made. This is particularly important for foreign acquisitions, new ventures, and new financing. These are all transactions in which corporations work closely with their investment bankers and other financial advisers. Only too often tax is left as an afterthought, with very expensive consequences.

Profit Diversion
This involves arranging for profits to arise in a low-tax rather than a high-tax country—taking proper account of all taxes ultimately payable. Blatant use of obvious tax havens is countered by controlled foreign corporation (CFC) legislation—but the corporation need not go out of its way to pay up to 60 percent tax in

somewhere like Japan. Profit diversion may mean deciding where to locate or expand a plant, or where to source production, given existing facilities. A more aggressive technique involves transfer pricing: adjusting the intercompany prices of goods (often including unfinished goods) or services, so as to move profits from a high-tax country to a low-tax country. This can be extended to intercompany interest payments, a subject discussed in more detail later.

Corporate tax rates in industrial countries vary widely. In Germany or Japan the total burden may approach or exceed 60 percent, compared with 34 to 45 percent (depending on state taxes) in the United States. In the United Kingdom there is a flat rate of 35 percent, while many territories, including Singapore and Ireland, seek to tempt industry with much lower rates or special tax breaks. This does not, of course, mean that the corporation should concentrate all its production in Ireland and ignore Japan; tax is not the only factor. The subject is complex and beyond the scope of this handbook, but financial planners need to educate general management about these general ground rules:

1. The object of the exercise is not to minimize tax, but to maximize after-tax profits—the bottom line. Costs, quality of the labor force, access to markets, and tariffs usually have more impact on this figure than tax rates.
2. In making the appraisal, after-tax profits should not be calculated on nominal or "quick reference book" figures, but on the basis of state-of-the-art tax planning. Some countries have high rates but a generously defined tax base with lots of breaks. Until 1986 the U.S. federal rate was 46 percent; it is now 34 percent but the tax burden on manufacturing profits has actually increased. There are as striking contrasts in and between other countries.
3. The aim is to maximize profits after all taxes—not just the immediate local ones. What will it cost to bring profits home, either as dividends or as capital gain? The right figure is not necessarily that reflected in consolidated accounts, nor the theoretical one assuming immediate distribution. We need to use a "discounting" approach, familiar to treasurers and corporate planners, but still little used by conventional accountants.

4. A manufacturing plant is there for a long time. Future tax rates and rules are an uncertainty. Watch tax trends, and if in doubt redo calculations on a range of future tax assumptions. Other things being equal, tax rates in different countries seem more likely to converge than diverge.
5. Finally, a nontax point that often emerges from tax analysis: take foreign currency uncertainties into account. A strong yen may be good news in translating the Japanese assets but bad news for the costs and profits of the Japanese factory. Calculating the trade-offs, and the real trading exposure, is complex, but rewarding.

Transfer Pricing. There is another way of diverting profits. How does one price goods (and services) transferred within a group? A U.S. company selling components to a Japanese affiliate wants a high transfer price; but selling to a tax-sheltered Irish one, it wants a low price. There may be tariff (and in some countries exchange control) aspects to be considered, but the general principle is clear enough.

An extreme version of this strategy would be for the Japanese manufacturing affiliate to sell to a tax-free Panamanian company at a very low price, leaving Panama to sell to a Canadian distribution company at a high price, making a tax-free profit in the middle at the expense of both countries.

The catch, of course, is the antiavoidance provisions; originally, these were used only against blatant tax-haven operations. In 1962 the United States began using its provisions more aggressively and generally, even on transactions with other high-tax countries where a successful reallocation would be at the expense of the foreign government and not the taxpayer. Other countries were forced to take similar action to protect their own revenue, and nowadays even the company that does not try to be clever may find itself caught in the cross fire between two or more rival tax authorities. The recent White Paper is likely to intensify these disputes.

Profit Extraction

If profits cannot be diverted, can they be extracted? If a royalty is paid from the foreign company to a U.S. parent, the royalty is (if the amount is "reasonable") deductible from host-country taxable profits. The relevant slice of profits is, therefore, extracted from the foreign company at no local tax charge.

The income is subject to a U.S. tax charge, but at what may now be a lower rate. What if the rights had been transferred from the United States to, say, Bermuda? Could the royalty deduction have been achieved without the U.S. tax charge? Bermuda has no double tax agreements and full withholding tax would be imposed. There might still be a net tax saving but could we do better? Until recently the answer was "Yes, by treaty shopping."

The technique was to use an intermediate company such as one in Holland. Royalties would flow from the local company to Holland tax free by treaty. There is no withholding tax from Holland to Bermuda (Dutch domestic law), but the group would have to leave a 7 percent margin to be taxed in Holland. (Practical horse trading with the Dutch.)

This procedure is becoming increasingly difficult as the United States and other countries renegotiate their treaties. In any case, Bermuda would be a "controlled foreign corporation" if owned by a U.S. parent.

Profit Distribution—Group Structure

If you have done what you can in the way of diversion and extraction you are left with profits actually earned in the high-tax country in which you do business. How do you bring this profit home? Typically the profits pay corporation tax and there is an additional level of withholding tax when dividends are paid. In the United States, for instance, the total burden is 53.8 percent. The old procedure by which the second layer of tax can be avoided by trading in the United States as a branch has been partly blocked by the branch tax provisions of the Tax Reform Act of 1986.

There are various ways of dealing with this problem. Some involve setting up intermediate holding companies in countries with double tax agreements with the benefit of reduced withholding taxes. Others involve postponing distribution, probably by the use of intercompany loans and hoping eventually to release a profit by way of a capital gain. Needless to say, there are antiavoidance provisions and a complex series of tax traps. Group structure is important as is financing.

TAX EFFICIENT CORPORATE FINANCE

Tax efficient corporate finance is a powerful but often overlooked technique. It is overlooked, perhaps, because it only works where there is close collaboration between corporate finance advisers, treasury managers, foreign-exchange specialists and international tax specialists. This does not happen naturally within the hierarchy of most organizations. The people concerned have different and sometimes incompatible temperaments and time horizons, and it can take a real effort from somebody close to the top to bring them together.

There are problems, and opportunities, that can only be solved or exploited by systematically looking at the related factors of international tax, exchange risk, interest, and inflation. There are cases where these problems have threatened the very survival of enterprises. In other cases, a very useful improvement in after-tax profits can be obtained by an integrated, professional approach to tax efficient treasury management. The treasury team can become a genuine profit center, making as much contribution as a plant employing thousands.

Financing and the Deduction of Interest

In general, if a company pays interest on money borrowed for a business purpose, the interest is deductible in computing taxable profits. Where there is a choice, an international group of companies prefers profits to accrue in that group company having the lowest effective rate of tax. The obvious corollary, sometimes overlooked, is that charges against income, such as interest, should be taken in a country having a high rate of tax.

The choice of where to take the deduction depends on more than a comparison of nominal tax rates. We need to know effective tax rates. A company with most of its activities abroad may have insufficient profits taxable at the parent level to support major borrowings; it should finance at the subsidiary level. A new project in a new country is unlikely to generate taxable profits for some years, and then parent company financing may be more appropriate. Interest received, including interest on intercompany loans, is taxable.

There are several applications of these important principles. Some are obvious. A group company with a 20 percent effective tax rate should lend at the maximum acceptable rate to an affiliate paying 50 percent—and vice versa. "Transfer pricing" rules limit the scope for this.

There are more opportunities for choosing the financial structure of a subsidiary. Where it is profitable, and in a high-tax country, exploit "thin capitalization" to the maximum permitted by local law to make up for start-up losses, borrow at home, and inject equity or preferred stock. In the United States there can be advantages in setting up a thinly capitalized corporation or in using a limited partnership or subchapter S corporation as a means of cutting out the corporate level of tax. Leasing or tax exempt loans can, or at least could, exploit differences in the tax status of different investors and different corporations.

All these techniques have their parallels in other countries although the rules and the opportunities are usually quite different. Even on the "single country" transactions it is worth taking a high-level specialist's advice. Do not assume that the latest wrinkles are known to everyone in town who is involved in tax compliance, or even planning, work. The cross-border angles are even more interesting. Dual resident companies are no more, and "double dip" leasing where accelerated depreciation and investment tax credits can be claimed in more than one country on the same asset are harder to negotiate.

Less aggressive, but still profitable, planning opportunities are still available. If a corporation has taxable activities in more than one country and in more than one currency how does it arrange the financing and the management of the foreign exchange risk, to maximize the after-tax profit?

Tax Fragmentation

Foreign exchange gains and losses on foreign currency loans are often similar in economic effect to interest, but the tax treatment can be very different. This "tax fragmentation" creates both problems and tax-efficient arbitrage opportunities.

Before TRA, Philip Kaplan, coeditor of the *Journal of Strategy in International Taxation,* wrote: "Present U.S. law on measuring income or loss following variants in the value of a foreign currency against the U.S. dollar is, in a word, a mess."

What has changed? In 1988 Stephen J. McGarry wrote: "Chaotic, unsettled, confused, multidirectional, inconsistent, illogical, complex, uncertain. These are but a few of the terms used in articles describing the taxation of exchange transactions."[4]

In most countries the tax treatment of foreign-exchange gains is neither simple nor rational. By international standards, the rules in the United States, to which the preceding quotes apply, are relatively straightforward. TRA is discussed in Appendix 1. Corporate taxpayers have to accept the risks of currency movements; they might feel entitled to expect that the tax treatment of the resulting gains and losses was symmetrical and predictible. This is not typically so. In the United Kingdom, the law on the tax treatment of foreign-exchange liabilities has been a public scandal at least since 1976. Appendix 2 explains the background, and is required reading even for those who have no major U.K. activities.

Planning for Groups of Companies

What happens when an international group of companies has foreign currency exposures with tax consequences in more than one country?

Step one must be to compute exposure in local currency in each country. This exercise must be thorough and accurate. A liability to pay Portugese escudos next month is not the same as a liability to pay in September next year and needs to be recorded separately.

Step two is to calculate group exposure in after-tax terms, treating each subsidiary in exactly the same way as if it were an independent company, taking account of tax factors in its country of residence but (at this stage) ignoring tax factors at parent-company level.

Step three is to centralize the information. The parent, or a fellow subsidiary, may have matching risks and it may be advisable

---

[4] Stephen J. McGarry, "The Taxation of Exchange Gains and Losses: A Road Map," *International Tax Journal* 14, no. 1 (Winter 1988), pp. 25–51.

to net out the exposure on a group basis before taking any steps to hedge.

A foreign-exchange exposure in one direction in a subsidiary may be matched by a risk in the opposite direction (or a hedging transaction may be deliberately set up) in a subsidiary in another country.

Armed with this information we can look at our overall strategy. It is easy enough to set out a schedule balancing these out in pretax terms—provided we have scheduled liabilities by maturity as well as by currency. Now tax comes into the analysis, and it is essential to continue the calculation in posttax terms. To take an obvious example: if there is a $10,000 exposure in a country with a 40 percent tax rate, a 10 percent movement in the exchange rate produces a gross loss (or profit) of $1,000, but this will be reduced by tax to $600. If the hedge is carried out through a tax-haven affiliate, it may only be necessary to hedge half the amount—$600.

Branches

Another complication arises where the same profit or gain is liable to tax in more than one country. The income and gains of an unincorporated foreign branch of a domestic company are normally subject to domestic tax. The same income is taxable in the host country, but in principle this tax is available as a credit. As each country calculates gains and losses in its own currency, however, this can produce anomalous results. Although (apart from banks) branches as such are relatively rare in international operations, the point is becoming increasingly important with the spread of controlled foreign corporation (Subpart F) legislation. This may, in certain circumstances, result in a foreign subsidiary being taxed transparently, as if it were a branch.

Because each country calculates tax in its own currency, this often results in corporations getting the worst of both worlds. The mechanics of these and other traps are set out in more technical writings.[5]

---

[5] See note 1.

Distortion of Double Tax Relief

Double tax relief, whether given unilaterally or by treaty, can be distorted by foreign-exchange fluctuations. This fourth type of tax fragmentation is more complicated but repays study. For instance, profits earned in a foreign branch are typically subject to tax in both countries, each of which makes the calculation in its own currency. The planning implications of this are more in the arithmetic than in the law, but some legal points are relevant. How are the profits of a foreign branch computed? Must we translate all transactions into home-country currency, or will the home revenue bureau accept the foreign currency computation, translating only the resulting profits? Is translation at average or closing rates? How do we calculate double tax relief? What rate of exchange is appropriate?

Gains and losses in a foreign subsidiary in the first instance, are taxed under host-country rules, which have their own traps and opportunities. This is not the end of the story. The gain may ultimately be taxed (or the loss relieved) when there is a dividend distribution or when the subsidiary is wound up or sold.

The United States, the United Kingdom, Canada, France, Germany, and Japan have legislation "deeming" the profits of controlled foreign companies to arise at parent level. Is a currency gain or loss realized by such a subsidiary to be treated as "subpart F" income or its equivalent? If so, it is immediately taxable at parent level. There is no corresponding provision for relieving a loss. This is another danger of nonsymmetrical treatment against the taxpayer.

Even if the profit is not "subpart F" income, and not subject to taxation at the parent level until there is a distribution, how is it treated for the purpose of tax-credit relief?

THE FINANCIAL SERVICES REVOLUTION

The financial services revolution is a worldwide phenomenon. Bankers, investors, and corporate treasurers must look beyond their own countries and watch developments in London, New York, Tokyo, and elsewhere for two reasons. First, they may give some guidance on what is, or ought to be, happening nearer home.

Second, every international transaction involves, by definition, regulatory and tax angles in more than one country. The shrewd banker or treasurer can exploit opportunities and needs to avoid problems at both ends.

The demarcations denoting banks, trust companies, stockbrokers, and insurance companies are fast disappearing. Liabilities are becoming securitized. Business operates in an international world, not one without frontiers, but one in which a dealing book may be passed on from London to New York to Tokyo to give a 24-hour market service. Financial markets are becoming increasingly flexible, innovative, and competitive. London's Big Bang and its equivalents are steps, though important ones, in the process. A growing range of new and imaginative financial services give corporate treasurers and investors exciting opportunities to manage their financial assets and liabilities, and to transfer the currency and interest rate risks inevitable in modern business.

Two features of the financial revolution alarm professional observers. First, tax law has not always kept up with these changes. There are still many gray areas and uncertainties, and with today's slim margins a relatively minor mistake in tax planning can turn a small profit or financial saving into a large loss.

There are some traps and opportunities here. A recent case involved an American parent with a major British subsidiary which had some £50 million of local sterling debt. Along comes a friendly merchant bank which suggests that this is a classic case for a swap. Swaps have ranked among the top "flavor of the month" financial products for some time. The American parent would take advantage of its top credit rating to raise a dollar Eurobond issue and then swap the proceeds into sterling at a saving of about 30 basis points on the cost of money. Not a dramatic saving, but $300,000 a year is worth a little powder and shot and generates some useful fees to the bank. Many companies would have jumped at it. This one was sensible enough to have the tax angles checked out. It turned out that they risked paying $5 million in tax as a result of tax fragmentation. Banks in both London and New York have been marketing, and some American and foreign companies have been buying financial products without proper consideration of the tax angles.

Second, banks and other financial intermediaries are becoming increasingly transaction-driven and correspondingly casual in their approach to the tax aspects of the financial products they sell. These may look very attractive in pretax terms but, in the context of the target company, often do not stand up to the scrutiny of the tax adviser. Only too often bankers at the sharp end may be product specialists, knowing that their promotion prospects and their bonuses depend on their ability to sell options, collars, swaps, Eurobond issues, or whatever. Unlike the old-style relationship banker, but like the hard-sell tax shelter or life insurance salesperson, they just want to pocket the commission and move on to the next transaction. They have no patience with boring old tax advisers who may actually hold up the deal for as much as 48 hours while the more detailed implications are being examined.

Part of the business of a bank is to take risks, generally small and calculated risks for a relatively modest margin. A close analysis of the tax aspects of products sometimes reveals that the risk aspects, too, have unsuspected subtleties. Bank regulators, charged with the protection of depositors, want to ensure that banks have an adequate margin of their own capital to cover the risks they are taking. In designing new financial products, banks may have a two-fold aim. First, they want to convince their corporate customers that the risk the bank is absorbing is greater than it really is so that they can charge a higher fee for the service. Second, they want to persuade the bank regulator that the risk is less than it is, so that they can push through a greater volume of transactions on a given committed capital base. This could, in fact, be a perfectly rational strategy for a bank provided that they know what they are doing and are not blindly copying the tactics of a rival bank. John Maynard Keynes once defined a sound banker as one who "when he is ruined, is ruined in a conventional and orthodox way along with his fellows, so that no one can really blame him."

APPENDIX 1: UNITED STATES TAXATION OF FOREIGN EXCHANGE GAINS AND LOSSES

This outline is intended for general guidance and not as a detailed statement of current law. It raises, rather than answers, questions.

UNITED STATES TAX TREATMENT OF
FOREIGN EXCHANGE

In the United States there have been in recent years many changes
in the tax treatment of foreign currency and financial instruments
culminating in the Tax Reform Act of 1986.

In concept, TRA brings a spirit of rationality and common
sense to the whole subject but in practice, problems remain. The
subject is developing rapidly as regulations are published, technical
corrections are discussed in Congress, and IRS attitudes become
clearer.

Each entity or "qualified business unit" (QBU) has a "functional currency" which is either the U.S. dollar or a local currency
in the case of a self-accounting branch. Very broadly, profits on a
QBU using a foreign functional currency are converted into U.S.
dollars using a "weighted average exchange rate" (whatever that
may mean). Translation is ignored unless and until the assets of the
entity are repatriated.

The second important concept is that of a "Section 988
transaction" where the taxpayer is "entitled to receive, or required
to pay, a sum denominated in a currency other than the functional
currency." As those who understand American tax appreciate, we
have to consider the source, character, and timing of any such
transaction. Generally this is straightforward but the more one
studies the small print, the more one sees possible anomalies,
mainly in the definition of source. It is also envisaged that certain
foreign-exchange gains and losses are treated as analogous to
interest, although in this case (as with so much of the Tax Reform
Act) we have to await regulations before we know exactly how it
works.

In the United States, long-term capital gains were, prior
to the 1986 Tax Reform, taxed at a lower rate—a maximum
of 20 percent for individuals, 28 percent, against 46 percent,
for corporations—than normal income or corporate profits.
Short-term gains have been taxed at normal income rates.
The holding period of 12 months to qualify for long-term treatment was reduced to 6 months for assets acquired after June 22,
1984 and before January 1, 1988. It was important to determine
whether a foreign currency transaction gave rise to a long-

term or short-term gain (or loss) or to regular income treatment.[1]

The Tax Reform Act reduced the personal maximum rate to 28 percent; corporations pay 34 percent. Capital gains are taxed as regular income with limited relief for capital losses. The lack of indexation relief means that the balance of the whole system is vulnerable to renewed inflation and may have significant tax planning implications. The distinction between income and capital gains may be less important than before, but other problems remain.

Section 1261 of the Tax Reform Act of 1986 deals with foreign currency transactions. It adds new sections 985, 986, 987, 988, 989 and 1092 (d)(7) to the Code, and repeals Section 1256 (e)(4).

Generally we are required for each qualifying business unit to determine the tax effect of Section 988 transactions undertaken in a currency other than the functional currency of that QBU. Where the functional currency is not the U.S. dollar, we have to translate to determine the U.S. dollar tax consequences.

QUALIFYING BUSINESS UNITS AND FUNCTIONAL CURRENCY

The functional currency in which the first calculations are made is either the U.S. dollar or "in the case of a qualifying business unit (QBU), the currency of the economic environment in which a significant part of such unit's activities are conducted and which is used by such unit in keeping its books and records." The concept is adapted from FASB 52. Where a QBU is operating in a foreign country, the taxpayer may, in certain circumstances, elect to use the U.S. dollar as the functional currency. It must then maintain its accounts in U.S. dollars, and use separate transaction accounting for nondollar transactions. (Section 985b) This is intended mainly for highly inflationary economies.

---

[1] For a discussion of prior law including case law which may still prove relevant, see John Chown, "The Tax of Foreign Exchange Fluctuations in the United States and the United Kingdom," *Journal of International Law and Economics* 16, no. 2 (1982), pp. 201–37.

SECTION 988 TRANSACTIONS

A Section 988 transaction is one in which the taxpayer is entitled to receive, or is required to pay, a sum denominated in a currency or currencies other than the functional currency of the entity [S.988 (c)(1)(A)]. This is sometimes referred to as a "nonfunctional currency" or NFC.

Section 988 begins: "Except as otherwise provided in this section, any foreign currency gain or loss attributable to a section 988 transaction shall be computed separately and treated as ordinary income or loss (as the case may be)."

Corporate treasurers should particularly note that the definitions include as Section 988 transactions "the acquisition of a debt instrument or becoming the obligor under a debt instrument." [S.988(c)(1)B(i)]. U.S. treatment was, and remains, symmetrical with regard to liabilities. Significantly, the definition of "debt instrument" includes "to the extent provided in regulations such term shall include preferred stock" [S.988(c)(4)].

We need to examine the following aspects of a foreign currency transaction or exposure:

1. The tax treatment of the transaction against the functional currency of the relevant entity (Section 988).
2. Where the functional currency is not the U.S. dollar, the tax consequences of translation or conversion.

There are, as before, the three "characterization" questions:

- Is the gain or loss capital or regular income?
- When is timing recognized?
- Is the source U.S. or foreign?

Capital or Income?

This is now less relevant than it was. However, although the rates are to be the same, the rules for loss offset are different. The general rule is that Section 988 transactions "shall be computed separately and treated as ordinary income or loss (as the case may be) [S.988(1)(a)].

The distinction between short-term and long-term capital gains is still important because a short-term capital loss is deductible from ordinary income. The holding period is now 12 months. Is a "short sale," where the sale predates the purchase, characterized as "short term"?

Timing

When is the gain or loss recognized? This only affects the timing of tax payments but this can be worth quite a few basis points on financing costs. Taxpayers will wish to so arrange matters that year-end losses on currency exposure can be recognized in the current year, while profits can be deferred. The straddle rules specifically limit certain postponement transactions.

Generally, a "closed and completed transactions" doctrine is adopted. Section 988 (c)(2) and (3) define "booking date" and "payment date" respectively. There must be a "realization event." The booking date is the date that the taxpayer:

- Acquires or becomes an obligor on a debt instrument.
- Accrues or otherwise takes into account an item of expense, gross income, or receipts.
- Enters into or acquires a forward or futures contract or option.

The payment date is the date that the taxpayer makes or receives payment on a debt instrument or item of expense, gross income, or receipts; in the case of a forward or futures contract or option, it is the date of completion.

Source

The United States has a modified "overall limitation" basis for calculating double tax relief. Where this basis applies, a U.S. company might have income from two sources:

	Income	Tax Rate Percent	Foreign Tax
Source A	$100,000	60%	$ 60,000
Source B	200,000	22	44,000
Total	$300,000		$102,000

In this case the total foreign tax is just 34 percent of total income. No U.S. tax would be payable and no credit is wasted. With per country limitation, an extra $24,000 would be payable on Source B, and the surplus credit on Source A would be wasted.

It is obviously desirable to characterize low-tax income as having a foreign, rather than a domestic, source and to offset losses or deductions, such as interest expense, against U.S. rather than foreign income.

The international tax planning strategies of U.S. parent companies depend on whether they have a surplus or a shortage of foreign tax credits.

They aim to characterize gains on exchange as foreign source (to increase the denominator in the limitation calculation) and losses as domestic. Under prior law (Sections 861 and 862) the passage of title rules could be manipulated and characterization was often at the choice of the taxpayer.

The rules have been changed considerably by TRA. Generally, profits may be treated for this purpose as foreign source even though no foreign country is claiming tax jurisdiction. We need to ask two questions, and the answers to both were changed by TRA.

Is a gain a domestic or foreign source? Under Section 904 which limits credit for foreign taxes paid, there used to be a presumption that the gain on the sale or exchange of capital assets outside the United States is a domestic source regardless of where title passes. The effect of this can be to restrict the denominator of the overall limitation calculation, and treatment is not symmetrical.

Similarly, is a loss to be allocated against domestic or foreign source income? Regulations under Section 861 also provide that certain expenses have to be allocated to domestic or foreign source income in computing the double tax credit. The Tax Reform Act of 1986, while retaining the concept of overall limitation, introduces a number of restrictions and special categories. Separate limitations apply to:

- Financial services income.
- Shipping income.
- Interest income subject to a foreign withholding tax of at least 5 percent.

- Dividends from non-CFCs for which an indirect credit can be claimed.
- Passive income, including certain foreign currency gains.

SUBSIDIARIES

Section 986 sets out the procedure for computing the tax liability of a U.S. shareholder of a foreign corporation. The profits must be calculated in the functional currency, and "when distributed, deemed distributed or otherwise taken into account" shall "be translated into dollars using the appropriate exchange rate."

FOREX GAINS AS INTEREST

Section 988(a)(2) states that "to the extent provided in regulations any amount treated as ordinary income or loss . . . shall be treated as interest income or expense (as the case may be)." Can such gains (not being "fixed determinable annual or periodical income") be treated as interest when received by nonresidents? It seems difficult to apply withholding tax, unless the transaction is associated with a swap, for example. Will the computation be on a realization or an accrual basis?

STRADDLES AND SWAPS

The general principles for dealing with straddles are found in Section 1256. Contracts marked to market were first enacted in 1981 and substantially amended in 1984. A "Section 1256 contract" means: "(1) any regulated futures contract; (2) any foreign currency contract; (3) any nonequity option; and (4) any dealer equity option."

Where the section applies, "each Section 1256 contract shall be treated as sold for its fair market value on the last business day of each taxable year."

Under TRA, Section 1256 transactions are excluded from the definition of Section 988 transactions. S.988(c)(1)(B)(iii) defines the latter to include: "Entering into or acquiring any forward contract, futures contract, option or similar financial instrument if such instrument is *not* marked to market at the close of the taxable year under Section 1256."

A key provision used to be S.1233(a) (antistraddle) which provides that "gain or loss from the short sale of property shall be considered as gain or loss from the sale or exchange of a capital asset to the extent that the property, including a commodity future, used to close the short sale constitutes a capital asset in the hands of the taxpayer." Section 1233(b) goes on to deal with the holding period rules. Section 1234A (introduced in 1981) brought into account as capital gains the profit or loss on the cancellation, settlement, or lapses of obligations, even though there is no sale or exchange.

APPENDIX 2: UNITED KINGDOM TAXATION OF FINANCIAL TRANSACTIONS

The United Kingdom has more than its share of tax traps and opportunities on financial transactions. Foreign groups with U.K. subsidiaries, branches, or ventures need to understand this. The sums at stake can be high; some of the opportunities can be available even to groups whose U.K. tax exposure is relatively small.

Since 1979 there have been major changes in U.K. taxation. In that year the first Conservative budget decreased the top rates of personal tax from 98 percent. The 1984 package phased out accelerated depreciation but reduced the rate of corporation tax from 52 percent to 35 percent, anticipating the U.S. 1986 tax reform. The 1984 package is already bringing in more revenue even than its supporters hoped and paved the way for the more general reductions in personal tax announced in March 1988. As in the United States, there is now in concept a simple two-rate system, 25 percent and 40 percent; in practice, this is complicated by National Insurance (social security) contributions.

Amid all the changes, one running sore remains: the irrational treatment of foreign-exchange transactions, particularly of liabilities. Many U.K. companies including subsidiaries of foreign companies are being unfairly taxed because of the lack of symmetry in the legislation. Others—now a growing minority—are now finding tax-saving opportunities because of the lack of rationality in the legislation.

Tax fragmentation is the technical term covering the different tax treatment of transactions having similar economic consequences, and it takes several forms. The first, and most serious, arises in the United Kingdom from the nonsymmetrical treatment of capital gains on assets and liabilities. The classic U.K. cautionary tale became a major scandal in 1976 when there was a sharp fall in the pound, but the relevant anomaly in tax law is still unamended.

As an example, assume a U.K. company had borrowed $12 million when the pound was $2.40, and bought an asset in the United States. A few years later, the pound being $1.20, the asset is sold for the same $12 million, and the loan is repaid. Commercially, there was neither gain nor loss. The U.K. Revenue assesses the company on a chargeable capital gain calculated as follows:

Disposal proceeds, $12 at $1.20	£10 million
Less cost of acquisition, $12 at $2.40	£5 million
Chargeable gain	£5 million
Tax on chargeable gain	£1.5 million

The hard-pressed taxpayer might well ask about relief for the exactly corresponding loss on the liability. Unfortunately, this is being treated as a "nothing"; there is no relief and the result is a tax charge of £1.5 million even where there is no economic gain. This is not a hypothetical example; real cases have cost British companies £1 billion or more.

The second type of tax fragmentation applies on assets as well as liabilities and arises from the relationship between interest and foreign currency risk. If sterling interest rates are 10 percent while DM rates are 4 percent, the market is expecting, and the forward market is offering, a 6 percent appreciation in the DM over the year.

A corporate treasurer who invests surplus sterling to earn interest suffers a 35 percent tax. If the treasurer buys a DM bond or other financial instruments, this may earn interest of 4 percent and is expected to produce a chargeable gain of 6 percent. Since the 1987 budget, chargeable gains are also taxed at 35 percent. Given that both interest and chargeable gains are now taxed the same 35 percent rate, does it matter? The short answer is "yes." Chargeable gains are eligible for indexation relief. If the company invests £1 million for a year at 10 percent interest, it pays tax on the whole amount. The return, after 35 percent tax, is £65,000. If invested in such a way that it realizes a 10 percent capital gain, the company enjoys indexation relief and pays tax only on the real gain, after inflation. Assuming inflation at 5 percent, the net return after tax is £82,500. This is worth the equivalent of 2.7 percentage points on the gross yield on the investment.

In dealing with these two types of tax fragmentation, one should be certain whether a foreign-exchange gain is a capital gain or regular income. In some cases, it is not simple. Those who have based their financial planning on the assumption that it was obvious that tax would be levied or tax relief given on the basis of the actual profit made or loss sustained have been seriously misled. In attempting to set up a transaction so that it receives capital gains treatment on a gain, a taxpayer may fail if there is a profit—but succeed only too well if there is a loss. This is perhaps the commonest relevant tax trap, and one which the good currency tax planner must avoid or, even better, turn into an opportunity.

The third, less important tax fragmentation depends on when a gain or loss is recognized. This only affects the timing of tax payments but at high rates of interest, or fine margins, this can be significant.

Double tax relief, whether given unilaterally or by treaty, can be distorted by foreign-exchange fluctuations. This, the fourth type of tax fragmentation, is more complicated but repays study. (In this case there are more angles in the United States than the United Kingdom.) Profits earned in a foreign branch typically are subject to tax in both countries, each of which makes the calculation in its own currency. The planning implications of this are more in the arithmetic than in the law, but some legal points are relevant. How are the profits of a foreign branch computed? Must we translate all transactions into home country currency, or will the home revenue bureau accept the foreign currency computation, translating only the resulting profits? Is translation at average or closing rates?

How do we calculate double tax relief? What rate of exchange is appropriate?

The United Kingdom, in common with the United States, Canada, France, Germany, and Japan, has legislation deeming that the profits of certain controlled foreign companies arise at parent level. In the U.K. this does not apply to capital gains. Is a currency gain or loss realized by such a subsidiary to be treated as apportionable income? If so, it is immediately taxable in at parent level. There is no corresponding provision for relieving a loss.

RECENT DEVELOPMENTS

Reverting to tax fragmentation cases, the U.K. Revenue bureau did in fact lose one case—on limited facts. Marine Midland Ltd., a U.K. Eurodollar bank with no sterling business, was partly financed by a $15 million subordinated loan from its U.S. parent. These funds were never converted into sterling but were lent, in the normal course of business, in dollars. By the time the loan was repaid in 1976 the pound had fallen from $2.55 to $1.78. The value of the $15 million asset had gone up from £5.9 million to £8.4 million. The Revenue sought to assess tax on this £2.5 million purely paper gain, while disallowing the exactly corresponding loss on the liability. The Revenue won at first instance, but were roundly defeated in the higher courts.

The point at issue was whether the company was to be taxed on this translation profit. The sum at stake was £1.25 million, but much larger amounts depended on this test case. The Court of Appeal and later the House of Lords, the British Supreme Court, found for the company, reversing a decision of the High Court. This gave comfort for some of the banks, but little for their corporate customers.

The Statement of Practice

Following the Marine Midland case, the Revenue issued a Provisional Statement of Practice (SOP) in January 1985, followed by a definitive version in February 1987. This did not solve the real problems, and the government now accepts this. Meanwhile, the

Statement of Practice is our best guide to the present state of the law.

The nonspecialist needs to read the document with care. A statement that "there is no exchange gain or loss for Case I purposes" must be read, not as a reassurance, but as a warning that there is probably a serious capital gains tax trap. The basis of SOP is "matching." In certain circumstances a gain on an asset is matched against a loss on a liability (or vice versa) but only for Case I purposes.

Generally, SOP does not give relief for capital transactions. The old problem remains. Paragraph 14 specifically permits long-term monetary assets to be matched against current liabilities in the same currency. Paragraphs 16–20 set out the basis of computation. It accepts that the extent of matching fluctuates within the accounting period but assumes "that the extent to which currency assets and liabilities are matched during an accounting period is reflected in the size of the net exchange difference debited or credited to the profit or loss account or in some circumstances to reserve."

The Working Group

Representative bodies who were consulted on various drafts of the Statement of Practice pointed out that the statement was no substitute for long overdue changes in the thoroughly unsatisfactory state of the law itself. Those of us mainly concerned were, therefore, pleasantly surprised to be invited to an informal discussion lunch at Revenue head office. We were asked to form a Working Group which would seek an agreed private sector solution and report back to the Revenue.

Previous initiatives had broken down because of differences of approach between the banks and commercial borrowers. The main task was to find an agreed solution that would deal with the main problem of tax fragmentation while not being unacceptably expensive to the Revenue. The aim was to provide a rational basis for future treatment. Also inevitably, a few major corporations who understood the anomalies and how to profit from them were reluctant to agree to any change. Nevertheless, the final document represents the consensus of those actually taking part in the discussions.

Meanwhile, matters have been delayed again. The key official on the Revenue side has been head-hunted by the International Monetary Fund (IMF), and it will take time for his successor to master the complexities of the subject.

Using Indexation

U.K. companies are now taxed at the same rate on income and capital gains. Capital gains tax is calculated after adjusting the cost basis for inflation during the holding period: indexation relief. Interest earned on bank deposits, or discounts on bills, suffer tax on the gross income with no allowance for inflation. If a corporation (or individual) invests spare cash in a fixed-interest security within the charge to capital gains tax (government securities and domestic "qualifying corporate bonds" are not), net after-tax yield is enhanced. At 4 percent inflation, an 8 percent deposit yields 5.2 percent net of 35 percent tax. A suitable 8 percent bond would produce 6.6 percent net—equivalent to an enhancement of 215 basis points in gross yield.

In its simple form this is "the angle that never was" for it was killed by a last minute amendment to the 1985 Finance Act. It can still be achieved in a more complicated way by using foreign bonds creating a synthetic sterling security by hedging the exchange risk. Specifically, there may be opportunities in routing surplus corporate cash through an otherwise taxpaying U.K. affiliate, with a substantial pickup in effective yields. Such transactions need handling with care, as the borderline between interest receipts and capital gains is not precisely drawn, and there are complications in the treatment of hedging transactions.

APPENDIX 3: AUSTRALIA AND NEW ZEALAND

Australia and New Zealand are two other territories with a lot of angles. Both are in the throes of major tax reforms and the examples are intended to give the flavor of the game rather than to make specific suggestions.

AUSTRALIA

Until 1985 Australia had no capital gains tax. Therefore, the definition of what was, and what was not, a capital gain was much disputed between the taxpayers and Revenue.

A leading case, *AVCO Financial Services Ltd.* v. *FC of T*, 82 ATC 4246 (FN/1) can best be regarded as a horror story. AVCO, a wholly owned subsidiary of the U.S. parent, was carrying on a consumer finance business in Australia. As such, it borrowed substantial sums for the purpose of its business. Its trading assets were mainly denominated in the local currency, Australian dollars, but some of its liabilities were in U.S. dollars. In November 1972 there was U.S. dollar-denominated debt of $23 million and Australian dollar-denominated debt of $10 million. Thereafter, the emphasis switched to Australian-denominated borrowings, and by November 1977 debt was $111 million (Australian) and $17 million (U.S.). However, in 1975 and 1976 it proved impossible to raise funds for planned expansion in the Australian market; the U.S. parent arranged a temporary increase in U.S. dollar borrowings.

For the first four years of the period considered, the Australian dollar was stronger than the U.S. dollar and the company made gains on repaying its U.S. dollar debt of $6 million in 1973. In 1975 and 1976 there were both gains and losses on different transactions, but in 1977 the company incurred a substantial loss over the 1976 Australian dollar devaluation. The figures were:

Year to 30 Nov.		A$ in Millions
1972	gain	175
1973	gain	1579
1974	gain	298
1975	net gain	243
1976	net loss	(126)
1977	loss	(2,800)

The company claimed that this loss should be on revenue account and accepted that this treatment should apply consistently over the six-year period. The Commissioner of Taxation, with no respect for consistency, actually assessed the company on gains in the years 1972–76 and disallowed the deduction for losses incurred in the years 1975–77.

The Supreme Court of New South Wales found for the taxpayer, holding that the borrowings were essential steps in the performance of its day-to-day activities, and therefore, not related to capital account. The gains were income, the losses deductible. The Federal Court allowed the commissioner's appeal and found that the transactions were consistently of a capital nature. Both courts at least required consistent treatment.

During the period none of the borrowings was from the parent company. The U.S. dollar borrowings were of two kinds: commercial paper was issued in the U.S. money market for 90- or 180-day periods. Formal term loans were arranged for periods of between one and five years with an average of about two and a half years. In many cases, the proceeds of borrowings were rolled over; the proceeds of the new borrowings were applied in repaying foreign borrowings, the entire transaction being carried on within the United States. The taxpayer did not treat any foreign exchange difference as a realization of foreign-exchange gain or loss until there was a final repayment.

The commissioner had based his submissions on *Commercial and General Acceptance Ltd (CAGA)*, v. *FC of T,* 75 ATC 4201; 77 ATC 4375 previously regarded as the authority on this point. It was held in *CAGA* that: "an exchange gain or loss on the repayment of moneys lent will always be a capital gain or loss and can never be taken into account in the assessment of income."

In the *AVCO* case, one of the three federal judges accepted this principle. Another found for the taxpayer. The third, while finding for the commissioner on the facts (that the borrowings were undertaken with a view to establishing or setting up the business of the company), reserved his position on the more general questions.

The 1985 Australian Tax Reform

In September 1985 the treasurer announced the introduction of a capital gains tax, of an imputation system, and of a credit relief system for taxing foreign-source income.

Capital gains tax applies only to assets acquired after September 19, 1985. The tax is indexed, but applies at full personal or corporate rates. Indexation is not symmetrical as it cannot be applied to increase a loss. Another asymmetrical feature of the tax is that, although capital gains are added to income gains (and can be offset by income losses) capital losses can only be carried forward (at a declining real value after inflation for which no adjustment is 'proposed) aginst future capital gains.

There will still be tax fragmentation but it will be the reverse of the previous rule. If the Australian dollar continues to fall, there will be tax relief on liabilities. There will be no corresponding tax on assets if the assets were acquired before September 20, 1985, while capital gains tax on assets subsequently acquired will in practice often be postponed.

Well advised treasurers of organizations should seek to preserve the tax-free status of any transaction showing a gain (in today's circumstances these will be foreign currency assets) while reorganizing post announcement any transactions expected to show a loss.

NEW ZEALAND

New Zealand has a long standing and clearly drafted provision (Section 71) specifically providing that exchange gains or losses on the repayment of foreign currency debt are assessible or deductible. More recently, New Zealand is going through a general tax reform on the U.S./U.K. "broader base/lower rates" model. New Zealand has also introduced an accrual basis of taxing financial transactions. This now seems to apply generally. The key legislation is Section 74 introduced by the ITAA in 1987. There is a history of attempts to bypass the legislation. Some provisions apply from October 23, 1986; those on debt defeasances on December 20, 1986; on variable debt from April 1987; and for shares and options from June 18, 1987.

The general principle is that calculations are made on a yield-to-maturity basis. The appropriate income (or charge against income) is calculated in respect to each year of assessment. When the instrument is disposed of or redeemed, there is a base price adjustment designed to ensure that the full economic gain is taxed but that it is not doubly taxed. There is a difference of treatment when a variation in price arises from a change in the credit status of the debtor.

APPENDIX 4: THE NATURE OF FOREIGN-EXCHANGE EXPOSURE

Foreign-exchange exposure is not just a single figure and certainly not the figure derived from traditional year-end accounts. The proper analysis needs to take account of the maturity of assets and liabilities; dollars receivable next month cannot be netted against dollars payable next year. Uncertain receipts and liabilities need to be taken into the model.

The simplest possible exposure results from imports or exports. For instance, a U.S. company is owed £1,000 (invoiced in sterling) by a British customer; this payment is expected to be made in three months' time. The spot rate of exchange is $1.80 and the U.S. company may therefore regard itself as being owed $1,800. If the rate of exchange falls to $1.70, it will in effect receive only $1,700. This could be an important loss of expected profit even for a high-margin manufacturing company; for a low-margin export merchant, which might have bought the goods for $1,750, the loss could be disastrous. The company might, therefore, sell £1,000 sterling for U.S. dollars three months forward, at the ruling market price of $1.78. This is the most elementary form of hedging and normally raises no tax problems. The loss or profit of the hedging transaction is a straightforward trading loss or gain and the U.S. company is taxed on the basis of the number of dollars it eventually receives. Even this very simple example reveals some significant points.

First, the company receives not $1,800 but $1,780—the cost of $20 is sometimes regarded as insurance against a possibly greater loss. The insurance analogy is, in fact, misleading. The correct procedure is to base quotations on the forward price ruling at the date of payment expected, not the spot price at the date of quoting. If the U.S. company wanted to be sure of receiving $1,500, it should have quoted a sterling price of £101 (i.e., $1,800 at $1.78). Currency risk needs to be appraised at the level of making pricing decisions.

The second problem is of timing. Unless the transaction is settled by a bill of exchange maturing on a specified date, the "forward sale" hedge will not be a perfect one. Trade debts are often settled on open account, and the U.S. supplier knows roughly when to expect payment but not exactly. In practice payment may be received at a different date and converted at a different rate from the rate of maturity of the forward contract.

The third problem arises even before the order is placed. Alfred Kenyon discusses the life cycle of currency exposure from conception to death. He discusses the antenatal period between "conception: when we commit ourselves to a mismatch" and "birth: when the commitment becomes a commercial or contractual reality: it has ceased to be unilateral."[1]

He also refers to this in a later chapter as "the worst problem, the tender period." The difficulty here is when the would-be seller has to quote a firm price in a foreign currency and the exchange rate may well move before the customer decides. There is a unilateral risk which cannot be covered by hedging. It is sometimes possible to shift it to a credit insurer such as the Exim Bank. Such agencies are well aware of the problem and have made helpful arrangements. There is a similar problem for parties to lawsuits where the settlement is to be in a currency other than that the plaintiff wants or the defendant may have to pay. This is an obvious application for options.

Exchange risks of a trading nature can also be hedged by altering the currency mix of assets and/or liabilities. For instance, the U.S. exporter in the first example could borrow £1,000 from its bankers, convert them into spot dollars and deposit the resulting $1,800 with the bank. When payment is received, the transactions would be reversed. The cost of hedging would then be the interest differential and because of interest arbitrage, the cost of the alternatives would (on a large scale) tend to be about the same.

---

[1] Alfred Kenyon, *Currency Risk Management* (New York: John Wiley & Sons, 1981).

When analyzing currency risk, it is particularly important to distinguish between anticipated and unanticipated changes. The systematic "interest parity" relationship as described in the dollar/yen example is an anticipated change. Anticipated changes give opportunities for systematic tax arbitrage of the type just outlined.

What about the unanticipated changes? Supposing, not too improbably, on recent experience, that instead of rising 4 percent against the dollar, the yen actually falls? There can be scope for tax planning, taking account of these timing rules. In the simplest terms you set up a long-term foreign currency asset, perhaps a bond (preferably an actual or synthetic zero coupon bond of the appropriate maturity) and then reappraise the position at the year-end. If you have a loss you precipitate it, if you have a gain you run it.

A variant of this is to set up an offshore subsidiary that takes exchange risks—probably on a hedge basis. If this makes a profit, the profit is an unrealized foreign gain which can be run indefinitely. If it makes a loss, the subsidiary can be wound up, so creating a loss that can be offset against the other gains.

In addition to the difference between anticipated and unanticipated exchange risk, there is another uncertainty—of the tax treatment itself. This, of course, is what keeps the likes of myself in business. Instead of merely putting a tax dimension onto currency risk management, we have to apply a risk management approach to international tax planning itself.

These problems are made worse, unnecessarily, by the tax system itself. Wherever there is uncertainty as to the outcome of a transaction, there is always a danger that the tax treatment is not symmetrical. The tax collector's share of the upside potential may be greater than the share of downside risk, which is a serious distortion of the odds. In currency risk management we can live with a tax charge of 35 percent, or whatever it is in our country of operation, provided that we have equivalent deductions for losses. But if the Internal Revenue Service (IRS) stands to take a higher (even slightly higher) proportion of the gains than its share of the losses, we are cleaned out just as surely as the gambler is cleaned out by the zero on the roulette wheel.

TYPES OF EXPOSURE

In a fascinating short paper based on the authors' experiences in managing Novo, the Denmark-based multinational, Arthur Stonehill, Niels Ravn, and Kare Dullum[2] identify and discuss four levels of currency exposure:

1. Transaction exposure: "outstanding accounts receivable, accounts payable, and unexecuted forward contracts."
2. Impact on "medium-term cash flows assuming *equilibrium* between foreign-exchange rates, national inflation rates, and national interest rates."
3. Impact on "the same medium-term cash flows but this time assuming *disequilibrium* between foreign-exchange rates, national inflation rates and national interest rates."
4. "Impact on long-run cash flows. . . . At this strategic level a firm must take into account the reaction of existing and potential competitors."

The authors define foreign-exchange economic exposure as "the possibility that the net present value of a firm's expected net cash flows will change due to an unexpected change in foreign exchange rates." They distinguish between the effective changes assuming equilibrium (level 2), assuming disequilibrium (level 3), and between foreign exchange rates, national inflation rates, and national interest rates. There are relationships between exchange rate movements on the one hand, and interest rate differentials (the Fisher effect) and inflation differentials (purchasing power parity). It may be important to distinguish between an exchange rate movement where one of the classical relationships actually holds, and one (more common these days) where it does not hold. The appropriate corporate strategy and the tax consequences could be very different indeed.

Suppose an American parent company has an operating subsidiary in Germany. From the treasurer's point of view, it has

---

[2] Arthur Stonehill, Niels Ravn, and Kare Dullum, "Management of Foreign Exchange Economic Exposure" in *International Financial Management*, 2d. (Stockholm: P. A. Norstedt & Soners, 1982).

current assets (net receivables and cash balances) on which there is a translation risk. There are also real assets (fixed assets and inventories) which need to be treated in a different way. So far so good. The group seems vulnerable to a fall, and will profit from a rise, in the dollar value of the deutsche mark.

But what if the German subsidiary is a major supplier of product to third markets? In such circumstances a strong DM which really and fairly exactly reflects lower German inflation rates will not affect the trading position. If, as happened in the late 1970s, the DM rises even more than relative price levels justify, what happens? Sure enough, the group makes a profit even allowing for tax on its translation exposure but it may find its German factory becoming uncompetitive in terms of costs. Its profits would be squeezed and the value of the going concern reduced by a strong deutsche mark. If this strength of the deutsche mark had been anticipated, the right strategy might be to move production away from Germany. An unanticipated rise might result in a loss on trade account exceeding the gain on purely financial account. The true exchange risk of the group may be the opposite of what was originally supposed.

PART III

THE MANAGEMENT DECISIONS

CHAPTER 12

FOREIGN-EXCHANGE RISK AND EXPOSURE

Maurice Levi
Josef Zechner

THE SEARCH FOR A DEFINITION

To co-opt a cynical turn of phrase of the great Alfred Marshall, "every short statement about foreign exchange exposure is misleading (with the possible exception of my present one)."[1] This difficulty of explaining what foreign-exchange exposure is becomes very apparent if we examine some likely contenders for a definition.

It is not at all uncommon to hear statements that: *Foreign-exchange exposure is the riskiness attributable to changes in exchange rates.*

Unfortunately for the utility of this brief definition, exchange-rate risk is not exchange-rate exposure. Exchange-rate risk is related to the uncertainty due to unanticipated changes in exchange rates. The word "unanticipated" is paramount because there is no risk from changes in exchange rates when exchange rates are always as expected because the situation is known at all times.

---

[1] Alfred Marshall, who was concerned with much weightier matters than those here, referred, of course, to economics.

Exchange-rate risk stems only from the fact that predictions are often incorrect. The degree of exchange-rate risk is therefore related to the accuracy of exchange-rate predictions, and this in turn is related to the statistical properties of exchange rates over time.[2]

While exchange-rate risk is related to the accuracy of exchange-rate forecasts, exchange-rate exposure is what is at risk. For example, if a U.S. firm has accounts receivable of £1 million, and there are no commitments to pay out any of these pounds, the U.S. firm has an exposure in British pounds of £1 million for the date when the pounds are due. We see from this example that exposure is measured in units of foreign currency and has a date. Foreign-exchange risk has a different measurement dimension (e.g., the variance or the standard deviation of the dollar value of an asset) and is not generally dated. The definition of exchange exposure in terms of risk is therefore wholly inadequate.

An alternative definition of exposure which would appear to overcome the difficulties of the previous definition might be: *Foreign-exchange exposure is the amount of foreign currency-based assets or liabilities that will be affected at particular future dates by unanticipated changes in exchange rates.*

This definition does offer the correct dimension of measurement in that it is a foreign currency amount. In addition, this definition does emphasize that exposure should be measured at a particular date and is due to uncertainty in exchange rates. Unfortunately, however, this definition is at the same time too vague and too narrow.

The vagueness of the definition surrounds the concept of foreign currency base. We might all accept the declaration of, for example, British government bonds—or "gilts" as they are locally known—as being foreign currency-based because their face value

[2] The necessary association of risk with the random component of exchange rates dates at least to a paper by W. Poole, "Speculative Prices as Random Walks: An Analysis of Ten Time Series of Flexible Exchange Rates," *Southern Economic Journal*, April 1968, pp. 468–78. The point is also poignantly made by M. Adler and B. Dumas, "International Portfolio Choice and Corporation Finance: A Synthesis," *Journal of Finance*, June 1983, pp. 925–84; M. Adler and B. Dumas, "Exposure to Currency Risk: Definition and Measurement," *Financial Management*, Summer 1984, pp. 41–50.

and coupons are stated in pounds. But what about British property such as land which generally only happens to be transacted in pounds; in principle, a buyer could pay for British property in U.S. dollars, and no doubt this has been done. Furthermore, what about British equities which, in open capital markets where capital can flow freely, might just as relevantly be priced in terms of risk from a U.S. investor's perspective as from a British investor's perspective. This means that we might be as justified to think of British equities as being U.S. dollar-based as being pounds-based. More generally, it makes little sense to think of assets or liabilities being exposed in terms of the location or currency of their "base," and not merely because it is difficult to determine the base.

The narrowness of the foregoing definition is closely connected to its vagueness. The definition refers to foreign assets and liabilities as being exposed to exchange rates whereas, in fact, all assets and liabilities, domestic and foreign, are exposed to exchange rates in at least two ways.

First, exchange rates in a special scaled form have an effect on the profitability of domestic firms that buy or sell abroad.[3] This is because exchange rates can have an effect on the operating profitability of exporting or importing firms, with depreciations helping exporters and hurting importers. Indeed, exchange rates also affect the operating profitability of firms that have nothing to do with buying or selling abroad but which compete with imports. This includes most firms. For example, U.S. machine tool manufacturers selling exclusively to U.S. customers are generally able to charge higher prices when the U.S. dollar depreciates vis-à-vis the Japanese yen or German deutsche mark. One might even say that suppliers to U.S. exporters, importers, or import competers are exposed to foreign-exchange risk through effects of exchange rates on derived demand.

Second, exchange rates frequently have a systematic effect on interest rates. For example, when the U.S. dollar is low, further

---

[3] The scaling that is required is to put changes in exchange rates into "real" terms. This is not the best place to describe the necessity or the methodology required to compute real exchange rates. The necessity and methodology for computing real exchange rates is described later in this chapter.

declines in its value can result in actual or anticipated action by the Federal Reserve to support the dollar. Actual or anticipated action that involves higher interest rates is likely to affect the value of a large range of securities in the United States, meaning that they are exposed to the exchange rate. Residents of Canada, Great Britain, and other countries have become familiar with their domestic securities being exposed to exchange rates in this way.

Yet another definition of exposure is: *Foreign-exchange exposure is the change in the home currency value of an asset or liability at a future particular date with respect to unanticipated changes in exchange rates.*

This definition casts exposure in terms of what mathematicians refer to as a "derivative."[4] The definition overcomes the problem attributed to the previous definition in that it can be applied to domestic just as well as to foreign assets and liabilities. Furthermore, this definition recognizes the necessity of dating exposure. Finally, the definition gives exposure the dimension of foreign currency.[5] It is, therefore, a useful definition.

There is an empirical counterpart to the definition of exposure as the change in the home currency value with respect to unanticipated changes in exchange rates. This definition is in terms of regression coefficients: *Foreign-exchange exposure in each currency is given by a regression coefficient on that currency in a multiple regression of exchange rates against the domestic currency value of an asset or liability.*[6]

The reason that regression coefficients may serve as measures of foreign exchange exposure is by no means obvious, and an explanation requires that we take a short detour.

---

[4] Since exposure is with respect to one particular exchange rate, while all other exchange rates and other factors are assumed to be constant, the definition can be thought of as the "partial derivative" of home currency value vis-à-vis the exchange rate. See Adler and Dumas, "Exposure to Currency Risk," for more on this definition.

[5] This final point is not obvious. We demonstrate it in the context of the following definition which is the empirical analogy to that presented here.

[6] See Adler and Dumas, "Exposure to Currency Risk."

A regression equation of assets/liabilities against exchange rates takes the form

$$V(\$) = \alpha + \beta_{\pounds}ER(\$/\pounds) + \beta_{\yen}ER(\$/\yen) + \ldots + \mu, \qquad (1)$$

where

$V(\$)$	= Asset or liability value in dollars
$ER(\$/\pounds)$	= Exchange rate, dollars per pound
$ER(\$/\yen)$	= Exchange rate, dollars per yen
$\beta_{\pounds}$	= Regression coefficient and exposure in pounds
$\beta_{\yen}$	= Regression coefficient and exposure in yen,

and where μ is the regression error. We can see from examining the regression equation that if there is an increase in $ER(\$/\pounds)$, which means a depreciation of the dollar, the coefficient $\beta_{\pounds}$ measures the extent to which there is an associated change in $V(\$)$, the dollar value of an asset or liability, and so on.[7] Thus, regression coefficients measure the effect of a change in exchange rates on the domestic currency value of an asset or liability. Only when $\beta_{\pounds}$ is zero is the asset not exposed to the pound. We see that exposure can be positive or negative depending on whether, for example, a positive change in the exchange rate causes an increase or decrease in the dollar value, $V(\$)$, of an asset or liability. This is as we would expect as the effect of exchange rates on firms with net exposed assets should be the reverse of those on firms with net exposed liabilities, and the effect on importers should be the reverse of those on exporters.

The first thing we notice about the use of regression coefficients as measures of exchange-rate exposure is that they have the correct dimension, that is, they are measured in units of the foreign currency. This is because the coefficients convert the exchange rates on the right side which are in units of $ per £ and $ per ¥ into a magnitude on the left side, $V(\$)$, measured in U.S. dollars.

---

[7] We are, of course, considering exposure from the perspective of a U.S. investor. The conversion to exposure for any other investor is a natural extension of Equation 1.

Therefore, the coefficient must be in £ or ¥ to cancel against the £ or ¥ in the denominator of the exchange rate.[8]

We also notice about regression coefficients as measures of exchange-rate exposure that they apply equally to domestic and foreign assets or liabilities. That is, the dependent variable, V($), can be the U.S. dollar value of a British asset or liability, or it could be the U.S. dollar value of a U.S. asset or liability. The U.S. asset could be the shares of a company buying goods from Great Britain, selling goods to Great Britain, or competing in the United States against imports from Great Britain. The U.S. asset could be a U.S. Treasury bond which could fall in market price following a depreciation of the dollar against the pound if the Federal Reserve raised interest rates to help prop up the dollar.

A major advantage of measuring exposure as regression coefficients is that they reflect any comovement between an exchange rate and the value of an asset or liability. It may happen, for example, that a depreciation of the pound is systematically associated with an increase in the pound value of a British asset. We might then find what is shown in Table 12–1. This table shows a situation where the pound value of an asset increases while the dollar value of the pound decreases in such a way that the dollar value of the asset is unchanged. In such a situation, the change in the exchange rate in Equation 1, that is ER($/£), has no effect on the dollar value of the asset, V($), which implies that $\beta_£ = 0$. That is, the asset is not exposed.

It is not by chance in our example that we have a full offset for the pound depreciation with the pound price of the asset. To explain why such a situation could occur, it is necessary to take a detour from discussing exposure.

---

[8] Economists are familiar with checking the units of measurement. The trick is to think of the left side of Equation 1 as $, and ER($/£) as $/£ and so on, so that:

$$\$ = \beta_£ \frac{\$}{£}, \$ = \beta_¥ \frac{\$}{¥}.$$

This means that $\beta_£$ must be in £ to cancel against the £, $\beta_¥$ must be in ¥ to cancel against the ¥, and so on for every exchange rate. We can note that the same thinking makes the previous definition one that is in terms of foreign currency. That is, if the change in home currency is in terms of dollars, and the change in exchange rate is in dollars per pound, the derivative has the dimension of pounds.

TABLE 12-1
Constancy of Dollar Values When the Exchange Rate Offsets Fully Any Change in Local Currency Value

	Exchange Rate	£ Value of Asset	$ Value of Asset
Before depreciation of £	$1.50/£	£1 million	$1.5 million
After depreciation of £	$1.25/£	£1.2 million	$1.5 million

THE PURCHASING POWER PARITY PRINCIPLE

In the absence of shipping costs, tariffs, and other impediments to international trade, goods and services must cost the same when measured in one currency, such as the U.S. dollar, wherever they are sold; otherwise there are opportunities for arbitrage.[9] This means that exchange rates must reflect the prices of traded goods in their local currencies. For example, if a bushel of wheat costs $3 in the U.S. and £1.5 in Britain, the exchange rate between dollars and pounds must be $2/£. Furthermore, it means that if the price level in pounds in Britain increases, for example, by 10 percent during a year, while the price level in the U.S. increases by 5 percent during the year, the U.S. dollar value of the pound must decline by 5 percent during the year; otherwise arbitrage opportunities would occur by year-end. More generally, we can claim:

Percent change in ($/£) = U.S. inflation − British inflation. (2)

Equation 2 is the purchasing power parity principle (PPP) stated in its dynamic form and can be applied to any exchange rate and the associated inflation rates.

Of course, in reality there are numerous reasons why PPP does not hold. Not all goods are traded or tradable, and there are shipping costs, tariffs, and other impediments to trade. It is, therefore, hardly surprising that the evidence on PPP is very poor,

---

[9] Of course, many services cannot be moved so that arbitrage is not possible. This is one of the reasons why the conditions we derive do not hold precisely, and why exchange rate risk therefore generally remains.

especially when we consider it over periods as short as a year.[10] The departures of movements of exchange rates from PPP as given in Equation 2 are an important source of risk.[11] Let us see the implications for exposure.

Exposure of Noncontractually Fixed Assets

In our understanding of exposure it is useful to distinguish between two classes of assets and liabilities: contractually fixed and noncontractually fixed assets. We define noncontractually fixed assets as assets with an uncertain future foreign currency value, with these including real assets like property, and claims on real assets like stocks.

Consider the situation of a U.S. investor buying British property. Suppose that during the course of the first year of holding the property the British rate of inflation is 20 percent while prices in the United States are, for simplicity, constant. If PPP holds exactly as in Equation 2, the number of dollars per pound will decline by 20 percent per annum, that is, there will be a depreciation of the pound of 20 percent per year. Table 12–1 can then be used to represent the situation for a property that is initially worth £1 million, and at an exchange rate of $1.50/£, is worth $1.5 million. After the British inflation rate of 20 percent and depreciation of the pound by 20 percent to $1.25/£, the property is worth $1.2 million, but at the depreciated exchange rate it is still worth $1.25 × £1.2 million = $1.5 million. What we find is that the comovement of the foreign currency value of an asset and the exchange rate that we assumed earlier is not by chance, but the result of PPP. Let us recall what this implies when we measure exposure by the regression coefficient as in Equation 1.

The change in ER($/£) is associated with no change in the dollar value of the asset, V($). Therefore, it must be that $\beta_£ = 0$. This means the asset is not exposed. That is, changes in the value

---

[10] See, for example, J. Frenkel, "The Collapse of Purchasing Power Parities in the 1970s," *European Economic Review*, May 1981, pp. 145–65.

[11] See R. Z. Aliber and C. Stickney, "Accounting Measures of Foreign Exchange Exposure: The Long and Short of It," *Accounting Review*, January 1973, pp. 44–57.

of the pound have no effect from the U.S. perspective. We find that the regression coefficient gives the correct answer.

In reaching our conclusion of no exposure, we assumed that:

1. Purchasing power parity holds exactly.
2. All British prices increase by 20 percent while no U.S. prices change.

Under these assumptions noncontractually fixed assets are not exposed to exchange risk and need not be hedged. But what are the implications of dropping these assumptions?

If PPP does not hold, as in general is the case, the value of noncontractually fixed foreign assets changes in terms of U.S. dollars as a result of changes in exchange rates. However, if PPP holds in terms of expected values, the deviations from PPP are random, that is, changes in exchange rates could as easily be larger as be smaller than inflation differentials. Then it is not possible to determine in advance how dollar values of assets or liabilities will change from a change in exchange rates. That is, there is no systematic effect of a change in exchange rates on dollar values. This implies that the regression coefficient is zero as regression coefficients measure the average or expected effect of exchange rates on dollar values. We can, therefore, say that by the regression coefficient definition there is no foreign-exchange exposure and therefore no need for hedging.[12] This situation occurs when departures from PPP are independent of changes in exchange rates. However, if departures from PPP are not independent of changes in exchange rates with, for example, depreciations of the pound more often than not reducing the dollar values of British real assets, then exposure does exist. We find that the existence and degree of exposure depends on the extent to which inflation might offset depreciation. This shows up in the regression coefficients that are smaller in absolute terms the greater the offset, that is, the nearer PPP is to holding.

In reality there is far more variation in exchange rates than in relative inflation rates so that exposure does exist; depreciations cause declining dollar values of foreign real assets and vice versa.

---

[12] There is, of course, risk in this case. However, this risk cannot be avoided.

Furthermore, the amount of exposure and therefore the size of any required hedge is given by the regression coefficients. However, we believe the practical value of using regression coefficients as a measure of exposure and required hedges is limited because the regression coefficients are estimated with error. This means some risk occurs purely from "regression risk." We shall return to this later.[13]

Turning to the second assumption used when reaching the unexposed nature of real assets, namely that all prices change at the same rate, we should note that without this assumption we have what is generally known as "relative price risk."[14] This risk exists because even if exchange rates change according to overall inflation rates, there may well be changes in the dollar values of particular real assets because for individual assets the law of one price might not hold; for example, for nontradable goods. However, risk due to changes in relative prices is not unique to the arena of international finance, and whenever it occurs it is very difficult to avoid. We mention it here only because it is sometimes believed that if PPP did hold exactly in every time period and the domestic inflation rate was certain, there would be no risk on noncontractual assets; their values would be predictable. However, in fact, PPP in terms of two indexes of prices leaves exchange risk for individual assets.

Although we have analyzed the exposure of noncontractually fixed foreign assets, our definition of exposure as the regression coefficients of exchange rates on the dollar values of assets or liabilities applies to domestic assets as well. As we have pointed out, the values of domestic assets or liabilities can also be affected

---

[13] Adler and Dumas, in "Exposure to Currency Risk," do not allow for any errors in regression coefficients because the regression coefficients are defined over a "state space" which involves a finite number of known potential outcomes. This situation does not correspond to the data over which actual estimation is made, which is actual realized outcomes measured over time. From such realized outcomes the true regression coefficients can never be known. In our opinion, the definition of exposure as the regression coefficients is correct only if it refers to the true coefficients. However, with the impossibility of knowing these, the practical value of the regression coefficient definition is diminished.

[14] See B. Cornell and A. Shapiro, "Managing Foreign Exchange Risk," *Midland Corporate Finance Journal*, Fall 1983, pp. 16–31; or A. Shapiro, "What Does Purchasing Power Parity Mean?" *Journal of International Money and Finance*, December 1983, pp. 295–318.

by changes in exchange rates. In fact, it is even difficult to define domestic versus foreign assets. For example, with world oil prices quoted in U.S. dollars the Canadian dollar value of Canadian oil clearly depends on exchange rates, and therefore, is exposed even to a Canadian owner of the oil.

EXPOSURE OF CONTRACTUALLY FIXED ASSETS

We define assets or liabilities whose foreign currency values are fixed at a given future date as contractually fixed foreign assets or liabilities, or more briefly, contractual assets or liabilities. For example, a Treasury bill is a contractual asset that promises to deliver a particular amount of a country's currency at a particular time. Alternatively, an account receivable of £1 million to a U.S. firm is also a contractual asset. Unlike the case of noncontractual assets, there can be no change in the amount of foreign currency to be received if exchange rates happen to change.

To understand exposure on contractually fixed assets, we need to explain the interest parity principle which states that the expected returns on assets of the same risk and maturity from different countries are the same. For example, if $1 invested in the United States provides after one year

$$\$(1 + r_A),$$

this must equal what is received, in dollars, from a similar investment in Britain.[15]

Each dollar buys the number of pounds given by

$$£ \frac{1}{ER(\$/£)}.$$

This number of pounds invested in Britain for 1 year provides the investor with:

$$£ \frac{1}{ER(\$/£)} (1 + r_B).$$

---

[15] This condition is based on the assumption that PPP holds and investors are risk neutral.

If the expected exchange rate next year is

$$E[ER(\$/£)]$$

then the expected number of dollars received back on the British security is

$$\$ \, \frac{E[ER(\$/£)]}{E(\$/£)} \, (1 + r_B).$$

Equating this to $\$(1 + r_A)$ gives

$$(1 + r_A) = \frac{E[ER(\$/£)]}{E(\$/£)} \, (1 + r_B).$$

Subtracting $(1 + r_B)$ from both sides:

$$(r_A - r_B) = \frac{E[ER(\$/£)] - E(\$/£)}{ER(\$/£)} \, (1 + r_B).$$

This says that the difference between two countries' interest rates is the expected percent change in the exchange rate. Because this is enjoyed on the principal and the foreign interest we hence have the term $(1 + r_B)$.

Consider the situation of a U.S. investor buying a sequence of one-year maturity U.S. or British Treasury bills. Let us suppose that the investor can count on interest parity holding each time the funds are rolled over. Let us further suppose that expectations of changes in exchange rates turn out to be correct over each time period. This situation is shown in Table 12–2 for an investor starting at time zero with $1.5 million in U.S. Treasury bills and £1 million in British Treasury bills, and with these amounts being reinvested at the constant interest rates $r_A = 5\%$ and $r_B = 10\%$. Table 12–2 shows that with interest parity holding each time the funds are rolled over, and with realized exchange rates always being equal to the expected exchange rates, the dollar value of the British Treasury bill grows at exactly the same rate as the dollar value of the U.S. Treasury bill. This means that because of interest parity, if exchange rates change as predicted there are no gains or losses as a result of changes in exchange rates. This also means that there is no exchange risk, and therefore that exposure on the British Treasury bill is zero.

TABLE 12-2
Equality of Dollar Values When Interest Parity Holds Exactly in All Periods and Exchange-Rate Expectations Are Correct (All T-Bills in $/£ Millions)

Year	U.S. T-bill	Percent Yield	British T-bill	Percent Yield	Exchange Rate[a]	Value of British T-bill
0	$1.5000	5%	£1.0000	10%	$1.5000/£	$1.5000
1	1.5750	5	1.1000	10	1.4318/£	1.5750
2	1.6538	5	1.2100	10	1.3667/£	1.6538
3	1.7364	5	1.3310	10	1.3046/£	1.7364
4	1.8233	5	1.4641	10	1.2453/£	1.8233
5	1.9144	5	1.6105	10	1.1887/£	1.9144
6	2.0101	5	1.7716	10	1.1347/£	2.0101

[a] These exchange rates are calculated according to the interest parity equation,

$$E[ER(\$/£)] = ER(\$/£) + ER(\$/£) \cdot \frac{r_A - r_B}{1 + r_B},$$

which is a rearrangement of interest parity as derived in the text.

When we drop the assumption that exchange rates are always correctly forecasted, we find that foreign-exchange risk and exposure appear. The risk occurs because the admission that exchange rates are not always correctly forecasted means uncertainty about future values of exchange rates, and exposure exists because a change in exchange rates that differs from predictions as embedded in interest rates means a change in the dollar value of pound assets. Indeed, unexpected changes in exchange rates cause changes in the dollar value of contractually fixed foreign assets that are of a size that is given by the foreign currency value of the foreign asset. Let us see this from the following example.

If on the first day after paying £1 million for the British Treasury bill the value of the pound versus the dollar were to decline unexpectedly by 1 percent, there would be a drop in the dollar value of the British Treasury bill by 1 percent. There is no compensation for this via higher British interest rates because the drop in the pound had not been expected. What we find is that the unexpected change in the exchange rate by 1 percent causes a 1 percent decline in the dollar value of the £1 million face value of the British Treasury bill. The full face value of the British bill is therefore exposed to the exchange rate, that is, the exposure is £1 million at the moment after the Treasury bill is purchased. Over time as the pound value of the British Treasury bill grows via reinvestment, the amount exposed grows so that after one year exposure is £1 million.

The degree of exposure is confirmed if we consider the size of the regression coefficient we would find in Equation 1. When the value of the pound drops by 1 percent from $1.500/£ to $1.4851 the moment after the British Treasury bill is purchased, the dollar value of the bill declines from $1.5 million to $1.4851 million. For this to occur the value of $\beta_£$ in Equation 1 must be $\beta_£$ = £1 million. Let us see how this is found.

From Equation 1[16]:

$$\text{Change in } V(\$) = \beta_£ \cdot \text{Change in } ER(\$/£),$$

that is,

($1.4851 million − $1.5000 million) = $\beta_£$($1.4851/£ − $1.5000/£)

or

$$\beta_£ = \frac{-\$0.0149 \text{ million}}{-\$0.0149/£}.$$

By canceling the $ sign and the minus sign,

$$\beta_£ = \frac{0.0149 \text{ million}}{0.0149/£},$$

that is,

$$\beta_£ = £1 \text{ million.}$$

We find that contractually fixed foreign assets are 100 percent exposed to unexpected changes in exchange rates. But what about contractually fixed domestic assets?

The nominal future dollar value of, say, a U.S. Treasury bill at the time of maturity clearly does not depend on exchange rates. Therefore, if we assume that the U.S. inflation rate is certain, or at

---

[16] The regression coefficients are "partial regression coefficients" which means that we hold all other exchange rates constant as we change any one exchange rate.

least independent of changes in exchange rates, the real future dollar value of a U.S. Treasury bill at the time of maturity does not depend on exchange rates either. Consequently, contractually fixed domestic assets are not exposed to exchange risk. Of course, the market value of the U.S. Treasury bill prior to maturity might depend on exchange rates if, for example, a dollar depreciation causes an increase in U.S. interest rates and consequent decline in market price. The U.S. Treasury bill is, therefore, exposed to exchange rates prior to maturity, but only because it is not a noncontractual asset during this time.

EXPOSURE AND THE HEDGING DECISION

So far we have argued that exposure to an exchange rate can be viewed in terms of the regression coefficient of that exchange rate on the domestic currency value of an asset or liability. We have demonstrated that both domestic and foreign noncontractually fixed assets are exposed to exchange risk, with the degree of exposure depending on the degree to which PPP holds. We have also demonstrated that contractually fixed foreign assets are 100 percent exposed whereas contractually fixed domestic assets at maturity are not at all exposed. But why is a knowledge of exposure important?

The amount of exposure to a particular exchange rate is important information for managers when making hedging decisions. Through hedging, managers attempt to insulate the value of assets or liabilities, or the total value of their firms, from unexpected changes in exchange rates. When managers know the amount of exposure, they can fully ensure against exchange risk by selling forward an amount of foreign currency equal to the asset's or liability's exposure. In this case, the future dollar value of the hedged asset or liability, that is, the value of the asset or liability plus the payoff from the forward contract, is independent of exchange rate changes. By definition, this means that exposure of the hedged asset is zero.

Managers must weigh the advantage from risk reduction against the potential cost of hedging. The expected cost of hedging in the forward market is equal to the difference between the expected future spot rate and the forward rate. If there were no transaction costs and investors were risk neutral, the expected future spot rate would equal the forward rate so the expected cost of hedging would be zero. In reality, however, there are risk premiums impounded in the forward rate, and there are transaction costs with these slightly higher on forward versus spot transactions, so that there is an expected cost of hedging.

Given a manager's cost-benefit analysis she or he might decide to hedge all or only part of an asset's exposure to foreign-exchange risk. To eliminate the effects of foreign-exchange risk on a contractually fixed foreign asset, the full future foreign currency value of that asset must be sold forward. In the case of noncontractually fixed foreign or domestic assets, a manager might have to sell forward more or less than the expected future foreign currency value of these assets since they can be exposed more or less than 100 percent; the exchange rate change can be partly offset or reinforced by changes in the foreign currency value of the asset.[17]

Hedging can eliminate all risk in the case of a contractually fixed foreign asset (recall that we assume that domestic inflation rates are certain). For noncontractually fixed assets the future domestic currency value is still risky even after hedging in the forward market. The remaining risk, however, is not related to unexpected changes in the exchange rate. Hence, given that we can exactly determine the amount of exposure of, say, a German stock, it is possible to eliminate all changes in the dollar value associated with changes of the exchange rate, but the future dollar value of the stock would still be uncertain.

There is empirical evidence that for foreign financial assets such as stocks and bonds hedging against foreign exchange risk substantially reduces the risk of international portfolios without significantly decreasing the dollar returns.[18] The typical exposure of foreign bonds is 100 percent because a 1 percent change in the exchange rate generally implies a 1 percent change in the dollar

---

[17] If depreciations, say of the British pound, generally coincide with a decrease in the pound value of a particular asset, this asset is more than 100 percent exposed to exchange risk.

[18] See J. Madura and W. Reiff, "A Hedge Strategy for International Portfolios," *Journal of Portfolio Management,* Fall 1985, pp. 70–74.

value of the bonds. This translates into a hedging strategy of selling forward, say, £1 million for each £1 million invested in British bonds. On the other hand, there is surprising evidence that stock portfolios might be even more than 100 percent exposed to foreign exchange risk.[19] This implies that a portfolio manager who has currently invested, say, £1 million in British stocks should be short in the forward market by more than £1 million.

EXPOSURE OF EXPORTERS AND IMPORTERS: AN EXPOSURE ON NONCONTRACTUAL ASSETS

It is well known that depreciations or devaluations have a favorable effect on exporters and an unfavorable effect on importers, and vice versa for appreciations or revaluations. What is perhaps not so well known is what determines the size of any gains or losses and hence the extent of exposure.

We can think of the value of a stock as being the present or capitalized value of expected future earnings, discounted at an appropriate required shareholder return for the risk of the stock in a diversified portfolio.[20] If we consider the discount rate to be unrelated to day-to-day changes in exchange rates, then changes in V($) due to changes in exchange rates are caused by changes in earnings, with the extent of exposure depending on the typical size of changes in earnings.

As with other real assets, the value of a stock does not change merely because exchange rates change. What it takes is a departure from PPP. For example, a 10 percent depreciation of the U.S. dollar when inflation in the United States exceeds inflation abroad by 10 percent does not help U.S. exporters' profitabilities. This is because from the perspective of foreign buyers, U.S. products are unaffected by the depreciation of the dollar.[21]

---

[19] See M. Adler and D. Simon, "Exchange Risk Surprises in International Portfolios," *Journal of Portfolio Management,* Winter 1986, pp. 44–53.

[20] According to the Capital Asset Pricing Model the risk is that contributed to the market portfolio.

[21] As before we assume all prices change at the U.S. inflation rate. This allows us to ignore relative price risk.

Only depreciation in excess of the amount warranted by PPP has positive effects. The exposure therefore results from the inability to correctly forecast whether future changes in exchange rates will exceed or fall short of parity changes. We call the change in exchange rates minus the inflation differential the real change in exchange rates. We can, therefore, say that exporters are exposed to uncertain future changes in real exchange rates.

A real depreciation can be viewed as shifting up the exporter's demand curve when plotted against the exporter's home currency. This is because the exporter could increase the home currency price by the amount of depreciation and still sell the same quantity; the price faced by foreign buyers in their currency is unchanged.[22] In general, the profit-maximizing response to the depreciation is not to increase the home currency price by the devaluation and leave foreign prices constant. Rather, an upward shift in the demand curve drawn against the exporter's currency suggests an increasing price less than the depreciation so as to increase quantity sold; with the price increased in domestic currency by less than the percent devaluation, prices in foreign currency are lower after devaluation. The effect of the upward shift in the demand curve is higher profits; with the profit increase being larger, the greater are the following:

1. The exporter's elasticity of demand.
2. The existing profitability of exports.
3. The ability to increase output.
4. The importance of domestic inputs.[23]

The effect of real exchange rates on exporters' profits is the result of what is frequently called "operating exposure."[24] The operating exposure facing importers works in the opposite direction. A real depreciation of the importer's home currency increases

[22] To be fully consistent with our discussion on real changes in exchange rates we should say a real depreciation shifts up the demand curve by more than the cost curves. Our simplification is to help picture the effect.

[23] The relevance of these factors is demonstrated in M. Levi, *International Finance: Financial Management and the International Economy* (New York: McGraw-Hill, 1983).

[24] For a discussion of the concept of operating exposure see E. Flood, Jr., and D. R. Lessard, "On the Measurement of Operating Exposure to Exchange Rates: A Conceptual Approach," *Financial Management*, Spring 1986, pp. 25–36.

import costs. The effect on profits depends on the extent to which these costs can be passed on to buyers.[25] This effect on importers' profits also depends on the elasticity of demand for the product; with the importer's profits reduced more, the greater is the demand elasticity.

If we have readily observable stock prices of exporters and importers, we can in theory compute the exposure from regression coefficients. We can find the extent to which stock prices change vis-à-vis each exchange rate, that is, the β's, and use these as exposure measures. This means that the complexities introduced by demand elasticities and production flexibilities can be ignored. Of course, in reality the measures of exposure include both exposure on contractual and other noncontractual assets and liabilities of the firm as well as its operating exposure. If what we want is the overall measure of exposure, what we are looking for are these coefficients. Because regression coefficients measure the overall exposure against each exchange rate, we might find exporters' or importers' coefficients to be zero even if they face extensive operating exposure if this is offset by contractual exposure. For example, an exporter might purposely incur debt in the currency of the sales market to reduce exposure; what is gained via devaluation on profitability is offset by losses on liabilities. Of course, to eliminate exposure in this way it is necessary to compare a "flow" effect on operating income to a "stock" effect on the balance sheet, requiring a complex analysis.

ACCOUNTING EXPOSURE

So far we have focused our discussion of exposure on the impact of a change in exchange rates on the market value of an asset or liability, or on the market value of a firm. In practice, managers are often more concerned about the effect of a stochastic future exchange rate on accounting profits or book values.

---

[25] Other factors relevant for exporters such as ability to increase output do not matter because we can usually assume importers can buy all they want to at the going seller's price. Of course, on a good which is imported and then finished before selling the other factors will matter.

There are several possible reasons why stable accounting profits or book values could be a relevant objective for management. First, it can be difficult to estimate the market value for certain assets or liabilities, and it can be even more difficult to estimate the systematic relationship between market values and exchange rate changes. On the other hand, book values are readily observable and the impact of exchange-rate changes on book values can be easily determined. Second, book values and accounting profits can have cash flow implications by determining the firm's tax liabilities or the managers' total compensation (via bonuses, for example).

In addition, in a world of incomplete information, accounting numbers are used as signals about the true or intrinsic value of the firm. For example, before a firm issues new securities, it might want to avoid the adverse impact of foreign-exchange losses on its income statements as this might depress the price at which the firm is able to sell the new securities to the market.

The concept and the definition of exposure carries over to accounting data in a very natural way. Building on the first section we can say that: *Foreign-exchange accounting exposure is the change in the home currency book value of a firm's net worth at a future particular date with respect to unanticipated changes in exchange rates.*

According to this definition, accounting exposure depends on the method used for translating the assets and liabilities of a foreign operation into the domestic currency. For example, if an asset is translated at the historical exchange rate, that is, the exchange rate prevailing at the time when the asset was acquired, then a change in the exchange rate at a future point in time will not affect the future book value of the asset. On the other hand, if the asset is translated at the current exchange rate, it is 100 percent exposed to exchange-rate changes (assuming that the foreign currency book value is independent of exchange-rate changes).

The standards for the translation of foreign currency-denominated financial statements and transactions of U.S.-based multinational companies are established in Financial Accounting Standards Board *Statement No. 52,* or *FASB No. 52.* According to *FASB No. 52* firms must use the current-rate method to translate foreign currency-denominated assets and liabilities into dollars. Revenue and expense items must be translated at either the exchange rate in effect on the date these items are recognized, or at a weighted average exchange rate for that period. Even without delving into the details of translation methods, we can say some things about exposure as measured in accounts.[26]

Operating exposure of exporters and importers cannot be reflected in balance sheets that are not forward looking. The noncontractual exposure that we have given the special name "operating exposure" cannot, therefore, be calculated from the balance sheets. Nor can the exposure faced by exporters' and importers' suppliers who are exposed via facing a derived demand dependent on exchange rates. Similarly, the exposure faced on any contractual or noncontractual asset or liability that happens to be priced in terms of the domestic currency cannot be seen from accounts that consider only "foreign" assets or liabilities as needing to reflect the exchange rate.

Whatever the accuracy of accounting rules for translating foreign assets and liabilities, if actual and potential shareholders can see through the accounts to the true economic effects, the market value of assets should be correct. This means that $V(\$)$ is correct in Equation 1 and there is, therefore, still reason to measure exposure by regression coefficients, provided we believe the estimated coefficients to accurately reflect true coefficients. Where the serious problem arises is where there are no market prices. This will be the case with real property and private companies. Exposure here might perhaps be calculated by a simulation. We could think, for example, of what would happen to foreign property prices in association with a number of possible changes in exchange rates and compute exposure in this way.[27]

---

[26] For a more extensive explanation of accounting effects see Aliber and Stickney, "Accounting Measures." Also see Cornell and Shapiro, "Managing Foreign Exchange Risk," for a discussion of the relationship between operating exposure and accounting exposure. For a discussion of translation standards see A. Shapiro, *Multinational Financial Management*, 2nd ed (Boston: Allyn & Bacon, 1986); and B. Carsberg, "FAS. No. 52—Measuring the Performance of Foreign Operations," *Midland Corporate Financial Journal*, Summer 1983, pp. 48–55.

[27] It might help to think in percent changes in exchange rates and foreign currency prices, rather than in absolute amounts. Indeed, as is argued in Adler and Simon, "Exchange Risk Surprises," it may well be necessary to estimate regression coefficients in percent changes in exchange rates and in V($) rather than as in Equation 1.

WHY BOTHER TO HEDGE EXPOSURE?

We have seen that by appropriate use of forward contracts it is possible for a firm to avoid all exposure and risk on contractual assets and all exposure and some of its risk on noncontractual assets. We may ask, however, whether a firm should bother to hedge when its shareholders can hedge themselves via the choice of an appropriate portfolio of assets or liabilities including the shareholders' own use of forward contracts.[28] Indeed, shareholders can diversify away any unsystematic risk, even that faced by exporters and importers which the exporters and importers themselves cannot avoid. For example, an investor can buy shares of both exporters and importers so that when exchange rates change, gains/losses on exporters are offset by losses/gains on importers. With such possibilities open to shareholders, we should consider why firms spend any resources on hedging.

The reason why it might be more efficient for firms than for shareholders to hedge exposure is that shareholders might not be well informed about the status of individual firms' holdings, for example, of accounts receivable in foreign currency and foreign-denominated debt. It may be expensive for firms to convey this information to shareholders and it may also put the firm at a strategic disadvantage.

Also along the lines of information, there may be an internal advantage of firms hedging if this provides them with better estimates of where they are making profits. Such information may be useful for the allocation of marketing budgets. For example, a multinational corporation with sales subsidiaries in a number of countries might want each subsidiary to remain hedged. Of course, it is possible to compute what profits would have been had the subsidiaries hedged, but it might be almost as cheap to actually hedge.[29]

---

[28] See G. Dufey and S. L. Srinivasulu, "The Case for Corporate Management of Foreign Exchange Risk," *Financial Management*, Winter 1983, pp. 54–62.

[29] The cost of hedging is lower than is often supposed. For example, because accounts receivable must eventually be sold spot if they are not sold forward, and because forward rates must be close to expected future spot rates—otherwise there is an expected return to speculation—the expected cost of hedging is merely the extra transaction cost of a forward versus a spot sale of foreign exchange.

Firms might have better access to markets used for hedging than their shareholders. The better access may be due to reputation or the typical size of order; shareholders' hedging needs may be small vis-à-vis those of firms with transaction costs declining with the size of order.

Another reason why it may be better for firms to hedge than to leave it to shareholders is that if the firms are vulnerable and fail, there are legal and other costs of reorganization. By the firms hedging and reducing the expected costs of bankruptcy, the shareholders may themselves be better off. We can also note that it has been argued that progressive taxes provide another reason for firms to hedge; a smoother income stream lowers total taxes.[30] Shareholder income streams are likely to be smoother than those of firms even if personal taxes are progressive because of the portfolio diversification shareholders are able to enjoy.

In conclusion, there are a number of reasons why firms may want to hedge foreign-exchange exposure. There is consequently good reason for them to maintain measurement of exposure, perhaps employing the method described in this chapter.

REFERENCES

Adler, Michael, and Bernard Dumas. "International Portfolio Choice and Corporation Finance: A Synthesis." *Journal of Finance,* June 1983, pp. 925–84.

———. "Exposure to Currency Risk: Definition and Measurement." *Financial Management,* Summer 1984, pp. 41–50.

Adler, Michael, and David Simon. "Exchange Risk Surprises in International Portfolios." *Journal of Portfolio Management,* Winter 1986, pp. 44–53.

Aliber, Robert Z., and Clyde P. Stickney. "Accounting Measures of Foreign-Exchange Exposure: The Long and Short of It." *Accounting Review,* January 1973, pp. 44–57.

Carsberg, Bryan. "FAS No. 52—Measuring the Performance of Foreign

---

[30] For an account of these and other reasons for hedging, see C. Smith and R. Stulz, "The Determinants of a Firm's Hedging Policies," *Journal of Financial and Quantitative Analysis,* December 1985, pp. 391–405; and A. C. Shapiro and S. Titman, "Why Total Risk Matters," *Midland Corporate Finance Journal,* Summer 1985, pp. 41–56.

Operations." *Midland Corporate Finance Journal,* Summer 1983, pp. 48–55.

Cornell, Bradford, and Alan Shapiro. "Managing Foreign-Exchange Risk." *Midland Corporate Finance Journal,* Fall 1983, pp. 16–31.

Dufey, Gunter, and S. L. Srinivasulu. "The Case for Corporate Management of Foreign-Exchange Risk." *Financial Management,* Winter 1983, pp. 54–62.

Flood, Eugene, Jr., and Donald R. Lessard. "On the Measurement of Operating Exposure to Exchange Rates: A Conceptual Approach." *Financial Management,* Spring 1986, pp. 25–36.

Frenkel, Jacob. "The Collapse of Purchasing Power Parities in the 1970s." *European Economic Review,* May 1981, pp. 145–65.

Levi, Maurice. *International Finance: Financial Management and the International Economy.* New York: McGraw-Hill, 1983.

Madura, Jeff, and Wallace Reiff. "A Hedge Strategy for International Portfolios." *Journal of Portfolio Management,* Fall 1985, pp. 70–74.

Poole, William. "Speculative Prices as Random Walks: An Analysis of Ten Time Series of Flexible Exchange Rates." *Southern Economic Journal,* April 1968, pp. 468–78.

Roll, Richard. "Violations of Purchasing Power Parity and Their Implications for Efficient International Commodity Markets." In *International Finance and Trade, vol. 1,* ed. M. Sarnat and G. P. Szego. Cambridge, Mass.: Ballinger Publishing Co., 1979.

Shapiro, Alan. "What Does Purchasing Power Parity Mean?" *Journal of International Money and Finance,* December 1983, pp. 295–318.

——. *Multinational Financial Management,* 2nd ed. Boston: Allyn & Bacon, 1986.

Shapiro, Alan C., and Sheridan Titman. "Why Total Risk Matters." *Midland Corporate Finance Journal,* Summer 1985, pp. 41–56.

Smith, Clifford, and René Stulz. "The Determinants of a Firm's Hedging Policies." *Journal of Financial and Quantitative Analysis,* December 1985, pp. 391–405.

CHAPTER 13

THE DEBT DENOMINATION DECISION

Robert Z. Aliber

The key decision in international financial management is the debt denomination decision. When borrowing, managers of firms must decide whether to sell new debt and bank loans denominated in their domestic currency or in a foreign currency. Domestic currency, for all practical purposes, is the currency in which the firm reports its income to its stockholders, or to its owners. For most purposes the relevant foreign currency is either the currency of one of the foreign countries in which the firm sells or produces, or the currency of one of the small number of countries in which the firm can borrow readily. The choice of currency for the denomination of debt and bank loans affects both the level and the variability of the firm's income because it impacts on net interest payments and foreign-exchange gains and losses.

The key elements in the debt denomination decision can be grouped into two sets. First, the market-factor set includes the interest rates on bonds and bank loans denominated in the domestic currency, the interest rates on comparable bonds and bank loans denominated in one of several foreign currencies, and the anticipated change in the exchange rate for each of these foreign currencies in terms of domestic currency. Second, the firm-specific factor set includes the foreign-exchange exposure associated with the various components of the firm's income statement and its balance sheet, the risk associated with individual foreign currencies, the risk of a portfolio of various foreign currencies, and the relation between the firm's total income and capital gain (or loss) from a change in the exchange rate at a time when the firm has a foreign-exchange exposure.

The central decision for the firm is whether the currency denomination of its debt and its bank loans should be managed to reduce or fully neutralize the foreign-exchange exposure of its income statement, or whether the currency denomination of its debt and bank loans should be managed to increase its net income, either by reducing its borrowing costs, or by increasing its foreign-exchange gains—at least in an anticipated sense. The inputs to this decision include both the market factors—the relation between the interest rates on comparable bonds denominated in different currencies and the anticipated change in exchange rates—and the firm-specific factors—the firm's attitude toward risk and the relation between the income associated with changes in the firm's foreign-exchange exposure and its total income. An individual firm might, and should, have different postures toward maintaining foreign-exchange exposures in different groups of currencies, because the market factors associated with each of these groups of currencies might differ. Two firms involved with the same group of foreign currencies may follow quite different policies when making the debt denomination decision because of differences in their attitudes toward risk.

The debt denomination decision for the firm is the mirror image of the portfolio decision of the investor. The key elements in the portfolio decision are all present in the debt denomination decision—the interest rates on comparable assets denominated in various foreign currencies and in domestic currency, the anticipated change in the exchange rate for each of these currencies in terms of domestic currency, the investor's attitude toward risk, and the risk associated with a portfolio of foreign currencies. The debt denomination decision has one element not usually associated with the portfolio decision—the firm may have revenues and costs in individual foreign currencies, and hence income or profits in these currencies. Similarly, to the extent that the firm's profits on its domestic production or sales are sensitive to changes in exchange rates, the firm has an income-statement exposure. Paradoxically, the firm may have an income-statement exposure even though it is not engaged in importing or exporting or any other international activities.

The measurement of the exposure of the firm's income statement is discussed in the next section of this chapter. Then the market factors are analyzed; the techniques for altering the foreign-exchange exposure of the firm's balance sheet, and the comparative costs of each technique are reviewed. Next the firm-specific factors are evaluated. Each of several strategies that a firm might adopt toward its foreign-exchange exposure are evaluated.

THE FOREIGN-EXCHANGE EXPOSURE OF THE FIRM'S INCOME STATEMENT

The key question for the firm involves whether the currency denomination of debt and bank loans should be managed to neutralize the foreign-exchange exposure of the income statement. Hence, the first element in the debt denomination decision involves estimating the exposure of several components of its income statement and the sensitivity of the firm's income in domestic currency to changes in exchange rates. Changes in exchange rates may lead to changes in the domestic income associated with royalties and license fees from foreign firms and the firm's foreign subsidiaries, the domestic income equivalent of the profits of the firm's various foreign subsidiaries as reported in the currencies of the countries in which these subsidiaries are organized, and the domestic income on its export activities. Similarly, changes in exchange rates may lead to changes in the domestic income of its domestic production and sales. Moreover, the profits of the firm's foreign subsidiaries—as reported in the currencies of the countries where they are organized—may be significantly affected by changes in exchange rates.

The measurement of the foreign-exchange exposure of these several activities is considered in turn. Consider the foreign-exchange exposure of the firm's royalty and licensing income, initially under the assumption that the payment of royalties and license fees is in the domestic currency and subsequently in a foreign currency. If the firm contracts to be paid royalty and licensing income in its domestic currency, it might seem that the firm does not have a foreign-currency exposure—instead the payor has the foreign-exchange exposure. If, however, the change in the exchange rate would cause the payor to go bankrupt or to become financially distressed so that it could not make its contractual payments, then the firm has a foreign-exchange exposure.[1] If the firm contracts instead to receive payment in a foreign currency, then the domestic currency equivalent of the scheduled receipts in the foreign currency will change whenever the exchange rate changes. The foreign-exchange exposure of a projected stream of receipts in each of several foreign currencies can be measured as the discounted present value of the anticipated receipts in each of these foreign currencies.[2]

Consider the exposure of the income on exports to various foreign countries. These export sales may be invoiced in the currency of the buyer or the currency of the seller. If the exports are invoiced in the currency of the buyer and the buyer's currency depreciates, the firm incurs a foreign-exchange loss and the domestic income attached to export sales declines. As a result, the unit volume of exports may decline as the price of these goods in the buyer's currency is increased relative to the price of similar or competitive goods produced in the buyer's country, or the profits per unit of export sales decline because the price in the buyer's currency is not increased by as much in percentage terms as the change in the exchange rate. In most cases, both export volume and profits per unit of export decline. Indeed, the firm has a foreign exposure on its exports unless the firm is able to increase its selling price in the foreign country by the same percentage amount as the change in the exchange rate and still maintain the volume of its sales. And the economic condition for being able to raise selling prices is that the firm has no effective competitors in the various foreign countries to which it exports.

---

[1] The analogy is the foreign-exchange exposure of the major international banks on their loans to Mexico, Brazil, and Argentina. These loans were denominated in U.S. dollars, German marks, or Japanese yen; the borrowers acquired the foreign-exchange exposure. But when the currencies of Mexico, Brazil, and Argentina depreciated sharply, the debt-servicing burden of the borrowing countries increased significantly and many went bankrupt.

[2] The interest rate used in the present value calculation is likely to be the host-country interest rate or to be based on this interest rate.

If export sales are denominated in the firm's currency, it might seem that the firm does not have a foreign-exchange exposure on these sales, but that the importer has the foreign-exchange exposure. However, the volume of the importer's purchases is likely to decline as the importer has to pay a higher price in its own currency for imports; the importer's sales may decline and its profits per unit of sales also may decline. Hence, the factors that lead to a foreign-exchange exposure when the exports are denominated in the firm's currency are the same as those when the exports are denominated in the importer's currency. In both cases, the exporter's exposure is the anticipated revenues in the foreign currency discounted to the present.[3]

The firm's foreign-exchange exposure on its export sales is the anticipated revenues in the foreign currency, or more precisely, the discounted present value of these revenues.[4] The appropriate interest rate is the market interest rate in the country in which the exports are sold.

Consider the exposure of the projected income of the firm's foreign subsidiaries. Initially, this income is estimated in the currency of the country in which the subsidiary is located, and then the domestic currency equivalent is determined on the basis of the anticipated exchange rate. If the foreign currency depreciates more rapidly than anticipated, the domestic currency equivalent of the subsidiary's income is smaller than anticipated. The anticipated income of these subsidiaries can be estimated under a number of assumptions about exchange rates at various future dates: the firm's exposure in each of these foreign currencies is the present value of the anticipated income in these currencies. The exposure of the income of the foreign subsidiaries differs from the exposure of royalty and licensing income in foreign currencies of the parent in one significant way—the income in each of the foreign currencies may vary as the foreign-exchange value of the currencies of

---

[3] A distinction must be made between the income-statement exposure on anticipated foreign sales and the balance-sheet exposure on sales-financing loans to the importers.

[4] The firm's foreign-exchange exposure on its export sales is not independent of whether the export sales are invoiced in the firm's currency or in the importer's currency. The rationale is that the volume of exports may decline more rapidly if the importer acquires the foreign-exchange exposure than if the exporter does.

the countries in which the subsidiaries are located varies. Thus, each of the foreign subsidiaries has its own foreign-exchange exposure and its income is sensitive to changes in the exchange rate.[5] The firm's exposure in each currency is the domestic currency equivalent of the anticipated profits of each of the foreign subsidiaries.

The firm may have an exposure on its income statement even though the firm does not participate in international trade. The income statement is exposed if profits on domestic sales are sensitive to changes in exchange rates, perhaps because the firm's products are competitive with imported goods or because one of the components to domestic production is imported. Changes in the exchange rates might lead to changes in the volume of domestic sales or to changes in the price and, hence, unit profits of domestic sales. The foreign-exchange exposure of export sales provides this analogy: if one or several foreign currencies should depreciate, then the domestic demand for imports may increase, and the firm may lose sales in its domestic market. If the firm responds to the loss of its market share by cutting prices, then its profits per unit of sales decline. The foreign-exchange exposure of domestic sales and revenues is measured as the foreign-currency equivalent where the foreign currency is that in which the sales are sensitive.

Each of the components in the foreign-exchange exposure of the income statement can be expressed in present value terms. Two factors complicate the estimation of the foreign-exchange exposure in present terms. The first is the estimation of the revenues associated with each of these activities. The second is the choice of the interest rate used in the present value calculation. The complication is that estimates of some of these components are less certain that estimates of others. (Despite the uncertainty, the firm's confidence in its ability to develop estimates of its future sales is likely to be greater than its confidence in its ability to develop estimates of future exchange rates.)

The firm may have an income-statement exposure in a number of foreign currencies. Eventually, the firm's managers view its

---

[5] To some extent, the foreign-exchange exposure of the foreign subsidiaries and of the parent may be offsetting.

foreign-exchange exposures in a portfolio context. Managers might group income-statement exposures in various foreign currencies; or instead they may determine that the firm's aggregate foreign income-statement exposure is the sum of its income-statement exposures in individual foreign currencies. To the extent that the foreign-exchange values of different national currencies are highly correlated, the income statement exposures in these currencies can be grouped.

MARKET FACTORS AND THE CURRENCY DENOMINATION OF A FIRM'S DEBT

Changes in the currency denomination of the firm's debt and bank loans can reduce or fully neutralize the exposure of its income statement. Alternatively, the currency denomination of the firm's debt and bank loans can be managed to increase the firm's foreign-exchange exposure to profit from anticipated changes in exchange rates. Moreover, efforts to arrange the currency denomination of a firm's debt and bank loans to reduce its net interest costs can alter its foreign-exchange exposure.

A firm with a foreign-exchange exposure increases the sensitivity of its income or its net worth and, perhaps, its market valuation to changes in exchange rates. Because many firms seek to minimize the variance in their income, managers may attempt to reduce their foreign-exchange exposures—if other things are equal. But other things are rarely equal—altering the foreign-exchange exposure may incur various costs. For the firm, the relevant trade-off is between the cost of reducing (or increasing) its foreign-exchange exposure and the benefits of having a smaller foreign-exchange exposure—or of not having any foreign-exchange exposure.

The firm can alter its foreign-exchange exposure through a variety of now traditional techniques, including leading-and-lagging, forward exchange contracts, futures contracts in foreign exchange, options on foreign exchange, and foreign-exchange swaps. And some more esoteric techniques are available and may be used when the traditional techniques are not available—these techniques include the pricing of commodity sales transactions, speculation in inventories or real assets, and various nonmarket swaps.

Consider a firm that alters its foreign-exchange exposure through the purchase of a three-month forward exchange contract. This transaction may reduce or fully neutralize the firm's exposure on its income statement or increase the firm's exposure. The cost of the purchase of a three-month forward contract is the difference between the amount of domestic currency in settlement of the forward contract and the amount of domestic currency realized when the foreign currency which is taken in delivery in the settlement of the forward contract is immediately sold for domestic currency. This "cost" can be negative or positive. This cost is closely approximated as the difference between the exchange rate in the forward contract and the spot-exchange rate on the date when the forward contract matures.[6] Computation of this cost always involves a comparison between the exchange rate used to effect a change in the firm's foreign exposure with the spot-exchange rate at some future date, usually on the date when the forward-exchange contract matures. If the forward-exchange rate and the spot-exchange rate at the maturity of the forward-exchange rate are not significantly different, there is no cost to altering the firm's foreign-exchange exposure by altering the currency denomination of its debt. And the flip side of this statement is that there is no anticipated gain from altering the firm's foreign-exchange exposure in anticipation of a profit from an anticipated change in the spot-exchange rate.

That the firm can alter its foreign-exchange exposure without cost may seem surprising and comparable to the proverbial free lunch, for even though firms would be willing to pay for the lunch, they are not required to do so. The story is that transactions of U.S. firms to hedge a long foreign-exchange exposure in the German mark, and of the German firms to hedge their foreign-exchange exposures in the U.S. dollar, tend to be offsetting. Hence, both groups of firms may be able to reduce their foreign-exchange exposures in their transactions with each other—and

---

[6] The difference between the cost computed from payments and receipts, and the approximation based on the exchange rate in the futures contract and the spot-exchange rate on the date when the forward contract matures is a set of transactions costs.

conceivably at no net cost. An insurance analogy is inappropriate because there is no intermediary in the forward-exchange market that shares in the risk-reduction activity; instead, the banks act as brokers in the forward-exchange market and marry the transactions of the U.S. firms with those of the German firms at a very modest charge—essentially the difference between their buying and selling rates for forward-exchange contracts with the two parties.

Similarly, assume managers alter the firm's foreign-exchange exposure through leading-and-lagging; the firm borrows in a foreign currency, converts these borrowed foreign funds into domestic currency, and uses the domestic funds to repay its domestic loans. As the firm's interest payments increase in one currency, and its interest payments decline in the second currency, there is likely to be an increase in its interest payments. Moreover, there is a change in the timing of the firm's foreign transactions—the firm enters into a spot-exchange transaction today rather than in three or six months. The cost of leading-and-lagging is the difference between the interest payments during the term of the loan and the amounts of foreign exchange realized on the date when the borrowed funds are converted and on the date when the borrowed funds are repaid. This amount can be approximated as the difference between the interest rate differential and the realized change in the exchange rate over this same interval. If the interest rates on the two loans are not significantly different from the change in the exchange rate in percentage terms, there is no cost to altering the firm's exposure. Again the free lunch question arises, and again the answer involves the impact of the hedging transactions of the U.S. firm and of the German firm on current exchange rates and interest rates. The mirror image of this proposition is that there is a cost to altering the firm's foreign-exchange exposure only to the extent that there is a difference between the two interest rates and the percentage change in the exchange rate. And if the U.S. firm incurs a cost in altering its foreign-exchange exposure, the German firm alters its exposure and at the same time realizes a profit—a free lunch.

Because exchange rate movements are volatile, individual forward contracts are poor predictors of the spot-exchange rate on the dates when the forward-exchange contracts mature. The central question is whether for a large number of forward-exchange contracts in each foreign currency, the forward-exchange rate is a biased or an unbiased predictor of the future spot-exchange rate. If the forward-exchange rate is an unbiased predictor, then the forecast errors on one side of the spot-exchange rate and the forecast errors on the other side of the spot-exchange rate more or less cancel each other out. The alternative result is that the forecast errors on one side of the spot-exchange rate are substantially larger than the forecast errors on the other side of the spot-exchange rate. If the alternative result is valid, the interpretation might be that investors demand, and receive, a risk premium.

The concept for estimating the costs of altering the firm's exposure is known as Fisher Open; it involves the relationship between interest rates on comparable assets denominated in different currencies and the realized change in the exchange rate over this same holding period. An alternative version is that the Fisher Open involves the relationship between the forward-exchange rate and the spot-exchange rate on the date of the maturity of the forward-exchange contracts. (These two versions would prove identical in measured costs if domestic and foreign assets were not significantly different in political risk.)

The residual or difference between the two versions can be considered a risk premium, a forecast error, or some combination of both. The forecast error reflects that predicting changes in exchange rates is a risky activity because the movements in spot-exchange rates from one period to the next and from one month to the next may be volatile. Investors do their best to forecast the next period's exchange rate, but frequently they are overwhelmed by unanticipated events and the resulting very large unanticipated movements in the spot-exchange rate. Some investors may be willing to increase their exposure to foreign-exchange risk only if they receive an additional payment—a risk premium—for incurring the risks associated with cross-border finance. The economic situation is that the larger the unanticipated movements in the exchange rate, the larger the forecast error and the larger the minimum required risk premium. In a world characterized by a variety of monetary and structural disturbances, there are likely to be large deviations from Fisher Open on a monthly or quarterly basis, with the result that any firm or investor maintaining an exposed position in foreign exchange is likely to realize a significant loss—or gain.

Firms and investors may seek to reduce or minimize their exposure to loss from changes in exchange rates because they believe the cost of the loss dominates the benefits of the gain— even if both are equally probable. Firms and investors would increase their exposure to loss from changes in exchange rates only if they anticipate a large gain in an expected value sense, or at least a savings in interest costs on borrowed funds from maintaining an exposed position in foreign exchange and carrying the associated risk. The implicit proposition is that the cost of reducing or eliminating the exposure is too high relative to the anticipated loss from maintaining an exposed position in foreign exchange and bearing the uncertainty associated with possible changes in the exchange rate. In effect, the firms and the investors carrying foreign-exchange exposures self-insure—they believe that the additional income from the savings in interest payments associated with maintaining a foreign-exchange exposure is adequate to compensate for the occasional foreign-exchange losses and for carrying the uncertainty associated with changes in exchange rates.

Fisher Open has been subjected to many tests, especially in the form of the proposition that the forward-exchange rate should be considered an unbiased (or a biased) predictor of the future spot-exchange rate. To a lesser extent, studies have been undertaken to assess the relationship between the difference in interest rates on comparable assets denominated in different currencies, and the observed change in the exchange rate. (If the interest rates are those on Eurodeposits, then the second test is identical with the first.) The general thrust of these studies is that on average forward rates are very close to being unbiased predictors of future spot-exchange rates. The economic rationale for this conclusion is that the firms in each of several countries use foreign-exchange contracts as a way to reduce their foreign-exchange exposures—and the sales of the German mark in the forward market by U.S. firms and the sales of U.S. dollars in the forward market by German firms tend to be offsetting.

The empirical observation that forward-exchange rates are unbiased predictors of future spot-exchange rates must be reconciled with the observation that there is a substantial difference among countries in real interest rates. The countries with low real interest rates are the capital-rich countries, while the countries with high real interest rates are the capital-poor countries. The difference in real interest rates can be thought of as the return required for the marginal investor for taking on a foreign-exchange exposure.

The combination of competition among the suppliers of these different financial instruments and arbitrage by firms and investors among those for altering exposure ensures that the costs to the firm or investor of using one of these techniques is not likely to differ by a large amount from the costs of some other technique. The cost of altering foreign-exchange exposure through the use of forward contracts and through the use of futures contracts is likely to be less than 0.1 percent in a major currency, and perhaps closer to 0.02 or 0.03 percent. Similarly, the cost of forward contracts and the cost of leading-and-lagging are not likely to differ by more than several tenths of 1 percent. Any difference between the cost of these two techniques means that there is a deviation from interest rate parity theorem and since this concept is based on arbitrage, any observed deviation implies that the financial assets or liabilities used for this comparison are less than perfect substitutes for each other.[7] Arbitrage may be constrained because of exchange controls. Or tax considerations may favor one technique for altering exposure rather than another.

The cost of each of the techniques for altering exposure is an opportunity cost. Hence, the cost of altering the firm's exposure can only be calculated after the end of the investment period, when the spot-exchange rate is known. The cost of altering the firm's exposure is the return for maintaining the exposed position during the period when the exchange rate changes.[8]

The costs of each technique for altering exposure may be compared in a present value analysis. For example, assume a U.S.

[7] There may be a difference between the cost of forward contracts and the cost of leading-and-lagging because the financial instruments denominated in different currencies used in leading-and-lagging are less than perfect substitutes for each other in terms of sensitivity to default or the exchange controls.

[8] An alternative—and incorrect—approach to measuring the cost of altering the firm's exposure involves the comparison between the today's forward-exchange rate and today's spot-exchange rate. This approach confuses the costs of two different techniques for altering foreign-exchange exposure.

firm wants to pay £10 million in two years. The U.S. firm can buy British pounds today for delivery in two years; in two years, the firm is obliged to deliver $3.5 million (on the assumption that the forward-exchange rate is $1.75 = £1.00). The present value of $3.5 million in two years can be obtained by using the firm's marginal cost of dollar funds as the interest rate. Alternatively, the firm might lead-and-lag; in this case, the firm uses present value analysis to determine the amount of British pounds that must be acquired today to compound to £2 million in two years; here present value analysis is applied to the British pound investment.

FIRM-SPECIFIC FACTORS AND THE CURRENCY DENOMINATION OF DEBT

If the managers of a firm were confident that Fisher Open would remain continuously valid, they would be indifferent about the currency denomination of its debt. The firm might have an income-statement exposure, but the managers would not be able to alter its aggregate foreign-exchange exposure by altering the currency denomination of its bank loans and debt. The managers of the firm are concerned about the currency denomination of its debt because they believe there are nontrivial differences from Fisher Open in an ex ante, or anticipated, sense. The inputs to the debt denomination decision include the risk aversion of the firm, the risk the firm associates with particular foreign currencies, the distribution of the firm's income-statement exposure by currency, and the significance of the potential foreign-exchange gains and losses to the firm's income, net worth, and market valuation.

Risk Aversion. Individual investors can be ranked by the risk premium that each requires for acquiring or maintaining exposure to loss—and to gain—from unanticipated changes in exchange rates. Similarly, individual firms can be ranked according to their willingness to bear the various cross-border risks.[9] The cliche that is the cornerstone of one view is that "We specialize in

---

[9] Finance theory stipulates that the managers of the firm should ignore risk in their borrowing and lending decisions. Individual investors can as a group neutralize the risk they associate with particular firms.

producing shoes or machine tools, not in speculating in the foreign exchange.'' This statement is a cop-out. Almost every firm that takes this view is implicitly speculating in foreign exchange because it has failed not only to devote any resources to measuring its foreign-exchange exposure but also to arrange the currency denomination of its debt so that its income statement is not exposed.

For the managers of the firm, the key question is how their risk aversion compares with the risk aversiveness of investors as a group and of firms as a group. In this context, risk aversion is firm-specific and should be distinguished from the risk that each firm encounters because of the set of currencies in which the firm has an income-statement exposure.

For firms and for investors, the relevant risk is that of a portfolio of foreign currencies rather than an individual foreign currency. The less strong the correlation among the changes in the exchange rates of these several foreign currencies, the greater the likelihood that some firms and investors acquire or maintain exposures in each of several different foreign currencies. For these firms and investors, maintaining exposure in a group of foreign currencies leads to a disproportionate increase in the returns relative to the risk; for the firm, the increase in the return is a result of the reduction in interest costs; for the investor, the increase in the return is a result of higher interest income. And by extension, the risk of exposures in various foreign currencies can be grouped with a variety of other financial and nonfinancial risks, on the basis of the same proposition that there is an unusually large increase in the returns relative to the increase in risk as long as the changes in the price of these assets is less than perfectly correlated.

Some firms may manage the currency denomination of their bonds and bank loans to reduce their exposure to foreign-exchange risk. In contrast, other firms may manage the currency composition of their debt so that the effect is an increase in their foreign-exchange exposure and increased sensitivity to gain and loss from changes in the exchange rates.

One difference among firms that affects their willingness to maintain a foreign-exchange exposure is that their risk aversion may differ. The greater the risk aversion, the less likely is the firm to knowingly maintain a foreign-exchange exposure.

National Domicile. Firms headquartered in different countries may have somewhat similar exposures of their income statements. Consider a U.S. firm with an income-statement exposure in the Canadian dollar and a Canadian firm with an income-statement exposure in the United States. Assume the size of each income statement exposure is similar. Both the U.S. and the Canadian firms are concerned about the debt denomination decision. The Canadian firm could reduce its foreign-exchange exposure by borrowing U.S. dollars, at least to the extent that the increase in the volume of U.S. dollar-denominated loans or borrowings offsets the U.S. dollar exposure of its income statement. The Canadian firm might increase its U.S. dollar borrowings so they exceed the volume of its exposure on its income statement to reduce interest costs; at the same time the firm can reduce both its exposure and net interest costs by borrowing U.S. dollars. In contrast, if the U.S. firm seeks to reduce the exposure of its income statement by borrowing Canadian dollars, it increases its net interest payments. The asymmetry reflects that the difference in interest rates on comparable assets is large relative to the anticipated change in the exchange rate.

Risk of Particular Foreign Currencies and the Portfolio Effect. Individual foreign currencies can be ranked by their riskiness. Risk might be measured by the volatility of the movement of the foreign-exchange value of individual foreign currencies, where the volatility might be measured as the range of movement or the standard deviation. Alternatively, the risk might be measured as unanticipated movement in the exchange rate, and either the range or standard deviation of the actual movement about the unanticipated movement.

The firm's attitude toward its exposure might be a function of the riskiness of particular currencies and the cost of altering its exposure. The algorithm is that the firm might maintain exposure in those currencies where the risk is low, and reduce its exposure in those currencies considered very risky. Moreover, this posture toward exposure in particular foreign currencies should be viewed in the context of a portfolio of currencies.

One implication of the portfolio argument is that the larger the firm and the more diverse the array of its foreign-exchange exposures, the stronger the case for maintaining these exposures for any given posture toward risk aversion. The rationale is that as the number of currencies in which the firm has income-statement exposures increases, the larger the impact of the inclusion of each additional currency on the firm's income relative to the impact on the riskiness of the firm's portfolio of currencies. The common-sense interpretation is that those firms with income-statement exposures in a diverse group of foreign currencies are best positioned to carry these exposures and "collect" the risk premium in the foreign-exchange market.

Materiality.   One principle of personal finance is that individuals can increase their incomes by carrying small risks rather than buying insurance against these risks. Thus, individuals may buy automobile and homeowner's insurance with large deductibles; the principle is that they minimize the total cost by self-insuring for small risks. Similarly, individuals may buy major medical insurance and self-insure the cost of smaller medical expenses. The implication is that firms might carry small or modest exposures to their income statements and hedge any exceptionally large exposures. The distinction between large and small is arbitrary and firm-specific; for each firm the question becomes how large a foreign-exchange loss it could accept during a quarter or a year, without having any unusual impact on its reported income or its market. The larger the firm, the larger the foreign-exchange exposure it might carry.

CONCLUSIONS

The key decision in the debt denomination decision is whether the firm should denominate its debt and bank loans in its domestic currency or in a foreign currency. The managers of the firm must decide whether the denomination of debt and bank loans should be managed to increase or reduce the foreign-exchange exposure of its income statement. Hence, they must first measure the components of the foreign-exchange exposure associated with royalty and licensing income, and the income of the firm's foreign subsidiaries, exports, and domestic sales. Then the managers must address the market factors associated with exchange risk and decide whether they believe that risk premiums are evident in the foreign-exchange market. The less convinced they are that risk premiums exist, the stronger the case for hedging the firm's foreign-exchange exposure. The flip side of this statement is that the more evident the risk premiums, the larger the possible cost of hedging exposure and the greater the return from carrying the exposure.

Several firm-specific factors affect the firm's posture toward carrying or hedging foreign-exchange exposure. A central one is its own attitude toward risk aversion. Moreover, the larger the array of currencies in which the firm has income-statement exposures, the more likely it is to view these exposures in a portfolio context. The firm might hedge only those exposures so large that the foreign-exchange losses could have a significant impact on earnings and market value.

REFERENCES

Aliber, Robert Z. *Exchange Risk and Corporate International Finance.* London: Macmillan, 1978.

Huizinga, John, and F. Miskin. "Inflation and Real Rates on Assets with Different Risk Characteristics." *Journal of Finance,* July 1984, pp. 699–714.

Levi, Maurice D. *International Finance: Financial Management and the International Economy.* New York: McGraw-Hill, 1983.

Levich, Richard N. *The International Money Market.* New York: JAI Press, 1979.

Makin, John H. "Portfolio Theory and the Problem of Foreign Exchange Risk." *Journal of Finance,* May 1978, pp. 517–34.

Oxelheim, Lars. *International Financial Market Fluctuations.* Chichester: John Wiley & Sons, 1985.

Papadia, F. "Forward Exchange Rates as Predictors of the Future Spot Rates and the Efficiency of the Foreign Exchange Market." *Journal of Banking and Finance,* June 1981, pp. 217–40.

Wihlborg, Claus. *Currency Risks in International Financial Markets under Different Exchange Rate Regimes.* Stockholm: Institute for International Economics, 1977.

CHAPTER 14

CURRENCY RISK MANAGEMENT

John F. O. Bilson

Most corporate executives believe that if their companies design good products, produce them efficiently, and market them effectively, the world will reward them with material success. This inward-looking perspective on corporate strategy is contradicted by the fact that the greater part of the variation in corporate wealth, as measured by market valuation, can be attributed to factors beyond the control of the company. The behavior of external risk factors—stock prices, interest rates, exchange rates, and commodity prices—are far more important determinants of market value than are internal factors relating to product development, production, and marketing.

There are two reasons why external risk factors are such an important component of the variation in market value. First, changing fundamental economic conditions like the breakdown in the Bretton Woods system of fixed exchange rates, the formation of the Organization of Petroleum Exporting Countries (OPEC) oil cartel, and the collapse of U.S. fiscal discipline have increased the volatility of external risk factors. Second, corporations that routinely spend millions of dollars on product development and advertising have been reluctant to invest in the management of external risk. As the experience of the American economy demonstrates, the consequences of this neglect have been immense.

Whether we consider the automobile industry, Silicon Valley, or the entire state of Texas, the failure to manage external risks has indeed disrupted, and occasionally destroyed, large segments of productive capacity.

The failure to manage external risks cannot be attributed to the absence of markets in which such risks can be traded. The rapid development of futures markets trading futures contracts on stock indexes, interest rates, currencies, and commodities permit corporations to insulate their market value by offsetting external risks at a low cost. In addition, external risks can be managed by taking advantage of interbank currency markets, the international swap market, and specialized instruments created by commercial and investment banks. The failure, I argue, can be more accurately attributed to the absence of a clearly defined program measuring risk exposure and defining who is responsible for the management of risk.

Currency risk management is an important component of an overall strategy of risk management. Based on current volatility levels, the dollar exchange rate can be expected to rise or fall against the other major currencies by approximately 6 percent over a calendar quarter. Because changes tend to average out, the expected change over a calendar year is currently around 12 percent. Currency volatility affects the profitability of export, import, and import competing activities. It is also important in determining the home currency values of assets and liabilities denominated in foreign currencies. Even though currency volatility is an important determinant of corporate wealth, it also offers the greatest possibilities for hedging because of the depth and breadth of the currency markets. Futures, forwards, options, and swaps can all be used to modify the inherent exposure of a corporation toward a desired level.

In this chapter, I discuss the most important components of an effective approach toward corporate foreign-exchange risk management. The first, and most important, component of the strategy is the allocation of responsibility for currency risk management. In almost all of the instances in which corporate wealth has been adversely affected by currency fluctuations, the corporation has failed either to specify who was responsible or to adequately supervise the management team.

The second component is the measurement of foreign-exchange exposure. In this area, corporations have faced a choice between an accounting approach with little economic content and an economic approach of intimidating complexity. I discuss an approach toward the estimation of economic exposure that is sensible in its precepts and manageable in its implementation.

The third component in the strategy concerns discretionary management of foreign-exchange exposure. As upper management typically prefers that managers hedge losses while leaving profitable positions exposed, it is necessary for managers to estimate the direction of the currency relative to the forward rate. Although the act of foreign-exchange forecasting is always difficult and occasionally humiliating, generally a modest knowledge of market direction should be preferred to no knowledge at all.

The immediate objective of this analysis is to create managers who understand the economic exposure of corporations to fluctuations in exchange rates and who have a systematic approach toward the management of the exposure. I have resisted the urge to go beyond this point into the mechanics of trading and the selection of trading instruments.

THE ALLOCATION OF RESPONSIBILITY

In the typical multinational corporation, the responsibility for foreign-exchange management is shared between the central treasury division and the divisional treasuries. The first question that arises is whether the performance of subsidiaries should be evaluated in dollars or the local currency. For senior management unaccustomed to foreign markets, a dollar-based performance evaluation has the virtues of simplicity and comparability with U.S. subsidiaries. However, given the volatility of exchange rates, the dollar-based system often means that the most important determinant of performance is the value of the currency. Local managers typically do not have the skills necessary to effectively manage this risk. As a consequence, they are often unduly influenced by local bank contacts whose motives are not necessarily compatible with the interests of the corporation.

The alternative structure permits divisions to be evaluated in the local currency while central treasury is given the responsibility for the management of foreign-exchange exposure. As many corporations have discovered, the implementation of the centralized approach is also fraught with difficulty. For example, central treasury hedges divisional net assets and income flows and the local currency appreciates against the dollar. The loss on the hedge is allocated to the division, which is required to make an immediate cash outlay to cover an appreciation in the dollar book value of local assets. Because the divisional management was not responsible for the hedge decision, they are reluctant to accept its cost. On the other hand, the central treasury is reluctant to accept a loss on their own books, as the position was motivated by hedge considerations.

The most effective solution to the responsibility problem involves the establishment of an internal forward market (IFM) for currencies within the firm. Although divisions are evaluated in dollars, they have the right—but not the obligation—to purchase or sell foreign currencies to the central treasury division at market-related forward prices. Central treasury makes a market for its services by consulting with the divisions on issues related to the measurement of exposure and hedge management procedures.

The most common benefit attributed to the IFM relates to the netting of transactions and the resulting reduction in transaction costs. To the extent that intracompany transactions are offset, the need to enter the interbank forward market is reduced. For example, a production facility in the United Kingdom sells to distribution facilities in Europe on a price list denominated in British pounds. The subsidiaries would like to purchase sterling to cover their exposure, while the production facility would like to sell sterling to cover their net income. By netting transactions, the total transaction costs of the company are reduced.

Even though netting is an important component of the IFM, it is probably secondary to the increased flexibility which the system gives to the subsidiaries. The IFM manager is often able to offer transactions and strategies that divisional management would not be able to obtain through conventional banking relationships. Interbank corporate foreign-exchange hedging is primarily designed to hedge short-term cash flows. The major part of the volume in the market is in forward contracts with a maturity of less than three months. Furthermore, banks are reluctant to allow nonfinancial subsidiaries to take positions in the forward market that are not related to anticipated cash flows or to net asset positions.

The increased flexibility of the IFM allows divisional managers to take longer dated forward or futures contracts that are less directly related to short-term cash flows. The net asset position, for example, could be hedged with a ten-year forward contract. Anticipated revenue and expenses could be hedged over a two-to-three-year period. Since the IFM is essentially a bookkeeping system, the divisional manager is protected from the cash-flow volatility that results from dealings with external markets.

An additional advantage results from the issue of compensating balances or margins. Most banks require compensating balances as a security against the provision of a foreign-exchange guideline. In the futures markets, daily margin requirements are typically 3 to 5 percent of the value of the position. However, to protect against cash-flow instability resulting from margin calls, margins should typically be kept above 10 percent. The difficulty with most margin policies is that the margin is kept in an instrument—cash or Treasury bills—that is not related to the instrument being hedged. Within the IFM framework, the margin covering the position can be the asset, revenue, or expense that is being hedged. Local cash balances can be released for other purposes.

The flexibility of the IFM can be illustrated with this hypothetical example. A division of a U.S. paper manufacturer in Seattle, Washington, is experiencing rapid growth in its Asian export markets because of the appreciation of the Japanese yen against the U.S. dollar. Instead of simply hedging anticipated revenue over a three-month period, the division locks in the competitive advantage by selling 10 years of anticipated revenue to the IFM. The 10-year forward would typically not be available through the interbank system because the size of the contract exceeds the capital of the division. Furthermore, the quarterly fluctuation in the value of the contract exceeds the net revenue of the division. Despite these problems, the strategy is appropriate for the division. If the yen should continue to appreciate, the division's export markets should experience continued growth. On the other hand, a reversal in the value of the yen would lead to profits on the short currency position that would offset the deterioration in the division's competitive position.

The IFM provides a flexible solution to the issue of responsibility. In contrast to the confrontational problems associated with centralized management, the IFM allows the divisional management the right to decide whether to hedge foreign currency positions. The central management team must view the divisions as a client base. By providing consulting and dealing services, the team should be viewed as a valuable asset rather than as an irritant manufactured by the head office.

The central management team should, in turn, be evaluated as a profit center within the corporation. Because of netting, the ability to deal in size, and the opportunities to hedge long-dated forwards with short-term positions and options, the activities of the group should generally be profitable. In the next two sections, I discuss two issues that should be important in the policy management of the IFM: the measurement of economic exposure and discretionary foreign exchange (FX) management.

ESTIMATING ECONOMIC EXPOSURE TO EXCHANGE RATES

Suppose a U.S. bank has made substantial dollar-denominated loans to the government of Mexico. Is the bank exposed to fluctuations in the Mexican peso? Although common sense would dictate that a large decline in the peso would lower the credit quality of the loan, most of the standard accounting approaches to the measurement of foreign-exchange exposure would consider the loan to be unexposed. At the other extreme, consider a loan denominated in a foreign currency which has a perfectly predictable rate of depreciation against the dollar of 10 percent per annum. Reflecting the crawling peg policy, local interest rates are 10 percent above U.S. rates. Despite the fact that the yield exactly compensates for the anticipated depreciation, this loan would be considered to be 100 percent exposed to the currency according to U.S. accounting standards.

Economic exposure is defined as the change in the economic value of an entity resulting from a change in the exchange rate. Accounting exposure is defined as the change in the book value resulting from a change in the exchange rate. The extent of accounting exposure depends basically on whether particular foreign assets and liabilities are translated into dollars using a current or a historical exchange rate. Under a monetary standard, real assets were translated using a historical exchange rate, while nominal assets were translated using the current exchange rate. As most foreign subsidiaries have real assets and nominal liabilities, the monetary standard resulted in large variations in the dollar value of liabilities without any compensating variation in the value of assets. In response to strong protest from American corporations, the Financial Accounting Standards Board (FASB) abandoned the monetary approach included in *FASB Statement No. 8* in favor of an all current methodology in *FASB Statement No. 52*. Within the all current methodology, all assets and liabilities are translated into dollars using the current (end of period) exchange rate.

Although *FASB Statement 52* has succeeded in reducing the level of tension in FX accounting, the foreign-exchange translation adjustment in the balance sheet is still only slightly related to the concept of economic exposure. The most important difference is that accounting approaches do not take account of the effect of exchange rates on business conditions. However, even so far as asset valuation is concerned, the economic approach relies on concepts alien to accounting practice. A bond, for example, would be considered to be exposed to unanticipated changes in exchange rates that are not reflected in interest rates while being protected from anticipated exchange-rate changes. The exposure of real assets depends on the extent to which the local currency value of these assets appreciates in response to a depreciation of the exchange rate. Issues relating to interest-rate parity and purchasing-power parity are difficult to incorporate into standard accounting methodology.

Although estimates of accounting exposure are generally considered to have little economic content, the economic approach is often thought to be too difficult and too imprecise to be useful. An appreciation of the yen, for example, should increase the market value of U.S. automobile manufacturers by increasing the price of Japanese imports. However, the size of the effect depends on whether the Japanese increase dollar prices, on whether the other currencies also appreciate, on the cross-elasticity of demand between Japanese and U.S. cars, on the extent of U.S. purchases of Japanese auto parts, and on many other factors. For a typical U.S. multinational engaged in many products and many markets, estimation of economic exposure appears to be impossible.

There is, however, a way around the impasse. In the equity markets, there are many specialists whose role is to estimate the effects of changing economic conditions on U.S. corporations. If an appreciation of the yen is good for General Motors, we should expect that the price of GM stock should increase by an amount equal to the present discounted value of the benefit. By relying on the equity markets, the corporation can cheaply and effectively measure its economic exposure to currency fluctuations.

Consider a portfolio containing a fundamental asset, K, and a potential hedge asset, X. The revenue from the portfolio is equal to the return times the value of the investment.

$$\text{Revenue} = R_k \cdot K + R_x \cdot X \qquad (1)$$

The level of investment in the hedge asset is chosen to minimize the variance of total revenue. Since forward or futures contracts do not require the placement of capital, we do not have to assume that capital placed in X must be subtracted from K. Minimizing the variance of revenue yields the following equation for X:

$$X = - b \cdot K \qquad (2)$$

The coefficient b is the regression slope coefficient obtained by regressing R_k on R_x. Assume that this coefficient is .1 and that the market value of the corporation is $100 million. A 10 percent depreciation of the currency results, on average, in a 1 percent decline in the market value of the firm. This predictable effect could be offset by borrowing 10 percent of the firm's capital in the foreign market and investing the funds in dollars.

The regression approach toward the measurement of FX exposure can be extended to include a multiplicity of risk factors. A typical regression would include stock indexes, interest rates, currencies, and important commodity prices. Care must be taken in implementing the approach to ensure that there have not been major changes in corporate structure during the estimation period or that the exposure estimates are dominated by a small number of extreme observations. Despite these caveats, the regression approach has proven to be a practical and efficient procedure for estimating economic exposure. In the case of the U.S. bank loans to Mexico, for example, there was a significant tendency for the return on equity to fall below the market return when the peso depreciated in the futures market.

As a more general illustration of the approach, Equation 3 summarizes the results of regressing the quarterly return, excluding dividends, on the Standard & Poor's 500 Stock Average (S&P 500), and on the quarterly returns on the three major currencies. The quarterly currency return is defined as $(S_{t+1} - F_t)/F_t$, where F_t is defined as the beginning-of-period three-month forward rate and S_{t+1} is the end-of-period spot rate.

$$R(S\&P) = .0191 - .2226*X(DM) + .1576*X(BP) + .3358*X(JY) \tag{3}$$
$$ (.0092) \quad (.2267) \qquad\qquad (.2072) \qquad\qquad (.3358)$$

The coefficients on the deutsche mark and sterling returns are of opposite signs and jointly are not significantly different from zero at the 5 percent level. Eliminating these two currencies leads to Equation 4:

$$R(S\&P) = .0202 + .2838*X(JY)$$
$$ (.0088) \quad (.0567) \tag{4}$$
$$\text{R-SQ} = .0759 \quad \text{Std. Error} = .0567$$
$$\text{Estimation Period: 1976Q1 - 1986Q4}$$

The results indicate a general tendency for the U.S. market to rally when the Japanese yen strengthens against the dollar. This exposure could be eliminated by redenominating debt from dollars to yen for 30 percent of the market value of the index. The standard error of the coefficient, given in brackets below the coefficient, defines the precision of the hedge ratio estimate. Using the two standard deviation rule, the true hedge ratio is estimated to lie between 20 percent and 40 percent. Finally, the R-squared statistic provides information about the contribution of the risk factor to total risk. In the case of the S&P 500, approximately 7.5 percent of the variance can be attributed to volatility in the yen.

The IFM structure discussed in the previous section is a method for consolidating the currency exposures of the various corporate divisions. The exposure measurement analysis in this section provides a base position in currencies for the entire corporation. By combining the two methods, the corporate treasury management should be able to create a hedge portfolio which is negatively correlated with the return on corporate equity. In the next section, I look at procedures for collecting and evaluating advice about taking discretionary positions in the foreign-exchange market.

DISCRETIONARY FOREIGN EXCHANGE MANAGEMENT

The international treasury manager is typically inundated with advice from banks, traders, and commercial services. Because of the difficulty of evaluating this advice, most of it is typically ignored. In this section, I first outline a simple model for foreign-exchange forecasting and then use this model to illustrate some general principles about the evaluation and use of advice.

The model utilizes three indicators to forecast currency returns: value, yield, and trend. Under most circumstances, the model prefers to buy undervalued, high-yielding, and upward-trending currencies. Conversely, the model prefers to sell over-valued, low-yielding, and downward-trending currencies. To implement the approach, it is first necessary to define the indicators empirically.

Value refers to the level of exchange rate in comparison to relative consumer prices. Although the purchasing-power parity doctrine has declined as a theory of exchange-rate determination as asset market conditions have increased in importance relative to physical commodity trade, there is still a tendency for exchange rates to reflect relative prices over a longer time horizon. For the value model, it is assumed that the rate of convergence is proportional to the log of the difference between the exchange rate and the relative consumer price index (CPI) after adjustment by a factor of proportionality.

Yield refers to the difference between short-term interest rates which, through the interest-rate parity theorem, is equal to the forward premium or discount on the currency. There are two distinct theories of the determination of interest-rate differentials. Most market commentators implicitly believe that interest rates are predominantly determined by domestic money-market conditions. Higher interest rates are typically attributed to either a tightening of domestic monetary policy or to the emergence of inflationary expectations. On the other hand, the international view is that interest-rate differentials reflect the expected appreciation or depreciation of the exchange rate. According to this view, an increase in domestic rates relative to world rates reflects a market expectation that the domestic currency will depreciate relative to other currencies.

Although efficient-market theorists often characterize asset prices using a martingale or random walk process, casual observation suggests that there have been significant longer-run trends in the exchange rates. One of the reasons why academic studies have not been able to discern trends using standard statistical methods is because of the use of linear time series models. The linear model assumes that a future trend is proportional to the size of the current trend. However, large moves in exchange rates must eventually reverse. Most technical trend-following models assume a constant expected future trend that is reversed when an objective is met. I account for this behavior with a model that discounts the past trend for its size.

$$\text{TREND} = X \cdot \exp(-\text{abs}(X)/\text{std}(X)) \tag{5}$$

In Equation 5, X is the rate of change in the exchange rate over the past quarter. The second term in the equation "discounts" the trend by its size relative to its past standard deviation. The value of the trend variable reaches its maximum when X is one standard deviation from zero, and falls asymptotically toward zero as X approaches infinity. The function is symmetric for positive and negative values of X.

Two features of the forecasting model should be pointed out. The first is that the concepts employed are simple and understandable in their trading implications. Value traders expand their positions as the exchange rate moves against the position. Yield traders typically hold stable positions. Trend traders cut losses and let profits run. The implications of the forecasting strategy for a trading pattern are as important as the forecast itself. The second feature is the diversification of advice. Even though each trading methodology is profitable in its own right, the periods of profitability are very different. The value strategy is most profitable in a trendless, volatile market; the yield strategy is profitable in a stable market; and the trend strategy is profitable in a trending market. By combining the three, a greater measure of stability can be achieved.

To combine the three advisory methodologies, the indicators are regressed on the actual ex-post return on a forward contract. The coefficients are estimated by multivariate regression using quarterly data for five currencies over the period from 1976 Q2 to 1987 Q1. In the estimation, the coefficients on each indicator are constrained to be the same for each currency. There are two reasons for this constraint. First, the quarterly returns are an extremely noisy series and it is necessary to be parsimonious to obtain stable coefficient estimates. Second, the constraint implies that forecasts of expected returns only reflect differences between the indicators, rather than differences between the coefficients.

The results of the estimation are as follows:

$$\text{Return} = \underset{(.0269)}{.0887 \cdot \text{PPP}} + \underset{(0.3233)}{1.1190 \cdot \text{YIELD}} + \underset{(.1854)}{.6289 \cdot \text{TREND}} \tag{6}$$

where: $\text{Return} = \ln(S_{t+1}/F_t)$

$\text{PPP} = \ln((P/P^*)_t) - \ln(S_t);$
$\quad P\,(P^*) = \text{local (US) CPI}$

$\text{YIELD} = \ln(S_t/F_t)$

$\text{TREND} = \text{Equation 5}$

In addition to the reported coefficients, individual constant terms are estimated to scale the relative prices to the exchange rate.

Each of the reported coefficient estimates are over three standard deviations from zero. Essentially, the results suggest taking 10 percent of the undervaluation of the exchange rate, 110 percent of the interest-rate differential, and 60 percent of the discounted trend. The combination of the three factors then defines the expected return on the currency. We can examine the forecasting ability of the model by regressing the actual return on the expected return for each currency.

B-pound   Actual =   .0002 + 1.1212 · Expected
                     (.0076) (0.3288)
        R-SQ =   .22 F(1,42) = 11.63 Sig. Level = .0014

D-mark   Actual =   .0004 + 0.7633 · Expected
                    (.0089) (0.4091)
       R-SQ =   .07 F(1,42) = 3.48 Sig. Level = .0691

J-yen   Actual =   .0020 + 1.2939 · Expected
                   (.0098) (0.4726)
      R-SQ =   .15 F(1,42) = 7.49 Sig. Level = .0090

F-franc   Actual =   .0006 + 1.0089 · Expected
                    (.0085) (0.3591)
       R-SQ =   .16 F(1,42) = 7.89 Sig. Level = .0070

S-franc   Actual =   .0012 + 1.4069 · Expected
                    (.0100) (0.3946)
       R-SQ =   .23 F(1,42) = 12.70 Sig. Level = .0009

With the exception of the DM all of the equations pass standard significance tests at the 1 percent level or better, and the slope coefficients are all greater than unity. Again with the exception of the DM, the equations typically account for between 15 and 25 percent of the quarterly variation in the actual return. The relatively poor performance of the DM is difficult to explain given that the best performing equation is the Swiss franc.

While statistical significance is reassuring, the real test from a treasury management perspective is the risk/return trade-off implied by the equations. To address this question, it is necessary to specify an expected utility function that will determine the positions taken in the currencies on the basis of the expected return and the covariance matrix of the regression residuals. A simple expected utility function is specified in Equation 7:

$$E(U) = E(r)'q - (\tfrac{1}{2}g) \, q'Vq \qquad (7)$$

In Equation 7, E(r) is an nxl vector of expected returns, q is an nxl vector of positions valued in dollars, V is the nxn covariance matrix of the residuals, and g is a risk aversion parameter. The first term in the equation E(r)'q is the expected profit on the portfolio of positions, while q'Vq is the anticipated variance of profits. The expected utility function states that the corporation's expected utility is directly proportional to the level of expected profit and inversely proportional to the variance of profits. The risk aversion parameter determines the corporation's tolerance for risk.

Minimizing the utility function through the choice of the q vector leads to the following set of linear equations:

$$\begin{array}{cc} V & q \\ (nxn)(nxl) \end{array} = g \begin{array}{c} E(r) \\ (nxl) \end{array} \qquad (8)$$

The risk aversion parameter is an arbitrary scaling factor that influences the total size of the positions taken but has no effect on the portfolio proportions or the risk/return trade-off. In the following simulations, this parameter has been set equal to $10,000. Positions were then calculated for each period along with the actual and expected profits on the position.

The average quarterly profit on the position was $9,164 and the standard deviation was $11,123. The ratio of average profit to the standard deviation was .82 which is high relative to other risky investments. For example, the ratio for the S&P 500 on a quarterly basis is approximately .35. Furthermore, the model has a tendency for outliers to be positive: all of the observations which were greater than 2 standard deviations from zero were positive. This is because the model tends to scale up positions where all of the return indicators agree.

As a guide to actual trading, the results reported here should be treated with considerable caution. The most important deficiency is that the estimates are all in-sample. The out-of-sample stability of the model is an important issue that cannot be addressed here. The second deficiency is that the model assumes that decisions are only made once a quarter. In an applied context, daily revisions are probably more appropriate. Finally, no attempt is made to take account of transactions costs, bid-ask spreads, or slippage.

Indeed, the purpose of this section is not to tout a particular approach to exchange-rate forecasting but to describe some general principles for forecast evaluation and use. I have demonstrated how the regression approach can be used to combine the different forecasts and how the results from the composite forecast can be used to construct a portfolio of positions. This procedure allows a strategy to be evaluated within the traditional risk/return framework of corporate finance rather than the academic standard of statistical significance.

CONCLUSION

Many aspects of currency risk management have not been covered in this chapter. In particular, no attention has been paid to the centralization of cash flows through international lock-box facilities; to the variety of instruments—swaps, options, and asset liability management—that can be used to manage foreign-exchange exposure; to the accounting and tax implications of foreign-exchange strategies; and to many other issues. However, the implementation of the three programs that we have discussed would put the average company well on the way to a reasonably sophisticated currency risk management system.

CHAPTER 15

EVALUATION OF EXCHANGE-RATE FORECASTS

Richard M. Levich

THE INTERNATIONAL
FINANCIAL ENVIRONMENT

With few exceptions, a system of pegged but adjustable exchange rates as specified under the Bretton Woods agreement dominated the post–World War II experience of all industrialized countries. Exchange-rate behavior under the Bretton Woods system was characterized by prolonged periods of minor oscillations around the peg, and a few large, discrete exchange-rate changes. In this environment, analysts focused their attention on balance of payments data and international reserves. A sustained payments imbalance along with substantial shifts in international reserve holdings increased the probability that a central bank could no longer support the pegged rate. As these pressures were slow to accumulate, analysts could be certain of the direction of the exchange-rate change. The magnitude of the change—that is, the amount required to restore payments balance and to halt international reserve flows—could be estimated from a purchasing-power parity (PPP) model or from other data. However, the ultimate decision to change the peg was fundamentally a political decision.

The great majority of countries today—105 out of 151 members of the International Monetary Fund (IMF)—have chosen to limit the price movements in their currencies.[1] Most of these countries have elected to peg their currency's value to the U.S. dollar, the French franc, the IMF's Special Drawing Rights (SDR), or to some other standard; eight countries participate in a cooperative floating agreement—the European Monetary System. For these currencies, exchange-rate forecasting must rely on much the same mixture of economic and political forecasting that was essential during the Bretton Woods period.

The introduction of floating exchange rates in the early 1970s marked a major systematic change for international financial markets. Exchange-rate behavior under the floating-rate system is characterized by relatively small exchange-rate changes that occur continuously as new information is received. Over time, however, these small changes can accumulate into exchange-rate movements that appear large relative to current differentials in economic aggregates such as money supply growth rates, inflation rates, or interest rates. This tendency for the exchange rate to "overshoot" the changes implied by current economic developments, as if the current exchange rate were changing to discount future, and as yet unobserved, economic developments, is one factor that has made exchange-rate forecasting an extremely difficult task.

Of the remaining 46 IMF member countries, only 18 countries are classified as "independently floating." However, this small group includes the United States, Japan, the United Kingdom, and Canada, major countries whose exchange rates, trade flows, and capital flows play a dominant role in international trade and investment.

The exchange rates of these countries are determined in highly competitive markets in which current prices reflect to a great extent what is currently known or expected to happen regarding a wide array of economic variables. A corollary of this view is that, in the short run, exchange rates are driven by "news" or unanticipated announcements of economic variables. To be sure, governments (i.e., central banks) continue to play a role in the foreign-exchange market through economic policy making and direct market intervention, but the impact of this role is difficult to assess.

---

[1] *International Financial Statistics* (Washington, D.C.: International Monetary Fund, May 1988).

Despite government intervention, the market price of foreign exchange may present an accurate reflection of what is known and what is expected to happen in the future. In this case, market prices themselves may reflect the best available implicit forecast. And it may be difficult to outperform this forecast if one is using generally available economic information and forecasting tools.

The Need to Forecast

It is sometimes claimed that corporations forecast exchange rates not because they have special expertise in doing so, but rather because exchange-rate forecasts play an important role in a wide variety of decisions. Obviously, any foreign borrowing or investment decision requires a forecast of future exchange rates so that future foreign cash flows can be converted into units of domestic currency and a comparable domestic cost of funds or return on investment can be computed. A currency forecast is generally required for the firm to manage its currency exposure, which results from current and planned holdings of foreign currency.

Currency forecasts can play a role in marketing, specifically with respect to pricing decisions. Suppose that a Japanese automobile selling for yen 1.35 million in Japan is priced at $9,000 in the United States when the exchange rate stands at yen 150/$. If the yen appreciates to yen 130/$, each U.S. auto sale will earn only yen 1.17 million. The Japanese firm is now worse off. Thus, their decision to raise U.S. prices depends on many factors, including the future yen-dollar exchange rate. From this example, one can also see that assessing subsidiary performance also requires exchange-rate projections.

Finally, exchange-rate forecasts can be valuable for long-range or strategic planning. If the real exchange rate is expected to change, a U.S. firm can maximize its dollar profits (revenues minus costs) by incurring costs in those countries where the currency has depreciated below its purchasing-power parity (PPP) level and by earning revenues in those countries where the currency has appreciated above its PPP level.

General Benefits from Forecasting

The forecasting process itself may be associated with other indirect benefits. Most forecasting services provide an extensive discussion of macroeconomic conditions for each country. These reports are a convenient way to see the broad trends in money markets, labor markets, and the markets for goods and services. Some services offer extensive computer libraries of macroeconomic data.

Forecasting services also enable users to judge the likely range of future currency values and to quantify the risks in maintaining open positions. Some services include a range forecast as part of their regular reporting. When a forecast range is not provided, a user might estimate one by allowing fundamental variables to vary over some likely range, thus generating a range of likely minimum and maximum currency values. The ability to specify a range for future exchange rates is an important part of many exposure management models that use a decision matrix approach.

Another way to judge the range of future exchange rates is to analyze a group of forecasts from several forecasting services or several forecasting models.[2] These forecasts reflect both different assumptions on future economic variables and different ways of modeling exchange rates.

General Problems Facing Forecasters

Research conducted over the last 15 years has shed considerable light on the subject of the economic determinants of the exchange rate.[3] Economists have been fairly successful in constructing models to explain cross-sectional exchange-rate differences—for example, why the U.S. dollar exchanges for roughly 1,200 lira but only 1.60 deutsche marks—and to explain the time series of exchange-rate developments on a quarter-to-quarter or year-to-year basis. Economists are also more clear on the fundamental economic variables that drive exchange rates, the channels through which these variables act, and the directional impact of changes in each variable.

---

[2] One such service is *Currency Forecasters Digest*, White Plains, New York.
[3] See Peter Isard, "Lessons from Empirical Models of Exchange Rates," *IMF Staff Papers,* March 1987, pp. 1–28; and Richard M. Levich, "Empirical Studies of Exchange Rates: Price Behavior, Rate Determination and Market Efficiency," in *Handbook of International Economics,* ed. P. Jones and R. Kenen. Amsterdam: North-Holland Publishing, 1985, for surveys of recent approaches to exchange rate modeling.

Despite these achievements, a number of key problems remain with respect to exchange-rate forecasting. Even though economists have had some success in explaining quarterly or yearly exchange-rate changes, the ability to explain day-to-day or week-to-week changes is much more limited. In part, this is because many of the variables that play a role in popular exchange-rate models, such as the money supply or national income, cannot be measured daily while other variables by their very nature, such as expected money supply growth, and expected inflation, cannot be observed directly. Furthermore, an economic theory that concludes that the spot rate is a function of some set of variables $(X_1, X_2, \ldots X_N)$, does not solve the forecasting problem even if the theory is valid. It only forces an analyst to forecast future values of $X_1, X_2, \ldots X_N$, which raises its own difficulties.

A related problem is that most forecasting models, especially those that are formalized, assume that the past economic data and relationships will remain relevant for the future. This can be a dangerous procedure in a world economy prone to frequent structural shocks. For example, technical forecasters often assume that past support and resistance levels will apply in the future. Econometric forecasters assume that regression equations estimated using historical sample data will remain valid for postsample predictions. These procedures fail when there is a fundamental or structural economic change. Until the structural change is recognized and the model is modified, a formal model will lead to biased predictions.

A special problem concerns long-term exchange-rate forecasting. Typically, forecasting services produce forecasts of nominal exchange rates. But for long-term investment decisions, the real exchange rate is the more relevant variable. When PPP holds, the nominal exchange-rate change is matched by the difference in inflation rates between the two countries so that there is no real exchange-rate change. Because we observe both positive and negative deviations from PPP, it is easy to construct examples in which a nominal exchange-rate depreciation or appreciation is associated with either a real depreciation or a real appreciation depending on the realized inflation-rate differentials between the two countries. The point here is that a nominal exchange-rate forecast can be completely accurate, and yet provide no information on the future real exchange rate. And it is the real exchange rate that influences both consumers' and producers' decisions concerning real goods and services.

Finally, an important corollary of the asset view of exchange rates and the efficient market principle is that exchange-rate changes are the result of unanticipated economic events, that is, news. By definition, it is impossible to forecast news. The implication here is that forecasters cannot expect to be successful in predicting exchange-rate movements relative to the anticipated trend. In this case, even forecasts that are very accurate might not help one to establish profitable positions because other financial market prices were free to adjust to reflect the same information.

OVERVIEW OF FORECASTING TECHNIQUES

In this section, we review some of the major exchange-rate forecasting techniques that have been introduced into the academic and professional literature. These techniques can be classified into two broad groups—economic models and pure forecasting models. Economic models are those that rely on a set of internally consistent assumptions regarding economic behavior. Pure forecasting models, on the other hand, involve numerical or statistical techniques intended to produce good forecasts, but not necessarily based on a clear or plausible economic model.

Economic Models—First Principles

Within the class of economic models, several further distinctions can be made: econometric versus judgmental models, single equation versus multiequation models, and flow versus stock models. We discuss each of these briefly.

The distinction between econometric and judgmental forecasting is somewhat artificial as the decision to accept one forecasting model and reject all the others clearly involves judgment. The most obvious difference between these two categories is that econometric forecasts are generated from an explicit numerical formula. The econometric forecaster's list of important driving variables and their weights are clearly stated. A judgmental forecaster might consider econometric estimates of important and quantifiable variables (e.g., the money supply or inflation rate). However, economic factors that are difficult to quantify (e.g., market sentiment or the chance of central bank intervention) are also considered. All of these factors are combined in some unspecified way to produce a judgmental forecast.

The judgmental approach offers the potential advantage of shifting quickly when structural (e.g., economic or political) change occurs. To be sure, there is a cost, since judgment can be wrong. Econometric forecasts, on the other hand, rely on stated, specific structural relationships that try to account for the systematic impact of variables on the exchange rate. But these relationships must be estimated from historical data. The cost here is that if economic structure has shifted, it takes some time before an econometric forecaster has sufficient data to account for the new structural environment in the forecasts.

Econometric forecasts are very often based on a single-equation model, and most of these are inspired by purchasing power parity or monetary models with additional variables added to suit the model-builder's preferences. The advantage of this approach is simplicity and the ability of the user to simulate other scenarios. The disadvantage of the single-equation approach is that the simple equation might not adequately represent the real world. Forecast errors might result even when the right-hand side variables are known with some confidence.

At the opposite extreme, some econometric advisory services prepare their forecasts using models based on several dozen to several hundred equations, sometimes allowing for interactions and feedback between economic regions. These complex models attempt to be a better reflection of the real world. But more regression coefficients and variables have to be estimated, so forecasting performance need not improve beyond the simple models. Moreover, when forecasting errors occur in a large model, it may be difficult to trace the source of the problem.

All economic models of the exchange rate posit that there is both a demand for and a supply of foreign exchange, and that an equilibrium price is one that equates the demand and supply of that currency. Until the 1970s, international capital flows were limited and, to a great extent, foreign-exchange transactions were believed to be associated with the flows of international trade in commodities and manufactured products. As a result, economic models focused on the demand and supply of currencies associated with balance of payments flows.

With the advent of floating exchange rates, exchange controls have been relaxed and international capital mobility has increased substantially. Investors are now free to shift large portions of their stock of assets (i.e., their wealth) from assets denominated in one currency, say, dollars, into assets denominated in another currency, say, yen. In this environment, an equilibrium exchange rate is one that induces investors to willingly hold the existing stock of financial assets denominated in the various currencies.

All modern economic models of foreign exchange-rate determination incorporate the principle of "stock" or "asset market" equilibrium. In great part, this feature helps to explain why exchange rates are both volatile and difficult to forecast.

Economic Models—Specific Examples

Recent papers by Isard and Levich have surveyed a variety of exchange-rate models that might be used for forecasting purposes.[4] In this section, we highlight some of the most popular models.

Purchasing-Power Parity.   Perhaps the most popular and intuitive model for forecasting exchange-rate behavior is represented by the theory of purchasing-power parity (PPP). The main idea of purchasing-power parity is that nominal exchange rates are set so that the real purchasing power of currencies tends to equalize. As a result, PPP suggests that in the long run, nominal bilateral exchange-rate changes tend to equal the differential in inflation rates between countries.[5]

To implement PPP as a forecasting model, one must first select a time period (t) and domestic and foreign price indexes (P and P*) so that PPP is satisfied.

---

[4] Ibid.

[5] Many writings on purchasing-power parity have been surveyed by Lawrence H. Officer, "The Purchasing Power Parity Theory of Exchange Rates: A Review Article," *IMF Staff Papers* 23 (March 1976); a more extended discussion is in Ronald I. McKinnon, *Money in International Exchange* (Cambridge: Cambridge University Press, 1979), chap. 6.

$$S_t = \frac{c\,P_t}{P_t^*} \qquad (1)$$

Period t is defined as the base period for our calculations.[6] The constant term c scales the price indexes to equal the exchange rate S_t. In a later period, if PPP remains true, the exchange rate in period t+n will be

$$S_{t+n} = \frac{c\,P_{t+n}}{P_{t+n}^*} \qquad (2)$$

Dividing Expression 2 by Expression 1 results in

$$\frac{S_{t+n}}{S_t} = \frac{P_{t+n}/P_{t+n}^*}{P_t/P_t^*} \quad \text{or}$$

$$S_{t+n} = S_t\,\frac{P_{t+n}/P_{t+n}^*}{P_t/P_t^*} \qquad (3)$$

Expression 3 suggests that the future exchange rate is equal to the current exchange rate adjusted for future domestic price changes relative to future foreign price changes. To take an example, let $S_t = \$0.60/\text{DM}$ and $P_t = P_t^* = 100$. If one thinks that over the next three years, U.S. inflation will be about 5 percent per year, while West German inflation will be roughly 2 percent per year, then the estimates of future price indexes are $\hat{P}_{t+n} = 115.76$ and $\hat{P}_{t+n}^* = 106.12$, where the circumflex denotes a forecast. From Expression 3 it follows that $\hat{S}_{t+n} = \$0.6545/\text{DM}$.

From the example, it is clear that two critical assumptions have been made. First, the exchange-rate forecast depends on accurate forecasts of both price indexes. This problem would exist even if PPP were known to be the true model of exchange rate determination. Second, it is assumed that exchange rates are determined in accordance with PPP. Put another way, PPP assumes that real exchange rates are constant.

---

[6] In practice, we may identify this as a period when the country was close to an international payments balance and also meeting its domestic policy targets. The determination of a proper base period or equilibrium exchange rate is discussed in John Williamson, "The Exchange Rate System," *Policy Analyses in International Economics*, No. 5, 2nd ed. (Washington, D.C.: Institute for International Economics, 1985).

Empirical evidence on PPP in the 1970s and 1980s shows that substantial and prolonged deviations from PPP were common among industrial countries. As a result, economists turned to monetary and portfolio balance models of exchange-rate determination.

Monetary Theory and Exchange Rates. Although PPP concludes that the exchange rate is the relative price of goods in two countries, the monetary approach leads to the conclusion that the exchange rate is the relative price of two moneys. The equilibrium exchange rate is the one at which the supplies (or stocks) of the two moneys are willingly held.

To implement the monetary approach as a forecasting model, we must first specify an explicit demand function for real money balances (M/P). A popular specification is

$$M/P = K \, Y^n \, e^{-ai} \qquad (4)$$

where Y represents real income, n is the income elasticity of demand for real money balances, i represents the nominal interest rate and a is the interest rate semielasticity of demand. (A time subscript t is suppressed.) If terms are rearranged in Equation 4, we have

$$P = M/(K \, Y^n \, e^{-ai}) \qquad (5)$$

Assuming that the same specification of money demand also applies in the foreign country, we can write

$$P^* = M^*/(K^* \, Y^{*n} \, e^{-ai^*}) \qquad (6)$$

where as before, an asterisk indicates the foreign country. For simplicity only we assume the elasticity terms are identical in both countries. We now draw on purchasing-power parity theory, substituting Expressions 5 and 6 into 1, resulting in

$$S = \frac{M}{M^*} \left(\frac{Y^*}{Y}\right)^n \frac{K^*}{K} \, e^{a(i - i^*)} \qquad (7)$$

In the context of Equation 7, a forecast of the future spot rate (S_{t+n}) would require forecasts of all the right-hand-side variables, plus estimates of n and a. These estimates could be taken from outside sources or from a regression analysis of Equation 7. To run such a linear regression, we would take the logarithm of Equation 7 to get

$$s = (m-m^*) + n(y^*-y) + (k^*-k) + a(i-i^*) \qquad (8)$$

where we use the convention that a lowercase letter represents the logarithm of a capital letter (e.g., $s = \ln S$). Equation 8 predicts that a 1 percent increase in the domestic money supply would be matched by a 1 percent depreciation of the exchange rate. It also predicts that the exchange rate (in \$/DM) is negatively related to domestic income, and positively related to domestic (nominal) interest rates.

Equation 8 represents the most basic version of the monetary approach to exchange rates. Variations on this model have incorporated the impact of traded and nontraded goods prices, real interest differentials, and current account balances.

Portfolio Balance Theory.   The portfolio balance approach extends the monetary approach by arguing that the relevant set of international assets that must be willingly held includes government-issued bonds as well as national money supplies. In the portfolio balance framework, the interaction between investors' demand for government bonds and governments' supply of bonds come together to determine the exchange rate. The portfolio balance approach to exchange rates thus bears a strong resemblance to the portfolio theory of securities markets, in which investor wealth (representing demand) bids for the supply of existing securities thereby determining their relative prices.

To implement the portfolio balance approach as a forecasting model, we must first specify an explicit demand function for domestic versus foreign-currency-denominated bonds. We assume that an investor will increase holdings of domestic bonds (B) relative to foreign bonds (F) as some positive function (G) of the expected relative rate of return on domestic bonds $[q = i - i^* - E(\triangle s)]$. This general specification can be written as

$$B_j/(S \; F_j) = G_j(q) \qquad (9)$$

where j refers to the demand of the jth investor and S, as before, is the spot exchange rate.

Two further assumptions are required to complete the model. First, we must specify the desired portfolio balance across all investors rather than just investor j. For simplicity, let us assume that all investors are identical so that Expression 10

$$B/(S\ F) = G(q) \tag{10}$$

describes preferences in the aggregate, and B and F are the net supplies of domestic and foreign-currency-denominated government bonds. Second, we need to specify a particular function for G, which for the sake of example we take as in Expression 11

$$B/(S\ F) = G(q) = \exp\{\alpha + \beta[i - i^* - E(\triangle s)]\} \tag{11}$$

Taking logarithms of Expression 11 and rearranging terms, we get

$$s = -\alpha - \beta[i - i^* - E(\triangle s)] + b - f \tag{12}$$

In Expression 12 an increase in the domestic interest rate or in the net supply of foreign bonds tends to appreciate the domestic currency, while the opposite is true of an increase in the foreign interest rate or an increase in the net supply of domestic bonds.[7]

The Generalized Asset Approach and the Role of News.   The monetary and portfolio balance approaches just reviewed suggest that the demand for currency depends on its qualities as a durable asset. If a currency is expected to continue offering services as a medium of exchange (i.e., transactions services) and as a store of value and unit of account (i.e., the choice for denominating portfolio wealth), then the currency will continue to be demanded. One property of financial assets that is associated with stocks and bonds is that their prices are forward looking, depending on future discounted cash flows. The same forward-looking property is true of exchange-rate pricing and it can be helpful in forecasting.

---

[7] In contrast, other models predict that an increase in the domestic fiscal deficit may lead to an increase in domestic interest rates, thus attracting foreign capital and appreciating domestic currency. For empirical evidence supporting this interpretation, see Martin Feldstein, "The Budget Deficit and the Dollar," in *NBER Macroeconomics Annual 1986*, ed. Stanley Fischer (Cambridge, Mass.: MIT Press, 1986). If the explanatory variables in Expression 12 are interrelated, then additional equations describing these relations are required.

In Equation 8, the interest differential term $a(i - i^*)$ appears. If covered interest parity holds, $(i - i^*) = f_t - s_t$, and if forward rates are assumed equal to expected future spot rates, $f_t = E(s_{t+1})$, then Equation 8 can be written as

$$s_t = z_t + a[E(s_{t+1}) - s_t] \tag{13}$$

where

$$z_t = (m - m^*) + n(y^* - y) + (k^* - k) \tag{14}$$

If we collect terms, we have

$$s_t = \frac{1}{1 + a} z_t + a\, E(s_{t+1}) \tag{15}$$

Expression 15 shows that the log of today's spot rate depends on today's economic variables (the z_t) plus an expectation of the spot rate in the next period. But from Expression 13, we can see that $E(s_{t+1})$ itself will depend on $E(s_{t+2})$, and that $E(s_{t+2})$ will depend on $E(s_{t+3})$, and so forth. By this process of forward iteration, we can show that

$$s_t = \frac{1}{1 + a} \sum_{k=0}^{\infty} \left(\frac{a}{1 + a}\right)^k E(z_{t+k}) \tag{16}$$

In other words, the current spot rate depends on the current expectation of all the important driving variables, (the z's), from the present ($t = 0$) into the indefinite future.

Expression 16 suggests that the current spot-exchange rate reflects what is presently known or expected to happen regarding future economic variables. As a corollary, the exchange rate deviates from its expected path only in response to unanticipated events. The implication of the asset market approach is that deviations between today's forward exchange rate and the future spot rate are the result of news (assuming no exchange-risk premium). In a regression format, we can write this as

$$s_t = a + b\, f_{t-1} + \text{``news''} + w_t \tag{17}$$

Intuitively, "news" could be modeled as the deviation between the realization of some important variable (z_t) and what had been widely expected by market professionals about that variable (z_t). The list of candidates for z_t could include the money supply, interest rates, current account, or the trade balance. Several empirical studies confirm that unanticipated changes in these important variables are significantly related to forward rate forecasting errors.[8] The implication of these results is that analysts who can forecast one or two key variables better than the market as a whole might be able to outperform the forward-rate forecast.

The Forward Rate as a Forecaster. An interest in the forward rate as a forecaster of the future spot rate is linked closely with the efficient market hypothesis, which states that market prices reflect available information. Because investors' expectations of the future spot rate are part of the available information set and these expectations should be reflected in market prices, under certain strict assumptions (which we outline shortly) it is correct to argue that today's forward exchange rate is an unbiased forecast of the future spot rate. When these strict assumptions are met, the forward rate would be a very attractive forecast to use—first, because it represents the collective wisdom of many well-informed, profit-seeking traders; second, because the forward rate is revised quickly as new information becomes available; and third, because the forward rate is a very inexpensive forecast to use.

To analyze the case for the forward rate ($F_{t,n}$) as a forecaster of the future spot rate (S_{t+n}), consider the error term, $e_{t,n}$ where

$$e_{t,n} = S_{t+n} - F_{t,n} \tag{18}$$

One interpretation of $e_{t,n}$ is that it is the forecast error of the forward rate against the future spot rate. Another interpretation of $e_{t,n}$ is that it represents the speculative profit for investors who buy forward contracts outright at $F_{t,n}$ and then sell their matured contracts in the spot market at S_{t+n}.

Since $e_{t,n}$ can be interpreted as a speculative profit, it is

---

[8] See Rudiger Dornbusch, *Exchange Rate Economics: Where Do We Stand?* Brookings Papers on Economic Activity, no. 1, 1980; Sebastian Edwards, "Floating Exchange Rates, Expectations, and New Information," *Journal of Monetary Economics,* May 1983, pp. 321–36; Craig Hakkio and Douglas Pearce, "The Reaction of Exchange Rates to Economic News," *Economic Inquiry,* October 1985, pp. 621–36; and Kishore Tandon and Thomas Urich, "International Market Response to Announcements of U.S. Macroeconomic Data," *Journal of International Money and Finance,* March 1987, pp. 71–84.

unlikely that $e_{t,n}$ would be consistently large and positive. The reason is that consistently large profits would attract forward speculators. Their purchases of forward contracts would increase $F_{t,n}$ and decrease $e_{t,n}$, thus removing profits. Similarly, it is unlikely that $e_{t,n}$ would be consistently large and negative. In this case, forward speculators would sell forward contracts: $F_{t,n}$ would decrease and $e_{t,n}$ would increase, thus removing losses.

A credible story seems to be that $e_{t,n}$ would be negative at some times and positive at others. In repeated trials over long periods of time, the average of $e_{t,n}$ should be a small number near zero. Furthermore, the time series of $e_{t,n}$ should not exhibit predictable patterns of positive and negative values. If patterns could be discovered, speculators could use this information to make unusually large profits.

As a technical matter, when the average value of $e_{t,n}$ is small and not statistically different from zero, the forward rate is considered to be an unbiased forecaster of the future spot rate.

The preceding discussion reflects an important subtlety. Equation 18 really represents a joint hypothesis: first, that the market can form rational and unbiased expectations of the future spot rate $[E(S_{t+n}) = S_{t+n}]$; and second, that the market elects to set its forward rate equal to that expectation $[F_{t,n} = E(S_{t+n})]$. The first hypothesis concerns the market's ability to divine the future; the second hypothesis involves a pricing model. Even if the first hypothesis is true, it may be that market participants include a risk premium when pricing the forward rate.[9] Violation of either hypothesis will break the simple and direct link between the forward rate and the future spot rate, and the error series in Equation 18 need not have a zero mean. Therefore, whether or not the forward rate is an unbiased forecast depends on two parts of a joint hypothesis being satisfied. An unbiased forward rate is not an inherent property of any economic system, even one that is in equilibrium and processes information efficiently.

---

[9] For an expanded discussion of risk premiums in the foreign exchange market, see Levich, "Empirical Studies"; and Robert Hodrick, *The Empirical Evidence of the Efficiency of Forward and Futures Foreign Exchange Markets* (Chur, Switzerland: Harwood Academic Publishers, 1987).

Pure Forecasting Models

The term *pure forecasting model* is used to describe a technique that is not built on a particular economic model of exchange rates. Sometimes, these are characterized as "black box" approaches in that users are given a set of forecasts, but the economic structure or rationale underlying them is not always clear. The advantage of a pure forecasting model is that it is selected because it produces good forecasts. The disadvantage is that to the extent that the approach is ad hoc, the approach can suddenly produce very bad forecasts. Of course, econometric forecasts may also perform badly when there is a change in structure, but the forecaster can be alert for these changes and adjust the model accordingly. A pure forecaster who works without an internally consistent underlying model might also try to account for changes in economic structure, but the linkages between the forecasts and the structure will be less clear.

Technical Models. So-called technical or momentum services advise their customers on the direction of exchange-rate movements in the very short run and correspondingly whether customers should hold long or short positions in particular currencies. Some technical forecasts may offer a point forecast of a future spot rate, but most commonly, the technical service offers only "buy and sell" signals.

Technical forecasts are typically based on a statistical analysis of recent exchange-rate behavior, although judgment may play an equally large role. Time series analysis is one effective way to identify patterns in economic data. A simple application of technical analysis to generate signals is the comparison of the current spot exchange rate to 7-day or 30-day moving averages of past rates. A more sophisticated application is the construction of an explicit time series model of the exchange rate based on past values of the rate (autoregressive terms) and past innovations in the series (moving average terms).

Although actual patterns may be observed in economic variables, traditional economists raise the efficient markets argument. If the path of exchange rates leaves a readable signal about future exchange rates, why do not interest rates (or exchange rates themselves) adjust to negate expected speculative profits from taking positions based on these signals? In response, technical analysts seem to argue that the foreign-exchange market is inefficient, largely because of institutional constraints.

Rosenberg has summarized many of these arguments, which seem to amount to a claim of insufficient speculative capital in the foreign-exchange market.[10] As an institutional matter, it is argued that large international banks and multinational corporations are permitted to hold small speculative positions relative to the enormous flow of foreign-exchange trading (perhaps, $300 billion per day). As a result, risky profit opportunities predicted by technical analysis are not quickly bid away. A related argument is the practice of central bank intervention which historically has "leaned against the wind," thereby slowing the adjustment of exchange rates to their ultimate levels.[11]

Several empirical studies that we review later in this chapter suggest that technical models may assist speculators in earning a favorable risk/return ratio. However, we cannot rule out the possibility that technical trading profits are simply the fair return for capital at risk.

Composite Models. A composite forecast is a forecasting rule based on two or more individual forecasts. A very simple rule could be applied to directional forecasts, as follows: if two services or forecasters issue buy signals, then buy; if two services issue sell signals, then sell; if the two services disagree, then take no position. The purpose of this rule is to weed out false signals and improve the chances for profitable positions. The rule could be extended to three or more services, but the chances that three (or

---

[10] Michael R. Rosenberg, "Is Technical Analysis Right for Currency Forecasting?" *Euromoney*, June 1981, pp. 125–31.

[11] Taylor has computed that central banks lost in aggregate more than $14 billion in the 1970s through foreign exchange intervention. This may be interpreted as a transfer to private speculators. See Dean Taylor, "Official Intervention in the Foreign Exchange Market, or, Bet Against the Central Bank," *Journal of Political Economy*, April 1982, pp. 356–68.

more) services would agree is small, which would reduce the amount of position taking.

The composite forecasting approach could also be applied to point forecasts generated by different economic models. If two forecasts, S_1 and S_2, capture or reflect different information, it may be possible to construct a new, composite forecast (S^c_t) that is superior to either forecast individually. One way to construct the composite is through a linear regression, such as

$$S^c_t = w_1 S_{1,t} + w_2 S_{2,t} + v_t \qquad (19)$$

As a regression equation, the weights w_1 and w_2 would be selected to minimize the forecasting error variance. Note that because w_1 and w_2 are estimated from historical data, we must assume that these weights remain applicable in a true forecast period. Expression 19 can easily be extended to a case where there are three or more forecasters. Candidates for the S_i include today's spot rate, today's forward rate (both publicly available information), a PPP forecast, and forecasts from professional advisory services.

The theoretical foundations of composite forecasting rest on two key points. First, it is assumed that different forecasters possess different information and different forecasting abilities. Market prices (in particular, the forward rate) reflect this information only to the extent that investors have actually bought or sold foreign exchange based on these forecasts. The composite approach seeks to combine available information in a more efficient manner. Second, the diversification principle suggests that a portfolio of forecasters reduces the risk of large forecast errors and improves forecasting accuracy relative to the record of an individual forecaster.

We include the composite approach under the heading of "pure forecasting approaches" because there is no obvious economic reason why two forecasters should exhibit or maintain a particular pattern of forecast errors. For example, if forecaster one's errors are generally twice as large and of opposite sign than those of forecaster two (e.g., 2 percent versus -1 percent; or -3 percent versus 1.5 percent) this would imply optimal weights $w_1 = 1/3$ and $w_2 = 2/3$ for unbiased forecasting. When the accuracy of either forecaster improves, this weighting system no longer produces unbiased forecasts. There are numerous econometric techniques for weighting and combining forecasts, several of which are explained in Bilson, Figlewski, and Figlewski and Urich.[12]

METHODS OF PERFORMANCE EVALUATION

How can one evaluate and choose among alternative currency forecasts? As in other similar problems (such as evaluating the performance of mutual funds managers or of individual subsidiaries or profit centers within a firm), evaluating foreign-exchange forecasting performance is a tricky procedure. Basically, one must establish a standard of performance and then calculate how a forecast compares to that standard. Selection of a reasonable standard is the key.

General Principles

Before going into greater detail, several general principles of performance evaluation are worth noting. First, there is a critical distinction between the fit of a model using historical data and the postsample, forecasting performance of the model. An econometric or composite forecasting model expressing the future spot rate as a function of certain X_i may be tailored to fit well throughout a historical sample. But a more meaningful assessment of the model can be made by analyzing its performance in a postsample period—based on either unconditional forecasts using the true values of the future X_i, or conditional forecasts using estimated values of the future X_i. Poor forecasting performance may be the result of an inability to forecast the X_i, but it also may be because the parameters of the model are imprecisely estimated or vary over time and require periodic reestimation.

---

[12] John Bilson, "The 'Speculative Efficiency' Hypothesis," *Journal of Business,* July 1981, pp. 435–51; Bilson, "Purchasing Power Parity as a Trading Strategy," *Journal of Finance,* July 1984, pp. 715–25; Stephen Figlewski, "Optimal Price Forecasting Using Survey Data," *Review of Economics and Statistics,* 1983, pp. 13–21; and Stephen Figlewski and Thomas Urich, "Optimal Aggregation of Money Supply Forecasts: Accuracy, Profitability, and Market Efficiency," *Journal of Finance,* June 1983, pp. 695–710.

A second general point is the importance of a loss function in selecting and evaluating forecasts. The forecast user must be able to specify the use of the forecast and the costs associated with forecast errors of varying magnitudes. For example, many corporate treasurers have a policy of limiting their forward positions to cases in which there are actual underlying business transactions. In this case, if the firm is long DM 1 million, the treasurer would consider a forward sale of up to DM 1 million, but nothing further. This firm might only be concerned with the forecaster's ability to predict depreciation in deutsche marks relative to the forward rate, because the firm's only decision is whether to sell deutsche marks on the forward market. This firm might evaluate forecasters on the basis of their buy/sell signals and ignore the magnitude of their forecast errors.

At the other extreme, international portfolio managers would be concerned about many currencies and the currency forecast could affect their allocation of funds across national stock markets. Actual portfolio performance would be affected by the magnitude of exchange-rate forecast errors as well as the correlation of errors across currencies.

The last general point concerns the selection of a standard or benchmark for performance. Ideally, we would like to judge whether or not a forecaster "beats the market." Unfortunately, there is no simple way to observe the market's expected future exchange rate. Market professionals participate in the forward market and it would be convenient to say that the forward rate reflects the "best" weighted average of the market's expectations. As we noted previously, however, this assumption reflects the joint hypothesis that the market makes a rational expectation of the future spot rate $[E(S_{t+n}) = S_{t+n}]$ and that the market elects to set its forward rate equal to that expectation $[F_{t,n} = E(S_{t+n})]$. In particular, the second hypothesis is false when the market includes an exchange risk premium in the forward rate. In this case, forecasters who outperform the forward rate should earn profits, but they may not be risk-adjusted profits. As a theoretical matter, then, beating the forward rate is not identical with beating the market. But beating the forward rate is still a formidable benchmark, and one that reveals whether forecasts lead to profits.

Performance Based on Accuracy

One approach to performance evaluation focuses on the forward-rate error, defined previously as

$$e_{t,n} = S_{t+n} - F_{t,n} \qquad (18)$$

One desirable property of a forecast is that its errors be small. However, even this simple criterion needs qualification. For example, if today's forward rate is \$1.50 and two alternative forecasts of the future spot rate are $S_1 = \$1.49$ and $S_2 = \$1.58$, if the actual spot rate turns out to be \$1.52, the forecast error associated with S_1 (−\$0.03) is smaller than the forecast error associated with S_2 (+\$0.06). However, forecast S_2 is superior in the sense that it leads investors to take long and profitable forward positions. That is, forecast S_2 leads to a "correct" decision.

To extend this example, a third forecast, $S_3 = \$1.64$, might also exist. Even though its forecast error is +\$0.12, it does not follow that this forecast is twice as bad as forecast S_2. If, for example, the firm is remitting a dividend to its U.S. parent and the firm is considering an all-or-nothing hedging decision, it will make the same decision using either S_2 or S_3 as a guide. So there is no additional cost associated with S_3's larger forecast error.

For some corporate purposes such as budgeting, the managers of a firm are concerned about the magnitude of forecast errors. Assuming risk-averse behavior, the users prefer a lower variability of forecasting errors. If the cost of forecast errors is proportional to the absolute magnitude of the error, that is, a linear loss function, then forecasters should be selected on the basis of mean absolute errors. If the cost of forecast errors is proportional to the squared magnitude of the error such as a quadratic loss function, then forecasters should be selected on the basis of mean squared errors. It is an empirical question whether these criteria can rank forecasters in similar order.

Usefulness as a Performance Criterion

In several previous examples, a firm might consider a forecast useful for hedging decisions even though it was less accurate than other available forecasts. If the magnitude of forecast errors can be ignored, we can evaluate a forecast by calculating the fraction of periods in which the forecast correctly predicts only the direction of exchange-rate movement. Direction is defined relative to a benchmark that could be either the forward rate or some other decision variable such as the forward rate plus a risk premium. In our earlier example, S_2 and S_3 were correct forecasts relative to the forward rate, while S_1 was an incorrect forecast. If the fraction of correct forecasts is unusually high, then one can conclude that the forecaster has expertise.

For example, suppose in a sample of 100 independent forecasts (n), we observe 60 correct forecasts (r), or a 60 percent track record. Using the binomial distribution, the probability is 2.3 percent of observing 60 or more correct forecasts assuming that the forecaster has no expertise. Statistically, this track record is too good to be the result of chance and indicates forecasting expertise.

The preceding percentage-correct methodology is discussed further in Levich.[13] When exchange-rate changes are not normally distributed (such as in a pegged exchange-rate regime with a large probability of no exchange-rate change and a small probability of a large change), modifications to the test are required. These are discussed in Krasker.[14] A more general test for the presence of market timing was developed by Henriksson and Merton and applied to the foreign-exchange market by Cumby and Modest.[15]

Profitability as a Performance Criterion

Another approach for evaluating forecasting performance is to calculate the stream of profits that an investor would earn by following the forecast. One would conclude that the advisory

[13] Richard M. Levich, "Analyzing the Accuracy of Foreign Exchange Advisory Services: Theory and Evidence," in *Exchange Risk and Exposure,* ed. R. Levich and C. Wihlborg (Lexington, Mass.: D. C. Heath, 1980).

[14] W. S. Krasker, "The 'Peso Problem' in Testing the Efficiency of Forward Exchange Markets," *Journal of Monetary Economics,* 1980, pp. 269–76.

[15] Roy Henriksson and Robert Merton, "On Market Timing and Investment Performance, II: Statistical Procedures for Evaluating Forecasting Skills," *Journal of Business,* 1981, pp. 513–33; and Robert Cumby and David Modest, "Testing for Market Timing Ability: A Framework for Forecast Evaluation," *Journal of Financial Economics,* September 1987, pp. 169–89.

service has expertise if the stream of profits (adjusting for risk) is high relative to alternative investments. Because one or two foreign-exchange positions might result in very large gains (or losses), the profitability criterion may result in a different ranking of forecasters than the percentage correct approach.

The emphasis on profits rather than returns is intentional. Although futures contracts have an explicit margin requirement, forward contracts do not. As a result, the return on investment concept is not defined. (A return can be computed under the assumption that the purchase of a forward contract equals the initial investment outlay.) The trade-off between expected profits from foreign-exchange speculation and risk is linear and proportional to the size of the open position. An investor holding $n = 0$ contracts has zero expected profit and zero risk. The expected profits associated with a position of $n = 2$ contracts is exactly double that for $n = 1$, as is the risk level.

Judging unusual profitability requires a benchmark. Ideally, this should be a suitable foreign-exchange risk pricing model. As there is little agreement on such a model, in practice most profitability comparisons are made vis-à-vis a well-diversified portfolio of equities.

Marginal Value of the Forecast

The performance evaluation methods reviewed earlier are intended to make an evaluation of an individual forecaster. The implicit task was to measure the value of the forecaster, and perhaps use this in deciding which single forecast to use. However, the traditional concept of economic value implies that one should measure the marginal contribution of a forecast to optimal decision making. Evaluation procedures that focus on forecasters individually might not measure their true economic value. Both overstatements and understatements of value would be possible.

For example, a speculator or a firm already has considerable public information at its disposal to construct its own exchange-rate forecast. A composite forecast based on the current spot rate and the current forward rate

$$S^c_{t+1} = w_1 \, S_t + w_2 \, F_t \tag{20}$$

represents one possible forecast based on public information. The economic, or marginal, value of a professional forecaster (S_{Pro}) could be measured by the statistical significance of the coefficient of w_3 in the equation

$$S^c_{t+1} = w_1 S_t + w_2 F_t + w_3 S_{Pro,t} \qquad (21)$$

The professional forecast might perform very well by itself, but in the context of Equation 21, if w_3 is small the forecast adds very little to what is already known. On the other hand, a poor individual forecast might be significant in the context of Equation 21 if it reflects information not captured in the other forecasts. The marginal value of S_{Pro} is high if it brings new information that can be incorporated with existing forecasts.

EMPIRICAL EVIDENCE ON FORECASTER PERFORMANCE

In this section, we review the empirical evidence on a variety of models that might be used for exchange-rate forecasting. We begin with a review of economic models, and then examine the results of technical and composite style forecasts. Levich and Isard offer a more extensive discussion of these issues.[16]

Economic Models

The empirical evidence on purchasing-power parity is, at best, mixed. Moreover, the evidence is sensitive to the countries, time periods, and price indexes that we select. Over long periods and during periods dominated by monetary disturbances, such as hyperinflation, PPP offers a fairly good description of exchange-rate behavior. However, over shorter time periods, say, 3 to 12 months, it has not been uncommon in the 1970s and 1980s to observe substantial exchange-rate changes—10 to 20 percent—unrelated to commodity price changes.

Even though PPP has been discredited as a useful description of exchange-rate behavior in the short run, many economic models

---

[16] See Isard, "Lessons from Empirical Models", and Levich, "Empirical Studies."

incorporate PPP as a long-run equilibrium property. Even though the deviations may be large and prolonged, currencies with floating exchange rates seem to have a tendency to oscillate around their PPP values. Thus, PPP may represent a useful anchor to keep in mind as deviations from PPP accumulate.

Tests of the monetary approach to the exchange rate have a history similar to the PPP results. In a study using data from the German hyperinflationary period of the 1920s, Frenkel finds results that are fully consistent with the monetary approach (Equation 8).[17] It is gratifying to see a theory supported by the data, but the results are not all that surprising given the dominance of monetary shocks during that period. In tests of the monetary approach for the 1970s and 1980s, studies by Backus, Dornbusch, and Frankel typically show poor results by the standard statistical criteria.[18]

The preceding studies tested the fit of the monetary model and its variations to in-sample data. In a more ambitious series of papers, Meese and Rogoff tested the ability of several popular economic models (including the monetary approach) to predict in a postsample period.[19] The authors conclude that even when the models perform well in-sample, they perform poorly in the post-sample period and fail to outperform the random-walk model or the forward-rate model in forecasting the spot rate. The devastation here is made more complete as the authors give their economic models the benefit of the doubt by using the actual ex post values of the X_i rather than using ex ante forecasts of them.

However, a subsequent paper by Boughton offers some hope by showing that portfolio balance models in general performed

---

[17] Jacob A. Frenkel, "A Monetary Approach to the Exchange Rate: Doctrinal Aspects and Empirical Evidence," *Scandinavian Journal of Economics* 78, no. 2, 1976, pp. 200–224.

[18] David Backus, "Empirical Models of the Exchange Rate: Separating the Wheat from the Chaff," *Canadian Journal of Economics,* 1984, pp. 824–26; Rudiger Dornbusch, "Exchange Rate Economics"; Jeffrey Frankel, "Tests of Monetary and Portfolio Balance Models of Exchange Rate Determination," in *Exchange Rate Theory and Practice,* ed. J. Bilson and R. Marston (Chicago: University of Chicago Press, 1984).

[19] Richard Meese and Kenneth Rogoff, "Empirical Exchange Rate Models of the Seventies: Do They Fit Out of Sample?" *Journal of International Economics,* 1983, pp. 3–24; and Meese and Rogoff, "The Out-of-Sample Failure of Empirical Exchange Rate Models: Sampling Error or Model Misspecification?" in *Exchange Rates and International Macroeconomics,* ed. J. Frenkel (Chicago: University of Chicago Press, 1983).

better than a random-walk model in postsample forecasts of the
$/DM and $/SDR exchange rates, although they did not perform
better in predicting the $/yen rate.[20] And a more recent study
by Somanath concludes that various models that incorporate a
lagged spot exchange rate outperform the random walk in a
postsample period.[21]

A series of papers by Levich analyzed the performance of
professional forecasters who use macroeconomic models to predict
exchange rates.[22] Levich concluded that individual services did
worse than the forward rate in terms of mean squared error. But
the services exhibited significant expertise in making "correct"
forecasts relative to the forward rate. There was, however, a
tendency for the overall forecaster performance to deteriorate as
the sample period extended into the 1982–83 period of the surprisingly strong U.S. dollar.

Technical Models

Several published studies have examined the profitability of various technical exchange-rate forecasting models. A study by
Dooley and Shafer reports the profits earned by following a "filter
rule" trading strategy for nine currencies on a daily basis over the
1973–81 period.[23] Their calculations are adjusted to reflect the

---

[20] James M. Boughton, "Exchange Rate Movements and Adjustment in Financial
Markets: Quarterly Estimates for Major Currencies," *IMF Staff Papers* 31 (September
1984), pp. 445–68.

[21] V. S. Somanath, "Efficient Exchange Rate Forecasts: Lagged Models Better than the
Random Walk," *Journal of International Money and Finance* 5, no. 2 (June 1986), pp.
195–220.

[22] Levich, "Analyzing the Accuracy"; Richard M. Levich, "Evaluating the Performance
of the Forecasters," and "Composite Forecasts," in *The Management of Foreign Exchange
Risk,* 2nd ed., ed. B. Antl and R. Ensor (London: Euromoney Publications, 1983).

[23] A filter rule is a mathematical rule that can be applied mechanically to produce buy and
sell signals. An *x* percent filter rule leads to the following trading strategy: "Buy a currency
whenever it rises *x* percent above its most recent trough; sell the currency and take a short
position whenever the currency falls *x* percent below its most recent peak." A filter rule thus
attempts to identify price momentum. See Michael Dooley and Jeffrey Shafer, "Analysis of
Short-Run Exchange Rate Behavior: March 1973–November 1981," in *Exchange Rate and
Trade Instability,* ed. D. Bigman and T. Taya (Cambridge, Mass.: Ballinger Publishing,
1983).

interest expense and income of short and long positions, and transaction costs are incorporated by using bid and asked foreign-exchange quotations. If the market were efficient, filter-rule profits adjusted to reflect the preceding costs should be a martingale process—that is, they should be free of serial correlation with an average profit of zero. Dooley and Shafer's results indicate that small filters (x = 1, 3, or 5 percent) would have been profitable for all currencies over the entire sample period, and for many of the subperiods analyzed. However, as there are losses for some filters in some cases, there appears to be an element of riskiness to these trading rules.

A similar study by Sweeney analyzed filter rules for 10 currencies over the 1973–80 period.[24] Sweeney reports that small filters tend to produce profitable trading strategies and that the results are consistent between two subsample periods. In many cases, the profits are significant at standard statistical significance levels, although not necessarily according to economic risk-return criteria.

A related paper by Goodman examined the performance of professional foreign-exchange advisers who issue buy and sell signals based on technical analysis.[25] Goodman reports that large profits in excess of the risk-free rate were generally available to users of these professional signals. There were also risks; the largest individual loss on one buy/sell signal was 2.4 times the initial 5 percent margin, and the largest sequence of losses was 2.9 times the initial margin. Goodman suggests that these risks are small for investors with enough capital to withstand intermittent losses and who use professional signals on a regular basis. To further bolster his case, Goodman reports that if investors use a composite signal based on two or more advisers, the risk-return trade-off improves.

The most recent study of professional technical services is by Cumby and Modest.[26] The authors evaluate seven services during

[24] Richard Sweeney, "Beating the Foreign Exchange Market," *Journal of Finance,* March 1986, pp. 163–82.

[25] Stephen Goodman, "Two Technical Analysts Are Even Better than One," *Euromoney,* August 1982, pp. 85–96.

[26] Cumby and Modest, "Testing for Market Timing Ability."

the 1979–84 period using the percentage correct methodology. The results are somewhat mixed with one set of tests showing strong evidence of market timing expertise when all available data are used.

Composite Models

Forecasting results based on a composite approach have been reported by Levich and Bilson. In his study, Levich estimated a composite model for an in-sample period running from 1974 to 1978, and applied the model to the 1978–79 period. Levich reports that for the nine currencies covered, a track record of 70 percent correct forecasts (one-month and three-month horizons) was achieved. These results are highly statistically significant.[27]

Bilson has investigated the performance of a variety of composite forecasting models. Bilson reported on a composite formed by spot and forward rates only, representing publicly available information (our Equation 20).[28] Bilson also examined a composite based on spot and forward rates plus a professional forecasting service (our Equation 21).[29] And Bilson built a composite with spot, forward, and PPP rates to estimate the marginal contribution of a PPP forecast.[30]

Bilson's initial study based on spot and forward rates only is the only study of the three that contains a postsample analysis, a one-year period with weekly positions.[31] This analysis shows that the composite forecast significantly outperforms the forward rate and leads to positive profits. The other studies by Bilson conclude that an additional forecast (either from a professional service or based on PPP) can make a significant marginal contribution to forecasting performance.

[27] Levich, "Evaluating the Performance" and "Composite Forecasts."
[28] Bilson, "The 'Speculative Efficiency' Hypothesis."
[29] Bilson, "The Evaluation and Use."
[30] Bilson, "Purchasing Power Parity."
[31] See Bilson, "The 'Speculative Efficiency' Hypothesis."

SUMMARY AND CONCLUSIONS

In this chapter, we have discussed several topics related to exchange-rate forecasting—how to forecast, how to evaluate forecasts, and the empirical evidence on forecasting performance. The conclusions we reach may seem somewhat contradictory. It appears as though many of the formal models of exchange rate determination are not immediately useful for forecasting future spot exchange rates. And as well, it appears that profit opportunities using simple technical models or other published models have been available, although these profits were not risk-free.

The recent wave of empirical studies focusing on the role of news in moving spot exchange rates offers some comfort.[32] These studies confirm that exchange rates seem to reflect everything that is presently known or expected to happen and that rates move quickly and in the predicted direction in response to news regarding the money supply, inflation announcements, interest rate shocks, and other macroeconomic events. These results suggest that economic theory is working, that is, exchange rates appear to move in understandable ways in response to news.

The conundrum for economists then is why economic models do not fit better when examining the relationship between exchange rates and macroeconomic variables over the floating exchange-rate period. The implication of these results for exchange-rate forecasters, however, is somewhat brighter. The forecaster who can predict one or two key variables better than the market as a whole might be able to outperform the forward-rate forecast.

REFERENCES

Backus, David. "Empirical Models of the Exchange Rate: Separating the Wheat from the Chaff." *Canadian Journal of Economics*, 1984, pp. 824–26.

---

[32] See note 8.

Bilson, John. "The 'Speculative Efficiency' Hypothesis." *Journal of Business,* July 1981, pp. 435–51.

————. "The Evaluation and Use of Foreign Exchange Rate Forecasting Services." In *Managing Foreign Exchange Risk,* ed. R. Herring. Cambridge: Cambridge University Press, 1983.

————. "Purchasing Power Parity as a Trading Strategy." *Journal of Finance,* July 1984, pp. 715–25.

Boughton, James M. "Exchange Rate Movements and Adjustment in Financial Markets: Quarterly Estimates for Major Currencies." *IMF Staff Papers* 31, September 1984, pp. 445–68.

Cumby, Robert, and David Modest. "Testing for Market Timing Ability: A Framework for Forecast Evaluation." *Journal of Financial Economics,* September 1987, pp. 169–89.

Dooley, Michael, and Jeffrey Shafer. "Analysis of Short-Run Exchange Rate Behavior: March 1973–November 1981." In *Exchange Rate and Trade Instability,* ed. D. Bigman and T. Taya. Cambridge, Mass.: Ballinger Publishing, 1983.

Dornbusch, Rudiger. "Exchange Rate Economics: Where Do We Stand?" *Brookings Papers on Economic Activity,* no. 1, 1980.

Edwards, Sebastian. "Floating Exchange Rates, Expectations, and New Information." *Journal of Monetary Economics,* May 1983, pp. 321–36.

Feldstein, Martin. "The Budget Deficit and the Dollar." In *NBER Macroeconomics Annual 1986,* ed. Stanley Fischer. Cambridge, Mass.: MIT Press, 1986.

Figlewski, Stephen. "Optimal Price Forecasting Using Survey Data." *Review of Economics and Statistics,* 1983, pp. 13–21.

Figlewski, Stephen, and Thomas Urich. "Optimal Aggregation of Money Supply Forecasts: Accuracy, Profitability, and Market Efficiency." *Journal of Finance,* June 1983, pp. 695–710.

Frankel, Jeffrey. "Tests of Monetary and Portfolio Balance Models of Exchange Rate Determination." In *Exchange Rate Theory and Practice,* ed. J. Bilson and R. Marston. Chicago: University of Chicago Press, 1984.

Frenkel, Jacob A. "A Monetary Approach to the Exchange Rate: Doctrinal Aspects and Empirical Evidence." *Scandinavian Journal of Economics* 78, no. 2, 1976, pp. 220–24.

Goodman, Stephen. "Two Technical Analysts Are Even Better than One." *Euromoney,* August 1982, pp. 85–96.

Hakkio, Craig, and Douglas Pearce. "The Reaction of Exchange Rates to Economic News." *Economic Inquiry,* October 1985, pp. 621–36.

Heriksson, Roy, and Robert Merton. "On Market Timing and Investment

Performance, II: Statistical Procedures for Evaluating Forecasting Skills." *Journal of Business,* 1981, pp. 513–33.

Hodrick, Robert. *The Empirical Evidence of the Efficiency of Forward and Futures Foreign Exchange Markets.* Chur, Switzerland: Harwood Academic Publishers, 1987.

International Financial Statistics. Washington, D.C.: International Monetary Fund, May 1988.

Isard, Peter. "Lessons from Empirical Models of Exchange Rates." *IMF Staff Papers,* March 1987, pp. 1–28.

Krasker, W. S. "The 'Peso Problem' in Testing the Efficiency of Forward Exchange Markets." *Journal of Monetary Economics,* 1980, pp. 269–76.

Levich, Richard M. "Analyzing the Accuracy of Foreign Exchange Advisory Services: Theory and Evidence." In *Exchange Risk and Exposure,* ed. R. Levich and C. Wihlborg. Lexington, Mass.: D. C. Heath, 1980.

———. "Composite Forecasts." In *The Management of Foreign Exchange Risk,* 2nd ed., ed. B. Antl and R. Ensor. London: Euromoney Publications, 1983.

———. "Evaluating the Performance of the Forecasters." In *The Management of Foreign Exchange Risk,* 2nd ed., ed. B. Antl and R. Ensor. London: Euromoney Publications, 1983.

———. "Empirical Studies of Exchange Rates: Price Behavior, Rate Determination, and Market Efficiency." In *Handbook of International Economics,* ed. R. Jones and P. Kenen. Amsterdam: North-Holland Publishing, 1985.

McKinnon, Ronald I. *Money in International Exchange.* Cambridge: Cambridge University Press, 1979.

Meese, Richard, and Kenneth Rogoff. "Empirical Exchange Rate Models of the Seventies: Do They Fit Out of Sample?" *Journal of International Economics,* 1983, pp. 3–24.

———. "The Out-of-Sample Failure of Empirical Exchange Rate Models: Sampling Error or Model Misspecification?" In *Exchange Rates and International Macroeconomics,* ed. J. Frenkel. Chicago: University of Chicago Press, 1983, pp. 67–112.

Officer, Lawrence H. "The Purchasing Power Parity Theory of Exchange Rates: A Review Article." *IMF Staff Papers* 23, March 1976.

Rosenberg, Michael R. "Is Technical Analysis Right for Currency Forecasting?" *Euromoney,* June 1981, pp. 125–31.

Somanath, V. S. "Efficient Exchange Rate Forecasts: Lagged Models Better than the Random Walk." *Journal of International Money and Finance* 5, no. 2 (June 1986), pp. 195–220.

Sweeney, Richard. "Beating the Foreign Exchange Market." *Journal of Finance,* March 1986, pp. 163–82.

Tandon, Kishore, and Thomas Urich. "International Market Response to Announcements of U.S. Macroeconomic Data." *Journal of International Money and Finance,* March 1987, pp. 71–84.

Taylor, Dean. "Official Intervention in the Foreign Exchange Market, or, Bet Against the Central Bank." *Journal of Political Economy,* April 1982, pp. 356–68.

Williamson, John. "The Exchange Rate System," *Policy Analyses in International Economics*, No. 5, 2nd ed. Washington, D.C.: Institute for International Economics, June 1985.

CHAPTER 16

FOREIGN-CURRENCY OPTIONS

Niso Abuaf
Stephan Schoess

A foreign-currency option is the right, but not the obligation, to buy or sell a specified foreign-currency contract. This could take the form of a spot, a futures, or even a forward contract.

Foreign-currency options, first introduced in 1982, are relatively new financial instruments. Since then, the trading of these instruments has grown dramatically. The demand for foreign-currency options by corporations and financial institutions is based on their desire to hedge financial and economic risks given the increased uncertainty about foreign-exchange rates and the inability to forecast them.

The Philadelphia Stock Exchange was the first exchange to introduce currency options trading. Options on the Australian dollar, British pound, Canadian dollar, German mark, Japanese yen, and the Swiss franc are traded on its floor. Options on futures contracts for these currencies are traded on the Chicago Mercantile Exchange. Foreign-currency options are also traded on the European Options Exchange in Amsterdam, the Montreal Exchange, the London International Financial Futures Exchange, and the London Stock Exchange. The contracts traded on these exchanges are standardized. Since, however, many corporate hedgers desire tailor-made contracts, an over-the-counter foreign-exchange options market also exists.

This chapter presents a general overview of foreign-currency options. We first review some basic concepts and definitions relevant to the foreign-currency options market. Second, we discuss the pricing of options. Finally, we describe some basic currency-option strategies for speculators and hedgers.

Basic Concepts

A call (put) option gives its owner (holder) the right to buy (sell) a specified financial instrument at a fixed price (exercise or strike price) before or at a certain future date (maturity or expiration). The buyer of the option pays the option price (premium) to the seller (writer, grantor).

A call or put option whose exercise price is the same as the spot price is termed *at-the-money*. A call (put) whose exercise price is below (above) the underlying spot price is termed *in-the-money*. A call (put) whose exercise price is above (below) the underlying spot price is termed *out-of-the-money*. An option owner only exercises an option if it is in-the-money.

Profit profiles at expiration of buying call and put options are given in Figure 16–1. The profit profiles of selling options are the mirror images, around the horizontal axis, of those for buying options. Put differently, the profits earned by the buyer of an option equal the losses for the seller, and vice versa.

At maturity, options are usually settled physically. That is, the grantor of the option delivers or receives delivery of the underlying financial instrument. Some over-the-counter options, however, are cash settled. No delivery of the underlying instrument takes place. Instead, the cash value of the option contract equaling the difference between the exercise price and the spot price is remitted.

The option premium is a function of the option's strike price, the spot exchange rate, the domestic and foreign interest rates, and the expected volatility of the relevant exchange rate. The following glossary reviews and expands on the preceding concepts.

Glossary

American option Any option that can be exercised on or before the expiration date.

arbitrage Taking advantage of a temporary price disparity between different options or between options and the underlying currency.

FIGURE 16–1
Profit Profile of Buying a Straddle

(a) Buying a call

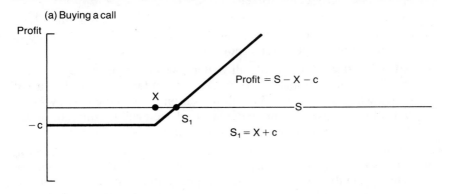

Profit $= S - X - c$

$S_1 = X + c$

(b) Buying a put

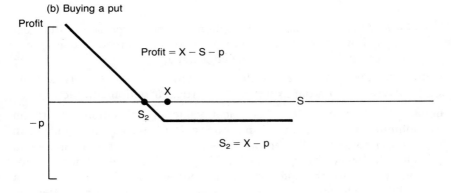

Profit $= X - S - p$

$S_2 = X - p$

(c) Buying a straddle

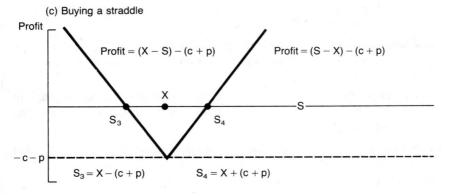

Profit $= (X - S) - (c + p)$ Profit $= (S - X) - (c + p)$

$S_3 = X - (c + p)$ $S_4 = X + (c + p)$

at-the-money   An option is at-the-money if the underlying currency is selling for the option's exercise price. The intrinsic value of the option is exactly equal to zero.

call option   A contract granting the right to buy a given underlying currency or currency-futures contract at a specific price for a stated period of time or at a stated point in time.

covered call writer   A covered call writer owns the underlying currency on which the option is written. Also considered covered is a call writer who has purchased a call option on the same currency as the call sold. The exercise price of the purchased call is equal to, or less than, the exercise price of the written call.

covered put writer   A covered put writer is short (owes) the underlying currency on which the option is written. Strictly speaking, the definition only applies to a put option writer who also bought put options that have an exercise price equal to or higher than that of the written put options.

curvature   A characteristic of an option or option spread position describing how rapidly the delta of an option or a spread changes when the spot rate changes. Also called gamma.

deliverable currency   The specific underlying currency that is actually deliverable upon the exercise of a particular option contract.

delta   The change in the theoretical value of an option due to an infinitesimal change in the spot rate, expressed as a percentage or in natural numbers. A deep in-the-money call (put) option has a delta close to 100 percent (-100 percent). Its value changes almost one for one (-1) with the spot rate. A far out-of-the-money option has a delta close to zero. A change of the spot rate has little or no effect on the value of the option. An at-the-money call (put) option has a delta near 50 percent (-50 percent).

delta long position   A position in options and/or underlying currency in which a small appreciation of the currency theoretically increases the net value of the position.

delta short position   A position in options and/or underlying currency in which a small depreciation of the currency theoretically increases the net value of the position.

European option   An option that can be exercised only on the expiration date and not before.

exercise   A right held by an option buyer. The buyer requests the call option writer to deliver the foreign currency at the stated price or requests the put writer to pay the exercise price for the delivered foreign currency.

exercise price   The price at which the call option buyer may purchase or the put option buyer may sell the underlying currency. Also called the strike price.

expiration date   The final date on which an option may be exercised. After the expiration date the option is worthless.

forecast volatility   A forecast of the volatility which an underlying currency spot, futures, or forward rate will exhibit in the future.

gamma   See curvature.

historic volatility   The observed volatility that an underlying currency spot, futures, or forward rate has exhibited.

implied volatility   The volatility that must be attributed to the underlying currency to equate the theoretical value of an option with its current market price.

in-the-money   An option is in-the-money when it has intrinsic value. A call option is in-the-money if the underlying currency's spot price is greater than the option's exercise price. A put option is in-the-money if the underlying currency's price is lower than the option's exercise price.

intrinsic value   For a call option the intrinsic value is the difference between the underlying currency's spot value and the exercise price. For a put option the intrinsic value is the difference between the exercise price and the underlying currency's spot value. Because options convey a right, but not an obligation, intrinsic value is always greater or equal to zero. Note, however, that the theoretical as well as the actual value of a European option can lie below its intrinsic value.

long option   An option that has been purchased.

option buyer   The purchaser of a call or put option.

option valuation model   The model is based on variables including the underlying currency's spot or futures rate, time to expiration, domestic and foreign interest rates, the exercise price, and the forecast volatility. The model develops theoretical valuations for individual options and provides information necessary to determine proper ratios for hedge positions. Typically, for European options the Black-Scholes model or modified versions are used. For American options, a modified binomial option pricing model of Cox, Ross, and Rubinstein is used.

option writer   The seller of an option who grants option privileges to the buyer in exchange for receiving the premium.

out-of-the-money   An option that has no intrinsic value. A call option is out-of-the-money when the exercise price is higher than the underlying currency's price. A put option is out-of-the-money when the exercise price is lower than the underlying currency's price.

parity   A call option is said to be at parity when the price of the option equals the current market price minus the exercise price. A put option is at parity when the price of the option equals the exercise price minus the current price of the underlying currency.

premium   The price of an option agreed upon by the buyer and seller. The premium is paid by an option buyer to the seller.

put option   A contract granting the right to sell a given underlying currency or currency-futures contract at a specific price for a stated period of time or at a stated point in time.

short option   An option that has been sold.

strike price   See exercise price.

theoretical value   The value of an option as given by an option valuation model.

time decay   Options are described as wasting assets. In most cases, the value of an option decreases as expiration approaches, all other variables remaining constant. Under some circumstances, characterized by low volatilities and large interest-rate differentials, the value of European-style currency options can increase as expiration approaches.

time value   The component of the option premium that reflects the remaining life of the option. The time value component is defined as the difference between the option premium and the option's intrinsic value.

uncovered call writer   A call writer is uncovered (naked) when the writer does not own the underlying currency on which the option is written or does not own a long call on the same currency with an equal or lower exercise price.

uncovered put writer   A put writer is uncovered (naked) when the writer does not hold a put on the same underlying currency with an equal or higher exercise price.

underlying currency   A spot, forward, or futures position/contract that underlies a particular option or option position.

volatility A measure of actual or expected price movement in an underlying currency over a specific time period. Volatility is expressed as the annualized standard deviation of daily exchange-rate changes.

PRICING

Options are viewed by the majority of the public as exotic and speculative instruments. This can partially be attributed to the pricing formula for options. The formula involves rather complex mathematics and is usually not well understood. In this section, we attempt to erase the myth about options by explaining the pricing mechanism on intuitive rather than rigorous mathematical levels. First, we discuss how currency option prices are quoted in the market and interpret these quotes. Second, we analyze the value and, therefore, the prices of options at expiration. For hedgers, the value of options at expiration is of greatest concern. Third, we attempt to describe the value of options before expiration on an intuitive level. Last, we discuss several propositions to clarify the relationship among prices for puts, calls, and the underlying currency as well as the price relationships among options with different exercise prices and expiration dates.

Quotations

In the United States option premiums are most often expressed as U.S. dollars or cents per unit of foreign currency (American terms). This is in contrast to the interbank spot and forward markets where most major currencies (except the British pound) are quoted in foreign currency units per U.S. dollar (European terms).

Quotation in American terms is standard in the major foreign-currency futures market—the International Money Market of the Chicago Mercantile Exchange (CME). The tradition has spilled over to the major foreign-currency option markets both within and outside of the United States.

Tailor-made foreign-exchange options are also traded in the interbank market. Prices for these options are usually quoted in

European terms. A user should double-check pricing conventions, especially when using the over-the-counter market or dealing in cross-currency options.

Exhibit 16–1 illustrates how *The Wall Street Journal* displays foreign-currency option prices. The table lists horizontally different expiration dates for calls and puts, and vertically different strike prices. The quotes refer to prices of the last transactions of the day. The letters "r" and "s" indicate options not traded and options not offered, respectively.

Though option premiums are usually quoted as described, traders in the interbank market also quote options in implied

EXHIBIT 16–1
Foreign Currency Options

Philadelphia Exchange
Wed., Apr. 19

Option & Underlying	Strike Price	Calls–Last			Puts–Last		
		Apr	May	Jun	Apr	May	Jun
50,000 Australian Dollars-cents per unit.							
ADollr	...78	s	r	r	s	r	0.90
80.11	...79	s	r	1.62	s	r	1.33
80.11	...80	s	0.80	1.22	s	r	r
80.11	...81	s	0.41	0.78	s	r	r
80.11	...82	s	0.18	r	s	2.55	r
31,250 British Pounds-cents per unit.							
BPound	167½	s	r	r	s	0.44	1.17
171.14	.170	s	r	r	s	1.15	r
171.14	172½	s	0.84	r	s	r	r
171.14	.175	s	0.29	0.80	s	r	r
50,000 Canadian Dollars-cents per unit.							
CDollr	...83	s	1.25	1.30	s	r	r
84.31	.83½	s	r	r	s	r	0.47
84.31	...84	s	0.49	0.69	s	0.33	r
84.31	...85	s	0.13	0.31	s	r	r
62,500 West German Marks-cents per unit.							
DMark	.. 50	s	r	r	s	r	0.03
53.73	...52	s	r	r	s	r	0.10
53.73	...53	s	r	r	s	0.14	0.30
53.73	...54	s	0.37	0.77	s	r	0.71
53.73	...55	s	0.10	0.35	s	r	r
53.73	...56	s	r	0.16	s	r	r
53.73	...57	s	r	r	s	r	3.19
250,000 French Francs-10ths of a cent per unit.							
FFranc	..16	s	0.78	r	s	r	r
6,250,000 Japanese Yen-100ths of a cent per unit.							
JYen	... 73	s	r	r	s	r	0.11
75.53	...74	s	r	r	s	· 0.07	r
75.53	...75	s	r	r	s	0.24	0.48
75.53	...76	s	0.45	r	s	0.55	r
75.53	...77	s	0.15	0.59	s	r	r
75.53	...78	s	0.06	0.34	s	r	2.40
75.53	...79	s	r	0.15	s	r	r
75.53	...80	s	r	0.10	s	r	r
75.53	...81	s	r	0.04	s	r	r
62,500 Swiss Francs-cents per unit.							
SFranc	..60	s	r	r	s	0.15	r
61.15	...61	s	r	r	s	r	0.67
61.15	...62	s	0.30	0.75	s	r	1.15
Total call vol.	20,827		Call open int.		320,485		
Total put vol.	7,351		Put open int.		353,287		

r–Not traded. s–No option offered.
Last is premium (purchase price).

volatilities. A typical quote for a three-month U.S. dollar option against the German mark might be: 11.5–11.8. This means that the dealer is willing to buy the option if its premium translates into an implied volatility of 11.5 percent. The dealer is willing to sell the option if the premium translates into an implied volatility of 11.8 percent.

Value at Expiration

At expiration, the value of any currency option is determined solely by the difference between the spot exchange rate and the exercise price. Because options entail the right, but not the obligation, to buy or sell a given amount of foreign currency, option values can never be negative. This holds not only at expiration, but also for the entire life of the option.

At expiration, a call option only has value if the spot exchange rate is higher than the exercise price. When this is the case, the holder exercises the option. The exerciser buys the foreign currency at the exercise price and sells the received foreign currency at the prevailing spot exchange rate. The call option holder's profit from this transaction equals the difference between the spot exchange rate and the exercise price. Therefore, the value of the call option at expiration must also equal the difference between the spot rate and the exercise price. Similarly, the value of a put option at expiration equals the greater of zero or the exercise price minus the spot price. The following table shows the expiration values as a function of the spot exchange rate for call and put options on the DM with an exercise price of $0.50/DM.

Spot Rate ($/DM) at Expiration	Expiration Value in $	
	Call	Put
.30	.00	.20
.35	.00	.15
.40	.00	.10
.45	.00	.05
.50	.00	.00
.55	.05	.00
.60	.10	.00
.65	.15	.00
.70	.20	.00

Suppose the spot rate at expiration is $0.35/DM. The call option buyer can purchase DM cheaper in the spot market than through the exercise of the option. The value of the option at expiration cannot be greater than zero. Suppose the spot exchange rate at expiration is $0.65/DM. The call option holder exercises the option and buys DM for $0.50 and then sells DM for $0.65, pocketing a profit of $0.15/DM. The call option cannot be priced less than $0.15/DM, otherwise arbitrage opportunities exist. Because the option is at its expiration, no one would be willing to pay more than $0.15/DM. The call option price at expiration equals exactly the greater of zero or the difference between the spot exchange rate and the exercise price.

Assume the spot rate at expiration is $0.35/DM. The put option holder exercises the option by selling DM for $0.50 and then buys the DM back in the spot market for $0.35/DM, pocketing a profit of $0.15/DM. The put option cannot be priced less than $0.15/DM, otherwise arbitrage opportunities exist. Because the option is at its expiration, no one would be willing to pay more than $0.15/DM. Suppose the spot rate at expiration is $0.65/DM. The put option buyer can sell DM at a higher price in the spot market than through the exercise of the option. The value of the option cannot be greater than zero. The value of the put option at expiration equals exactly the greater of zero or the difference between the exercise price and the spot exchange rate.

Once the option value at expiration is known, the profit on any option position can be calculated by accounting for the initial investment for option buyers or cash receipts for option writers. Ignoring the time value of money, the profit at expiration for options buyers is the option value at expiration minus the option purchase price. The profit at expiration for the option seller is the option selling price minus the option value at expiration. Typical option profit profiles are given in parts (a) and (b) of Figure 16–1.

Value before Expiration

To calculate the value of a call or put option at expiration is easy. Before maturity, however, we do not know what the spot price will be at expiration. We can, nevertheless, assign probabilities to various possible maturity spot prices, compute the corresponding call values, and then discount these values to the present. That is, we can compute the value of a call or put option before expiration as the probabilistically discounted net present value of its future value. Complex as this might seem, most of the widely used option-pricing models simulate this procedure.

Of these, the Black-Scholes (B-S) options pricing model is the most commonly used. This model was originally developed for pricing European options on nondividend paying stocks. It can be extended to apply to stocks continuously paying dividends, foreign exchange, commodities such as oil and gold, and even debt instruments—albeit crudely.

First, we attempt to demystify the B-S model by stressing the intuition behind its derivation. Though we do present the B-S formula, we do not use mathematical concepts more sophisticated than simple algebra. Second, by using the B-S formula and intuitive arguments we discuss how various input parameters affect foreign-currency option prices.

The Black-Scholes Currency Options Pricing Model

The basic idea behind the Black-Scholes approach to pricing options is that option portfolios can be replicated by buying or selling a certain proportion of the underlying instrument and by borrowing or lending money. If the replicating portfolio is identical to the desired option portfolio, and one can price the replicating portfolio, then one can also price the option portfolio.

Specifically, buying a call option is identical to buying a certain proportion of the underlying instrument (the delta) and borrowing money to finance the transaction. Analogously, buying a put is identical to selling a proportion of the underlying instrument and lending the proceeds.

The mathematical derivation of the preceding is beyond the scope of this chapter. The intuition, however, is fairly straightforward. If an investor is long a call option, the return on the investment increases drastically as the underlying instrument appreciates. Put differently, a call option holder's returns resemble the returns of a leveraged portfolio.

The value of any currency option depends on six variables: domestic interest rate (i), foreign interest rate (i*), time to expiration (t), current spot rate (S), exercise price (K), and expected volatility (σ). These six variables are the inputs to the B-S currency options pricing model. In theory, the domestic interest rate is the risk-free rate, and the foreign rate is the Eurodeposit rate. In practice, both the domestic and foreign rates are given by the corresponding Eurorates. Of the six price-determining variables, five are readily observable. Only expected volatility is unknown and has to be estimated. The output of this model can be either the price of a European call (C), or the price of a European put (P). Put differently, the B-S model can be thought of as a black box:

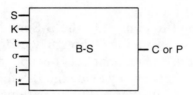

where the input variables are on the left side of the box and the output variable (the option price) is on the right side.

Interestingly, the box is frequently used in a mode where one of the input variables, σ, changes places with the output, C or P:

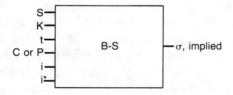

In this mode, the output is referred to as the implied volatility, as opposed to the expected volatility, which is an input variable to the first mode. Options traders use implied volatilities to devise hedging, speculative, and trading strategies. Implied volatility is a quantification of the market's estimate of the underlying currency's future price movements.[1]

---

[1] To pick a simple example, let the DM/$ rate be DM 2.00/$, and the implied volatility be 10 percent. Assuming that the logs of exchange rates behave as a random-walk model, the market's 68 percent and 95 percent confidence levels for the DM/$ rate one year out are DM 1.90–2.10/$, and DM 1.80–2.20/$, respectively.

If the world were deterministic, the value of the call would be the greater of zero or:

$$C = Fe^{-it} - Ke^{-it} \tag{1}$$

where F is the forward rate in domestic currency units per foreign currency and e represents the natural number such that e^{-it} (e^{it}) stands for continuous discounting (compounding). Because of the interest-rate parity theorem, the forward rate is a function of the spot rate and the domestic and foreign interest rates:

$$F = Se^{(i - i^*)t} \tag{2}$$

Rewriting Equation 1, we have:

$$C = Se^{-i^*t} - Ke^{-it} \tag{1*}$$

Similarly, if the world were deterministic, the value of the put would be the greater of zero or:

$$P = Ke^{-it} - Fe^{-it} \tag{3}$$

Rewriting Equation 3 we have:

$$P = Ke^{-it} - Se^{-i^*t} \tag{4}$$

So, in a deterministic world, the value of the call is the greater of zero, or the discounted value of the forward price minus the strike price. Similarly, the value of the put is the greater of zero, or the discounted value of the strike price minus the forward price.

The B-S model is a modified version of this formula. The modification is there because the world is not deterministic, and adjustments for probabilistic outcomes must be made. These adjustments lead to the B-S foreign-currency option pricing formula:

$$C = Fe^{-it} N(d_1) - Ke^{-it}N(d_2) \tag{5}$$

where:

$$d_1 = (\ln (F/K) + (\sigma^2/2)t)/\sigma t^{0.5}, \text{ and}$$

$$d_2 = d_1 - \sigma t^{0.5}$$

N is the cumulative distribution of the stardard normal probability distribution function and ln is the natural logarithm. Note that i and i* are continuously compounded interest rates.

The formula for put options can be derived using the formula for call options and the option parity theorem (see the upcoming section on put-call price relationships for more details):

$$P = Ke^{-it} N(d_3) - Fe^{-it}N(d_4) \qquad (6)$$

where:

$$d_3 = (\ln (F/K) + (\sigma^2/2)t)/\sigma t^{0.5}, \text{ and}$$

$$d_4 = d_3 - \sigma t^{0.5}$$

The Sensitivity of Option Prices to Changes in Input Variables

The best way to understand option pricing and the B-S formula is to examine what happens to C and P as S (or F), K, t, σ, i, and i* change in value one at a time.

Underlying Foreign-Currency Price. The higher the underlying foreign-currency price (S or F), the higher (lower) the value of the call (put). This can be easily seen from the deterministic formulations 1* and 4, and also holds for the B-S formula. As S or F approach zero, C approaches zero, and P approaches the present value of the exercise price. As S or F approach infinity, C approaches infinity and P approaches zero.

The magnitude of the effect of changes in exchange rates on option prices depends to a large extent on the level of the spot rate relative to the exercise price. The price effect of a given change in the spot rate for (far) out-of-the-money options is (very) small. Prices of deep in-the-money options change by nearly the same amount as the spot rate. For at-the-money options, prices tend to change by one unit for every two unit change in the spot rate.

The sensitivity of option prices to changes in the spot rate (the delta) is not only a function of the level of the spot rate relative to the exercise price but also a function of the volatility level. As a general rule, the following holds: For out-of-the-money options, the option price sensitivity with respect to changes in the spot rate increases as volatility increases. For in-the-money options, the option price sensitivity decreases as volatility increases. Intuitively, the delta can be interpreted as the probability that the options will be in-the-money at expiration. Assume a far-out-of-the-money option. If volatility is low, the probability for this option to be in-the-money at expiration approaches zero. If volatility is high, the out-of-the-money option has a greater chance of being in-the-money at expiration. Thus, the price sensitivity of out-of-the-money options increases as volatility increases. For deep in-the-money options, the opposite holds. If volatility is low, the option has a very high probability of staying in-the-money throughout its life. On the other hand, if volatility is high, the probability of being in-the-money at expiration is lower. Thus, the price sensitivity of in-the-money options decreases as volatility increases.

Strike Price. The higher the strike price, the lower (higher) the value of the call (put). Again, this can be readily seen from the deterministic formulations. As K approaches zero, C approaches S, and P approaches zero. Intuitively, a call with a zero strike price is like the underlying instrument.

An option's price sensitivity with respect to the exercise price depends on how far in- or out-of-the-money the option is and also on the volatility level. The arguments here are virtually identical to those discussed in the preceding section.

Expected Volatility. The expected volatility of future spot price changes is an important variable in option pricing. It is the only variable which is unknown and has to be estimated. If currency prices were fixed, all (European-style) currency options would be either worthless if out-of-the-money or would be priced at the discounted value of the difference between the forward price and exercise price for calls or between the exercise price and forward price for puts. It is volatility which gives options the additional value. The higher the volatility of the spot exchange rate, the greater the uncertainty, and as a result the higher the prices for puts and calls. In addition, as explained earlier, the price sensitivity of options with respect to changes in volatility is also dependent on the time to maturity and the relative position of the spot exchange rate to the exercise price.

Domestic Interest Rate. Assume that the spot rate and the foreign interest rate do not change with a change in the domestic interest rate. As domestic interest rates rise, the value of a call (put) increases (decreases). This can be readily seen from the deterministic formulations 1* and 4. This is the pure interest-rate effect.

As i rises, the present value of K declines so that the call price increases. The value of the call is equivalent to the cost of maintaining the hedge portfolio which consists of delta units of the underlying currency and borrowed money. As interest rates rise, the cost of maintaining the hedge portfolio rises, leading to a rise in the call price.

The value of a put decreases as i increases because the cost of the hedge portfolio of a put which shorts the underlying currency decreases. That is, the hedge portfolio on a put earns more interest as i increases, lowering its overall cost.

A change in the domestic interest rate, however, usually influences both the spot and the forward-exchange rate. These changes lead to a change in the option price. The effect on option prices depends not only on the extent of the change in the domestic interest rate but also on the change's relative impact on the spot and forward rates.

Suppose that a change in the domestic interest rate does not alter the current spot rate. This implies that an increase in the domestic interest rate either increases the forward premium or decreases the forward discount of the foreign currency. Given a constant spot rate, an increase in domestic interest rates leads to an increase in call option prices and a decrease in the prices of put options on the foreign currency. Similarly, a decrease in domestic interest rates decreases call option and increases put option prices on the foreign currency.

An investor may view a long foreign-currency position and a call-option position as alternatives to profit from anticipated appreciations of the foreign currency. An increase in the domestic interest rate increases the carrying costs of holding the foreign currency more than the carrying costs for the call option. This increases the attractiveness of call options and thus their value. A similar argument holds for put options. An investor may view a short foreign-currency (long domestic-currency) position and a put-option position as alternatives to profit from anticipated depreciations of the foreign currency. An increase in the domestic interest rate increases the opportunity costs of carrying a put option because the investor does not earn the higher interest on the domestic currency. Thus, the price of put options falls with an increase in domestic interest rates and rises with a decrease in these rates.

Suppose, now, that changes in domestic interest rates leave the forward rate constant. If so, increases (decreases) in domestic interest rates lead to spot depreciations (appreciations) of the foreign currency. The effect on call and put prices is undetermined. If the call option is in-the-money, an increase (decrease) in the domestic interest rate will lead to decline (increase) in call prices. The same holds for the price of put options.

As changes in domestic interest rates usually affect both spot and forward rates simultaneously, the preceding effects offset each other, at least partially. Hence, the pure interest effect usually dominates. The effect of changes in interest rates on option prices is positively correlated to the length of the options life.

Foreign Interest Rate.   According to Formulations 1* and 4 an increase in foreign interest rates, given a constant spot rate, decreases (increases) call (put) option prices. For a constant forward rate, Equations 1 and 3 indicate that a change in the foreign interest rate does not affect call and put option prices. In particular, any news such as a change in foreign interest rates affects both spot and forward rates simultaneously and in the same direction. Therefore, in all likelihood, a change in foreign interest rates affects option prices only to the extent that the underlying currency's value changes.

Time to Expiration.   Everything else constant, option values usually decline as time passes. The holder of an American option with a longer time to maturity has all the rights that a holder of an option with a shorter time to maturity has. In addition, he has the rights for a longer period. Therefore, the price of an American option with longer maturity has to be greater than the price of an option with shorter maturity. This, however, is not always true for European options.

The longer the time to expiration, the higher the value of a call on nondividend paying stock. A European call with a longer time to maturity offers everything that a European call with a shorter time to maturity offers. Hence, it should be more expensive.

The above holds because an investor would not want to prematurely exercise a European call on nondividend paying stock. An investor exercising such a call prematurely would lose the option's time value. To avoid this loss, the investor would rather sell the call in the open market. If the stock pays dividends, however, the situation might be different. On the ex-dividend date, the call option holder not only loses time value, but also intrinsic value. If the expected loss in intrinsic value is larger than the loss in time value, a dividend-paying stock's call should be exercised prematurely.

The change in the value of a European put on nondividend-paying stock with respect to a change in time to expiration is ambiguous. Two opposing effects are at work. Because of the time value of money, it is better to early exercise a put. This leads to the conclusion that the longer the time to expiration, the less valuable the put. On the other hand, as it increases, the likelihood of the put price ending in-the-money increases, raising the value of the put. Because these two effects operate in opposite directions, the overall effect of a change in t on the put price is ambiguous.

Options on foreign currencies are like options on stocks which pay dividends continuously. In a deterministic world, the effects of changes in time to maturity on option prices are mostly ambiguous. As time to expiration increases, the value of a call (put) on a foreign currency trading at a discount decreases (increases) or stays at zero. The same effect would lead to ambiguous results for options on currencies trading at a forward premium.

Time decay of an option is, in addition, a function of the volatility level and the ratio between the current spot rate and the exercise price. In general, time decay for deep in-the-money options is small. Time decay for at-the-money options increases as expiration approaches. The time decay for out-of-the-money options is most severe in the beginning of their lives and decreases as expiration approaches. Absolute time decay (and correspondingly the total time value) increases with an increase in volatility. However, in relative terms (ratio of time value of total premium), distinctions have to be made about whether the option is out-of-the-money or in-the-money. In relative terms, time decay decreases for out-of-the-money options as volatility increases. On the other hand, time decay increases in relative terms for in-the-money options as volatility increases.

Put - Call Price Relationships

Though an option buyer has the right, but not the obligation, to deliver or receive foreign exchange and a forward contract must be delivered or reversed, the two contracts are linked in many ways. Various combinations of puts, calls, forward (or futures) contracts, and lending or borrowing can substitute for one another. Thus, some basic relationships between prices for options and forward exchange contracts can be established. Strictly speaking, these relationships only hold for European options. However, for most practical purposes, few American options are exercised before the expiration date. American options are almost always more valuable "alive" than "dead" and thus are kept alive. To the extent that the premature exercise right of American options is not used and is hence worthless, the following relationships also apply to American options.

1. A position of buying a call option (C) with an exercise price of K and selling a put option (P) with an identical exercise price and expiration date is equivalent to buying a forward contract at a forward-exchange rate K:

$$C\ (K) - P\ (K) = \text{Forward contract (K)}$$

As the spot-exchange rate is above K on the expiration date, the gains on the long call position match those on the forward contract. The put expires worthless. As the spot-exchange rate is below K on the expiration date, the losses on the short put position match those on the forward contract. The call expires worthless.

2. The difference between the value of a call and a put option with the same expiration date and identical exercise prices K equals the discounted value of the difference between the forward/futures rate (F) and the exercise price (put-call parity):

$$C\ (K) - P\ (K) = (F - K)/(1 + r)^t$$

Traders regard the preceding as a result of two arbitrage transactions. The reversal combines buying a call and selling a put option with identical strike prices and selling the foreign currency forward for the same expiration date. The conversion combines buying a put and selling a call option with identical strike prices and buying the foreign currency forward for the same expiration date.

3. The prices for put and call options with identical expiration dates and exercise prices equal to the forward/futures rates (F) are the same:

$$C\ (F) = P\ (F)$$

This follows immediately from the previous proposition, since:

$$F - K = 0$$

4. Prices of call and put options with the same expirations but different exercise prices are related to the discounted value of the exercise prices' difference:

$$C\ (K_1) - P\ (K_1) + P\ (K_2) - C\ (K_2) = (K_2 - K_1)/(1 + r)^t$$

This can simply be derived by summing up two put-call parity equations. The correct relative pricing of call and put options with different exercise prices is maintained by boxes. Boxes contain positions of long call/short put at a given exercise price and short call/long put at a different exercise price.

5. At any date before maturity, an American call option (C_A) must sell for at least the difference between the spot rate (S) and the exercise price. An American put option (P_A) must sell for at least the difference between the exercise price and the spot rate:

$$C_A\ (K) \geqslant S - K, \text{ and}$$
$$P_A\ (K) \geqslant K - S$$

If the call options sell for less, an investor could buy the option, immediately exercise the option, receive the foreign currency, and sell it in the spot market to earn a riskless profit.

6. A European call or put option may be priced below the intrinsic value (S − K for calls, K − S for puts). The longer the time to maturity, the larger the difference between domestic and foreign interest rates, and the lower the volatility, the more likely that European options are valued below their intrinsic value. European put options on foreign currencies trading at a forward premium and European call options on foreign currencies trading at a forward discount can be priced below intrinsic value.

7. At any time before maturity, an in-the-money call option (put option) must be priced at least at the discounted value of the difference between the forward price and the exercise price (the exercise price and the forward price):

$$C (K) \geqslant (F - K)/(1 + r)^t, \text{ and}$$
$$P (K) \geqslant (K - F)/(1 + r)^t$$

If the call is underpriced, an investor can buy the call, sell the currency forward at F, and exercise the call option if in-the-money at expiration. This arbitrage transaction increases the value of the call option.

The possibility for combining put and call positions, having different exercise prices and expiration dates, with forward/futures contracts and lending or borrowing is almost endless. For each of these possibilities, an arbitrage equation and lower and upper bounds for prices could be formulated. For most practical purposes, the preceding relationships suffice.

CURRENCY-OPTION STRATEGIES

A foreign-currency option is a powerful tool for managing risk in today's volatile foreign-exchange market. It can be used by participants in an almost unlimited number of ways. The existence of calls and puts and a wide array of exercise prices and maturity dates allows a versatility unequaled by other financial instruments. Currency options enable international firms and investors to hedge contingent and noncontingent foreign-exchange exposures, to tailor international portfolio results in new ways, and to take a view on the direction and volatility of exchange-rate movements. This section describes some of the most often used currency-option strategies.

Speculation

Options are versatile tools not only for the purpose of hedging foreign-currency exposures but also for speculation. Options allow investors to speculate both on directional moves in exchange rates and on exchange-rate volatilities.

Suppose an investor expects the British pound to appreciate or depreciate against the U.S. dollar. Conventional strategies such as buying or selling the British pound in the spot, forward, or futures market expose the investor to large potential losses in case of an unfavorable movement in the exchange rate. Because options give the holder the right, but not the obligation, to buy or sell foreign exchange, the potential loss of a long option position is limited to the premium paid. On the other hand, the profit potential is unlimited and reduced only by the premium paid.

Direction. Assume an investor expects an appreciation of the British pound against the U.S. dollar. The investor could buy British pounds in the spot or forward/futures market. The final outcomes for all these alternatives will be identical if the interest-rate parity condition holds. With a long position in the British pound, profits materialize if the British pound appreciates as anticipated. On the other hand, losses are realized if the British pound depreciates.

The investor can use at least two options strategies. First, the investor can sell a put option on the British pound, receiving a premium. If the pound appreciates, the put option expires worthless and the investor's profits are limited to the premium received. If the pound depreciates, the holder of the put exercises it and the investor delivers U.S. dollars (buys British pounds) at the stated exercise price. The received premium (partially) cushions the investor's losses. Second, the investor can buy a call option on the British pound, paying a premium. If the British pound appreciates, the investor profits. However, profits are reduced by the initial premium paid, compared to a spot, forward, or futures position. If the pound depreciates, losses are limited to the premium paid.

Options are analogous to insurance contracts. Call options used as uncovered (naked) long positions in foreign currencies protect the holder from large losses if the value of the underlying currency decreases. Put options used as uncovered (naked) short positions in foreign currencies protect the holder from large losses if the value of the underlying currency increases.

To demonstrate this principle, consider the following scenario and prices:

$$S = \$1.4000/\pounds$$
$$F_{90} = \$1.3880/\pounds$$
$$90 \text{ day } 1.4000 \text{ Call} = .0280$$
$$90 \text{ day } 1.4500 \text{ Put} = .0714$$

The investor expects an appreciation of the British pound and is willing to take a long position of £1 million. The total premium to be paid for the call option is $28,000 ($.028/£ premium), and the premium received for the in-the-money put option is $71,400 ($.0714/£ premium). Because spot, forward, and futures positions give identical outcomes, we assume that the investor buys £1 million forward for 90 days at the prevailing forward rate of $1.3880/£. The following table shows profits and losses as a function of the spot rate on maturity date for the three investment alternatives.

Profit/Loss Comparison
(in U.S. dollars)

Future Spot Rate ($/£)	Forward Contract 1.3880/£	Sell in-the-Money Put–Premium: $71,400	Buy at-the-Money Call–Premium: ($28,000)
$1.2000	−$188,000	−$178,600	−$ 28,000
1.3000	− 88,000	− 78,000	− 28,000
1.3500	− 38,000	− 28,600	− 28,000
1.3880	0	+ 9,400	− 28,000
1.4000	+ 12,000	+ 21,400	− 28,000
1.4500	+ 62,000	+ 71,400	+ 22,000
1.5000	+ 112,000	+ 71,400	+ 72,000
1.6000	+ 212,000	+ 71,400	+ 172,000

Interest income earned on the premium received is not considered. Thus, the outcomes for the short-put option position are downward biased, whereas, the results for the long-call option position are upward biased.

The insurance characteristics of the long-call option position is obvious. The maximum loss is limited to the total premium paid. The flexibility of using any exercise price for the call and put position gives the investor a large variety of possibilities. Also note that none of the alternatives is dominant. Each has a unique profit-loss profile. The forward strategy is preferred for large appreciations of the British pound, while the call-buying strategy is superior for large depreciations. The put-selling strategy is the best for in-between outcomes.

For obvious reasons, an investor expecting a depreciation of the British pound would compare these strategies: selling forward, buying puts, and selling calls.

Volatility. Options also can be used to profit from anticipated exchange-rate volatilities, independent of the direction of exchange-rate movements. We discuss some of these strategies next.

Straddles

A straddle is formed by simultaneously buying or selling puts and calls. The purchase of a straddle is equivalent to buying both a put and call with identical strike prices and expiration dates. The sale of a straddle is equivalent to selling both a put and a call.

Straddles are bought or sold when management has specific expectations about the future variability of exchange rates, but not about the direction of those movements. Specifically, management buys a straddle when it believes a currency will either appreciate or depreciate beyond a specific point.[2]

Similarly, a straddle is sold if management thinks that currency movements will be limited within a specific range. For example, management may sell a straddle if it thinks that the volatility of a certain currency will drop below market expectations, possibly because of expected central bank intervention. Conversely, management may buy a straddle if it expects volatility to rise above market expectations—as the result, for example, of expected increases or decreases in money supply growth.

Figure 16–1 shows the profit profile of a long straddle position. To see why a straddle provides this payoff profile, remember that the purchase of a straddle is equivalent to the simultaneous purchase of a call option and a put option with identical terms. The profit profile of buying a call option at exercise price X is illustrated

---

[2]As shown later, this point is a function of the exercise prices of the individual options in the straddle, and the option premiums.

by part A in Figure 16–1. At spot-exchange rates X and lower, the call is not exercised. The loss of this position equals the price of the option. At spot-exchange rates above S_1, the option is sufficiently in-the-money to more than cover its cost. Between X and S_1, the option is in-the-money, though not by enough to cover its cost. Similarly, part B illustrates the profit profile of buying a put option.

Part C in Figure 16–1 illustrates the profit profile of a straddle purchase. It is constructed as the vertical sum of parts A and B. The price of the straddle incorporates the market's assessment of the variability of the exchange rate. The buyer of the straddle thus profits only if the exchange rate moves plus or minus a certain percentage, $[(S-X)(100)/X]$, or $[(X-S)(100)/X]$ beyond X. The seller of the straddle accepts that risk for a lump sum.

The profit profile of selling a straddle is the mirror image of part C around the horizontal axis. Writing a straddle is quite risky because the investor is writing both a naked call and a naked put. The investor has no protection against large moves in the value of the currency in either direction, thus exposing himself to potentially large losses.

As Figure 16–1 suggests, buying a straddle is equivalent to buying insurance, with a deductible, against large movements either up or down in the value of the underlying instrument. Profit opportunities or bargains exist, however, only if this insurance (1) can be bought for less than its fair actuarial value, or (2) can be sold for more than its fair actuarial value.

The most important determinant of the fair actuarial value of this insurance is the expected volatility of the underlying currency. If one's expectation of this volatility is higher than the market's, one buys this insurance. But, if one's expectation of this volatility is lower than the market's, one sells this insurance.

Spreads

A spread is the simultaneous purchase of one option and sale of another on the same underlying instrument in which the two options differ only in time to expiration and/or in strike price. Vertical spreads are formed by varying only the strike price; horizontal spreads (also called time or calendar spreads) are formed by varying the time to maturity. These spreads are so named because quotes for options differing in exercise prices are listed vertically and quotes for options differing in maturities are listed horizontally.

When traders think that certain options are mispriced, they try to make a profit by establishing a spread—that is, by buying the low-priced option and selling the relatively high-priced one. The following example, using three-month and six-month foreign-exchange options (FXO), illustrates how traders detect arbitrage opportunities.

First, the implied volitilities of three-month and six-month FXOs are calculated by using the option-pricing models together with current market prices to "back-out" the market's implicit estimate of expected volitility. Second, the implied volitility of three-month FXOs is used to compute the theoretical value of six-month FXOs. If the theoretical value of six-month FXOs is higher than the current market value, then six-month FXOs must be relatively underpriced compared to three-month FXOs, at least theoretically. The trader thus buys six-month FXOs and sells three-month FXOs.

But this is not an entirely riskless activity. First, a spread might incur a loss. The maximum loss is called the basis of the spread, and is discussed in further detail later. Second, volatility may not be a stationary process—that is, the relationship between the volatility of three-month and six-month FXOs may change over time—creating potential losses for spread positions.

Horizontal Spreads

Figure 16–2 shows the profit of a horizontal spread formed by selling a three-month call and by buying a six-month call, both at the same exercise price. The profit profile, at expiration, of selling a three-month call is straightforward and is presented in part A. The profit profile, at three months, of buying a six-month call is given in part B. (The broken lines are the asymptotes of the profit profile.) The solid line represents the actual profit profile, reflecting the fact that options command a time premium. The profit profile of the spread, at three months, is the vertical sum of parts A and B. The maximum loss of the spread equals the premium of the six-month call minus the premium of the three-month call. This is called the basis of the spread.

FIGURE 16-2
Profit Profile of a 6-3 Month Spread

A. Profit profile at expiration of selling a 3-month call

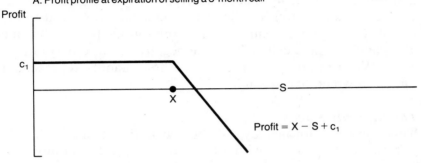

Profit = $X - S + c_1$

B. Profit profile at 3 months of buying a 6-month call

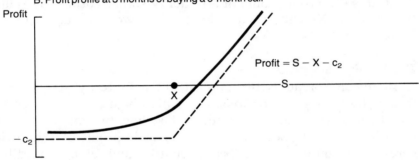

Profit = $S - X - c_2$

C. Profit profile at 3 months of a 6-3 month spread

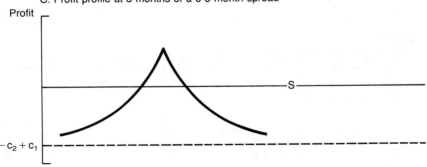

The Simple Vertical Spread

The simple vertical spread is formed by buying an option with one exercise price (X_1) and selling another option with the same maturity date as the first, but a different exercise price (X_2). Figure 16–3 depicts the profit profile of buying a call at X_1, and selling a call at X_2 (X_2 greater than X_1). The profit profile from selling a call at X_1 and buying a call at X_2 is the negative counterpart of Figure 16–3. When referring to spreads, the first quantity represents the option in which one is long.

The Butterfly Spread

This spread is formed by selling two options, one with a high exercise price and one with a low exercise price, and buying two options at an exercise price in between the two. Figure 16–4 illustrates the profit profile of a butterfly spread formed by selling two calls at X_1 and X_3, and by buying two calls at X_2 ($X_1 > X_2 > X_3$; $X_2 = (X_1 + X_3/2)$).

The Sandwich Spread

A sandwich spread is the opposite of a butterfly spread. It is formed by buying two options, one with a high exercise price and one with a low exercise price, and selling two options at the exercise price in between the two. The profit profile of a sandwich spread formed by buying calls at X_1 and X_3, and selling two calls at X_2 is the negative of Figure 16–4 and is given in Figure 16–5.

FIGURE 16–3
Profit Profile of a Simple (X-X) Vertical Spread (also called a bull spread)

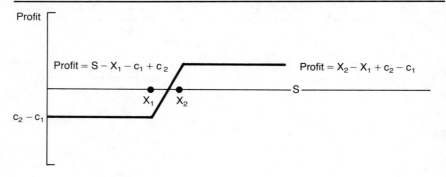

FIGURE 16–4
Profit Profile of a Butterfly Spread (a short butterfly position)

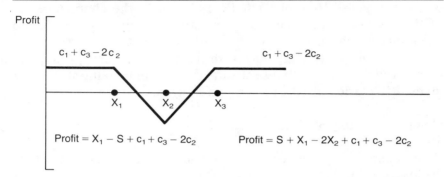

The profit profiles of sandwich and butterfly spreads somewhat resemble those of straddles. The difference is that, unlike straddles, sandwich and butterfly spreads limit the potential profits and losses. Like straddles, sandwich and butterfly spreads can be used to take positions when one's expectation of the future volatility of a currency's change is different from that of the market's.

Other Strategies

In addition to the preceding, there is a wide variety of option strategies, including diagonal spreads (a combination of vertical

FIGURE 16–5
Profit Profile of a Sandwich Spread (also called a long butterfly position)

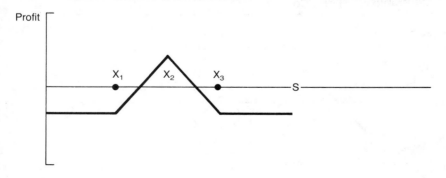

and horizontal spreads), bull spreads, bear spreads, condors, strangles, call and put ratio spreads, and call and put ratio back spreads. Figures 16–6 through 16–10 highlight the characteristics of these various strategies. An investor uses these strategies to make directional, or volatility bets, or to exploit mispriced instruments. As each strategy has a different risk-return profile, an investor picks the one that best suits the economic outlook and the investor's particular risk-return preferences.

Hedging Contingent Payables/Receivables

Contingent foreign-currency receivables arise as the result of disposals of foreign subsidiaries, uncertain foreign sales, uncertain dividend remittances from abroad, and a host of other situations.

FIGURE 16–6
Profit Profile of a Bear Spread

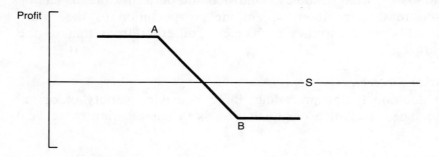

FIGURE 16–7
Profit Profile of a Long Condor

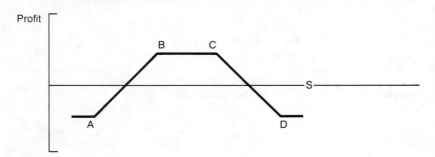

FIGURE 16–8
Profit Profile of a Long Strangle

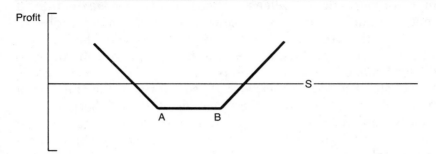

FIGURE 16–9
Profit Profile of a Call Ratio Spread (a call ratio backspread is the mirror image of this)

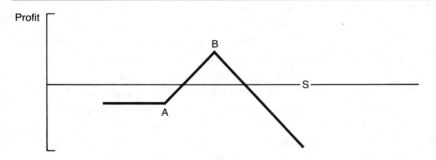

FIGURE 16–10
Profit Profile of a Put Ratio Spread (a put ratio backspread is the mirror image of this)

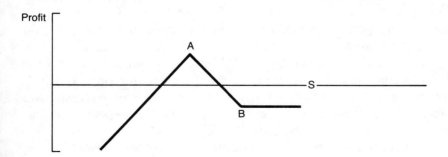

The most often used example for contingent receivables involves the case of a bidding firm. In hedging contingent receivables, the simple forward sale of foreign exchange equal to the sum of the bid is not a solution to the risk problem because the bidder's foreign-exchange exposure is contingent upon acceptance of the bid.

If the bid is accepted after the firm sells forward the foreign-exchange sum of the bid, the firm is hedged. If, however, the bid is not accepted and the firm has already sold forward the anticipated amount of foreign currency, the firm ends up with a short position in the foreign currency. Ex post the firm has taken a speculative rather than a hedged position. If the foreign currency appreciates, the firm takes a loss. Yet, if the firm does not sell forward the anticipated foreign currency and the bid is accepted, the firm finds itself with a long foreign-currency position. In this situation, it takes a loss if the foreign currency depreciates.

Options can solve these problems because the exercise of options is voluntary and contingent upon prevailing economic conditions. There are two methods of hedging receivables: buying a put option on the foreign currency, or selling the foreign currency forward and simultaneously buying a call option. Because of put-call parity, the methods generate identical results.

In the first case, buying a put option, the timing, quantity, and the exercise price of the option contract should correspond to the forward contract that would have been bought if the firm had a noncontingent foreign-currency receivable. But this is not always possible with respect to the timing. American options provide some flexibility only if the timing range—but not the exact date—of the contingent foreign-exchange receivables is known. The quantity and strike prices can take on a range of values depending on management's desired risk/return profile. Especially with respect to the quantity, some caution is in order. Firms bidding on a regular base know from experience that only a portion of the bids are accepted. Hedging each bid to the full amount is equivalent to "over-insurance." This can turn out to be costly for the bidding firm. Consequently, the firm should only cover a portion of the full bid. This portion should either approximate the average probability of bids being accepted or the expected probability of acceptance of the specific bid.

The premium on the put option is sometimes viewed as the cost of buying insurance against possible exchange-rate fluctuations in case the bid is accepted. If the bid is accepted and the foreign currency depreciates, the firm offsets the loss in the value of the foreign currency by exercising the put option.

In fact, however, the put option also provides additional profit opportunities. If the foreign currency depreciates and the bid is rejected, the hedger can exercise the option and profit by selling the foreign exchange for dollars. (Of course, if the foreign exchange appreciates, the firm lets the put option expire in either case.) So the option premium consists of an investment value and a hedging value. Only the hedging value of the option premium should be incorporated into the cost of submitting the bid—provided, of course, that this hedging value can be calculated.

As another hedging technique, the firm can sell the foreign currency forward and simultaneously buy a call option on the foreign currency. Obviously, the quantities, exercise prices, and maturity dates should match. If the bid is accepted and the foreign currency depreciates, the forward transaction hedges the firm, and the call expires worthless.

In the event that the foreign currency appreciates, the firm's forward contract covers its receipts, and it exercises the call option at a profit. If the bid is rejected and the foreign currency appreciates, the calls fully hedge the firm's short forward position. Should the foreign currency depreciate, the firm lets the call option expire and buys spot foreign currency to cover its forward position.

Contingent payables in foreign exchange come about through stock tender offers, merger and acquisition tenders to foreign companies, pending foreign law suits, anticipated foreign dividend payments, etc. These situations are properly hedged through the use of foreign-currency options, just as in hedging contingent receivables. Again, there are two corresponding techniques: buying a call option on foreign exchange, or simultaneously buying the foreign-currency forward and buying a put option. Our earlier comments on hedging contingent receivables apply correspondingly to the case of hedging contingent payables.

Hedging Payables and Receivables

The use of foreign-currency options to hedge noncontingent accounts payable and receivable creates outcomes that could not be constructed with more traditional instruments. The following section describes the use of five basic option strategies to hedge foreign-currency-denominated accounts payable.

Buy an at-the-money call option. This is the classic insurance policy for a company anticipating a foreign-currency-denominated payable. The chosen exercise price of the call option equals or approximates the current spot rate. This strategy protects the firm against any appreciation of the foreign currency as the call option provides the holder with the right to buy the foreign exchange at the exercise price. At the same time, the strategy allows the firm to participate in opportunity gains should the foreign currency depreciate. For this option, the firm pays a predetermined premium.

Many firms still view options differently from other insurance products. In general, premiums for automobile, health, or fire insurance are not viewed as wasted should the accidents not occur. On the other hand, firms continue to view an option premium as wasted should the foreign currency depreciate, that is, should the accident not occur. The firm, however, is always better off with a depreciated value of the foreign currency and a wasted option premium than with an appreciated value of the foreign currency and a nonwasted option premium.

Buy an out-of-the-money call option. Insurance premiums can be reduced by assuming some of the insurer's risks. This is the basic idea behind the deductible clause in property and health insurances. If a firm is willing to accept the risk of a limited adverse move in the exchange rate, it can buy a call option with an exercise price above the current spot rate at a lower premium. This out-of-the-money call option provides—depending on the exercise price—insurance against a large appreciation of the foreign currency. The higher the deductible, that is, the greater the difference between the exercise price and the current spot exchange rate, the lower the premium.

Buy a bull spread. Another way to reduce the net premium is to combine long and short option positions. For example, a firm that does not expect the foreign currency to appreciate sharply might want to buy a call option with an exercise price at or near the current spot rate and simultaneously sell a call option with a higher exercise price. The premium received for the sold call option reduces the net premium to be paid. With this strategy, the firm is protected against any appreciation of the foreign currency up to the exercise price of the written call. On the other hand, the position allows for full participation in opportunity gains should the foreign currency depreciate. The flexibility in the choice of exercise prices allows for a hedge which precisely reflects the exchange rate anticipations of the firm.

The described strategy is known as a 1:1 bull spread in the options industry. The strategy is directly comparable to any cap insurance contract.

Buy a fence. There is no real insurance analogy for this strategy. It is based again on the desire of a firm to lower the net premium to be paid by assuming some of the risk or by giving up some of the profit potential.

A firm that does not expect the foreign currency to depreciate sharply might consider buying a call option with an exercise price at or near the current spot exchange rate and simultaneously selling a put option with a lower exercise price. Again, the combination of a long and a short position reduces the net premium to be paid. The strategy protects the firm from any appreciation of the foreign currency. On the other hand, opportunity gains from a depreciating foreign currency are limited by the exercise price of the written put option. Any depreciation below the exercise price of the put option does not benefit the firm.

The preceding strategy is also known by other names such as a range forward. Variations on the basic fence strategy allow for choices of exercise prices or of ratios between bought calls and written puts.

One version chooses the exercise prices for call and put options so that the net premium equals zero. This can be accomplished at an exercise price equal to the forward rate. However, this would just create a synthetic forward contract. In practice, exercise prices are chosen in such a way that both options are out-of-the-money and correspond to the risk/return trade-off for the client.

A second version is also constructed to end up with a net premium of zero. However, the firm pays for the protection against an appreciation of the foreign currency by giving up a certain proportion of the profit should the foreign currency depreciate. The strategy requires that the exercise prices for calls and puts are identical and that fewer puts are written than calls are bought. To end up with a net premium of zero, the bought call options must be out-of-the-money and, because of identical exercise prices, the puts must be in-the-money. The client either specifies the participation rate or the strike price for the call options.

Sell puts. If a firm believes that current option premium levels overestimate future exchange-rate volatilities, it might consider selling put options to cover its foreign-currency payables. This strategy provides fixed gains relative to a forward contract should the foreign currency depreciate. It protects the firm against any appreciation of the foreign currency only to the extent of the premium income received. However, should the foreign currency depreciate, losses on the put will offset gains on the payables.

To clarify the previously described strategies, consider the following example:

$$
\begin{aligned}
\text{90 day account payable} &= \text{£1 million} \\
S &= \$1.4000/\text{£} \\
F_{90} &= \$1.3880/\text{£} \\
\text{90 day 1.40 call} &= .0280 \\
\text{90 day 1.45 call} &= .0105 \\
\text{90 day 1.50 call} &= .0050 \\
\text{90 day 1.30 put} &= .0060 \\
\text{90 day 1.45 put} &= .0714
\end{aligned}
$$

Table 16–1 summarizes the U.S. dollar outflows on expiration as a function of future spot rates. In addition to the five option strategies, results for a do-nothing strategy and a forward contract strategy are included.

These five strategies offer solutions to most foreign-currency exposure positions. The same principles apply for hedging foreign-currency-denominated receivables. The corresponding strategies are buy at-the-money puts, buy out-of-the-money puts, buy a bear spread, buy a fence, and sell calls. For hedging receivables, puts are used instead of calls and vice versa.

TABLE 16–1
U.S. Dollar Cash Outflows for £1 Million Payable

Future Spot Rate ($/£)	Open Position	Forward Position at 1.3880	Buy ATM £ Call Long 1.40 Call at .0280 Premium Paid: $28,000	Buy OTM £ Call Long 1.45 Call at .0105 Premium Paid: $10,500	Buy Bull Spread Long 1.40 Call at .0280 Short 1.50 Call at .0050 Net Premium Paid: $23,000	Buy Fence Long 1.40 Call at .0280 Short 1.30 Put at .0060 Net Premium Paid: $22,000	Sell Put Short 1.45 Put at .0714 Premium Received: $71,400
1.25	$1,250,000	$1,388,000	$1,278,000	$1,260,500	$1,273,000	$1,322,000	$1,378,600
1.30	1,300,000	1,388,000	1,328,000	1,310,500	1,323,000	1,322,000	1,378,600
1.35	1,350,000	1,388,000	1,378,000	1,360,500	1,373,000	1,372,000	1,378,600
1.40	1,400,000	1,388,000	1,428,000	1,410,500	1,423,000	1,422,000	1,378,600
1.45	1,450,000	1,388,000	1,428,000	1,460,500	1,423,000	1,422,000	1,378,600
1.50	1,500,000	1,388,000	1,428,000	1,460,500	1,423,000	1,422,000	1,428,600
1.55	1,550,000	1,388,000	1,428,000	1,460,500	1,473,000	1,422,000	1,478,600

Interest income forgone or received due to option premiums is not considered.

Table 16–1 demonstrates that virtually every option recommendation is an in-between solution to a foreign-exchange exposure problem. For example, if the firm buys an at-the-money call it will be worse off compared to an open position if the foreign currency depreciates. It also will be worse off compared to a forward contract hedge if the foreign currency appreciates. So the option hedge is a compromise: not as good as the best scenario and not as bad as the worst scenario.

A second result worth emphasizing is the transaction nature of the option hedge: you get something and you give up something. Compared to other instruments, options do not create better or superior hedges under all circumstances. Options allow for hedges, with distinct risk/reward characteristics.

Hedging Noncash-Flow Exposures

Experience during the last decade has shown that sudden, unexpected large movements in exchange rates have significant and possibly devastating effects not only on the domestic currency value of foreign income streams but also on the domestic currency value of foreign-currency-denominated net asset or liability values. Treasurers of international firms and managers of international portfolios try to limit this foreign-exchange (translation) exposure through hedging. Hedging net asset or liability values with conventional instruments, however, can create very undesirable cash-flow positions.

Suppose a firm or a portfolio manager faces a foreign-currency net asset position. To cover the exposure, the manager sells the foreign currency forward at the current forward rate. Several scenarios are possible:

1. *Net asset value constant, foreign currency depreciates:* Assuming a relative long-term outlook, the foreign-currency-denominated net asset positions are not liquidated. The depreciation of the foreign currency leads to a reduction in the domestic value of the foreign-currency net asset value. This is an unrealized (non-cash flow) book loss. This book loss is offset (partially or more than, depending on whether the foreign currency trades on a forward discount or premium) by gains in the forward contract. To fulfill the obligation of the forward contract, the manager buys the foreign currency in the spot market. Thus a cash-flow gain is realized. The total position consists of a (non-cash flow) unrealized book loss which is offset by a realized (cash flow) gain.

2. *Net asset value constant, foreign currency appreciates:* The appreciation of the foreign currency leads to an increase in the domestic value of the foreign net asset position. The firm has an unrealized (non-cash flow) book gain. To fulfill the obligation of the forward contract, the firm buys the foreign currency in the spot market. Thus a cash-flow loss is realized. The total position consists of a (non-cash flow) unrealized book gain which is offset by a realized (cash flow) loss. From a cash-flow point of view, this outcome is highly undesirable.

3. *Net asset value declines, foreign currency appreciates:* Given the hedging strategy, this scenario leads to the worst outcome. Depending on the relative size of the currency appreciation versus the decline in the foreign-currency asset value, the domestic value of the foreign net asset value may decline, stay constant, or increase. If the percentage appreciation of the foreign-currency value is smaller than the percentage depreciation of the foreign-currency-denominated net asset value, the firm suffers an unrealized (non-cash flow) book loss. Again, the firm has to buy the foreign currency in the spot market to cover its obligations from the forward contract. The total position, therefore, might consist of an unrealized (non-cash flow) book loss and a realized (cash flow) loss. From a cash-flow point of view, this outcome is most undesirable.

The use of option strategies can diminish most of the problems associated with hedging net asset or liability positions denominated in foreign currencies. Each of the option strategies presented in the previous section can be employed.

In addition, the flexibility of exercise prices allows for specific custom tailoring. We use a hedge constructed with an at-the-money put option to point out the differences between a forward hedge and an option hedge. This is analyzed using the same scenarios.

1. *Net asset value constant, foreign currency depreciates:* The firm faces an unrealized (non-cash flow) book loss due to the decline in the domestic value of the foreign net asset position. Because the purchased put option is in-the-money at expiration, the firm realizes a cash-flow gain on the option position. This gain, though, is smaller than for the corresponding forward hedge because of the premium paid.

2. *Net asset value constant, foreign currency appreciates:* The firm has an unrealized (non-cash flow) book gain as the domestic value of the foreign net asset value increases. At expiration, the put option being out-of-the-money expires worthless. Except for the original cash outflow for the paid premium, there will be no potentially unlimited cash-flow losses as in the case of the forward hedge position. The main characteristic of an option— giving a right but not the obligation—makes this outcome possible.

3. *Net asset value declines, foreign currency appreciates:* Again the combination of both effects might lead to an increase, decrease, or constant domestic value of the foreign-asset position. The cash outflows on the hedge transaction are again limited to the original option premium paid. No further cash-flow losses are possible.

Aside from providing a multitude of possible risk/return characteristics, option strategies manage cash-flow problems associated with hedges for net asset and liability positions in a superior way.

Foreign-currency options are a potent instrument for coping with today's highly volatile financial environment. Options enable managers to (1) hedge contingent foreign-currency exposures; (2) take a view on the direction and volatility of exchange-rate movements while limiting downside risk; (3) tailor risk-return outcomes in ways previously impossible; and (4) fine-tune the level or currency risk one is willing to accept over a specific period of time. Options, though, are no substitute for omniscience. Trading spot or forward-outright positions with perfect knowledge and forecast will always outperform foreign-currency options as a hedge. The value of options to their users increases with the level of uncertainty.

Option strategies complete financial markets by allowing players to buy or sell contingent payoff streams. The quantity of possible variations in the structuring of option positions and hedges opens new possibilities for financial managers. Their flexibility, creativity, and potential to custom-tailor virtually any risk-return profile requires that financial managers study the instrument and use it when appropriate.

CHAPTER 17

CAPITAL INVESTMENT AND MANAGEMENT IN GLOBAL BUSINESSES

Christine R. Hekman

A handbook of international financial management can presumably be expected to prescribe financial solutions to global business management problems that do not arise in the management of domestic businesses. It follows that a handbook chapter describing investment acquisition and management should describe methods of analysis and investment selection in addressing such uniquely international challenges.

This chapter identifies and examines those uniquely international challenges and recommends a method for evaluating global investment opportunities. In sum, it addresses the following questions:

What distinguishes a global business from a domestic business?

How do global considerations change investment acquisition and management?

How can investment acquisition, divestiture, and restructuring opportunities be analyzed in a way that recognizes the importance of international factors?

GLOBAL AND DOMESTIC BUSINESSES: CHARACTERISTIC DIFFERENCES

A global business is simply a business that faces opportunities to capitalize on differences between domestic and foreign economic conditions. These differences may present themselves as opportunities to enter foreign markets, to source from foreign production sites, or to invest abroad through foreign subsidiaries. Differences may also present themselves as challenges from competitors who pursue such opportunities. Because they are uniquely foreign, such opportunities exploit conditions that exist in the foreign economy, but are absent domestically.

Foreign investment opportunities are often experienced as intrusions of global realities. An example of one such intrusion is the recognition that not all production locations and markets are equivalent. Some locations may provide low-cost production while costs of production are relatively high in other locations. In this case, management of investment opportunities recommends sourcing from low-cost locations and selling into high-return markets.

Thus, the decision to expand into foreign markets or to source from a foreign location is driven by the anticipation of differences between foreign and domestic economic conditions. Specific differences might be dissynchronies between foreign and domestic business cycles, or dissimilarities between foreign and domestic populations, raw material resources, industrial or financial structures, or economic or legal infrastructure. Investment in the global, as opposed to the domestic, business opportunity is recommended when the positive foreign aspects outweigh the negative.

After commitment to investment in a global business, continued success depends on performance. Thus, investment in global businesses represents an attempt to capitalize on national differences; global business investment performance depends on continuation of those differences.

As increasing numbers of corporations commit to international investments, the national economic system becomes globalized. As a result, the process by which domestic businesses and markets are transformed into global businesses and markets is called globalization. This transformation of businesses and markets may proceed through increasing dependence on foreign production or sourcing, through expanding participation in foreign markets, or through cross-border investment. However, the end result is that the performance of the national economic system comes to depend heavily on foreign economic events.

As globalization proceeds, changes in foreign economic conditions intrude with increasing frequency on domestic investment and production management. This intrusion of global factors and the increased sensitivity to foreign events of formerly domestic businesses may also be accomplished indirectly through the actions of foreign or domestic competitors who source or sell abroad.

In summary, the distinctive characteristic of a relatively attractive global investment is that its value derives from differences between foreign and domestic business environments and opportunities. It follows that the subsequent performance of a global investment is noticeably sensitive to those changes in foreign economic conditions that differ from domestic changes. In other words, the characteristic feature of a global business is the sensitivity of its performance to distinctively foreign economic events. Only businesses which are somehow insulated from, and therefore insensitive to, changes in foreign conditions are strictly domestic.

MEASURING DIFFERENCES BETWEEN GLOBAL AND DOMESTIC INVESTMENT OPPORTUNITIES

The differences between foreign and domestic businesses and economic conditions are frequently structural, complex, and comprehensive. However, from the perspective of corporate investment analysis, their manifestation is straightforward and quantifiable. National differences in economic structural and business conditions are reflected in differences between foreign and domestic wages, costs, and prices.

For example, a complex accumulation of historical factors results in a range of differences between national populations. In countries where that history results in a relative abundance of skilled labor, the structural differences translate into relatively low wages. From a corporate investment perspective, those countries are viewed as low-cost production centers.

Similarly, a country that boasts relatively affluent and developed consumers and developed advertising and distribution systems may represent extremely attractive markets to some corporations. In these markets, product prices significantly exceed those in the domestic market. In sum, the factors that make the markets attractive, and the extent of the attraction, are summarized in the excess of prices in the foreign markets to prices in the domestic market.

Of course, foreign markets and foreign production and sourcing possibilities can be rated against domestic and other foreign opportunities only when product prices and production costs are stated on a comparable basis. This normalization of prices and costs to a single-currency standard is accomplished quite simply.

Prices and costs in one foreign location can be compared to prices and costs in other foreign locations and to domestic prices and costs by translating all into a common currency. In effect, relevant foreign costs and prices are translated into domestic currency equivalents. The exchange rate used for the translation is that projected to be in effect at the time the costs are to be incurred or the returns are to be achieved.

Thus, the relative desirability of foreign production locations depends on the differences between the domestic currency equivalents of translated production costs. Similarly, foreign markets are considered relatively attractive to the extent that translated revenues are expected to exceed revenues from domestic sales.

Finally, although a single cost component might be relatively low in one country, or prices in a particular product segment might be relatively high, the aggregate advantage of operating in a particular location determines the appeal of the opportunity. The net aggregate benefits of uniquely foreign production or market characteristics, as summarized in potential revenues and costs, are attractive only by comparison with the aggregate net profit projected for domestic and other foreign alternatives.

Thus, differences in national business and economic environments are reflected at the most basic level as differences in a common currency translation of foreign wages, costs, and prices. These differences imply relatively attractive foreign investment opportunities when the net effect of distinct foreign factors—aggregate net profit—is larger than profits forecast for investment in comparable domestic opportunities. Finally, aggregate net profit for investment opportunities is measured as the amount by which the domestic currency equivalent of revenue exceeds the equivalent of costs.

The value of a global investment is the value of the opportunity which it represents. This opportunity is the potential for increasing profits or returns by expanding markets or operations beyond domestic economic constraints. The expansion may be undertaken in an attempt to reduce costs, increase revenues, or both.

These incremental profit opportunities represent superior foreign conditions as captured in relatively high or low revenues or costs. Foreign costs and revenues are relatively high or low as compared to domestic alternatives when foreign wages and prices are translated into domestic currency equivalents. Finally, the net dominance of the foreign opportunity depends both on the magnitudes of the cost and price differentials and the relative importance of the various differentials to the particular investment context.

VALUING GLOBAL INVESTMENT OPPORTUNITIES

Differences between global and domestic investment opportunities depend, at base, on differences between foreign and domestic business and economic conditions. Also, those fundamental differences that signal investment opportunities are reflected in wages, prices, and costs differing from domestic wages, prices, and costs, after translation to a domestic currency basis.

However, the decision to commit resources to a foreign or global business investment depends on more than positive differences in foreign profits. A commitment to invest requires that the current value of these profit differences exceed, by a substantial margin, the initial investment requirement.

The model used to relate the values of net profits to investment cost for domestic investments is the net present value model. Even though the same basic model is also a powerful tool for the evaluation of global investment opportunities, its use in these situations requires the ability to assess the distinctively international aspects of the investment. At each point in time the measure of these distinctions is the amount by which the net profit from the global investment exceeds net profit from the alternative domestic investment. Thus, the incremental value of a global investment is the value of capitalizing on distinctive foreign economic and business conditions.

Consider Tables 17–1 through 17–5 as illustrations of both these concepts and the technique by which the value of commitment to global business can be measured. The tables describe expected performance for a series of investment opportunities and display the values which accrue to each.

The investment illustrations include an investment relying on and solely influenced by domestic conditions and events. Also

TABLE 17–1
Investment Forecast and Analysis (Domestic Investment Opportunity—$ millions)

Profitability and income	
Revenue	$100.0
Cost of goods sold	70.0
Gross margin	30.0
Operating expenses	10.0
Other expenses	5.0
Net income before tax	15.0
Tax expense	7.2
Net income	$ 7.8
Initial investment required	45.0
Measures of performance	
Total costs—excluding tax	85.0
Gross margin (%)	30.0%
Net margin—before tax (%)	15.0
Net margin—after tax (%)	7.8
Return on investment—before tax	33.3
Return on investment—after tax	17.3
Investment value	
Value of revenue	$625.9
Value of costs—including tax	577.1
Value of costs—excluding tax	532.0
Value of tax expense	45.1
Value of profits—before tax	93.9
Value of profits—after tax	48.8
Net investment value	$ 3.8

included are a series of alternative investments, each of which depend, in different ways, on foreign environment aspects which differ from those in the domestic environment.

Differences between the expected investment performances reflect the effects of the different economic environments. Differences between the values of the various investment opportunities represent the incremental values of each progressive commitment to globalization.

To begin, consider the base case—a strictly domestic investment. The investment described in Table 17–1 represents an opportunity to expand a domestic business by serving additional domestic markets through domestic sourcing and production.

An important underlying assumption, and one which becomes very important as the sensitivities of investment performance to changes in economic conditions are considered, is that the revenue and costs attached to the expansion are truly independent of events occurring abroad. On reflection, it is clear that this is an extremely strong, and perhaps unsupportable assumption, if the example is presumed to be at all relevant in today's world. Even though the assumption of independence from foreign factors makes this a domestic investment, it also requires that the business be insulated both directly and indirectly from the foreign environment. That is, not only direct revenue and expenses but also the condition of the target customers, suppliers, and competition is assumed exempt from foreign factors that would even indirectly affect the illustrated investment.

Potential applicability aside, consider Table 17–1, as an example of a strictly domestic investment. Annual after-tax profit on the domestic business expansion is expected to be 7.8 percent of revenue, or $7.8 million. With an initial investment of start-up capital of $45 million, the expected return on investment is 17.3 percent. For simplicity, we assume that the cash flow stream is just equal to the stream of profits and that the capital will be used for 20 years and then abandoned. At that time, the abandonment costs will just equal salvage costs.

With these simple assumptions about the investment's maturity and cash flow, and assuming that alternative and roughly equivalent investment opportunities provide internal investment

TABLE 17–2

Investment Forecast and Analysis (Foreign Investment Opportunities: Access to Foreign Markets—10 Percent Effective Price Premium)

	Functional Currency	Exchange Rate (FC/$)	Equivalent
Profitability and income			
Revenue	FC440.0	4.0	$110.0
Cost of goods sold	280.0	4.0	70.0
Gross margin	160.0	4.0	40.0
Operating expenses	40.0	4.0	10.0
Other expenses	20.0	4.0	5.0
Net income before tax	100.0	4.0	25.0
Tax expense	48.0	4.0	12.0
Net income	FC 52.0	4.0	$ 13.0
Initial investment required			$ 45.0
Measures of performance			
Total costs—excluding tax	FC340.0		$ 85.0
Gross margin (%)			36.4%
Net margin—before tax (%)			22.7
Net margin—after tax (%)			11.8
Return on investment—before tax			55.6
Return on investment—after tax			28.9
Investment value			
Value of revenue			$688.5
Value of costs—including tax			607.2
Value of costs—excluding tax			532.0
Value of tax expense			75.1
Value of profits—before tax			156.5
Value of profits—after tax			81.4
Net investment value			$ 36.4

yields of 15 percent, we can assess the current values of the revenue, cost, profit, and cash flow streams.[1]

The revenue stream is valued at $625.9 million, the stream of expenses (excluding taxes) at $532 million, and the cash flow or net profit stream at $48.8 million. Because the initial capital investment

---

[1] Standard financial management texts review basic valuation techniques. Key components of the method are assessment of future cash flow expectations and the discount rate. This rate captures comparability with other investments with respect to risk. In other words, investment or project risk is reflected in the discount rate.

requirement is $45 million, the net present value of the opportunity for domestic expansion is $3.8 million.

Now proceed to consider the foreign investment possibilities for enhancement of value and return as described in Tables 17–2 through 17–5. The progression of examples represents increasing levels of commitment to and connection with foreign environments.

The first foreign investment opportunity, demonstrated in Table 17–2, is the opportunity to enter a foreign market and to supply that market through domestic production. This opportunity may have arisen either through some actual change in the business environment or simply through a change in management's perception of either the business or the environment.

As described in Table 17–2, the value of expected performance on entry into the foreign market is $36.4 million. This is the amount by which the value of profits from investment in expansion into foreign markets, $81.4 million, exceeds the initial investment requirement of $45 million.[2]

For our purposes, however, the important aspect of the investment is the amount by which its value exceeds the value of

---

[2] In these examples, the standard methods of valuing international investments are used. These methods are described in Alan C. Shapiro, *Multinational Financial Management* (Boston: Allyn & Bacon, 1986); and Maurice Levy *International Finance: Financial Management and the International Economy* (New York: McGraw-Hill, 1983). There are two key aspects of international investment analysis. First is that the cash flows to be valued are domestic currency equivalents of foreign cash flow expectations. The second is that the discount rate is to be adjusted from the discount rate appropriate for comparable domestic investments in risk.

While this risk adjustment is still controversial, there are basically two offsetting arguments with regard to the direction of the adjustment. To the extent that foreign currency investments increase the risk to the investor's portfolio, the investment must command a greater risk premium and discount rate than the domestic investment. For example, foreign exchange risk may require a risk premium relative to a comparable domestic investment. However, modern portfolio theory teaches that only those risks which are not diversifiable within a domestic portfolio effectively increase risk.

To offset added risk, if international investment activity diversifies an investor's portfolio, that investment effectively reduces the portfolio's risk. In this case, the applicable discount rate should be *lower* rather than higher for the international investment.

In my judgment, given the controversy and the likelihood that each effect is, in itself, small and offsetting, the same discount rate can be used for investments in international marketing and manufacturing as for otherwise similar domestic marketing and manufacturing investment.

investment in domestic expansion. That excess or difference is the value of access to the foreign market.

The incremental value of expanding into foreign markets compared with domestic expansion is the net foreign investment value of $36.4 million less the net domestic investment value of $3.8 million, or $32.6 million. This increment is the difference between the stand-alone values of the domestic expansion and foreign market expansion investments. It is also the net incremental value of access to a foreign market relatively more attractive than the domestic market. For incremental value of $32.6 million, this corresponds to the difference between the dollar equivalent of value of revenue from the foreign market ($688.5 million), and the value of domestic market revenue ($625.9 million), adjusted for the difference in taxes ($75.1 million less $45.1 million).

The source of the after-tax revenue differential is the difference between the domestic currency equivalent of revenues from foreign sales in Table 17–2 and revenues for the strictly domestic investment. As shown in Table 17–2, the annual revenues from the foreign market participation are forecast at $110 million, an increment of 10 percent above the $100 million forecast for expansion in the domestic market.

In economic terms, prices in the foreign market are relatively high, or the foreign currency is overvalued relative to the domestic currency and to prices in the two markets. Because production for both investments is sourced domestically, costs are not affected by the currency misvaluation. Thus, gross margins for the entry into the foreign market exceed domestic gross margins by 30 percent and net income exceeds domestic net income by 70 percent.

This same 70 percent excess of foreign over domestic net income is directly reflected in the relative values of the profits. The value of foreign profits exceeds the value of domestic profits by 70 percent, or $81.4 million.

In other words, foreign currency overvaluation translates directly into excess profits and value for the type of foreign market participation illustrated in this example. Companies which source foreign sales from domestic markets can benefit substantially when the foreign currency is or becomes overvalued relative to the domestic currency and foreign and domestic prices. The valuation model translates the effects of currency valuation on relative prices, margins, and incomes, into assessments of investment values.

Finally, comparing the values of various investment opportunities reveals the values of underlying differences in the investments. In this case, the comparison is used to isolate the uniquely and distinctively foreign investment characteristics and to measure the potential value those differences represent.

The magnitude of this effect of price and currency valuation on the value of participation in foreign markets is further illustrated by the example in Table 17–3. The opportunity illustrated here is

TABLE 17–3

Investment Forecast and Analysis (Foreign Investment Opportunities: Access to Foreign Markets—20 Percent Effective Price Premium)

		Functional Currency	Exchange Rate (FC/$)	Equivalent
Profitability and income				
Revenue	FC	480.0	4.0	$120.0
Cost of goods sold		280.0	4.0	70.0
Gross margin		200.0	4.0	50.0
Operating expenses		40.0	4.0	10.0
Other expenses		20.0	4.0	5.0
Net income before tax		140.0	4.0	35.0
Tax expense		67.2	4.0	16.8
Net income	FC	72.8	4.0	$ 18.2
Initial investment required				$ 45.0
Measures of performance				
Total costs—excluding tax	FC	340.0		$ 85.0
Gross margin (%)				41.7%
Net margin—before tax (%)				29.2
Net margin—after tax (%)				15.2
Return on investment—before tax				77.8
Return on investment—after tax				40.4
Investment value				
Value of revenue				$751.1
Value of costs—including tax				637.2
Value of costs—excluding tax				532.0
Value of tax expense				105.2
Value of profits—before tax				219.1
Value of profits—after tax				113.9
Net investment value				$ 68.9

structurally identical to that illustrated in Table 17–2, but the magnitudes differ. Here, the configuration of domestic and foreign prices and currency valuation translates into foreign prices exceeding domestic prices on a common-currency basis by 20 percent. For purposes of illustration, assume that this investment represents the potential for entry into another and even more attractive foreign market.

In this second foreign market, gross margins exceed domestic gross margins by 20 percent or the equivalent of $20 million, and income exceeds domestic income by 130 percent or $10.4 million. As a result, the stand-alone value of the foreign investment is $68.9 million, an excess of $65.1 million over the domestic investment. This value also reflects an excess of $32.5 million over the investment in expansion into the foreign market with the 10 percent price and revenue premium.

This example is useful for two reasons. First, the exercise illustrates the method by which expectations about currency valuation and relative prices are reflected in investment analysis. It should be clear from these examples that distinctively international factors, such as currency valuation and attractive foreign markets, can be assessed and valued as increments to the traditional investment valuation process. In fact, incremental valuation forces the analysis to focus on the underlying, structural, and strategic elements of the differences between the domestic and foreign investments.

Second, comparison of the second and third examples demonstrates the effects of changes in the underlying strategic advantages on the relative values of the investments. In simple, and perhaps overly stark terms, the comparative example demonstrates both possible magnitudes of the sensitivity of investment value to changes in foreign factors and a powerful method for studying and forecasting that sensitivity. In the example, the $32.5 million difference between the net investment value at a 20 percent market premium and the net investment value of $36.4 million at a 10 percent market premium is the sensitivity of the performance and value of the investment to a change in the foreign price premium.

Tables 17–4 and 17–5 illustrate the effects and methods of valuing another form of foreign investment advantage—low-cost sourcing. In these examples, investment opportunities are pre-

TABLE 17–4

Investment Forecast and Analysis (Foreign Investment Opportunities: Access to Foreign Markets—10 Percent Effective Price Premium; 3.5 Percent Total Effective Cost Reduction)

		Functional Currency	Exchange Rate (FC/$)	Equivalent
Profitability and income				
Revenue	FC	440.0	4.0	$110.0
Cost of goods sold		280.0	4.0	70.0
Gross margin		160.0	4.0	40.0
Operating expenses		32.0	4.0	8.0
Other expenses		16.0	4.0	4.0
Net income before tax		112.0	4.0	28.0
Tax expense		53.7	4.0	13.4
Net income	FC	58.2	4.0	$ 14.6
Initial investment required				$ 45.0
Measures of performance				
Total costs—excluding tax	FC	328.0		$ 82.0
Gross margin (%)				36.4%
Net margin—before tax (%)				25.5
Net margin—after tax (%)				13.3
Return on investment—before tax				62.2
Return on investment—after tax				32.4
Investment value				
Value of revenue				$688.5
Value of costs—including tax				597.4
Value of costs—excluding tax				513.3
Value of tax expense				84.1
Value of profits—before tax				175.3
Value of profits—after tax				91.1
Net investment value				$ 46.1

sumed to offer not only access to attractive foreign markets but also the possibility of sourcing at the foreign location.

The examples illustrated in these tables assume that costs of foreign sourcing undercut costs of domestic sourcing. At the same time, prices and revenues reflect access to relatively attractive foreign markets. Thus, these investments represent opportunities to sell into and source from foreign locations. On the market side, Table 17–4 is directly comparable to Table 17–2, with foreign prices and revenues exceeding domestic prices and revenues by 10

TABLE 17–5

Investment Forecast and Analysis (Foreign Investment Opportunities: Access to Foreign Markets—20 Percent Effective Price Premium; 3.5 Percent Total Effective Cost Reduction)

		Functional Currency	Exchange Rate (FC/$)	Equivalent
Profitability and income				
Revenue	FC	480.0	4.0	$120.0
Cost of goods sold		280.0	4.0	70.0
Gross margin		200.0	4.0	50.0
Operating expenses		32.0	4.0	8.0
Other expenses		16.0	4.0	4.0
Net income before tax		152.0	4.0	38.0
Tax expense		73.0	4.0	18.2
Net income	FC	79.0	4.0	$ 19.8
Initial investment required				$ 45.0
Measures of performance				
Total costs—excluding tax	FC	328.0		$ 82.0
Gross margin (%)				41.7%
Net margin—before tax (%)				31.7
Net margin—after tax (%)				16.5
Return on investment—before tax				84.4
Return on investment—after tax				43.9
Investment value				
Value of revenue				$751.1
Value of costs—including tax				627.4
Value of costs—excluding tax				513.3
Value of tax expense				114.2
Value of profits—before tax				237.9
Value of profits—after tax				123.7
Net investment value				$ 78.7

percent. Table 17–5 compares to Table 17–3 with foreign revenue enhancement of 20 percent.

In both of these examples, there are two cost categories—production inputs and operating and other expenses. In the examples, the domestic equivalents of these two cost categories are independent of each other. Specifically, direct costs of foreign production conform to the costs of domestic production. As a result, the common-currency equivalents of direct production costs are identical at $70 million for both the foreign and domestic production expansions.

In contrast to the neutrality of production costs, operating and other expenses for production in the foreign location are relatively low. They are forecast at FC 32 and FC 16 million respectively, so that the domestic currency equivalents undercut domestic operating and other expenses, at forecast exchange rates, by 20 percent.

Even though the assumptions about the relative behaviors of foreign costs are arbitrary, they are likely to reflect reality in one important respect. That is that a share of production costs, often a substantial share, is pegged to world cost levels. For these inputs and costs, speculation and arbitrage of the production inputs is so complete, and the process by which the commodities are traded and priced is so efficient, that common-currency costs are the same regardless of the production location.

The examples assume that all costs of production fall into this category of world-traded goods. However, operating and other expenses do not. In these examples, differences between foreign and domestic operating and other expenses generate a relative advantage for foreign location of production.

As shown earlier, standard valuation methods are powerful tools for assessing the extent to which these opportunities for foreign sourcing enhance the total value of the investments. The value of the investment described in Table 17–4, which is directly comparable to Table 17–2, is $46.1. This exceeds the value of investment from Table 17–2 ($36.4 million) by $9.7 million. The source of the added value is capitalization of the $3 million annual, pretax cost differential, less capitalization of the $1.4 million difference in annual tax expense.

Table 17–5 expands the analysis beyond the case of low-cost foreign production and 10 percent market premium to a market premium of 20 percent. In this final example, net investment value rises to $78.7 million, an increment of $74.9 million over the domestic investment and an increment of $32.6 million over the foreign manufacturing investment with a 10 percent market premium. Of course, the value added by the higher market premium in this case, is identical to the increment between investment 2 and investment 3.

Thus, comparison of Tables 17–4 and 17–5 to Tables 17–2 and 17–3 yields a measure of the incremental value of the foreign production opportunity. Comparison of Tables 17–2 and 17–3 to Table 17–1, the base case domestic investment, demonstrates the value of access to the foreign market under two different assumptions regarding relative prices and revenues.

Finally, the approach to valuing foreign investment opportunities, whether these reflect underlying advantages of access to attractive markets or to low-cost sources of supply or both, is effectively an incremental approach. By considering foreign opportunities either as increments to or substitutes for domestic expansion opportunities, we focus the analysis on the distinctly international or foreign aspects of the investment. As we later show, the framework that measures and values the international investment as an incremental marketing or manufacturing opportunity is also useful as a tool for managing the risk of global investments.

SOURCES OF VALUE IN GLOBAL BUSINESS INVESTMENTS

The preceding examples illustrate the concepts discussed in the first several sections of this chapter. That is, foreign investments are distinguished from domestic by many factors. The net effects of these distinguishing elements are differences in translated wages and prices, and the incremental values offered by global investment are simply the capitalized values of wage and price differentials.

It is clear from the examples that the net value added by the distinctively different foreign elements can be further decomposed into two major categories. The first is the extent of wage and price deviation, or the magnitude of the effects of the market or production advantages. The second is the relative importance of each category of divergence in the total investment structure. In the examples, differences between market premiums of 10 percent and 20 percent were valued to illustrate the effects and measurement of magnitude differences. As the differences in magnitudes were relatively large and the margins on the investment were sizable, the total effects of the added premium was also large. In sum, increasing from a 10 percent premium over the domestic market to a 20 percent premium induced an increase in value of $32.5 million. (The investment opportunities and the implied premium over domestic investment values are summarized in Table 17–6.)

The second factor determining the extent of foreign value enhancement is the relative share of the divergent price or cost component in the total investment. This factor was illustrated in the differences between the investments which relied on domestic and foreign production. The foreign production opportunity resulted in a premium of $9.7 million.

The source of the premium was the lower cost of operating and other expenses in the foreign production operation. Costs of goods sold were maintained, for both production opportunities, at world price levels. Thus, the foreign production advantage came from other cost categories. The important point is that the divergent cost categories amounted to nearly 15 percent of total costs. This proportion, together with the amount of divergence, 20 percent, determined the net advantage. Clearly, the net foreign advantage would have been increased substantially if the proportions were reversed so that 85 percent of costs, rather than 15 percent, enjoyed a 20 percent advantage.

GLOBAL INVESTMENT OPPORTUNITIES: IDENTIFYING STRATEGIC COMPONENTS

In addition to actual valuation analysis, for purposes of supporting investment commitment decisions, the analysis demonstrated earlier can be used to explore the strategic nature of foreign investment. This use of the approach simply requires organization of the analysis to emphasize the incremental nature of the investment components. A sample reorganization of the analyses is presented in Table 17–6.

Table 17–6 displays analytical valuation results for each investment as increments to the domestic investment alternative. With this incremental approach, the uniquely foreign strategic components of the various investments are emphasized and valued.

TABLE 17–6
Incremental Value Enhancement—Premium over Domestic Investment

	Foreign Market Domestic Market and Production (Table 17-1)	Foreign Market Expansion- 10% Market Premium (Table 17-2)	Foreign Expansion- 20% Market Premium (Table 17-3)	Foreign Production 10% Market Premium (Table 17-4)	Production 20% Market Premium (Table 17-5)
Revenue	$100.0	$10.0	$ 20.0	$10.0	$ 20.0
Non-tax costs and expenses	85.0	0.0	0.0	(3.0)	(3.0)
Tax expense	7.2	4.8	9.6	6.2	11.0
Net Income	7.8	5.2	10.4	6.8	12.0
Return on investment—before tax	33.3%	22.3%	44.5%	28.9%	51.1%
Return on investment—after tax	17.3%	11.6%	23.1%	15.1%	26.6%
Value of revenue	625.9	62.6	125.2	62.6	125.2
Value of costs—excluding tax	532.0	0.0	0.0	(18.7)	(18.7)
Value of tax expense	45.1	30.0	60.1	39.0	69.1
Value of profits—after tax	48.8	32.6	65.1	42.3	78.8
Net Investment Value	$3.8	$32.6	$65.1	$42.3	$74.9

For example, investment 2 offers foreign market expansion worth an increment of $32.6 million. Investment 3 offers market expansion worth an incremental $65.1 million. Comparison of the various valuation categories highlights the revenue streams as the sources of the added value.

Investments 4 and 5 add $42.3 million and $74.9 million, respectively, to the domestic investment option. Consideration of the valuation components shows that the source of the added value is a combination of low-cost production and attractive foreign market possibilities. Comparison among the components shows the share of the added value which is supplied by each of the investment components. For Investment 4, $32.6 million is due to the attractive foreign market and $9.7 million is due to low-cost foreign production.

Finally, while the examples are evaluated on the assumption that the price and cost advantages of the foreign investments persist indefinitely, such persistent advantage is unrealistic. Moves to further expansion, either by one's own corporation or by competitors is sure to drive away the advantage eventually.

Therefore, a final and major consideration that must be added to the valuation and measurement analysis is the duration of the advantage. Clearly, the more persistent the advantage is expected to be, the greater the net effect of the incremental value of the foreign project. The less persistent the advantage, the less substantial is the added value.

MANAGING GLOBAL INVESTMENT COMMITMENTS

The preceding analysis is useful not only for purposes of investment valuation but also as a powerful tool of investment performance evaluation. In this capacity, the numerical frameworks should be seen as performance benchmarks.

The groundwork for this discussion was laid in earlier sections when the differences between Tables 17–2 and 17–3 were shown through sensitivity analysis as well as a comparison of two distinct investments. There the value differential was seen as the change in the value of the investment in the event that the foreign-market premium increased from 10 percent to 20 percent. Such an increase in premium could be due to foreign consumers' incomes or to changes in foreign-exchange rates which were not offset by changes in either foreign or domestic prices and revenues.

The same concept of sensitivity is applicable to the other examples. For instance, the foreign market and foreign production advantages of investment 3, will decline to a net advantage equivalent to investment 2, if foreign production costs move toward world levels. Thus, the difference between Tables 17–2 and 17–3 represents the sensitivity of investment 3 to the tendency of foreign costs to return to world levels.

FOCUSING ON THE INTERNATIONAL FACTOR

The analysis for global business investment and management recommended and described in this chapter utilizes the power of an incremental approach. The approach depends on the following three factors for distinguishing foreign from domestic investment opportunities and for determining the size of the foreign advantage:

The uniquely foreign aspects of particular investment opportunities are identified by comparing that investment to a similar domestic investment.

The many and varied differences in the investments are captured in differences between current and future expected costs and prices, in domestic currency, and the translated equivalents, in domestic currency, of foreign prices and costs.

The net foreign investment advantage depends on the magnitude of differences in prices and costs, the persistence or duration of such differences and the relative importance to the investment of the market or production components affected by the differences.

Combining measures of these factors, through the approach described in this chapter yields both measures of investment value and benchmarks for evaluation of subsequent performance. Of course, the measure of value should be compared to investment cost to determine the feasibility of committing corporate resources to the project.

The benchmark analysis can be applied after the commitment to the investment is complete. With the benchmark, the effects of changes in foreign economic conditions on the value and performance of the investment can be monitored and evaluated. Finally, the analytical framework, and the understanding of the strategic components it implies, can be a powerful initial analysis in the development of hedging strategy.

REFERENCES

Aliber, Robert Z. *Exchange Risk and Corporate International Finance.* New York and London: Macmillan, 1978.

Hekman, Christine R. "Evaluation of Risk in International Portfolios." *The Handbook of International Investing,* ed., Carl Beidleman. Chicago: Probus Publishing, 1987.

_____. "Don't Blame Currency Values for Strategic Errors: Protecting Competitive Position by Correctly Assessing Foreign Exchange Exposure." *Midland Corporate Finance Journal* 4,3 (Fall 1986), pp. 45–55.

_____. "Measuring Foreign Exchange Exposure: A Practical Theory and Its Application." *Financial Analysts Journal,* September–October 1983, pp. 59–65.

Levi, Maurice. *International Finance: Financial Management and the International Economy.* New York: McGraw-Hill, 1983.

Shapiro, Alan C. *Multinational Financial Management.* Boston: Allyn & Bacon, 1986.

Stern, Joel M., and Donald H. Chew, Jr. *New Developments in International Finance.* New York: Basil Blackwell, 1988.

CHAPTER 18

FOREIGN-TRADE FINANCE

Geoffrey E. Wood

The methods by which firms finance their international transactions have only recently been studied. Just a few years ago, the complexity of the financial decisions associated with trading overseas was little understood, except by individual skilled practitioners. The descriptions given by economists and other students of business practice were crude, based on assertion rather than analysis or examination of the facts.

This chapter starts by setting out what this "received wisdom" was. It proceeds to display some analysis which casts doubt on the universal validity of that wisdom. That, in turn, leads to discussion of what is done and examination of what can be done and why it is useful to do it.

TRADITIONAL BELIEFS

Although in the past economists had often written about the forward-exchange market, they actually paid little attention to the users of it. They were much concerned with what they imagined to be more important matters, such as its influence on monetary policy. When it came to foreign trade, they naively assumed the traders made use of "vehicle currencies."

By this was meant that all—or at any rate most—international trade was invoiced in one or two actively traded currencies. The reason for this, it was asserted, was that such currencies could readily be converted to whatever currency the firm actually wished to hold, with no problems of lack of marketability or large buy-sell spreads. These currencies were called vehicles because they carried, so to speak, transactions between firms in countries neither of which necessarily used the vehicle as a home currency. They were the currencies of a third country, one irrelevant to the parties in the transaction except insofar as the currency of that third country was very marketable.

Now, the marketability of a currency is obviously important. But regarding it as the dominating feature in the trade-financing decision is surely extreme. This suspicion prompted Sven Grassman, in 1973, to examine a detailed sample of Swedish foreign trade.[1] His results were quite inconsistent with the previously accepted view.

GRASSMAN'S FINDINGS

Grassman found that, by and large, exports were invoiced in the exporter's currency. That is, Swedish exports were invoiced in the Swedish krona; exports to Sweden from other countries were invoiced in the home currency of the exporter. For example, exports from South Africa to Sweden were invoiced in the South African rand.

There were, however, some important exceptions to this general rule. Exports to, as well as imports from, the United Kingdom and the United States were invoiced predominantly in British pounds or U.S. dollars. The currency of the trading partner was, for all practical purposes, used not at all in trade with Eastern Europe and the less developed countries (LDCs). Fuel was invoiced primarily in British pounds.

Grassman reported these findings but did not devote much time to analysis of them. Discussion of why this pattern emerged, and the possibilities open to foreign traders, had to await other

---

[1] S. Grassman, *Exchange Reserves and the Financial Structure of Foreign Trade* (London: Saxon House, 1973).

studies. What Grassman really did was to prompt people to think about a previously generally accepted belief.

An initial reaction was, of course, that Sweden was, in some way usually left unspecified, "different." Nevertheless, other studies were carried out—by Magee; Grassman again; Brittan; Page; the U.K. Department of Trade; Carse, Williamson, and Wood; and subsequent to that, by other authors following up these studies.[2] All of these found results not identical to those Grassman had found for Sweden, but certainly sufficiently close to them, and sufficiently far from the traditional view, to prompt detailed analysis of the foreign-trade financing decision.

It is useful now to set out this analysis, as it highlights the issues any treasurer has to consider when deciding on foreign-trade financing. That leads to an examination of what is usually done and a brief discussion of the advice sometimes given by "professional" advisers. (The reason for the quotation marks envisages later in the chapter.) That, in turn, prepares the way for concluding remarks.

BACKGROUND DESCRIPTION OF TRADE-FINANCING PROCEDURES

It is useful to set out the stages of a transaction, both "real"—in the sense of being concerned with the behavior of the goods (or services)—and financial. This is because we can then expose the principles in the financing decision. As the actual financial instruments that can be used are continually evolving, an understanding of the principles is essential so that we can make the right choices from the continually evolving menu.

The time profile of a typical foreign-trade transaction is

---

[2] S. P. Magee, "U.S. Import Prices in the Currency-Contract Period," *Brookings Papers on Economic Activity*, no. 1, 1974; S. Grassman, "Currency Distribution and Forward Cover in Foreign Trade: Sweden Revisited, 1973," *Journal of International Economics*, May 1976, pp. 151–63; S. Brittan, "Trade Figures May Be Wrong," *Financial Times*, 21 February 1977; S. A. B. Page, "Currency Invoicing in Merchandise Trade," *National Institute of Economics Review*, August 1974, pp. 25–37; United Kingdom, Department of Trade, *Trade and Industry*, 5 May 1978; and S. Carse, J. Williamson, and G. E. Wood, *The Financing Procedures of British Foreign Trade* (Cambridge: Cambridge University Press, 1980).

displayed in Figure 18–1. The real events shown in the top portion of the figure normally occur in the sequence shown, although even this statement requires qualification: t_P may precede t_I and even t_E, in exceptional cases where the importer takes delivery of the shipment unusually early, before it arrives in the importer's country. The process always starts with an order placed at a time t_O; typically this is also the time at which the contract is signed, although sometimes a number of orders may be placed under a single contract. At some subsequent time t_E the goods are delivered by the exporter to the port and are registered with the customs of the exporting country. After a delay that may vary from a few minutes in the case of countries with a common frontier to several months where a long sea voyage is involved, the goods are registered by the customs of the importing country at a time t_I. The importer takes delivery of the goods at a time t_D, typically though by no means invariably after a further brief delay. Trade statistics compiled on the customary transactions basis relate to the trade transactions registered by the customs authorities on the dates t_E and t_I.)

The financial events shown in the bottom portion of Figure 18–1 can vary even more than the real events of the top portion. The contract, which is normally signed when the order is placed at t_O, includes provisions governing the financial side of the transaction. These may be divided into (1) specification of the sum that is to be paid, expressed in a particular currency (the invoice currency); and (2) stipulation of a method to determine the date (t_B) on

FIGURE 18–1
Time Profile of a Foreign Trade Transaction

Real Events			
Order placed t_O	→ Date of exportation t_E	→ Date of importation t_I	→ Date of delivery t_O
Financial Events			
Order placed t_O	→ Purchase of forward cover t_F	→ Start of term of payment t_A	→ Payment occurs t_P → Payment due t_B

on or by which payment should be made. The latter can be subdivided into (1) choice of method of settlement (also known as a form of payment or form of contract), that is, the legal form to be used in acknowledging the financial obligations of the buyer; and (2) choice of a term of payment which is the period from the time (t_A) when the exporter demands payment by dispatching an invoice, presenting documents, or requiring acceptance, up to t_B. The contract does not govern the fourth topic which is of interest, namely, whether cover is sought in the forward market; whether to seek such cover is a unilateral decision faced by a party with an exposed foreign-exchange position. Presumably a firm taking out forward cover normally does so at a time t_F shortly after the order is placed. However, there certainly exist circumstances under which t_F might occur later, even after the start of the term of payment t_A—notably if exchange rates, or the firm's expectations thereof, change after t_O in a way that alters the balance of advantage perceived by the firm between holding an open or a covered position.

Methods of settlement take a wide variety of legal forms. It is convenient to group these into three economic categories, depending on whether they allow the buyer a period of credit and, if so, whether or not this period is flexible.

No Credit

Under a typical contract of this type, the buyer has to pay for the goods as soon as they are ready for delivery and cannot take possession until doing so. In this case t_D, t_A, t_P (the date when payment is actually made and received—we ignore any minor discrepancy between the two), and t_B are coincident, as shown in Figure 18–2 (with the date of delivery t_D added, for the case of a typical contract of this type).

FIGURE 18–2
Financial Events in a Foreign Trade Transaction

$$t_o \qquad (t_p) \qquad t_D = t_A = t_P = t_B$$

The legal forms of contract that fall in this category are cash on delivery, cash against documents, payment of bills against documents, sight documentary credits, and payment in advance. In the last case—which seems to be very rare in practice—t_B and t_P occur before t_D. It is far more common for the buyer to be allowed a few days' grace to check the shipment for quality, which means that t_B and t_P occur slightly after t_D and t_A.

Fixed Credit

Contracts involving a fixed period of credit given to the buyer fall into two main categories: those settled by a single payment and those involving a series of installment payments.

The legal forms of payment with a fixed period of credit and a single payment are the acceptance bill, the term bill, and time documentary credits. Under the first of these, for example, the exporter draws a bill with a fixed term (and expressed in the same currency as the invoice) on the importer. This is delivered at the same time as the goods, which the importer is allowed to receive only if accepting the bill; this implies a guarantee to pay the bill's holder when the bill matures. The exporter may then hold this bill or sell it, for example, to a bank, in which case to receive payment (less some discount) before the buyer pays. The bank, rather than the exporter, would then be providing the credit to the importer—although the exporter would continue to bear the risk of the importer defaulting. Or, the exporter could seek cover from the Export Credits Guarantee Department (ECGD) in the United Kingdom or a foreign equivalent such as the EXIM Bank in the United States. In the typical case just described, t_D and t_A are coincident and are followed after a fixed length of time by t_P and t_B, which are also coincident: this typical sequence is illustrated in Figure 18–3. In some cases, however, the start of the term of payment may be measured from the date of invoice or dispatch of

FIGURE 18–3
Sequence of Events for Imports

$$t_O \quad (t_P) \qquad t_D = t_A \qquad t_P = t_B$$

documentation rather than on sight or acceptance of a bill or documentation, in which case t_A would precede t_D.

Contracts involving installment payments normally require an advance payment for a portion of the cost prior to dispatch of the goods at t_E, followed by a series of payments (often also made with bills) after receipt of the goods at t_D. This method is commonly used for payments for capital goods.

Variable Credit

A typical example of a contract involving flexibility of the period of credit is the sale on open account. At some date t_A (which is normally close to t_E) the seller sends an invoice specifying the date t_B (which normally falls after t_D) by which payment is due. The buyer is given freedom to settle within that period, although a discount may be offered for early or prompt payment. Thus t_P normally precedes t_B, as shown in Figure 18–4. However, due to the lack of formal documentation the seller would find it difficult to invoke legal sanctions against a purchaser who delayed payment for a limited period beyond the due date, so that t_P can in practice follow t_B on occasion. Because of the weakness of the sanctions available against a purchaser who postpones payment, open account is a technique that should be used only in transactions involving trading partners between whom there is a good deal of trust. On the other hand, it is administratively the simplest procedure, so that one would certainly find it employed where the necessary trust exists and there are no countervailing disadvantages.

A procedure sometimes employed when two firms have frequent transactions is for the account to be settled at regular intervals, for example, on the last day of each month. Another practice sometimes regarded as a variant of open account is

FIGURE 18–4
Period of Credit Definitions

$$t_O \quad (t_P) \quad t_A \quad t_D \quad t_P \quad t_B$$

consignment, where an importer agrees to make payment when, but only when, selling a shipment. This certainly results in a credit term that is variable from the standpoint of the exporter, but it is not clear that it provides the same scope as does the typical form of open account.

It is useful at this point to define more precisely what is meant by the "period of credit," for it is, in fact, a highly ambiguous concept.

1. The "term of payment" is the period of time stipulated in the contract; for example, "30 days on open account" or "60-day bills." It is the time allowed to the importer, measured from the date t_A when payment is first demanded. This concept is represented by $(t_B - t_A)$ in Figure 18–4.

2. The "credit term" is the realized version of concept A. It is the period from the start of the term of payment to the date when payment is actually received, or $(t_P - t_A)$.

3. The "credit term" is a revised concept. One criticism of the preceding concepts is that they measure the start of the period of credit by an event that is to some extent arbitrary—the date of invoice, documentation, or acceptance. In particular, the date when the invoice for an open account transaction is dispatched is not in itself of any significance. Consider an exporter selling goods with a normal transit time of 30 days; whether invoices are sent out at t_E with a 60-day term of payment, or 20 days later with a 40-day term, is inconsequential, but concepts 1 and 2 would both register a longer period of credit in the former case. To correct for this, it is natural to replace t_A by t_D, the date of delivery. We have made this change to concept 2 to get concept 3, but have not made a similar revision to concept 1, mainly because the use of concept 1 is traditional. (It would be simple to calculate a similar revised concept of the term of payment by subtracting the excess of 2 over 3 from 1, should it appear useful.) The revised concept of the credit term is $(t_P - t_D)$.

4. The "credit period" is Grassman's term for the period that elapses between the time the goods are registered by

customs and the date that payment is made or received.[3] For exports this is $(t_P - t_E)$, and for imports it is $(t_P - t_I)$. Credit periods for exports tend to exceed those for imports, because of the time $(t_I - t_E)$ taken in transit. (From the point of view of statisticians and occasionally analysts of balance-of-payments markets, one important reason for being interested in credit periods is that their variations lead to deviations between measuring trade balances on a transactions basis or on a payments basis.)

In addition to these four concepts of the period of credit, one can identify the time between the order date t_O and the date payment is made t_P. This provides a measure of the total period of time during which traders could have been exposed to exchange risk, as well as illuminating the minimum possible period within which the trade balance can be expected to respond positively to an exchange-rate change. We call this the contract period.

One other element of a firm's environment influencing its trade-financing practices consists of the exchange control regulations to which it is subject. In the United Kingdom for example, these were quite strict until 1979. In general, U.K. exporters were required to convert any foreign currency they received into sterling immediately. The only exception concerned firms that received exchange control permission to open a foreign currency (or "hold") account, which could be granted where a firm had sufficiently regular export/import business. Up to 10,000 such accounts were approved (with some firms maintaining more than one account, in more than one currency). Firms with such accounts were generally authorized to credit certain classes of foreign currency receipts to their accounts, but obliged once a month to sell to a bank for sterling any excess of their balances over known payments due during the following month. In addition to the rule requiring immediate conversion of foreign currency receipt into sterling, U.K. exporters were limited to granting export credit for a maximum period of six months, unless a longer period was specifically approved by the Bank of England or the

---

[3] Grassman, *Exchange Reserves*.

contract was insured by ECGD. Exporters could sell their expected receipts forward immediately after they fixed the date that a foreign-currency payment would fall due.

A U.K. importer who had to pay a supplier in foreign currency could buy that currency only when about to make the payment. There is again, of course, the limited exception that applied to those firms authorized to maintain hold accounts. Importers could take forward cover as long in advance of an expected payment as they wished and up to six months beyond the expected date of importing the goods. They were not restricted as to the length of export credit that they accepted, but only with the specific permission of the Bank of England could they pay for any import in advance of its shipment to the United Kingdom. Such permission was normally given only for certain imports of raw materials and capital goods.

These regulations allowed very little scope for U.K. residents to vary the timing of purchases or sales of foreign currency relative to the date of payment or receipt. Holders of foreign-currency accounts had some flexibility in this direction, by running down the end-month balances below the permitted maximums and by varying the proportions of their receipts and payments passed through the accounts within the month, but the total potential effects of such operations were believed to be of fairly modest size.

The exchange control regulations applied to all firms legally resident in the United Kingdom—including the local branches of foreign-owned multinationals. It is important to understand the regulations when trading with a country subject to exchange controls. They can very substantially affect decisions with regard to the financial aspect of the transactions.

Incentives

As noted earlier, the four degrees of freedom in the financial side of trade transaction are choice of the invoice currency, whether to seek forward cover, the method of settlement, and the length of credit to be allowed and the proportion of it to be taken up.

It is useful to start by analyzing trade between independent firms, that is, excluding trade between branches of the same multinational corporations (MNC); it is assumed that both trading partners are located in countries with a convertible currency. We start from the premise that firms engaged in foreign trade seek certainty in their domestic currency. One should, as a first approximation, expect trade-financing practices to differ radically between two categories of goods, labeled "tradables 1" and "tradables 2." The first comprises products with some degree of product differentiation whose price is set by their producers, while the second group consists of those goods whose prices are determined by demand and supply on worldwide markets. Cars are a typical example of tradables 1 and wheat of tradables 2. More generally, the distinction is very close to that between manufactures and primary products.

A producer of tradables 1 has costs that are largely specified in the domestic currency. Hence the producer can reduce the risks by setting a price in the domestic currency and allowing inventories rather than price to vary so as to clear the market in the short run. To fix price in the domestic currency, the producer has to invoice exports in that currency, which of course throws the burden of exchange-rate risk onto the importer. There are two main ways in which the importer may be able to reduce this risk: by gaining some freedom to choose the timing of the payment and by covering the position in the forward market. Where the exporter has sufficient confidence in the trading partner, one would expect the exporter to be willing to give the partner the advantage of buying on open account, with the associated freedom to select the time when payment will be made, rather than tying the importer down by a formal contract to make payment on a specified date. (One would also expect to find considerable forward covering in this type of trade.) However, one should not necessarily expect all transactions to be covered (even partially) forward; first, because traders sometimes wish to hold open positions for essentially speculative reasons, and second, because transactions costs (buy/sell spreads) are slightly wider in the forward than in the spot market, so that the period for which the risk is borne may be too brief to make the extra expense worthwhile.

The situation is very different for tradables 2. Exporters are price takers who do not have the market power to fix domestic-currency prices, but simply have to accept the going international price in the currency in which the market operates. They have no particular incentive to invoice in their own currency, because (unlike the producer of tradables 1) the value of their inventories cannot be protected by an administered price. On the other hand, importers of tradables 2 have an interest in being invoiced in the same currency as other traders in the same product. They can offset "exchange risk" (the risk that the firm bears through having an open position in foreign exchange) by "price risk" (the risk that the price of the goods the firm has in inventory may change). For example, a 10 percent depreciation of sterling can be expected to raise the sterling price of wheat by about 11.1 percent; that is, to leave its dollar price unaffected, except to the surely second-order extent that the sterling depreciation alters the world balance between demand and supply. An importer who has already con-tracted to buy wheat at a fixed-dollar price, therefore, has the exchange risk neutralized by price risk and does not need forward cover.

Under these circumstances there are significant gains if trans-actions are invoiced in international money, or what is often referred to as a vehicle currency, and competitive pressures force exporters to offer such invoices. Where a commodity is traded on a central international market, like the Chicago wheat market or the London tea market, one might furthermore expect to find the vehicle currency used being the currency of the country where the market is located. As all the major commodity markets are located in either the United States or Britain, the vehicle currencies may be taken as the dollar and sterling.

However, where the vehicle currency is not the exporter's own currency, the exporter bears exchange risk by invoicing in the vehicle currency. Any exporter in this position has an incentive to avoid adding to this risk by allowing the importer to choose the exact timing of payment. Although less likely to give credit, when the exporter does, this is more likely to be through a formal instrument payable in a precisely specified number of days. This also aids the exporter in covering the position forward if so desired.

Consider now how these conclusions need to be modified in the case of trade between two branches of a MNC. The essential difference between the two cases is that, for the MNC as a whole, it does not matter which branch bears the exchange risk. Thus, one would not expect multinationals exporting tradables 1 to another branch of the same corporation to display the same anxiety to invoice in domestic currency as in the case of transactions between independent firms. On the other hand, the incentives for invoicing tradables 2 are unaffected, as the importer bears no ''net exchange risk'' (i.e., price risk offsets exchange risk) in any event.

When a multinational is trading internally, it does not matter (except perhaps for distortions caused by taxation) which branch of the firm bears the exchange risk. This fact does not mean that multinationals are indifferent to exchange-rate changes or never take forward cover. On the contrary, if they come to believe that one currency is going to depreciate relative to another, they have exactly the same incentive as any other agent to shift funds from the depreciating to the appreciating currency. What is special about the position of a MNC is not the incentives it faces but its ability to respond to those incentives, in particular by leading-and-lagging trade payments between branches in countries with currencies expected to depreciate and appreciate. Exchange control, unless it be draconian, cannot prevent the acceleration of a payment due to a branch in a strong-currency country by a branch in a weak-currency country, nor the retardation of payments in the opposite direction. The desire to maximize opportunities for profiting through leading-and-lagging is a factor, additional to administrative simplicity, and without the offsetting risk of bad faith by the partner, which would make one expect to find intra-MNC transactions settled on open account. Alternatively, if the forward rate does not reflect the spot rate that the MNC expects to see in the future (either because it takes a different view to other market operators or, no doubt more important, because of central bank support for the forward rate), it may be able to achieve the same objective by buying forward cover. This tends to be particularly attractive if the branches' respective liquidity positions make further variations in the timing of payment inconvenient. In times when no dramatic rate change is expected, however, a multinational trading internally would not be expected to take forward cover.

Consider finally in which ways the previous conclusions should be modified in the case of trade with a country having an inconvertible currency. The fact that it is inconvertible means there is no market in that currency abroad. An exporter selling to such a country could, therefore, not rely on being easily able to convert earnings in that currency into the home currency. Hence, the exporter will surely be invoiced in the home currency (for tradables 1) or in a vehicle currency (for tradables 2). Conversely, the fact that there is no market in such a currency accessible in their own country means that it would be inconvenient to firms that imported from such a country if their purchases were invoiced in the currency of the exporter. Imports from such countries, while following the normal rule in the case of tradables 2, would deviate from the normal pattern in the case of tradables 1; in order to compete, the exporter would be obliged to forgo the advantages of invoicing in the home currency. If the exporter's own currency is pegged to a vehicle currency, there would be some convenience to using that as the invoice currency; but, because that convenience gain would presumably be less than that normally gained by an exporter through invoicing in the home currency, one might expect to find invoicing in the importer's currency (which is the most attractive policy to the clients) more frequent.

The preceding discussion contains a series of specific conclusions. For convenience, we summarize them as follows:

Currency of Invoice

Conclusion 1: Tradables 1 exported to an independent firm from a country with a convertible currency are invoiced in the exporter's currency.

Conclusion 2: Tradables 2 are invoiced in a vehicle currency (dollars or sterling).

Conclusion 2A: The vehicle currency used for invoicing commodities traded on an international market is the currency of the country where the international market for the commodity in question is located.

Conclusion 3: Tradables 1 exported to another branch of the same MNC are less likely to be invoiced in the home currency of the exporter than are tradables 1 exports sold to an independent firm.

Conclusion 4:   Tradables 1 imported from countries with inconvertible currencies are invoiced in either sterling or dollars, with the sterling or dollars invoiced proportion being higher than in imports from countries with convertible currencies.

Use of the Forward Market

Conclusion 5:   Importers of tradables 1 invoiced in a foreign currency are more likely to cover forward than are importers of tradables 2 invoiced in a foreign country.

Conclusion 6:   Except when the central bank is supporting the forward rate, intra-MNC transactions are less likely to be covered forward than are transactions between independent firms.

Method of Settlement

Conclusion 7:   Sales on open account or similar terms, other than within an MNC, are more common (1) for transactions invoiced in the exporter's currency, and (2) the longer the two partners to the transactions have been trading with one another.

Conclusion 8:   All transactions between the branches of a MNC are settled on open account.

THE EVIDENCE

The preceding section has set out the choices available to a firm engaged in foreign trade and suggests what rational responses to these choices would be. As a confirmation of whether the preceding analysis is a useful guide, it is useful to look at the evidence on how firms actually behave.

It is helpful to go through the preceding conclusions in turn. The results are drawn largely from Carse, Williamson, and Wood.[4] This examination confirms whether the previous outline of the questions a firm engaged in foreign trade has to face is reasonably complete. The conclusions are considered in the order established earlier.

Conclusion 1

Our first conclusion is strongly supplied by the data. The exporter's currency is almost universally used in such transactions.

Conclusion 2

Concerning the use of a vehicle currency, conclusion 2 is the traditional hypothesis in this area. And curiously, although the evidence is consistent with it, the support is not all that strong. It does, however, become somewhat stronger when one looks exclusively at primary commodities. The conclusion must, however, inevitably be that the advantages of using a vehicle currency are rather modest and are readily outweighed by other factors.

Conclusion 2A

The evidence is that goods are invoiced in the currency of the market in which they are traded, but the sample which leads to this conclusion is so small that no statistical significance can be claimed for this result. Its main purpose is to help support the analytical discussion of the trade conclusion: multinationals make very restricted use of the forward market. (They do use it, which is of some surprise.)

Conclusion 7

This conclusion was in two parts: the first relates to use of open account when the exporter's currency is that of the invoice. The data support this strongly except for the United Kingdom. With

---

[4] Carse, Williamson, and Wood, *Financing Procedures*.

regard to the influence of the time companies have been trading with each other, this is indeed a significant determinant of the use of open account—which is the predominant method of settlement by the time firms have been trading with each other for more than two years. What is, perhaps, striking about this result is just how quickly open account is used—the direction of movement to it is as expected.

Conclusion 8

The conclusion that MNCs universally use open accounts was not supported, although there was a clear tendency to use flexible credit terms. Perhaps local branches of MNCs have some degree of self-interest.

The concludes our summary of the empirical work. By and large, it suggests that the analytical framework set out for reaching conclusions on the factors relevant to financial decisions in a company's foreign trade are reasonably complete. Before concluding by setting out the implications of these for the treasurer of such a company, a look at the advice of professional advisers is useful to place their role in perspective.

Professional Advisers

Firms sometimes approach banks to seek advice on foreign-trade financing. Regrettably, the advice given (on the basis of a survey reported in Carse, Williamson, and Wood) is not always optimal.[5] This is particularly important because generally inexperienced foreign traders went to banks for advice. The advice, although not optimal, was conservative and focused on avoiding circumstances where losses would show and being little concerned about losses which existed but did not show on the balance sheet, as compared to an available alternative.

U.K. banks appear generally to advise complete forward cover and the use of some formal settlement document, such as

---

[5] Carse, Williamson, and Wood, *Financing Procedures*, pp. 180–81.

bills of exchange. Open account should only be used with "long established partners or a large and well-known company."

Foreign banks in the United Kingdom were much less conservative; they sought to give optimizing advice, rather than cautious, risk-avoiding-at-all-costs advice. They expected their clients to be much more active in foreign-exchange management than did the British banks.

The rule seems to be: choose your advisers carefully.

PRACTICAL IMPLICATIONS

This chapter has laid out an analytical framework which can serve two purposes. It exposes the decisions that are inevitably involved, explicitly or not, in the financing of a foreign-trade transaction. And it gives guidance on the factors relevant to reaching these decisions. This chapter does not, it should be stressed, say precisely which instruments should be used—that is a continually evolving matter.

The first question foreign traders should consider is whether they and their trading partners are subject to any form of exchange controls. If the answer is "yes," then the trade financing decision is inevitably circumscribed, and in some circumstances determined, by these controls. In the absence of such controls, however, traders have a series of decisions to make.

The first is, do they wish to be exposed to foreign-exchange risk *with regard to the transaction?* (Note the emphasis—in the absence of exchange controls, such exposure can always be taken in the absence of trade.)

Suppose the answer is no. Then the exporter invoices in the home currency or covers the exposure—if the first course is ruled out—by competitive pressures, for example. The method of covering chosen should, of course, be the cheapest at the time.

The cover can include not only some financial transaction to offset the trade one but also, if the nature of the goods is suitable, the holding of an inventory roughly equal in value to the exposure.

An important influence on the decision is surely the view taken of the likely course of the exchange rate. This is important not only if the exporter has a clear expectation that the rate is going to change but also if he has not. The expectation that the rate will fluctuate quite unpredictably on some reasonably narrow band is consistent with not taking cover if one trades sufficiently regularly for the fluctuations to be offset.

This leads to the next matter, once foreign-exchange exposure has been decided. What method of settlement is to be used? Is it to be formal, giving little flexibility with the benefit of assured payment and the possible loss of competitive edge? Or is it to be informal—open account, for example—and thus requiring a high degree of trust? Factors such as knowledge of the market and of the trading partner, and of competitive conditions in the market, are relevant here.

Finally, a note of caution is in order. These financing decisions may seem peripheral to the main business of producing the goods and getting the orders. They are subsequent to these, but they are certainly not peripheral. Firms that had everything else right have gone into bankruptcy as a result of inadequate foreign-exchange exposure management. These decisions are far too important to be allowed to be reached by default.

REFERENCES

Brittan, S. "Trade Figures May Be Wrong." *Financial Times,* 21 February 1977.

Carse, S.; J. Williamson; and G. E. Wood. *The Financing Procedures of British Foreign Trade.* Cambridge: Cambridge University Press, 1980.

Grassman, S. *Exchange Reserves and the Financial Structure of Foreign Trade.* London: Saxon House, 1973.

————. "Currency Distribution and Forward Cover in Foreign Trade: Sweden Revisited, 1973." *Journal of International Economics,* May 1976, pp. 151–63.

Magee, S. P. "U.S. Import Prices in the Currency-Contract Period." *Brookings Papers in Economic Activity* 1, 1974.

Page, S. A. B. "Currency Invoicing in Merchandise Trade." *National Institute of Economics Review,* August 1974, pp. 25–37.

United Kingdom, Department of Trade. *Trade and Industry.* 5 May 1978.

CHAPTER 19

PROJECT FINANCE

Michel G. Maila

In the fourth century B.C., some lenders in Athens granted loans solely against the security of a seaborne cargo. When ships were lost at sea, debtors were under no obligation to repay the loan whether or not they owned other assets, and creditors often suffered total loss of the funds they had lent.

This type of loan is among the earliest precursors of modern-day "project financing" and highlights its two central features:

- The limited-recourse nature of the contractual obligation of the borrower to the lender.
- The broad interpretation of the term *project* to include not only its conventional connotation of construction or development activity but also any economic undertaking requiring investment of a significant amount of capital, usually over a number of years.

In colloquial use, project financing refers to any financing notionally destined to fund an investment program. In the financial community, however, project financing has come to be used in the

* The views expressed here are those of the author and should not be interpreted or construed as representing or repleating those of his employer.

more restricted sense of limited-recourse lending. That is, a financing whereby the borrower's obligation to pay and the lender's right to recover all amounts due under the contractually agreed financing arrangements are clearly circumscribed to specific activities or assets of the borrower to the exclusion of all others.

The key concepts involved in this type of lending are highlighted in the definition of project financing given by the Financial Accounting Standards Board (FASB) in the United States:

> The financing of a major capital project in which the lender looks principally to the cash flows and earnings of the project as a source of funds for repayment and to the assets of the project as collateral for the loan. The general credit of the project entity is usually not a significant factor, either because the entity is a corporation without other assets or because the financing is without direct recourse to the owners of the entity.[1]

HISTORICAL OVERVIEW

The first modern form of limited-recourse financing on a significant scale emerged in the late 1920s and early 1930s when banks in the United States began making "production loans" to petroleum producers. These were primarily short- to medium-term loans (one to three years) secured only by a mortgage over an onshore field's proven, producing reserves of oil or natural gas. As reservoir engineering techniques improved, American and Canadian banks felt comfortable extending longer-term loans against producing reserves and accepting less than full collateral as security for these loans. Such was the case in most petroleum "production payment" loans arranged in the United States during the 1950s and 1960s, where only a portion of future production was dedicated to debt repayment. Moreover, the lender was unable to access non-dedicated cash flow (or to foreclose on the producing property) if the dedicated cash flow fell short of the borrower's obligations. This lending was primarily tax-driven and declined considerably in

---

[1] Financial Accounting Standards Board *Statement No. 47*, March 1981.

the United States as a result of the enactment of the Tax Reform Act in 1969.

Notwithstanding this development, the project-financing approach developed substantially and was refined considerably in energy financing during the 1970s and 1980s. It was also increasingly adopted, within and outside North America, in other sectors and in a variety of projects or transactions requiring sizable capital investments.

From lending against onshore producing reserves, energy financiers graduated to limited-recourse financing of the riskier development of proven, nonproducing offshore reserves. Examples outside the Americas include the North Sea and offshore Australia, to cite two provinces that have witnessed a great deal of project-financing activity for hydrocarbon field development over the past decade or so.

The willingness of banks and other lenders to assume a variety of technical, economic, and political risks has also extended to pipeline finance, mine development, petrochemical installations, power stations, and cogeneration projects.

Outside the extractive industries, limited-recourse financing techniques are increasingly prevalent in any situation that permits identification and segregation of future cash flows and, hence, reliance on them for debt service. Generic applications in the industrialized world include leasing, leveraged buy-outs, and any discrete manufacturing or processing project. Applications have been frequent and widespread in real estate development, mortgage-backed securities financing, tanker finance, aircraft financing, paper mills and newsprint plants, amusement parks, mass-transit systems, trade finance (forfaiting), infrastructure projects (such as tunnels and bridges), and in the telecommunications industry for cable television and, more recently, satellite financing.

In developing countries, multinational institutions (such as the International Finance Corporation and various regional development banks) have been the most active foreign lenders on a project basis, particularly in the import-substituting and export sectors of these countries' economies. A portion of that project lending, particularly over the past decade or so, has taken the form of cofinancing in conjunction with commercial banks.

THE DEMAND FOR LIMITED-RECOURSE FINANCING

The main determinants of the demand for limited-recourse financing by corporations and other project sponsors vary considerably across countries and within economic sectors depending primarily on:

- The sponsors' degree of risk aversion.
- The sponsors' financial condition.
- The nature and efficiency of the financial markets to which the sponsors have access.
- The legal jurisdictions as well as the accounting and tax environments in which the sponsors and the lenders operate.

Risk Transfer

Notwithstanding the diversity of institutional and contractual arrangements, the sponsors' desire to transfer risk to limited recourse creditors is the most prevalent motivation for project financing. In contrast to conventional, corporate debt which can be backed unequivocally by "the full faith and credit" of the borrower, project financing typically involves a deliberate allocation of most of the risks associated with a given venture among the borrower, lender, and third parties. (Relevant third parties include product off-takers committed to purchase the project's output under "take-or-pay" contracts, insurers providing cover against specified hazards, the sponsor's joint venture partners, the project's operators and contractors, as well as regulatory bodies in the relevant jurisdictions.)

The risk transfer to the lenders is rarely a complete and all-encompassing one so that nonrecourse (as opposed to limited-recourse) financing is generally a misnomer. The rationale is that, in the limit, any comprehensive and total risk transfer would imply that the nonrecourse lender is the residual risk-bearer, that is, effectively an equity holder.

Why would corporations and project sponsors wish to transfer risk? In many cases, the answer is that project financing is the only option; the aspiring borrower is a "one-project" entity and although the company may stand behind the corporate debt, the loan is, de facto, a limited-recourse financing. In fact, the criterion used in some commercial banks to determine whether a loan opportunity is to be handled by a corporate lending officer or by a project finance officer is the answer to the following question: "Would the borrower survive if the project failed?"

In other cases, the demand for risk transfer arises from either exogenous or self-imposed constraints on the financing and investment decisions of a corporation. Typical instances of the internal constraints are

- Limits as to the overall monetary exposure of the corporation to a given project.
- Covenants in bond indentures or other financing documentation precluding (or imposing significant restrictions on) the raising of further pari-passu (equal-ranking) corporate debt or the issuance by the parent company of further guarantees covering the indebtedness of its subsidiaries.
- Limits on the magnitude, type, and maturity profile of the corporation's cross-border exposure to various countries, whether established by management or required by shareholders.

How do these three illustrative constraints give rise to a demand for project financing? In the first case, complying with corporate diversification guidelines could well be achieved by selling to other parties a portion of the firm's equity interest in the project; but this route involves forgoing the upside potential of the project; that is, the potentially significant opportunity cost of greater than anticipated returns from the project. In contrast, a limited-recourse financing could shelter the firm from a number of risks and delineate its monetary exposure under various scenarios, thus obviating the need for a partial divestiture of its equity interest and enabling it to retain the full upside potential of the project.

In the second case with restrictive covenants, a subordinated loan to the parent company or, more effective in terms of recourse limitation, a stand-alone financing for a single-purpose project subsidiary may well be the only means available to the corporation to leverage a given project while remaining in compliance with its covenants.

In the third case, with country exposure constraints, a limited-recourse financing can be designed to mitigate specific political risks such as the imposition of impediments to repatriation of funds, adverse changes in the tax régime, license revocation, and expropriation by the host government. For projects in "high-risk" developing countries (particularly since the early 1980s) the implication has often been that, were it not for such risk-mitigation, the investment opportunity would have been forgone.

As for the binding exogenous constraints that can dictate the need for risk transfer, they tend to emanate from two sources:

1. Regulatory authorities charged with a well-defined oversight responsibility over the financial affairs of companies operating in a particular industry (e.g., utilities).
2. Directly from governments intent on circumscribing the role of the public sector (whether as a provider of funds or as a risk-bearer) in major infrastructure projects.

A recent, prominent example of the operation of the latter constraint relates to the Channel Tunnel project whereby the insistence of the British and (to a lesser extent) the French governments that the venture should be an entirely private-sector one necessitated the arrangement of a limited-recourse financing of £5 billion sterling.

From a corporate standpoint, the deliberate transfer of risk via limited-recourse financing presupposes a detailed risk assessment that takes into account not only constraints on financial decisionmaking but also the financial condition of the corporation and the degree of risk aversion of its management. The decision to transfer risk via project financing also involves finely balanced judgments as to the attractiveness of the cost-benefit configuration associated with that financing. Are the extra costs (discussed next) justified by the benefit of reduced risk? Are lenders underestimating or underpricing risks, thus giving rise to a profitable arbitrage opportunity for the corporate treasurer?

In fact, it is unlikely that risk transfer would be the sole objective of a financing strategy. Accordingly, corporate treasurers are likely to face multiple and often complex trade-offs among competing objectives which have to be resolved within a specific institutional context.

Other Motives

Apart from risk transfer, a wish list of the objectives sponsors strive to achieve via a project financing usually includes most, if not all, of the following:

- To maximize the project's rate of return on equity.
- To maximize the debt capacities of the project and of the corporation while protecting the corporation's debt ratings.
- To minimize taxes on project and project-related income.
- To optimize accounting treatment given consolidation and disclosure rules.
- To perfect the contractual limitation of recourse in respect to the risks transferred to third parties and to facilitate hedging of remaining exposures.

The objectives relating to leverage and return on equity are fairly standard and generic. Achieving those relating to tax, optimal disclosure and accounting treatment, debt rating impact, and perfection of recourse limitation is, however, highly specific to the jurisdiction and time period. In an Anglo-Saxon legal framework, for example, sponsors can reinforce the de jure limitation of recourse (as contractually agreed between lenders and the borrower in a loan agreement) via a de facto segregation of the project's assets in a distinct, limited-liability company. This separate, stand-alone legal entity is then charged with the single purpose of undertaking and operating the project and is the one formally contracting the debt, thus keeping the sponsors one step removed from the creditors.

In addition to perfecting the limitation of recourse, the single-purpose entity mechanism can serve as a means for corporate treasurers to achieve other, less tangible and often largely cosmetic goals. One such objective has on occasion been to keep debt off the balance sheet (consolidation and disclosure rules permitting) with a view to maximizing overall debt capacity and to minimizing any adverse impact on the corporation's debt ratings. Another one has been to achieve a so-called synergistic leverage effect whereby it is alleged that, as a result of the closer scrutiny accorded by lenders to the debt capacity of individual projects, the sum of limited-recourse project loans would be greater than the corporate debt capacity of the firm owning or consisting of these projects.

Such institutionally driven motivations for limited-recourse financing tend, at best, to be transient and difficult to quantify although there are notable exceptions such as the exploitation of tax advantages through leasing.[2] It is difficult, however, not to be skeptical about the impact on the cost of capital and hence on the fundamental value to shareholders of such accounting effects. Such skepticism is particularly well founded in the case of well-developed financial markets characterized by broad financial disclosure requirements, vigilant rating agencies, and well-informed investors and financial intermediaries.

As for the more fundamental objectives pursued by sponsors (such as maximizing leverage and return on equity), it is possible conceptually to subsume most of them under a single decision rule; for example, "maximize post-tax, risk-adjusted value." However, unavoidable trade-offs among some of these goals arise in practice; they must be dealt with as effectively as feasible, given the market-driven and institutional constraints facing project sponsors.

To illustrate some of these trade-offs, consider the two apparently congruent goals of maximizing the amount of limited-recourse debt raised against a project and maximizing the return on the sponsor's equity in it. The prospects of achieving the latter goal would clearly be enhanced by significant cash throw-offs to the sponsor in the early years of the project's operation. This in turn requires negotiation of a project financing with the following structural elements: a relatively small proportion of project cash flow dedicated to debt service particularly in the early years, an extended final maturity, and a repayment schedule skewed toward the distant future. When faced with such requirements, however, potential limited-recourse lenders would not be willing to provide maximum loan value; that is, to maximize the amount of limited recourse debt. The rationale is twofold:

1. Because lenders base their loan value decisions on the expected amount of cash flow available for debt service,

---

[2] For example, in the United States production payments were brought into the balance sheet as debt pursuant to FASB 19 (December 1977). In 1981 FASB 47 dealt with the disclosure in financial statements of take-or-pay contracts, throughput contracts, and other unconditional purchase obligations typically associated with project financing arrangements.

the lower the debt service dedication rate, the lower the loan value, other things being equal.[3]

2. To the extent that risk-averse lenders perceive (as they usually do) that uncertainty increases with time, the longer the average life of the loan, the lower the loan value they are prepared to grant.

Another significant trade-off from the treasurer's standpoint can arise between perfecting the limitation of recourse and facilitating the hedging of residual risks. Consider the case of a sponsor using the single-purpose entity mechanism to finance a project giving rise to exposure to foreign-exchange risk. Assume further that the limited-recourse lenders are not willing to assume this risk in its entirety. Under those circumstances, the loan agreement would include various financial ratio covenants and/or hedging requirements designed to minimize the borrower's (and ultimately the lenders) exposure to exchange risk. Even without delving into any detailed consideration of consolidation and translation rules, it should be clear that such constraints are unlikely to facilitate exposure management at the corporate level. In fact, it is likely that, under such a scenario, the difficult task of reconciling and managing accounting and economic exposures to exchange risk is likely to be exacerbated by the differing perspectives on this issue adopted by lenders and by the borrower's parent company. Because their concern is centered around cash flow available for debt service in the relevant currency, project lenders would be focusing exclusively on the borrower's economic exposure, whereas the sponsor would be attending to both accounting and economic dimensions on a consolidated basis.

No discussion of the determinants of the demand for project financing would be complete without mention of the extra costs to the sponsors inherent in this type of financing. The bulk of these additional costs consists of higher interest margins, or spreads, on funds borrowed, commitment fees (usually calculated in reference

---

[3] Cash flow available for debt service is usually subjected to sensitivity analysis to ascertain its resilience with respect to a number of potentially adverse developments. The loan value is then derived judgmentally by applying a cover (or protection) ratio (typically greater than one and smaller than two) to the discounted net present value of projected cash flows.

to the maximum amount to be made available by the lenders), and front-end fees (typically expressed as a percentage of the amount of financing arranged, underwritten, and/or eventually taken up by financial intermediaries).

The size of these incremental borrowing costs—relative to the often notional pricing of a "classical" corporate debt benchmark—varies with the nature and magnitude of the risks transferred to lenders and the risk-adjusted return negotiated for the specific financing at hand. As project financing is tailor-made financing par excellence, comparing risks and risk premiums across situations is fraught with methodological pitfalls. Accordingly, it would not be possible—even if enough of the required, usually confidential data were made available—to make any cogent generalizations about an average risk/return pricing grid, let alone about the appropriateness in some actuarial sense, of the risk premium paid to lenders for assuming a particular set of risks.[4]

Given the complexity of limited recourse financings (relative, say, to a corporate loan or even to a public issue of debt securities), transaction costs also tend to be significant. These take the form of direct external costs for legal, technical, and financial advisory services and of indirect costs in management time expended in negotiating, documenting, and implementing the financing structure. In most financial markets, a large proportion of these transaction costs is fixed so that there are definite economies of scale in borrowing on a limited-recourse basis.

THE SUPPLY OF LIMITED-RECOURSE FINANCING

The main arrangers and suppliers of limited-recourse financing have been the major commercial and investment/merchant banking groups in North America, Europe, and the Far East. Other financial intermediaries such as multinational institutions, insurance companies, venture capital firms, and to a lesser extent,

---

[4] A rough indication of the magnitude of these incremental borrowing costs may, however, be gleaned from the experience, in North America and in the Euromarkets, with project financing and leveraged acquisition financings where the "average" risk premium since the mid-1970s has fluctuated between 25 and 250 basis points per annum for senior debt and up to 250 basis points more for "mezzanine" and subordinated debt instruments.

export credit agencies, have also played a role. On occasion, financially strong commercial companies have been induced by their weaker joint-venture partners to provide limited-recourse financing for their share of project costs in return for incentives (such as stock options, warrants, or royalties) usually structured in relation to the degree of future profitability of the venture.

The supply of limited-recourse financing has increased significantly over the past decade or so, primarily as a result of the following factors:

- The attractive risk-adjusted returns associated with arranging, underwriting, and to a lesser extent, participating in such financings.
- The increased confidence of the major players in their ability to identify, assess, and assume risk.
- The development—often on an ad hoc basis—of hedging and insurance products that allow limited-recourse lenders to neutralize or at least mitigate certain risks at an acceptable cost.
- The greater familiarity with limited-recourse financing techniques in many of the world's financial markets; this has spawned a considerable number of new entrants on the supply side.

Not surprisingly, the interaction of the "learning curve effect" within the community of established practitioners of project finance and of the "new entry effect" has led to a highly competitive supply situation in many applications. The result has been, in general, twofold: assumption by lenders of greater risks and erosion of the risk premium over time. The history of hydrocarbon field development and pipeline financing in the North Sea is a case in point. In the 1970s, limited-recourse loans for these offshore projects were generally characterized by the following features:

- Assumption by lenders of limited technical and economic risks only after completion of the project.[5] Accordingly, the

---

[5] In the project-financing jargon, completion has two dimensions: *physical or technical* completion (which refers to successful commissioning of all facilities and equipment as well as passing specified performance/production tests particularly where take-or-pay offtake or throughput contracts are involved), and *economic* completion that usually involves meeting a minimum coverage ratio.

borrower typically provided a completion undertaking usually secured by a corporate guarantee issued either by the borrower or, if not sufficiently creditworthy, by a third-party guarantor—for example, the borrower's parent company, a joint-venture partner, or the government.

- Where the lenders deemed the security package to be insufficient and the risks significant, the risk premium would consist of a spread of about 150 to 250 basis points over the lenders' cost of funds and of an "equity kicker" such as a royalty interest calculated in relation to the field's production or to the associated stream of future revenues.

Over time however—and specifically since the early 1980s—most precompletion risks have become easily bankable; contingent equity-type rewards to senior lenders have all but disappeared, security arrangements are now more flexible, and spreads have fallen to the 60-to-140-basis-point range.[6] To a certain extent, these developments constitute an appropriate market response to the reduced risk profile associated with the well-tested technology and improved performance of these projects particularly in cost overrun control and timely completion.[7] It is arguable, however, whether competitive pressures have not pushed returns down to a level that is no longer commensurate with the risks borne by limited-recourse lenders or, in many cases, with the returns accruing to equity holders for bearing essentially the same risks.

RECENT DEVELOPMENTS AND TRENDS

The preceding discussion suggests that, at least in some applications of limited-recourse financing, the line between debt and

---

[6] These trends have not been arrested by the oil price collapse of 1986 or by the subsequent volatility of hydrocarbon prices.

[7] On the other hand, the history of large-scale projects across a wide spectrum of industries and sectors continues to exhibit instances of significant miscalculation and unexpectedly poor performance even in cases involving proven technology. The well-publicized overruns and delays in the construction of the Seikan tunnel in Japan and, more recently, the expansion of the Mongstad refinery in Norway are cases in point.

equity has become increasingly blurred. The traditional, textbook classification of debt and equity instruments rests essentially on three distinguishing features:

1. The order of priority of these instruments in on-going access to cash flow or rank order of repayment-redemption on liquidation.
2. The nature and number of independent exit routes (or ways out of their exposure) available to the holders of the instruments.
3. To a lesser extent, the contingent or noncontingent nature of the returns accruing to them, particularly in sharing the upside potential of the project or situation.

The priority ranking of various claims has invariably been well defined, in a formal sense, in limited-recourse financing situations; witness the precise delineation between senior debt, mezzanine debt, and equity in leveraged buy-outs. Moreover, holders of debt claims have generally obtained a security interest over the assets being financed on a limited-recourse basis as a second way out of their exposure, the first exit route being, of course, repayment from projected cash flows. However, in a fundamental sense, limited-recourse lenders remain to a varying degree, joint, residual risk-bearers along with the sponsors or the equity investors. The rationale is that priority positions and security interests are, at best, of limited value in a situation where anticipated cash flows do not materialize. A relevant analogy from everyday experience is that of the cold comfort one derives from being first in line in the queue outside a theater when it is known that tickets for the best seats—if not all the seats—have already been sold!

The position of the limited-recourse creditor relative to the equity holder is even less favorable in situations where the borrower is a diversified conglomerate. Under those circumstances, the equity holder can often rely on the negative, or at least imperfect, correlation between the various activities of the sponsor to mitigate the exposure to any given project; limited-recourse lenders, however senior, cannot by definition derive any such benefit.

The competitive pressure to become stake-holders alongside of sponsors and equity investors has recently extended not only to financial institutions with the growth of debt-to-equity conversions in a number of developing countries but also to third parties such as contractors. This is particularly the case in developing countries where traditionally, contractors have sought to limit both their country exposure and their involvement in projects beyond the construction phase. In recent years, however, many contractors have been induced to become residual risk-bearers by the governments of developing countries facing external borrowing constraints. A prime example of this trend is the "build-operate-transfer" model recently developed in Turkey, Chile, and elsewhere in the Third World. Under these schemes, contractors have undertaken not only to build infrastructure and power projects on time and within budget but also to own and/or operate them for a considerable number of years. More significantly, they have committed to seek payment for their construction and management services solely out of project cash flow and to transfer ownership of these ventures to the host government authorities at a predetermined time.

Another noteworthy trend is the unbundling of the various components inherent to a limited-recourse financing structure on the basis of the comparative advantage enjoyed by various financial market participants. In line with the securitization and disintermediation trends witnessed in the world's major capital markets since the late 1970s, the "funds provision" function of financial intermediaries has been uncoupled from their risk-bearing role with these two tasks increasingly being allocated to separate parties within the context of an integrated project financing structure. For instance, the funding function can be provided as a credit enhancement service by entities enjoying superior credit ratings; they would issue, on behalf of the project sponsor, tradable securities on the money and capital markets at the most competitive rates available. To the extent that the credit-enhancing institution is not willing to take "project risk," it is itself the recipient of a guarantee of the sponsor's obligations from the ultimate limited-recourse risk-bearers, that is, those entities best suited to evaluate and assume project risk.

The growing use of efficient mechanisms for division of labor among various participants in a limited-recourse financing illustrates the coming of age of the discipline. One of the challenges ahead for practitioners and corporate treasurers alike is to further develop the project financing paradigm to incorporate more flexibly and effectively the capital market instruments and risk management products appropriate to the limited-recourse financing at hand.

CHAPTER 20

FOREIGN CURRENCY AND U.S. INCOME TAXES

Howard S. Engle
Mark T. Campbell

PART I—BACKGROUND

This chapter provides an introductory survey of relevant U.S. federal income tax law as it affects U.S. corporations with either foreign currency transactions or non-U.S. business operations. It introduces the principles of U.S. income taxation as they apply to foreign currency matters in general, as well as helps develop the reader's intuition as to how those principles might affect specific financial decisions influenced by foreign currencies and their fluctuations.

The U.S. tax law continues to be a rapidly evolving area. The Tax Reform Act of 1986 and its successors brought massive changes to the U.S. taxation of international business transactions both clarifying old concepts as well as introducing new ones. This chapter is based on the U.S. law, regulations, and Internal Revenue Service interpretations in effect as of March 26, 1989. These provisions may differ substantially from the pre–1987 law. Because the U.S. tax law is so complex and constantly changing, the reader should consult with a tax adviser before entering into any actual transactions.[1]

Overview of the U.S. International Tax System

The U.S. tax rules governing foreign currency matters are only part of a much broader U.S. tax system governing the whole area of international business. The first part of this chapter provides a brief overview of the general principles of U.S. taxation to place specific foreign currency rules in their proper context.

With the Tax Reform Act of 1986, the international arena has simultaneously become more certain and more complex. Prior to the act, some topics had never been addressed by legislation. There was case law, but it tended to be inconsistent, with judicial support for virtually any position but certainty about none. The Tax Reform Act of 1986 addressed many unclear issues, but also signaled the beginning of legislation by regulations. The act authorized a series of voluminous regulations that address numerous issues with general rules, exceptions to the general rules, and exceptions to the exceptions.

The Foreign Tax Credit and Its Limitation

The United States taxes its residents on their worldwide income computed in U.S. dollars. A U.S. corporation is defined as being resident in the United States and is taxed currently on its taxable income, which includes not only all income earned directly by the corporation but also dividends, interest, and royalties when received from non-U.S. subsidiaries. Generally, U.S. taxation of the profits of foreign subsidiaries is deferred until those profits are repatriated to the U.S. parent.

U.S. corporations, whether directly conducting business in other countries as a branch or indirectly through a subsidiary, are

---

[1] For more tax technical areas of the law see White, *Taxation of Foreign Currency Transactions under the Tax Reform Act of 1986*, International Bureau of Fiscal Documentation (May 1987), pp. 206–14; and David P. Zaiken, Frederic E. White, and Frederick E. Wooldridge, "Handling the Treatment of Foreign Currency Under Tax Reform," *Journal of Taxation* 67 (September 1987), p. 168. See also the provisions of the Revenue Act of 1987 and the Technical and Miscellaneous Revenue Act of 1988.

typically subject to tax on their local income by foreign governments. To eliminate the possibility of double taxation of the same income, the U.S. tax law provides a foreign tax credit system whereby a U.S. taxpayer may annually elect to claim a credit against U.S. income taxes for foreign income taxes previously paid abroad.

The U.S. taxpayer can claim a direct credit for foreign taxes paid directly by the corporation or an indirect credit for taxes paid by certain foreign subsidiaries.

U.S. taxpayers, however, are not permitted to claim foreign tax credits against U.S. tax on U.S. source income. They are instead subject to a foreign tax credit limitation that prevents U.S. taxpayers from applying foreign tax credits in excess of the U.S. tax on foreign source taxable income to offset U.S. tax on U.S. source income. For instance, if a U.S. taxpayer subject to a 34 percent U.S. tax has already paid a 50 percent foreign income tax on foreign source income, it cannot claim the 16 percent (50 percent − 34 percent) excess foreign tax credit as a credit against the U.S. tax on purely U.S. source income.

To compute the foreign tax credit limitation, the law provides a set of definitions and rules to calculate the portion of total taxable income that is foreign source taxable income. These complex rules specify whether gross income such as gross profit on sales, dividends, interest, and royalties are from U.S. or foreign sources. Similar rules exist to determine whether expenses incurred by a U.S. taxpayer such as interest and R&D should be deducted from foreign source gross income to arrive at foreign source taxable income. In general, the foreign tax credit limitation is equal to the U.S. tax on foreign source income and is computed as follows:[2]

$$\text{Foreign Tax Credit Limitation} = \text{Total U.S. Tax} \times \frac{\text{Foreign Source Taxable Income}}{\text{Total Worldwide Taxable Income}}$$

---

[2] See Sections 861–864 and Section 904(d).

The foreign tax credit limitation is zero for a U.S. taxpayer with a taxable loss.

Excess Foreign Tax Credits

A U.S. taxpayer has excess foreign tax credits in a taxable year if its available foreign tax credits exceed its foreign tax credit limitation. Generally this occurs if the foreign taxes paid on its foreign source income exceed the U.S. tax on the same income. Such excess foreign tax credits can be carried back two or forward five taxable years to offset U.S. tax on foreign source income in other taxable years. A taxpayer with creditable foreign taxes less than its foreign tax credit limitation is said to have excess foreign tax credit limitation and can absorb excess foreign tax credits from other years to offset U.S. tax on that year's foreign source taxable income. The excess foreign tax credits can be absorbed only to the extent of that year's excess foreign tax credit limitation.

In a simplified fashion, Figure 20–1 illustrates the operation of the U.S. foreign tax credit system on a dividend from a subsidiary to a U.S. corporate parent. The subsidiary functional currency (FC) earns FC 1 million of pre-tax profits and pays a local tax of 30 percent when the exchange rate is FC = $1.50.

If the subsidiary's after-tax profits are distributed immediately, the U.S. parent receives cash of $1,050,000 (FC 700,000 × $1.50/FC). If the U.S. parent elects to claim a foreign tax credit to compute the U.S. tax on the dividend, the cash dividend income is then grossed up by the underlying foreign tax credit to arrive at foreign source taxable income. This total amount of cash and foreign tax credit is the U.S. equivalent of local pre-tax income, that is, $1,500,000 = $1,050,000 + $450,000 = FC 1,000,000 × $1.50/FC. Such a dividend is also said to have an effective foreign tax rate of 30 percent = $450,000/$1,500,000.

The gross U.S. tax is computed on this gross amount and a credit is allowed for foreign taxes paid, leaving a net U.S. tax due of $60,000. As the local tax rate was 4 percent less than the U.S. rate (34 percent − 30 percent), this $60,000 brings the total tax burden on the income up to 34 percent, that is, $60,000 = 4% × FC 1,000,000 × $1.50/FC.

Discussed more fully later is the case where the cash is

FIGURE 20–1
Illustration of Foreign Tax Credit System

Foreign Subsidiary Results		Taxes Paid When FC = $1.50
Pretax profits	FC 1,000,000	
Local taxes at 30 percent	(300,000) =	$ 450,000
Dividend distributed	FC 700,000	

U.S. Tax Computations

	Dividend Distributed When	
	FC = $1.50	FC = $1.00
Cash dividend received	$1,050,000	$ 700,000
Foreign tax credit gross-up	450,000	450,000
Foreign source taxable income*	$1,500,000	$1,150,000
U.S. tax at 34 percent	510,000	391,000
Foreign tax credit	(450,000)	(391,000)†
Net U.S. tax due	$ 60,000	$ 0
Excess foreign tax credits		$ 59,000

* Assumes no deductions allocated or apportioned to foreign source taxable income and no withholding taxes on remittance.
† Subject to foreign tax credit limitation.

distributed when the local currency has fluctuated with respect to the dollar.

Foreign Tax Credit Baskets
The natural response of taxpayers with excess foreign tax credits is to attempt to generate low-taxed foreign source income. In so attempting to circumvent the foreign tax credit limitation, taxpayers have found some types of foreign source income, such as interest or other types of passive income, comparatively easy to generate. To prevent taxpayers from artificially converting U.S. source income into foreign source income on which the tax can be offset by excess foreign tax credits, each item of a taxpayer's

foreign source income is allocated to separate foreign tax credit *baskets* depending on the nature of the income. Each basket of foreign source taxable income is then subject to its own separate foreign tax credit limitation calculation made with respect to both the income and foreign taxes only in that basket. This prevents the offset of excess foreign tax credits from one basket against the U.S. tax on other low-tax foreign source income.

There are separate foreign tax credit baskets for passive income such as interest, as well as high withholding tax interest, financial services income, shipping income, dividends from certain less-than-50 percent-owned corporations, and so forth. Income not part of a separate basket is part of the residual or active income basket that generally includes active business income.

The law and regulations also provide complex provisions which *look through* certain intercompany payments, such as interest, royalties, or dividends, to determine the underlying nature of the income and assign the income to the appropriate foreign tax credit basket. Needless to say, these rules impose a heavy compliance burden on U.S. taxpayers many of whom rely on sophisticated software to correctly account for all these items.[3]

International Tax Planning

The international tax planner's objective is to minimize the worldwide tax burden on income. The first step is to minimize local taxes on income by earning and reinvesting profits in low-taxed jurisdictions and by minimizing profits earned in high-taxed jurisdictions. In deciding where to earn and reinvest profits, the United States can be considered as just another country.

Next, to the extent foreign taxes are paid, planners expend considerable effort to ensure that they are fully creditable against U.S. taxes. Taxpayers also generally attempt to maximize the amount of their income allocated away from the separate foreign tax credit baskets into the residual active income basket. For purposes of this chapter, all foreign source income is assumed to be

---

[3] As employees of Arthur Andersen & Company, we are partial to *International Manager™*, Arthur Andersen & Company's comprehensive International Tax Planning and Compliance System for U.S. Multinational Corporations.

active business income, all of which is eligible for the same foreign tax credit basket.

Abandon All Hope Ye Who Enter Here . . .
Alas, taxation is a highly technical discipline with a well-deserved reputation for having its own arcane jargon. In this initial discussion, we have endeavored not to overwhelm readers with Internal Revenue Code section numbers, regulations, and revenue rulings. Unfortunately, while they are sometimes painful, section numbers are part of the conceptual shorthand necessary to understand the tax system. We therefore apologize in advance for the use of such abominations as "Section 1256 contracts" but they are the easiest part of the price we pay for a civilized society.

Functional Currency

It is usually convenient to account for the results of business activities in terms of a base or home currency, and U.S. law requires every U.S. taxpayer and each of its qualified business units to determine their home or functional currency. A qualified business unit is defined as a separate and clearly identified unit of trade or business conducted by a taxpayer that maintains its own separate books and records. For example, a foreign branch of a U.S. corporation could constitute a qualified business unit and have a functional currency separate from its U.S. dollar-based home office.[4]

   The functional currency tax concept closely mirrors the financial accounting principles promulgated in *FASB Statement No. 52* and is intended to constitute the most meaningful unit of measure for assets, liabilities, and operations of a business entry. A business unit's functional currency should, therefore, be the currency in which it primarily conducts its business. There may also be different functional currencies for tax and financial statement purposes.

---

[4] Section 985 and Temporary Regulations thereunder, Notice 88–101.

In general, for tax purposes, a qualified business unit's functional currency is either of the following:

The U.S. dollar.

The currency of the economic environment in which a significant part of the unit's activities are conducted and which is employed by the unit for purposes of keeping its books and records.

A qualified business unit is required to use the U.S. dollar as its functional currency if the unit's activities are primarily conducted in dollars. A taxpayer can elect to use the U.S. dollar as the functional currency of a qualified business unit, if the unit maintains its books and records in U.S. dollars or uses a translation method that approximates U.S. dollar-based accounting. Taxpayers operating in hyperinflationary economies can elect to use the U.S. dollar as their functional currency without being required to maintain their books and records in U.S. dollars.[5]

PART II—UNHEDGED FOREIGN-CURRENCY TRANSACTIONS

Section 988 Transactions

Section 988 Transactions Defined
U.S. taxpayers frequently engage in transactions whose financial outcome is wholly or partially determined by fluctuations in foreign exchange rates. For tax purposes, most of these transactions are treated under Section 988 which governs most foreign currency transactions, both hedged and unhedged.

Section 988 transactions are those unhedged transactions where the amount the taxpayer is entitled to receive or required to pay is denominated in a nonfunctional currency or is determined by reference to the value of one or more nonfunctional currencies.

---

[5] See Temporary Regulation Sections 1.985–1T and 1.985–2T.

Thus, a qualified business unit with a French franc functional currency could enter into a U.S. dollar transaction which for the branch constitutes an unhedged Section 988 transaction.

Section 988 transactions are by definition limited to:

Disposing of a nonfunctional currency.

Acquiring a debt instrument or becoming an obligor on a debt instrument denominated in a nonfunctional currency.

Accruing (or otherwise taking into account for tax purposes) any item of gross income, receipts, or expense to be received or paid after the date on which it is taken into account.

Entering into or acquiring any forward contract, futures contract, option, or similar financial instrument.[6]

Section 988 transactions do not include transactions such as:

The use of a nonfunctional currency to establish a demand or time deposit or similar instrument in the same currency or the conversion of such an instrument into another similar instrument in the same nonfunctional currency.

Receivables and payables that have a maturity date of 120 days or less.[7]

Exchange gains and losses attributable to nonpreferred stock investments.

Certain regulated futures contracts and nonequity options.

Inventory.

Fixed assets.[8]

Treatment of Section 988 Transactions

The base premise of Section 988 is that changes in exchange rates are principally a function of interest rate differentials between currencies and that, therefore, exchange gains and losses should be taxed as ordinary income or expense rather than capital gains and

---

[6] Section 988(c)(1)(B).

[7] S. Rep. No. 313, 99th Cong., 2d Sess. (1986) p. 460.

[8] Section 988(c)(1)(B) provides the general definition of Section 988 transactions but see also Section 988(c)(1)(C).

losses.[9] Such ordinary income or expense may, in turn, be specifically treated as interest income or expense as set forth in future regulations.[10]

Generally, any foreign currency gain or loss attributable to a 988 transaction must be computed and treated separately as ordinary income or loss and as interest to the extent provided in regulations. The total Section 988 gain or loss from any transaction, however, cannot exceed the total transaction gain or loss.[11]

Following the general closed and completed transaction tax principle, a foreign currency gain or loss is also not recognized for Section 988 purposes until the entire transaction is closed and completed. Thus, any inherent Section 988 gain or loss on a long-term receivable may fluctuate over time and is not recognized for tax purposes until the receivable is ultimately collected.

Figure 20–2 illustrates the operation of the Section 988 rules. The overall economic gain or loss on the transaction is decomposed and treated as arising from two sources: foreign currency fluctuations and the underlying transaction. The tax law then treats the foreign currency ordinary gain or loss separately from the transaction gain or loss, but foreign currency gain or loss cannot exceed the overall transaction gain or loss. The residual transaction gain or loss is treated as a separate transaction gain or loss taxed according to its own fundamental nature. For instance, in Figure 20–2 any transaction gains are capital, while a foreign currency gain or loss is ordinary and subject to the special Section 988 rules.

The U.S. or foreign source of a Section 988 foreign currency gain or loss is determined by the residence of the qualified business unit on whose books the item is properly reflected. Thus, the Section 988 gains and losses of a U.S. taxpayer other than a foreign branch are generally U.S. source. The gains and losses of a non-U.S. qualified business unit would generally be treated as foreign source.[12]

---

[9] Section 988(a)(i)(A).
[10] Section 988(a)(2), this regulation had not yet been issued at the date of this writing.
[11] Section 988(b).
[12] Section 988(a)(3).

FIGURE 20–2
Transaction Limitation on Foreign Currency Gain/Loss

Facts:
   U.S. dollar taxpayer buys a bond for £100 when £1 = $1 and sells it later for £200.

Tax Results:

	Bond Sold When the Value of £1 Equals		
	$.25	*$.75*	*$2.00*
£200 sales proceeds	50	150	400
Tax basis in bond	(100)	(100)	(100)
Gross gain (loss)	(50)	50	300
Source of gain/loss			
£200 transaction gain	25	75	200
Foreign currency	(75)	(25)	100
	(50)	50	300
Tax treatment of gain			
Transaction	0	50	200
Foreign currency	(50)	0	100
	(50)	50	300

To maximize their foreign source income, U.S. taxpayers would generally prefer that Section 988 foreign currency loss transactions be recognized by U.S. taxpayers and that Section 988 foreign currency gain transactions be recognized by non-U.S. qualified business units.

Non-Section 988 Transactions
Foreign currency transactions that do not fall within Section 988 are subject to the confused pre-Tax Reform Act rules which were based on case law.[13] These rules are largely based on the separate

---

[13] *Corn Products Refining Co.* v. *Comm.*, 55-2 USTC ¶ 9746, and *International Flavors and Fragrances, Inc.*, 36 TCM 260. *Hoover Co.* v. *Comm.* 72 T.C. 206 (1979), acq. 1984–1 C.B. 1.

transaction principle which holds that foreign currency gains and losses should be accounted for separately from any other gain or loss on a transaction, but which permits taxpayers to take a variety of positions with respect to the nature and source of the income or loss.

Foreign Currency-Denominated Loans

Foreign Currency-Denominated Obligations

Section 988 rules can be illustrated by their application to foreign currency-denominated loans. If a foreign currency loan is not hedged, and Section 988 foreign currency gain or loss on the repayment or receipt of the principal amount of the loan is treated as ordinary interest income or expense having the same source as the residence of the qualified business unit. The residence of a qualified business unit is the country in which its principal place of business is located. Unless it can be shown otherwise, a U.S. corporation is a U.S. resident. A foreign corporation is not a U.S. resident, unless is has a permanent establishment in the United States, or has income effectively connected with a U.S. trade or business.[14] Thus, a U.S. taxpayer would recognize U.S. source ordinary income or loss from Section 988 gains or losses arising from the payment or collection of a foreign currency obligation.

Each interest obligation on the loan is itself treated as its own separate Section 988 transaction. Each accrual of foreign currency-denominated interest income or expense is made at the average exchange rate between functional and nonfunctional currencies for the period. To the extent the actual value of making or receiving an accrued interest payment differs from the accrued amount, the difference is a separate Section 988 gain or loss.

Curiously, interest and the Section 988 gains or losses arising from the interest are sourced differently. That is, interest income is generally U.S. or foreign source depending on the residence of the payer while any foreign currency gain or loss on the interest payment itself is sourced by the residence of the taxpayer. Thus, the interest income received by a U.S. person from a non-U.S.

---

[14] Section 988(a)(3)(B).

person is treated as foreign source income eligible for foreign tax credit treatment, but any foreign currency gain or loss on the principal amount of the loan or the accrued interest income would be treated as a U.S. source gain or loss.[15]

U.S. taxpayers, therefore, should generally prefer to maximize foreign source interest income by lending in weak currencies. Weaker currencies have nominally higher foreign source interest income which would be financially offset by a U.S. source foreign currency loss. Regulations to be issued may provide for the recharacterization of interest and principal payments with respect to obligations denominated and certain hyperinflationary currencies.[16]

Foreign Currency Loans with Original Issue Discount

Obligations issued at a discount from their stated redemption price are said to have original issue discount (OID) and are subject to special tax rules which treat the OID as interest.[17] In the case of any debt instrument, the portion of the OID allowable as a deduction to the issuer or taxable by the recipient for any taxable year is accrued on a yield to maturity basis.[18]

When the debt has an OID amount that is measured in foreign currency terms, the accrued OID income or expense is computed initially in the foreign currency. The relevant amount for any accrual period is then computed in dollars using the average exchange rates for the period. Any foreign currency exchange gain or loss is computed by comparing the total dollar income or expense accruals to the fair market value of the foreign currency when actually received or paid.[19]

Intercompany Loans

Look through provisions. A number of special income tax provisions apply to loans between related parties but not to loans between independent parties. As discussed earlier, interest income

---

[15] Sections 862(a)(1) and 865(a)(1).
[16] Section 989(c).
[17] Section 1273(a)(1).
[18] Section 163(e).
[19] S. Rep. No. 313, 99th Cong., 2d Sess. (1986) p. 461–62.

from unrelated foreign sources is initially treated as passive basket foreign source income. This reflects the relative ease with which taxpayers can invest in foreign obligations and create foreign source income. By placing such income in a separate passive foreign tax credit basket, the U.S. tax thereon generally cannot be offset by excess credits generated in other separate foreign tax credit baskets.

U.S. taxpayers and their non-U.S. subsidiaries, however, also invest in related foreign subsidiaries' debt for valid business reasons such as centralized cash management or lower borrowing rates. Therefore, special rules for looking through interest received from related parties assign the interest income into the appropriate foreign tax credit basket based on the preinterest expense nature of the foreign subsidiary's income. Thus, if a foreign subsidiary is engaged in active business operations, its interest when received by a related company is reclassified from passive basket income into active basket income. Interest income from controlled foreign subsidiaries can, therefore, be an attractive low-taxed foreign source income that can absorb other excess foreign tax credits.[20]

There are limits to this strategy. If the foreign subsidiary has passive income, the related party interest income received by the parent must first be characterized as passive basket to the extent that the foreign subsidiary has passive income. Temporary regulations issued in September 1988 require that the foreign subsidiaries maintain a thrid party debt-to-equity ratio similar to that of the U.S. parent.[21] If this ratio falls below the prescribed level, interest expense is directly allocated to the related party interest income, effectively eliminating the low-taxed foreign source income and the enhanced foreign tax credit limitation.

Under these rules, a natural planning technique would be to maximize the amount of loans by a U.S. parent to controlled foreign subsidiaries and to attempt to denominate such loans in the weaker of the lender's or borrower's functional currency. This maximizes the amount of nominal interest income treated as foreign source income and if the lender were the U.S. parent, would treat any foreign currency losses as U.S. source losses.

---

[20] Section 904(d)(3)(E).
[21] Reg. Section 1.861–9T.

Certain related party loans, however, are subject to a special resourcing rule. These rules apply if the loan is denominated in a foreign currency and the loan has an interest rate which is 10 percentage points higher than the equivalent U.S. rate. For foreign tax credit purposes only, the related party loan must then be marked-to-market annually with the interest income received from the foreign subsidiary treated as U.S. source income to the extent of any loss recognized when the loan is marked-to-market. This rule operates to reduce the generation of foreign source income in hyperinflationary economies.[22]

Interest allocation.   For purpose of calculating the foreign tax credit limitation, U.S. taxpayers must also allocate some of their U.S. expenses such as interest and R&D against foreign source income. This rule is based on the assumption that cash within a U.S. corporation is fungible and that management has a great deal of flexibility as to the source and use of funds. Interest expense is, therefore, assumed to be attributable to all activities and property regardless of any specific purpose for incurring the debt. Consequently, some portion of a corporation's U.S. interest expense is deemed incurred to finance the company's investment in its foreign operations and should be charged against foreign source income. In addition, as discussed previously, the regulations may require specific allocation of U.S. interest expense to interest income received from related foreign subsidiaries. The effect of these allocations is, of course, to reduce the U.S. corporation's net foreign source income and thereby the foreign tax credit that can be claimed.[23]

Arm's-length interest rate.   The U.S. tax law recognizes taxable income and expense among related corporations based on the premise that foreign subsidiaries under U.S. control are independent entities dealing at arm's length. To maintain that premise, an arm's-length rate of interest must be charged on a loan advance between members of a group of controlled entities.[24]

If the loans are denominated in dollars, the interest rates are

---

[22] Section 988(a)(3)(C).
[23] See the Temporary Regulations under Section 861 for the allocation of interest rules.
[24] Section 482, and Treasury Regulations, and Section 7872.

tied to the applicable federal rates for similarly termed loans. The safe haven interest rates do not apply to any loan or advance the principal of interest of which is expressed in a currency other than the U.S. dollars. In the case of a debt instrument, the proceeds or repayment of which is denominated in a foreign currency, the applicable federal rate shall be a foreign currency rate of interest analogous to the applicable federal rate used for U.S. debt instruments.[25]

U.S. Tax Treatment of Swaps

Although no one area of the tax law specifically governs foreign currency or foreign currency interest-rate swaps, generally for tax purposes swap transactions are not treated as loans. Because no funds advance from one party to the swap to the other party, the amounts paid or received under a swap arrangement are not taxed as interest payments, but are instead treated as ordinary business income and expense.

Consequently, for U.S. tax purposes, swap income or expense is treated as ordinary in nature and included in taxable income when recognized. Swap transactions that are components of hedge transactions may be subject to the special rules discussed later.[26]

PART III—HEDGING TRANSACTIONS

Hedging insulates a taxpayer from the financial risk arising from foreign currency fluctuations in the context of a number of transactions, including:

Receivables or payables denominated in foreign currencies.

Dividends and royalties receivable from foreign currency affiliates.

---

[25] Proposed Reg. Section 1.1274–6.

[26] In January 1987, the IRS issued notice 87–4 I.R.B. 1987–3, 7 which discusses the source rules for federal income tax purposes of swap income and swap expense attributable to United States dollar-denominated interest rate swaps where one of the contracting parties has its residence in the United States and has the United States as its functional currency. This notice does not cover issues regarding income or expense from the disposition of the swap agreement. These sourcing rules apply only to United States dollar-denominated interest rate swaps.

Equity investments in foreign branches or subsidiaries with foreign currency.

Long-term loans denominated in foreign currencies.

Long-term sales contracts or purchase commitments denominated in nonfunctional currencies.

Taxpayers hedge by entering into offsetting positions in the same foreign currencies so that the effects of foreign currency fluctuation on one leg of the transaction are fully or partially offset by opposite effects on the other leg.

For tax purposes, hedges are governed by a maze of different statutes, some of which are not yet operative and others of which were not originally enacted to apply to foreign currency transactions. Some of these rules, such as the Section 1256 and straddle rules, were originally intended to correct perceived abuses in the commodities areas and have been extended to the foreign currency area. As these rules sometimes unexpectedly apply to common foreign currency transactions, they are discussed later.[27]

988 Hedging Transactions

The Tax Reform Act of 1986 defined a 988 hedging transaction as any transaction entered into by the taxpayer primarily to reduce the risk of foreign currency exchange-rate fluctuations with respect either to property held or to be held by the taxpayer, or to borrowings made or to be made, or to obligations incurred or to be incurred by the taxpayer and identified by the taxpayer or the IRS as being a 988 hedging transaction. This broad definition includes hedges of assets and liabilities that could yield either capital or ordinary gains and losses. Foreign currency swaps may also be included in this definition.[28]

To the extent provided in regulations that are not yet issued, if a 988 hedge is identified as such on the date it is entered into, all positions in the hedging transaction are to be integrated, treated as a single transaction, and treated consistently for purposes of

---

[27] See also Andrea S. Kramer, *Taxation of Securities, Commodities, and Options*, 1986.

[28] Section 988(d)(2). The law refers to 988 hedges rather than Section 988 Hedges.

determining the character, source, and timing of the income of loss. Thus, transactions which on their own would generate U.S. source income or loss if part of a 988 hedge, can acquire foreign source income characteristics.[29]

For example, a U.S. taxpayer with a yen dividend receivable may wish to hedge any risk arising from dollar-yen fluctuations. Assume the taxpayer enters into a contract to sell the yen forward, and that at the time the dividend is received, the taxpayer has a gain on the forward contract but a loss on the value of the dividend. Absent a 988 identification of the hedge on the day it was entered into, the gain on the forward contract might be treated as a U.S. source while the decline in the yen value of the dividend would produce an undesirable reduction in foreign source income. A 988 identification however, would recast the forward contract gain from U.S. source into foreign source ordinary income, restoring the U.S. taxpayer to his original tax position.

It should be noted first that the 988 hedging rules apply to a transaction only when the taxpayer has identified them as such on the same day the hedges are entered into. Only the IRS can make a retroactive identification of a transaction as part of a 988 hedge. Second, the general 988 hedging provisions are not available until the IRS issues the regulations. Until then, the pre-Tax Reform Act of 1986 rules continue to apply. Foreign currency hedging transactions constitute straddles or Section 1256 contracts. As discussed later, these transactions may then be subject to the mark-to-market or the loss deferral rules.

Integrated Synthetic Transactions

Some hedging transactions are such perfect hedges that all risk from foreign currency fluctuations or cross fluctuations is eliminated. In the Tax Reform Act of 1986, Congress provided that a special set of Treasury regulations were to be promulgated to specially treat fully hedged transactions which together make up an integrated economic package through which the taxpayer has assured itself of a cash flow that does not vary with movements in exchange rates.

---

[29] Section 988(d)(1).

For instance, if a U.S. dollar functional currency taxpayer issues yen-denominated debt but through a series of sterling-yen swap arrangements hedges out all net economic exposure to yen-sterling exchange movements, it has in effect converted a yen borrowing into a sterling borrowing. Under the special rules for integrating certain hedging transactions, all the components of such a fully hedged foreign currency borrowing would be treated as the equivalent of a single currency borrowing, that is, sterling. Any special tax rules governing the separate components of the swap transition would be ignored. The U.S. dollar functional currency taxpayer would then be treated as issuing purely sterling debt.[30]

Foreign Currency Contracts

General Section 1256 Rules

Foreign currency contracts such as foreign currency options, forwards, and futures contracts, are subject to their own complex tax rules in both the commodities and international tax areas. The basic rules were introduced in 1981 and related principally to interbank and exchange traded instruments in the commodities industry. They have been subsequently modified and in 1986 were integrated with the new foreign currency rules.

The general rules for foreign currency contracts are contained in Section 1256, which defines a Section 1256 contract as including regulated futures contracts, any foreign currency contracts, and certain foreign currency options.[31] A regulated futures contract is defined as a contract generally traded on a U.S. qualified board of exchange.[32] A foreign currency contract is any contract which requires delivery of, or the settlement of which depends on the

---

[30] In January 1987, the IRS issued Notice 87–11 I.R.B. 1987 4, announcing that it will issue regulations under Section 988(d) regarding fully hedged currency transactions. The notice specifies that the regulations to be issued will set forth the consequences of integrating and treating as a single transaction all transactions that comprise a fully hedged Section 988 transaction that is an integrated economic package. The notice can also be relied on for transactions entered into after December 31, 1986.

[31] The authors wish to thank Paul M. Daugerdas of Arthur Andersen & Co. for his assistance in the Section 1256 and straddle areas.

[32] Section 1256(b)(1), (2), and (3).

value of, a foreign currency in which positions are traded through regulated futures contracts and traded in the interbank market. Most, but not all, contracts in major foreign currencies are 1256 contracts.[33]

Section 1256 contracts are subject to two special tax provisions. First, these contracts are marked-to-market, that is, at the end of each taxable year any accrued but unrecognized gain or loss is included in current taxable income. Second, all gain or loss from a marked-to-market Section 1256 contract, regardless of its holding period, is deemed to be 60 percent long-term and 40 percent short-term capital gain or loss. Thus, any unrealized appreciation or loss on the contracts is annually recognized for tax purposes on an accrued basis as 60 percent long-term and 40 percent short-term capital gain or loss.[34]

Interaction with the 988 Hedging Rules

Inevitably, a number of exceptions to the general Section 1256 mark-to-market rules are important as the 988 hedging rules are not yet fully in effect. Because these sections interact in a complex fashion, Figure 20–3 diagrams the conceptual interrelationships between Section 988 and Section 1256.

If any foreign currency contract, regardless of whether Section 1256 applies, is part of a 988 foreign currency hedge, then the provisions of Section 988 override both the Section 1256 mark-to-market and 60 percent/40 percent capital gain provisions. If a foreign currency contract is part of such a 988 hedge, then for U.S. tax purposes it will be integrated with the underlying transaction and take on its source and character. However, if the contract is part of a synthetic transaction, then, as part of the integration of the entire transaction, its nonfunctional currency characteristic may be entirely eliminated.[35]

Foreign currency contracts may not be part of a 988 hedge either because the contract is not part of a hedge or it would be part of a 988 hedge, but the 988 regulations are not yet issued.

---

[33] Section 1256(g)(1) and (7).
[34] Section 1256(a).
[35] Section 988(d)(1).

FIGURE 20–3
Overview of U.S. Taxation of Foreign Currency Contracts

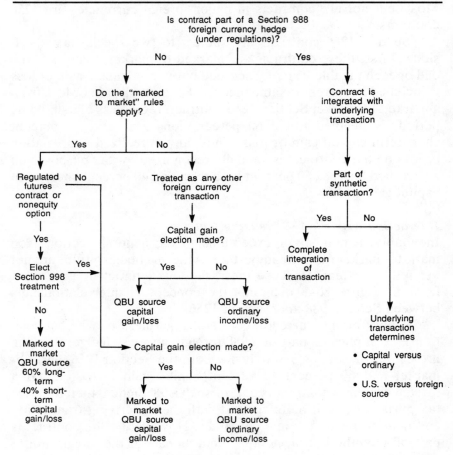

Interaction of Section 988 and Section 1256 Rules

Foreign currency contracts not governed by the 988 hedging rules may be subject to the Section 1256 mark-to-market rules previously described. Contracts subject to Section 1256 are then split into two types: those contracts traded on exchanges such as regulated futures contracts or listed options and all other foreign currency contracts.

The first type of contract is then subject to the full Section 1256 rules whereby the gain or loss from the foreign currency contract is marked-to-market at each year-end, and the gain or loss treated as 60 percent long-term and 40 percent short-term capital gain or loss. The source of the gain or loss is a U.S. source, assuming the taxpayer is a U.S. taxpayer. A special election is available to treat the gains and losses on traded foreign currency contracts as Section 988 gains and losses without affecting the mark-to-market requirement.[36]

Foreign currency Section 1256 contracts not traded on exchanges continue to be subject to the mark-to-market regime but their gain or loss is treated as arising under Section 988.[37]

Section 1256 rules may not apply to a contract for a number of reasons. First, Section 1256 rules would not apply in any case if the foreign currency contract is not of a specified currency. Second, Section 1256 has its own currency hedging exception. This exception applies only if the transaction is entered into in the ordinary course of business primarily to reduce the risk of currency fluctuations with respect to property or borrowings, the gain or loss on such transactions is treated as ordinary income or loss, and such transactions are clearly identified on the day entered into. It is more difficult to qualify for this hedging exception than a 988 hedge because it requires an ordinary income transaction but it is currently available.[38] Also, Section 1256 hedges do not provide for consistent treatment with respect to the source of the underlying transaction.[39]

Finally, the Section 1256 rules may be modified if it is a straddle loss deferral, if the contract is part of a mixed straddle, or if the taxpayer opts for the general Section 988 transaction rules to apply.[40]

Transactions Not Subject to the 988 Hedge or Section 1256 60/40 Percent Rules

If the Section 1256 rules do not apply, the foreign currency contract is treated as any other foreign currency transaction and gain or loss from the foreign currency contract is, in general,

---

[36] Section 988(c)(1)(D).
[37] Section 988(c)(1)(B)(iii).
[38] Section 1256(e).
[39] Section 1256(a).
[40] Sections 1256(d) and new 988(c)(1)(D)(ii).

ordinary and sourced by the residency of the taxpayer.[41] There is also a special election available whereby a taxpayer can identify, on the date entered into, a capital asset foreign currency contract otherwise yielding 988 ordinary income as producing only capital gain or loss. This election is intended for foreign currency speculators or taxpayers with other capital losses.[42]

Straddles

Tax Straddle Defined

As with the rules under Section 1256 governing foreign currency contracts, the straddle rules also came into the law as a result of transactions on the commodities exchanges. The original purpose of the straddle legislation was to limit certain perceived tax avoidance transactions whereby tax on certain income could be indefinitely deferred. The most unfortunate aspect of the straddle rules is that they can often apply without the taxpayer being aware of, or even intending to have a straddle in place.

For tax purposes, the term *straddle* means any two offsetting positions with respect to personal property.[43] A taxpayer holds offsetting positions with respect to personal property if holding one position substantially diminishes a taxpayer's risk of loss from holding the other position.[44] For these purposes, the term *personal property* means only personal property which is actively traded.[45] Shares in foreign subsidiaries would therefore not normally be considered to be a part of a straddle. The term *position* means an interest, including a futures or forward contract or option on personal property.[46] A position can include an obligation in non-functional currency denominated debt.[47]

Straddles are thus very broadly defined. A straddle can exist where a taxpayer hedges foreign currency loans. There are also

---

[41] Section 988(a)(3).
[42] Section 988(a)(1)(B).
[43] Section 1092(c)(1).
[44] Section 1092(c)(2)(A).
[45] Section 1092(d)(1).
[46] Section 1092(d)(2).
[47] Section 1092(d)(7)(A).

broad related persons rules providing that if a taxpayer has straddle positions held by any two subsidiaries, the straddle rules may apply.[48]

Treatment of Straddles

The purpose of the straddle rules is to prevent taxpayers who are at no economic risk from shifting taxable income from one time period to another. The tax straddle rules only operate when the loss leg of a straddle is closed out in one taxable year and the gain leg is closed out in a later year. The straddle rules do not deny deductibility of the loss on the closed loss leg, but rather defer its deductibility until the offsetting gain position is also closed out and recognized. Once the gain leg is closed out and the gains recognized for tax purposes, then the loss is also recognized for tax purposes.

Interrelationship between Section 1256 and Foreign Currency Rules

The tax rules governing straddles are even more convoluted than the rules of Section 1256 foreign currency contracts. The straddle rules are also interrelated with the Section 1256 foreign currency contract rules as well as the Section 988 foreign currency transactions rules. Figure 20–4 provides a conceptual overview of the U.S. taxation of foreign currency straddles.

First, if the straddle is part of a 988 hedge—as with Section 1256 contracts—the 988 hedge provisions completely override the tax straddle rules. Thus, if the loss leg is recognized before the gain, it is recognized for tax purposes, even if the gain leg is still open.[49]

The next test is whether or not the straddle contains a Section 1256 contract. There can be straddles without Section 1256 contracts, as might be the case with offsetting cash and payables denominated in the same nonfunctional currency. If the straddle does not contain any Section 1256 contracts, the straddle rules would automatically apply to defer recognition of the loss leg for tax purposes until the gain leg is recognized.

---

[48] Section 1092(d)(4)(A).
[49] Section 988(d)(1).

FIGURE 20–4
Overview of U.S. Taxation of Foreign Currency Straddles

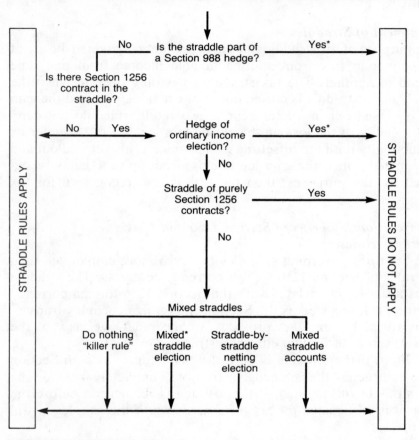

* "Mark-to-market" rules do not apply.
† Including "same day on, same day off" identified mixed straddles.

    If the straddle does contain a Section 1256 contract, a series of other provisions could apply to override the straddle rules. First, if there is a Section 1256 hedge of ordinary income assets which overrides the Section 1256 rules, the straddle rules are also overriden.[50] This means that if the taxpayer is hedging ordinary

---

[50] Section 1092(e).

income type assets with Section 1256 contracts, then the straddle rules do not apply to defer the recognition of the loss before the gain side of the straddle.

Second, it is possible to construct straddles consisting of only Section 1256 contracts. The straddle rules do not apply to such contracts because accrued losses and gains are recognized annually by the mark-to-market rules.[51]

If the straddle consists of a Section 1256 contract and a non-Section 1256 interest, it is deemed to be a mixed straddle. A taxpayer with a mixed straddle has a number of options. It can do nothing, which invokes the killer rule, as well as make the mixed straddle election under Section 1256(d), which prevents the operation of Section 1256 that allows the straddle rules to apply. The benefit of this mixed straddle election is that it avoids the mark-to-market rules, however the 60/40 percent characterization rules also do not apply. A taxpayer can also elect to maintain a mixed straddle account where all transactions including non-Section 1256 positions are marked-to-market daily.[52]

When there is a difference between capital gains and ordinary income tax rates however, the most favorable tax rate benefit is generally achieved by employing the straddle by straddle identification option, where each straddle is separately identified and tracked and the net gain, if attributable to a Section 1256 leg receives 60/40 percent treatment.

Some Common Hedging Transactions

Transaction Exposures
As discussed earlier, taxpayers can be constantly exposed to risk from various forms of foreign currency transactions. This exposure arises when receivables, payables, or loans are denominated in foreign currencies which fluctuate with respect to the taxpayers' functional currency. These exposures can also exist more insidiously in long-term purchase commitments or sales contracts where the purchase price or sales price is denominated in nonfunctional currencies.

---

[51] Section 1256(a)(1).
[52] See the Temporary Regulations under Section 1092.

Taxpayers seek to hedge their foreign currency exposures on these transactions by entering into various forms of forward currency contracts or even borrowing long-term debt denominated in the appropriate foreign currencies. These transactions can be subject to widely different tax treatment depending on actions taken or not taken by the taxpayer, sometimes on the very day on which the transactions occur. For instance, when the 988 hedge rules are operative, a taxpayer could elect, on the day on which the hedge is entered into, to have these special rules apply to all aspects of the transaction. The Section 1256 rules would then not apply to a foreign currency contract and the straddle rules would also not apply to defer recognition of the loss leg.

If a Section 988 election is not or cannot be made, and the transaction yields ordinary income, the taxpayer can still opt under Section 1256 to have the hedge treated as a hedge of an ordinary income item. Here, too, the identification must be made on the very date that the transaction is entered into and must be clearly indicated as such in the taxpayer's books and records. If a Section 1256 hedge treatment is appropriate, again neither the general Section 1256 nor the straddle rules would apply to any part of the transaction.

If neither one of these characterizations is appropriate, the Section 1256 rules apply to any foreign currency contracts and the straddle rules apply to defer the loss leg of the transaction. That means that the gain or loss on the contract is 60 percent long-term and 40 percent short-term U.S. source capital gain or loss. The gain or loss on the other side of the contract is subject to the general rules of Section 988, which characterize the gain or loss as ordinary and as U.S. source interest income or expense. The straddle rules also apply to defer recognition for tax purposes of the loss side of the straddle until the gain side is recognized.

Subsidiaries

The tax treatment of hedges of shares in foreign subsidiaries is unsettled. Under pre-1986 Tax Reform Act law, gains or losses from foreign currency contracts entered to hedge the foreign currency exposure of the equity investments in the shares of foreign subsidiaries were generally treated as capital gains or losses. Because these transactions were hedges of capital asset properties, the normal or ordinary income Section 1256(e) hedge rules were not available. In addition, because shares of subsidiaries generally do not qualify as personal property for purposes of the straddle rules, the straddle rules generally did not apply to these transactions.[53]

The situation was further complicated in 1981, however, when Section 1256 was amended. As part of a debate surrounding a change to Section 1256, Senators Robert Dole and Daniel Patrick Moynihan implied that the Section 1256 ordinary income hedge rules were intended to apply even to hedges of shares of foreign subsidiaries. If such is the case, a taxpayer could elect to exempt any gain or loss on foreign currency contracts from the normal Section 1256 rules and thereby also be exempt from the straddle rules.[54]

The situation was further muddled by the provisions of the Tax Reform Act of 1986 which introduced the 988 hedging rules which can apply to capital asset hedging transactions not covered under the Section 1256 rules. Although these new rules are not yet in effect, the effect of these provisions would be to treat the gain or loss on the foreign currency contract as being the same nature and source as the underlying asset it seeks to hedge. If the hedged asset is a long-term investment in a foreign subsidiary, there is a question as to whether or not the gains or losses on the regulated currency contract should be deferred until the investment in the shares of the subsidiary is liquidated. If so, the foreign currency gain or loss becomes, in effect, merely a semipermanent adjustment to the U.S. parent's tax basis in the foreign stock.[55]

PART IV—BUSINESS OPERATIONS CONDUCTED IN FOREIGN CURRENCIES

U.S. corporations conduct business operations outside the United States using a number of different legal structures such as branches, partnerships, and corporations. A branch is merely a

---

[53] Section 1092(d)(3)(A).
[54] See Section 1256(f)(1), *Hoover Co.* v. *Comm.*, Supra.
[55] Tax Reform Act of 1986 Conference Committee Reports at P. II-665-667.

division of a U.S. company conducting day-to-day business operations in a foreign country. The income of a branch is typically taxed currently by the foreign jurisdiction under local tax principles and then again currently by the United States at the U.S. corporate level. Branch earnings are subject to current U.S. tax whether they are distributed or not. Overseas business operations conducted through partnerships are essentially taxed as branches of the partner.

U.S. corporations more frequently conduct their foreign operations using foreign corporations. The income of foreign corporations is taxed locally when earned but is generally not subject to tax by the United States until distributed as a dividend back to the U.S. parent. The U.S. taxation of undistributed earnings is not deferred however when they arise from certain passive sources, or when they are deemed distributed as dividends by being invested in certain U.S. property such as loans to the U.S. parent.

Branches and International Partnerships

Each branch that is a qualified business unit with a nondollar functional currency computes its current U.S. taxable income in two steps. First, it computes its income or loss in its own functional currency using U.S. tax accounting principles. Second, it translates that income or loss into U.S. dollars using a weighted average exchange rate for the period over which the income or loss is accrued.[56] Because the taxable income or loss is computed on current earnings only, unrealized branch translation gains and losses are not included in taxable income.

If they are to be credited, foreign income taxes paid by each qualified business unit are translated into U.S. dollars using the historical exchange rates in effect at the time of actual payment.[57]

When a foreign branch remits earnings to the U.S. home office, the amount of U.S. dollars received may not be the amount of U.S. dollars of income previously included on its U.S. tax return. This results in an exchange gain or loss, computed in a

---

[56] Section 987.
[57] Sections 987(4) and 986(b).

manner very similar to that on a dividend from a foreign subsidiary. After 1986, remittances of foreign branch earnings or transfers involving branches with different functional currencies are treated as paid pro rata out of post-1986 accumulated earnings of the branch. Exchange gains and losses on such remittances are deemed to be ordinary instead of capital and treated as U.S. or foreign source income depending on the underlying income, which generated the accumulated profits.[58]

Foreign Subsidiaries
The U.S. shareholder of a foreign corporation is taxed on a cash distribution from a non-U.S. corporation if the foreign corporation is deemed to have positive earnings and profits, an item similar to financial statement retained earnings. After the Tax Reform Act of 1986, a foreign corporation's earnings and profits (E&P) must be calculated in its functional currency and accounted for separately from pre-1987 E&P. The E&P is then translated into dollars at the exchange rate in effect on the date the distribution is included in the taxable income of the U.S. parent. As the E&P is accounted for in the subsidiary's own functional currency, no translation of the foreign subsidiary's balance sheet into dollars is required so that E&P is not adjusted to reflect unrealized balance sheet translation gains and losses.[59]

Accumulated foreign taxes paid by the foreign corporation are accounted for in U.S. dollars and are translated into U.S. dollars using the historical exchange rate in effect as of the date of payment. Any refund of a foreign tax is translated using the rate in effect as of the payment date.[60]

Distributions of positive E&P carry with them underlying foreign taxes which can be claimed as credits against U.S. tax on the dividend. The amount of foreign tax credits associated with a specific dividend is computed on a pooling method and is equal to

---

[58] Section 987(3).
[59] Section 986.
[60] Sections 986(b)(1)(B)(ii) and 989(c)(4).

that portion of accumulated foreign taxes that the dividend paid bears to that subsidiary's accumulated E&P.[61] Or, alternatively,

$$\frac{\text{Foreign Tax Credit}}{\text{in Dollars}} = \frac{\text{Dividend in Functional Currency}}{\text{Accumulated E\&P in Functional Currency}} \times \frac{\text{Accumulated Foreign Taxes in Dollars}}{}$$

Figure 20–1 illustrates the operation of the system. The foreign subsidiary earns FC 1 million in pre-tax profits and pays a local 30 percent income tax of FC 300,000 when the exchange rate is FC 1 = $1.50. If the exchange rate is the same when the dividend is distributed, the U.S. corporation owes an additional $60,000 in U.S. tax to bring the total tax burden up to 34 percent. The effective foreign tax rate of this dividend is 30 percent = $450,000/$1,500,000, or the ratio of foreign tax credit to the sum of dividend income plus foreign tax credit.

If, the exchange rate falls to FC 1 = $1.00 when the dividend is paid, the dividend amount falls in value but the foreign tax credit computed at the historical exchange rate remains unaffected. The effective tax rate on the dividend therefore rises from 30 percent to 39.1 percent = ($450,000/$1,150,000); when the dividend is subject to U.S. tax, it generates excess foreign tax credits.

Fluctuations in Effective Foreign Tax Rates

These changes in effective foreign tax rates can occur because the foreign currency gain or loss on the undistributed earnings and profits is taxed in the United States essentially as another form of dividend income. The foreign taxing jurisdiction in terms of its own currency perceives no such gain or loss and does not tax or tax benefit the foreign exchange gain or loss. In the Figure 20–1 example therefore, there is no reduction in local taxes for the foreign currency loss.

These rules thus introduce an asymmetry between the U.S. tax treatment of undistributed earnings, the value of which fluctuates with foreign currency exchange rates, and foreign tax credits,

---

[61] Section 902(a).

the value of which is fixed at historical exchange rates. For example, in Figure 20–1, the foreign currency depreciates with respect to the U.S. dollar reducing the value of the dividend while holding the foreign tax credit constant and increases the effective foreign tax rate. In this case, the higher effective tax rate causes the dividend to generate excess foreign tax credits. If the foreign currency were to appreciate with respect to the U.S. dollar, the exchange gain would be treated as additional untaxed dividend income, the effective foreign tax rate would therefore fall, and the dividend would generate additional excess foreign tax credit limitation.

Figure 20–5 shows how foreign currency appreciation and depreciation with respect to the U.S. dollar, affect the effective foreign tax rate of undistributed earnings and profits. The system values foreign tax credits at their historical fair market value and

FIGURE 20–5
Exchange Rate Changes and Effective Foreign Tax Rates on Dividends

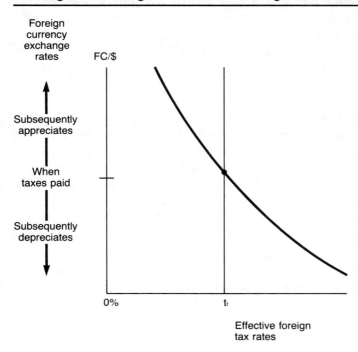

earnings at their current value. This historical valuation, however, is achieved at the cost of fluctuating dividend-effective foreign tax rates.

Pre-1987 Earnings of Foreign Subsidiaries

The foreign tax credit translation rules in effect before the Tax Reform Act of 1986 were different and continue to apply to undistributed pre-1987 earnings. Under the old rules, an annual E&P and foreign tax credit calculation was made in the subsidiary's functional currency. This resulted in annual layers of accumulated earnings and profits as well as their associated layers of foreign tax credits. Both E&P and foreign tax credits were accounted for in the same functional currency. As dividends were paid out of these E&P layers on a last-in first-out basis, layer by layer calculations were made to determine the foreign tax credits (and effective foreign tax rate) that accompanied each dividend.

The earnings and profits, and the underlying foreign tax credits were then translated into U.S. dollars at the foreign exchange rate in effect on the date of distribution. The historical exchange rate when the taxes were paid therefore had no effect on the undistributed foreign tax credits actually claimed. This system tended to preserve the effective foreign income tax rates in effect when the earnings were earned so that effective foreign tax rates did not fluctuate.

These earnings and profits rules are still in effect if foreign subsidiary retains earnings and profits earned prior to 1987. In addition to the old general rules, there was also a special set of rules for income deemed distributed. Income can be deemed distributed and, therefore, taxable for instance if it arises from passive sources, is invested in U.S. assets, or was accumulated in a foreign subsidiary sold by one U.S. person to another. These special earnings and profits rules, under Section 964, allowed the calculation of earnings and profits, and foreign taxes in U.S. dollars. This calculation allowed the inclusion of unrealized translation losses in the annual earnings and profits calculations.[62]

---

[62] Sections 902(c)(6) and 964.

Both of these systems of earnings and profits now coexist with the new Section 988 series of earnings and profits rules. Ordering rules determine which system is used to compute the amount of the deemed paid credit received with a dividend. As a general rule, the most recent earnings and profits are deemed to be distributed first. The deemed paid foreign tax credit is computed using the pooling method, that is, the weighted average as adjusted for foreign exchange effects. Only if a distribution exceeds the total earning and profits accumulated after 1986 is the layering approach considered. Then that portion of the deemed-paid credit is computed using the annual tax rate for each year in reverse order (i.e., first 1986, then 1985).

Remittance Decision

Foreign currency fluctuations affect the U.S. tax costs of a multinational firm by constantly changing the effective foreign tax rates on undistributed foreign earnings. In this environment, a U.S. parent of profitable foreign subsidiaries must constantly determine the optimal financing of its foreign subsidiaries. One of these financing decisions is whether the subsidiary should distribute those profits as dividends for reinvestment in the United States or alternatively reinvest local after-tax profits. This dividend or no dividend decision affects the debt-to-equity structures of both foreign subsidiaries and their U.S. parents. Naturally, once profits are distributed back to the United States, both the foreign profits and the U.S. profits subsequently generated by those foreign profits are subject to direct U.S. tax. Ideally this dividend decision should produce optimal after-tax financial results to the U.S. parent.

The real world dividend decision is generally made in the uncertain context of both nontax management or cash flow considerations, as well as the U.S. parent company's other tax planning around items such as expiring foreign tax credits or allocation of interest expense. In this context it may be difficult to appreciate the interaction of foreign currency fluctuation and taxes; therefore, the remaining portion of this chapter compares repatriating or reinvesting foreign earnings in an environment of complete certainty.

Some Assumptions

This analysis occurs in a financial environment of both perfect interest rate parity and tax predictability and focuses on how two local country variables, local income tax rates and local interest rates, affect the dividend decision. Interest rate parity assumes that the differences in interest rates between two currencies are perfectly compensated for by anticipated changes in the foreign-exchange rate. Initially there are no anticipated tax or interest rate shocks to the system.

Classical income tax systems are assumed so that the local income of a U.S. or foreign subsidiary is subject only to a flat marginal income tax. The after-tax foreign profits are then subject to a flat withholding tax, if any, when distributed back to a U.S. parent. Withholding taxes are not explicitly analyzed here since it can be shown that whatever their rate, they do not affect the fundamental analysis. Every foreign income tax is assumed to be fully creditable in the United States.[63]

The U.S. parent company is assumed to determine its foreign tax credit position first based on its nondiscretionary income. That is, the U.S. parent determines if it is in an excess foreign tax credit position or excess limitation position before any of the discretionary dividend income is considered. It is also assumed that it remains indefinitely in that foreign tax credit position regardless of the payment or nonpayment of discretionary dividends.

In Figure 20–6, any country, including the United States, can be shown as a point corresponding to the combination of its local income tax rate expressed as a percentage, and the local interest rate for some comparable debt. The combination for the U.S. company is shown as t_{us} and i_{us}, where t_{us} is the U.S. marginal income tax rate and i_{us} is the U.S. interest rate.

Excess Foreign Tax Credit Limitation for the U.S. Parent

If the U.S. parent is in a long-term excess foreign tax credit limitation position, intuitively all foreign subsidiaries with local income tax rates greater than the U.S. rate should distribute their earnings currently for reinvestment in the United States. For

---

[63] Countries with imputation systems such as the Federal Republic of Germany and the United Kingdom do not strictly meet this flat marginal tax rate requirement.

FIGURE 20–6
U.S. Parent with Excess Foreign Tax Credit Limitation

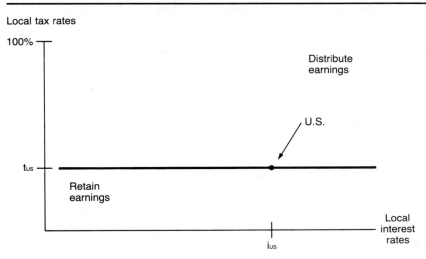

instance, if the U.S. tax rate is 34 percent and a foreign country's tax is 50 percent, a dividend of after-tax earnings generates excess foreign tax credits of 16 percent which can be claimed against other taxes owed to the United States. The after-tax earnings and excess foreign tax credit themselves generate more earnings which accumulate faster on an after-tax basis in the United States than if they were retained in a high-taxed local country. Conversely, all foreign subsidiaries with local tax rates less than the U.S. tax rate should retain their earnings for local reinvestment.

Foreign subsidiaries with local income tax rates equal to the U.S. income tax rate are indifferent as to whether to reinvest or distribute their earnings because the after-tax profits are the same. For instance, assume that the U.S. tax and interest rates are 34 percent and 8 percent and that the corresponding rates in a foreign country are 34 percent and 10 percent, respectively. If the initial exchange rate is FC 1 = $1 and the interest rate parity holds, the anticipated exchange rate one period later is $(1 + 10\%)/(1 + 8\%) =$ FC 1.0185 = $1. This means the depreciation of the FC with respect to the dollar is perfectly compensated for by the 2 percent higher interest rate that can be earned by investing in FC-denominated debt.

If the subsidiary has FC 10,000 of pre-tax earnings, and immediately distributes the after-tax cash and earns U.S. interest thereon, the after-tax results after one period are:

Immediate Dividend

Cash flow		
Pre-tax income	FC	10,000
Foreign tax at 34 percent		(3,400)
Dividend to the United States	FC	6,600
U.S. parent dividend income		$ 6,600
U.S. interest income at 8 percent		528
U.S. tax on the interest at 34 percent		(180)
End of period after-tax cash		$ 6,948

If the funds were retained, reinvested locally and then the total after-tax proceeds dividended back to the U.S. parent, the results would be as in the following table.

Reinvest Profits

Cash flow		
Pre-tax income	FC	10,000
Foreign income tax at 34 percent		(3,400)
After-tax earnings		6,600
Foreign interest income at 10 percent		600
Foreign tax on the interest at 34 percent		(224)
Cash dividend to United States	FC	7,036
U.S. parent dividend income FC 7,036 ÷ $1.0185/FC		$ 6,908
Utilization of excess foreign tax credits computed below		40
End of period after-tax cash		$ 6,948
U.S. tax computation		
Dividend income		$ 6,908
Foreign taxes FC 3,400 at 1 FC = $1		3,400
Foreign taxes FC 224 at 1.0185 FC = $1		220
U.S. taxable income		$10,528
U.S. tax at 34 percent		$(3,580)
Foreign tax credits		3,400
Foreign tax credits		220
Excess foreign tax credits		$ 40

The U.S. parent is, therefore, indifferent whether the earnings are left overseas or distributed back to the United States because, on an after-tax basis, the financial effects of any foreign currency fluctuation are perfectly compensated for. It can also be shown that this effect holds in general.

Because the U.S. parent is indifferent to the strength or weakness of the foreign currency, in Figure 20–6, all countries below the horizontal line should retain their earnings and not make distributions, while all countries above the line should make the distributions for investment in the United States.

U.S. Parent with Excess Foreign Tax Credits

When the U.S. parent is in an excess foreign tax credit position, the dividend decision depends on not only the local tax rate but also the local interest rate. A U.S. company in a long-term excess foreign tax credit position is essentially taxed as if it pays no marginal U.S. taxes on incremental foreign source income and receives no U.S. tax benefit for any foreign source losses. Any additional U.S. tax on incremental foreign source income is offset by excess foreign tax credits. Any foreign source loss does not affect net U.S. tax due and yields only more excess foreign tax credits. For such a U.S. parent, therefore, the marginal tax rate on foreign earnings is really only the marginal foreign tax rate including any withholding taxes.

By taxing a dividend at its fair market value when actually received, U.S. tax law treats foreign exchange gains and losses from undistributed subsidiaries' earnings as foreign source income. However, since these same foreign exchange gains and losses are not recognized by the local tax authorities, they are exempt from local income taxation and can be included in the foreign tax credit computation as zero-taxed foreign source income or loss.

For instance, consider our previous example of a U.S. parent with an excess foreign tax credit limitation. If the profits were distributed immediately and reinvested in the United States, the after-tax cash flow to the U.S. parent would still be $6,948. But for an excess foreign tax credit parent, the after-tax cash flows are different if the funds are reinvested and distributed one year later. If the U.S. parent is in an excess foreign tax credit position, the after-tax cash flow is not $6,948 because only $6,908 cash is received. This difference is solely because the U.S. parent cannot obtain a benefit for the $40 in excess foreign tax credits.

Figure 20–7 begins the analysis for a U.S. parent company with continuing excess foreign tax credits subject to a U.S. interest rate of i_{us} and a U.S. tax rate of t_{us}. If a foreign subsidiary is generating income subject to a local tax rate lower than the United States and the local interest rate is lower than the United States, the earnings should be retained and reinvested in the foreign subsidiary. The lower tax rate permits faster accumulation of earnings and a lower interest rate implies the foreign currency is appreciating with respect to the dollar. The dollar value of the accumulating earnings therefore steadily increases. Thus, all earnings of foreign subsidiaries subject to local income tax rates less than the United States and interest rates less than the United States should be retained by the foreign subsidiaries and not distributed.

Conversely, all earnings of foreign subsidiaries with local tax rates higher than the United States and local interest rates greater than the United States should be immediately distributed. The

FIGURE 20–7
U.S. Parent with Excess Foreign Tax Credits

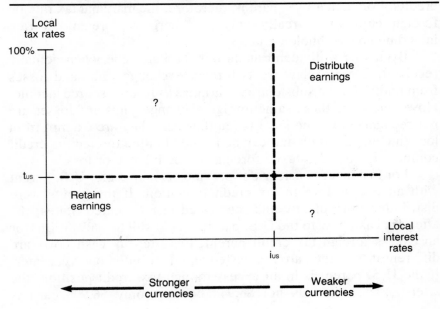

reason is a higher foreign tax rate slows the accumulation of after-tax profits and a higher interest rate implies the dollar value of the after-tax profits will be falling.

However, it is more difficult to resolve countries with either currencies weaker than the dollar and tax rates lower than the United States or alternatively currencies stronger than the dollar with higher tax rates. At these interest rates, the benefits of a lower local income tax rate may or may not be offset by the cost of foreign exchange losses.

Taxpayers should be indifferent to those combinations of tax and interest rates where the after-tax local yield on interest adjusted for the appreciation or depreciation of the local currency with respect to the dollar equals the U.S. after-tax yield on U.S. interest. It is possible, based on the specific values of i_{us} and t_{us}, to calculate the combination of local tax and interest rates at which a U.S. parent with excess foreign tax credits is indifferent to distributing or reinvesting the foreign subsidiary earnings.

Figure 20–8 illustrates the locus of such countries where distributing or reinvesting local profit yields the same after-tax return to a U.S. parent. Companies in countries to the upper right

FIGURE 20–8
Distribution/Retention of Local Earnings

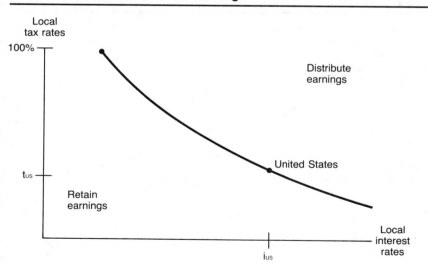

of the line should generally distribute their earnings while those to the lower left reinvest them. Companies with the same interest and tax rates as the United States can either distribute or retain their earnings.

Figure 20–9 shows some illustrative countries; this figure is not drawn to scale.

Unfortunately, real decisions are not so simple. This analysis isolates the foreign currency components of the calculation but does not consider a number of other factors, especially the effect of the expense allocation on the foreign tax credit limitation. A highly leveraged U.S. parent company may have a strong bias toward the repatriation of earnings, notwithstanding any tax savings.

Pre-1987 Earnings and Profits

The preceding discussion is based on the general rules governing E&P generated after 1986. It is also possible to similarly analyze the factors governing the distribution or retention of pre-1987 earnings, which may remain in a number of foreign subsidiaries. In fact, the curve governing pre-1987 E&P whatever the parent's foreign tax credit position is the same curve for post-1986 E&P

FIGURE 20–9
Sample Countries

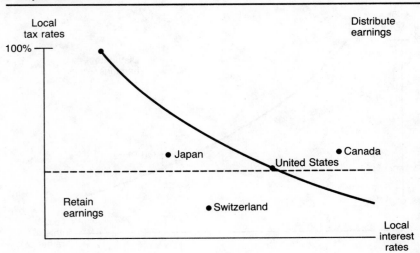

with the parent in an excess foreign tax credit position. However, pre-1987 E&P can only be distributed after all post-1986 E&P has been distributed, and the local earnings generated from accumulated pre-1987 E&P are all treated as post-1986 E&P.

Shocks to the System

Figure 20–10 shows the effect of a reduction in U.S. marginal corporate tax rates such as occurred with the enactment of the Tax Reform Act of 1986 whereby companies in more foreign countries should be distributing their earnings because with a lower tax rate, the United States becomes a more tax-attractive location to do business. U.S. parents in an excess limitation position now repatriate the profits of subsidiaries in countries with tax rates between 34 percent and 46 percent. U.S. parents with excess foreign tax credits also have their dividend indifference curves shift down, resulting in more countries which should make dividend distribution to the United States.

Similarly, Figure 20–11 shows the impact of a rise in U.S. interest rates whereby a weaker U.S. dollar may increase the number of countries where reinvestment is preferred. Such a U.S.

FIGURE 20–10
Decrease in U.S. Tax Rate

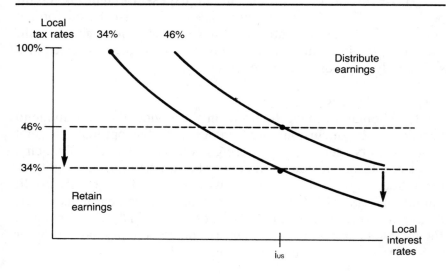

FIGURE 20–11
Increase in U.S. Interest Rate

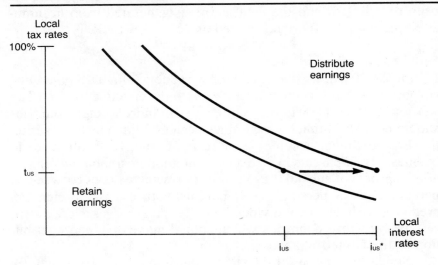

interest rate change shifts the point for the United States right-ward. This does not affect the decisions of a U.S. parent with excess limitations because only local tax rates determine the decision.

However, a U.S. parent in an excess foreign tax credit position is affected, as the appreciation of undistributed foreign currency earnings is untaxed foreign source income. It will, therefore, retain earnings in some countries that are converted into sufficiently appreciating currency countries.

Some Conclusions
First, although we have focused on the dividend or no dividend decision, the conclusions are analogous to the optimal marginal debt-to-equity decision for foreign subsidiaries. The financing needs of a local subsidiary can either be satisfied through equity or local debt. For a U.S. parent with excess foreign tax credit limitation Figure 20–6 can be recast from retained earnings versus dividend earnings into marginal equity or marginal debt. Similarly, Figure 20–8 can be recast as marginal debt and marginal equity for U.S. parents with excess foreign tax credits.

Second, this analysis suggests that for tax purposes, U.S. parents with excess foreign tax credit limitation are indifferent to whether currencies are weaker or stronger with respect to the dollar but are sensitive solely to changes in U.S. and local tax rates. U.S. parents with excess foreign tax credits must balance both interest and tax rates to remain in an optimal capital structure. Occasionally they must distribute or not distribute in apparently counterintuitive situations.

PART V—CONCLUSION

First, we have demonstrated that metaphysical tax concepts have a real impact on the after-tax financial performance of the firm and can convert financially optimal transactions into suboptimal transactions. Because taxes do affect financial decisions, firms must inevitably adjust their financial strategies to accommodate these forces.

Second, the complexity of the tax and financial consequences of these transactions requires not only careful prestructuring but also close observation to obtain the optimal financial results. It is important to track a large volume of information, both to substantiate the positions taken on a company's tax return, and to properly fine-tune a company's operations. Sophisticated computer software has become the only realistic solution to this problem.

CHAPTER 21

COUNTRY RISK EVALUATION

Thomas J. Trebat

INTRODUCTION TO COUNTRY RISK EVALUATION

Country risk arises when debt service payments are somehow dependent on the actions of government. Country risk evaluation concerns the likelihood that residents of a country will be able and willing to meet external payment commitments to foreign creditors. Country risk encompasses sovereign risk which is the special case in which the sovereign (the government or one of its agencies) is the direct obligor of an external liability and private risk when the obligor is a nonsovereign foreign resident, that is, a private, individual firm.

Whether the ultimate obligor is the sovereign or a private corporation, in the final analysis, the creditor must look to a single source of repayment: the future foreign-exchange earnings of the country. If the sovereign is unable to discharge its external obligations because of an economic crisis and consequent foreign-exchange shortfall, private corporations may not have access to the foreign exchange needed to service their external debt either. This risk arises even in cases in which the private sector obligor has adequate liquidity measured in domestic currency, that is, even when the creditworthiness of the private borrower is not in question. Because of this, the terms *country risk* and *sovereign risk* are often used interchangeably.

638

But although all so-called cross-border claims give rise to country risk, the distinction between sovereign risk and private risk remains important. Obligations incurred by private firms and corporations also expose foreign creditors to more ordinary commercial or credit risks in addition to the underlying country risk. These credit risks are not independent of the actions of the sovereign in the sense that poor government policies can weaken business conditions and exacerbate the risk of lending to private corporations.

Institutional arrangements in international lending also make it important to maintain a distinction between sovereign lending and lending to private corporations. The great developing country debt crisis of the 1980s has drawn new attention to the fact that the property rights of sovereign lenders are ill defined. Private sector lenders may have recourse to the legal system, including bankruptcy courts, to define, enforce, and protect their claims. Lenders to sovereigns, including government-owned corporations operating on a commercial basis, find themselves in a legal gray area when conditions arise that make it impossible for the sovereign to discharge all external obligations. In such cases, it is often impossible to define the loss that has been incurred by the creditors or to establish a hierarchy of creditor claims to parcel out the loss.

The concept of country risk arises most readily in the context of international lending. International commercial banks must weigh the extent to which loans on the balance sheet and commitments to extend credit in the future expose the bank to country risk. They must come to grips with the question of whether or not the bank's capital position is adequate in view of the risk of default, that is, whether the projected rate of return on international lending is justifiable in the light of the country risk. This requires an understanding and appreciation of the importance of political, social, and economic factors on the ability of countries to meet debt service payments. Country risk evaluation attempts to provide for the intelligent layman a compact framework for thinking about these factors and judging their relevance for business decisions.

The development of country risk evaluation in banks lagged during that period in time when an effective early warning risk system was most sorely needed. It was not until late in the international lending boom of the 1970s that country risk evaluation became integrated into the decision-making processes of the largest international banks and, even then, only under pressure from supervisory authorities in various industrial country governments. High rates of return on international lending and a long history of negligible loan losses on sovereign borrowings lulled many banks into a false sense of security. Most international lending prior to the 1970s involved claims on residents of industrial countries where sovereign risk considerations seemed remote. No major cases of international defaults had occurred since the 1930s when, in any case, the bond markets rather than the commercial banks were the major creditors.

The rapid growth of international lending to developing countries throughout the world, but particularly in Latin America, forced banks to upgrade their ability to understand country risks. The resources dedicated to staff development and information gathering increased steadily at many large banks as the lending boom crested in the early 1980s and then gave way suddenly to a reverse tide of debt reschedulings in the rest of the decade.

The legacy of this period is that large international banks have honed their skills in detecting and acting on the early indicators of country risk. If this knowledge is preserved for future generations of managers, improved country risk evaluation will mitigate the next boom and bust cycle in international lending. In the meantime, the techniques and lessons from country risk evaluation will be useful to both banks and to other international corporations as they seek to understand the risks involved in acquiring cross-border claims in the 1990s and beyond.

A CONCEPTUAL FRAMEWORK
FOR EVALUATION

Country risk evaluation rests heavily on economists' ability to analyze a country's balance of payments. The net external asset position of a country results from a history of balance of payments outcomes. The ability to service external debt in a timely fashion depends on the volume and rate of growth of exports.

The economic assessment of country risk rapidly becomes more complex when one considers that the balance of payments accounts are really only part of global supply and demand relations within an economy. A deficit in the current account of the balance of payments of an economy results in a buildup of a country's external debt or a drawdown of its international reserve assets. In a broader context, the current account deficit reflects a situation in which domestic demand exceeds aggregate domestic supply. The excess domestic demand becomes a demand for foreign goods and services which are paid for via the export of IOUs from corporations and government agencies resident in the country.

Because the buildup of external debt is rooted in macroeconomic trends in the economy as a whole, the economist must look beyond simple ratios drawn from the balance of payments and external debt statistics. Government economic policies and their impact on economywide trends in demand and supply must be on the center stage of the analysis of country creditworthiness.

Governments fashion economic policies to win elections or otherwise to prolong themselves in power, not to reassure external creditors anxious to see a reasonable balance over time in the country's economy. So to say that country risk evaluation is concerned with economic policies in a country is also to say that it is concerned with the push and pull of politics and how this affects the choice of economic policies.

Balance of payments problems and debt servicing difficulties occur as a result of both economic and political forces. Therefore, country risk evaluation involves a blending of the insights and techniques of both economics and political science. The following discussion of a stylized balance of payments crisis provides a way to see how these factors fit together.

Understanding a Debt Service Crisis

A debt service crisis results from a complex interaction of political and economic forces, stemming from both internal and external sources.[1] The interaction of conflicting political and economic

---

[1] This section draws heavily on an article that I wrote with my colleague, Lawrence J. Brainard: "The Role of Commercial Banks in Balance of Payments Crises: The Cases of Peru and Poland." Paper presented to the International Conference on Multinational Corporations in Latin America and Eastern Europe. Bloomington, Indiana, March 5–8, 1981.

factors generates what can be called a policy cycle which consists of a series of identifiable stages. These include:

1. The formulation of the political goals of the government and the initial impact of these goals on the economic behavior of individuals, firms, and the government itself.
2. The appearance of foreign-exchange shortages and other signs of economic disequilibriums.
3. A balance of payments crisis characterized by the severe depletion of foreign-exchange reserves and serious debt servicing difficulties.
4. Economic stabilization and recovery.

The policymakers of the economic regime take as a given the primacy of their political goals, particularly prolonging the regime's or the party's or the ruling elite's permanence in power. With this goal uppermost in mind, a tendency arises to either overestimate resources available in the economic system to meet these goals or to underestimate the adjustment effort needed to counter external shocks. Typically, the regime promises too much to too many social groups; eventually aggregate demand overwhelms the output limits of the economic system. Inflation, shortages, balance of payments deficits, and mounting external debt are all signs of the market disequilibriums produced by such policies.

The policy response of the regime to the appearance of economic imbalances is key to the propagation of the policy cycle. The politicians' concern for political goals, combined with their excessive optimism and limited knowledge of the economy's resource constraints, makes them slow to recognize and react to warning signs of problems, such as a growing shortage of foreign exchange or rising inflationary pressures. Monetary, fiscal, and exchange rate policies are not properly aligned as the political costs of economic adjustment are deemed excessive.

The process is carried to a point at which economic stresses overburden the political system, thus producing a crisis both political and economic. The crisis leads to fundamental changes in economic policy designed to reduce the stresses and strains caused by economic disequilbrium and to move the economy closer to an economic equilibrium. These changes are likely to include changes in the top political leadership of the country.

The link of this policy cycle to external borrowing and a foreign debt crisis can now be drawn. Borrowing allows policymakers two possibilities: (1) to attract additional resources to help achieve their specific policy goals; and (2) to use external resources to mitigate economic problems, thus postponing effective (and politically costly) adjustment.

The policy cycle for borrowing countries can now be set out. It consists of five discreet stages, each associated with different lender behaviors.

Low Levels of Borrowing.   The policy cycle is generated by the inconsistency of the regime's political goals with the country's economic situation: its economic system and resource endowment. During this phase of early debt accumulation, foreign borrowings are used primarily to help meet the specific goals of the regime. Reasoning that policymakers will adjust before debt levels become excessive, banks are usually willing lenders to the country during this phase of the cycle.

Rising External Debt.   Economic imbalances worsen as policymakers prefer to avoid painful economic adjustments rather than risk losing political support. They remain hopeful that economic problems over time are manageable and see foreign borrowing as the best way to bridge the gap between domestic expenditures and incomes. Commercial banks remain willing lenders, acting in the belief that policymakers will make promised economic reforms in time to head off a debt crisis. Banks do turn more cautious, however, insisting on more favorable lending terms such as higher interest spreads and shorter tenors.

Crisis Phase.   The cumulative effects of the economic imbalances and the inability of policymakers to contain them lead to a serious economic crisis. An external shock of some sort—a decline in the terms of trade or a rise in world interest rates—can hasten the onset of the crisis. The crisis is triggered in part by a restriction in the flow of new credits from commercial banks that finally react to evident economic problems, particularly excessive debt levels. The lenders at first limit their new credit exposure, then cease to lend, then seek ways to reduce exposure as quickly as possible, often by pulling in short-term lines of credit.

Rescheduling Phase. Policymakers are forced to come to grips with the economic crisis and lack of foreign financial support. Efforts are made to stem foreign-exchange outflows deepening the economic crisis. Foreign-exchange controls are placed on domestic residents. Principal repayments to foreign creditors are halted and interest arrears may be allowed to accumulate. Banks are forced to reschedule loan repayments and possibly to refinance interest as well. They may agree as well to keep open limited amounts of foreign trade lines.

Stabilization and Recovery. Fundamental economic and political changes are made in the country to reduce the economic imbalances which led to the debt crisis. Commercial banks and other lenders continue to play a mostly passive role limiting their activity to refinancing past loans and maintaining short-term lines. However, some creditors perceive that permanent political and economic changes have occurred and begin again to provide credit.

Summing up, five stages of borrowing have been identified in the policy cycle ranging from early borrowing to a full-fledged debt crisis to economic recovery. From the lender's viewpoint, the purpose of country risk evaluation can be restated as sifting through political and economic intelligence to identify correctly these stages in any given country and to adjust lending policies accordingly. Certain economic and political indicators are useful in this task. These are summarized in the following section.

BASIC TECHNIQUES OF COUNTRY ASSESSMENT

Professional economic and political judgments are indispensable in the country risk evaluation, but the basic concepts used by the analyst can and should be readily understood by all participants in the country risk decision-making process.

Most country risk meetings revolve around a structured report prepared by an analyst or a team of analysts. The information and assessments of the analysts typically are grouped in the following categories:

1. Domestic economy.
2. Balance of payments and external financing.
3. Economic policy assessment.
4. The political environment.
5. Summary overview and assessment.

The first three topics involve a review of economic and financial information, the fourth expressly treats the political risk factors, while the final summary should be a view integrating both economic and political views. The summary section should also contain the analyst's recommendation on the practical business issues to be decided at the country risk meeting.

More quantitative in nature, the economic concepts used in the country risk report are more readily summarized. Their use and interpretation in an actual country review are illustrated in the country worksheet of Korea included as an appendix. The worksheet typically summarizes the recent five or so years of economic history and project the main economic variables for at least the next year or two.[2]

The Domestic Economy

Gross national product (GNP) or gross domestic product (GDP) and the related concept of per capita GDP (lines 1 and 3 on the worksheet) are commonly used indicators of economic size and comparative economic development. GDP is a rough measures of the value of goods and services produced by a country in a given year. Recent and projected future changes in real GDP (line 3) give clues to the success or failure of economic policy in lifting national output and income over time.

Proper interpretation of GNP growth rates requires awareness of other economic indicators. A high growth rate of GDP is a positive indicator, provided it is not associated with rising inflation or a growing trade deficit. A low or negative growth rate may also

---

[2] In this section, I have relied on materials provided by Lawrence J. Brainard.

be a positive sign, if it reflects policy measures to curb inflation or imports.

Gross fixed investment (line 4) and its real rate of growth (line 5) give clues to the sources of economic growth and the likelihood of future growth. It measures the value of investment in the country's fixed assets—its capital stock in machinery and equipment, buildings, and housing. The economist looks at trends in fixed investment relative to GDP to determine the country's degree of effort in replacing worn-out capital and adding new capacity to the economy. A low investment share, say, 15 percent or less of GDP could indicate a lack of investment opportunities (possibly because of high real interest rates) and poor economic growth prospects. A high rate investment of 25 percent or more usually indicates a dynamic economy, but it could also be a warning of overambitious plans which are being financed by foreign credit. Furthermore, the simple indicator tells nothing of the efficiency with which resources are being invested in the economy. A look at other indicators is needed.

A series of other indicators permit a fuller evaluation of the quality of government economic policy and its impact on the balance of payments. The ratio of the public sector deficit to GNP (line 6) provides an international comparative benchmark of the size of the government's deficit. The public deficit measures the size of total government borrowings (whether from foreign or omestic creditors) to cover shortfalls between revenues and expenditures. The higher the deficit, the greater the pressure of government spending on interest rates and the higher the risk that borrowing shortfalls will be financed by printing money. A high deficit adds to overall aggregate demand which could decrease exports and add to imports, adversely affecting the balance of payments.

Indicators of the nature of government financial policies are also found in the statistics on money supply growth (line 8) (here interpreted as M-1) and domestic credit (line 7). These summarize recent growth trends in overall liquidity in the economy and the growth of lending by commercial banks and the monetary authorities to the public and private sectors. When interpreted in the light of data and inflation and interest rates, these indicators reflect the degree of slackness or tightness in government monetary policy.

Relatively high rates of growth of these aggregates can be a sign of future inflation and balance of payments problems.

Rounding off the list of indicators of trends in the domestic economy are data on consumer prices (line 9) and the unemployment rate (line 10). In practice, both indicators are notoriously unreliable. Consumer prices can be manipulated by government price controls; unemployment data are frequently unavailable and rarely comparable from one country to another. Taken in conjunction with other indicators, however, they contribute to an assessment of the relative success or failure of economic policy and the pressures of domestic expenditures and output on inflation and the balance of payments.

Balance of Payments and External Finance

The core of country risk evaluation is in applied balance of payments analysis. The balance of payments is a summary tabulation of credits and debits between residents of one country and all nonresidents, that is, the rest of the world, during the course of a year. Special significance attaches to the current account balance (line 11) whether expressed in dollars or in percent of GDP (line 12). This aggregates the credit and debit items deriving from exports and imports of goods (merchandise trade on lines 13–17), services (banking, insurance, tourism, shipping, interest, and dividends on lines 18–22), and net official and private transfers (government grants, private gifts, and other remittances on line 23.)

The current account balance is identically equal to the change in the country's stock of net international assets. Expressed in terms of national income accounting, the current account balance is the difference between domestic savings and domestic investment in a given year. A current account deficit indicates that investment exceeds savings from domestic sources, hence the country is importing savings from the rest of the world. The country's stock of external liabilities must increase.

Trends in the export and import components of the balance of payments are affected by external shocks, particularly a deterioration in the country's international terms of trade. This can be produced by changes in international prices of particular commodities—for example, oil or grain, which are important in a country's export bill—or by sharp increases in international interest rates applicable to the country's external debt. A world recession leading to a decline in demand for the country's exports is another example of an external shock.

Export and import data are closely monitored for indications of success or failure in boosting foreign exchange earnings and improving debt servicing capacity over time. High rates of export growth (line 15) are usually a positive sign, especially in connection with high rates of investment as this may indicate that economic growth is export-led. High rates of import growth (line 17) could be a negative sign, especially if associated with growing current account deficits. Service payments (line 21) include payments of interest on external debt and, thus, are an indicator of the country's vulnerability to external interest rate shocks.

The capital account of the balance of payments indicates the financing for the net change in the country's international asset position signaled by the current account balance. As such, it records inflows and outflows of such financing items as direct foreign investment (line 25), net long-term financing (line 24) and net short-term capital transactions (line 26). The distinction between long-term and short-term capital flows is usually made on the basis of the original maturity of the underlying financing item. Financing items with a maturity of more than one year are grouped in the capital account. The short-term capital account tends to be a catch-all category which includes short-term trade financing and errors and omissions. "Balance" in the balance of payments is assured by the net change during the year of the international reserves of the central bank or monetary authority, the total balance (line 29) item in the worksheet.

Indicators of International Liquidity

Accumulated balance of payments flows results in a stock of international assets and liabilities. Indicators of international assets (or reserves) and liabilities (or debt) are summarized in the second page of the typical worksheet.

Gross foreign assets (lines 30–35) is one view of the stock of liquid foreign exchange available to the banking system of the country for purposes such as servicing debt obligations. Central bank reserves (line 32), here defined to exclude gold holdings, is one of the most important measures as liquidity available to the central bank is frequently the main criterion used by the sovereign in the decision to suspend external debt payments. In practice, it is often necessary to go beyond this summary indicator of central bank liquidity to inquire about the structure of reserve assets. How much foreign exchange is freely available in the form of cash versus longer-term foreign assets less readily transformed into cash? What part of the reserve position results from short-term borrowings by the central bank? How far is the central bank willing to draw down cash reserves in the event of a payments crisis? Expressing reserves as a percentage of imports (line 33) sheds light on this issue, with three to six months of import coverage usually considered a minimum.

It is often important to consider other sources of foreign-exchange liquidity in addition to central bank reserves. The sovereign may have recourse to International Monetary Fund (IMF) drawings (line 34) providing emergency balance of payments loans conditioned on economic reform. IMF borrowings are available to member countries of the fund up to a multiple of the country's fund quota which is determined as a function of the country's size. Residents of the country (whether official or private sector residents) may acquire claims on western banks. To some extent, this indicator measures the "capital flight" which has occurred, although data coverage is spotty at best for most countries. Net foreign assets of the commercial banks (lines 35–37) describe the net foreign-exchange position of the country's own banks and, as such, permit an assessment of the net foreign-exchange position of the banking system as a whole.

Indicators of external indebtedness are grouped in lines 38–46. Total external debt (line 38) is as comprehensive a measure as possible of total liabilities of residents with respect to nonresidents. It is broken down into short-term debt (line 39) and medium-term debt, with one-year original maturity in the loan instrument again being the cutoff point. A high level of short-term debt is a negative sign indicating the country's vulnerability to sudden shifts in the sentiment of creditors. Debt to western banks (line 40) is an indicator of the part of the debt that is on ordinary commercial terms as opposed to debt to multilateral lenders and official lenders, often available to countries on "soft" terms.

Commonly used ratios, often interpreted with the help of rules of thumb, relate a country's external indebtedness to its ability to pay. The ratio of debt to exports (line 41) relates the total debt to the annual flow of export earnings. Total debt in excess of 1.5 to 2 times exports is usually a reliable indicator of imminent debt servicing difficulties. The debt service ratio (line 45) draws a relationship between the amounts of interest and amortization payments and annual exports. The rule of thumb that has emerged is that the risk of default rises sharply when the debt service ratio exceeds 20 percent of exports.

Political Risk Assessment

The fundamental dynamics of the policy cycle are provided by politics; hence, the critical importance of the political risk assessment in the overall country review.[3] The key question is whether the political system in the country provides support for those economic policies that maintain creditworthiness over the longer term. Judgment must rest on quantitative intelligence about social and political institutions, but the qualitative interpretation of these data is the crucial element in the analysis.

In contrast to the economic indicators just reviewed, indicators of political risk are inherently more difficult to define. Two temptations must be avoided. The first is to react to the complexity of the subject by delving into excessive detail on politics and society which can hinder decision making. The second and more dangerous is to react to complexity by throwing one's hands in the air, relying only on the most casual empiricism—hunches or intuition—to come to conclusions about the political risk.

A structured approach to political risk can be built on an understanding of the economic dynamics. Is the political environment supportive of the economic policies needed to maintain or recover creditworthiness?

---

[3] A basic reference on political risk assessment is William H. Overholt *Political Risk,* (London: Euromoney Publications, 1982).

From this vantage point, political analysis of country risk proceeds to group and assess intelligence in the following categories:

Country Leadership.   The top leadership must be assessed as to its competence, honesty, and particular economic ideology. Other important considerations include the stability in office of the leadership and likely successors in the event change is probable.

Government Institutions.   A positive sign is the existence of government institutions staffed by competent technocrats able to implement economic policies on the basis of adequate information. A happy medium is desired between entrenched bureaucracies who resist needed economic reforms and demoralized institutions handicapped by political interference. It is particularly important to assess those institutions responsible for the implementation of economic policy: the central bank, the ministry of planning, the ministry of finance, the agencies responsible for foreign trade policies.

Social Environment.   Political risk is attenuated by a lack of severe social divisions which could produce tumultuous political change and radical restructuring of the economic rules of the game. Social fractures along economic, racial, religious, or ethnic grounds must be assessed. The economic strategies of the main opposition political groups, such as nonruling political parties, should also be taken into account.

International Relations.   The country's approach to multi-lateral cooperation is often of critical importance. Positive indicators are commitments to freer international trade flows, a track record of support for and cooperation with the IMF and the World Bank, and a welcoming attitude to foreign direct investment.

USING THE COUNTRY RISK EVALUATION

Even the best country risk assessments are of little use unless managers can find a way to integrate the information and opinions of the report into the corporate decision-making process. The country risk meeting provides the setting for discussing and criticizing the evaluation and drawing the implications of the evaluation for lending policies. The purpose of the country risk meeting is to reach a "bottom line" assessment of how the corporation's viewpoint on country risk should be translated into a country limit decision providing guidance to lending officers.

Because of the complexity of country risk evaluation, it is not realistic to suppose that an analyst's report can or should be the sole basis for corporate policies. Hard and fast "scores" or foolproof country rating systems are neither possible nor desirable, in part because assumptions inevitably play a large role in any analysis and these need to be questioned.

The meeting format should allow each of three types of participants to express their viewpoints on the country risk and its relation to the business opportunities presented. These would include the senior officers, usually credit officers with ultimate decision-making authority, line officers who have the best perspective on actual business opportunities, and the analysts responsible for preparing the economic and political assessments.

The purpose of the meeting should be to review the written assessments of the risk environment in a given country and to contrast the conclusions with the types of business opportunities present. Many meetings, for example, on Organization for Economic Cooperation and Development (OECD) countries such as Japan and West Germany, can be quite abbreviated in all respects because the country risk (as opposed to credit risks) of doing business is negligible. Other countries reviewed are so clearly at the opposite end of the country risk spectrum—for example, countries such as Bolivia, Nicaragua, and Zaire—as to make any business opportunities hardly worth discussing.

The most important country meetings concern the large number of countries in that vast middle ground between those with gilt-edged credit ratings and those in outright default. With respect to these middle countries, opinions within the bank about the perceived risk may differ between analysts and line officers. A certain amount of creative tension can be generated as opposing viewpoints on the risk environment and its consequences for bank business are argued in the presence of senior management.

One can see from this description of meeting dynamics that success is directly dependent on a significant commitment of senior management time to the preparation and evaluation of arguments. For this reason even though country risk systems are designed to save on management time and expense by compressing the complexity into a single score or a forced ranking system, they can be quite costly in the long run by discarding valuable information.

For example, it might be appropriate and profitable to do business in countries which would receive a low risk score in a quantitative system. The particular business being considered in the country might deal adequately with the perceived risk or be special in nature; for example, financing of a vital import for the country or lending that is collateralized by funds held outside the country. By the same token, it might be a mistake not to question lending to countries that may rate highly on a quantitative scale, but whose standing could decline if certain assumptions prove unwarranted.

The outcome of the country risk meeting is a decision on the limit of exposure to the country in question that the corporation can accept. The overall limit refers to an aggregate exposure of the corporation to the country in question. It refers to all cross-border claims, including those arising in branches and subsidiaries of the corporation. Credit extensions beyond the amount stipulated in the aggregate exposure limit are not permitted.

In fact, this overall limit is comprised of several sublimits applicable to different businesses. Specific sublimits typically refer to the amount of medium-term credits (i.e., credit of more than one year original maturity) and commitments to extend medium-term credit. Other sublimits may be established for short-term lending, for loans to specific sectors in the country (e.g., to banks or private indigenous corporations) that could be considered particularly risky, and for total funded outstandings at any point in time (as opposed to the total of outstandings and commitments governed by the aggregate limit).

If all views are aired properly, the country risk meeting should end with a consensus among all parties concerned about bank policies with no need for a formal vote. One of the following decisions about the country limit should result from the meeting:

1. No change in the limit is justified because the limit as it stands is adequate for current and projected levels of business; from a strict business viewpoint of risk and reward, full utilization of the limit is not justified.
2. Limit is reaffirmed as a binding limit; no further extensions of credit or commitments to lend will be permitted.
3. Limit is reduced; outstandings will have to be reduced over a period of time.
4. Limit increased.
5. Limit reduced to amounts outstanding on a declining balance basis—typically the case of a country approaching a balance of payments crisis.
6. Limit decision deferred; more information is needed.

The decisions reached at the country risk meeting usually govern corporate policy for the next year or so. In cases in which opinions within the corporation differ sharply, or where deterioration of creditworthiness is in the offing, monitoring procedures should be established at the conclusion of the meetings and follow-up meetings should be scheduled at appropriate intervals.

SPECIAL PROBLEMS IN COUNTRY RISK MANAGEMENT

Short-Term versus Long-Term Assets.   Banks commonly react to a deteriorating country risk by shortening the tenors of bank exposure. Tighter limits are placed on medium-term assets and the bank's portfolio shifts toward short-term lending. The rationale is often along the lines that shorter tenors allow a closer monitoring of the risks because the portfolio is turning over more often. A quicker exit from the country also becomes possible in the event the country experiences debt service delays.

In general, short-term transactions are somewhat less risky extensions of credit. Many of these are trade related so that additional safety is provided in the form of the actual goods being shipped. However, shortening the portfolio in the light of increased country risk can lead to a false sense of security, especially as many other bank lenders to the country are likely to react in a similar fashion.

The result of this supposedly risk-averse behavior by banks can be perverse. If many lenders shorten the tenor of their credits, the country's debt profile is likely to worsen as the country must more frequently roll over large amounts of debt. Economic problems that would be manageable when debt is rolling over slowly can suddenly become unmanageable if creditors jointly shorten tenors and even seek to protect their individual positions by seeking repayments of some of these credits at maturity.

A buildup in short-term debt preceded all of the major debt reschedulings in Latin America in the early 1980s. While some of the short-term creditors may have obtained repayments prior to actual halts in principal repayments, most did not. Trade credits in Brazil, Argentina, Chile, and other debtor countries were essentially locked in after rescheduling. Money-market deposits in branches of Brazilian, Argentine, and Mexican banks were also caught up in the reschedulings and, de facto, converted into medium-term credits.

Obtaining Information. The issue of how and where to obtain economic and political information used in country evaluations often arises. Analysts generally can look to two sources for basic data and interpretations of the risk environment; publications that specialize in country economic and political data and in-country interviews with experts and local observers.

Certain standard publications contain essential and relatively up-to-date statistics for many countries on a comparable basis. These include the *International Financial Statistics* published monthly by the International Monetary Fund, *The Balance of Payments Yearbook,* also published by the fund, and the World Bank's authoritative *World Debt Statistics.* Data collection methods have improved, but analysts usually need to supplement these written sources with publications by the country's central bank and more specialized publications on national or regional economic and political problems. The Institute of International Finance (IIF) in Washington, a private organization set up in the wake of the debt crisis by a large number of international banks, is also consolidating its reputation as an authorative source of country risk studies. Individual country studies are regularly produced and updated, frequently on the basis of in-country visits by the IIF staff.

CONCLUSIONS ON COUNTRY
RISK EVALUATION

Country risk evaluation has gained stature and credibility in the wake of the debt reschedulings of the 1980s. But the methods of evaluation are far from foolproof and often rest on assumptions that need to be questioned and on data that is sketchy or unreliable. Success rests heavily on the commitment of time and resources by the senior management of the bank to make the system work.

With the benefit of hindsight, it is important to guard against certain problems that beset country risk evaluation systems and contributed to the severity of the debt crisis. Some of these would include the following:

1. Seeing the big picture. Country risk evaluations and country meetings run the risk of becoming too narrowly focused on the economic policies and business opportunities in the country being examined. Potential adverse impacts on country creditworthiness stemming from world macroeconomic trends, the so-called systemic factors, must always be taken into account in thinking about what could go wrong. No factor was as important in triggering the Latin debt crisis as the unprecedented rise in U.S. interest rates in 1980–81. The consequences of U.S. anti-inflation policy were not properly taken into account in evaluating the debt servicing prospects of the less developed countries (LDCs).

2. Choosing private rather than public sector exposure. The experience with the Latin reschedulings, in particular, revealed some of the pitfalls in lending to private sector corporations in the debtor countries. Economic policy measures taken by the sovereign to head off impending debt difficulties—tight money policies, devaluations, and cuts in public investments—acted to undermine the ability of the private sector corporation to service its external debt well before a general rescheduling of the public sector debt occurred.

3. Avoiding the herd mentality. Banks tend to reach the same conclusions and take the same actions on lending policies. A bank's decision to increase exposure to a given country should be done by considering that other banks are likely to do the same, possibly leading to a rapid increase in the country's debt. Similarly, a decision to reduce exposure or to exit the country can be frustrated by the simultaneous policy actions of competitor banks. The herd mentality in lending was never more apparent or damaging than in the simultaneous decisions of many banks to suspend new credits to all Latin American countries in the immediate aftermath of the Mexican payments default of August 1982.

4. Choosing the bias toward optimism. The views of line officers responsible for marketing and booking country lines are an integral part of the country evaluation process. But senior management must guard against the natural tendency of line officers to minimize the long-term country risks in their haste to lock in short-term profits.

5. Monitoring decisions. By its very nature, country limit decisions must be based on considerable uncertainty. Decisions to increase the limit or to leave it intact in cases in which country creditworthiness is under suspicion should be complemented by monitoring procedures—periodic updates, for example—that provide a check on critical assumptions.

APPENDIX: A Sample Country Worksheet

KOREA: Key Economic Indicators (Revised Last: 03-09-88)

	Average 1977–1981	1982	1983	1984	1985	1986	1987	1988e
Domestic economy								
1. Gross domestic product ($BB)	55	71	77	83	85	100	121	148
2. Real growth (percent ch)[a]	6.6	5.7	10.9	8.6	5.4	11.9	12.5	7.5
3. Per capita GDP ($)	1463	1797	1920	2055	2066	2416	2876	3483
4. Gross fixed investment (percent GDP)	29.9	29.3	30.3	30.2	29.7	30.3	30.9	
5. Real growth (percent change)	7.9	5.0	13.7	11.9	8.0	17.5	16.3	
6. Government fiscal deficit (percent GDP)	-2.1	-3.1	-1.1	-1.2	-1.3	-0.1	-1.3	
7. Domestic credit (percent change)	35.3	25.1	16.0	13.1	17.7	14.6	9.9	
8. Money supply (M1, percent change)	21.4	45.6	17.0	0.5	10.8	16.6	14.7	18
9. Consumer prices (percent change)	34.5	7.3	3.4	2.3	2.5	2.3	3.2	4
10. Unemployment rate (percent)	6.2	6.0	5.4	4.9	4.9			
Balance of payments ($MM)								
11. Current account balance[b]	-3038	-2650	-1606	-1372	-887	4617	9854	8294
12. Percent GDP	-5.5	-3.8	-2.1	-1.6	-1.0	4.6	8.7	5.6
13. Merchandise Trade (net)	-2933	-2594	-1763	-1036	-19	4206	7659	5948
14. Exports	15069	20879	23204	26335	26442	33913	46244	53252
15. Percent change	21.6	1.0	11.1	13.5	0.4	28.3	36.3	15.3
16. Imports	-18002	-23473	-24967	-27371	-26461	-29707	-38585	-47304
17. Percent change	24.1	-3.4	6.4	9.6	-3.3	12.3	29.8	24.2
18. Services (net)	-522	-555	-435	-877	-1446	-628	977	1146
19. Receipts	4853	7477	7179	7317	6664	8052	10011	11888
20. Percent change	34.8	13.3	-4.0	1.9	-8.9	20.8	24.3	13.3
21. Payments	-5375	-8032	-7614	-8194	-8110	-8680	-9034	-10742
22. Percent change	37.6	-1.0	-5.2	7.6	-1.0	7.0	4.1	16.0
23. Transfers (net)	417	499	592	541	578	1039	1200	1200

24. Long-term capital (net)	2441	1797	1791	3012	2295	-2571	-8777	
25. Long-term direct inv.	41	-76	-57	73	200	325	418	
26. Short-term capital (net)	1188	858	-421	-1080	-1216	-1969	722	
27. Identified short-term capital (net)	1473	2159	524	-189	-333	-1422	-462	
28. Errors and omissions	-284	-1301	-945	-891	-883	-547	1184	
29. Total balance	591	5	-236	560	192	207	2104	
International Liquidity ($MM)								
30. Gross foreign assets[c]	5657	6954	6878	7619	7717	8012	9162	14500
31. Annual change	-1201	97	-77	741	99	294	1150	5338
32. Central bank reserves	2859	2807	2347	2754	2869	3320	3584	4289
33. Reserves, percent imports G&S	12.2	8.9	7.2	7.7	8.3	8.6	7.6	7.4
34. International Monetary Fund, percent quota	*	446.1	279.3	345.5	296.7	283.9	179.8	
35. Net foreign assets of commercial banks	-2613	-7829	-7984	-9323	-11019	-9844	-6013	
36. Assets	2798	4147	4531	4865	4848	4692	5578	
37. Liabilities	5411	11976	12515	14188	15867	14536	11591	
38. Total debt	*	37083	40378	43053	46762	44510	35945	29935
39. Short-term debt	*	12427	12115	11425	10732	9256	8646	8623
40. Owed to commercial banks	*	22133	24397	26673	29654	27225	19563	14166
41. Net debt/export ratio	*	1.1	1.1	1.1	1.2	0.9	0.5	0.2
42. Debt service	*	5970	2860	6900	7304	8851	8898	8381
43. Principal	*	2201	2533	3031	3449	4991	5725	5598
44. Interest	*	3769	327	3869	3855	3860	3173	2783
45. Debt service ratio (percent)	*	21.1	9.4	20.5	22.1	21.1	15.7	12.9
46. Gross financial requirements[d]	*	4948	4062	5144	4435	668	-3661	2642
Memo Items								
47. Population (MM)	37.55	39.33	39.93	40.51	41.06	41.57	-42.07	42.49
48. Foreign-exchange rate, won per US$	562.48	748.80	795.50	827.40	890.20	861.40	-792.30	760.00

a Base year 1980.
b Current account numbers based on *International Financial Statistics* and imports are calculated in F.O.B. terms.
c Sum of lines 32 and 36. Excludes gold holdings.
d Defined as line 43 minus line 10 plus line 31.
e Forecast.

REFERENCES

Brainard, Lawrence J. "The Foreign Debt Problem and the International Firm." *Handbook of International Business,* 2d ed., ed. I. Walter. New York: John Wiley & Sons, 1988.

Brainard, Lawrence J., and Thomas J. Trebat. "The Role of Commercial Banks in Balance of Payments Crises: The Cases of Peru and Poland." Paper presented to the International Conference on Multinational Corporations in Latin America and Eastern Europe. Bloomington, Indiana, March 5–8, 1981.

Cline, William. *International Debt: Systematic Risk and Policy Response.* Washington, D.C.: Institute for International Economics, 1984.

Dillon, K. Burke, et al. *Recent Developments in External Debt Restructuring.* Occasional Paper No. 40. Washington, D.C.: International Monetary Fund, 1985.

Dillon, K. Burke, and Gumersindo Oliveros. *Recent Experience with Multilateral Official Debt Rescheduling.* World Economic and Financial Surveys. Washington, D.C.: International Monetary Fund, 1987.

Friedman, Irving. S. *The World Debt Dilemma: Managing Country Risk.* Philadelphia: Robert Morris Associates, 1984.

Heffernan, Shelagh A. *Sovereign Risk Analysis.* London: Allen & Unwin, 1986.

Hering, R. J., ed. *Managing International Risk.* Cambridge: Cambridge University Press, 1983.

Kindleberger, C. P. *Manias, Panics, and Crashes: A History of Financial Crises.* New York: Basic Books, 1978.

Walter, Ingo. "Country Risk, Portfolio Decisions, and Regulation in International Bank Lending." *Journal of Banking and Finance* 5, 1981, pp. 77–92.

CHAPTER 22

FINANCIAL INNOVATION

Ian A. Cooper

Corporate financial officers are now confronted with a plethora of alternatives for the management of financing, hedging, and liquidity. New borrowing alternatives such as junk bonds, capped floating rate notes, and convertible bonds with investor put options have increased financing choices considerably from the simple traditional choice between equity and bank debt. At the same time, many local financial markets have ended restrictive agreements and barriers to entry. As a result, financial management has become more dynamic and competitive both domestically and internationally.

Currency options and futures, forward rate agreements, and interest rate options have expanded the range of possibilities for hedging exposure to interest rate and currency fluctuations. Swaps have made it possible to change the currency or rate structure of debt instruments independently of the market of issue. This expanded opportunity set has resulted from a flood of financial innovation over the last 20 years. The purpose of this chapter is to examine some of these innovations, to describe what has caused them, and to provide a framework for evaluating their usefulness.

TRENDS IN INNOVATION

Globalization

Table 22–1 documents two important trends in international credit and capital markets in the 1980s. International markets have experienced rapid growth during this period. This is part of the trend called globalization whereby the growth of international money markets, debt markets, and equity markets has led to the increasing integration of world financial markets.

Typical transactions representative of this trend are:

1. A British industrial company issues commercial paper in New York and swaps it for fixed-rate sterling debt.
2. A Dutch company has its equity simultaneously listed on all the major European and North American stock markets.
3. Futures on U.S. Treasury bonds are traded in both London and Chicago.

In many cases this globalization of financial markets is occurring in parallel with the globalization of product markets. The traditional structure of financing, whereby a corporation is financed with funds raised in its domestic capital market in its own currency, is rapidly disappearing.

TABLE 22–1
Growth of Selected International Credit and Capital Markets ($ billions)

Year	1981	1983	1985
International bonds and notes	44	72	163
Syndicated Eurobank loans	97	52	22
Note issuance facilities	1	3	49

Source: Bank for International Settlements, 1986.

Securitization

A second trend within the globalization of markets is the increasing use of securities such as bonds, notes, and commercial paper rather than direct bank lending. Intermediation services can be provided in two ways. Banks can act as intermediaries that accept deposits and make loans. Borrowing and lending transactions consist, in this case, of contracts with banks. Alternatively, intermediation can occur through traded markets. Borrowers sell debt contracts as pieces of paper (securities) and lenders buy these pieces of paper. Examples of such securities are commercial paper, Euronotes, collateralized mortgage obligations, Eurobonds, certificates of deposit, and property income certificates.

Such securitization brings with it the benefit of liquidity, as long as the secondary markets maintain liquid market-making structures. Liquidity of secondary markets offers the opportunity for more active management of assets and liabilities and the potential for rapid restructuring of risks in response to economic events.

Risk Management

Another development associated with the desire for more active risk management and portfolio restructuring is the innovation of derivative agreements such as swaps, currency options, forward rate agreements, and caps. These derivative products generally fall into two categories: contracts locking in rates for future transactions and contracts limiting the rate at which future transactions will be made, but not precommitting a particular rate. In the former category are forward contracts, futures contracts, and swaps; in the latter category options, caps, and convertible debt. Related to the development of products such as forward contracts and options are innovations in security design that embed forward and option contracts in debt market instruments. Examples of this instrument are "heaven and hell" bonds and capped floating-rate notes.

The risks that are managed with these instruments are those arising from the volatility of interest rates, exchange rates, bond prices, and equity prices. A necessary condition for these instruments to be useful is that the associated market rates and prices are volatile. Currency options, for instance, were not necessary under the fixed exchange regime. The explosion in these markets has been the most dramatic of any new instruments.

A final trend that combines the features of forward and option contracts with the benefits of securitization is the rapid growth of traded financial futures and option markets. This is the area where the growth in the volume of transactions has been most spectacular. The volume of trading in many financial futures markets now eclipses the volume in the cash market underlying the futures contract. This is due to the attractive combination of risk management and the liquidity of a secondary market that enables rapid and cheap transactions.

It is tempting to underestimate the importance of the financial futures markets, since much of the trading volume seems not to be directly related to the provision of financial services to the nonbank sector. They are, however, crucial to the innovators and market-makers of other new instruments. Almost all financial innovation involves exposure to risks of exchange-rate and interest-rate fluctuations. The financial futures markets facilitate the hedging of this risk and, therefore, speed the pace of innovation.

Competition and Regulation

These three trends: globalization, securitization, and derivative instruments have occurred hand in hand. As an example, many international debt issues are combined with swap transactions and would not be made if it were not possible to use a swap to restructure the risk. Thus, all are part of a trend toward liquid, competitive, and sophisticated international capital markets. Table 22–2 summarizes the changes that are occurring and the instruments that are the vehicles for these changes. The scale and scope of these changes is will documented in detail elsewhere.[1]

From the point of view of economic policy, these new

---

[1] See "Recent Innovations in International Banking" (Basel, Switzerland: Bank for International Settlements, 1986); and I. Cooper, "Innovations: New Market Instruments," *Oxford Review of Economic Policy* 2 (1986), pp. 1–13.

TABLE 22–2
Financial Market Trends and Related Instruments

Trend	Old World	New World	Main Instruments
Globalization	Fragmented	Integrated	Euromarkets swaps
Securitization	Illiquid	Liquid	Securitized loans
Risk management	Passive	Active	Futures/forwards options

instruments have important consequences. They blur the distinctions between different segments of financial markets both domestically and internationally and they lead to increased competition. This introduces into financial institutions exposures that cannot be analyzed and regulated in conventional ways.

To strike a balance between the freedom to compete and regulation of the banking system has always been difficult. This is made all the more difficult by the new instruments which transcend conventional distinctions between different segments of the global financial markets. Definitions of such terms as *money, bank, risk,* and *swiss franc borrowing* are all being rapidly revised or discarded.

NEW INSTRUMENTS

There are very few completely new instruments: "Many of the financial innovations . . . already existed in one form or another for many years before they sprang into prominence. They were lying . . . like seeds beneath the snow, waiting for some change in the environment to bring them to life."[2]

For instance, parallel loans and back-to-back loans, precursors of the instrument now known as the swap, were used throughout the 1970s as a way around the United Kingdom's exchange controls.

---

[2] M. Miller, "Financial Innovation: The Last Twenty Years and the Next," *Journal of Financial and Quantitive Analysis* 21 (1986), pp. 459–71.

What is new is the scale and scope of the use of these instruments. Swap volume has increased from an insignificant amount to hundreds of billions of dollars over the last 10 years. Financial futures volume is now tens of thousands of billions of dollars. Options are now traded on equities, bonds, interest rates, currencies, and commodities. Each year new instruments appear and the international scope of the revolution is extended.

An exhaustive categorization of the new instruments is not attempted here. Many are idiosyncratic and transient. Those that persist fall into four main categories: forward contracts, futures contracts, securitized loans, and option contracts. Often these features are embedded in other securities, as is the case with currency convertible bonds where a long-dated currency option is contained in a bond. This categorization is useful because the motivations behind the innovations in each category are similar, as are the techniques used by their creators to price and hedge them.

Forward Contracts

Every banker and treasurer is familiar with the foreign-exchange forward market. It is a standard means of hedging foreign-exchange risk for banks and corporations. The foreign-exchange forward contract can be thought of simply as an agreement to make an exchange of currencies at a prespecified price at some future date. For instance, a three-month contract to buy £10 million at $1.65 obligates the holder to make this transaction when the contract matures.

If this contract is held to maturity, the holder can make or lose money at the maturity date. The amount made or lost depends on the spot sterling rate at that time. Table 22–3 shows the net payoff to the holder of this forward contract. If, for instance, spot sterling is at $1.60 when the contract matures, the holder buys £10 million

TABLE 22–3
Net Payoff to Holder of Forward Contract to Buy £10 at $1.65

Spot rate at maturity ($)	1.55	1.60	1.65	1.70	1.75
Net payoff ($ million)	−1.0	−0.5	0.0	+0.5	+1.0

at \$1.65 and sells it at \$1.60, resulting in a net loss of \$500,000. Of course, if the forward contract is being used for hedging purposes, there is an offsetting gain on the transaction which is being hedged with the forward contract.

The key financial characteristic of the forward contract is that its payoff is simply proportional to the difference between the forward rate in the contract and the market price at the maturity date. A significant innovation along these lines has been the forward rate agreement (FRA), whereby the forward contract is on an interest rate. For instance, a six-month FRA on three-month London Interbank Offered Rate (LIBOR) pays, six months from now, the difference between the three-month LIBOR and the FRA rate.

A treasurer who will be paying taxes six months from now will need to borrow three-month money at that date and can lock in the borrowing rate. The treasurer simply enters into a FRA to receive the difference between LIBOR and the FRA rate. Six months from now the treasurer borrows (at LIBOR say) and receives or pays the settlement amount on the FRA, resulting in a net borrowing cost equal to the FRA rate.

There are long-dated currency forward contracts available in the form of currency swaps. They are also included as a component of the redemption payment of heaven-and-hell bonds. The latter are an interesting example of a bond-market innovation that consists of a packaged forward contract and a normal bond. Table 22–4 shows the structure of the IBM Credit Corporation's yen-linked notes due 1995.[3] The holder of the bond essentially buys a package consisting of:

1. A straight dollar bond.
2. A 1995 forward contract to buy dollars at 169.

The attraction of the package to the investor is the rate in the embedded forward contract. An investor attempting to execute a 10-year forward sale of yen directly would be charged a large premium for default risk. In this case, however, IBM need not

---

[3] For a more detailed description of this bond, see R. Mason, "Innovations in the Structures of International Securities," Credit Suisse–First Boston, 1986.

TABLE 22–4
Forward Contract Embedded in Heaven and Hell Bond

	This Bond	Straight Bond	1995 Forward Contract
Coupon	$10.75	$10.75	
Principal	$200–16,900	$100	$100–16,900

worry about default risk, because if the yen appreciates the forward contract is effectively settled out of the redemption proceeds of the bond.

Swaps

Swaps are forward contracts for streams of cash flows rather than single payments.[4] A standard currency swap consists of an agreement to exchange payments of fixed interest in one currency for fixed interest in another currency with an exchange of principal at the maturity of the swap. A standard interest-rate swap consists of an agreement to exchange floating interest-rate payments for fixed-interest payments in the same currency.

Table 22–5 shows the cash flows for simple currency and interest-rate swaps. As separate transactions, swaps are not that interesting. Combined with bonds, however, they have the effect of converting one type of borrowing to another. Thus part C of Table 22–5 shows the conversion of a fixed-rate note to a synthetic floating-rate note. In this case the net borrowing cost is 20 basis points below LIBOR.

Until recently, this type of liability swap transaction has been the dominant use of swaps. It has been used to take advantage of anomalies in debt markets to generate low net borrowing costs. Now swaps are used as standard medium-dated forward contracts to restructure the risks of asset and liability portfolios.

---

[4] For a detailed but clear explanation of swaps, see J. Price and S. Henderson, "Currency and Interest Rate Swaps," *Butterworths*, 1984.

TABLE 22-5
Swap Cash Flows

A.   Currency swap, 3 years, 4% DM for 7% dollars at 2 DM/$

Year	1	2	3
Payment (DM)	−8	−8	−208
Receipt ($)	+7	+7	+107

B.   Interest-rate swap, 3 years, LIBOR for 7% dollars

Year	1	2	3
Payment	7−LIBOR	7−LIBOR	7−LIBOR

C.   Fixed-rate 6.8% note combined with interest-rate swap

Year	1	2	3
Note payment	−6.8	−6.8	−106.8
Swap payment	7−LIBOR	7−LIBOR	7−LIBOR
Net payment	−(LIBOR−0.2)	−(LIBOR−0.2)	−(LIBOR−0.2)−100

Although swaplike transactions have existed at least since the mid-70s, volume prior to 1982 was very small. Now volume is hundreds of billions of dollars each year. The innovation which caused this explosion was not the swap transaction itself, but the structuring of the swap contract to limit default risk exposure. This is most obvious in the interest-rate swap illustrated in Table 22–5, part B. The contract is written as an exchange of net cash flows which exclude principal payments. This significantly limits the default risk exposure of market-maker banks. As a result, liquid markets now exist for standard interest-rate swaps with maturities up to 12 years and low bid/ask spreads.

As with swaps, a major problem with forward contracts is default risk. This is the greatest obstacle to liquid long-dated forward markets. It is quite simple to estimate the order of magnitude of this risk. For instance, with a currency forward contract, the size of the risk is related to the possible range of spot currency rates at the maturity date of the forward contract. To

TABLE 22–6
Two Standard Deviation Confidence Limits for Dollar/Sterling Exchange Rate ($/£)

Maturity (years)	1	5	10	20
Upper limit	2.01	2.59	3.10	4.03
Lower limit	1.35	1.06	0.87	0.68

estimate this range we can use four empirical observations about dollar/sterling exchange rate behavior:[5]

1. Successive changes are statistically independent.
2. Changes are roughly lognormally distributed.
3. The change over a single year has a standard deviation of approximately 10 percent.
4. The mean rate of change is approximately zero.

If the rate is currently $1.65, two standard deviation confidence limits for the rate are at different future dates given in Table 22–6. The seller of a 20-year forward contract for £10 million at $1.65 would, at the maturity date, be owed $24 million as a settlement payment if the spot rate is $4.03. Thus, the potential default could be as large as $24 million.

This risk must be compensated in the forward contract rate. It is the reason that bid/ask spreads in the long-dated forward markets are so wide. A paradox which arises from this is that the forward contracts which are potentially most useful, those which hedge large risks, are also the ones where the default risk problem is greatest, and the buy/sell spreads are greatest.

Financial Futures

There is, however, another way of dealing with the default risk of forward contracts and this has led to the most significant new

---

[5] See Chapter 23.

instrument, as measured by volume: financial futures. Financial futures are forward contracts that are

1. Standardized.
2. Traded.
3. Collateralized with margin.
4. Resettled daily.

In terms of their uses, they fulfill all the functions that forward contracts fulfill. Short-dated futures contracts are also close substitutes for cash market transactions. Thus, the innovation in financial futures has little to do with the payoff structure of the instrument but rather is an innovation of a market-making and risk control structure.

Financial futures are now traded on currencies, interest rates, bonds, and equities. The volume in some futures markets is now greater than that of the underlying instrument. The nature of the futures market innovation can be seen from Table 22–7. This shows a set of hypothetical currency rates over a three-month period and the resulting cash flows arising for the purchaser of a forward contract and a futures contract.

The futures contract is settled each day. As long as the holder of the futures contract has enough margin in the account to settle

TABLE 22–7
Forward Contract and Futures Contract; Three-Month Sterling Contract, Equal Interest Rates

Day	0	1	2	..	88	89	90	
Spot rate (¢/£)	165	163	161	...	148	150	149	
Forward rate (¢/£)	165	163	161	...	148	150	149	
Futures rate (¢/£)	165	163	161	...	148	150	149	
Cash flows								Total
Buy forward	0	0	0	...	0	0	−16	−16
Buy futures	0	−2	−2	...	+1	+2	−1	−16

the maximum daily move (in this case two cents) there is no risk of default. If the holder of the contract is unable to remargin the position for the next day, the contract is simply closed with no resulting default. In the case of the forward contract, settlement is not made until maturity so the seller of this contract is exposed to a potential default of 16 cents at the maturity date.

For hedging purposes, the two contracts are almost identical. Note that, in this case, each contract lost 16 cents over its life, so that they would have had identical effects if used for hedging purposes. In the case of exchange-rate futures, the futures contracts compete directly with the established forward markets. In the case of some bond futures, equity futures, and interest-rate futures, no parallel forward markets exist. In these latter cases, the innovation of the financial futures markets has considerably enhanced the possibilities for hedging.

Options and Instruments Containing Options

The Chicago Board Options Exchange opened trading in U.S. equity options in 1973. In the same year Black and Scholes published their seminal option valuation article.[6] Options are now traded on equities, currencies, interest rates, and bonds. In addition there are caps, floors, options on swaps, range forward contracts, currency convertible bonds, and a whole host of other options either sold by banks or embedded in securities.

Options and instruments containing options are probably the most widely misunderstood of the financial innovations. At one level, the characteristics of options are simple to understand. To illustrate the key feature of options, consider the purchase of a three-month call option on sterling. Assume that sterling is at $1.65, dollar and sterling interest rates are 8 percent, and the three-month forward rate is $1.65. Such an option might cost three cents.[7]

---

[6] F. Black, and M. J. Scholes, "The Pricing of Options and Corporate Liabilities," *Journal of Political Economy* 81(3), May 1973, pp. 637–54.

[7] For a simple exposition of options see W. Sharpe, *Investments* (Englewood Cliffs, N.J.: Prentice-Hall, 1985). For a more advanced treatment, see J. Cox and M. Rubinstein, *Options Markets* (Englewood Cliffs, N.J.: Prentice-Hall, 1985).

TABLE 22–8
Payoffs to Holder of Call Option on £, Exercise Price 165¢

Spot rate at maturity (¢)	155	160	165	170	175
Gross payoff to option (¢)	0	0	0	5	10
Net payoff to option (¢)	−3	−3	−3	2	7
Net payoff to forward contract (¢)	−10	−5	0	5	10

Table 22–8 shows the gross and net payoff to the holder of this option. It also shows the net payoff to a forward contract. The difference between the two lies in the limited loss possible with the option contract. There are many situations where this characteristic is desirable. The classic example used for currency options is that of an exporter tendering for a contract in a foreign currency. If forward cover is taken and the contract is not awarded, the exporter could potentially lose a large amount as a result of the hedging strategy. If option cover is taken, this loss is limited to the amount paid for the option—the option premium.

Options also exist embedded in bonds. For instance, the CEPME issue of 1984 maturing in 1996 contained the option for the holder to take either of the two redemption payments:

1. $100 per $100 of face value
2. £72.62 per $100 of face value

The holder will take the alternative which has higher value at the maturity date. Table 22–9 shows that this bond is equivalent to a straight dollar bond plus a call option on sterling.

TABLE 22–9
Payoffs to CEPME Currency Convertible Bond

Exchange rate at redemption (¢/£)	120	130	140	150	160
Payoff to bond ($)	100	100	102	109	116
Payoff to straight bond ($)	100	100	100	100	100
Payoff to call option ($)*	0	0	2	9	16

* Call on sterling with exercise price of 1.377 $/£

TABLE 22–10
Cap, Floor, and Collar Payoffs to Borrower

LIBOR (percent)	4	6	8	10	12	14
10 percent cap pays (percent)	0	0	0	0	2	4
7 percent Floor pays (percent)	−3	−1	0	0	0	0
Collar pays	−3	−1	0	0	2	4

Another option innovation has been the cap with its related instruments, floors and collars. A borrower who issues a seven-year floating-rate note is exposed to the possibility that rates will rise. To protect against this eventuality the borrower can now buy protection in the form of a cap. The cap ensures that the interest paid will never be more than the prespecified cap rate. To achieve this, the seller of the cap agrees to make a payment equal to the difference between the floating rate and the cap rate whenever the former is higher on a rate-setting date. The holder of the cap has, therefore, purchased a sequence, or strip, of options on the floating rate.

Table 22–10 shows the payoff to a cap and to two related instruments, floors and collars. The collar is, essentially, a means of allowing the cap purchaser to pay for the cap without charging an upfront fee. Instead of a fee, the cap seller agrees to take compensation in the form of a payment whenever the floating rate falls below a certain level (the floor). The collar amounts to the simultaneous purchase of a call option and sale of put option by the collar buyer. If the collar rates are set correctly, the collar seller does not need to charge for the collar, as the sale of the cap is (more than) fully compensated by the floor.[8] Similar transactions are the range forward contract in foreign exchange and the mini-max transaction on interest rates.

---

[8] A fairly sober summary of this financial engineering is provided in C. Smithson, "A LEGO Approach to Financial Engineering," *Midland Corporate Finance Journal* 4 (1987), pp. 16–28.

Securitized Loans

The final category of instruments is securitized loans. This includes commercial paper, Eurobonds, Euronotes, collateralized mortgage obligations, pass-thorugh and pay-through securities, and property income certificates. Here the innovation is simple. Rather than borrowing by loan agreements with financial institutions, corporations and institutions borrow by selling securities.

The trend here is to substitute market-based intermediation for institution-based intermediation. Apparently the relative efficiency of these two types of intermediation has shifted. Securities markets provide liquidity in the form of the ability to sell the securities should one not wish to hold them any longer. Banks provide, in this context, services such as monitoring and controlling borrowers. The rate difference for a borrower between securitized borrowing and direct bank borrowing is determined by the relative advantage to a lender of the liquidity of a traded security and the benefit of having a bank performing the monitoring and control function. It appears that this balance has shifted in favor of securitized borrowing for a large group of borrowers.

Here, again, what is new is the scale of use of securitized borrowing and its penetration into segments such as mortgages that are traditionally the preserve of institutional as opposed to market intermediation.

Structured Bonds

Many bonds consist of packages of components that can, in principle, be split apart and sold separately or put together in innovative packages. An early example of this was the "stripping" of U.S. Treasury bonds to sell the coupon stream and the principal repayment separately. More recent examples are bonds that pay the coupon in a different currency to the principal (dual-currency bonds), forward swaps, repackagings of perpetual floating-rate notes, and bonds with stepped coupons. Each of these gives rise to a debt instrument with an innovative cash flow profile.

In a competitive market with low transactions costs, no tax anomalies, and no restrictions on trading, these transactions should not give rise to much added value.[9] International debt markets contain, however, restrictions and anomalies which can make it profitable to provide debt instruments tailored to particular investor clienteles or tax rules. In many cases, part of the value added from these structured debt instruments is captured by the issuer, resulting in a lowered cost of funds. The availability of swaps to transform the liability into its desired form while locking in the reduced cost has greatly facilitated this activity.

PROCESS INNOVATIONS

In addition to innovative new financial instruments is innovation in the process of treasury management; it has both complemented and competed with some of the new instruments. Corporations and national agencies have become increasingly willing to undertake activities previously the exclusive preserve of financial institutions. Treasury departments have adopted sophisticated financial techniques, which technology has made feasible at reasonable cost.

Marking-to-Market

As market interest rates vary, the present value of fixed-rate debt varies. Thus assets or liabilities with fixed rates change in present value, even though these gains or losses may not be recognized by the accounting system until a transaction occurs. Similar considerations apply to property assets, foreign currency contracts, and pension fund assets. Although reported financial statements must be in the form prescribed by law, internal management accounting can include financial reports based on the current market values of these assets and liabilities. This marking-to-market facilitates decision making and is useful also in determining transactions,

---

[9] For the first analysis of a repackaging transaction, see M. H. Miller, and F. Modigliani, "Dividend Policy, Growth, and the Valuation of Shares," *Journal of Business* 34, October 1961, pp. 235–64.

such as swaps, which are designed to precipitate the recognition of an economic gain in published financial accounts.

Marking-to-market has also resulted in a significant related innovation: increased use of margining as a means of controlling default risk. It can also be related to the increasing use of high apparent leverage in buyouts and low-grade debt transactions, where the leverage is based on the economic value of future cash flows rather than the balance sheet value of assets.

Economic Hedging

Allied to the notion of marking-to-market is the recognition that the hedging of accounting exposures may not adequately protect the economic value of the corporation's equity. To the extent that fluctuations in balance sheet values or reported income do not fully reflect the impact of exchange-rate or interest-rate fluctuations on the economic value of assets and liabilities, it may be necessary to undertake hedging transactions that offset those economic exposures. Some of these exposures are cash flow risks of the type that are hedged by forward rate agreements or caps; others are asset risks that can be hedged by using long-term financing instruments tailored to the asset profile.

Risk Measurement

Because many innovative transactions require a balancing of risk and reward, it is frequently necessary to measure the risk component of the transaction in a precise way. Precise measures of the volatility of prices in particular markets are now used as standard means of communicating about risk. In debt markets, duration is increasingly used as a measure of interest-rate risk. In options markets, prices are converted to equivalent implied volatilities to facilitate comparison of prices.

Synthetic Transactions

In some cases, the new instruments that are available can be approximately synthesized by using a substitute market. One important area where this is possible is options. Rather than buying a currency option outright, it is possible to approximately duplicate the characteristics of the option by a series of transactions in the spot, forward, or futures foreign-exchange markets. The simplest strategy which achieves some of the characteristics of an option is a stop-loss order. More sophisticated variants include the so-called delta strategy which is based on an options model such as Black and Scholes.[10] The choice for a potential option purchaser of whether to buy the option outright or perform the alternative synthetic strategy involves considerable sophistication in weighing the relative costs of the two alternatives, and the extent to which the synthetic strategy fully replicates the purchase of the outright option.[11]

AN EXAMPLE: THE SWAP MARKET

In this section, the evolution of the swap market is examined, as an example of the development of an innovation. Table 22–11 gives an overview of the phases in this development. Early swaps prior to 1980 took the form of parallel loans circumventing exchange controls. Volume was small, and the transactions were tailed to the requirements of the counterparties and time-consuming to construct. The parallel loan arrangement is cumbersome and directed at avoidance of particular regulation. It is, therefore, inefficient for general use. Nevertheless, its form is essentially that of a swap: an agreement between two counterparties to exchange specified streams of cash in the future.

In the early 1980s it was realized that this general structure could be used to arbitrage anomalies in interest rates between different currencies and between floating and fixed borrowing rates in the same currency. The types of anomaly that gave rise to the swap opportunity are illustrated in Table 22–12.

Using the currency swap opportunity illustrated in Table 22–12, part A, as an example, the swap opportunity arises when

---

[10] Black and Scholes, "Pricing of Options," 1973.
[11] M. Rubinstein and H. Leland, "Replicating Options with Positions in Stock and Cash," *Financial Analysts Journal* 37 (July–August 1981), pp. 63–72.

TABLE 22–11
Evolution of the Currency and Interest-Rate Swap Market

Date	Phase	Market Arrangement	Approximate Volume
1970s	Arbitrage of regulation	Parallel loans	Small
1980–81	Arbitrage of market anomalies (1)	Intermediated agreements	Small
1982–83	Arbitrage of market anomalies (2)	Intermediated with bank inventories	$20 bn
1984	Standardized traded swaps	Market-making on standard contracts	$100 bn
1985	Derivative agreements on swaps (forward swaps, swaps options)	Market-making on standard contracts	Small

borrowers wish to borrow in markets in which they face relatively uncompetitive rates. If, in this example, borrower A wishes to have a Swiss franc liability and B a dollar liability, each is borrowing in the market where they receive, relative to each other, the least advantageous rate. The swap is a vehicle whereby each can have its liability denominated in the currency it desired, while raising funds in the relatively advantageous market. This swap is illustrated in Figure 22–1.

TABLE 22–12
Market Anomalies Giving Rise to Swap Opportunities

A: Currency Swap Anomaly: Fixed five-year borrowing rate		
Borrower	SF	US$
A	7.0%	15.0%
B	7.5	16.5

B: Interest Rate Swap Anomaly: Five-year $ borrowing rate		
Borrower	Fixed	Floating
A	15.0%	LIBOR
B	16.5	LIBOR + 0.5%

FIGURE 22–1
Currency Swap Structure

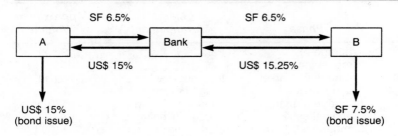

Each borrower, through the swap, pays the other's liability, with an adjustment to enable each to gain from the transaction. In addition, an intermediary bank guarantees the payments, arranges the swap and takes a fee. The net gains in this case are shown in Table 22–13. The total gain is split between the three participants in the transaction. The total gain is equal to the difference between the 1.5 percent borrowing rate differential in US$ and the 0.5 percent borrowing rate differential in SF. The notion that lies behind the swap is that these differentials should be the same because they are the price of the same thing: the difference in the quality of the two borrowers. Since they are not the same, an opportunity for arbitrage is presented.

The next developments in the swap market were not related to the instrument itself, but to the market-making structure. Finding two counterparties that wish to enter the same swap at the same time is an inefficient way to run the swap market. Banks became increasingly willing to accept one side of the swap transaction and

TABLE 22–13
Net Gains from the Swap

Party	Borrowing Cost without Swap	Borrowing Cost with Swap	Gain
A	SF 7.0%	SF 6.5%	0.5 %
B	US$ 16.5%	US$ 16.25	0.25
Bank			0.25
			1.00%

hold this in their inventory until they could match the other side. This is risky unless the currency or interest-rate risk arising from the unmatched swap can be hedged. With forward and futures contracts on currencies, interest rates, and bonds, it is possible to eliminate much of the risk of interest-rate or currency fluctuation, so the banks become increasingly willing to hold inventories of temporarily unmatched swaps.

It was a short step from this to the stage where some banks became willing to make continuous quotations on standard types of swaps without worrying about eventually matching the counter-parties. Several banks now do this on a wide variety of swap transactions. This development has been the final element enabling the phenomenal recent growth of the swap market. Some swaps are now a commodity product similar to foreign exchange forward contracts. Swap quotations are continuously available and execution is virtually instantaneous.

Such standardization and liquidity has made it possible to develop derivative products on the back of swaps. Options on swaps and forward swap agreements are natural extensions of the swap market. The experience in writing and trading swaps has also facilitated expansion of the variety of swaps: swaps of equity for debt, swaps of commodities for financial assets, and swaps of peculiar bonds.

The swap market is instructive, in that it illustrates some general features of financial instrument innovations:

1. Initially, the instument was invented in response to anomalies produced by regulation and differences between sectors of the global financial market.
2. Growth was facilitated by the availability of other financial instruments for hedging risk.
3. Explosive growth became possible when a liquid market-making structure arose.
4. Growth of this market enabled the development of other derivative markets based on it.

Although all of these are not common features of all innovative new market instruments, they represent common features of many of the most important innovations. Some innovations, however, do not proceed beyond the initial stage of arbitraging anomalies. Zero-coupon dollar bonds are a good example of this. The U.S. tax authorities had a tax accrual rule that used simple rather than compound interest. A large market temporarily developed to take advantage of this. When the rule was changed, the market contracted.

CAUSES OF INNOVATION

Evidence on the causes of financial innovation is very limited. Some innovation is fragmented, opportunistic, and caused only by tax rules and regulation. Other innovation consists of introducing instruments that generate fundamentally new and useful risk-sharing possibilities, such as options. In other cases, such as the example of swaps given in the previous section, innovation occurred initially in response to various market regulations and anomalies and generated a new risk-sharing contract, in the form of a medium-term forward contract to exchange cash flow streams. A list of these reasons for financial innovation is given in Table 22–14. Evidence that imperfections and regulations are the major sources of financial innovation is given in Ben-Horim and Silber.[12]

All the reasons listed in Table 22–14 represent desirable characteristics of the innovated financial instruments, such as swaps, futures, options, and securitised mortgages. The interesting thing is, however, that every item in the list was just as good a reason for innovating twenty years ago as it is now. There was potentially as much money in arbitraging the Swiss central bank's control of the Swiss franc debt market in 1966 as there is in 1986. The risk-sharing gains from offering equity index futures were potentially as great in 1956 as they are now. In seeking the cause of innovation, this list cannot explain the most striking feature: the explosive recent growth.

Table 22–15 lists aspects of the financial markets which have changed significantly over the last 10 years. Of these, the last three,

---

[12] M. Ben-Horim and W. Silber, "Financial Innovation: A Linear Programming Approach," *Journal of Banking and Finance* 1 (1977), pp. 277–96.

TABLE 22–14
Proximate Causes of Innovation

1. Arbitrage regulations and imperfections.
2. Facilitate risk-sharing and hedging.
3. Reduce transaction costs and provide liquidity.
4. Compete against cartelized markets or other high cost markets.
5. Avoid restrictions on short-selling.
6. Give leverage and facilitate speculation.

sophistication, competition, and regulators' attitudes are more endogenous than exogenous variables. Regulation, for instance, has been loosened in response to the destruction of the status quo. The competition that has caused this has been created by the ability to compete in innovative ways across traditional market barriers. The threat caused by this has required investment in more sophisticated instruments and techniques by the threatened institutions. Even the volatility of financial market rates can be viewed as an endogenous response to the reduced ability of governments and central banks to control capital flows.

One exogenous shift that has taken place is the technology software that is available to run markets in financial instruments. Without fast, efficient, and sophisticated computer and telecommunications systems it was impossible to run, for instance, highly liquid and competitive global markets for currency options. Now it is possible to do so, and this fundamentally useful hedging and risk-sharing instrument is an important financial tool.

An interesting illustration of this feature of innovation is the financial futures market. The conventional analysis of commodity

TABLE 22–15
Ultimate Causes of Innovation

1. Volatility of interest rates, exchange rates, equity prices.
2. Computer/telecommunications capabilities.
3. Global pattern of financial wealth.
4. User education/sophistication.
5. Financial intermediary competition.
6. Regulator's attitudes.

futures or forward contracts is in terms of their addition to market opportunities for those wishing to hedge commodity price risk. It is tempting, by analogy, to think of financial futures market as performing a similar role; that is, allowing the transfer of financial risks in a way that cannot be achieved without the existence of these instruments.

This analogy is, in many cases, completely misleading. There is a great difference between a farmer selling forward a grain crop that has not yet been harvested, and a corporation selling forward a currency that will be received at some future date. The difference is that the farmer has no alternative market available in which to hedge, whereas the corporation does. It is well known that an American corporation that wishes to hedge the receipt of yen six months from now can simply borrow yen for six months and switch them at the spot dollar/yen exchange rate now (and, if so desired, lend the dollar receipts at the dollar interest rate for six months).

This trade, which creates a synthetic forward currency contract, is simple to perform and is available without the existence of explicitly traded currency forward or futures contracts. It is identical, in its impact on the risk exposure of the corporation, to the explicit forward and futures on financial instruments must, therefore, lie in more than the general desirability of hedging particular financial risks. To illustrate this further, Table 22–16 presents some stylized facts about financial futures markets.

Consider first points 1 and 2 in Table 22–16. A close approximation to a short maturity financial futures contract can be obtained by buying (or selling) the underlying asset and borrowing (or lending). Yet most of the volume in the financial futures market is concentrated in the short maturity.

TABLE 22–16
Aspects of Financial Futures Markets

1. Futures can be approximately synthesized from other existing securities.
2. Most volume is concentrated in the near maturity.
3. Most trades are by transactors who have no intention of taking delivery of the underlying security.
4. A large proportion of trades are arbitrage of very small discrepancies within the market or between markets.

Why does this happen? The alternative synthetic trade just referred to is not costless and not available to everyone. Some may be faced by large transaction costs in executing the trade, others may be prevented from shorting the underlying asset, and the cost of borrowing may be more expensive for some than for others. The role of the financial futures market in this case is not the creation of an economically new contract, but making low transaction costs, shorting, and leverage available to a larger group.

This perspective also makes clear the role of traders who are speculating, scalping, or arbitraging. Their transactions add to the liquidity of the marketplace. Since their activity tends to be concentrated in one contract, the near maturity, the liquidity is maximized. It also highlights the real usefulness of the futures contract. It does not create a genuinely new security, in terms of the price which is being traded, but it makes low spread, fast execution, leverage, and short positions available to transactors who could otherwise not get them. How valuable these are depends largely on the characteristics of the spot market and the restrictions on those who are interested in the asset.

EVALUATION OF INNOVATIONS

From the point of view of the treasury function of a corporation or a financial institution, innovations are useful if they enable the treasury to achieve its objectives more efficiently. Most treasury decisions concern raising funds, investing liquid balances, and hedging risks. Innovations are, therefore, useful if they lower the overall cost of funds, raise the overall risk-adjusted rate of return on liquid balances, or improve the hedging of exposures.[13]

Innovations That Reduce the Cost of Funds

Innovations such as liability swaps and zero-coupon bonds frequently result in lower all-in borrowing costs than conventional

---

[13] I. Cooper and J. Franks, "The Measurement of Treasury Performance," *Midland Corporate Finance Journal* 4 (1987), pp. 29–43.

methods of borrowing. In many cases, this gain is a pure arbitrage gain with no offsetting risks. In some cases, however, care must be taken that the reduction in borrowing costs is not being achieved at the expense of increased risk. In the case of swaps, for instance, the cost reduction usually results from making a debt issue in a market where rates are relatively favorable, combined with a swap to give a net liability with the desired currency or interest rate configuration. If the net cost of the debt issue and the swap is lower than the cost of borrowing directly in the desired form, the transaction is deemed to have lowered the cost of funds.

There is, however, a difference between borrowing directly in a particular currency and borrowing indirectly by borrowing another currency and swapping the liability. In the latter case, the borrower is exposed to the risk of default by the swap counterparty. Care must be taken to ensure that the gain resulting from the liability swap is sufficient to compensate for this increased risk. Similar considerations arise from uncertainty about future tax rates or tax rules in tax-driven innovations. They may reduce borrowing costs given the current tax treatment, but expose the borrower to risks concerning the future tax treatment of the transaction.

Another risk in the use of innovations that lowers the cost of funds concerns the use of yields as an all-in measure of the cost of debt. Innovations such as zero-coupon bonds, stepped coupon bonds, and bonds that contain investor options to extend the life cannot be compared with traditional full-coupon bonds on the basis of yield alone. These structured bonds have different cash-flow profiles (and therefore different durations) than conventional bonds, and care must be taken that a reduction in cost, as measured by yield, is not being purchased at the price of increased exposure to interest-rate risk.[14]

Innovations That Improve Hedging

Innovations such as currency options, caps, and forward rate agreements have considerably expanded opportunities for hedging

---

[14] S. Schaefer, "The Problem with Redemption Yields," *Financial Analysts Journal* 33 (July/August 1977), pp. 59–67.

currency and interest-rate exposure. This has occurred in parallel with an increase in the sophistication with which hedging strategies are formulated and implemented. In particular, there has been a shift toward hedging economic exposure rather than accounting exposure, and improved monitoring of whether hedging actually achieves its stated purpose.

To evaluate innovations that improve hedging, the following steps are important:

1. Quantification of the risk to be hedged.
2. Measurement of the ability of the hedging instrument to hedge the risk.
3. Evaluation of the cost of the proposed hedging method against alternatives.

As an example, consider the use of a currency futures contract to hedge the exchange-rate risk involved in a stream of revenue to be made in a foreign currency. Step one consists of forecasting the volatility of the currency rate and the uncertainty about the amount of foreign currency to be received. Step two consists of measuring the amount of this risk that can be eliminated by the specific hedging transaction under consideration. Step three consists of comparing the possible outcomes of this hedging strategy with other strategies such as a tailor-made forward contract, borrowing the foreign currency to create a synthetic forward contract, or covering using a currency option to eliminate exposure to uncertainty about the quantity of foreign revenue.

These comparisons require some sophistication, in that the hedger must be able to balance transaction costs, mishedging risks, and the price paid for the hedge. Frequently, cover using options provides a more complete hedge but at a higher cost and greater transaction costs. In some cases, there may be other strategies available to the more sophisticated treasury operations, such as the creation of synthetic optionlike hedging strategies by active trading of futures markets.

One feature of many of these innovations that offer improved hedging is that the financial institutions selling the hedging instruments are themselves hedging their exposure by an offsetting transaction. Thus a forward rate agreement can be hedged by a pair of borrowing and lending transactions that span the two dates of the agreement. As many corporations now have access to borrowing markets at terms which are at least as fine as those of some banks, it may, in certain cases, pay the corporations to do the financial engineering themselves, rather than trying the engineered product.

LIMITS TO INNOVATION AND POTENTIAL PITFALLS

Much financial innovation contains the seeds of its own destruction. For instance, arbitrage through swaps of regulations effectively segmented the global debt market; now it has had the impact of increasing the integration of that market and reducing the anomalies on which the arbitrage was based. In its wake has come the problem of large swap portfolios which are potentially exposed to significant counterparty default risk.[15] Other innovation has appeared to be profitable only when it has caused rates to move in a favorable direction. In some cases, it is not even possible to assess the true profitability of innovation because the opportunity cost of the capital involved is not subtracted before the "profit" is computed.[16]

It is instructive in considering the limits to innovation to consider some areas where innovation has made little impact. As an example, currency options on administered exchange rates such as the Saudi riyal/dollar rate have proved difficult to write at a reasonable price. This is because most of the techniques that market-makers use to hedge the options that they sell are reliable only when rates are relatively free to move in response to market forces and do not jump by large amounts.[17] In this case, the problem in providing the instrument is the inability of market-makers to hedge their resulting exposure.

---

[15] D. Shirref, "Turning down the Gaz de France Swap Credit Exposure," *Risk,* December 1987, pp. 28–29.

[16] K. Yokio and P. Hubbard, "Zaitech: The Japanese Perspective on Financial Engineering," *Journal of International Securities Markets* 2 (Spring 1988), pp. 67–72.

[17] This is also the reason that some options market participants experienced problems on Black Monday.

Another currency option innovation that has not proved successful is the "syndicate forward." Potential demand for this contract arises when tendering in a foreign currency. Forward contracts do not provide the appropriate cover, because they commit the hedger to settle the contract whether the tender is or is not successful. What is needed is a forward contract that is conditional on the tender being successful. A syndicate forward is an attempt to do this, in the form of a currency forward contract that is taken by a group, each of which is tendering on the contract, and then allocated to the successful member of the group. The problems with this contract arise because each member of the syndicate may not wish to hedge into the same currency, and there are problems for each member in revealing the amount it wishes to cover. As a substitute, many of these exposures are covered by currency options. These are simple to write, as they are contingent on a financial market rate rather than on an event over which one of the parties to the contract has some control. By using a currency option, however, the hedger is effectively buying more insurance than is needed.

These two examples illustrate an important feature that potentially limits the design of new instruments. Most of the successful innovations so far have been contracts that are contingent on the behavior of financial market rates traded in relatively competitive and open markets. Many of the problems for which innovative solutions are now needed have to do with phenomena that cannot be easily dealt with in this way. Problems of default risk, liquidity, administered rates, moral hazard, and adverse selection cannot be easily handled by the analysis and new instruments that have proved so fruitful over the last 20 years.

REFERENCES

Bank for International Settlements. "Recent Innovations in International Banking." Basel, Switzerland: Bank for International Settlements, 1986.

Ben-Horim, M., and W. Silber. "Financial Innovation: A Linear Programming Approach." *Journal of Banking and Finance* 1, 1977, pp. 277–96.

Cooper, I. "Innovations: New Market Instruments." *Oxford Review of Economic Policy* 2, 1986, pp. 1–13.

Cooper, I., and J. Franks. "The Measurement of Treasury Performance." *Midland Corporate Finance Journal* 4, 1987, pp. 29–43.

Cox, J., and M. Rubinstein. *Options Markets*. Englewood-Cliffs, N.J.: Prentice-Hall, 1985.

International Monetary Fund. *1986 International Capital Markets: Developments and Prospects*. Washington, D.C.: International Monetary Fund, 1986.

Kane, E. "Policy Implications of Structural Changes in Financial Markets," *American Economic Review* 73, May 1983, pp. 90–100.

Mason, R. "Innovations in the Structures of International Securities." Credit Suisse–First Boston, 1986.

Miller, M. "Financial Innovation: The Last Twenty Years and the Next." *Journal of Financial and Quantitative Analysis* 21, 1986, pp. 459–471.

Nomura Research Institute. *The World Financial Markets in 1995*. Nomura Research Institute, 1986.

Price, J., and S. Henderson. "Currency and Interest Rate Swaps." *Butterworths*, 1984.

Rubinstein, M., and H. Leland. "Replicating Options with Positions in Stock and Cash." *Financial Analysts Journal* 37, July–August 1981, pp. 63–72.

Saunders, A., and L. White, eds. *Technology and the Regulation of Financial Markets: Securities, Futures, and Banking*. Lexington, Mass: Lexington Books, 1986.

Schaefer, S. "The Problem with Redemption Yields." *Financial Analysts Journal* 33 July/August 1977, pp. 59–67.

Shirref, D. "Turning down the Gaz de France Swap Credit Exposure." *Risk*, December 1987, pp. 28–29.

Sharpe, W. *Investments*. Englewood Cliffs, N.J.: Prentice-Hall, 1985.

Silber, W. "Innovation, Competition, and New Contract Design in Futures Markets." *Journal of Futures Markets* 2, 1981, pp. 125–55.

———. "The Process of Financial Innovation." *American Economic Review* 73, May 1983, pp. 89–95.

Smithson, C. "A LEGO Approach to Financial Engineering." *Midland Corporate Finance Journal* 4, 1987, pp. 16–28.

Telser, L. "Why There Are Organized Futures Markets." *Journal of Law and Economics* 24, April 1981, pp. 1–22.

Van Horne, J. "Of Financial Innovations and Excesses." *Journal of Finance* 40, July 1985, pp. 621–31.

Yokio, K., and P. Hubbard. "Zaitech: The Japanese Perspective on Financial Engineering." *Journal of International Securities Markets* 2, Spring 1988, pp. 67–72.

CHAPTER 23

EXCHANGE-RATE VOLATILITY

Christian C. P. Wolff
Cecilia G. Reyes

Since 1973 when the Bretton Woods fixed-parity system was abandoned, the nature of exchange-rate volatility has changed considerably. Before that time exchange rates of the U.S. dollar vis-á-vis currencies of major industrial countries were fixed at an official rate and adjustments took the form of infrequent discrete jumps in the level of an exchange rate. After 1973 exchange rates have been allowed to adjust more or less continuously in response to market forces. Monetary authorities in most major industrial countries, however, intervene in currency markets from time to time when they observe developments deemed to be undesirable.

A number of European countries were concerned about the very high level of exchange-rate volatility in the years directly following the abandonment of the Bretton Woods system. Their concern was the basis for the foundation of the European Monetary System (EMS) in 1979. Member states of the EMS are bound to keep the level of their exchange rates within a certain range of values relative to one another. An incipient move beyond the range, therefore, should urge the monetary authorities of the two countries in question to intervene in the market. These institutional aspects of the behavior of exchange rates are, of course, reflected in the pattern of exchange-rate volatility.

In the academic options-related literature the word *volatility* takes a very specific meaning, which we also use throughout this chapter. When employing the word *volatility,* we refer to the standard deviation of the continuously compounded exchange-rate return. If we define r_t to be this continuously compounded exchange rate return at time t (as is explained in detail later), then its standard deviation σ is given by the formula

$$\sigma = \sqrt{\sum_{t=1}^{T} (r_t - \mu)^2/T} \qquad (1)$$

where T is the number of periods for which r_t is measured and μ is the mean of the set of T measurements. Thus volatility is a concept with a sharper focus than just variability.

WHY IS VOLATILITY IMPORTANT?

Impact on Corporate Profits

Whenever a company has streams of costs or revenues denominated in foreign currencies, exchange-rate volatility generally influences corporate profits. For instance, a U.S. importer of foreign-made goods often sees dollar profits decline when the foreign currency in question strengthens relative to the dollar. Of course, a high level of exchange rate volatility implies a relatively high probability of "good" outcomes as well as "bad" outcomes. Although increased exchange-rate volatility does not usually have an important impact on the size of expected or average profits, it does lead to greater uncertainty. A company may, therefore, choose to hedge its foreign-exchange risk using some of the financial contracts explained in earlier chapters.

Foreign-Exchange Options

Foreign-exchange options are a significant financial innovation whose market has grown dramatically in recent years. Several exchanges like the Chicago Board of Options Exchange (CBOE) and the Philadelphia Stock Exchange in the United States, London International Financial Futures Exchange (LIFFE) and the London Stock Exchange in the United Kingdom and the European Options Exchange in Amsterdam now trade standardized put and call option contracts on major currencies. In addition, a significant over-the-counter market operates through major banks and other financial institutions, where option contracts are tailor-made to the requirements of customers. Option contracts provide a significant instrument to protect the holders against or provide exposure to foreign-exchange-rate volatility.

The concept of exchange-rate volatility is crucially important for the valuation of currency options. Garman and Kohlhagen built on previous option pricing results to value European foreign-exchange call and put options.[1] It is interesting to inspect their valuation formulas to see the link with volatility. If we let C denote the value of a European call and P the value of a European put (both in dollars per unit of foreign currency), their results read as follows:

$$C(S,T) = \exp(-r_f T)SN(x + \sigma\sqrt{T}) - \exp(-r_d T)KN(x) \qquad (2)$$

$$P(S,T) = \exp(-r_f T)S[N(x + \sigma\sqrt{T}) - 1] \\ - \exp(-r_d T)K[N(x) - 1] \qquad (3)$$

with

$$x = \frac{\ln(S/K) + [r_d - r_f - (\sigma^2/2)]T}{\sigma \sqrt{T}} \qquad (4)$$

Here the notation is as follows:

S = the spot price of the underlying currency (dollars per unit of foreign currency)

K = the exercise price of the option (dollars per unit of foreign currency)

T = the time to expiration of the option

r_d = the domestic (dollar) riskless rate of interest

r_f = the foreign riskless rate of interest

σ = the (constant) volatility of the currency

N(.) = the cumulative normal distribution function

exp = the base of the natural logarithm

---

[1] Mark B. Garman and Steven W. Kohlhagen, "Foreign Currency Option Values," *Journal of International Money and Finance* 2 (1983), pp. 231–37.

The interesting thing about these pricing formulas for the purposes of this chapter is the fact that every single ingredient of the valuation formulas (2) through (4) is observable, except the volatility. There is predictable relationship between volatility and the prices of both put and call options. As volatility increases, the price of a put as well as the price of a call increases. This is because greater volatility simply increases the probability that an option will end up in-the-money at maturity. Because the volatility is the only relevant determinant of option values in the preceding formulas we cannot observe, every actually observed option value implies a certain level of volatility. Using the option pricing formulas, we can solve numerically for this implied volatility or implied standard deviation (ISD). Currency option values, therefore, can give us useful information about the market's assessment of exchange-rate volatility during the period to expiration of the options.

Volatility was assumed to be constant in the preceding formulas. In reality volatility can change over time. Next, we outline some evidence on this issue and briefly discuss the pricing of currency options when volatility is not constant.

International Portfolios

International diversification of equity portfolios is usually aimed at a reduction in portfolio risk (standard deviation of portfolio return). Provided that stock returns in various countries are less than perfectly correlated, an investor spreading holdings across different stock markets to a certain extent is normally better off than an investor who does not diversify internationally. This is reflected in a higher expected-return-to-risk ratio.

A complication arising in this context is the presence of exchange-rate risk (volatility). For international diversification to be desirable, the reduction in risk obtained from investing in foreign stocks should not be offset by the additional exchange-rate risk that arises from holding assets denominated in foreign currencies. Thus, exchange-rate volatility and the degree of correlation between exchange-rate returns and stock returns are important considerations when constructing international portfolios of shares.

Volatility and Systematic Risk

A crucial implication from the capital asset pricing model (CAPM) in the context of the domestic capital market is that not all risk is priced in an equilibrium structure of security prices. The risk (standard deviation of return) of a security can be divided into diversifiable or nonsystematic risk, which is not priced, and nondiversifiable or systematic risk, which is reflected in equilibrium security prices. The bottom line here is that risk that can be diversified away by holding a variety of securities is not be priced in the market.

Similarly, it stands to reason that not all exchange-rate volatility represents risk of the systematic variety in an international context. Unfortunately, we do not have a model of international asset pricing that is as widely received and useful as the CAPM is for domestic capital markets. Building an international asset pricing model is inherently more difficult than constructing a purely domestic model, for at least three reasons:

1. Capital asset pricing models generally assume that all investors have the same investment opportunity set. Barriers to international investments lead to investors in different countries facing different return distributions.
2. Whenever there are deviations from purchasing-power parity, investors in different countries perceive different real return distributions.
3. Investors in different countries generally consume different baskets of goods. These consumption differences make perceived real returns dependent on which investor's perspective is taken: every investor thinks in terms of his or her own consumption basket.

A number of international asset pricing models have been developed which capture aspects of the preceding difficulties. So far, however, we do not have a generally accepted model of international asset pricing to help us to identify the systematic component of exchange-rate risk in an international context.[2]

---

[2] For references, see Rene M. Stulz, "Pricing Capital Assets in an International Setting: An Introduction," *Journal of International Business Studies* 16 (1985), pp. 55–74.

EMPIRICAL EVIDENCE ON EXCHANGE-RATE VOLATILITY

"A flexible exchange rate need not be an unstable exchange rate" according to Milton Friedman.[3] In recent years a considerable amount of empirical evidence on exchange rate volatility has been generated. In this section we provide an overview of this evidence. In addition to presenting some basic statistics and graphs, we discuss in some detail a recently developed class of econometric models that has proved very useful for modeling the pattern of exchange-rate volatility over time.

Statistics

To get a feel for the data, we first present some basic statistics concerning the continuously compounded exchange-rate return, r_t:

$$r_t = \ln (S_t/S_{t-1}) = \ln (S_t) - \ln (S_{t-1}) \tag{5}$$

where S_t is the level of the spot exchange rate at time t. The variable r_t is usually the variable of interest in empirical research on exchange rates and currency options. In Table 23–1, we provide descriptive statistics on the distribution of r_t for a number of currencies measured relative to the U.S. dollar.

The statistics in Table 23–1 are based on daily exchange-rate data taken from the Barings International Database maintained by the Institute of Finance at the London Business School. All trading days from January 1975 through November 1986 are included in the sample (3,005 observations). The rates are quoted relative to the U.S. dollar and represent middle quotes at the opening of the business day in London (8:15 A.M.).

The mean returns in all cases are very small, consistent with the empirical fact that changes in the levels (or logarithms) of exchange rates are almost entirely unpredictable for currencies of major industrial countries. The second column in the table contains

---

[3] Milton Friedman, *Essays in Positive Economics* (Chicago: University of Chicago Press, 1953), p. 173.

TABLE 23–1
Descriptive Statistics on Exchange-Rate Returns

Currency	Mean $(\times 10^{-3})$	Standard Deviation $(\times 10^{-2})$	Skewness	Kurtosis
Sterling	0.160	0.715	−0.310[a] (0.685)	7.593[a] (0.212)
S. franc	−0.142	0.868	−0.083 (3.286)	8.999 (0.247)
Yen	−0.205	0.645	−0.394 (0.525)	7.948 (0.190)
F. franc	0.129	0.751	0.061 (4.466)	8.688 (0.270)
Guilder	−0.034	0.732	−0.279 (0.899)	7.768 (0.267)
Deutsche mark	−0.062	0.742	−0.189 (0.300)	7.768 (0.257)

[a] Standard errors of estimates in parentheses.

Source: Cecilia G. Reyes, "The Distribution of Daily Foreign Exchange Rate Changes." Working Paper, London School of Business, 1987.

standard deviations of exchange-rate returns. These are measurements of exchange rate volatility in the period at hand. For these currencies volatility was about $0.75 \times \sqrt{252} = 11.9$ percent per annum. In the third column the skewness of the distribution of exchange-rate returns is reported, with standard errors of estimates in parentheses. As the skewness measurements are relatively small, also in relation to the standard errors, we can conclude that the distribution of exchange rate returns is approximately symmetric. In the fourth column we present coefficients of kurtosis. A normal distribution would have a coefficient of kurtosis of three. Kurtosis in excess of three implies that the distribution at hand is more peaked than the normal and has fatter tails than the normal. All coefficients of kurtosis reported are significantly greater than three; thus, we can conclude that the distribution of exchange-rate returns does indeed have more pronounced tail areas than the normal distribution, in combination with a more peaked shape at the center of the distribution.

Graphs

Oftentimes a simple graph of a set of data gives a much better impression than tables filled with statistics. In Figures 23–1 through 23–3 the exchange-rate returns have been plotted from 1969 through 1987 for three major currencies relative to the U.S. dollar.

It is interesting to note the difference in exchange rate behavior pre-1973 and post-1973. In the earlier part of the sample, exchange rates were governed by the Bretton Woods fixed-parity system. In that period exchange-rate returns were usually zero, but once in a while there would be a devaluation or revaluation, as indicated by the spikes in the graphs. Exchange-rate volatility increased dramatically in the post-1973 period. Market participants as well as academics were caught off guard by this tremendous degree of volatility. Not surprisingly, an increased demand arose for financial instruments that allow companies, individuals, and portfolio managers to hedge foreign-exchange rate risk. Figures 23–1 through 23–3 capture another feature of exchange rate volatility: volatility comes in waves. That is, large exchange-rate

FIGURE 23–1
Daily Log Price Relatives of Deutsche Mark

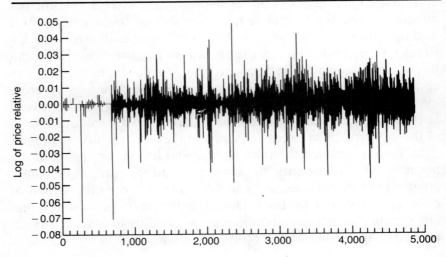

FIGURE 23–2
Daily Log Price Relatives of Japanese Yen

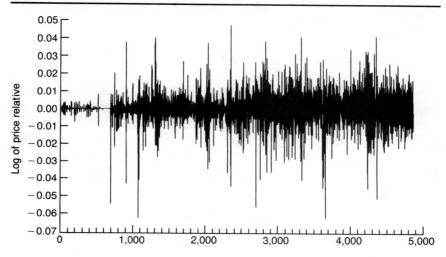

FIGURE 23–3
Daily Log Price Relatives of Pound Sterling

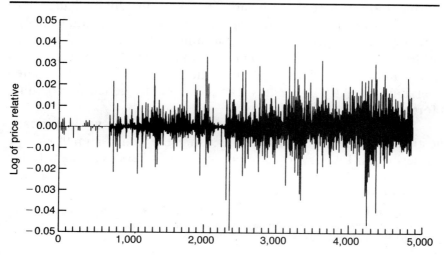

returns tend to be followed by large returns and small exchange rate returns tend to be followed by small returns. This is an important consideration when trying to forecast exchange-rate volatility in the short run.

Models of Exchange-Rate Volatility

When studying exchange-rate volatility, it is useful to try to capture its properties in a formal model. In recent years, a new class of econometric models has become available; it is ideally suited to do just that. These models are autoregressive conditional heteroskedastic (ARCH) models, first developed by Engle.[4] The simplest ARCH model of exchange-rate volatility takes the following form:

$$r_t|I_{t-1} \sim N(0, v_t) \tag{6}$$

with

$$v_t = a_o + a_1 r_{t-1}^2 \tag{7}$$

The exchange-rate return at time t, r_t, conditioned on all information that was available to market participants at time $t-1$ (I_{t-1} represents this set of information) is assumed to be normally distributed with zero mean and with a variance (i.e., squared volatility) v_t, which varies over time. In the preceding simple formulation v_t depends linearly on the squared exchange rate return on the previous trading day. Thus, the magnitude of the previous exchange-rate return determines the conditional variance of today's return. This characteristic of the ARCH model captures the feature that exchange-rate volatility comes in waves. Estimated versions of ARCH models can be used to generate volatility forecasts.

Quite recently, a number of researchers have empirically estimated models of this nature using the general methodology described in Engle.[5] Some references are Bollerslev, Hsieh, Hsieh

[4] Robert F. Engle, "Autoregressive Conditional Heteroscedasticity with Estimates of the Variance of United Kingdom Inflation," *Econometrica* 50 (1982), pp. 987–1008.

[5] Engle, "Autoregressive."

and Wolff, and Reyes.[6] The empirical results generally show that ARCH models capture important features of exchange-rate volatility. So far, however, the models do not completely account for the pronounced kurtosis in the distribution of exchange-rate returns mentioned earlier. Hsieh established that the distribution of exchange rate returns differs across days of the week.[7] One explanation for this feature of the data could be that news revelations relevant to the foreign-exchange market (such as money supply announcements) are not equally distributed across days of the week.

Every estimated ARCH model implies a time series of volatility estimates for the period of estimation. An example of such a time series of volatilities is provided in Figure 23–4.

Figure 23–4 is based on an ARCH model which was estimated for the sterling/dollar exchange rate data for which summary statistics were presented in Table 23–1. The time period is January 1975 through November 1986. Note how much the estimated level of volatility fluctuates over time, reaching a low of about 0.3 percent per day and a high of about 3 percent per day. The estimated model on which Figure 23–4 is based takes the form:

$$r_t | I_{t-1} \sim N(0, v_t) \tag{8}$$

$$v_t = a_o + \sum_{i=1}^{15} a_i \, r_{t-i}^2 \tag{9}$$

Thus, realized exchange-rate returns from the previous 15 trading days are allowed to impact on our forecast for today's volatility. Maximum-likelihood estimates of coefficients, together with associated standard errors, t-statistics, and P-values, are reported in Table 23–2.

---

[6] Tim Bollerslev, "A Conditionally Heteroskedastic Time Series Model for Speculative Prices and Rates of Return," *Review of Economics and Statistics* 69 (1987), pp. 542–47; David A. Hsieh, "The Statistical Properties of Daily Foreign Exchange Rates: 1974–1983," working paper, University of Chicago (1985); David A. Hsieh and Christian C. P. Wolff, "Exchange Rate Volatility and Fat Tails in the Statistical Distribution of Foreign Exchange Rate Changes," working paper, University of Chicago and London Business School (1987); and Cecilia G. Reyes, "The Distribution of Daily Foreign Exchange Rate Changes," working paper, London Business School (1987).
[7] Hsieh, "The Statistical Properties."

FIGURE 23–4
Time Series of Volatility for Sterling/U.S. Dollar Exchange Rate

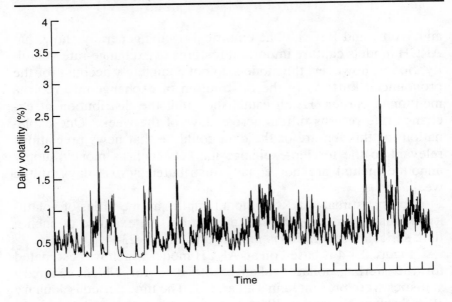

TABLE 23–2
Estimated Coefficients in an ARCH Model of the Sterling/Dollar Exchange Rate

Coefficient	Value	Standard Error	t-Statistic	P-Value
a_0	0.261	0.018	14.51*	0.000
a_1	0.459	0.030	15.48*	0.000
a_2	0.338	0.034	9.86*	0.000
a_3	0.272	0.037	7.35*	0.000
a_4	0.233	0.044	5.31*	0.000
a_5	0.185	0.059	3.13*	0.002
a_6	0.219	0.050	4.36*	0.000
a_7	0.210	0.048	4.39*	0.000
a_8	0.202	0.044	4.60*	0.000
a_9	0.258	0.041	6.27*	0.000
a_{10}	0.328	0.048	6.89*	0.000
a_{11}	0.329	0.042	7.88*	0.000
a_{12}	0.121	0.067	1.82	0.068
a_{13}	0.209	0.048	4.39*	0.000
a_{14}	0.120	0.082	1.45	0.146
a_{15}	0.075	0.113	0.66	0.509

* Indicates statistical significance at the 1 percent level.

The coefficient values show the estimated pattern of persistence in exchange rate volatility. Most coefficients are statistically significantly greater than zero. These positive coefficient values confirm our earlier observation that large exchange-rate returns tend to be followed by large returns and small exchange-rate returns by small ones.

We now have two independent models to forecast exchange-rate volatility. We already established that implied standard deviations incorporated in currency option prices are a reflection of the market's assessment of exchange-rate volatility during the period to expiration of the option. The ARCH models presented in this section form a second, independent class of models that can be used for volatility forecasting. It would be interesting to compare the empirical forecasting performance of the two strategies. To our knowledge, such a comparison has not been undertaken to date.

TIME-VARYING VOLATILITY AND THE PRICING OF OPTIONS

When the pricing of currency options was discussed earlier in this chapter, it was assumed that exchange rate volatility (σ) is constant over time. Based on the empirical evidence in the previous section, however, we cannot escape the conclusion that volatility varies over time. One would, therefore, be interested in an option pricing model that allows for time-varying volatility. Hull and White have recently devised a pricing formula for European call options when volatility is stochastic.[8] They need to make a number of assumptions to derive their result. It is beyond the scope of this chapter to present a detailed analysis of option pricing with time-varying volatility. It is useful, however to summarize briefly the empirical evidence to date on this issue.

Hull and White show that the traditional fixed-volatility Black-Scholes call option pricing formula overvalues at-the-money op-

---

[8] John Hull and Alan White, "The Pricing of Options on Assets with Stochastic Volatilities," *Journal of Finance* 42 (1987), pp. 281–99.

tions and undervalues deep in- and out-of-the-money call options.[9] The range over which overpricing by the Black-Scholes formula takes place is for stock prices within about 10 percent of the exercise price. The magnitude of the pricing bias can be up to 5 percent of the Black-Scholes price. Hull and White obtained these numerical results for the case of a call option on a security with a stochastic volatility that is uncorrelated with the security price. When there is a positive correlation between the security price and its volatility, out-of-the-money options are underpriced by the Black-Scholes formula, while in-the-money options are over-priced. When the correlation is negative, the effect is reversed.

SUMMARY AND CONCLUSION

In this chapter we have discussed the importance of exchange-rate volatility and implications for financial decision making. The recent experience with exchange-rate volatility was documented extensively and some new statistical tools for modeling volatility were discussed. Finally, we explored some issues related to the pricing of currency options under various assumptions with regard to the time pattern of the volatility of the underlying currency. Much of the research discussed in this chapter was undertaken quite recently and we expect that these issues will continue to fascinate researchers and practitioners alike.

REFERENCES

Black, Fischer, and Myron Scholes. "The Pricing of Options and Corporate Liabilities." *Journal of Political Economy* 81, 1973, 637–59.

Bollerslev, Tim. "A Conditionally Heteroskedastic Time Series Model for Speculative Prices and Rates of Return." *Review of Economics and Statistics* 69, 1987, pp. 542–47.

Engle, Robert F. "Autoregressive Conditional Heteroscedasticity with

---

[9] Fischer Black and Myron Scholes, "The Pricing of Options and Corporate Liabilities," *Journal of Political Economy* 81 (1973), pp. 637–59.

Estimates of the Variance of U.K. Inflation." *Econometrica* 50, 1982, pp. 987–1008.

Friedman, Milton. "The Case for Flexible Exchange Rates." In *Essays in Positive Economics*. Chicago: University of Chicago Press, 1953.

Garman, Mark B., and Steven W. Kohlhagen. "Foreign Currency Option Values." *Journal of International Money and Finance* 2, 1983, pp. 231–37.

Hsieh, David A. "The Statistical Properties of Daily Foreign Exchange Rates: 1974–1983." Working Paper, University of Chicago, 1985.

Hsieh, David A., and Christian C. P. Wolff. "Exchange Rate Volatility and Fat Tails in the Statistical Distribution of Foreign Exchange Rate Changes." Working Paper, University of Chicago and London Business School, 1987.

Hull, John, and Alan White. "The Pricing of Options on Assets with Stochastic Volatilities." *Journal of Finance* 42, 1987, pp. 281–99.

Reyes, Cecilia G. "The Distribution of Daily Foreign Exchange Rate Changes." Working Paper, London Business School, 1987.

————. "Time Series Processes for Exchange Rate Volatility." Working Paper, London Business School, 1988.

Stulz, Rene M. "Pricing Capital Assets in an International Setting: An Introduction." *Journal of International Business Studies* 16, 1985, pp. 55–74.

PART 4

THE ENVIRONMENT

CHAPTER 24

PATTERNS OF CAPITAL FLOWS

Brendan Brown

Just as international trade in goods has a strong regional bias—for example, there is much more intensive trade between the West European economies than between them and the outside world— so it is with international trade in financial assets of different currency denominations. Foreign borrowing and lending in deutsche marks, for instance, is at its most intensive in Western Europe, rather than, say, in North America.

The one common factor behind the regional bias of both types of trade is transaction costs, where these are broadly defined to also include transport costs. The ease of selling goods is greater to markets less than one hour away than to those halfway around the world; market information about consumer preferences and distribution networks can be established at relatively low cost. Similarly, it is easier for Europeans—especially when dealing in small size—to make international transactions in, say, deutsche marks, than it is for Japanese or Americans.

There is, however, an additional important factor behind the regional concentration of trade in international monies. This is risk. Usually currencies of countries in the same economic region belong to one zone between whose members exchange-rate volatility is less than with outsiders. (In turn, these zonal formations usually have their ultimate source in a regional concentration of trade.) Thus for a French or Dutch investor or borrower, the exchange risk incurred in borrowing or lending deutsche marks is considerably less than U.S. dollars—hence, their bias of currency choice toward the mark.

CURRENCY ZONES AND POLES

In the contemporary world, there are two great currency zones—the U.S. dollar zone and the DM zone. Both contain an inner zone within which exchange risk is particularly low and an outer zone. The inner dollar zone consists of U.S. and Canadian dollars; the inner DM zone of the deutsche mark, Swiss franc, Dutch guilder, Austrian schilling, and the Belgian franc. In the outer dollar zone are found currencies of the Latin American nations and of the Asian newly industrialized countries (NICs). Outer DM-zone currencies include the French franc, Italian lira, and British pound.

The statistical characteristic of a zone lies in a comparison of correlation coefficients. Currencies e_i ($i = 1$ to n) lie in a zone with respect to currency D if it is true that the correlation of exchange-rate changes between D and the various e_i ($\rho_{e_i\text{-}D,e_j\text{-}D}$), is significantly greater than the correlation of exchange-rate changes between E and the various e_i, ($\rho_{e_i\text{-}E,e_j\text{-}E}$), where E is the largest of the e_i. In Table 24–1, D is the U.S. dollar, and the various e_i are the Dutch guilder, French franc, and British pound; E is the deutsche mark.

TABLE 24–1
Correlation Coefficients (three-month exchange-rate change)

	Deutsche Mark/Dollar		
	1974–87 HI	*1974–79*	*1980–87 HI*
Guilder/dollar	0.98	0.92	0.99
Guilder/deutsche mark	0.05	−0.03	0.04
Franc/dollar	0.90	0.65	0.97
Franc/deutsche mark	−0.29	−0.53	−0.14
Pound/dollar	−0.61	−0.45	−0.65
Pound/deutsche mark	0.54	0.60	0.51
Yen/dollar	0.64	0.33	0.77
Yen/deutsche mark	0.44	0.63	0.35

The Japanese yen is the outsider. Correlation coefficients are presented for three-month changes over the years 1974–87; in addition, coefficients are shown for two subperiods, 1974–79 and 1980–87.

It is clear from the table that both the Dutch guilder and French franc belong to a DM zone in that $\rho_{Dfl\text{-}\$,DM\text{-}\$}$ is substantially greater than $\rho_{Dfl\text{-}DM,DM\text{-}\$}$ and similarly for $\rho_{Ffr\text{-}\$,DM\text{-}\$}$ compared to $\rho_{Ffr\text{-}DM,DM\text{-}\$}$. The strength of the zonal formation has been greater in the second than in the first period, doubtless in large part reflecting the formation of the European Monetary System (EMS). By contrast, in the years 1974–79, both the British pound and Japanese yen could have been characterized as belonging to the dollar zone in that they were more bound to the dollar in their movement against the mark than they were bound to the mark in their movement against the dollar. Since 1980 both currencies have fallen out of the dollar zone. The bare statistics show that the yen has become closer than the pound to the mark. In more recent subperiods not illustrated, however, the pound has become more of a DM currency.

Zones are defined with respect to exchange-rate changes over a specified period, say, one month, three months, one year, or more. It is quite possible for currencies to form a zone with respect to changes up to one year, for example, and not beyond. This is because the relative strength of different forces behind exchange-rate change varies according to the length of the period considered. In particular, differential inflation rates are an important factor in explaining long-run but generally not short-run exchange-rate changes. Inflation rates do not usually show the same (if any) order of regional interdependence as do some other forces operating on currencies—for example, the business cycle.

The high degree of economic interdependence of countries within a region usually lies in the intensity of trading relationships between them. In turn, real exchange-rate change between a nation's currency and that of others in the same region normally has greater economic impact than change of the same order against outsider currencies. Many investors are aware of these differential impacts; for example, the especially powerful influence of intra-DM zone exchange-rate change on inflation and the trade balance of any member country.

This awareness of investors helps limit intrazonal exchange-rate fluctuation. For example, many investors realize that a 10 percent appreciation of the deutsche mark against other European Community (EC) currencies would have a greater impact on the German trade balance and on other EC trade balances (in the opposite direction) than would a similar change in its exchange-rate relative to the dollar. This awareness is reflected in a greater elasticity of demand for the deutsche mark with respect to changes in its rate relative to other European currencies rather than to the dollar.

The task of stabilizing the dollar against EC currencies, despite the natural volatility of these transzonal exchange rates, would have involved huge sacrifice of monetary independence. The various shocks which the United States has successively emitted to the international economy—the Carter monetary boom, the Volcker squeeze, the Reagan budget buster, and the Baker devaluation—have been very large. These shocks have incidentally increased the cohesion of zonal formations by raising the correlation between changes in the exchange rates of nondollar currencies relative to the dollar.

Indeed, the common exposure to dollar shock makes changes in the yen-dollar rate significantly correlated (over short- and medium-term periods) with changes in the rate between EC currencies and the dollar. This common exposure is responsible for the correlation being substantially greater than that between changes in the yen-mark rate and in the mark-dollar rate, despite the particularly strong economic interdependence between the United States and Japan (see Tables 24–2 and 24–3).

TABLE 24–2
Exports to the United States ($ billions)

	Percent Share in OECD GDP 1982	1983	1984	1985	1986
Inner DM Zone	13.6	21.5	27.4	30.2	36.0
Outer DM Zone	21.0	37.1	42.0	43.2	48.8
Japan	14.0	42.8	60.2	65.6	80.7
Asian NICs	(1.8)	28.6	37.5	37.3	45.8

TABLE 24–3
Asian NICs' Trade with Japan and United States in 1986 ($ billions)

	Exports to		Imports from	
	United States	*Japan*	*United States*	*Japan*
Asian NICs				
S. Korea	12.8	5.3	5.8	10.5
Taiwan	19.8	4.7	5.1	7.9
Singapore	4.7	2.5	3.3	4.8
Hong Kong	8.8	1.5	3.0	7.1
Total	46.1	14.0	17.2	30.8

Yet the yen cannot be described even abstractly as a member of the DM zone; $\rho_{DM-\$,Y-\$}$ is significantly less than $\rho_{DM-\$,e_i-\$}$ (the correlation coefficient between short-run changes in the mark-dollar and in any other DM-zone currency, e_i, relative to the dollar). The distance of the yen from the DM-zone can be explained by the much greater trade of Japan with dollar-zone countries than with the EC and in turn the considerable synchrony between U.S. and Japanese business cycles.

The DM and dollar zone each contain a currency pole—the DM and U.S. dollar respectively. The pole currency has a strong influence on other currencies in the zone in their motion against outsiders—greater than these other currencies' influence on the pole currency. The basis of polar power is economic dependence. For example, behind the polar power the deutsche mark wields over the Dutch guilder lies the greater share of Germany—and those small countries highly dependent economically on Germany—in Dutch trade; Holland's share in German trade is smaller. Thus a unilateral revaluation, say, of the deutsche mark against all currencies, would have a great economic impact on the Dutch economy; in particular, it would raise the threat of inflation, by bringing a jump in import prices and in prices of tradable goods generally, and by ultimately fueling monetary growth through an improved trade balance. In order to avoid these ill-effects the Hague would probably revalue the guilder in the deutsche mark's wake. By contrast, a unilateral revaluation of the guilder would not bring pressure on Bonn to change the Federal Republic's currency policy.

The deutsche mark's polar power in the DM zone is accentuated by the fact that the Federal Republic is surrounded by several smaller economies in each of whose trade (as in the Dutch example) it is dominant; each of these has a strong interest in tying its currency to the mark, thereby making their monetary policies subservient to Bundesbank policy. The countries include the other members of the inner DM zone.

Thus, for example, the deutsche mark exerts some polar power with respect to the French franc, even though France and the Federal Republic are not in themselves unequal trade partners. France, unlike the Federal Republic, does not have a number one position in the trade of the small countries on its frontier. The deutsche mark's power with respect to the French franc is derived from the fact that the Federal Republic, together with other members of the inner DM zone (considered in aggregate) have a much larger share in France's trade than France has in the trade of inner DM-zone countries with the outside world (see Table 24–4).

The polar power of the deutsche mark gives Bonn a degree of monetary hegemony and lies behind the frequent description—albeit less frequent now than a decade ago—of the currency map as

TABLE 24–4
Inner DM-Zone Countries' Trade with the Federal Republic and France 1985 (in percentage of total trade)

	Federal Republic		France		Inner DM Zone	
	X^a	M^b	X	M	X	M
Belgium	18.7%	21.0%	19.0%	15.1%	36.0%	42.6%
Netherlands	30.0	22.2	10.4	9.0	46.7	36.6
Austria	30.2	41.1	5.4	3.6	41.5	50.2
Switzerland	19.7	30.6	8.4	11.1	28.2	42.8
France	14.3	16.5	—	—	32.0	33.9
Federal Republic	—	—	11.9	10.6	26.0	22.9
Outer DM zone	16.1	17.9	—	—	35.1	35.7

[a] This is the percent of the given country's exports to the Federal Republic.
[b] This is the percent of the given country's imports from the Federal Republic.

bipolar. In the bipolar world, the deutsche mark dominates the movement of most other West European currencies against the dollar, at least over short-run periods. The deutsche mark is the clear number two international money in the world, and potential switches in investment demand between the mark and dollar are greater than between the dollar and any other currency.

The bipolarism of the 1970s and 1980s based on the mark-dollar axis has antecedents in previous eras—notably the years of hegemony for the French franc-dollar axis from September 1931— when Britain left the gold standard, while France, Belgium, Holland, Switzerland, and a group of countries in Eastern Europe remained on gold—until September 1936 when the French franc was devalued and the gold bloc finally broke up. Then, there were the last three years before the outbreak of World War II, when sterling was at "the opposite end of the pole" to the U.S. dollar; during much of that time, the French franc was pegged to sterling.[1]

Could the world of the late 1980s be evolving beyond the bipolarism that marked the 1930s or the decade or more that followed the demise of the Bretton Woods system? There are two pointers in that direction: first, the growing financial power of Japan; and second, the greater competition for the deutsche mark in Europe from the French franc and British pound.

The Japanese yen faces considerable handicaps, however, in any bid to bring bipolarism to an end, albeit that on the basis of 1982 weights, Japan and the inner DM-zone countries are approximately equal in economic size at around 14 percent of the total Organization for Economic Cooperation and Development gross domestic product (OECD GDP). But Japan is not surrounded, as is the inner DM zone, by large countries in each of whose trade it is dominant and which are ready to accept its monetary lead.

True, Japan has strong trade relations with the Asian NICs (South Korea, Taiwan, Singapore, and Hong Kong), but these are collectively of much smaller economic size (less than one sixth of the Japanese GDP) than the outer DM zone (one and a half times the inner DM zone GDP), and for each of them, Japan is less

---

[1] See B. D. Brown, *The Flight of International Capital* (London: Croom Helm, 1987), chap. 1 and 2; and *Monetary Chaos in Europe* (London: Croom Helm, 1987), chap 5.

important than the United States as a trading partner. Moreover, there is no counterpart political framework, analogous to the EC, in which the monetary hegemony of Japan could be disguised; and there are strong political obstacles to the Asian NICs explicitly accepting yen dominance. In sum, the Bundesbank has important monetary influence over a wider economic area than does the Bank of Japan.

The existence of the outer countries around the inner DM zone provides a "first layer" of international demand for the deutsche mark that has no counterpart in the case of the Japanese yen. For investors in the outer zone, the deutsche mark has the appeal of being of much lower risk than the U.S. dollar and also denominating highly liquid money and bond markets. German government bonds, for example, proved a magnet to European savings during the mid-1980s, in that their bearer form and exemption from withholding tax made them highly attractive compared to most other EC government bonds. The imposition of withholding tax from end-1988 in the Federal Republic was a blow, but the Euro-DM bond market remains the most liquid of Euro bond markets denominated in European currencies.

For investors in the world outside the DM zone, the existence of the outer-zone countries around the inner DM zone expands the hedging justification for holding marks in their portfolio. Mark assets are not just a low-risk store of value for future consumption of goods coming from the inner DM zone, but also from France, Britain, Italy, and other outer-zone countries. Market liquidity and tax advantages are two factors making the deutsche mark an attractive alternative to a direct hedge in francs, liras, or pounds.

THE DOLLAR'S POLAR POWER

The fact that the mark's function as a store of value has a base in the whole DM zone—an area more than double the economic size of Japan and considerably less sensitive to most types of U.S. shock—is an important element in the defenses around mark-dollar bipolarism. Many of the varieties of U.S. shock that hit the international economy pull the Japanese economy along a common path with the United States and away from Europe. As a corollary, the effect of U.S. shock at such times is greatest on the flow of capital between the mark and dollar. Examples of such shock include sudden turns in the U.S. business cycle or a change in U.S. monetary policy.

The emergence of the U.S. economy from recession tends to be associated with an increased force of capital inflows into the United States from the rest of the world, particularly Europe, as U.S. interest rates rise from their recession low points and fears of deliberate devaluation as a recession-countering measure by Washington recede. The interest rate advantage brought to the dollar by U.S. economic recovery is likely to be more vis-á-vis the mark than vis-á-vis the yen. Japanese exports to the United States and to economies highly geared to the U.S. economy such as the Asian NICs account for 6 percent of the GDP, compared to 2 percent for the DM zone. This means that U.S. recovery has a much greater stimulatory effect on the Japanese than on the European economy. Hence, Japanese interest rates are also likely to move upward in the wake of the U.S. recovery—leaving European rates behind. Similarly, at a time of U.S. economic contraction, Japanese interest rates would tend to follow U.S. interest rates down more closely than do European rates.

In sum, the U.S. business cycle is likely to have a greater influence on capital flows in and out of DM-zone countries than on Japan—the DM-zone capital account weakening by more than the Japanese in the early stage of a U.S. business recovery and strengthening by more when the U.S. economy slides into recession. In consequence, the yen would tend to be less weak than the mark relative to the dollar in the U.S. upswing, and less strong in the downswing. Adding to the relative insensitivity of the yen to the U.S. business cycle is the fact that there is a more powerful offset in the case of Japan than for the DM-zone countries to capital account weakness during U.S. recovery in the form of an improving trade balance (increased exports to the United States and to the Asian NICs) and to capital account strength during the recession in the form of a worsening trade balance.

Just as the yen tends to move with the dollar vis-á-vis the mark with respect to U.S. business-cycle fluctuations, so it does with respect to U.S. inflation risk. The yen is more likely than the mark to be submerged by U.S. inflation shock—meaning the mark is at the opposite end of the pole to the U.S. dollar at a time of rising fear of U.S. inflation. The yen's vulnerability here again stems from the particular interdependence of the U.S. and Japanese economies. A given fall of the U.S. dollar, on impact, has a greater recessionary influence on Japanese than European industry. Thus, the political pressure on Tokyo from within to ease monetary policy in the wake of a sharp dollar fall (due to increased fear of U.S. inflation, probably triggered by the Federal Reserve following a high-risk easy monetary policy) will be greater than on Bonn. By the same token, the mark is viewed as a better hedge than the yen against U.S. monetary excess—equivalently, it enjoys a greater degree of independence from Washington than the yen.

Overall, the U.S. dollar can be described as possessing polar power with respect to the Japanese yen in its movement against DM-zone currencies. This, in turn, undermines any bid by Japan to replace the deutsche mark as the opposite end of the pole to the U.S. dollar in a bipolar system. This is not to suggest, however, that there is a symmetry of power between forces at the mark and dollar ends of the pole. For example, a change in U.S. monetary policy exerts greater leverage on Bonn and other DM-zone capitals to follow suit than conversely—even though the United States and DM zones are of approximately equal economic size.

In part, the explanation lies in the greater importance of trade with the dollar zone for the DM-zone countries (the average of exports and imports coming to 4 percent of zonal GDP) than of trade with DM-zone countries for the United States (1.5 percent of GDP). The inequality is due to the transcontinentality of the dollar zone, which overall encompasses a much larger economic area than the DM zone; the transcontinentality stems from the U.S. position as the largest trading partner of Latin America and of the Asian Pacific—a dominance the DM zone does not enjoy with respect to important economic areas outside Europe.

The relatively small share of DM-zone countries in U.S. trade means that fluctuations of the dollar against the EC currencies has greater impact on the European than the U.S. economy—implying a correspondingly greater pressure on European central banks to bend domestic monetary policy toward U.S. policy than conversely. This power asymmetry is furthered by the fact that the Bundesbank does not have the same degree of monetary hegemony over the DM zone as the Federal Reserve has over the United States. In particular, central banks in the outer DM zone are usually content in times of turbulence on the mark-dollar axis to let their currency under natural forces swing by somewhat less than the mark. Hence the German economy is buffeted not just by a change in the mark-dollar rate but also by a lesser change in the mark's rate against outer DM-zone currencies when the United States emits a monetary shock lessening the Bundesbank's power of resistance.

The natural forces responsible for the outer DM-zone countries being able to steer their currencies somewhat away from the mark in the preceding circumstances include first, the tendency of the mark to bear a disproportionate share (relative to the size of the German economy) of shifts in international demand for the dollar. Second, some outer DM-zone countries such as Britain and Italy trade more with the United States (measured relative to their economic size) than do the inner DM-zone countries. The proportions respectively are Italy 2.75 percent, Britain 3.5 percent, and inner DM zone 2.5 percent.

Both natural forces are on the wane, and so correspondingly is the asymmetry between the power of the Federal Reserve to influence European monetary conditions and of DM-zone central banks (collectively) to influence U.S. monetary conditions. For example, the new (post-1970) generation of EC members are increasing the proportion of their trade with the EC; in addition, some of the new entrants have converted their currencies to being DM rather than dollar linked, so in turn increasing the proportion of older EC members' trade with DM-zone countries. Removal of exchange controls, financial market liberalization, and adoption of anti-inflation policies, have increased the competition within Europe to the mark as an international money. Hence, swings in monetary taste to and away from the U.S. dollar are likely to have less of a lopsided impact on DM-zone currencies; instead they should tend to respond more closely together.

By the same token, however, the expansion of the DM zone and the increased competition for the DM, have brought new checks to German monetary hegemony in Europe. The British pound and French franc can at times exert strong influence on the mark in its motion against outsiders. Moreover, there is the

possibility of the outer DM-zone members jointly refusing to follow
the monetary lead of Bonn (rather than being divided and led),
forcing the latter into either a unilateral parity adjustment, or a
change in policy. Bipolarism today should be seen in terms of the
U.S. dollar at one end of the pole, and at the other, the DM,
surrounded by first, the inner DM-zone and second, the outer
DM-zone currencies, able themselves to exert force.

Even in the 1970s, when deutsche mark hegemony in Europe
was at its peak—the French franc and British pound being subject
to exchange restrictions and high inflation—Paris, rather than
Bonn, sometimes held the key to European currency affairs. In
summer and autumn 1971, Paris's adamant refusal to join in a
common float of EC currencies was based in part on a dislike of
"DM nationalism" and in part on a preference for a gold-based
international monetary order. This led Bonn to unwillingly accept a
resuscitation of fixed exchange rates with the dollar (at the
Smithsonian, December 1971). Faced with a choice between
floating the deutsche mark unilaterally and so confronting German
exporters with considerable exchange risk not only against the
dollar but also against the currencies of the other EC countries, or
accepting the risk of U.S. inflation being imported via a fixed
exchange rate with the dollar, Bonn opted for the latter.

By spring 1973 the risk of U.S. inflation and its importation
had increased, while the chances of France getting its way in
international monetary reform had dwindled. Paris and Bonn
finally agreed on a common EC float. But it was not a float always
dominated by the mark. Already in January 1974, Paris demonstrated its power of independent action and its power to influence
the mark, by pulling the franc out of the "snake" in the middle of
the first oil crisis.[2] The possibility that France might abandon its
policy of financing the oil deficits over the medium term by official
borrowing abroad, largely in dollars, led briefly to a simultaneous
fall of the mark against the dollar. Investors feared that the franc
would pull down the mark, given the importance of France in
German trade.

---

[2] The Snake arrangement is described in the following chapter.

EXAMPLE OF ZONAL ANALYSIS—THE DEUTSCHE MARK

The advent of the European Monetary System (1979) has increased Europe's monetary independence of the United States in that two outer EC-zone countries, France and Italy, accepted the aim of greater stability, at least over short-run periods, of their currencies vis-à-vis the deutsche mark. EMS has also increased the likelihood of the French franc exerting polar power at times on the deutsche mark (insofar as Bonn is now ready to bend its own monetary policy toward achieving exchange-rate stability within the EMS rather than having frequent changes of parity, especially of the key mark-franc rate).

The EMS has also been responsible for spreading the "burden of adjustment" to German payment imbalances more widely among the DM-zone countries. For example, consider the situation where the German current account is in large surplus, while that of the outer DM-zone countries is in rough balance. As a corollary, the combined public and private savings rate is likely to be relatively high in the Federal Republic and, in turn, real interest rates on marks to be less than on outer DM-zone currencies and on the dollar. The resulting strong demand from the Federal Republic for foreign financial assets would be concentrated on other DM-zone currencies rather than the dollar, given their relatively low exchange risk.

In turn, the outer DM-zone countries, faced with a substantial German investment demand for their currencies, would be pushed ultimately into running current account deficits and so absorbing the capital inflows from marks. The push would come from a combination of lower (than otherwise) interest rates (stimulating domestic spending) and of currency adjustment (their currencies following the mark upward). The descent of the outer DM-zone countries into deficit and its financing by capital inflows from the inner DM zone mean that the German current account can remain in considerable surplus and yet not be a source of disequilibrium in international payments. Thus, the deutsche mark settles at a lower overall effective exchange rate against other currencies (and at a lower bilateral rate vis-à-vis the dollar) than in the case where the outer DM-zone currencies were on a dollar standard and exchange risk thereby hindered the recycling of the German surplus within the DM zone.

An example can be drawn from the experience of 1986–87. In 1986 the German current account had a huge surplus of DM 76 billion. The inner DM-zone countries had a combined surplus of DM 115 billion. By contrast, the outer DM zone countries had only a DM 15 billion surplus. Interest rates, both in nominal and real terms, were correspondingly higher in the outer zone countries than in the Federal Republic (one factor here being the relatively tight fiscal policy in the latter). The interest-rate differential lay behind a huge outflow of funds from the Federal Republic into the outer DM-zone countries, mainly in the form of (1) corporations in these countries increasing their liabilities in marks at the expense of domestic currencies (these operations explained the large outflow of funds from the Federal Republic to the Euro-DM marketplaces of London and Luxembourg) and of (2) German investors buying high-yielding bonds in France, Britain, Italy, Denmark, and in European Currency Units (ECUs) in preference to lower yielding German bonds.

The inflow of funds from the Federal Republic into the outer DM-zone countries was a potential stimulus to economic activity there; the inflow also helped prevent the outer DM-zone currencies from lagging far behind the deutsche mark in its ascent against the dollar. Both factors would draw the outer DM-zone countries into bearing a larger share of the adjustment by the DM zone as a whole toward reducing its current account surplus with the rest of the world, even though this was mainly attributable to the inner DM-zone countries.

Incidentally, the measures of currency liberalization taken by France and Italy during 1986–87 expanded the "sustainable" size of the DM zone's current account surplus (and of the surplus, in particular, of the Federal Republic). Both countries lifted long-standing controls on direct and portfolio investment abroad by domestic residents. In turn, pent-up demand from these countries for foreign investments was released—particularly those in the United States. Increased demand for dollar assets from the outer DM zone would be a source of upward pressure on interest rates in these countries—in turn, drawing capital in from the deutsche mark. Recycling of the German surplus into the outer DM zone to finance a bulge there in capital exports to the United States would reduce the pressure for external adjustment on the German economy, meaning a lesser appreciation of the deutsche mark.

EXAMPLES OF ZONAL ANALYSIS—THE DOLLAR AND YEN

The need to consider capital flows by zone when analyzing the motion of the key mark-dollar axis has been illustrated earlier for the European end of the pole. There are counterpart examples for the U.S. end. For example, at the time of the debt shock during the summer of 1982, there was much comment about how a "seizing up" of loans to Latin America and other developing countries would lead to a strengthening of the U.S. dollar in that the capital account of the U.S. balance of payments would be strengthened.

What the argument failed to acknowledge was the fact that most of the U.S. foreign lending of the late 1970s and early 1980s had simply financed round-tripping within the dollar zone, especially in the last 18 months before the crisis broke. A large counterpart to the lending had been huge inflows of flight capital into dollar investments from dollar-zone countries in the Third World—in particular, Latin America, Hong Kong, and the Philippines. As the lending was cut back, the inflow of flight capital would lose force; so would the export boom for U.S. corporations to Latin America. The end of the export boom might intensify the U.S. recession causing dollar interest rates to come under new downward pressure, itself negative for the dollar.

Another example of the need for zonal analysis—including both the DM and dollar zones—is predicting the response of the mark-dollar rate to "oil shock." It is not sufficient to look at the impact of a big change in the oil price on the external accounts of the United States and Federal Republic in isolation. Rather, analysts should consider the impact of the oil price change on the current account of the dollar zone as a whole—including North and South America, and the Asian NICs—and of the DM-zone countries, which like the dollar zone includes both energy exporters and importers. There are also capital account impacts to consider. How would the Organization of Petroleum Exporting Countries (OPEC) divide their funds between currencies? What would be the effect of the oil price change on investment opportunities and, thereby, interest rates in the two zones? For example, there is an argument that an oil price hike could raise the relative investment attractions of the United States, given the importance of its oil industry.

Japan must be incorporated as an outsider in zonal analysis. In the oil example, Japan stands out as the principal casualty of a big rise in the oil price (unlike the DM and dollar zones, Japan has no indigenous energy supplies). Given that its trade is highly oriented toward the dollar zone, its export drive to pay for oil (powered probably by a cheaper yen) would be more at the cost of the dollar zone than of the mark zone's current account—tending to undermine the dollar relative to the mark.

Critics may argue that the need to incorporate Japan into the analysis of the mark-dollar rate reveals an inadequacy of the bipolar framework for analysis. They could point out further that Japan, far from being a zonal "outsider" to the bipolar system, has emerged as a larger recorded capital exporter than the DM zone as a whole, surely invalidating any claim of the mark-dollar axis to dominate world finance.

There are, however, powerful counterarguments to the criticism. It is surely possible for zonal analysis to take account of countries outside the two zones, of which Japan is the largest. The Japanese yen does not exert polar power with respect to either the dollar or mark zone, and so the mark-dollar axis can be considered as an independent starting point for zonal analysis. Moreover, even in the peak year of Japan's net capital exports— $86 billion in 1986—this total was only a little ahead of the DM zone's net recorded capital exports of $60 billion. Account should also be taken of the estimated $25 billion investment in dollar financial assets by banks in Switzerland and Luxembourg on behalf of largely European clientele (made out of income accruing to portfolios in the given year) which escapes incorporation in balance of payments statistics (see Table 24–5). Finally, deviations from the "steady-state" flow of capital exports brought about by cyclical or monetary fluctuations in the United States are likely to be considerably greater for the DM zone than for Japan (albeit that on the steady state Japan could, in principle, be a larger capital

TABLE 24-5
Sources and Uses of Foreign Savings in Dollars ($ billions)

	1985	1986	1987
Sources			
International investment income[a]	37	24	25
Invisible export payments[a]	12	12	12
Japanese purchases of dollar bonds and notes[b]	35	44	18
Recorded bond purchases from Europe	7	3	4
Flight capital	12	12	12
Direct and equity investment in United States	20	41	40
Reserves of:	12	43	45
industrial countries (except the United States)			
developing countries[c]—fuel exporters	7	−19	−5
nonfuel exporters	16	32	25
Total	158	192	176
Uses			
Net financing in dollars by:[d]	2	−3	3
industrial countries (except the United States)			
developing countries[c]—fuel exporters	4	10	6
nonfuel exporters	16	12	15
others[e]	−3	0	0
U.S. direct and equity investment abroad	22	33	20
U.S. current account deficit	117	140	132
Total	158	192	176

[a] Accumulating in tax havens and offshore centers, nonreported in balance of payments statistics, and invested in dollar bonds, notes, and deposits.
[b] Excludes bond purchases covered in the forward market or by estimated short-term borrowings.
[c] Same nomenclature used as in the IMF statistics except that Taiwan (private and public sector) is included here.
[d] Bond purchases and reserve accumulation shown under sources are not netted from the total. (Bond purchases not under sources are netted).
[e] Communist countries (calculation is net of reserve changes).

exporter than the DM zone, given its particularly high savings rate).

ZONAL INVESTMENT PATTERNS

The larger size of transzonal exchange risk—for example, mark-dollar—than of intrazonal exchange risk such as franc-mark is responsible for a regionalization of investor and borrower choice with respect to currency of denomination. This is especially true where the horizon of decision making is short. The differential between transzonal and intrazonal exchange risk tends to narrow with length of the period over which it is considered, as real exchange-rate change—which is potentially less within than between zones—usually explains a shrinking proportion of total exchange-rate change. The other explanatory variable, differential inflation, is often no less volatile between countries in the same zone as in two different zones. Hence, short- and medium-term investors and borrowers within the DM zone view DM-zone currencies as lower risk than the U.S. dollar, and weight them much more heavily in their portfolios (of assets to liabilities) than do most dollar-zone residents.

The advent of floating exchange rates between the dollar and the DM-zone currencies in the early 1970s gave a fillip to the international growth of the deutsche mark and other European currencies. So long as the dollar-DM zone rates had remained pegged, investors and borrowers in Europe strongly favored the U.S. dollar, given the greater liquidity of dollar than other currency markets (in deposits, notes, and bonds). Once exchange risk was unleashed, however, this far outweighed liquidity considerations in the formation of currency choice.

Still, in their new enthusiasm for European currency placements, investors found that the "name spread" available was limited. In general, there were few issues in European currency bond markets by top international borrowers from outside the DM zone. In the interest of diversifying credit risk, investors found themselves driven into accepting transzonal exchange risk. Seeing greater exchange risk in the dollar, European borrowers would have preferred to raise almost all their funds in DM-zone currencies; but they found themselves driven to issuing substantial amounts of dollar paper because of the limited absorptive power of DM-zone markets for their bonds at their customary credit-rating. Thus, for example, following the first and second oil shocks, many European governments raised finance in dollar bond markets even though deutsche mark or Swiss franc finance would have been of lower risk.

The innovation and growth of currency and interest-rate swap markets have reduced the impediment of credit risk diversification to regionalization of investor and borrower choice in currency. For example, dollar-zone-based prime borrowers, noticing the especially low margins over government bond yields at which they could obtain finance in, say, deutsche mark or Swiss franc bond markets (the low margins reflecting a scarcity of their paper issued there to date) were able to indirectly obtain dollar finance on cheaper terms than available from a direct dollar bond issue, by entering into a currency swap with a DM-zone borrower. Effectively, the dollar-zone borrower swaps, say, a note issue in deutsche marks, with a European borrower who in turn has issued dollar debt (induced to do so by the attractive swap terms available for converting this into deutsche mark debt).

The range of names available to investors in DM-zone currencies is increased by the swap transactions described. The potential for DM-zone borrowers to assume DM-zone currency debt without paying higher than prime rates is extended in that they can obtain this via a dollar-zone proxy borrower, while themselves using the full potential of dollar-zone markets for their name. It is probable that the new scope for zonalization of currency choice has been of greater importance to borrowers than investors—in that a significant share of the latter have long-term horizons and are hence less narrowly concerned with short-term exchange risk than borrowers. Insofar as European borrowers were more constrained (prior to swaps) in their ability to raise DM-zone finance at prime rates than were U.S. borrowers to raise dollar finance at prime rates—a difference explained by the greater depth of U.S. markets than European—the innovation could have been a factor of support for the dollar by bringing a net switch of international borrowing from dollars to DM-zone currencies.

Swaps have brought a symmetric advantage to investors vis-à-vis borrowers, by contrast, in the area of variety of currency choice within a given zone. International bond markets in some of the smaller currencies which have grown up in the 1980s owe their existence to swaps. For example, few well-known prime international borrowers have a natural demand for finance in minor currencies such as Danish kroners, Canadian dollars, Australian dollars, ECUs, Italian liras, or even French francs and British pounds. Yet investors can gain from diversifying currency risk and see advantage in including a significant amount of minor currencies in their portfolios; some, moreover, are drawn by the speculative attraction of high coupons in the minor markets.

The excess demand for minor currency bonds sometimes presents international borrowers with an arbitrage opportunity. They can issue a bond in the minor currency, say liras; then they swap the proceeds into their preferred currency, say dollars, and obtain an interest cost cheaper than that on a direct issue in dollars. The counterpart to the swap would probably be Italian borrowers, located normally by an investment bank, interested in fixed-rate lira finance and ready to obtain this by taking on first a dollar liability, then swapping this for liras. The incentive to both sides to enter into the swap is cost-saving—stemming from the ability of the prime international borrower to issue lira debt on very keen terms (probably at a margin below yields on Italian government debt), itself explained by the scarcity of high-quality names in the lira sector.

The type of swap transaction just described has been instrumental to lowering tax barriers to international diversification of investment. For example, in the mid-1980s British government bond markets suffered in international competition with the German government bond market because of the exemption of the latter from withholding tax. International demand for pound bonds—particularly from Switzerland and Luxembourg—was concentrated on Euros rather than governments, causing the Euro-government bond yield differential to be exceptionally low and even sometimes in favor of governments. Before the advent of currency swaps, there were very few issues available in Euro-pounds, explained in large part by the lack of natural issuers among prime international borrowers. Later, issuers were attracted to the pound sector of the Eurobond market because of the sometimes attractive swap opportunities (which stemmed at first from the low yields on Eurobonds relative to government bonds) greater normally than those obtainable in the deutsche mark sector where Eurobonds have no tax advantage over the government sector. In general, swaps have contributed to an expansion of Eurobond markets in sectors where government bonds are subject to withholding tax, and conversely.

TRANSZONAL RISKS IN PERSPECTIVE

The preceding discussion of how the differential between trans-zonal and intrazonal exchange risk promote regional preferences in currency choice and of how markets cater to this should not be taken to imply that exchange risk is a huge deterrent to transzonal capital flows, especially those driven by investors with long-term horizons. Indeed, it is striking how one of the oldest relationships in the theory of international capital flows—that between the U.S. business cycle and the transatlantic movement of capital—continues to hold under the regime of floating exchange rates as under fixed rates.

In the era of fixed exchange rates between the dollar and other major currencies, dollar strength or weakness in response to cyclical or other factors was sublimated into swings in the U.S. official reserve balance—made up principally of gold flows and changes in dollar holdings by foreign central banks. With the advent of floating exchange rates between the dollar and other major currencies in early 1973, there were grounds for expecting cyclical influences on the dollar to wane. After all, why should international investors assume considerable exchange risk to obtain the short-term income advantages that are opened up periodically by the European business cycle being out of phase with the United States? Yet so far, with the important exception of 1977–78 when U.S. monetary risks loomed large and there were fears of runaway U.S. inflation, exchange risk does not appear to have been a substantial impediment to the capital flows responsible for the procyclicality of the dollar vis-à-vis the DM-zone currencies.

The secret of the U.S. business cycle's continuing strong influence on the dollar, despite evidence of considerable transzonal exchange risk, lies largely in a cyclicality of long-run expectations. In a business upswing, investors revise upward their assessment of the natural rate of interest in the economy—the rate consistent with an absence of inflationary pressure at full capacity output. In the gloom of a downturn, investors come to believe that the economy has lost its dynamism and that interest rates will have to stay at a permanently lower level than in the past for full employment to be reattained and maintained. A change in the natural rate implies a sustained change in the income advantage to be gained on

U.S. assets over a long period of time, making it worthwhile to assume the risk of effecting transzonal shipments of capital.

Changes in the level of interest rates expected over a long period of time—often associated with a changed assessment of a country's natural interest rate—are, of course, reflected more faithfully in the bond market than in the short-term money market. Hence, real bond yield differentials rather than short-term interest rate differentials are the prime mover behind transzonal capital flows. And there have indeed been significant swings in the natural rate differentials between Europe and the United States.

For example, in Western Europe's miracle years of late 1950s and early 1960s, interest rates and bond yields there were considerably higher than in the United States. The deutsche mark, freed of all restriction by 1958, became a center of attraction. The Bundesbank was faced with a growing dilemma of how to reconcile the external stability of the mark with domestic stability. The experience of the first half of the 1980s was the mirror image of this earlier period. Many investors were convinced that Reaganomics had pushed the U.S. economy into permanently higher gear, while Europe was smitten with "Euro-sclerosis." Consistent with this hypothesis, the natural rate of interest in the United States would have risen substantially above that in Europe, and large capital flows across the Atlantic to finance the U.S. miracle could be expected on a long-term basis. Just as the mark had been the European focal point of inflows in the late 1950s and early 1960s, it was in the early 1980s the largest source of outflows.

The possibility of substantial swings in the future in the differential between the natural rate of interest in the mark and the dollar zones is based on the assumption that within a zone natural interest rates in the member countries are held together by strong economic interdependencies and a high interest-elasticity of intrazonal capital movements. This is a powerful reason for long-term investors who look far enough into the future for cumulative interest income advantage to be a generous counterweight to exchange risk to invest in the other zone. For example, an investor in the DM zone can hedge against a fall in the natural interest rate in the EC, that is, a fall in the return to savings over a prolonged period, by holding U.S. dollar paper. In the event of the EC natural rate of interest falling and this not being fully matched by a fall in the U.S. natural rate of interest, the investor would score an exchange gain on the dollar holdings brought about by the increased long-term interest rate differential in the dollar's favor. This type of hedging function of transzonal investment is arguably one of the strongest motives behind transzonal diversification of money and bond holdings.

CHAPTER 25

THE EUROPEAN
MONETARY SYSTEM

Hans Genberg

The intent of this chapter is to review the evolution of the European Monetary System (EMS) for the purpose of identifying the forces that work toward monetary integration within Europe as well as those that tend to restrain this process. By doing so it is possible to evaluate the likelihood of future developments toward monetary unification within the European Economic Community (EEC) and eventually within Europe as a whole. To understand the creation of the EMS it is necessary to consider the development of economic integration within the EEC more generally. The first section of this chapter gives a brief historical perspective on this process. It is shown that closer monetary cooperation among the EEC countries has always been considered important in this context. But while the merit of such cooperation has always been admitted at an intellectual level, the progress toward its achievement has been slow. It is in fact possible to argue that external events, notably international financial instability associated with the U.S. dollar, were needed to provide the impetus for significant progress.

After the historical description, the main economic features and the principal institutions of the system are discussed in the next section. The exchange-rate mechanism that makes the EMS a fixed exchange-rate area is the nucleus. It is maintained by a set of support mechanisms that include interventions in the foreign-exchange markets, the use of a divergence indicator as a signal of the need for domestic policy adjustments, and communitywide credit facilities. A safety valve in the form of a procedure for parity realignments is also described.

Other institutional features of the system are also taken up in the following section, notably the definition and use of the ECU European Currency Unit (ECU) both at the official level and by the private sector.

The last part of the chapter reviews the contribution the EMS has made toward the achievement of monetary stability in Europe and discusses some issues that bear on the likely evolution of the system. It is shown that the relative fixity of exchange rates has been beneficial to the member countries on two accounts. On the one hand, it is likely that the reduction of exchange-rate fluctuations has diminished the uncertainty associated with international trade. On the other hand, the leadership of the German Bundesbank within the system together with its anti-inflationary policies has been an important factor behind the reduction in inflation within the EMS countries.

The chapter ends with an analysis of the implication of the complete liberations of capital movements scheduled to take effect within the EEC in 1992. It is argued that this liberation may lead to a substantial move toward monetary unification in Europe if the political will can be found to give up national control over the conduct of monetary policy.

A HISTORICAL PERSPECTIVE

Economic Integration within the EEC

The European Monetary System is to a large extent the logical and inevitable consequence of economic integration in the European Economic Community. The Treaty of Rome establishing the EEC was signed in March 1957 and entered into force on January 1, 1958. The treaty signified the start of a process of increased integration of the economies of the member countries.[1] The process began with the creation of a common market for the purposes of trade in goods. This entailed a gradual elimination of tariffs between the member states and the creation of a common external tariff both of which lead to a significant expansion of intracommunity trade and hence an increase in the sensitivity of each country to economic disturbances and policy actions in partner countries.

The Rome treaty also provided unrestricted movement of labor across the national borders. A number of measures designed to facilitate such movements were adopted, notably the provision that acquired social security rights could be transferred between countries. Although actual migration of labor has not to date been substantial (presumably due to language, cultural, and similar natural barriers), the potential increase in labor mobility that this aspect of the treaty entails is a further element that binds the community countries together.

The process of economic integration was given a further push in 1985 when the heads of state of the member countries endorsed a recommendation put forth by the commission of the EEC that calls for a completion of the internal market by 1992.[2] If this actually takes place, trade in services (e.g., banking, insurance, and transport) as well as goods between members will be totally unhindered, movements of capital as well as labor will be unconstrained, and a number of laws and regulations affecting economic life will be harmonized. Some of the consequences of the 1992 plan are discussed further later, but it is worthwhile mentioning that increasing the sphere of economic interdependence between the community countries reduces considerably the degree of monetary autonomy of individual central banks and increases the net benefits of monetary integration.

---

[1] The original six signatories of the treaty were Belgium, France, Germany, Italy, Luxembourg, and the Netherlands. The community was enlarged to nine members in 1973 when Denmark, Ireland, and the United Kingdom joined, to ten in 1981 with the addition of Greece, and finally to the current membership of twelve with the joining of Portugal and Spain in 1986.

[2] The so-called Single European Act. See Council of the European Communities, *Single European Act and Final Act,* Brussels: Office for Official Publications of the European communities, 1986.

Precursors to the EMS

Although the Rome treaty contained provisions for cooperation in the sphere of monetary and exchange-rate policy, few concrete proposals for institutional developments were undertaken to further such cooperation until the end of the 1960s. Several reasons can be found for this relative lack of progress. On the one hand, the Bretton-Woods system of fixed but adjustable parities seemed to work tolerably well at least until the latter half of the decade. This meant, first of all, that one aspect of monetary integration (fixed exchange rates) was already operating; and second, that shocks originating outside the EEC had a relatively uniform impact on the individual members. The external environment was thus not unfavorable enough to make greater cooperation within the community seem necessary. Another reason for the lack of progress on the monetary front can be ascribed to internal developments, especially concerning the community agricultural policy. This policy was predicated on stable exchange rates between the members and parity changes were hence difficult to accommodate. This may have created the illusion of de facto exchange rate union despite the lack of institutional support for such a union.[3]

The conditions that induced a certain degree of indifference vis-à-vis greater monetary integration within the EEC gradually disappeared toward the late 60s. External disturbances, mainly in the form of inflationary impulses from the United States, created tensions within the community as countries differed in their responses to these impulses. Internal factors and events (e.g., the May 1968 events in France) also tended to induce divergent policies among the members. In an environment of highly integrated financial markets, such divergences rapidly led to substantial capital flows and pressures in the foreign-exchange markets. Realignments of parities in 1969 put an end to the fixity of intra-EEC exchange rates and provided new arguments for

---

[3] See J. van Ypersele (with the collaboration of J. C. Koeune), *The European Monetary System: Origins, Operation and Outlook,* Brussels: Commission of the European Communities, 1985, p. 36.

those who aspired to achieve true monetary integration within Europe.[4]

Concrete plans for the realization of this goal were, however, not easily agreed on. The major hurdle was a difference of opinion concerning the appropriate sequencing of the steps leading to monetary unification. One group of countries maintained that coordination of economic policies leading to a convergence of the economic performance of the member countries was a necessary prerequisite to successful exchange-rate and monetary cooperation. Another group of countries felt that agreement and collaboration on the exchange-rate front would itself bring about the necessary coordination of economic policies.[5] The plan that was finally presented reflected a compromise between these two opposing views in that policy coordination and exchange rate-monetary cooperation would be pursued in parallel.[6] The plan also contained proposals for institutional changes and aspirations with a longer-term horizon. Specifically, it called for the eventual establishment of a European Monetary Cooperation Fund (EMCF) that could administer the existing short-term monetary support facility and that could in a later stage provide medium-term financial assistance and manage the community's foreign-exchange reserves. It also set permanently fixed exchange rates and complete freedom of capital movements as ultimate goals for the community. We shall see that these goals are still very much in the forefront of discussions even though progress toward their realization is slow and uncertain.

As it turned out, the Werner plan as such was not implemented. Significant further progress toward monetary integration occurred only with respect to its exchange-rate aspects, namely the narrowing of the margins of fluctuations between the EC currencies. A reason for this might be events in the global monetary

---

[4] The French government devalued the franc by 11.1 percent in August and the German authorities revalued the mark by 9.3 percent in October.

[5] Those who subscribed to the views of the former group became known as "economists" and those who accepted the latter argument acquired the label "monetarists." The latter label has nothing in common with the more familiar usage according to which a monetarist is typically a person who puts great emphasis on the supply of money in the context of the conduct of monetary policy.

[6] The so-called Werner plan submitted to the Commission of the EEC in October 1970.

arena that forced the hands of decisionmakers in the community. Two developments in 1971 are particularly relevant in this context: first the August 15 decision of President Richard M. Nixon to "close the gold window," that is, to suspend the convertibility of the dollar into gold; and second, the Smithsonian Agreement of December 17–18 which on the one hand involved a realignment of the parities of the main currencies and, on the other hand, increased the permitted margins of fluctuations from .75 percent around the dollar parity to 2.25 percent. This implied that the maximum fluctuation of any two European currencies vis-à-vis each other could reach 9 percent if one of them moved from the top to the bottom of the permitted range relative to the dollar while the other moved from the bottom to the top. Faced with the possibility of fluctuations of this magnitude, the central banks of the six EEC countries concluded an agreement in Basle on April 10, 1972, which limited the fluctuations of the community currencies to half of that allowed in the Smithsonian Agreement. These European currencies would thus be constrained to move within the "snake" (defined by the Basle Agreement) which itself would be required to stay within the limits of the "tunnel" specified by the Smithsonian Agreement.

As implied, the snake agreement was mainly concerned with exchange-rate stability per se. Not much was done to ensure that the policy convergence necessary for its survival would be forthcoming. It is not surprising then that the arrangement would experience a somewhat turbulent existence.[7] For instance, one of the original members, Italy, withdrew from the arrangement at an early stage. Another, France, withdrew after about two years to return one year later only to withdraw again after an additional ten months. Several countries joined (the United Kingdom and Denmark) or became associated (Norway and Sweden) and later withdrew from the arrangement (the United Kingdom, Norway, and Sweden). Again it may be argued that failure to agree on

---

[7] For detailed but succinct descriptions, see van Ypersele, *The European Monetary System*, p. 43, or N. Thygesen, "The Emerging European Monetary System: Precursors, First Steps and Policy Options," in R. Triffin, ed., *EMS: The Emerging European Monetary System,* offprint from the *Bulletin of the National Bank of Belgium,* 1979, p. 125.

common policy responses to external events (this time, the 1973–74 oil shock) prevented the achievement of exchange-rate stability within Europe. Sovereignty with respect to monetary policy had the upper hand. Once more, however, increasingly strained relationship between the European currencies and the dollar would "come to the rescue" and provide an impetus to renewed integration efforts. Fluctuations of the dollar subsequent to the decision in March 1973 to "let the snake out of the tunnel"[8] created tensions within Europe as speculation against the dollar was not evenly spread among the community currencies. The movements of the dollar took particularly dramatic proportions in 1977 and 1978 which no doubt increased significantly the motivation of European leaders to push ahead toward increased monetary integration and agree on the creation of a European Monetary System in December 1978. Thus, while the logic of the European Community provided a constant impetus toward the establishment of some form of formal monetary cooperation, the timing of the agreement when it eventually came was highly dependent on external events.

The Establishment of the EMS

Several plans for strengthening the snake arrangement were discussed within the commission during the 1974–77 period without much success. A high-level political initiative and commitment seemed needed for a breakthrough to be possible.[9] Such an initiative came during the meeting of the European Council in Copenhagen in April 1978 when French President Valéry Giscard d'Estaing and German Chancellor Helmut Schmidt jointly launched the idea of a European Monetary System. At a subsequent council meeting in Bremen the ministers of finance of the EEC countries were asked to design a system that: (1) assigned an important role to a European Currency Unit; (2) had exchange-rate rules at least as stringent as those in the snake; and (3) could be assured of substantial financial backing through a

---

[8] That is, to let the community currencies float jointly against the dollar.

[9] For an analysis of the political aspects of the establishment of the EMS, see P. Ludlow, *The Making of the European Monetary System*, London: Buttersworth's European Studies, 1982.

scheme of reserve pooling. Such a system was elaborated and submitted to the European Council of Brussels on December 5 and 6, 1978, at which time it was also adopted. Operations of the new European Monetary System started on March 15, 1979. All nine members of the EEC at the time joined the EMS.[10] On June 10, 1985, Greece signed the EMS Agreement. Like the pound, however, the drachma is not part of the exchange-rate mechanism. Neither of the two most recent members of the EEC, Spain and Portugal, have joined the EMS.

MAIN CHARACTERISTICS AND INSTITUTIONS

Like the snake arrangement, the principal intent of the EMS is the maintenance of stable exchange rates between the member countries. To achieve this aim, a number of supporting features have been built into the structure of the system, among them the so-called divergence indicator the purpose of which is to provide an early-warning signal to policymakers indicating the need to align policies with the other members of the system. Another feature introduced to support the aim of exchange-rate stability are the various credit facilities available to EEC members. Some of these are intended to provide funds for use directly in interventions on the foreign-exchange markets, while the purpose of others is to provide more general support for the financing of external payments imbalances. The original agreement establishing the EMS also contained provisions for the establishment of certain institutional features intended to reinforce the monetary integration of the members. The European Currency Unit is one of these features and the European Monetary Fund (EMF) is another. Although the ECU was indeed created from the very beginning and has taken on a certain significance within the system, the EMF has not yet been established. In the remainder of this section we describe in some detail the main characteristics of the EMS alluded to earlier to show how they make the EMS differ from the snake arrangement.

---

[10] The United Kingdom decided not to participate in the exchange-rate mechanism of the system and allowed the pound to float.

The Exchange-Rate Mechanism

The exchange-rate mechanism (ERM) in the EMS consists of three elements: (1) a requirement that participating currencies should be kept within specified ranges around their bilateral parities; (2) supporting mechanisms for the achievement of this aim; on the one hand, a set of credit facilities that can be drawn on to finance interventions in the foreign-exchange market, and on the other hand, a divergence indicator that signals the need to undertake additional policy measures to correct external imbalances; and (3) a safety valve that consists of realignment of the parities. Each of these is discussed in turn.

Bilateral Parity Ranges
Intervention rules in the ERM are defined in bilateral parity ranges between EEC currencies. These bilateral parity ranges are calculated from declared central rates expressed in terms of the ECU.[11] For instance, in February 1988 the central rate of the French franc (FF) was 6.90403 FF/ECU and that of the deutsche mark (DM) was 2.05853 DM/ECU See Table 25–1. The bilateral parity rate between the mark and the franc was, therefore, 2.960 FF/DM. As the maximum fluctuation permitted within the system is 2.25 percent, it follows that the bilateral parity range for the two currencies is 2.894–3.027 FF/DM.[12] The rules of the exchange-rate mechanism stipulate the central banks concerned must intervene with unlimited amounts at these margins to prevent further divergences from the central rates.

Supporting Mechanisms

Interventions.   As already noted, countries that participate in the exchange-rate mechanism of the EMS are required to intervene at the margins of the bilateral parity ranges to prevent further deviations from the central rates. These obligatory interventions

---

[11] For a discussion of the definition and uses of the ECU for other purposes than central rate quotations, see the following section.

[12] The maximum fluctuation for the Italian lira is 6.0 percent.

TABLE 25–1
Bilateral Central Rates and ECU Central Rates (February 1988)

	Belgian Franc	Danish Krone	Deutsche Mark	French Franc	Guilder	Irish Pound	Italian Lira
Belgian franc	—	0.185	0.048	0.163	0.055	0.018	39.94
Danish krone	5.407	—	0.262	0.880	0.295	0.098	188.94
Deutsche mark	20.621	3.814	—	3.353	1.126	0.373	720.53
French franc	6.150	1.137	0.298	—	0.310	0.111	214.89
Dutch guilder	18.309	3.386	0.888	2.977	—	0.331	639.75
Irish pound	55.284	10.224	2.681	8.990	3.020	—	1931.74
Italian lira	0.0286	0.0053	0.0014	0.0047	0.0016	0.0005	—
European Currency Unit	42.458	7.852	2.059	6.904	2.319	0.768	1483.58

are carried out in the partner's currency and may potentially be of unlimited amounts. The foreign exchange needed to carry out the interventions are obtained from the corresponding central bank under the so-called very short-term financing facility. The resulting claims or liabilities are settled in ECUs subject to certain limitations described later.

Interventions may also be carried out before a currency reaches one of the bilateral margins. These interventions are not obligatory and the needed foreign exchange could not be obtained under the very short-term financing facility until recently.[13] Because member central banks have been restricted with respect to the amount of a partner's currency they may hold, the intramarginal interventions have often been carried out in U.S. dollars.

Credit Facilities. To assist countries in maintaining their international payments obligations within the EMS, several credit facilities exist[14] and function under the management of the European Monetary Cooperation Fund[15] in some cases and with the member central banks in others. Mention has already been made of the very short-term facility established to provide central banks participating in the exchange-rate mechanism with foreign exchange required for interventions to maintain the bilateral parities. In principle, this facility is unlimited in size and has a duration of 45 days renewable for three months.

The short-term monetary support is a quasi-automatic facility intended to help the financing of temporary balance-of-payments deficits. Credits under this facility are administered by the member central banks and can be obtained for a maximum of nine months. Medium-term financial assistance may be given to countries with

---

[13] New rules allowing the use of this facility for intramarginal interventions were adopted at a meeting of the EEC finance ministers in Nyborg, Denmark, on September 13, 1987.

[14] Except for the very short-term facility these credit facilities were established within the EEC before the creation of the EMS. As a consequence, with this one exception, they are available also to EEC countries that do not belong to the exchange-rate mechanism. With the establishment of the EMS, the scope of the credit lines was enlarged.

[15] The European Monetary Cooperation Fund was created in 1972 for the purpose of furthering European monetary integration. The French acronym FECOM (Fonds Européen de Coopération Monétaire) is perhaps more frequently used than its English counterpart.

more durable balance of payments difficulties. Credits may be extended for periods between two and five years and they always carry some form of conditionality relating to the economic policy adjustments of the borrowing country. Maybe this is why very little use has been made of this form of assistance.

The Divergence Indicator and Macroeconomic Policy Adjustments.

Like any fixed exchange-rate system, policies other than interventions in the foreign-exchange markets may be used to maintain the external value of a currency. In particular, it is important that domestic monetary policy be consistent with the monetary policies pursued in the other countries. To determine whether such consistency exists within the region, it is useful to have a measure that indicates when a particular country's overall policy stance diverges from that of its partners. The divergence indicator developed within the EMS is meant to serve this purpose. Loosely speaking, it is calculated as a weighted average of the movement of a given currency vis-à-vis all other currencies in the system. More formally,[16] if

ECU_i = the current ECU rate of currency i
ECU_i^{par} = the central ECU rate of currency i
ECU_i^{max} = the maximum (or minimum) ECU rate consistent with maintaining bilateral parities[17]

then the divergence indicator for currency i (DI_i) is

$$DI_i = \frac{ECU_i - ECU_i^{par}}{ECU_i^{max} - ECU_i^{par}}$$

It is clear that the maximum value of the divergence indicator is 1.0 in which case the country in question would be under the obligation to intervene against all other currencies to avoid violating the bilateral parities. Before that occurs, however, when the indicator reaches 75 percent there is a presumption that the country takes

---

[16] See van Ypersele, *The European Monetary System*, pp. 53–57, for a clear description of the details of the required computations together with a numerical example.

[17] This maximum or minimum would occur if the currency was at the upper or lower bilateral intervention margin vis-à-vis all other currencies within the system.

action to avoid further movements.[18] The measures taken would, in addition to intervention against several of the partner currencies, involve changes in domestic monetary policy to support the interventions in the foreign-exchange market. Such modification of national monetary policy would, as a rule, prevent incompatibilities in monetary conditions between the member countries.

Apart from being an early-warning signal, the divergence indicator is also meant to provide a certain amount of symmetry of adjustment within the EMS. In a fixed exchange-rate area, typically the country with a weak currency feels the greatest pressure to align its domestic policies to those of the strong-currency country, be it only because of the limitation on foreign-exchange holdings. The divergence indicator and the presumption to modify domestic policy when it reaches the 75 percent threshold is meant to place the "burden" of adjustment on the "errant" country whether or not its currency is weak relative to the rest of the group. As we shall see, however, the actual working of the EMS seems to have lead to convergence of policies toward those of the hardest-currency country, Germany. To a large extent the divergence indicator has not played the role assigned to it.

Safety Valve: Realignments of Central Rates
A fixed exchange rate implies a loss of autonomy with respect to monetary policy that is inversely proportional to the size of the country. In addition, to the extent that asymmetries exist in the functioning of the system, even countries that are relatively large may lose effective control over their monetary policy. For instance, if Germany prevents its balance of payments position from having an influence on its domestic money supply or interest-rate level, it may effectively determine the monetary policy of all countries of the EEC that belong to the exchange-rate mechanism.[19] Large countries like France would have to subordinate

---

[18] Note that the 75 percent limit may be reached without any bilateral parity being reached.

[19] This point of view is taken in F. Giavazzi and A. Giovannini "Models of the EMS: Is Europe a Greater Deutschmark Area?" in R. Bryant and R. Portes, eds., *Global Macroeconomics: Policy Conflict and Cooperation*, Basingstroke: Macmillan, 1987, pp. 237–265.

their policies to the requirement of the fixed exchange rate. It is not difficult to imagine that the implied loss of sovereignty might be difficult to accept. As a consequence, realignments of the parities have occurred more or less frequently.

Parity realignments may also be thought of as justifiable responses to needed changes in relative prices due to real disturbances such as changes in the relative price of oil, technological innovations, or dissimilar fiscal policies. Although adjustment of nominal parities alone cannot provide a long-term solution to conflicts that may arise from such disturbances, they may make the adjustment process less onerous.

The safety valve of parity adjustments has been used quite regularly since the launching of the EMS. In all, 11 realignments have taken place, each one typically involving several currencies as Table 25–2 indicates.[20]

The fact that realignments have taken place can be interpreted both as a weakness and a strength of the EMS. It represents a weakness in the sense that it reflects a failure to achieve the required convergence of economic performance. Given the divergences however, the smoothness with which the realignments have taken place signifies a considerable degree of flexibility and adaptability of the system that was lacking in the snake arrangement. It is to be expected that further realignments will be undertaken at regular intervals in the future unless a much more significant degree of policy convergence is achieved.

The European Currency Unit

The European Currency Unit was created at the same time as the EMS itself. We have already seen how it is used for the purpose of defining central rates for each of the currencies participating in the exchange-rate mechanism and for the calculation of the divergence

---

[20] H. Ungerer, O. Evans, T. Mayer, and P. Young, "The European Monetary System: Recent Developments," Occasional Paper no. 48, International Monetary Fund, 1986, pp. 32–33, contains an informative table showing the underlying macroeconomic causes of the realignments as well as the role of the divergence indicator and the bilateral parity ranges as signals for the adjustments.

TABLE 25–2
Realignments of Central Rates (devaluation (−) and revaluation (+)
against other currencies)

Date	Currencies Involved	Size (Percent)
September 24, 1979	Danish krone	−2.9%
	Deutsche mark	+2.0
November 30, 1979	Danish krone	−4.8
March 22, 1981	Italian lira	−6.0
October 5, 1981	Deutsche mark	+5.5
	French franc	−3.0
	Dutch guilder	+5.5
	Italian lira	−3.0
February 22, 1982	Belgian franc	−8.5
	Danish krone	−3.0
June 14, 1982	Deutsche mark	+4.25
	French franc	−5.75
	Dutch guilder	+4.25
	Italian lira	−2.75
March 21, 1983	Belgian franc	+1.5
	Danish krone	+2.5
	Deutsche mark	+5.5
	French franc	−2.5
	Dutch guilder	+3.5
	Irish pound	−3.5
	Italian lira	−2.5
July 22, 1985	Italian lira	−8.0
April 7, 1986	Belgian franc	+1.0
	Danish krone	+1.0
	Deutsche mark	+3.0
	French franc	−3.0
	Dutch guilder	+3.0
August 4, 1986	Irish pound	−8.0
January 12, 1987	Belgian franc	+2.0
	Deutsche mark	+3.0
	Dutch guilder	+3.0

Source: van Ypersele, p. 81 and Ungerer, et al. (1986), pp. 32–33, and 35.

TABLE 25–3
Composition and Value of the European Currency Unit

Currency	Amount	$ Spot Rate[b]	$ Value[a]
Belgian and Luxembourg franc	3.85	0.0283	0.109
Danish krone	0.219	0.154	0.034
Deutsche mark	0.719	0.592	0.426
Greek drochma	1.150	0.00741	0.009
French franc	1.31	0.175	0.229
Dutch guilder	0.256	0.527	0.135
Irish pound	0.00871	1.577	0.014
Italian lira	140.0	0.000804	0.113
British pound	0.0878	1.762	0.155
European Currency Unit	1.0	1.224	1.224

[a] As of February 11, 1988.
[b] Measured as dollars per currency unit.

Source: *Financial Times.*

indicator. It was also expected that the ECU would take on three other functions within the system; as a means of settlement between member central banks, as a reserve asset, and as a unit of account. Each of these is discussed briefly below. In addition to being used by official EEC institutions, the ECU has become the cornerstone for a number of financial instruments created by the private sector. Some of the reasons for this development as well as some examples are also given.

The Definition of the ECU

The ECU is a synthetic monetary unit that is defined as a basket of all the member currencies. The number of units of each national currency included in this basket is reported in column 2 of Table 25–3.[21] To calculate the value of the ECU in any given currency, one simply uses the bilateral exchange rate of that currency and each individual component (column 3) to calculate the contribution of that component to the value of the ECU (column 4). The total

---

[21] Notice that the Greek drachma (DR) and the British pound sterling (UK£) are included in the definition of the ECU despite the fact that neither of these two currencies participate in the exchange-rate mechanism of the EMS.

value of the ECU is then, of course, the sum of the values of the individual components.

Official Supply and Uses

The ECU does not exist as a physical entity. The supply of ECUs for official purposes is created through automatically renewed three-month swaps between the member central banks and the European Monetary Cooperation Fund. The central banks deposit 20 percent of their gold and 20 percent of their U.S. dollar reserves and are credited with the corresponding amount of ECUs. As of the second quarter of 1986, 46.4 billion ECUs had been created in this way.[22]

ECUs are used as settlements of debts arising from interventions at the bilateral exchange-rate margins. As already noted, such interventions are carried out in community currencies supplied by the corresponding central banks in exchange for ECUs. The creditor bank may, however, refuse to accept settlement in ECUs on amounts that exceed 50 percent of the total value of the debt. Furthermore, the relative increase in intramarginal interventions, that for reasons already explained tend to be carried out in dollars, has reduced the use of the ECU for settlement purposes even further.[23]

The fact that the ECU cannot be used directly for intervention purposes, and the limits on a central bank's obligation to accept them for debt settlements has diminished the attractiveness of the ECU as a reserve asset. Recent changes have been introduced concerning the interest rate received on net ECU holdings, making them depend on money-market rates in the countries whose currencies make up the ECU basket rather than on official discount rates. These changes, and the attempts to increase the acceptability of the ECU for settlement purposes, are intended to encourage

---

[22] Ungerer, et al., "The European Monetary System . . .", p. 30. The amount of ECUs created fluctuates from day to day as a result of variations in the price of gold and of the dollar in terms of the ECU.

[23] The amendments of the EMS Agreement adopted on July 1, 1985, contain provisions that make it possible to draw on ECU holdings even for the purpose of financing intramarginal interventions.

the substitution of ECUs for other assets as international reserves. At present, however, this has reached rather limited proportions.

The main official use of the ECU is then as a unit of account. Within the EMS this relates not only to the definition of central rates and the divergence indicator in the exchange-rate mechanism but also to the various credit facilities of the European Monetary Cooperation Fund as described later. Furthermore, all financial activities of the EEC such as those related to the budget, the Common Agricultural Policy, the European Development Fund, and the European Investment Bank are denominated in the ECU.

Private Supply and Uses

Uses of the ECU by the private sector has grown rapidly since the creation of the EMS. Although strictly speaking completely autonomous, the development of the private ECU market owes much in fact to its official counterpart and to official encouragement and incentives. In turn, the growth of private utilization of the ECU may stimulate further developments at the official level.

It is now possible to find financial instruments of almost any type denominated in ECUs. Banks create sight and time deposit accounts for individuals and corporations. Personal loans as well as major syndicated loans are available. Bond issues and floating-rate notes can also be found on the market. Even ECU-based credit cards and traveler's checks exist. A number of reasons can be found for the rapid development of these instruments. Being defined as a weighted average of a number of currencies, the ECU provides a certain amount of protection against the risk of exchange-rate fluctuations. It would, of course, be possible to construct baskets that are tailor-made to the needs of each individual investor or borrower, but the widespread adoption of a common basket is likely to reduce the transactions costs of this type of currency diversification. The existence of an official unit has, therefore, undoubtedly fostered the private adoption of a standard basket.

Favorable treatment given to ECU-denominated financial instruments in countries that engage in controls on international capital movements is also likely to have a positive influence on the growth of the private ECU market. Also, the supply of ECU-denominated deposits is less subject to national monetary control which may provide banks with an incentive to prefer such deposits.

In addition to its use in financial transactions, the ECU has been employed in commercial contexts mainly as a unit of account and as an invoice "currency." With the development of credit card facilities and checking accounts, it does not seem impossible that the ECU might develop into an medium of exchange for certain transactions. This, in turn, would have significant implications for the process of monetary integration in the EEC as it would constitute a step toward the use of one common currency within the community. The use of privately created ECUs for transactions would, of course, also create difficulties with respect to monetary control and monetary sovereignty, an issue to be discussed in the last section of this chapter.

The European Monetary Fund

From the outset it was meant that the EMS would in due course reach an "institutional phase" that would pave the way for an eventual monetary union within the EEC. This phase would in part entail the establishment of a European Monetary Fund (EMF) to assume the functions of the EMCF in a first stage. Eventually the EMF would evolve into a European central bank entrusted with the customary functions of such an institution. The institutional phase would also entail "the full utilization of the ECU as a reserve asset and as a means of settlement. It [would] be based on adequate legislation at the Community as well as the national level."[24] The desire was to commence the institutional phase not later than two years after the entering into force of the EMS, that is, not later than March 1982.

For reasons that are not difficult to understand, the institutional phase of the EMS has yet not begun. Giving up national monetary sovereignty to a European central bank is a decision that goes far beyond those that have been implemented as part of the

---

[24] Resolution of the European Council on December 5, 1978, on the establishment of the European Monetary System (EMS) and related matters.

EMS, such as the exchange-rate mechanism. It requires amendments to national legislations and changes in the EEC treaty, both of which are politically sensitive subjects that governments are reluctant to tackle. Even less far-reaching institutional changes, such as the permanent pooling of reserves within the existing EMCF,[25] authorizing the EMCF to issue ECUs against national currencies or against itself, and permitting it to intervene directly on the foreign-exchange markets, would require legislative changes difficult for national parliaments to accept.

In addition to the political obstacles to further development of the EMS, there remains the debate between those who view convergence of economic performance as a prerequisite to institutional reform and those who argue that institutional reform would promote economic convergence. This debate precedes the creation of the EMS, described earlier, and is still at the center of controversy.

IMPLICATIONS FOR ECONOMIC PERFORMANCE AND FOR THE CONDUCT OF ECONOMIC POLICY

The preceding sections have described the background, creation, and institutions of the EMS. In this final part of the chapter, the functioning of the system since its inception and its implications for the conduct of economic policy are discussed. It can be argued that the EMS has indeed been as conducive to monetary stability within the EEC as its promoters hoped, and that this stability is mainly the result of increased convergence of monetary policies within the system. Furthermore, as a result of the dominant role assumed by the German Bundesbank, the EMS has functioned as an effective anti-inflationary arrangement for the EEC as a whole.

The liberation of capital flows implied by the adoption of the "Single European Act" is going to provide a challenge for the system. Either monetary unification will have to be intensified

---

[25] To replace the current swap arrangements.

(with the attendant loss of autonomy of individual countries' central banks) or there will be a breakdown of the EMS taking the form of more frequent parity adjustments.

The EMS, a Zone of Monetary Stability?

One of the goals of the founders of the EMS was to create a "zone of monetary stability" in Europe. Has this been achieved? To answer this question it is necessary to define monetary stability. At a fundamental level it should be related to the evolution of real economic activity. Monetary stability then simply means that monetary developments do not hinder the international or national allocation of resources. With this general concept in mind, it is possible to evaluate more specific definitions of monetary stability.

One of the most frequently used measures of the success of the EMS relates to the reduction in exchange-rate fluctuations between members of the exchange-rate mechanism it has been associated with.[26] A number of empirical studies have shown that this reduction can be observed almost independently of the exact measure that is being used and the countries being examined.[27] Bilateral nominal and real exchange rates between pairs of ERM countries have been less variable than between non-ERM countries, or between ERM and non-ERM countries. Effective exchange rates, that is, rates that are trade-weighted averages of bilateral rates, have shown less variability for ERM countries than for non-ERM countries whether measured in real or nominal terms. Does this evidence imply that efficient resource allocation

---

[26] It is not trivially true that nominal exchange rates have become less variable within the EMS as a result of the operation of the exchange-rate mechanism. First of all, there are possibilities for fluctuations within the margins. Second, since the mechanism allows for parity adjustments, and since such adjustments have taken place with some regularity, it is possible for the overall outcome not to be a net reduction in variability.

[27] See, for instance, P. De Grauwe and G. Verfaille, "Exchange Rate Variability, Misalignment and the European Monetary System," International Economics Research Paper no. 54, Centrum Voor Economische Studien, Katholieke Universiteit Leuven, 1987; K. Rogoff, "Can Exchange Rate Predictability be Achieved without Monetary Convergence? Evidence from the EMS." European Economic Review, vol. 28, 1985, no. 1–2, pp. 93–115; and Ungerer et al., "The European Monetary System . . .", for examples of such studies.

has been encouraged within the EMS? Not necessarily, because the effect of a reduction in exchange-rate fluctuations on real economic activity is likely to depend on the way in which the reduction is brought about. Consider two polar cases. In the first, reduced exchange-rate variability is brought about by more stable and compatible monetary and fiscal policy in the countries in question. In this case, the reduced exchange-rate uncertainty should be associated with better real economic performance measured, perhaps, by an increase in the volume of international trade between the two countries. Suppose instead that reduced exchange-rate variability is obtained through direct controls on capital flows that allow the authorities temporarily to maintain a certain degree of exchange-rate stability in spite of the inconsistent policies. Thus, one might well expect resource allocation to deteriorate and international trade in goods and services to diminish.[28]

Have exchange-rate fluctuations in Europe been reduced by policy convergence or by the imposition of controls? The available evidence points more forcefully in the former direction even though both factors have undoubtedly been in operation. On the one hand, Ungerer calculates measures of convergence for variables such as money supplies, short-term interest rates, inflation rates, unit labor cost, and fiscal deficits for all ERM countries as well as a number of other industrial countries. On the basis of these measures, the authors conclude that "there has been progress within the EMS toward economic convergence in domestic monetary policies and inflation rates, particularly in the more recent years."[29] On the other hand, a number of authors (e.g., Giavazzi and Giovannini) have pointed out that several EMS members, notably France and Italy, resort to controls on capital movements for the purpose of preserving some degree of domestic monetary

---

[28] The fact that the empirical research has not been able to find a significant relationship between the volume of international trade and exchange-rate variability may be a reflection of this theoretical ambiguity. Most of this research does not in fact distinguish between different sources of exchange-rate variability even though one should expect this distinction to be crucial.

[29] Ungerer et al., "The European Monetary System," p. 27. It is noteworthy that they also state that convergence has not been achieved with respect to fiscal policies.

autonomy.[30] These capital controls appear to have permitted postponement of parity realignments and, therefore, contributed to exchange-rate stability.

To determine which of the two sources of exchange-rate stabilization has been dominant, one might look at the evolution of intra-EMS trade. De Grauwe and Verfaille find that reduced exchange-rate variability within the EMS has had a positive influence on this trade; this suggests that policy convergence has been the dominant source of exchange-rate stability and that the EMS, therefore, has developed into a zone of relative monetary stability.[31]

The EMS as a DM Zone

The maintenance of fixed exchange rates between a group of countries requires at a minimum harmonization of their monetary policies. This requirement does not in and of itself say anything about around which country's monetary policy the harmonization takes place. Institutional arrangements, inherent asymmetries, and differences in the size of countries have to be considered. In spite of attempts to prevent EMS institutions from becoming a source of dominance of one country, size considerations and asymmetries inherent in almost any fixed exchange-rate arrangement has made Germany the de facto monetary policymaker among the countries belonging to the exchange rate mechanism. Given domestic institutional arrangements, this state of affairs may well suit the other members as it allows them to import a degree of discipline in monetary management that would be difficult to achieve without an external constraint.

It is clear that the sheer size of the German economy automatically gives the Bundesbank a certain power to dictate monetary conditions within the EMS. But the stable and anti-inflationary policies followed by the Bundesbank gives it additional strength for at least two reasons. First, the conservative monetary policy tends

---

[30] F. Giavazzi, and A. Giovannini, "The EMS and the Dollar," *Economic Policy: A European Forum,* no. 2, April 1986, pp. 456–74.

[31] De Grauwe and Verfaille, "Exchange Rate Variability."

to strengthen the DM within the margins of fluctuation allowed by the exchange-rate mechanism. The French franc and the Italian lira, to mention only the currencies of the next two largest countries in the ERM, will by definition tend to weaken. The relative currency movements are reflections of an improving balance of payments position in Germany and a deteriorating one in the other countries. In a symmetric system, German policy should have to expand and French and Italian policies contract to re-establish external balance in each country. But it is a well-known fact that surplus countries can avoid, or at least postpone, such adjustments more easily than deficit countries. The deficit countries must allow interventions in the foreign-exchange market to have an impact on domestic monetary conditions both to prevent an eventual depletion of reserves and, more important, to prevent a continuous external deficit from encouraging expectations of currency realignments and precipitation of exchange crises. The surplus country, on the other hand, can with less fear of undesirable side effects prevent interventions in the foreign-exchange market from influencing domestic monetary conditions by so-called sterilization operations. The outcome then is that the monetary policy of the strong-currency country is largely unconstrained by the fixed exchange-rate arrangement, and that potential deficit countries harmonize their policies around those of the surplus country. In the EMS context, Germany thus emerges as a leader.

A second set of considerations may also lead to the emergence of German leadership. Central banks are typically supposed to safeguard the real value of the domestic currency, that is, to avoid inflation. But domestic institutional constraints may prevent the realization of this goal; for instance, when lack of sufficient independence forces the monetary authorities to finance excessively expansionary fiscal policies. An external constraint in the form of an exchange-rate commitment within an even broader cooperative arrangement like the EEC may allow the monetary authorities to withstand internal pressures for expansionary policies. Monetary discipline can thus be imported. An independent Bundesbank with a record and reputation for policies conducive to price stability may thus emerge as a leader because other countries find this arrangement to be in their own interest.

Although there can be no doubt that Germany has, in fact, become a leader within the ERM with respect to monetary management, it is less clear which of the two explanations for this leadership is most relevant, the asymmetry argument or the self-interest of the partners' central banks. As long as attitudes toward price stability and monetary discipline remain unchanged in the potential deficit countries, the exact reason for German leadership does not matter. But suppose more political pressure to expand is brought on the French and Italian monetary authorities. Asymmetry within the EMS would in this case lead to one of two possible outcomes: either the fixed exchange rates are maintained with France and Italy being forced to adjust, or the system breaks apart due to inconsistencies among monetary policies. If the reason for German leadership is instead the acquiescence of the other central banks, then a halt to this acquiescence may lead to more inflationary policies within the EMS. Moves to create a European Central Bank in which each member country would have a more equal decision-making power may be viewed as a means to enforce greater symmetry and, at the same time, give more weight to pressures for more expansionary monetary policies.[32] It is not surprising that the initial reaction of the Bundesbank to this proposal is less than enthusiastic.

Some Implications of the 1992 Plan

In a meeting in December 1985, the heads of state of EEC countries endorsed a recommendation of the commission that calls for a completion of the internal market by 1992.[33] That recommendation covers a wide range of topics that are not directly related to the operation of the EMS and that are, therefore, not discussed here. A major aspect of the 1992 plan does, however, have a direct bearing on the future of the monetary system in the EEC, and this is the complete removal of controls on capital movements between countries. It has already been remarked that such controls have

---

[32] See, for instance, D. Gros and N. Thygesen, "The EMS: Achievements, Current Issues, and Directions for the Future," Brussels: Centre for European Policy Studies, 1988.

[33] The so-called Single European Act.

been used, notably by France and Italy, to postpone realignments in the presence of divergent monetary policies. It is only possible to combine two of the following three features of an international monetary arrangement: fixed exchange rates, complete freedom of capital movements, and monetary autonomy in individual countries. This suggests three possible consequences of the 1992 Plan.

The first is that capital movements will not be liberalized and that the system will continue to function more or less as it currently does. The letter of the Single European Act would be maintained despite the break from its spirit by altering the nature of capital controls so that they are consistent with the new rules. The second possibility is that fixed rates and freedom of capital movements will be adopted and that monetary autonomy is given up even to an greater extent than it already is. This is the hope of those who view the 1992 plan as an important step toward further monetary integration within Europe and, indeed, toward a European Monetary Union. The final possibility is that capital mobility is adopted but that monetary autonomy is not relinquished. This would imply either more frequent recourse to realignments within the ERM or the adoption of floating rates between the member countries.

The last of the three possible scenarios would, of course, mean the end of the EMS and hence represent a major failure of economic integration within the EEC. In view of the political commitment in the member countries toward the EEC, and in view of the achievements already made, the breakdown scenario seems unlikely.

It is clear that the second solution will be politically difficult to implement. Monetary autonomy is not easily relinquished. It implies giving up one instrument available to policy makers for economic stabilization. Moreover, it is likely that a certain degree of fiscal policy harmonization will be necessary to supplement a closer integration of capital markets. Widely different fiscal deficits in member countries will either imply a very uneven, and hence perhaps unacceptable evolution of external indebtedness if the deficits are financed by foreign borrowing, or a strain on monetary cooperation if the deficits are financed by money creation. As already noted, convergence of fiscal policies has not been achieved within the EMS to date. Substantial progress may be required on this front if the second 1992 scenario is to succeed. Given the likely difficulties in achieving such progress, the first possibility, maintenance of the status quo with more hidden controls on capital movements, remains a real possibility. It is not unrealistic to suppose that such hidden controls might do more damage to the allocation of resources than more clearly defined restrictions presently in force. International business may become somewhat more difficult to conduct as administrative barriers become more prevalent. For this reason, and because the breakdown solution would certainly bring more monetary instability to Europe, the scenario involving greater monetary unification is undoubtedly the most conducive to a stable international business environment. It remains to be seen if enough political resolve exists for this solution to be carried through.

CHAPTER 26

THE LINKAGES BETWEEN NATIONAL STOCK MARKETS

Philippe Jorion

This chapter studies the links between national equity markets and their implications for portfolio choice and corporate financial management. It focuses first on the diversification benefits from a presence across national stock markets; and second on issues related to the pricing of assets across national borders because such pricing determines the cost of capital.

The benefits from going international basically stem from low correlations between stock prices from different markets. The gains from diversification are similar to those that accrue within domestic markets and exist even when there is no mispricing of assets. There is compelling evidence, however, that diversification benefits are much stronger across international stock markets than within domestic markets. This is so because economic disturbances are often country-specific, and do not necessarily affect foreign stock markets. In statistical terms, international stock markets display relatively low correlations, which indicates that international diversification has the potential to substantially reduce overall portfolio risk. The first section in this chapter presents the case for international diversification by illustrating how portfolio risk is affected by the inclusion of foreign investments.

These results have to be analyzed carefully in light of a changing global financial environment that can lead to shifts in the linkages between stock markets. It is especially important to examine the stability of these comovements, and better still, to analyze the underlying macroeconomic factors creating the links between national stock markets. A better understanding of the causes of associations would provide a means to forecast future correlations, given projected changes in the global economic environment. These issues are examined in the second section.

The question of pricing is not only more difficult to analyze rigorously but also much more important. Over the last two decades, the essential contribution of academic research in finance has been to develop theoretical models of asset pricing and to test their empirical validity. These models provide a relationship between return and risk; this can be used to determine either required rates of returns from the viewpoint of investors, or the cost of capital for particular projects from the viewpoint of corporate financial management. When applied to international capital markets, these models have to specifically account for two added distinguishing features of the international environment: first, exchange rate risk; and second, barriers to the movement of capital. These factors can lead to segmentations of capital markets. Segmentation implies that factors priced in one market may not be priced in another because investors perceive risk differently; it may be due to differing consumption patterns, or restrictions on foreign investments. The last section presents the empirical evidence on segmentations in world capital markets and illustrates the implications for international financial management.

THE BENEFITS FROM INTERNATIONAL DIVERSIFICATION

If the movements in national stock markets are imperfectly correlated, then investors should be able to reduce their risk without sacrificing expected returns by international diversification. Early papers by Grubel and Levy and Sarnat have used ex post analysis of efficient sets to demonstrate how the risk-return trade-off could have been improved through foreign investments.[1] These results,

---

[1] H. G. Grubel, "Internationally Diversified Portfolios: Welfare Gains and Capital Flows," *American Economic Review* 58, December 1968, pp. 1200–1314; and H. Levy and M. Sarnat, "International Diversification of Investment Portfolios," *American Economic Review* 60, September 1970, pp. 668–75.

however, are only suggestive of the gains from international diversification, as ex post estimates are substituted for unobservable expectations, which in the context of portfolio optimization inevitably overstates the benefits from diversification.[2] Much more convincing is the approach of Solnik, who shows that equally weighted portfolios with increasing numbers of common stocks achieve a much faster and greater reduction in risk when foreign stocks are included.[3] Other writers, such as Agmon, Solnik, and Lessard display the potential for risk reduction by regressing individual stock returns on a national factor and a world factor.[4] It is usually found that national factors are much more important than world factors; again this strongly suggests that international diversification could be beneficial.

To illustrate the benefits from international diversification, take the case of a U.S. investor who, instead of staying fully invested in the U.S. stock market, ventured to allocate half of the investment to the Japanese stock market over the period 1979–86. As it turns out, this choice would have been superior not only to restricting the investment to the U.S. stock market but also to allocating everything to the Japanese stock market.

Table 26–1 describes historical stock market data. Over the period January 1978 to December 1986, the U.S. stock market, as defined by Morgan Stanley Capital International (MSCI), would have yielded an annualized growth of 17 percent with an annual volatility of 14.6 percent. Over the same period, the Japanese stock market grew by 21 percent in yen terms. Because foreign stock prices have to be translated in dollars, the movement in the $/yen

---

[2] The issue is whether such results could have been obtained on the basis of ex ante information. P. Jorion, "International Portfolio Diversification with Estimation Risk," *Journal of Business* 58 (July 1985), pp. 259–78, provides some evidence that ex post sample averages are very poor predictors of future returns, and that portfolios based on ex ante information systematically perform more poorly than anticipated in terms of expected returns.

[3] B. Solnik, "Why Not Diversify Internationally Rather than Domestically?" *Financial Analysts Journal* 30, July 1974, pp. 48–54.

[4] T. Agmon, "The Relations among Equity Markets: A Study of Share Price Co-movements in the United States, United Kingdom, Germany, and Japan," *Journal of Finance* 27, September 1972, pp. 838–55; B. Solnik, "The International Pricing of Risk: An Empirical Investigation of the World Capital Market Structure," *Journal of Finance* 29, May 1974, pp. 48–54; and D. Lessard, 1974. "World, National, and Industry Factors in Equity Returns," *Journal of Finance* 29, May 1974, pp. 379–91.

TABLE 26–1
The Benefits from International Diversification Based on Ex Post Data (January 1978–December 1986)

	U.S. Market ($)	Japanese Market (Yen)	Exchange Rate (Yen/$)	Japanese Market ($)	Half-invested, U.S. + Japanese Markets ($)
Return:					
Annual Growth	17.0	21.0	-2.4	24.0	20.5
Risk					
Annual Volatility	14.6	14.4	12.1	21.2	14.0

exchange rate increased this return from 21 to 24 percent per annum and the annual volatility from 14.4 to 21.2 percent. Thus higher returns have been accompanied by higher risk levels for this foreign investment. On the other hand, the historical correlation coefficient between these two stock markets is very low, on the order of 0.2. As a result, the risk of a portfolio divided equally between these two markets is only 14 percent, which is even lower than the risk of the U.S. market alone.[5] Because of this diversification effect, it may be advantageous to invest in foreign stock markets even with a projected rate of return lower than that of the U.S. market.

In practice, the risk-return trade-off has to be formulated in ex ante expectations, which may be different across investors. If we are willing to accept these ex post measures as substitutes for expectations, further conclusions can be reached. Clearly, the strategy of naive diversification would have been superior to holding the U.S. market, since it produces a higher return of 20.5 percent versus 17 percent, at a lower risk level. In addition, it is likely that a U.S. investor would prefer to be invested in each market rather than just in Japan, because the average investor would not accept a marked increase in volatility from 14 to 21.2 percent for a 3.5 percent increase in expected return.[6]

The low correlation coefficient is the driving factor behind this result. Low correlations imply that investors should optimally diversify across markets, up to the point where the addition of other assets produces a marginal reduction in risk, because the remaining stocks have a high correlation with the original portfolio.

---

[5] This is derived from computing the variance of the equally invested portfolio as $\sigma^2 = (1/2)^2\sigma^2_{US} + (1/2)^2\sigma^2_{Jap} + 2(1/2)^2\rho\sigma^2_{US}\sigma^2_{Jap}$ where σ_{US}, σ_{Jap} are the volatilities of the U.S. and Japanese stock markets and ρ is the correlation coefficient.

[6] Assume a typical risk aversion of 2, which means that the investor is indifferent between a risk-free asset and a risky asset with a volatility of 15 percent and a risk premium of $2(.15)^2 = 4.5$ percent. In this case, increasing the volatility from 14.0 to 21.2 percent would require an additional risk premium of $2[(.212)^2 - (.140)^2] = 5$ percent, which is more than the 3.5 percent pickup in return from moving the portfolio into Japanese shares only.

THE COMOVEMENTS BETWEEN
EQUITY MARKETS

To ascertain the benefits from diversification across equity markets, we now focus on the correlations between national stock indexes. This can be considered the first step in a top-down global asset allocation, the next step being the evaluation of correlations between individual stocks. This approach can also be justified by the results of Eun and Resnick, who have shown that the correlations within each market could be reasonably assumed to be constant.[7] Because a strong country factor seems to influence the return generating process, we examine the structure of the comovements between equity markets.

Tables 26–2, 26–3, and 26–4 present correlation coefficients for 18 value-weighted national equity indexes constructed by MSCI. Correlations are reported for a fixed exchange-rate period, 1959–70, and two flexible exchange-rate periods, 1971–78 and 1979–86. The first thing to notice from these tables is that the coefficients of correlation are relatively low. The median correlation coefficients are 0.21, 0.37, and 0.33 for the periods 1959–70, 1971–78, and 1979–86 respectively. These comovements are much weaker than those between U.S. industry indexes. For instance, the median correlation coefficient among the 10 Frank Russell industry indexes was 0.64 from 1980 to 1985. Therefore, a necessary condition is in place for international diversification to be useful.

Further, these benefits do not seem to disappear as time passes. A comparison of the relative magnitudes of correlations across subperiods reveals that correlations increased slightly from the fixed exchange-rate period to the first floating rate period, but that correlations actually decreased, on average, between the period 1971–78 and 1979–86. A number of barriers to the movement of capital were lifted in the latter period, notably in Britain and Japan, but this did not lead to closer movements among stock markets.

---

[7] C. Eun and B. Resnick, "Estimating the Correlation Structure of International Share Prices," *Journal of Finance* 39, December 1984, pp. 1311–24.

TABLE 26–2
Correlation Coefficients between National Stock Markets (January 1959–December 1970)

	AUSL	AUS	BEL	CAN	DK	FRA	GER	ITA	JAP	NET	NOR	SPA	SWD	SWI	U.K.	U.S.
Australia	1.00															
Austria	.00	1.00														
Belgium	.17	.14	1.00													
Canada	.24	.21	.46	1.00												
Denmark	.10	.10	.07	.15	1.00											
France	.13	.20	.48	.30	.13	1.00										
Germany	.18	.45	.41	.31	.06	.38	1.00									
Italy	.11	.30	.30	.20	.18	.31	.39	1.00								
Japan	.12	.09	-.01	.15	.15	.12	.15	.09	1.00							
Netherlands	.18	.13	.56	.53	.07	.41	.50	.26	.13	1.00						
Norway	.19	.21	.43	.35	.25	.27	.29	.20	.14	.27	1.00					
Spain	.13	-.06	.03	.12	.17	.22	.01	.01	.03	-.05	.18	1.00				
Sweden	.37	.08	.36	.40	.21	.24	.30	.18	.05	.30	.34	.17	1.00			
Switzerland	.21	.34	.50	.42	.15	.51	.62	.41	.14	.65	.37	.00	.30	1.00		
United Kingdom	.40	.01	.30	.28	.07	.23	.26	.21	.05	.37	.22	.06	.30	.24	1.00	
United States	.19	.17	.49	.78	.03	.26	.37	.21	.10	.62	.22	.01	.35	.47	.27	1.0
World	.29	.22	.57	.79	.08	.38	.50	.34	.16	.68	.30	.04	.42	.58	.45	.9
	AUSL	AUS	BEL	CAN	DK	FRA	GER	ITA	JAP	NET	NOR	SPA	SWD	SWI	U-K	US

TABLE 26–3

Correlation Coefficients between National Stock Markets (January 1971–December 1978)

	AUSL	AUS	BEL	CAN	DK	FRA	GER	H-K	ITA	JAP	NET	NOR	SNG	SPA	SWD	SWI	U.K.	U.S.
Australia	1.00																	
Austria	.19	1.00																
Belgium	.33	.51	1.00															
Canada	.60	.14	.38	1.00														
Denmark	.29	.49	.49	.27	1.00													
France	.44	.35	.64	.45	.29	1.00												
Germany	.27	.50	.66	.22	.33	.50	1.00											
Hong Kong	.27	.34	.40	.24	.40	.29	.28	1.00										
Italy	.21	.13	.43	.18	.20	.43	.35	.13	1.00									
Japan	.26	.42	.46	.28	.44	.41	.49	.45	.33	1.00								
Netherlands	.39	.50	.75	.46	.47	.57	.68	.41	.30	.49	1.00							
Norway	.34	.26	.54	.35	.30	.41	.30	.18	.31	.07	.41	1.00						
Singapore	.36	.31	.46	.38	.43	.37	.34	.47	.18	.50	.47	.28	1.00					
Spain	.22	.32	.45	.14	.33	.32	.35	.22	.26	.30	.38	.24	.16	1.00				
Sweden	.30	.40	.59	.33	.38	.34	.41	.19	.19	.34	.46	.37	.33	.35	1.00			
Switzerland	.41	.38	.72	.42	.38	.60	.67	.34	.42	.45	.73	.40	.49	.29	.48	1.00		
United Kingdom	.42	.19	.55	.45	.35	.56	.38	.31	.31	.34	.61	.31	.55	.17	.37	.56	1.00	
United States	.56	.10	.42	.71	.27	.39	.26	.28	.16	.31	.49	.42	.44	.16	.35	.46	.47	1.0
World	.60	.28	.60	.71	.41	.58	.51	.33	.34	.57	.70	.45	.59	.31	.44	.61	.65	.8
	AUSL	AUS	BEL	CAN	DK	FRA	GER	H-K	ITA	JAP	NET	NOR	SNG	SPA	SWD	SWI	U-K	US

TABLE 26–4
Correlation Coefficients between National Stock Markets (January 1979–December 1986)

	AUSL	AUS	BEL	CAN	DK	FRA	GER	H-K	ITA	JAP	NET	NOR	SNG	SPA	SWD	SWI	U.K.	U.S.
Australia	1.00																	
Austria	.03	1.00																
Belgium	.19	.46	1.00															
Canada	.56	.18	.27	1.00														
Denmark	.24	.23	.44	.28	1.00													
France	.25	.50	.62	.37	.31	1.00												
Germany	.20	.65	.61	.29	.41	.60	1.00											
Hong Kong	.32	.13	.19	.25	.20	.16	.23	1.00										
Italy	.25	.20	.37	.31	.35	.42	.29	.33	1.00									
Japan	.27	.23	.43	.21	.26	.37	.38	.18	.42	1.00								
Netherlands	.32	.39	.58	.54	.48	.59	.64	.39	.37	.40	1.00							
Norway	.36	.24	.48	.41	.37	.50	.39	.29	.15	.13	.53	1.00						
Singapore	.28	-.07	.14	.33	.21	.07	.10	.32	.13	.13	.26	.24	1.00					
Spain	.21	.23	.30	.23	.19	.37	.34	.12	.43	.40	.31	.14	-.06	1.00				
Sweden	.28	.20	.32	.31	.38	.32	.37	.28	.36	.31	.39	.29	.22	.28	1.00			
Switzerland	.34	.53	.65	.46	.51	.62	.77	.29	.30	.41	.69	.50	.19	.29	.48	1.00		
United Kingdom	.44	.26	.50	.57	.38	.51	.48	.33	.39	.30	.62	.42	.28	.38	.36	.52	1.00	
United States	.31	.14	.31	.66	.34	.41	.36	.14	.25	.20	.59	.34	.36	.11	.36	.49	.48	1.0
World	.47	.32	.56	.72	.46	.62	.58	.30	.47	.62	.76	.44	.35	.37	.48	.69	.69	.8
	AUSL	AUS	BEL	CAN	DK	FRA	GER	H-K	ITA	JAP	NET	NOR	SNG	SPA	SWD	SWI	U-K	US

Figures 26–1 and 26–2 display the comparative performance of four major markets, measured in dollars and with dividends reinvested, over the latter periods. This cursory evidence confirms that these markets display a remarkable degree of independence.

When comparing the correlation coefficients in Tables 26–2 to 26–4, note that all these numbers measure true correlations with estimation error. Addressing the issue of stability of comovements has to account for sampling variability in the data. Figure 26–3 illustrates this point by plotting a time-series of correlation coefficients between the U.S. and Japanese markets, estimated each month from the previous 48 months of data—a trailing correlation. At first sight, there seems to be some instability in the estimated coefficients, which vary from a low of 0.2 to a high of 0.5. But plotting a 95 percent confidence interval around the correlations reveals that these movements are not inconsistent with sampling

FIGURE 26–1

Performance of Stock Markets: 1971–1978 (indexes measured in U.S. dollars)

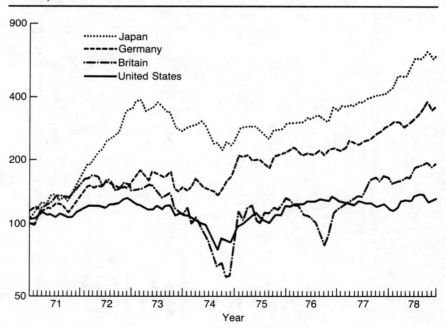

FIGURE 26–2
Performance of Stock Markets: 1979–1986 (indexes measured in U.S. dollars)

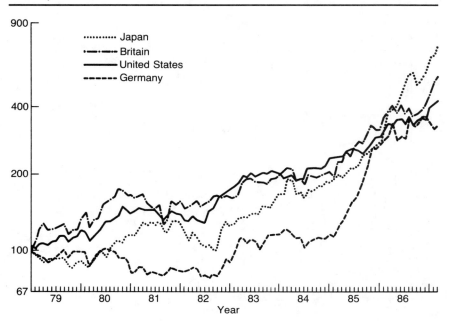

variation. Figure 26–3 indicates that the correlation between the U.S. and Japanese markets is relatively stable over time and certainly has not increased. This is an important result because in practice the effectiveness of international diversification rests on the stability of the comovements between equity markets.

Next, it is useful to explain the pattern of covariations in terms of a small number of factors. Reducing the pattern of covariation to a few factors allows one to focus on the fundamental macroeconomic variables influencing national stock returns. As shifts in national economic policies or in patterns of world trade or capital flows can alter these comovements, a good understanding of the linkages between equity markets is important. Looking more closely at the correlations in Tables 26–2 to 26–5, it appears that a large proportion of the comovements can be explained by a world factor, because of mainly positive correlation coefficients that

FIGURE 26–3
Stability of Correlation: U.S.–Japan Markets (four-year trailing correlation and 95 percent confidence interval)

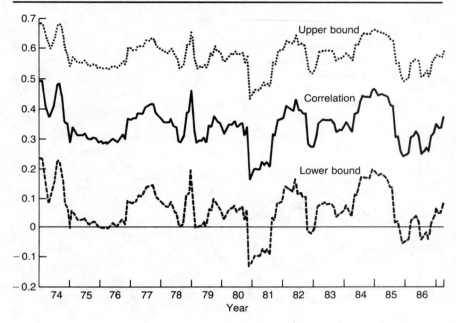

reflect global economic trends. In addition, there seem to be regional effects, with higher correlations between some markets.

To analyze more formally patterns of covariations, factor analysis can be used. Briefly, this technique of multivariate analysis decomposes the correlation matrix into the effect of a number of common factors and a residual matrix. Ripley first applied this method to monthly equity returns covering the period 1960–70.[8] It was found that most of the covariation was attributable to three factors interpreted as a "well developed market" factor, a "Lon-

---

[8] D. M. Ripley, "Systematic Elements in the Linkage of National Stock Market Indices," *Review of Economics and Statistics* 55, August 1974, pp. 356–61.

TABLE 26–5
Factor Analysis of National Equity Returns

	January 1971– December 1978			January 1979– December 1986		
	Rotated Factor Pattern			Rotated Factor Pattern		
	Factor 1	Factor 3	Factor 3	Factor 1	Factor 2	Factor 3
Australia	0.15	0.73*	0.16	0.02	0.65*	0.30
Austria	0.41	−0.09	0.64*	0.77*	−0.15	0.14
Belgium	0.74*	0.30	0.43	0.72*	0.15	0.31
Canada	0.12	0.84*	0.12	0.23	0.74*	0.17
Denmark	0.23	0.17	0.66*	0.43*	0.34	0.23
France	0.61	0.44	0.20	0.71*	0.17	0.33
Germany	0.68*	0.09	0.41	0.82*	0.11	0.26
Hong Kong	−0.01	0.24	0.72*	0.05	0.46*	0.31
Italy	0.63*	0.15	−0.02	0.12	0.21	0.76*
Japan	0.24	0.16	0.71*	0.24	0.08	0.68*
Netherlands	0.58*	0.40	0.48	0.64*	0.49	0.26
Norway	0.54*	0.42	−0.03	0.53*	0.49	−0.03
Singapore	0.07	0.49	0.62*	−0.05	0.69*	−0.03
Spain	0.52*	−0.02	0.29	0.18	−0.03	0.76*
Sweden	0.50*	0.25	0.31	0.26	0.37	0.42*
Switzerland	0.63*	0.41	0.35	0.78*	0.34	0.24
United Kingdom	0.34	0.59*	0.29	0.41	0.54*	0.37
United States	0.13	0.84*	0.15	0.36	0.67*	0.03

Percentage of variance explained by unrotated first three factors:
| | 42.4% | 9.5% | 7.1% | 39.5% | 10.3% | 7.4% |

* Asterisk denotes the highest value for the correlations between the markets and the factors.

don dependent" factor, and a "United States–Canada" link.[9] Similarly, Hilliard applied spectral analysis to daily data covering the announcement of the Organization of Petroleum Exporting Countries (OPEC) embargo and found that the correlations be-

---

[9] Comparable results were found by D. B. Panton, V. P. Lessig, and O. M. Joy, "Comovements of International Equity Markets: A Taxonomic Approach," *Journal of Financial and Quantitative Analysis* 11, September 1976, pp. 415–32.

tween equity markets were suprisingly low, except within North American and continental European areas.[10]

Table 26–5 presents the factors extracted from the correlation matrix estimated over the periods 1971–78 and 1979–86. The entries in each column represent loadings—correlations between markets and factors—with the highest entry marked by an asterisk. Two groups of countries are clearly apparent. One group is associated with continental European countries, while the other consists of the United States, Canada, Britain, and Australia. The third factor has no clear interpretation because the factor loadings change over time. Noteworthy of these markets moving independently is the Japanese stock market. The fact that the factor decomposition was similar across subperiods lends further support to the hypothesis that correlation coefficients are relatively stable over time.[11]

Some of these results can be interpreted in terms of patterns of trade, real activity, and fiscal and monetary policies. The close integration of European economies provides a natural explanation for the common movements in European stock markets. In addition, the pegging of exchange rates within the European Monetary System imposes some coordination of monetary policies implying a higher correlation between exchange rate and interest rate innovations. The linkage between the United States and Canadian stock markets, on the other hand, can be traced to the close economic ties between these two countries, which have the highest volume of bilateral trade in the world.

These findings should help us to optimally diversify across national equity markets. Generally, diversifications are most effective when investing across markets with low correlations. If the pattern of correlation matrix can be satisfactorily explained exactly

---

[10] J. Hilliard, "The Relationship between Equity Indices on World Exchanges," *Journal of Finance* 24, March 1979, pp. 103–13.

[11] This conclusion was also reached by Philippatos et al. who dispute the findings of Maldonado and Saunders that relationships across stock markets are unstable. See G. Philippatos, A. Christofi, and P. Christofi, "The Intertemporal Stability of International Stock Market Relationships: Another View," *Financial Management,* 1984, pp. 63–69; and R. Maldonado and A. Saunders, "International Portfolio Diversification and the Intertemporal Stability of International Stock Market Relationships, 1957–78," *Financial Management* 10, Autumn 1981, pp. 54–63.

by only three factors, say, then the investment opportunity set could be reduced to three assets; this considerably simplifies portfolio choice. If one had the choice to invest in three countries, it would be optimal to choose three markets from each group identified by factor analysis. For instance, investing in U.S., German, and Japanese markets would provide considerable diversification benefits. Further investment should go to those markets such as the Scandinavian countries that exhibit mostly specific movements.

SEGMENTATIONS IN INTERNATIONAL CAPITAL MARKETS

Empirical studies of international capital markets have left the issue of segmentation versus integration largely unresolved. Yet the question of national or international pricing of assets has crucial implications for financial decisions. Segmented markets imply that foreign securities may appear mispriced. For instance, with segmented markets, the firm's cost of capital is a function of project locations. As a result, multinationals may be able to reap substantial benefits from foreign investment over and above the pure diversification benefits previously discussed. Exploiting these anomalies is one of the challenges of international financial management.

Integration can be defined as a situation where investors earn the same risk-adjusted expected return on similar financial instruments in different national markets. Segmentation of international financial markets, on the other hand, means that assets are priced differently in each market. For example, if one is willing to accept the capital asset pricing model (CAPM) as relevant, expected returns in each market are determined by their systematic risk vis-á-vis the domestic market. Therefore, an investor who has the opportunity to scan various markets for value finds that expected returns on foreign assets may not be consistent with the domestic risk-return trade-off. In other words, foreign markets appear mispriced.

High correlations between national stock markets do not necessarily imply integration of capital markets. Two stock markets, such as those of the United States and Canada, can be highly correlated while expected returns on Canadian common stocks could be, say, 2 percent lower than for similar U.S. assets. This would be proof of segmentation of these markets, the finding of which has considerable interest both for the purpose of investment and issuance of capital.

The major hurdle in identifying mispriced foreign stocks is that risk has to be controlled. A first approach to detect obvious segmentations is to focus on investments with little market risk, such as short-term deposits in the same currency with the same maturity, but located in different capital markets. Deposit rates in the domestic and offshore markets, for instance, allow one to directly measure the effect of barriers to the movement of capital. Figure 26–4 compares domestic and Euro-French franc interest

FIGURE 26–4
Effect of Capital Controls (French franc interest rates: Euro and domestic)

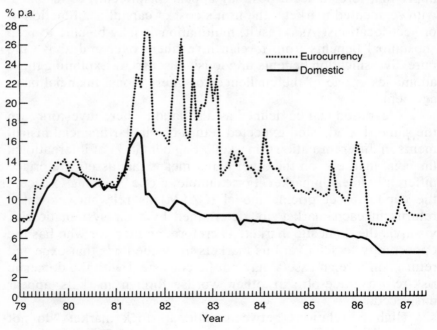

Source: World Financial Markets.

rates. The assets are identical in all respects except location.[12]
Thus, the wide interest rate differentials observed after 1981 can
only be attributed to barriers to the movement of capital; in this
case, restrictions on the outflow of capital from France. This is a
clear-cut case of segmentation, because similar assets earn different returns in different markets. Such examples are not rare. In
1973 German domestic rates were about 6 percent higher than the
Euromarket because of restrictions on the inflow of capital. Also,
capital controls restricted the inflow of capital into Japan between
1975 and 1978, while outflows were restricted over the periods
1973–74 and 1979–80. Multinationals with foreign operations have
the unique ability of being able to exploit these segmentations by
borrowing in the market with the lowest cost of capital.

The recent growth of the currency swap market is also
evidence of segmentations in world financial markets. Currency
swaps are usually explained in terms of comparative advantage.
For instance, some U.S. multinationals are able to raise capital in
foreign markets at a very low spread over riskless issues. When
hedged into dollars, this spread can be much lower than what the
company would have to pay by borrowing in the United States.
These opportunities arise because of investors' differing perceptions of credit risk in different markets, that is, segmentations.
Once the market recognized these discrepancies, these quasi-
arbitrage opportunities have been reduced because of the sheer
volume of transactions in the currency swap market.

Directly determining the extent of segmentation of national
stock markets, on the other hand, is a much more difficult matter.
A few models in international finance explicitly incorporate the
effect of barriers to the movement of capital on the pricing of
stocks but tests of integration of international stock markets have
usually been inconclusive.[13] A major issue is that these empirical

---

[12] And possibly some credit risk.

[13] Such as those proposed by F. Black "International Capital Market Equilibrium with
Investment Barriers," *Journal of Financial Economics* 1, December 1974, pp. 337–52; M.
Adler and B. Dumas, "Optimal International Acquisitions," *Journal of Finance* 30, March
1975, pp. 1–20; and R. Stulz, "On the Effect of Barriers to International Investment,"
Journal of Finance 36, September 1981, pp. 923–34. A good review can be found in M. Adler
and B. Dumas, "International Portfolio Choice and Corporation Finance: A Survey,"
Journal of Finance 38, June 1983, pp. 925–84.

tests are always joint tests of integration/segmentation, and of a particular asset pricing model, and of particular assumptions concerning the pricing of exchange-rate risk, which may be viewed differently across nationalities if consumption baskets differ. Thus, it will never be clear whether any empirical result reflects segmentation or an inappropriate model of pricing of risk or inadequate assumptions about exchange-rate risk.

In addition, definite results are seldom possible with stock market data. This is because expected returns are hard to identify when stock market returns are so volatile. The empirical researcher needs either large amounts of data or very powerful statistical methods. Indeed, Jorion and Schwartz, using a maximum-likelihood estimation technique, reject the hypothesis of integration between the U.S. and Canadian stock markets, when a priori, one would have expected these two markets to be quite integrated.[14] Indeed, a perusal of Tables 26–2 to 26–4 indicates that the Canadian stock market is consistently most highly correlated with the U.S. stock market. High comovements, however, do not necessarily imply market integration.

Over the period 1968 to 1982, Canadian stocks seem to have been priced according to their domestic systematic risk instead of their global systematic risk. Some insight into the sources of segmentation are also provided in this study. Market imperfections can be classified into two categories. The first, *information barriers,* is related to the difficulty of obtaining information about foreign stocks and the differences in the depth and quality of financial reporting due to differences in accounting disclosure requirements. The second category, *legal barriers,* stems from differential juridical status between domestic and foreign investments, such as tax considerations, restrictions on the foreign ownership of securities, and restrictions on foreign investments for pension funds.

To distinguish between these possible causes of segmentation, Jorion and Schwartz separate the sample of Canadian firms between firms interlisted in both markets and firms solely listed in

---

[14] P. Jorion and E. Schwartz, "Integration versus Segmentation in the Canadian Stock Market," *Journal of Finance* 41, July 1986, pp. 603–14.

Canada.[16] Because these firms are subject to the same disclosure requirements as U.S. firms, the information argument is much weaker than for purely domestic firms. The authors found that interlisted firms behave similarly to purely domestic firms. This evidence suggests that *legal* barriers have been the primary source of segmentation over this time period. Another interpretation is that Canadian stocks, which are for the most part resource-oriented, are exposed to different factors than U.S. stocks, and thus are priced differently, as the arbitrage pricing theory would suggest.

The implications of such results are illustrated in Table 26–6, which reports summary statistics for the U.S. and Canadian stock markets over the period 1979–86. With a correlation of 0.66, the systematic risk of the Canadian stock market relative to the U.S. market is $\beta_{CA}^{US} = \rho_{US,CA}\sigma_{CA}^2/\sigma_{US}^2 = 0.66 * 22.2/14.5 = 1.02$. Therefore, the minimum return required by a U.S. investor, based on the domestic CAPM, is $E(R_{CA}) = R_f + \beta_{US}[E(R_{US}) - R_f]$. Assuming a risk-free rate of 10 percent, this yields $E(R_{CA}) = 10.0 + 1.02 * [16.8 - 10.0] = 17.0$. A 17.0 percent rate of return would thus be a minimum compensation for the risk of the project, as perceived by the U.S. investor using the CAPM. If the projected return on Canadian stocks is assumed equal to the historical average, say 15 percent, then the Canadian stock market would appear overpriced. This descrepancy could be explained in terms of the legal barriers previously reported. For instance, Canadian pension funds cannot invest more than 10 percent of their assets in foreign securities. These legal restrictions could lead to artifically low expected returns in the Canadian stock market. From the viewpoint of equity funding, the implication is that, over this time period it would have been cheaper to float Canadian shares rather than U.S. shares.

Using the same reasoning, one can find the minimum required return on other stock markets. It appears that most of the risk of the Japanese and German stock markets is U.S.-diversifiable risk. Despite the exchange-rate volatility, the total systematic risk is very low for these markets. The minimum return required by the U.S. investor is 12 percent and 13.8 percent, for the Japanese and

[16] Ibid.

TABLE 26-6
Computing Expected Returns in Segmented Markets Based on Ex Post Data (January 1979–December 1986)

	Average Return	Volatility	Correlation with U.S. market	Systematic Risk (U.S. Beta)	Minimum Return with Segmented Markets
United States	16.8	14.5	1.00	1.	16.8
Canada	15.0	22.2	0.66	1.02	17.0
Japan	23.8	21.1	0.20	0.29	12.0
Germany	18.7	22.1	0.36	0.55	13.8

German markets, respectively. If this is below the projected return, then these markets would be considered undervalued according to this model.

CONCLUSIONS

Expanding horizons to the international environment is a difficult but potentially rewarding process for financial managers. In today's global financial environment, limiting oneself to the domestic market can only be justified after a conscious decision based on careful examination of the additional risk and rewards from going international.

The benefits from international diversification stem from two sources. First is the pure diversification effect, due to weak linkages between stock markets. These low correlations allow one to reduce overall portfolio risk to a much greater extent than by restricting the menu of assets to domestic securities. Historically, correlations have remained low and relatively stable across national stock markets, which strongly suggests that this risk reduction could have been achieved in the past and can be achieved in the future.

Second is the possibility of mispricing due to market segmentations, which imply that risk is perceived and priced differently across national stock markets, independently from the issue of statistical comovement. Identification of mispricing in international stock markets has proved difficult so far, but there is evidence from other asset markets that segmentations do occur. As the growth of the currency swap market has shown, these segmentations can substantially lower the cost of capital. Such opportunities will be reaped by the first international financial managers to recognize these segmentations.

APPENDIX: DATA SOURCES

The primary source of data is Morgan Stanley Capital International, which provides monthly stock indexes for 18 national stock markets, as well as spot rates and dividend yields. Data for Hong Kong and Singapore start in 1970 only. These indexes are relatively comparable since they are constructed using the same methodology and exclude interlisted stocks. To compute returns in the foreign currency, dividends were assumed to be the latest dividend yield divided by 12. Because no dividend data are available before 1971, returns before 1971 do not include dividends. Dollar returns are computed after conversion of the foreign currency prices into dollars at the latest spot rate.

REFERENCES

Adler, M., and B. Dumas. "International Portfolio Choice and Corporation Finance: A Survey." *Journal of Finance* 38, June 1983, pp. 925–84.

———. "Optimal International Acquisitions." *Journal of Finance* 30, March 1975, pp. 1–20.

Agmon, T. "The Relations among Equity Markets: A Study of Share Price Comovements in the United States, United Kingdom, Germany, and Japan." *Journal of Finance* 27, September 1972, pp. 838–55.

Black, F. "International Capital Market Equilibrium with Investment Barriers," *Journal of Financial Economics* 1, December 1974, pp. 337–52.

Eun, C., and B. Resnick. "Estimating the Correlation Structure of International Share Prices." *Journal of Finance* 39, December 1984, pp. 1311–24.

Grubel, H. G. "Internationally Diversified Portfolios: Welfare Gains and Capital Flows." *American Economic Review* 58, December 1968, pp. 1299–1314.

Grubel, H. G., and K. Fadner. "The Interdependence of International Equity Markets." *Journal of Finance* 26, March 1971, pp. 89–94.

Hilliard, J. "The Relationship between Equity Indices on World Exchanges." *Journal of Finance* 24, March 1979, pp. 103–13.

Jorion, P. "International Portfolio Diversification with Estimation Risk." *Journal of Business* 58, July 1985, pp. 259–78.

Jorion, P., and E. Schwartz. "Integration versus Segmentation in the Canadian Stock Market." *Journal of Finance* 41, July 1986, pp. 603–14.

Lessard, D. "International Portfolio Diversification: A Multivariate Analysis for a Group of Latin American Countries." *Journal of Finance* 28, June 1973, pp. 619–33.

———. "World, National, and Industry Factors in Equity Returns." *Journal of Finance* 29, May 1974, pp. 379–91.

Levy, H. and M. Sarnat. "International Diversification of Investment Portfolios." *American Economic Review* 60, September 1970, pp. 668–75.

Maldonado, R., and A. Saunders. "International Portfolio Diversification and the Intertemporal Stability of International Stock Market Relationships, 1957–78." *Financial Management* 10, Autumn 1981, pp. 54–63.

Panton, D. B.; V. P. Lessig; and O. M. Joy. "Comovements of International Equity Markets: A Taxonomic Approach." *Journal of Financial and Quantitative Analysis* 11, September 1976, pp. 415–32.

Philippatos, G.; A. Christofi; and P. Christofi. "The Intertemporal Stability of International Stock Market Relationships: Another View." *Financial Management,* 1984, pp. 63–69.

Ripley, D. M. "Systematic Elements in the Linkage of National Stock Market Indices." *Review of Economics and Statistics* 55, August 1974, pp. 356–61.

Solnik, B. "The International Pricing of Risk: An Empirical Investigation of the World Capital Market Structure." *Journal of Finance* 29, May 1974, pp. 48–54.

———. "Why Not Diversify Internationally Rather than Domestically?" *Financial Analysts Journal* 30, July 1974, pp. 48–54.

Stulz, R. "On the Effect of Barriers to International Investment." *Journal of Finance* 36, September 1981, pp. 923–34.

CHAPTER 27

DEBT PROBLEMS OF DEVELOPING COUNTRIES

Lawrence J. Brainard

The current international debt crisis dates from the Mexican default in August 1982. Individual developing countries encountered debt problems in preceding years and debt reschedulings were common enough. But these isolated situations did not rival the Mexican debt problems in scope, nor did they lead to a systemic crisis with significant effects on the international financial system. Within a short time, the shock waves from the Mexican default spread to other developing countries, leading to similar defaults. By the end of 1983, some 35 developing countries had defaulted on some or all of their external debt. In orders of magnitude, the debts of these countries totaled some $600 billion at the end of 1987, out of a total indebtedness of developing countries that measured about $1.0 trillion.

HISTORICAL PRECEDENTS

The historical record is replete with examples of debt defaults by sovereign states. Foreign lending, mostly bond issues floated in the London market, was prominent during 1870–1913. Another cycle of foreign bond lending, this time led by American institutions, emerged during 1924–30. In his assessment of the patterns of these lending episodes, Charles Kindleberger characterized British lending in the 1870–1913 period as demand driven and anticyclical, slowing down during periods of strong investment demand in the United Kingdom and rising during recessions, as domestic demand fell off. American lending in the twenties, by contrast, was supply driven and procyclical—rising and falling in tandem with the domestic business cycle, as a rise in savings fed increases in both domestic and foreign investment. Kindleberger concluded that the anticyclical British pattern of lending acted to stabilize the world economy. The patterns in the twenties—sustained by inexperienced American newcomers to the international lending business—destabilized the world economy and acted to aggravate the worldwide effects of the 1930s Depression.[1]

The current cycle in foreign lending dates from the late 1960s. In many ways, its origins reflect the experience of the twenties—it was supply driven, procyclical in character and sustained by a group of neophytes to the business of long-term international lending, the commercial banks. Financial innovations introduced in the late 1960s stimulated the supply of international loans by reducing the risks facing commercial banks in such lending. The Eurodollar roll-over loan, with its variable interest rate based on a short-term interest rate, typically six-month London Interbank Offered Rate (LIBOR), facilitated long-term international lending by reducing the risk of interest-rate fluctuations for the lenders.

Bond financing was restrained by the limited supply of long-term funds available for investment in such securities. Fixed-rate bank lending was inhibited by the risks posed by funding fixed-rate, long-term claims with short-dated deposit liabilities. The Eurodollar roll-over loan reduced a bank's risk of mismatched interest maturities of their assets and liabilities; given their easy access to short-term Eurodollar deposits, the banks gained a comparative advantage in such lending. The ease of arranging syndicates of lending banks allowed an increase in the size of individual credit transactions, further reducing financing costs to borrowers. For the

---

[1] Charles P. Kindleberger, "The Cyclical Pattern of Long-Term Lending," in *Theory and Experience of Economic Development: Essays in Honour of Sir W. Arthur Lewis*, ed. M. Gersovitz et al. (London: Allen & Unwin, 1982), pp. 300–302.

first time, commercial banks engaged in large-scale foreign lending for their own portfolios; in previous periods, the banks had acted primarily as underwriters rather than as investors or lenders.

TRENDS IN FOREIGN LENDING

During the 1960s foreign direct investment accounted for over half of the net flows to developing countries; official flows, such as official export financing and World Bank loans, made up most of the remainder.[2] By 1973, the eve of the rapid expansion in lending to developing countries, the share of direct investment in net financing flows had declined to 20 percent; private lending, mostly from commercial banks, accounted for a 27 percent share. (See Table 27–1.)

The oil price hike in 1973 led to substantial global financial imbalances highlighted by the Organization of Petroleum Exporting Countries (OPEC) surplus; a significant portion of these imbalances were intermediated by the commercial banks. Within the context of sharp increases in total net financing flows to the developing countries up to 1981, the share of commercial bank lending rose markedly, to 45 percent in 1974–79 and a peak of 60 percent in 1980–81. The share of long-term lending from official institutions remained in the 20–30 percent range, but sharp drops in the shares of foreign direct investment and other nondebt-creating flows were evident.

With the onset of the debt crisis in 1982, net financial flows to developing countries fell sharply and the share of commercial bank lending dropped precipitously. In 1986, for example, commercial bank lending accounted for only 2 percent of total flows, as banks sought to reduce exposure to many developing countries and a handful of countries (primarily Asian countries such as South Korea, Thailand, and Malaysia) repaid bank debt and shifted

---

[2] David J. Goldsborough, "Investment Trends and Prospects: The Link with Bank Lending," in *Investing in Development: New Roles for Private Capital?* ed. Theodore H. Moran (New Brunswick, N.J.: Transactions Books for the Overseas Development Council, 1986), p. 174.

TABLE 27-1

Developing Countries Net Foreign Funding Sources (1973–86)

	1973	1974–76[a]	1977–79[a]	1980–81[a]	1982–83[a]	1984–85[a]	1986 preliminary
Total (in $ billion)	$21.0	$43.2	$66.7	$131.8	$80.5	$66.1	$54.3
Sources (in percents)							
Direct investment	20%	12%	11%	9%	14%	15%	16%
Other non-debt-creating flows[b]	26	18	16	11	17	25	36
Long-term borrowing from official creditors	27	23	29	20	38	36	46
Private creditors[c]	27	46	44	60	32	24	2
of which bonds	5	5	5	1	3	7	7

[a] Annual average.

[b] Official transfers, special drawing right (SDR) allocations, and valuation adjustments.

[c] Principally from commercial banks; including also bond issues and suppliers' credits; banks purchased or refinanced some of the bonds and suppliers' credits.

Sources: *World Economic Outlook*, Table 40 (1985) and Table A43 (1987) (Washington, D.C.: International Monetary Fund), *Foreign Direct and Portfolio Investment in Developing Countries* (Washington, D.C.: International Finance Corporation, June 1984); *International Capital Market*, Table 4 (Washington, D.C.: International Monetary Fund, 1986).

borrowing to the international bond markets. Declines in flows of direct investment and official long-term lending were also recorded, though the relative shares show increases given the overall decline in total flows.

CHARACTERISTICS OF BANK LENDING

Financial Structure of Loans

The vehicle that permitted the rapid expansion of bank lending was the general-purpose Eurodollar roll-over loan. The term of such loans was typically 7 to 10 years, with floating-rate pricing based on a spread over a reference interest rate, usually six-month LIBOR. Every six months, for example, the loan would be repriced based on the current reference rate. Banks could eliminate risks of interest maturity mismatching on their books by locking in funding on the roll-over date for the relevant period; for example, six months. Depending on the banks' interest-rate expectations until the next roll-over date, they could also manage the mismatch by funding with deposits whose maturities were shorter or longer than the relevant period.

As the supply of Eurodollar deposits beyond six months is rather limited, the funding mismatch usually involved shorter-dated deposits. The problems of liability management for the banks were for practical purposes limited to risks of interest-rate fluctuations out to one year; the banks could access a growing interbank market in Europe, as well as arbitrage funds from the U.S. money market. By contrast, the borrowers assumed the risk of interest-rate fluctuations over the life of the loan; financial innovations to hedge such risks, such as interest-rate swaps and options, were developed only in the 1980s, too late to benefit most borrowing countries.

A few loans were structured as project credits with the repayment legally secured with cash flows or assets which the financing created. Such credits involved detailed technical analyses and complicated legal arrangements which increased the cost and limited the flexibility of the borrowers. Most sovereign borrowers were able to negotiate interest rates on general-purpose borrowings identical to those on project credits. General-purpose financing, thus, predominated in international lending due to the flexibility and cost advantage for sovereign borrowers. The borrower sometimes indicated that certain borrowings would be used for specific purposes, but the legal contract of a general-purpose financing did not give the lending banks rights to any specific cash flow; debt service payments—including interest and principal payments—were to be made out of the country's foreign-exchange earnings.

Country Risks

Whether a given foreign loan represents a claim on a public or private obligor, the foreign exchange necessary to service the debt must pass through the country's central bank. All such loans, therefore, are subject to cross-border transfer risk or country risk. The ability or willingness of the country's central bank to make such foreign-exchange payments imposes an additional risk for banks in cross-border lending to private borrowers. Such country risk comes on top of the risk that the obligor is able to service such debts in the local currency equivalent of the external loan.

Legal Structure of Loan Agreements

The typical Eurodollar loan agreement sought to protect the banks' rights to receive income and principal by:

- Selection of English or New York law that generally affords better protection of the creditor's rights.
- Waiver of sovereign immunity that allows the creditors to sue a sovereign over commercial disputes.
- Cross default, which means that default on one loan would render all other loans by the lender to the same debtor due and payable.
- Pari passu treatment of lenders (pro rata sharing clauses), which acts to prevent preferential payment to one or several defined creditors at the expense of other creditors.
- Negative pledges that restricted the ability of the borrower to pledge assets, such as the country's foreign-exchange reserves, to other creditors.

With the benefit of hindsight, it is clear that such legal agreements define rights which have turned out to be very uncertain in the context of the crisis that actually emerged after 1982. The loan agreements are private contracts, to be sure. This effectively prevents their invalidation, for example, by congressional legislation. The agreements provided no monitoring of the debtor's foreign cash flow and no controls over such flows, such as by the creation of sinking funds or similar structures; no possibility of conversion of the claims into domestic assets was foreseen. The only way private lenders can enforce their rights is by extreme actions, such as bringing legal attachments to a sovereign debtor's international assets or trade, thereby disrupting the ability of the sovereign to carry on normal international trade and payments.

A parallel with the U.S. Chapter XI bankruptcy code cannot be drawn for a sovereign debtor. In a Chapter XI bankruptcy proceeding, the courts determine a debtor's ability to pay and enforce such judgments, having access to the debtor's assets. For a sovereign debtor, the option of a bankruptcy proceeding does not exist. Sovereign debt problems must be worked out in the context of longer-term cooperation among the debtor government and its creditors, including private banks, official export agencies, and multilateral institutions. Within this context, the banks need to provide continuing flows of new credits to a number of countries to permit servicing of the debt.

There are doubts whether the banks could effectively enforce their rights through legal attachments: (1) the costs of seizure may be considerable; (2) the assets available to be attached may be rather modest and would have to be shared with other creditors; and (3) political pressure would likely be brought against such actions by other creditor or debtor governments. These considerations, though, are somewhat beside the point. The likely purpose of bringing attachments would be to force negotiations that would give banks a better settlement. Banks would be able in most cases to cause considerable disruption to trade flows by bringing attachments, even if the value of the assets attached is modest compared to their claims.

On one hand, the banks can defend their rights against invalidation. On the other, the banks' rights to income from debtor countries is ill-defined not only in relation to other creditors but also in relation to the country's foreign income, exchange reserves, and other external or domestic assets. In short, the legal structure of general-purpose lending to sovereigns has proved seriously deficient. In itself, this constitutes a strong reason to believe that such general-purpose lending will not have a significant role to play when developing countries' access to international credit markets is restored in the future.

REASONS FOR THE SURGE IN LENDING

Lending Decisions by the Banks

The oil price hike in 1973 played a key role in creating the major international financial imbalances that emerged during the 70s. But the creation of these imbalances does not explain why banks entered lending to developing countries so eagerly. These reasons reflect a number of other factors.

Financial innovation lowered the cost of such lending by reducing funding risks for the banks and by reducing the cost of entry into such lending. In the past, international bonds were sold to large numbers of individual and institutional investors; the costs of setting up a distribution network for such securities was significant. Eurodollar syndications, however, brought a wide network of banks—both large and small—into the business. The major syndicating banks could tap their network of correspondent bank relationships creating a tailor-made distribution network. Costs of entry for small banks were modest, only the costs of accessing Eurodollar deposits, either through a London or other offshore branch. In addition, the expansion of total credit was not restrained by legal reserve requirements, such as existed in domestic financial markets.

Detailed current data on banks holding rescheduled debt show the wide dispersal of claims among banks—only about 35 percent of the total debt is owed U.S. banks; the rest is spread widely among other international banks. And although there is a clear concentration of the debt in large banks, the number of small creditors in most of the major rescheduling countries runs into the hundreds. The number of bank creditors ranged from 90 banks in the Dominican Republic to over six hundred banks in the case of Mexico.

Competitive pressures were intense during the 1970s. Many of the U.S. banks suffered substantial domestic loan losses in the 1974–75 recession; the profits available in sovereign Eurodollar lending were a strong attraction. In 1976–77, for example, over 50 percent of the profits of the major U.S. money center banks came from international activities.[3] Initial successes bred a herd instinct; the rush of new entrants acted to depress lending margins, thus reducing profits on any given deal. In turn, the banks' effort to sustain and increase overall profitability undermined traditional credit disciplines, as loan maturities lengthened and credit standards were compromised.

Banks seriously underestimated the country risks involved in such lending. Two factors were at work here. One was a simple fallacy of composition. It was easy enough to imagine that an individual country could get into payments difficulties, such as Turkey did in 1977. And it was also easy to imagine how such a country got out of its difficulties—by tightening economic policies and by increased external support from major creditor governments. But few analysts were able to anticipate the implications of an international financial crisis, such as that which actually occurred with sharp increases in real interest rates, precipitous declines in export prices, no new bank lending, and little in the way of increased official lending.

The problem was not a lack of data on developing countries or faulty risk evaluation techniques, though both left room for improvement. The banks' mistake was in restricting their assessments to individual borrowing countries; they missed the fact that the policies of the industrial countries, the less developed country (LDC) borrowers, and the banks themselves were undermining the stability of the overall international system.[4]

---

[3] Committee for Economic Development, *Finance and Third World Economic Growth* (Boulder: Westview Press, 1988), p. 139.

[4] Lawrence J. Brainard, "More Lending to the Third World? A Banker's View," in *Uncertain Future: Commercial Banks and the Third World,* ed. R. Fineberg and V. Kallab, (New Brunswick, N.J.: Transactions Books for the Overseas Development Council, 1984), pp. 33–36.

Guttentag and Herring have termed these shortcomings "disaster myopia"—banks acted as if the probability of a major shock affecting their international loan portfolios were zero.[5] To be fair to the banks, though, they were not really aware they were being used; they were not the only ones who believed that major industrial countries would act to address the weaknesses in the world monetary system. Rather than dealing with weaknesses in the international financial markets, though, governments sought to encourage others—the commercial banks, the World Bank, and the International Monetary Fund (IMF)—to step into the breech. This acted to transform one economic disequilibrium—the OPEC surplus—into a different one—the LDC debt crisis; the result was persistent economic disequilibriums and continuing instabilities in international financial markets and recurring crises of the global economy.

A second problem was encountered when banks evaluated individual countries. In the inflationary environment of the times, a country's success in economic management appeared more substantial than it really was. The success of many countries in boosting exports reflected in large part the inflationary stimulus to prices and demand in the importing regions. The ability of such countries to manage their debt burdens in a less inflationary world was overestimated. Optimistic judgments, though, tended to become self-validating as new loans confirmed a country's creditworthiness and this perception generated even more new loans. It was difficult for the banks' country-risk analysts to argue with success and the judgment of the markets, though many did so. In many respects, the only real constraint on sovereign borrowing was the willingness of the banks to grant new credits.

Shortcomings of International Economic Policies

After the oil price shock in 1973, commercial banks played an indispensable role in providing the needed funds to countries facing huge financing needs. In so doing, the banks helped the interna-

---

[5] Jack M. Guttentag and Richard J. Herring, *The Current Crisis in International Lending* (Washington, D.C.: Brookings Institution, 1985), pp. 2–3.

tional economy avoid a severe and prolonged economic depression. Given the rigidities of working through the official financial institutions such as the IMF, the private recycling effort was seen by the major governments as a desirable development. But after 1976, the continuation and rapid expansion of such lending quickly became undesirable. After complimenting the banks for aiding in the recycling of OPEC surpluses during 1974–76, though, the major industrial governments were reluctant to rein in bank lending.[6] Bank regulatory agencies in the major countries were slow to recognize these undesirable trends and they reacted too late to discourage such bank lending.

Banks interpreted the silence of the authorities as tacit approval to continue lending to developing countries. They believed that the major industrial countries were firmly committed to maintaining the health and viability of the international economic system should a challenge similar to the 1973–76 OPEC surplus problem reemerge.

For their part, however, governments were busily abandoning past economic priorities given to balance-of-payments adjustments in favor of growth promotion. It was easy to lose sight of the need for balance-of-payments adjustment by the developing countries— LDC exports were rising rapidly, debt ratios were stable or were rising only moderately and there was a belief in high rates of return to investment in developing countries. These factors influenced industrial countries to encourage sustained high resource inflows to bolster rates of domestic investment and growth in the developing countries. In this context, the shift from public to private financing of development was generally viewed as a healthy development for the developing countries and the world economy.[7]

What was missing was the perception that nobody was really responsible for maintaining the overall stability and integrity of the international financial system. When Federal Reserve Board Chairman Paul Volcker finally decided to tackle the U.S. inflation

---

[6] David F. Lomax, *The Developing Country Debt Crisis* (London: Macmillan, 1986), pp. 19–27.

[7] Anne O. Krueger, "Debt, Capital Flows, and LDC Growth," *American Economic Review*, May 1987, pp. 159–60.

problem in October 1979, little thought was given to the possibility that such moves could fuel a world debt crisis. Other countries followed Volcker's lead by tightening fiscal and monetary policies. Countercyclical policies which had succeeded in 1974–76 were abandoned in favor of a war on inflation. And by this time, the banks' exposure to the developing countries was already high; instead of meeting the increased demand for financing as in 1974–76, banks restricted lending.

In summary, the interaction between bank lending and economic policies of the major industrial countries acted to create an unsustainable lending cycle, followed by severe contractionary pressures:

1974–76: Anticyclical economic policies implemented by the industrial countries, coupled with anticyclical lending by the banks was successful in countering the deflationary effects of the oil price hike and the OPEC surplus.

1976–79: Procyclical growth policies implemented by the industrial countries led to accelerating inflation, falling real interest rates, and a worldwide boom in investment and economic growth; sharp increases in lending by commercial banks acted to amplify the magnitude of the cycle.

1980–81: Anti-inflationary policies implemented by the industrial countries resulted in sharp declines in growth, commodity prices, and significant hikes in real and nominal interest rates; banks restricted new lending, thus aggravating the contractionary effects of the cyclical downturn.

Policy Failures in Developing Countries

The logic of recycling the OPEC surpluses to the developing countries depended on achieving balance-of-payments adjustments, albeit after a period of several years of financing current-account deficits. In the environment emerging after the 1974–76 recession, developing countries faced low or negative real interest rates and few effective disciplines on their borrowing policies. Strong political forces lined up behind continued financing of current-account deficits rather than painful economic adjustments and reduction of the deficits. Major oil-exporting countries, such as Mexico, Venezuela, and Nigeria, also increased external borrowing, despite a significant increase in export revenues.

The results of recycling were frequently halfhearted attempts at adjustment, together with continued financing of increases in investment as well as consumption. Under these circumstances, it is not surprising that economic mismanagement of one kind or another characterized their domestic policies. The political calculus of any country's leaders includes many noneconomic priorities, ranging from prestige projects, subsidies for special-interest groups, and increased growth and employment via an expansion of government spending. The easy access to external financing acted to weaken the economic constraints on such political expenditures.

Economic mismanagement, by itself, was not the cause of the excessive borrowing during 1977–81; adverse external economic factors and overlending by the banks were also contributing factors. But such mismanagement is a major impediment to the changes needed for developing countries to deal with their current debt problems. The period of easy money and low real interest rates contributed to a conviction among many LDC politicians that policies implemented during the late 70s were basically sound and politically desirable, but were thwarted by adverse economic developments, that is, recession, declines in commodity prices, record high real interest rates, and restricted lending by banks. There is good evidence in support of these views, but there were also serious policy shortcomings in most debtor countries. Adjustment policies recommended by the IMF and World Bank since 1982 focus on the harmful effects of statist policies that crowd out the private sector and on the inefficiencies generated by bloated bureaucracies and endemic corruption in many of the debtor countries. But the fund and bank cannot force radical changes in such policies; changes must come from each country's political leadership.

SCOPE OF THE CURRENT DEBT CRISIS

Since 1980 over 35 developing countries have been unable to service their foreign debt and have asked their creditors for a rescheduling or refinancing of their obligations. These countries fall into two distinct groups: first, the middle-income countries of Latin America, Asia, North Africa, and Europe; and second, the mostly poor countries of sub-Saharan Africa. (In Table 27–2, Nigeria and the Ivory Coast probably belong with the middle-income countries, though they share many characteristics with the other African countries.) A third group, including countries such as Bangladesh, and some very poor countries in Africa, have not

TABLE 27–2

Developing Countries Whose Foreign Debt Has Been Renegotiated since 1980 ($ billion, end 1987)

	Estimated Total Debt		Estimated Total Debt
Latin America	**$432.7**		
Argentina	60.0	Guyana*	$0.9
Bolivia	5.1	Honduras*	2.3
Brazil	123.7	Jamaica	4.2
Chile	21.7	Mexico	106.9
Colombia	17.1	Nicaragua*	4.7
Costa Rica	4.9	Panama	4.8
Cuba*	4.2	Peru	17.5
Dominican Republic	3.9	Uruguay	5.9
Ecuador	10.7	Venezuela	34.2
Africa	**$101.2**		
Gabon*	1.9	Nigeria	$29.1
Ivory Coast	12.4	Senegal*	2.7
Liberia*	1.4	Sudan*	8.0
Madagascar*	2.6	Tanzania	4.1
Malawi*	1.0	Togo*	1.0
Mauritania*	1.5	Zaire	8.2
Morocco	20.9	Zambia	7.1
Asia	**$28.6**		
Philippines	28.6		
Europe	**$67.7**		
Poland	39.2	Yugoslavia	$22.6
Romania	5.9		
Total all countries	**$630.2**		

* 1986.
Note: The data refer to total debt as of end-1987; the debts renegotiated amount to less than the total because certain debts were exempted from renegotiation.

Source: Institute of International Finance.

rescheduled debts, but they face debt problems similar in most respects to the second group of poor countries.

The debt problems of the poor countries derive largely from poverty, heavy dependence on commodity export earnings, weak economic management capabilities, and relatively limited economic prospects. Most of the indebtedness of these countries is owed official institutions and governments; debts to commercial banks are small. The management of their debt problems lies primarily with the governments and official institutions; there is a strong presumption that in the future they will remain dependent on official grants and concessional lending. Bank lending to these countries will likely be limited to traditional, short-term trade financing. Most countries have been successful in maintaining the servicing of such credits, even though medium- and long-term indebtedness has been rescheduled.

By contrast, the middle-income countries borrowed heavily from banks. For the most part these countries possess substantial human and natural resources, which point to good development prospects given appropriate conditions. The management of their debt problems not only poses many complex challenges, the size of their debt threatens substantial financial loss to creditor banks and possible instability of the international financial system. For these reasons, official debt management efforts have largely focused on these countries.

U.S. POLICIES FOR MANAGING THE DEBT CRISIS

Austerity and Adjustment—The Initial Phase

When the wave of defaults swept over Latin America in late 1982 and early 1983, the major industrial governments faced two related problems. One was the possibility that the defaults could threaten the stability of the international financial system. The other was the economic crisis within the debtor countries, as severe austerity measures, necessitated by the cutoff of external financing, were introduced. At the time these problems emerged, central banks throughout the industrialized world were committed to tight money policies, seeking to prevent a reoccurrence of double-digit inflation. Unlike the response to the 1974–75 recession, the option of reflation through Keynesian-type injections of government spending was not adopted. Instead, disinflation was the order of the day; record levels of positive real interest rates prevailed.

Within this framework of anti-inflationary policies, the United States acted to evolve a cooperative approach to managing the debt crisis. Though many proposals were offered at the time—for examples, see Bergsten, Cline, and Williamson—the option of imposing an orderly default on the various creditors and debtors was ruled out.[8] The bulk of the defaulted debt was owed to private commercial banks; such defaults would have threatened the financial viability of a number of banks, especially the large money center banks in the United States. At the end of 1982, the exposure of the nine U.S. money center banks to 15 major debtor countries measured 197 percent of these banks' capital. There was also a fear that the default option would bring havoc to a world economy just beginning to recover from a long and severe recession; such a result would have reflected poorly on the new Reagan presidency.

The cooperative approach, described by the U.S. Treasury as its Five-Point Program, relied on the following elements: (1) United States and world economic recovery; (2) economic austerity by debtor countries; (3) IMF lending with strict conditionality; (4) rescheduling and new money from commercial banks; and (5) short-term bridge financing, as required, from major industrial governments. These measures were designed in the short-term to contain the potential financial crisis associated with the debt defaults. The domestic economic problems of the debtor countries, in turn, were to be addressed over time by austerity measures and renewed world growth.[9]

The U.S. economic recovery got under way in 1983, fueled by a strong fiscal stimulus resulting from the implementation of substantial tax cuts. Given the tight monetary stance of the Federal

---

[8] C. Fred Bergsten, William R. Cline, and John Williamson, *Bank Lending to Developed Countries: The Policy Alternatives* (Washington, D.C.: Institute for International Economics, 1985).

[9] Lawrence J. Brainard, "Managing the International Debt Crisis: The Future of the Baker Plan," *Contemporary Policy Issues* 5 (July 1987), p. 66.

Reserve, inflows of foreign capital acted to push up the value of the dollar to record levels in 1983–84. A widening trade gap and increasing reliance on foreign savings resulted, and domestic growth exceeded all expectations. The intent of the debt management policy was to buy time on the expectation that the U.S. recovery would lead to broadly based world economic expansion. Growth promised opportunities for the banks to strengthen their capital and reserve positions, as well as increased demand for developing countries' exports.

The U.S. Treasury judged the initial results of the Five-Point Program as successful. Although obstacles were encountered in Brazil and Argentina, the Mexican success in 1983–84 acted to confirm the Treasury's support of the approach. Mexico rescheduled all its current debt maturities and also secured agreement from over six hundred banks to two new money agreements—$5.0 billion in March 1983 and $3.8 billion in April 1984. The economic turnaround was impressive. From a record current account deficit of $14.0 billion in 1981, Mexico was able to achieve surpluses of $5 billion in 1983 and $4 billion in 1985. There was also welcome news from the banks. The exposure of the nine U.S. money center banks to 15 major rescheduling countries, measured as a percentage of primary capital, declined steadily, from a peak of 197 percent at end-1982, to 121 percent at end-1986.

Phase Two—Multiyear Reschedulings

During 1984 U.S. policy for the debt crisis moved into a new phase defined by multiyear rescheduling agreements (MYRAs). MYRAs comprised the rescheduling of four to six years of future maturities, rather than the one or two years included in agreements during 1982–83.

The move to MYRAs was described by the Federal Reserve and the International Monetary Fund as a move from day-to-day crisis management to a more normalized process that would in the future lead to voluntary new lending by the banks. Policymakers feared that the developing countries would abandon efforts at austerity unless the incentives for going along with the debt policy were strengthened. An unstated objective of this new approach was to get the Federal Reserve and the IMF out of an active, behind-the-scenes role in arranging the various new money packages from the banks. Instead of the usual strict conditionality of the IMF standby agreements, the debtor countries could look forward to enhanced surveillance. This was a modification of the IMF's usual Article IV consultation, but with semiannual rather than annual reviews and without performance targets. Where country conditions did not as yet call for a MYRA, however, the standard of strict conditionality still applied.

For their part, banks were encouraged to reward the successful countries with lower interest rate spreads and the elimination of rescheduling fees. The banks' incentive for going along with these changes was the expectation that they would not be asked for new money in association with the MYRAs. The first MYRA was concluded with Mexico during the second half of 1984 and similar agreements with Ecuador, Yugoslavia, Venezuela, and Uruguay followed in 1985.

As conceived and sold to the banks and the debtor countries, the multiyear rescheduling approach reflected an unjustified optimism by the official sector about the future based on a profound ignorance of the reality of the debt problems in individual countries. The approach failed to spell out the responsibilities that each of the participants—the banks, the debtor countries, the IMF and World Bank, and the industrial countries—must shoulder to ensure success.

The approach was silent on how short-term gains from IMF austerity programs could be translated into medium-term economic progress. The role of the World Bank, best qualified to identify such changes, was not highlighted. There was no structure set up to deal with the possibility of future difficulties, whether due to adverse external changes or policy shortcomings in the debtor countries.

A more telling indictment of the MYRA approach came in the 1984 bank negotiations with Mexico. Although no new money was requested, the Mexican negotiators presented economic projections that pointed out the need for some $15–20 billion in new money from banks over the succeeding five-year period. Rather than address these issues in the negotiations, the Mexicans were told by the U.S. government and the banks that the new money issue could be addressed at a later date, if required. The banks then proceeded to disband their advisory committee and economic subcommittee, which had originally been set up to monitor ongoing developments in Mexico. Inasmuch as the MYRA approach had originally been presented to them publicly by both Paul Volcker, chairman of the Federal Reserve, and Jacques de Larosiere, managing director of the IMF, the banks were inclined "to take the money and run," rather than to argue for a different approach.[10]

Phase Three—The Baker Plan

The MYRA initiative was a failure. At the time when the initial successes of the early austerity programs should have been consolidated and translated into meaningful medium-term programs, the U.S. Treasury, the Federal Reserve, and the IMF were all seeking to take themselves out of active involvement in directing the debt management process. Banks, meanwhile, were unprepared and unwilling to assume a leadership role. These conditions created a leadership vacuum.

The introduction of the Baker Plan in October 1985 represented a tacit admission that phase two policies were not working. In the short space of a year, and before the 1986 oil price declines, Mexico's MYRA had failed—a request for new money had already been put on the table for negotiation, and other key countries such as Argentina, the Philippines, Peru, and Brazil failed to show progress in continuing economic adjustment.

Former Treasury Secretary James Baker's Program for Sustained Growth contained three key elements:

1. Implementation of structural economic adjustment measures in debtor countries and adoption of market-oriented policies for growth.
2. Increased and more effective structural adjustment lending by the World Bank and other multilateral development banks with continuation of the IMF's central role.
3. Increased lending by private commercial banks in support of comprehensive economic adjustment programs.

---

[10] For details, see Brainard, "Managing the International Debt," pp. 67-9.

The Baker Plan covered 15 major debtor countries owing an estimated $437 billion at the end of 1985. The plan projected $29 billion in net additional financing for these countries over a three-year period, 1986–88—$20 billion from the banks and $9 billion from the multilateral development banks (over and above a sum of $11 billion already planned for the period).

The Baker Plan reflected an awareness of the shortcomings of the MYRA approach. For one, it underlined the need for a revival of economic growth in debtor countries through medium-term structural changes. Also, by offering the prospect of substantial external financing, it sought to provide stronger inducements to countries to continue economic adjustment efforts and full servicing of interest obligations. And it spelled out specific roles for commercial banks, debtor countries, and international institutions.

Crucial elements, however, were missing from the plan. The role to be played by the United States and other industrial countries was unclear. Active leadership by the United States was essential for the plan to work. Instead, the World Bank was put forward with enhanced responsibilities. But the World Bank, by itself, lacks sufficient political clout to implement the needed policy changes in the debtor countries. And the banks were dismayed to find out that the Treasury planned no institutional mechanism to coordinate its new initiative. Without a new institutional framework among the debtor countries, the banks and the international institutions to coordinate the working out of medium-term programs for economic adjustment (along with their financing), Secretary Baker's initiative remained little more than conversation piece, lacking a concrete means of implementation.

Another flaw evident in past U.S. debt-management policies was that little attention was paid to the international environment and its effect on such policies. Economic recovery since 1983 in the rest of the world was dependent on increased exports to the United States. While administration economists were congratulating themselves on the success of Reaganomics, Germany and Japan sought to capitalize on the opportunities offered by an overvalued dollar and strong U.S. consumer demand; export-led growth allowed them to reduce inflation and budget deficits while their current account surpluses soared.

As the Baker Plan was being introduced and discussed in early 1985, the United States' ability to sustain the world economy and its accumulated debt burdens was being constrained. Domestic political pressures at this time caused the Treasury to redirect its attention to the dollar problem and the U.S. trade and budget deficits. The emergence of these problems led to efforts by the United States to respond by pursuing dollar devaluation and by urging Japan and Germany to stimulate their domestic economies.

By 1986 the record showed mixed progress in dealing with the financial and development aspects of the debt crisis. But further progress appeared more and more threatened by the worsening environment for world economic growth and a weakened commitment to adjustment on the part of the debtor countries. In a sense, debt-management policies had come full circle, back to the 1982 concern of insuring adequate world economic growth to work out developing countries' debt problems. The future success of the Baker Plan (and any successor program) seems as much dependent on sustaining a healthy world economic environment as it is on the effectiveness of internal economic reforms in the debtor countries. What is changed, though, is that the United States is no longer able by itself to provide the leadership that it provided in 1982. And on top of these worries, developing countries faced growing internal political pressures to weaken economic adjustment policies in favor of debt relief, either through negotiation or unilateral action.

MODIFYING THE BAKER PLAN

Contingent Lending and the Menu of Options

The first test of the Baker Plan came in Mexico, which concluded negotiations for a package of new loans from the IMF and World Bank in June 1986. The banks and the Mexican authorities agreed some weeks later on debt rescheduling and new money totaling over $7 billion. These agreements reflected several noteworthy developments. The United States played a key role in the negotiations, including a secret visit to Mexico City by Paul Volcker for discussions with the Mexican president, Miguel de la Madrid. Though the close involvement of the administration and the Federal Reserve reduced the scope for banks to influence the overall package, it is doubtful that the deal could have been accomplished without such involvement.

Another aspect of the program was Mexico's commitment to the World Bank—as called for in the Baker Plan—to implement far-reaching structural changes in budgetary and trade policies. In addition, the commitments from the IMF and commercial banks included contingent elements under which certain performance targets would be modified and new money commitments disbursed if oil prices moved below $9 a barrel or if growth failed to attain an agreed level during 1987. Another innovation was a provision allowing banks to convert their claims into local equity, so-called "debt-equity" conversions.

The Mexican deal was a significant achievement, providing clear support for the original Baker Plan approach. A major shortcoming, though, was that it took over six months to garner sufficient bank support for the new money package. In the end, a significant number of smaller bank creditors failed to come into the agreement—mostly U.S. regional banks—and some of the U.S. money center banks had to top up the facility to meet the agreed minimum sum.

In February 1987, as the Mexican agreement was finally being put in place and negotiations with Argentina were beginning, Brazil declared a unilateral suspension of interest servicing on its medium- and long-term bank debt. To facilitate the banks' agreement to the Argentine new money request, the bank advisory committee agreed on a menu of options to offer the creditor banks. The menu included provisions for debt-equity swaps and an exit bond, designed to appeal to banks wanting out of future new money commitments. The alternative participation instrument, as it was called, had a below-market interest rate and longer final maturity than the debt being rescheduled. Other innovations included a facility fee for banks that signed up quickly for new money, the inclusion of bonds and trade financing commitments as part of each bank's new money commitment, and banks were able to deduct from their base exposure (used to calculate each bank's new money commitment) any of such debt forgiven, provided the forgiveness was certified by the Argentine central bank.

The new money package for Argentina was successfully completed, though a number of small banks stayed out and only three banks opted for the exit bonds. The success of another new money deal, though, provided support to the overall approach of the Baker Plan, now modified by the menu of options. The weak link in the approach proved to be the lack of effective economic adjustment measures ultimately by the Argentine authorities.

Bank Strategies in Flux

Despite the success of the menu of options approach in facilitating bank financing packages, the viability of the debt-management process continued to be questioned. By 1987, five years after emergence of the debt crisis, few believed that new money was anything more than a creative approach to partial interest capitalization. The larger banks supported the new money deals because they had to—formal interest capitalization would have required setting aside large reserves—and as long as they got back more interest than they put in via new money, it was in their interest to support the process. But many of the smaller and medium-sized banks were opting out of new money commitments, increasing the burden on the remaining banks.

In May 1987 Citicorp management decided to set aside $3 billion in its general loan loss reserve, bringing the reserve up to 25 percent of their rescheduled loan exposure. In their public discussion, Citicorp officials explained that the decision did not alter their bank's commitment to the debt restructuring and new money process, provided the underlying adjustment programs were viable and the debtor agreed to market terms. The move was said to strengthen the menu approach by its support of debt-equity swaps and to restore more discipline to the rescheduling process. Any concessionary agreements or debt-relief schemes were to be strongly resisted. The reasons for the reserve reflected: (1) a general deterioration in the quality of developing country debts; (2) an increase in global economic uncertainties; and (3) a desire by Citicorp to begin putting the developing country debt issue on the side, to concentrate on working their other basic banking businesses.

Whatever the public explanation, analysts saw additional strategic reasons for the move. By taking an initiative that would force other, more heavily exposed banks to follow, Citicorp was strengthening its competitive position to pursue new banking initiatives in the areas of interstate banking and capital markets. With all the major U.S. banks at a 25 percent reserve level, the relative weaknesses of certain of the other banks' capital positions would be evident. By deciding on an aggressive policy to raise equity, sell assets, and to restructure their balance sheet by disposing of LDC debt for cash and equity, Citicorp was announcing that it was a winner, able to prosper during the coming shakeout of the U.S. banking system. Instead of bank cooperation that had marked the early years of the debt crisis, it now seemed that the survival of the fittest was becoming the driving force in bank relations.

Two effects were seen immediately after the Citicorp move. One was a substantial decline in prices for LDC debt in the secondary market, ranging between 10 and 20 cents in terms of discount from par. This market is a very thin market and there was apprehension that an increased supply of debt would be coming onto the market. A second result was to introduce drift into the rescheduling activities of the banks. LDC debt was becoming part of the competitive relationships among the banks; gone was the notion that all the banks were in the same boat.

Whatever the motives behind the Citicorp reserving action, the substantial increase in bank reserves revealed some of the inherent contradictions of the Treasury and Federal Reserve policies on international debt management. Most bank strategies were clearly focused on finding a way out of the debt problem, with its continuing pressures to lend new money. But the success of the Baker Plan continued dependent on keeping the banks in as significant lenders to the LDCs. The banks' reserving action reduced the official sector's influence on bank behavior and on the debt-management process overall.

Banks want out to get on with other, more lucrative activities; many do not want to be in the LDC lending business. Most U.S. regional and European banks had set aside reserves of 50 percent or more by the end of 1987, and many seem willing to accept large discounts on the debt to be able to refocus their energies on new banking opportunities elsewhere. The value likely to be realized by such banks in giving up their claims is clearly different from the value of the debt that other banks remaining in the rescheduling process expect to realize over the longer term.

These developments had clear implications for the official debt strategy. Given the diversity in banks' positions, it became essential to offer banks a range of options in order to secure their continued support of financing packages. In this regard, the evolution of the *menu* approach represented a pragmatic departure by the bank advisory committees (which negotiate the financing packages) from the Baker Plan's undifferentiated view of bank strategies.

NEW OPTIONS FOR MANAGING THE DEBT

Key Elements of the Debt Strategy

Prospects that a modified Baker Plan would be able to solve the debt problems of the developing countries diminished during 1987–88. Pessimism grew about future new money bank packages. Bank strategies for providing reserves for the debt evolved rapidly as major U.S. regional banks moved beyond Citicorp's initiative to hike reserve levels to over 50 percent of the debt by early 1988. Even though the Mexican and Argentine new money packages were successfully arranged during 1987, and a Brazilian financing package in mid-1988 brought a formal end to the moratorium, the growing divergence among bank strategies on LDC debt posed formidable obstacles to future new money packages.

A second, essential component of the debt strategy—effective adjustment policies in the developing countries—received less attention, but there was little to be encouraged about here either. Although indicators of economic performance reflected a continuing modest growth in real gross national product (GNP), fiscal management appeared to weaken as inflation worsened dramatically, particularly in Mexico, Brazil, and Argentina. Meanwhile, export volumes in 1987 for the group of 15 heavily indebted countries remained below the 1985 level (Table 27–3).

The overall impression from the data is one of gradual, if unspectacular, progress in economic growth, continued low levels of investment, a disappointing lack of sustained improvement in

TABLE 27–3

Indicators of Economic Performance: 15 Heavily Indebted Developing Countries*

	1969–78	1979–81	1982–83	1984	1985	1986	1987
Growth of real gross domestic product (GDP)	6.1	3.9	−1.6	2.3	3.8	3.8	2.5
Investment (percent of GDP)	n.a.	24.8	19.4	16.6	17.1	17.8	17.1
Consumer price inflation	28.5	46.9	73.6	118.4	121.8	77.2	116.2
Central government fiscal balance (percent of GDP)	n.a.	−2.3	−5.5	−3.6	−3.4	−4.8	−6.5
Export volumes	2.8	1.9	0.2	9.2	2.1	−0.3	4.1
Terms of trade	4.0	6.7	−3.6	2.6	−2.4	−18.2	−0.1
Non-oil commodity prices	9.3	2.0	−1.3	2.5	−10.8	1.5	−2.1
Current account (percent of export of goods and services)	−16.0	−23.1	−23.4	−1.0	−0.2	−11.9	−6.1
Net private borrowing ($ billion)	n.a.	44.0	12.9	1.1	−4.7	−11.5	−4.4
External debt (percent of export of goods and services)	n.a.	184.7	279.8	271.7	289.6	347.9	336.7

* Argentina, Bolivia, Brazil, Chile, Colombia, Ecuador, Ivory Coast, Mexico, Morocco, Nigeria, Peru, Philippines, Uruguay, Venezuela, and Yugoslavia.

Source: *World Economic Outlook*, Appendix Tables A5, A7, A11, A19, A24, A28, A29, A35, A42, A50. (Washington, D.C.: International Monetary Fund, 1988).

fiscal balances, and a further worsening in these countries' debt burden in the face of declines in non-oil commodity prices and in their terms of trade. There were, to be sure, major success stories:

1. Chile's economic boom in 1987–88 based on improved copper prices, strong investment and a successful debt-equity program which had reduced bank debt over 25 percent;

2. Mexico's rapid expansion of manufactured exports, up over 40 percent in both 1986 and 1987;

3. Brazil's impressive $19 billion trade surplus in 1988.

Despite such achievements, the stagnation of economic growth in key countries contributed to a growing pessimism about prospects for these countries. This was particularly evident in Brazil and Mexico, where growth faltered as policy makers battled serious inflation problems.

One result of these developments was that proposals multiplied for adopting new approaches to LOC debt management, especially some form of debt relief. Despite the popularity of debt relief as a solution to countries' debt problems, it is doubtful that generalized debt relief, by itself, really provides the solution that its proponents claim. Brazil's unilateral suspension of interest payments on its medium-term bank debt during 1987 should have provided evidence that debt relief could improve a country's economic performance, especially investment. In fact, economic performance and overall public confidence in economic management in Brazil deteriorated throughout 1987, resulting in a sharp reduction in economic growth and accelerated capital flight. Had economic policies been sound in the first place, the need for new loans or some form of debt relief in Brazil's case would have been lessened, if not rendered unnecessary altogether.

The Brazil experience suggests that debt relief through unilateral actions does not lead to a revival of investment confidence and economic growth. The argument that debt relief is essential before sound economic policies can be adopted seems contradicted by this example. The suspension of interest payments to banks undermined the confidence of other investors, both domestic and foreign. The February 1987 moratorium, ended in 1988, imposed losses on the economy variously estimated at between $1.5 billion to $4.5 billion, and by undermining confidence in economic policy, the moratorium gave rise to sustained annual losses by way of increased capital flight.

The link between commercial bank creditors and potential domestic or foreign investors is that both look to the same source of payment—the income flow created by the country's economic growth.[11] An investor who sees the government trying to force one group of creditors to take a loss unwillingly must conclude that there is a risk of sharing in the loss in one way or another—possibly by higher taxes on a successful investment, by restrictions on repatriation of profits or on access to foreign exchange, or even by partial repudiation of domestic government debt via currency reform. Thus, a new investor risks sharing in the loss being forced on another group of creditors.

To be compensated for this risk, a potential investor in the debtor country demands a high rate of return on any new investment, whether in new projects or in domestic financial instruments. The result is that domestic interest rates are pushed up, crowding out new investments in the country and compounding the government's fiscal deficit. Decreases in foreign investment and increased capital flight further aggravate the problem. A vicious circle of low investment and low growth takes hold. By undermining investors' confidence, mandated or unilateral debt forgiveness compounds this vicious circle.

Obstacles to Debt Relief

Even if the Brazilian case does not prove the need for debt relief, neither does it prove that debt relief is not needed in other countries. Certain low-income countries that borrowed heavily from banks have little hope of meeting their full interest obligations, even assuming the best of economic policies. And, as already noted, adverse changes in the world economic environment or a breakdown of the new money process would undermine the debt strategy.

---

[11] Michael P. Dooley, "Market Valuation of External Debt," *Finance and Development,* March 1987, pp. 6–7.

Given that debt relief may be desirable in certain countries or under certain circumstances, how can it best be implemented? A consideration of the practical aspects of implementating debt relief suggests that any scheme—whether comprehensive or partial—must surmount many obstacles.

The essence of any debt relief scheme is (1) a mechanism to determine current value of the debt, that is, the loss or discount from par; (2) a procedure to share out the losses in an acceptable way among the various creditors; and (3) a means to pass on debt relief to the debtor. Ideally, such a scheme should include equitable burden sharing among the various parties. It should also be efficient in the sense that it maintains the integrity of international financial flows to developing countries and provides for a revival of sound economic growth in these countries. Although many schemes have been proposed, none have so far been able to deal in a satisfactory way with the complexities of the problem faced by the middle-income debtor countries.

One problem already noted is that the legal rights of the private bank creditors to part of the sovereign's income or assets are ill defined. Despite this problem, economic theory on property rights suggests that it would still be in the interests of the creditor and debtor to negotiate a settlement. The real difficulty comes from the existence of multiple creditors—large numbers of diverse banks, as well as governments, the IMF, the World Bank, and other multilateral development banks. All the banks are locked into sharing (pari passu) clauses. Thus, a debt relief settlement agreed by one group of banks could be blocked by other more exposed banks who may worry that such a deal could set a precedent for other countries and, thereby, threaten their viability. The real obstacle here is the complexity of intercreditor relations more than the legal uncertainties.

One proposed way around these problems is for governments to get out of the debt-management business, forcing the banks to negotiate debt settlement with debtor countries unable to pay full interest due. But governments and multilateral institutions have strong interests in continuing credit relations with debtor countries. An overt attempt to isolate bank creditors would set off intercreditor warfare, making everyone, particularly the debtor country, worse off.

In such a situation, the banks would have the ability to disrupt a country's trade and finance by bringing legal attachments and by canceling short-term trade financing, which for most countries still remains in place. Neither the governments nor the multilateral institutions are structured to provide countries financial services such as clearing of international payments of short-term trade finance. This approach makes everyone worse off—not a desirable form of equitable treatment—and the result is not an efficient one.

A second approach starts from the opposite extreme by proposing to eliminate the bank claims. Governments would buy out the banks' claims at a discount and pass on the benefit to the debtor countries. The governments would set up and fund some type of debt-discounting agency, an International Debt Discounting Corporation (IDDC), and then devise a mechanism for passing on debt relief to the debtor country. Although this approach requires substantial public funding, it is favored by many because debt relief might easily be tied to World Bank and IMF programs which include appropriate economic conditionality. The banks would get out, albeit at a cost, but disruption to a country's ongoing trade and financial flows would likely be minimized.

On the surface, the IDDC approach seems to meet the criteria of equitable burden sharing and efficiency. A number of practical difficulties, though, remain. One is the cost to the taxpayer; this cost could be very large, raising public concerns of a bank bailout. Assuming that the governments fund an IDDC, though, how will the value of the debt be determined? The banks cannot be forced to accept a cheap buyout. The prices of LDC debt in the secondary market would likely rise as soon as the IDDC begins to operate and there would be incentives for free riders to stay out of the scheme as long as prices are rising.[12] Thus, it would be impossible to buy the debt cheaply, making the plan less feasible for budgetary reasons. If IDDC purchases of debt are restricted to reduce its cost to the public budget, then the benefits of the buybacks for the debtor would be meager.

Approaches which lie between these two polar alternatives must confront the difficulty of defining the various intercreditor

---

[12] Dooley, "Market Valuation," p.8.

rights in a debt relief scheme. The problem comes in determining equitable burden sharing, that is, the comparability of the sacrifice or give-up that each party brings to the deal. A complex set of tradeoffs among all the creditors confronts the negotiation of such schemes.

Banks might prefer interest-rate relief, without future commitments of new money, and with some sort of official guarantee on their residual principal and interest claims. Governments frequently grant interest relief in the context of reschedulings of their own credits, but by capitalization of interest, not by reduction of principal or interest. The IMF, World Bank, and other multilateral development banks have exempted themselves from rescheduling, but they would continue lending new money. How should the banks' interest-rate relief be compared with interest capitalization and new-money commitments from governments and multilateral lenders?

Ideally, the debt-relief scheme should provide a comprehensive definition of the losses facing each of the creditors. Otherwise, one group of creditors or the other would not support the scheme. Given these differing positions among creditors, though, the concept of equitable burden sharing is not only difficult to define, it could prove problematic to quantify in the context of negotiations worth billions. If this were not enough, the governments would point out that they pay part of the costs of debt relief granted by the banks via tax credits for such losses and they are responsible for providing supplementary capital to the multilateral lending institutions. On the other hand, the banks would claim that their debt relief acts to enhance the value of the claims held by the governments and multilaterals.

Any debt-relief mechanism also must confront problems with efficiency criteria. The basic problem is how to determine who should receive debt relief and how much is needed. Because public funds for debt relief are limited, should such funds be allocated to the poorest countries—who need it the most—or to middle-income countries—who may require more relief in the aggregate and who also may be able to use such relief more efficiently? Other worries concern the practical difficulty of securing acceptable economic performance from the debtor countries. A too-easy access to debt relief would create a moral hazard as it rewards the laggards and penalizes those who are making an effort to perform. A related risk is the free rider or contagion effect. Countries able to pay might be tempted to seek debt relief because others are receiving relief.

The moral hazard and free rider problems might be dealt with in the context of a global, top-down mechanism, with agreed criteria for debt relief. But agreement on such criteria would be difficult at arrive at for reasons already mentioned. A country-by-country, or bottom-up mechanism avoids this problem, but a contagion effect could easily force a global approach.

Mechanisms for Partial Debt Relief

The development of a secondary market for LDC debt since 1983 reflected the fact that certain creditors were willing to sell their claims at prices that represented substantial discounts from par value. The growth of this market has, in turn, encouraged approaches to debt relief that allow the debtor to benefit from such discounts. The most successful mechanism developed to utilize these discounts has been the debt-equity swap. Swaps were originally developed during 1983–84 in Brazil—in a program later discontinued—as a simple conversion of debt to equity at par. The potential benefits of using secondary market discounts soon became evident. All the existing programs now utilize a mechanism that effectively gives the country a substantial part of the existing secondary market discount.

Rescheduling agreements prevent countries from selective repurchases of their own debt. The agreements stipulate pro rata distribution of any repayment to all bank creditors, making selective debt repurchases infeasible, unless specific waivers are obtained from the banks. The repayment of the debt with local currency, though, was not likely to interest the majority of banks and it used no scarce foreign exchange. In 1984–85 Chile was the first country to persuade the banks to amend their rescheduling agreement to provide a formal debt-equity program for the original creditor or a nonbank foreign investor. A parallel program was also introduced for Chilean residents. The success of Chile's debt-equity program, which in three years converted $3 billion or 25 percent of the original 1982 bank debt, encouraged many other countries to introduce similar programs. Though with only some $7 billion converted in debt-equity programs in all countries by the end of 1987, the sums are still modest in the context of total LDC debt.

Because repayment is in local currency for debt-equity swaps, few problems in intercreditor relations emerged. As a rule, banks were willing to allow individual banks to seek repayment in such swaps as no outflow of foreign exchange was involved (dividend remittances were typically prohibited for a number of years). To the extent that nonbank foreign investors used the program, increased investment was likely to follow, thus improving the country's growth prospects. And the country would benefit by reducing total foreign debt and by realizing part of the secondary market discount on the debt. A successful debt-equity program would, therefore, enhance the value of the claims held by the remaining banks.

The main obstacles to debt-equity swaps have come on the side of the debtor. Swaps have domestic monetary consequences, depending on how the local currency is generated and whether public or private debt is converted. The biggest concern has been the potential inflationary consequences of conversions of public sector debt, given the existence of large fiscal deficits in many countries. This has limited the role for swaps in countries where inflation is an overriding concern of the government.[13] In any case, foreign investors perceive substantial risks in new equity commitments in many countries and the scope for such investments in some countries is constrained by the small size of the local market. On balance, debt-equity conversions appear likely to play a positive, albeit limited, role in providing debt relief to debtor countries.

Other initiatives developed during 1987 focused on mechanisms facilitating repurchases of discounted debt. Bolivia received agreement from its bank creditors to repurchase a substantial part

---

[13] For a discussion of this and related issues, see Willian R. Cline, *Mobilizing Bank Lending to Debtor Countries,* (Washington, D.C.: Institute for International Economics, 1987), pp. 45–49.

of its debt, using grant aid received from several industrial countries. Approximately 50% of the country's $670 million in bank debt was repurchased at a price of 11% of par value.

In December 1987 Mexico announced a novel program to repurchase up to $20 billion of its bank debt using a defeasance scheme. The debt—tendered at a discount in an auction by the bank—was converted into 20-year bonds, whose principal was collateralized by U.S. government zero-coupon bonds maturing in 20 years. The cash to buy the zero-coupon bonds came from Mexico's reserves. In effect, the defeasance scheme spreads the effective repurchase of the debt over the 20-year period, but Mexico gets the immediate benefit of the discount determined by the auction. Although the banks have the nondiscounted portion of their principal collaterized, they still face an interest-rate risk over the 20 years (the floating interest rate spread on the bonds was set at $1\frac{5}{8}$ percent over LIBOR compared with $\frac{13}{16}$ percent over LIBOR on the original debt) and they have to take an immediate write-off on the debt equal to the discount determined by the auction. The results of the bond swap, however, were disappointing. Mexico reduced their debt only $1.4 billion, at a cost almost twice that hoped for (a discount of 30 percent instead of the desired 50 percent).

The fundamental obstacle facing such repurchase schemes relates to the intercreditor problems discussed earlier. As Bolivia's case illustrates, where the market discount on a country's debt is large and bank debt relatively small, banks appear inclined to waive the pro rata repayment restriction in their rescheduling agreement. This suggests that mechanisms to facilitate debt repurchases by the poorest countries are feasible if support from donor governments and concessional loans from multilateral agencies can be secured.

In Mexico's case, the assumption of the bond swap was that Mexico would continue to pay full interest on its old debt. For this reason, the overall attractiveness of such a scheme to banks remaining as creditors is limited. The Mexican initiative should be viewed more as a sophisticated exit bond mechanism for smaller creditors than as a mechanism likely to appeal to its major creditors. Whether or not large creditor banks participate in such schemes does not detract from their usefulness. The voluntary exit of banks through such mechanisms is in everyone's interest. The exiting bank is free to concentrate on other strategic priorities, the country benefits by sharing in the discounted market value of the debt, and large bank creditors who decide not to participate gain from the country's improved ability to service the remaining debt.

Prospects for New Initiatives

A final consideration is who will likely take new initiatives for managing the debt problem—the banks, the major industrial governments, the multilateral institutions, or the debtor countries themselves?

The banks substantially increased reserves for LDC debt during 1987. If the evolution of individual bank strategies makes the provision of new bank lending to developing countries unlikely, the overall debt strategy will falter; this means that even higher reserves would be required. It would seem to be in the banks' interest, therefore, to sustain the debt strategy in two principal ways. One is by developing improved exit mechanisms for banks willing to sell their claims at substantial discounts. A second is by creating ways to enhance their new money commitments, by providing senior creditor status or some form of security to their new-money commitments.

The industrial countries are preoccupied with their own budget and trade problems. The United States will resist any debt initiatives which involve substantial commitments of public funds, given the budget deficit, the huge commitments already made to solve the domestic savings and loan crisis, and the political liability of being seen to bail out the banks and the debtor countries. The United States and other governments would likely commit public funds only when key countries are threatened by serious domestic instability or when the entire debt management effort is seen to collapse. This suggests that the governments will place a priority on sustaining the key elements of the current debt strategy with changes that are evolutionary rather than radical in nature.

The debtor countries may be tempted to force the issue, as Brazil did in February 1987, by suspending debt servicing to banks. But Brazil's moratorium produced an acceleration in capital outflows; indebted countries, though, need inflows of new capital to support a revival of economic growth. Experience suggests that a restoration of confidence is most likely to result from sound economic policies and reforms. Given such confidence, potential investors—including the country's own citizens—are more likely to respond positively, reinforcing a virtuous circle of economic growth. Economic programs built on cooperative relations with bank creditors and voluntary market-oriented mechanisms to provide effective cash-flow relief have the best chance of attaining these goals.

REFERENCES

Bergsten, C. Fred; William R. Cline; and John Williamson. *Bank Lending to Developing Countries: The Policy Alternatives.* Washington, D.C.: Institute for International Economics, 1985.

Brainard, Lawrence J. "Managing the International Debt Crisis: The Future of the Baker Plan." *Contemporary Policy Issues* 5, July 1987, pp. 66–75.

_____."More Lending to the Third World? A Banker's View." In *Uncertain Future: Commercial Banks and the Third World,* ed. Richard Feinberg and Valeriana Kallab. New Brunswick, N.J.: Transactions Books for the Overseas Development Council, 1984.

Cline, William R. *Mobilizing Bank Lending to Debtor Countries.* Washington, D.C.: Institute for International Economics, 1987.

Committee for Economic Development. *Finance and Third World Economic Growth.* Boulder: Westview Press, 1988.

Dooley, Michael P. "Market Valuation of External Debt." *Finance and Development,* March 1987, pp. 6–9.

Feldstein, Martin; Herve de Carmoy; Koei Narusawa; and Paul R. Krugman. *Restoring Growth in the Debt-Laden Third World.* New York: The Trilateral Commission, 1987.

Goldsborough, David J. "Investment Trends and Prospects: The Link with Bank Lending." In *Investing in Development: New Roles for Private Capital?* ed. Theodore H. Moran. New Brunswick, N.J.: Transactions Books for the Overseas Development Council, 1986.

Guttentag, Jack M. and Richard J. Herring. *The Current Crisis in International Lending.* Washington, D.C.: Brookings Institution, 1985.

Kindleberger, Charles P. "The Cyclical Pattern of Long-Term Lending," in *The Theory and Experience of Economic Development: Essays in Honour of Sir W. Arthur Lewis,* ed. Mark Gersovitz et al. London: Allen & Unwin, 1982, pp. 300–312.

Krueger, Anne O. "Debt, Capital Flows, and LDC Growth." *American Economic Review,* May 1987, pp. 159–64.

Lomax, David F. *The Developing Country Debt Crisis.* London: Macmillan, 1986.

APPENDIXES

APPENDIX A.   TABLES

TABLE 1
National Income in Current U.S. Dollars (Billions)

	1970	1975	1980	1984	1985	1986	1987
Industrial countries	$1821.1	$3464.7	$6386.4	$6781.5	$7136.0	$8059.1	$4800.7
Australia	25.4	45.7	95.4	187.4	260.5	293.1	313.4
Austria	12.7	33.0	67.3	55.6	57.0	81.5	102.0
Belgium	23.3	57.4	109.3	70.5	73.3	103.8	
Canada	77.0	147.3	227.8	295.9	300.3	313.4	357.6
Denmark	14.7	34.2	58.7	47.4	50.8	71.9	88.2
Finland	9.5	23.9	43.0	42.7	45.3	58.7	
France	130.3	306.1	582.9				
Germany	166.0	371.3	720.6	540.9	549.7	787.8	
Greece	9.6	20.1	38.1	30.9	30.3	39.1	42.4
Iceland	0.4	1.1	2.8	2.3	2.4	3.3	
Ireland	0.6	1.6	3.9	12.0	12.8	10.8	
Italy	92.8	171.4	358.0	311.4	319.4		
Japan	176.5	433.2	922.4	1079.7	1142.3	1683.8	
Luxembourg	0.7	2.3	4.7	3.6	3.8	5.3	
Netherlands	31.7	79.0	152.6	111.7	113.0	157.3	191.9
New Zealand	4.7	8.7	21.5	58.4	78.5	89.6	
Norway	9.6	24.0	47.4	46.2	49.3	58.6	69.2
Portugal	6.0	14.1	23.4	17.1	18.6		
Spain	33.2	95.3	187.8	134.9	142.3	200.4	
Sweden	29.9	65.3	109.1	81.6			
Switzerland	19.0	50.2	94.9	86.8	88.7	128.8	
United Kingdom	19.8	42.9	87.0	214.6	237.5	221.1	
United States	927.4	1436.6	2428.1	3349.9	3560.1	3750.7	3636.1

Source: International Monetary Fund, *International Financial Statistics*, various issues, calculated with period average exchange rates (Table III).

TABLE 2
National Income as Percentage of Total Industrial Country Income

	1970	1975	1980	1984	1985	1986
Australia	1.4%	1.3%	1.5%	2.8%	3.7%	3.6%
Austria	0.7	1.0	1.1	0.8	0.8	1.0
Belgium	1.3	1.7	1.7	1.0	1.0	1.3
Canada	4.2	4.3	3.6	4.4	4.2	3.9
Denmark	0.8	1.0	0.9	0.7	0.7	0.9
Finland	0.5	0.7	0.7	0.6	0.6	0.7
France	7.2	8.8	9.1			
Germany	9.1	10.7	11.3	8.0	7.7	9.8
Greece	0.5	0.6	0.6	0.5	0.4	0.5
Iceland	0.0	0.0	0.0	0.0	0.0	0.0
Ireland	0.0	0.0	0.1	0.0	0.0	0.0
Italy	5.1	4.9	5.6	4.6	4.5	0.1
Japan	9.7	12.5	14.4	15.9	16.0	20.9
Luxembourg	0.0	0.1	0.1	0.1	0.1	0.1
Netherlands	1.7	2.3	2.4	1.6	1.6	2.0
New Zealand	0.3	0.3	0.3	0.9	1.1	1.1
Norway	0.5	0.7	0.7	0.7	0.7	0.7
Portugal	0.3	0.4	0.4	0.3	0.3	
Spain	1.8	2.8	2.9	2.0	2.0	2.5
Sweden	1.6	1.9	1.7	1.2	1.2	
Switzerland	1.0	1.4	1.5	1.3	2.0	1.6
United Kingdom	1.1	1.2	1.4	3.2	3.3	2.7
United States	50.9	41.5	38.0	49.4	49.9	46.5
Industrial country total	100.0%	100.0%	100.0%	100.0%	100.0%	100.0%
	1,821.1	3,464.7	6,386.4	6,781.5	7,136.0	8,059.1

Source: Calculated from Table 1.

TABLE 3
Exchange Rates (Units Foreign Currency per U.S. Dollar)

	1970	1975	1980	1984	1985	1986	1987
Australia	1.1	1.3	1.1	0.9	0.7	0.7	0.7
Austria	26.0	17.4	12.9	20.0	20.7	15.3	12.6
Belgium	50.0	36.8	29.2	57.8	59.4	44.7	37.3
Canada	1.0	1.0	1.2	1.3	1.4	1.4	1.3
Denmark	7.5	5.8	5.6	10.4	10.6	8.1	6.8
Finland	4.2	3.7	3.7	6.0	6.0	5.1	4.4
France	5.6	4.3	4.2	8.7	9.0	6.9	6.0
Germany	3.7	2.5	1.8	2.9	2.9	2.2	1.8
Greece	30.0	32.1	42.6	112.7	138.1	140.0	135.4
Iceland	0.9	1.5	4.8	31.7	41.5	41.1	38.7
Ireland	2.4	2.2	2.1	1.1	1.1	1.3	1.5
Italy	625.0	652.8	856.4	1757.0	1909.4	1490.8	1296.1
Japan	360.0	296.8	226.7	237.5	238.5	168.5	144.6
Luxembourg	50.0	36.8	29.2	57.8	59.4	44.7	37.3
Netherlands	3.6	2.5	2.0	3.2	3.3	2.5	2.0
New Zealand	1.1	1.2	1.0	0.6	0.5	0.5	0.6
Norway	7.1	5.2	4.9	8.2	8.6	7.4	6.7
Portugal	28.8	25.6	50.1	146.4	170.4	149.6	140.9
Spain	70.0	57.4	71.7	160.8	170.0	140.1	123.5
Sweden	5.2	4.2	4.2	8.3	8.6	7.1	6.3
Switzerland	4.4	2.6	1.7	2.4	2.5	1.8	1.5
United Kingdom*	2.4	2.2	2.3	1.3	1.3	1.5	1.6

* U.S. dollar per British pound.

Source: International Monetary Fund, *International Financial Statistics*, various issues.

TABLE 4

Percentage Change in Exchange Rates

	Annual Averages			From Previous Year			
	1970–1974	1975–1979	1980–1983	1984	1985	1986	1987
Australia	5.4	-4.8	-5.1	2.2	-20.3	-4.3	4.5
Austria	-6.2	-6.3	8.1	11.4	3.4	-26.2	-17.2
Belgium	-4.7	-5.4	15.4	13.0	2.8	-24.8	-16.4
Canada	-1.9	3.7	1.3	4.9	6.2	1.5	-4.3
Denmark	-3.9	-2.8	15.0	13.5	2.2	-23.7	-15.5
Finland	-2.1	0.7	9.7	7.9	3.2	-18.2	-13.2
France	-1.2	-2.1	16.2	14.7	2.7	-22.8	-13.3
Germany	-7.9	-6.6	9.0	11.8	3.2	-26.2	-17.1
Greece	0.0	4.4	24.4	28.0	22.5	1.3	-3.3
Iceland	2.7	29.6	64.6	27.6	31.0	-1.0	-5.9
Ireland	-0.5	-2.1	-11.3	-12.8	-1.8	25.2	11.2
Italy	1.0	5.6	16.8	15.7	8.7	-21.9	-13.1
Japan	-3.8	-5.1	2.3	0.0	0.4	-29.4	-14.2
Luxembourg	-4.7	-5.4	15.4	13.0	2.8	-24.8	-16.4
Netherlands	-5.7	-5.5	9.5	12.6	3.4	-26.2	-17.1
New Zealand	4.7	-5.7	-9.9	-13.4	-13.8	4.0	13.5
Norway	-4.8	-1.7	9.8	11.8	5.4	-14.1	-8.8
Portugal	-2.3	14.3	23.4	32.1	16.4	-12.2	-5.8
Spain	-3.7	3.6	21.3	12.1	5.8	-17.6	-11.8
Sweden	-2.9	-0.6	16.1	7.8	4.0	-17.2	-11.0
Switzerland	-7.2	-10.5	6.1	11.9	4.7	-26.8	-17.2
United Kingdom	-0.5	-1.4	-7.5	-11.8	-3.0	13.1	11.6

Source: Calculated from Table 3.

TABLE 5
Money Market Interest Rates (Annual Averages in Percent per Annum)

	1975	1980	1981	1982	1983	1984	1985	1986	1987
United States	5.82	13.36	16.38	12.26	9.09	10.23	8.10	6.81	6.66
Canada	. . .	13.28	18.14	14.35	9.62	10.91	9.57	9.30	8.03
Australia	9.49	10.34	12.07	13.90	9.50	10.84	14.70	15.75	13.06
Japan	10.67	10.93	7.43	6.94	6.39	6.10	6.46	4.79	3.51
Belgium	4.68	11.22	11.47	11.44	8.18	9.47	8.27	6.64	5.67
Denmark	6.47	16.93	14.84	16.36	12.03	11.47	9.97	9.09	9.88
Finland	. . .	12.35	11.46	11.66	14.67	16.50	13.46	11.90	11.19
France	7.92	11.85	15.30	14.87	12.53	11.74	9.93	7.74	7.98
Germany	4.41	9.06	11.26	8.67	5.36	5.55	5.19	4.57	3.72
Ireland	10.71	16.39	16.20	17.65	14.45	12.93	11.87	12.28	10.84
Italy	10.64	17.17	19.60	20.16	18.44	17.27	15.25	13.41	11.51
Netherlands	4.17	10.13	11.01	8.06	5.28	5.78	6.30	5.83	5.16
Norway	7.62	11.16	12.35	13.91	12.27	12.67	12.29	14.15	. . .
Spain	6.70	15.46	16.56	17.21	19.40	12.60	11.60	11.50	16.07
Sweden	7.83	12.17	14.35	13.29	10.85	11.77	13.85	10.15	9.16
Switzerland	2.75	2.29	2.93	1.32	1.84	3.34	3.75	3.17	2.51
United Kingdom	6.08	15.62	13.12	11.36	9.09	7.62	10.78	10.68	9.66

Source: International Monetary Fund, *International Financial Statistics*, various issues.

TABLE 6
Government Bond Yields (Average Yields to Maturity in Percent per Annum)

	1975	1980	1981	1982	1983	1984	1985	1986	1987
United States	7.99	11.46	13.91	13.00	11.11	12.52	10.62	7.68	8.38
Canada	9.04	12.48	15.22	14.26	11.79	12.75	11.04	9.52	9.95
Australia	9.75	11.65	13.96	15.35	14.33	13.83	14.10	13.56	13.47
Japan	9.20	9.22	8.66	8.06	7.42	6.81	6.34	4.94	4.21
New Zealand	6.33	13.29	12.83	12.91	12.18	12.57	17.71	16.52	15.69
Austria	9.61	9.24	10.61	9.92	8.17	8.02	7.77	7.33	6.91
Belgium	8.54	12.04	13.71	13.56	11.86	11.98	10.61	7.93	7.83
Denmark	13.10	17.66	18.92	20.39	14.46	13.93	12.01	10.76	11.19
France	9.49	13.03	15.79	15.69	13.63	12.54	10.94	8.44	9.43
Germany	8.50	8.50	10.38	8.95	7.89	7.78	6.87	5.92	5.84
Ireland	14.64	15.35	17.26	17.06	13.90	14.62	12.64	11.07	11.27
Italy	11.54	16.11	20.58	20.90	18.02	14.95	13.00	10.52	9.65
Netherlands	8.79	10.21	11.55	10.10	8.61	8.33	7.34	6.35	6.38
Norway	7.29	10.27	12.31	13.20	12.86	12.16	12.58		
Sweden	8.79	11.74	13.49	13.04	12.30	12.28	13.09	10.26	
Switzerland	6.44	4.77	5.57	4.83	4.52	4.70	4.78	4.29	4.12
United Kingdom	14.39	13.79	14.74	12.88	10.81	10.69	10.62	9.87	9.48

Source: International Monetary Fund, *International Financial Statistics*, various issues.

TABLE 7
Equity Market Price Index (1980 = 100)

	1970	1975	1980	1984	1985	1986	1987
Australia	61.7	40.4	100.0	117.0	143.5	193.4	277.6
Austria	86.9	107.1	100.0	88.8	169.4	211.8	180.4
Belgium	94.0	108.0	100.0	154.0	171.0	246.0	290.0
Canada	45.8	49.9	100.0	110.2	130.5	143.9	168.0
Denmark	53.0	89.0	100.0	401.0	416.0	419.0	351.0
Finland	52.9	108.2	100.0	295.0	253.4	386.5	627.2
France	68.8	65.7	100.0	155.8	182.0	280.6	323.5
Germany	106.7	101.4	100.0	150.4	199.9	270.4	249.0
Ireland	43.2	48.3	100.0	105.5	149.3	234.4	338.5
Italy	145.8	94.8	100.0	171.9	286.7	667.4	642.7
Japan	34.5	65.7	100.0	172.1	210.2	279.2	412.9
Luxembourg	21.0	48.1	100.0	102.3	151.8	229.9	209.3
Netherlands	118.8	107.4	100.0	196.7	254.6	327.7	328.8
New Zealand	85.0	72.0	100.0	263.0	310.0	527.7	n/a
Norway	88.0	87.0	100.0	202.0	267.0	282.0	341.0
Spain	178.1	260.1	100.0	161.7	204.1	415.7	597.7
Sweden	60.0	87.0	100.0	394.0	367.0	599.0	715.0
Switzerland	122.0	85.3	100.0	132.1	171.8	209.3	216.6
United Kingdom	49.8	47.6	100.0	196.2	242.2	300.5	396.8
United States	67.9	71.7	100.0	134.7	154.5	194.9	246.0

Source: International Monetary Fund, *International Financial Statistics*, various issues.

TABLE 8
Percentage Changes of Equity Prices

	Annual averages			From previous year		
	1970–1974	1975–1979	1980–1983	1984	1985	1986
Australia	–13.2	20.4	11.2	–16.3	16.2	38.5
Austria	14.5	8.4	–14.3	–7.2	172.0	33.0
Belgium	4.7	9.2	–8.6	5.4	67.7	71.9
Canada	–2.7	19.2	7.6	–10.9	12.2	7.4
Denmark	14.7	3.7	23.6	–36.8	57.8	–0.4
France	–4.9	24.2	–5.9	2.0	78.4	76.0
Germany	1.2	10.5	–0.3	–7.5	131.5	33.5
Italy	–11.0	3.7	11.4	5.6	127.6	105.9
Japan	19.2	19.0	15.6	15.7	41.9	98.1
Netherlands	–6.3	18.7	6.1	6.4	54.2	35.8
Norway	25.6	41.8	0.3	–2.4	64.3	–5.2
Spain	11.2	–12.9	–15.6	27.3	44.7	112.8
Sweden	3.9	8.1	28.2	–23.1	53.8	63.0
Switzerland	1.7	18.0	–1.6	–13.5	102.5	31.6
United Kingdom	–11.6	27.5	7.9	0.6	46.3	21.9
United States	–5.3	14.5	11.4	1.0	27.2	13.4

Source: Calculated from Table 7.

TABLE 9
Equity Valuation (U.S. $ Billions)

	1970	1975	1980	1984	1985	1986	1987
Australia	$25.9	$ 22.9	$ 59.7	$ 51.6	$ 62.5	$ 77.7	$ 132.4
Austria	0.8	1.4	1.9	1.4	4.0	5.3	6.3
Belgium/Luxembourg	6.1	2.8	10.0	12.2	20.9	36.3	49.6
Canada	—	49.5	113.3	116.3	146.9	166.3	244.0
Denmark	0.9	2.8	4.0	6.3	13.1	15.1	19.5
France	22.9	34.5	52.8	40.2	78.5	149.5	185.2
Germany	28.0	51.5	71.3	78.1	179.0	245.9	254.6
Italy	10.5	11.5	25.0	23.3	64.7	140.8	127.9
Japan	42.5	135.1	356.6	616.8	909.1	1,746.2	2,895.4
Netherlands	11.4	15.6	24.5	31.1	51.6	73.3	90.9
Norway	1.0	1.4	2.6	4.1	9.8	9.6	16.6
Spain	11.7	29.4	16.3	11.7	18.7	41.6	73.1
Sweden	4.5	9.5	12.2	19.3	29.8	48.5	63.3
Switzerland	9.7	18.6	45.5	42.5	90.3	132.4	165.2
United Kingdom	76.2	77.7	189.7	219.2	328.3	439.5	727.8
United States	—	683.6	1,240.0	1,593.2	1,955.5	2,203.2	2,870.5

Source: Morgan Stanley Capital International, *Capital International Perspective*, various issues.

TABLE 10
Percentage Change of Equity Valuation

	Annual Averages			From Previous Year		
	1971–1975	1976–1980	1981–1984	1985	1986	1987
Australia	-2.6	32.0	-2.7	21.1	24.3	70.4
Austria	15.0	7.1	-5.3	185.7	32.5	18.9
Belgium/Luxembourg	-10.8	51.4	4.4	71.3	73.7	36.6
Canada	—	25.7	0.5	26.3	13.2	46.7
Denmark	42.2	8.6	11.5	107.9	15.3	29.1
France	10.1	10.6	4.8	95.3	90.4	23.9
Germany	16.8	7.7	1.9	129.2	37.4	3.5
Italy	1.9	23.5	-1.4	177.7	117.6	-9.2
Japan	43.6	32.8	14.6	47.4	92.1	65.8
Netherlands	7.4	11.4	5.4	65.9	42.1	24.0
Norway	8.0	17.1	11.5	139.0	-2.0	72.9
Spain	30.3	-8.9	-5.6	59.8	122.5	75.7
Sweden	22.2	5.6	11.6	54.4	62.8	30.5
Switzerland	18.4	28.9	-1.3	112.5	46.6	24.8
United Kingdom	0.4	28.8	3.1	49.8	33.9	65.6
United States	—	16.3	5.7	22.7	12.7	30.3

Source: Calculated from Table 9.

TABLE 11
Corporate Taxes (1987)

	Tax Rate (highest, %)	Loss Carry Forward (in years)	Withholding Tax		
			Dividends	Royalties	Interest
Austria	55	7	20	20	—
Belgium	48	5	25	25	25
Canada	44.34	7	25	25	25
Denmark	50	5	30	30	—
France	42	5	25	33.3	25
Germany	64	5	25	25	25
Italy	46.4	5 (IPREG only)	32.4	21	15
Japan	42	5	20	20	20
Netherlands	42	8	25	—	—
Norway	50.8	10	25	—	—
Spain	35	5	20	20	20
Sweden	52	10	30	—	—
Switzerland	34.8	2–6	35	—	35
United Kingdom	35	unlimited	—	25	25
United States	34	15	30	30	30

Source: Arthur Andersen & Co., *Western Europe . . . A Tax Tour*, London, 1987.

TABLE 12
Long-Term External LDC Debt (U.S. $ Millions)

	1970	1975	1980	1981	1982	1983	1984	1985
Argentina	5182	6581	16774	22736	27113	35838	37086	40179
Brazil	5138	23725	56711	64657	73303	81006	87835	91094
Chile	2576	4374	9433	12666	14004	14996	17266	17465
Colombia	1582	2744	4599	5939	7178	8163	9417	10945
Indonesia	2908	10363	18113	19449	21714	25085	26662	30435
Ivory Coast	268	1008	4863	5131	6325	6107	6305	7100
Korea	2019	6289	18530	21897	24080	27464	30256	35756
Mexico	5966	15608	41287	53325	59742	81559	88571	89010
Nigeria	572	1143	5335	7615	9926	12936	12536	13432
Peru	2658	5077	7431	7417	8605	10243	11077	11869
Philippines	1495	2805	9049	10438	12158	13704	14323	16559
Thailand	727	1352	5802	7224	8455	9656	10911	13268
Venezuela	965	1494	14054	14952	17124	17751	22449	21800

Source: World Bank, *World Debt Tables*, various issues.

APPENDIX B. PROFILES OF
INTERNATIONAL LENDING AGENCIES

AFRICAN DEVELOPMENT BANK
GROUP (AFDB)

Address: B.P. 01–1387, Abidjan 01, Cote d'Ivoire

Established: 1964

The African Development Bank Group consists principally of the African Development Bank and the African Development Fund, plus several smaller special-purpose funds, such as the Nigeria Trust Fund. The Bank and the Fund correspond to the Group's hard and soft windows, respectively. They are legally and financially separate, but are administered by the same board of governors.

The AFDB seeks to promote regional cooperation and development of member states through the financing of investment projects. Nonproject loans (sometimes, but not always, in conjuction with the World Bank), equity participation, and technical assistance are also provided. The Bank loans are repayable over 12 to 20 years at prevailing market rates, while Fund loans are repayable over up to 50 years with only service charges.

The Bank and Fund are both financed through capital subscriptions of members. Subscriptions of non-African members are limited to 33 percent of the total in the Bank, and to 50 percent in the Fund.

ASIAN DEVELOPMENT BANK (ADB)

Address: 2330 Box 25 Boulevard,
Pasay City, Philippines

Established: 1966

The Asian Development Bank was established at the recommendation of the United Nations Committee for Asia and the Far East, to promote regional cooperation and accelerate the development of regional member countries. Priority is given to poorer members.

The ADB has both regional and nonregional members. Nonregional members include Canada, the United Kingdom, the United States, and West Germany. The Bank is financed by the capital subscriptions of members.
Periodicals:

ADB Quarterly Review (quarterly)
Asian Development Review (semiannual)

INTER-AMERICAN DEVELOPMENT BANK (IDB)

Address: 1300 New York Avenue, N.W., Washington, D.C., 20577, U.S.A.

Established: 1959
The Inter-American Development Bank was established by the Organization of American States to promote regional cooperation and development of Latin American members. The IDB makes and guarantees loans for projects and export financing. Most loans are for 10–15 years, but there is also a soft-loan facility (the Fund for Special Operations) that offers longer term loans at concessional rates.
Periodicals:

IDB: Monthly News from the Inter-American Development Bank (monthly)
Socio-Economic Progress in Latin America (annual)

INTERNATIONAL BANK FOR RECONSTRUCTION AND DEVELOPMENT (IBRD) / WORLD BANK

Address: 1818 H Street, N.W., Washington, D.C., 20433, U.S.A.

Established: 1944
The International Bank for Reconstruction and Development, or World Bank, was created, together with the International Monetary Fund, over the course of a series of conferences concluding in

the United Nations Monetary Conference at Bretton Woods. The original purpose of the IBRD was to mobilize capital for postwar European reconstruction. The focus gradually shifted to lending to developing country members for investment projects, where sufficient private capital could not be obtained.

The IBRD is financed by member country subscriptions. The IBRD (then) issues bonds and notes.

IBRD loans are medium to long term at prevailing interest rates. The bulk of the loans are made to governments, but some are made to the private sector with host-country guarantees. The IBRD is complemented by the International Development Association and the International Finance Corporation (see below).

Although most IBRD loans continue to be for "traditional" projects, the use of nonproject lending has become increasingly important in the 1980s. The IBRD's nonproject lending seeks to encourage and enable adjustments in countries' sectoral and macroeconomic policies.

Periodicals:

Abstracts of Current Studies (annual)

Finance & Development (quarterly, published jointly with the IMF)

World Bank Economic Review (quarterly)

World Bank Research News (quarterly)

World Bank Research Observer (semiannual)

World Development Report (annual)

INTERNATIONAL DEVELOPMENT ASSOCIATION (IDA)

Established: 1960

The International Development Association is the soft window that complements its hard window affiliate, the IBRD. However, the IDA is legally and financially independent of the IBRD.

IDA loans are long term (up to 50 years) and typically have a 10-year grace period for repayment. Loans are free of interest, but there is a service charge of .75 percent per year. Eligibility for IDA loans is determined according to a weighted quota system, whereby poorest countries are given priority.

INTERNATIONAL FINANCE CORPORATION (IFC)

Established: 1956

The International Finance Corporation is, like the IDA, legally and financially independent of the IBRD. The IFC aims to promote the development of local capital markets and private industry by offering technical assistance, financing preinvestment studies, and providing loans and equity capital. Loans do not require host government guarantees.

INTERNATIONAL MONETARY FUND (IMF)
Address: 700 19th Street, N.W., Washington, D.C., 20431, U.S.A.

Established: 1944
The International Monetary Fund was created, together with the IBRD, over the course of a series of conferences concluding with the United Nations Monetary Conference at Bretton Woods.

The main objective of the IMF is to stabilize exchange rates through the coordination and regulation of members' foreign exchange policies. Until the early 1970s, this was manifested in the Bretton Woods System, in which all member-countries calculated the foreign-exchange value of their money according to the same method and in reference to a common gold standard. Central banks were charged with intervening in foreign-exchange markets to maintain agreed upon rates.

The removal of the U.S. dollar from the gold standard led to a switch from fixed to floating exchange-rates for most industrial countries. The IMF continues to promote the stability of exchange-rates through surveillance and consultations, whereby the IMF closely monitors member countries' exchange policies and advises members in periodic reviews.

An important secondary activity of the IMF is to provide short-term loans to member countries to meet balance of payments difficulties. The conditions under which the IMF can make such loans are articulated in the General Agreements to Borrow. Until 1983, only the main industrial-country members (plus Switzerland) were eligible for these loans, but eligibility was expanded to include all member countries in response to the debt crisis.

Periodicals:

Finance & Development (quarterly, published jointly with the IBRD)

IMF Staff Papers (quarterly)

IMF Survey (semimonthly)

World Economic Outlook: A Survey by the Staff of the International Monetary Fund (annual)

INDEX

DATE DUE